Acknowledgments

We would like to thank the Editorial Board for their time
and dedication to the creation of this book.

Marek McKenna
Shaka Rawls

TABLE OF CONTENTS

Section 1
The Colonial Period: 1492–1754

The May Flower.

The Colonial Period

KEY TERMS

- Age of Exploration (p. 9)
- Albany Plan of Union (p. 22)
- Bacon's Rebellion (p. 15)
- Cahokia (p. 4)
- Cash crop (p. 14)
- Eastern Woodlands Native Americans (p. 6)
- Enlightenment (p. 23)
- Frontier (p. 18)
- Great Awakening (p. 23)
- Indentured servant (p. 17)
- Jacques Cartier (p. 11)
- John Winthrop (p. 13)
- Line of Demarcation (p. 10)
- Mayflower Compact (p. 12)
- Mercantilism (p. 16)
- Metacom's War (p. 22)
- Middle Passage (p. 15)
- Mound builders (p. 8)
- Pilgrims (p. 12)
- Ponce de Leon (p. 10)
- Puritans (p. 11)
- Quakers (p. 13)
- Salem witch trials (p. 22)
- Samuel Champlain (p. 11)
- Slave society (p. 20)
- Social hierarchy (p. 21)
- Triangle trade (p. 15)
- Virginia Company (p. 14)
- William Penn (p. 13)

Long before Europeans arrived, the Americas were home to thriving cities. One of these developed between A.D. 1100 and A.D. 1400 a few miles northeast of present-day St. Louis, Missouri, on the Illinois side of the Mississippi River. **Cahokia** was a man-made earthen city. It was the capital of the Mississippian culture and served as a flourishing economic, ceremonial, political, and religious center.

Cahokia was accidentally discovered in the early 1960s during the construction of the Interstate highway system. It has been designated as a UNESCO World Heritage Site and a U.S. National Historic Landmark.

Cahokia's villages had palisades (wooden fences) to protect the inhabitants and the city had open communal plazas, ceremonial buildings, flat-topped temple mounds, round-topped burial mounds, and row houses. It also had vast acreages of land used for agriculture. Cahokia had a hierarchal society that utilized slave labor and practiced human sacrifice. Its inhabitants established trading networks with areas as far away as the Gulf of Mexico and present-day Minnesota.

In A.D. 1250, 100,000 people may have lived in Cahokia. By 1400, the site was abandoned. Scholars are unsure of the reason for Cahokia's decline. Some suggest human-caused deforestation or over-hunting. Others believe Cahokia was conquered or experienced some kind of epidemic.

NATIVE AMERICANS OF THE EASTERN WOODLANDS

Human migration to the present-day United States began over 12,000 years ago, across the Bering Strait from northern Asia into present-day Alaska. When Europeans arrived in the Americas in the 1500s, the hemisphere was home to numerous peoples and cultures.

FIGURE 1.1 Map of pre-Columbian North American Indian territories.

An old longhouse.

Eastern Woodlands Native Americans lived in the vast area east of the Mississippi River. They are referred to as "woodlands" people because they lived in wooded and forested areas near streams and lakes. Eastern Woodlands people inhabited areas from Maine to Florida and from the Atlantic shores to the Mississippi River. They were divided into three main groups—the Northeast Woodlands, Southeast Woodlands, and Far North Woodlands. The groups had much in common. They were hunters, gatherers, and fishers, using the products of nature for food and clothing, weapons and shelter, and tools. They lived in villages of various sizes. Festivals and religion were part of their daily lives. The groups also exhibited differences. Some were semi-nomadic and traveled to hunt for food. Others built more permanent villages. Housing types ranged from longhouses to round houses to wigwams. Some clans were patriarchal (ruled by men) while others were matriarchal (ruled by women).

> **EASTERN WOODLANDS NATIVE AMERICANS** People living in the area east of the Mississippi River at the time the European settlers arrived on the North American shores.

The Iroquois

The Iroquois are one Northeast Woodlands group of Native Americans. The Iroquois Confederation consisted of five tribes—the Senecas, Onondagas, Oneidas, Mohawks, and Cayugas—and inhabited areas of present-day New York. The confederation had a representative central government and may have had a written constitution. All decisions reached by the representatives had to be unanimous. The central government only debated major issues—leaving local issues to be decided by local councils.

Iroquois society was structured around the clan. Men ruled the clans but each clan had a clan mother head, a female who helped rule. When a couple married, they joined the wife's clan; a person could not marry within the same clan. Religion was important. They believed in a great spirit, the creator of all things. They also believed in good and evil spirits and in the afterlife.

Iroquois men were hunters, fishers, and gatherers. They trapped small animals for food and used canoes, nets, and traps for fishing. Canoes were used for water travel, and walking was the main method of land travel. Women planted and harvested agricultural products. Corn, beans, and squash were dietary staples. Clan members tapped maple trees for syrup to sweeten food and make candy. Excess food was stored in clay pots and buried near Iroquois houses.

Iroquois homes were either wigwams, round houses, or longhouses constructed of young trees. Because the Iroquois believed trees were sacred, they used only the parts of the tree they needed. The Iroquois built round houses by bending trees into round shapes and placing tree bark over the rounded shape. Dried grass or thatch was then placed over the bark. All round houses had a small hole in the center of the roof to allow smoke to escape. Longhouses, also framed by using young trees, were rectangular and covered with pieces of bark sewn together. Each longhouse had a center hall with rooms on both sides. They had sleeping platforms and storage shelves on the walls. The rafters were used for storing food, such as dried and smoked fish, corn, and squash. Several related families lived together in each longhouse.

Festivals were important to the Iroquois. The Green Corn Festival, thanking the gods for the bountiful harvest, was usually celebrated in late summer or early fall after the corn had ripened on the stalks.

The Ojibwa

The Ojibwa, or Chippewa, was another group of Northeast Woodland Native Americans. This group originally inhabited the Atlantic coastal area but migrated to the Lake Superior region, settling in the present-day states of Michigan, Minnesota, and Wisconsin. Chippewa communities were called tribes, and each tribe was politically independent. Men were hunters and women farmed, cultivating wild rice that grew in the northern waters. The methods they used to thrash the rice stalks and collect the grain in their birch bark canoes are still used today—people paddle canoes into the northern waterways to participate in the age-old tradition of ricing.

Ojibwa homes, like the homes of the Iroquois, were made of frames of young saplings with birch bark coverings. Their clothing, like the clothing of the Iroquois, was made from animal hides. The Ojibwa used picture messages rather than writing to communicate and had little formal government. They lived in villages during the summer, while they gathered and stored food, and camps in the winter.

Seminoles

The Southeast Woodlands groups included the Cherokee, Seminoles, Creeks, Choctaw, Chickasaw, and Mississippians. The Florida Everglades were home to the Seminoles. Seminole men hunted, and women prepared food for the entire village to eat in the communal eating house. Their food included wild plants that grew in and around the swampy, tall-grass areas of southern Florida. Seminoles also ate alligators, snakes, and other animals of the Everglades. Seminole clans were named for things in nature, and children belonged to their mother's clan.

Seminole villages usually consisted of no more than one eating house, one storage house, and twelve homes called *chickees*. Homes were built in a circle with a central open area inside the circle. Seminole families had several homes because they often moved and did not remain in any one place for long. Their homes were built on platforms, with the floor approximately three feet above the ground. The roofs were slanted and the interiors had little furniture. Beds, called *comfortables*, were made of hides and blankets that were rolled and hung in the rafters during the day.

Seminoles believed that animal spirits guided them. When a family member died, the family would permanently vacate the chickee and bury the dead family member in a coffin surrounded by clothing and cooking utensils. As a society, the Seminoles adhered strictly to rules. Punishment for violating rules often consisted of inflicting scars on the offender. The Seminole were excellent carvers, made musical instruments such as flutes and rattles, and used small drums for ceremonial purposes.

The Corn Dance Festival and Hunting Dance Festival were times of celebration for the Seminoles. At these events, the gods were thanked and honored for bountiful crops and the abundance of wildlife used for food, clothing, and utilitarian items. Seminoles traveled on foot, following animal trails, or by extensively decorated canoes.

The Cherokee

The Cherokee, another major Southeastern Woodland group, lived in the present-day areas of South Carolina and Georgia. They, like the other Eastern Woodland groups, were hunters, fishers, gatherers, and farmers. Their staple food item was corn, but they also grew beans and squash and gathered berries, nuts, and wild plants. Cherokees had a chief for war and a chief for peace. A council served as a governing group. Women were permitted to serve as members of village councils.

Cherokee villages were often located near streams and were protected and surrounded by walls of tall poles. From 200 to 500 inhabitants lived in each village, and each village had between 30 and 60 homes. The communities had central plazas and a central square. Each Cherokee family had two homes in two different villages. One was a rectangular and airy summer home. The other was a round winter home made of wood, covered with mud, and topped with a bark roof.

The Cherokees were artisans and made colorfully designed baskets, clay pots, carved pipes, masks, and beads. They worshiped the deer god and prayed to animal spirits.

The Mississippians

MOUND BUILDERS Native Americans who built ceremonial and trading sites, such as Cahokia.

The Mississippians were a Native American culture that flourished in what is now the Midwestern, Eastern, and Southeastern United States. They were known as the **mound builders** because they built large earthwork pyramid mounds, such as those discovered at Cahokia. The Mississippian culture declined rapidly, perhaps as a result of epidemics following early contacts with Europeans.

Far North Woodlands Native Americans

The Far North Woodlands Native Americans consisted of the Northern Algonquian language group, the Woodland Cree. The Algonquians lived along the eastern seaboard and Canada in the present-day areas of New England, New York, and New Jersey. The Powhatans of Virginia were members of the Algonquian group. The first Europeans met the Algonquians when they arrived in Virginia and New England. The Algonquians built seasonal homes and lived in longhouses and wigwams. The men hunted in the forests and fished the local rivers. The Algonquian women gathered berries and nuts and planted crops.

The Woodland Crees were a tribe of the Algonquian language group and lived in the forested areas of the East Coast. The men fished and hunted for food and clothing. They fashioned horns from the bark of trees to attract large animals, and they made fish hooks from bone. The Cree women were gatherers. The Cree homes were made from the bark of the birch trees, and they traveled in birch bark canoes.

It is believed that the Native American population was between 40 million and 100 million at the time of early European exploration of the Western hemisphere. There was a wide diversity of cultures among the native people. Tribal relations were fluid, and the territories, languages, and allegiances of the Native Americans changed regularly, just as territories, languages, and allegiances changed regularly among the nations of Europe.

EARLY EXPLORERS

The **Age of Exploration** was a period of competition, conquest, and discovery for European nations. Marco Polo, a Venetian explorer, returned from Asia with stories of the area's wealth, and European leaders initiated efforts to reach the remote lands. Advancements in science and technology, such as triangular sails, the compass, the astrolabe, and the sextant, aided the voyages of discovery in the 1400s and 1500s. The invention of the printing press also allowed information about science and technology to be printed at a fraction of the cost of handwritten documents and distributed beyond localities. Exploration was desirable for many reasons—wealth, power, prestige, the expansion of empires, and religious freedom in the time of the Protestant Reformation in Europe.

In 1487, under the Portuguese flag, Bartholomeu Dias led an expedition to establish trading relations with India. The voyage lasted over a year, and although Dias did not reach India, he is credited with being the first European to sail around the Cape of Good Hope at the southern tip of Africa. Approximately ten years later, Vasco da Gama, another Portuguese navigator, led an expedition around the Cape of Good Hope and reached India. His expedition took nearly eleven months. In 1500, Pedro Cabral was the first European to arrive in the present-day country of Brazil, which he claimed for Portugal.

AGE OF EXPLORATION A period of competition, conquest, and discovery for European nations lasting from the mid-1400s to the end of the 1500s.

The Spanish were interested in exploring the New World to obtain wealth, increase their empire, and spread Catholicism. In 1492, the Spanish king and queen financed Christopher Columbus, an Italian, to sail to the New World to discover a trade route to the Indies and claim land for Spain. Upon Columbus's

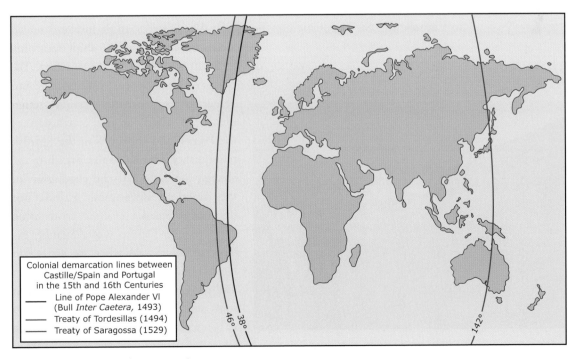

Colonial demarcation lines between Castille/Spain and Portugal in the 15th and 16th Centuries
— Line of Pope Alexander VI (Bull *Inter Caetera*, 1493)
— Treaty of Tordesillas (1494)
— Treaty of Saragossa (1529)

FIGURE 1.2 The Line of Demarcation.

LINE OF DEMARCATION
The line dividing Spanish and Portuguese possessions in the New World.

PONCE DE LEON The first Spanish explorer to arrive in Florida and Puerto Rico, where he established the first Spanish settlement.

return to Spain in 1493, the Pope of the Roman Catholic Church issued a **Line of Demarcation** that divided the lands in the New World between Spain and Portugal. The line, which approximately followed a line of longitude, gave the area of what is today Brazil to Portugal and most of the remainder of the New World to Spain. A year later, the line was adjusted to provide more of the New World land to Portugal.

Spanish conquistadors explored parts of the present-day United States. **Ponce de Leon** established the first settlement in Puerto Rico and visited Florida. Francisco Vasquez de Coronado discovered the Grand Canyon while searching for Cibola, the "Seven Cities of Gold" in the present-day American Southwest. Hernando De Soto explored America's southeast and the lower Mississippi River regions. Other Spanish explorers reached into present-day areas of Texas, Arizona, New Mexico, and Kansas.

Great Britain was an important participant in the Age of Exploration. English navigator Sir Francis Drake was the first to sail from the Atlantic Ocean to the Pacific. In 1584, Sir Walter Raleigh founded Roanoke Island, a Virginia colony where Virginia Dare, the first English child in the New World, was born. The colony was deserted but was reestablished by Sir Richard Grenville's arrival at Roanoke in 1586. In 1607, a group of gold-seeking English entrepreneurs were given a charter by King James I. They landed near the James River and established Jamestown, the first permanent English settlement in America.

THE COLONIAL EXPERIMENTS
Spanish in Florida

Ponce de Leon was the first Spanish explorer to arrive in Florida. He was searching for the mythical "fountain of youth." He landed near the present-day city of St. Augustine and continued exploring the East Coast south to the Keys. St. Augustine was built to protect the Spanish from enemy ships and from Native Americans. St. Augustine was formally settled as a Spanish colony in 1565 by Pedro Menendez de Aviles. The Spanish established a series of missions in the area to convert Native Americans to Catholicism. St. Augustine also became a designated Spanish fort and served as a stopping point for ships returning to Spain with New World treasures. The cities of Tallahassee, Gainesville, and Pensacola were original Spanish settlements. In 1763, at the conclusion of the French and Indian War, the Spanish relinquished Florida to the British in exchange for Cuba. At the conclusion of the American Revolution, Florida was returned to Spain.

Hernando Desoto was a Spanish explorer seeking gold when he arrived in Florida in 1539. He and his men did not find gold but followed Native American trails and explored the southeastern part of present-day United States and the lower Mississippi. He sent scouts as far as present-day Chicago.

Castillo de San Marcos in St. Augustine, Florida. Construction was started in 1672 by Spanish settlers.

The French

French settlement of the New World was different from the Spanish and English settlements. The English arrived in the New World to establish colonies and settlements and develop the area. The Spanish built forts, Christianized the natives, and shipped the mineral wealth of the New World to Spain. France, in contrast, centered its economic activity on trading in pelts and furs in Canada and in the Mississippi and Ohio River valleys. As a result, the French aligned themselves with Native Americans, did not sustain large centers of population, and made efforts to keep the land in its natural state. In the early development of Canada, the French attempted to use a system of quasi-feudal land grants to encourage men of good social standing to settle the area. The successful fur trade, however, was an impediment to permanent settlement under the land grant practices.

Giovanni Verrazano was the first explorer sent by the French king to assess the possibilities of wealth in the New World. Verrazano's 1524 voyage of exploration took him to the New York harbor and bay area, where he recorded his observations. Verrazano's voyage extended north to present-day Maine.

Ten years later, in 1534, **Jacques Cartier** made the first of three voyages seeking gold and a northwest passage to the Pacific Ocean across present-day Canada. Instead of gold, he discovered the Gaspe Peninsula, located at the outlet of the St. Lawrence River. He claimed the area for France. Cartier's second voyage took him to the area of the present-day city of Montreal. On his third trip, he again navigated the St. Lawrence but failed to discover gold or the desired passageway.

In 1603, **Samuel Champlain** set foot on the North American continent. He spent a few years in the area of Nova Scotia attempting to determine a good location for a French settlement. He explored parts of the New York state area and the lake that was later named for him. Champlain's explorations extended to the area near present-day Boston that the English would later settle and call Massachusetts Bay Colony. In 1608, Champlain and a small group of colonists founded Quebec. Champlain, who was referred to as the "Father of New France," found the wealth in New France, but the wealth was not gold. It was the lucrative business of trapping, fur trading, and fishing.

JACQUES CARTIER A French explorer who, in the 1500s, sought a northwest passage across present-day Canada to the Pacific Ocean.

SAMUEL CHAMPLAIN A French explorer who founded Quebec in 1608.

PURITANS Anglicans who settled Massachusetts Bay Colony in the 1600s.

NEW ENGLAND: THE PURITANS

Puritans were Protestants who believed the official Church of England needed to be purified. Some of the Puritans were separatists who believed they should renounce the Church of England. Other Puritans were non-separatists who wanted to reform the church. Puritans believed in compacts or covenants between God and God's followers. They also believed in predestination—that is, they thought that all events were willed by God.

Full membership in the Puritan church was open to those, the *elect*, who testified about their personal experience

Plymouth Plantation, Massachusetts.

with God. Full members of the church were called freemen in the Puritan communities. Puritans believed everyone should read the Bible, including women, and their colonial laws required schools to be established in order to teach children to read. In smaller communities children were taught in homes. Home schools were called "dame schools." In larger communities, regular schools were established. Harvard, the first college in America, was a Puritan college.

The twenty-year period from 1620 to 1640, when Plymouth, Salem, Massachusetts, and Massachusetts Bay Colony were settled, has been called the Great Migration because more than 20,000 people came to New England during this time. Settlers during the Great Migration were families who wanted to create permanent homes, rather than adventurers seeking wealth and discovery.

Plymouth Colony

A group of separatists left England in the early 1600s to sail to Holland, where they believed they could practice their religion without oppression. Finding it difficult to provide economically for their families, they sought and obtained a land grant from the King of England to settle the northern part of Virginia. Because they traveled a great distance for religious purposes, the group became known as **Pilgrims**. The Pilgrims left Holland in 1620, sailed to the New World on the *Mayflower*, and arrived at Plymouth Rock, in Cape Cod, Massachusetts in November of the same year. Realizing they had been granted land in northern Virginia and that they had landed off-course due to storms, the group wrote an agreement explaining the purpose of the Plymouth settlement and their obligations to each other in the new land.

The Pilgrim men addressed their obligations to each other in the **Mayflower Compact**. In the Compact the men explained that they were undertaking a voyage to plant the first colony in northern Virginia for the glory of God and their king and to advance the Christian faith. They agreed to commit themselves to a political body that they would establish. The covenant provided that the men agreed to establish laws and a constitution for the general good of the colony and that they would submit to and obey the agreement.

The Pilgrims planted basic crops such as corn, squash, wheat, and peas but also traded fish and furs with the Native Americans because the rocky New England soil was not conducive to an agricultural community. The Pilgrims were unable to grow what they needed to survive, and during the first year nearly half of the settlers died. In addition to relying on the Native Americans for trade, the Pilgrims were greatly helped by a Native American named Squanto. Before the Pilgrims arrived, in 1605, Squanto had been kidnapped by an English sea captain, George Weymouth, who took him to England where he learned English. When he returned to Massachusetts in 1619, he befriended the Pilgrims and taught them how to successfully grow crops. He also served as their translator with other Native American groups in the area.

William Bradford, the governor of Plymouth colony, kept a journal, recording the voyage of the *Mayflower* and the founding of Plymouth. From this comprehensive history of the settlement, we know that Plymouth colony became self-sustaining after a few years but did not become as prosperous as Massachusetts Bay Colony. Plymouth colony's influence gradually declined, and it became part of Massachusetts Bay Colony.

PILGRIMS The group of English separatists who settled Plymouth Colony for religious purposes.

MAYFLOWER COMPACT An agreement among the men on the Mayflower to commit themselves to a political body and to establish laws and a constitution for the colony they founded.

Massachusetts Bay Colony

In 1630, the king of England granted a charter to a group of Puritans who had formed the Massachusetts Bay Company. The charter was for the settlement of land along the Massachusetts Bay. The grant gave the Puritans land from the Charles River, near Boston, to the Atlantic Ocean between the north latitudes of 40 and 48 degrees. The company's charter referred to economic opportunities in metals the Puritans hoped to find in the New World. The Puritans, however, were also very interested in establishing religious communities where they could implement the reforms they believed were needed in the Anglican Church.

John Winthrop, a Puritan trained as a lawyer, led the group of nearly 1,000 to Massachusetts. On board the *Arbella,* the flagship for the group, Winthrop wrote a sermon describing the covenant the Puritans had made with God to establish a Christian Community.

The colonists arrived in Massachusetts and permanently settled the Boston area. They called their settlement Massachusetts Bay Colony. The government was located in Boston. Winthrop became governor of the colony, and the colony held annual elections. Freemen, who were church members, were permitted to vote. The minister was considered the most important individual in Massachusetts Bay Colony. The colony was not tolerant of others' religious beliefs, and did not permit non-Puritans to participate in government.

JOHN WINTHROP A Puritan lawyer who became governor of Massachusetts Bay Colony.

MID-ATLANTIC: THE QUAKERS

William Penn was a member of the Anglican Church but became a member of the Society of Friends (**Quakers**) while he was a student at Oxford University. Because of his Quaker beliefs, Penn was expelled. In 1681, King Charles II gave Penn a grant of 45,000 acres of land south and east of New Jersey to repay a debt owed to William's father. Penn, who believed in social, religious, and political equality, colonized the land with other Quakers and non-Quakers who wanted to migrate to escape the religious and social oppression they had encountered in England.

Quakers believed in equality for all, and unlike the Puritans, believed that everyone could experience personal salvation. The Society of Friends became known as Quakers because during religious services they seemed to shake—or quake—with enthusiasm. Quakers dressed plainly and were pacifists who opposed war and did not participate in military service. Quakers also permitted women to participate in religious services. The Quakers saw their colony as a "Holy Experiment" where everyone could experience religious equality.

Penn believed the Native Americans owned the land he had been granted and paid them for it. He then sold the land to those Europeans who wanted to settle it. The area was named Sylvania, meaning *woods*, but was later called Pennsylvania, meaning *Penn's Woods*. The land the Quakers settled was fertile and excellent for growing grain. Colonists established family farms, and grain became the primary crop. As a result, Pennsylvania became the "bread basket" of the colonies.

Philadelphia, a prosperous merchant center, eventually became Pennsylvania's most important city. The city's name, which means the *City of Brotherly Love*, reflected the Quakers' religious beliefs. Philadelphia's deep harbor and accessibility to the interior also helped the city grow. By the end of the American Revolution, Philadelphia was the largest city in the colonies.

WILLIAM PENN A Quaker who founded Pennsylvania.

QUAKERS Members of the Society of Friends who settled Pennsylvania to escape persecution. They believed in equality for all, pacifism, and personal salvation.

Statue of William Penn, Philadelphia City Hall.

ENGLISH IN THE CHESAPEAKE
The Virginia Company

In 1606, King James I of England granted English businessmen a charter for the **Virginia Company**, a joint stock company, to settle the area of Virginia. Individuals purchased shares that allowed them to take part in the financial success of the endeavor. The Virginia Company was responsible for appointing officials and providing settlers, ships, and supplies to produce a profit in the New World.

In 1607, the company established Jamestown, the first permanent settlement in America, and named the colony after the king. John Smith became governor. During the first few years the colonists had little time to make a profit because they were struggling to survive the harsh conditions of the New World. Although tobacco later became the "gold" the settlers were looking for, the industry was in its infancy. The Virginia Company did so poorly that the king revoked its charter because of increasing debts and their failure to find wealth. Despite the financial failures, they did succeed in establishing a European population in the Chesapeake Bay area.

Tobacco

John Rolfe, an English settler, brought tobacco seeds from South America and planted them in the Chesapeake region in 1612. Maryland's and Virginia's land and climate were conducive for growing tobacco, and soon it became a **cash crop**, grown for sale. Colonial tobacco was soon selling briskly in England, where they preferred its sweeter flavor to the stronger tobacco, mostly from Spain, that was popular in Europe. The colonies exported tobacco to Europe, the Caribbean, and South America. However, as the popularity of the product grew in Europe, England imposed laws limiting exports. The colonists had to send all tobacco to England, where it would be taxed and then sent on to other destinations.

Tobacco became so important in the Chesapeake region that the coast was referred to as *Tobacco Coast*. Tobacco leaves were even used as currency to pay debts and taxes and make purchases. Tobacco exports helped expand the region's shipbuilding industry and generally shaped the area's colonial life. Plantation owners also began using African slaves as cheap labor. In order to prevent great price volatility, the tobacco industry was regulated but regulations favored the elite plantation owners and became a source of social unrest.

Tobacco harvest.

Indian Wars

The English settlers experienced several conflicts with Native Americans. One of the first such conflicts was with the Powhatans, who were living in the area of Jamestown when the colonists arrived. The Powhatans saw the English settlers as trespassers. Tensions between the settlers and the Powhatans escalated, culminating in a 1622 Powhatan attack that killed more than 300 Jamestown residents. This conflict was one reason the Virginia Company's charter was revoked.

Another conflict occurred during the 1670s. At that time, the governor of Virginia, William Berkeley, was cultivating friendly relations with Indian tribes. At the same time, Virginia planters were experiencing depressed prices for tobacco and were struggling financially. When Berkeley failed to retaliate against some Indian border raids, resentment boiled over. Nathanial Bacon, an English plantation owner, demanded the Virginia House of Burgesses enact legislation that favored plantation owners, and he challenged the governor's profitable dealings with the Native Americans. Bacon rallied several hundred followers. The racially mixed group, including poor whites and blacks, attacked some peaceful Indian tribes and then marched on Jamestown, the capital. The legislature passed the legislation Bacon demanded, but Bacon's forces burned the town.

Bacon died from dysentery, and his forces lost momentum. The legislature repealed most of the laws Bacon had demanded. However, the alliance of poor whites and poor blacks in **Bacon's Rebellion** frightened the ruling class and prompted a hardening of the slavery system. The rebellion also caused England to recall Berkeley as governor of Virginia.

BACON'S REBELLION A rebellion in Virginia demanding legislation that would provide financial relief for tobacco planters.

THE SLAVE TRADE

Slave trade was a lucrative business—one that played a central role in the development of the colonies. The development of the colonies, and in particular the development of their tobacco plantations, created a huge need for manual labor.

African Slave Trade

The African slave trade, which began during the 16th century, provided the needed workers for cash crop plantations. The Portuguese were the earliest Europeans to use slaves to work in their colonies. English slave traders obtained most of their slaves from West Africa and West-Central Africa. African merchants and kings captured and traded people in return for European products such as rum, iron pots, copper, and firearms.

The slave trade was part of the **triangle trade** that became important for the economic growth of the colonies. Ships, filled with rum manufactured in New England distilleries, went to Africa. After the rum was unloaded, the ships were loaded with slaves. Most ships then sailed to the Caribbean, landing in Brazil, Barbados, Bermuda, Jamaica, or other Caribbean islands controlled by the British. There the slaves were sold to work on the sugar cane plantations. Sugar cane and molasses from the plantations were then shipped to New England for use in the rum distilleries. Some slave ships sailed directly from Africa to the colonies. Each ship held between 200 and 600 slaves, and each journey across the ocean took nearly two months.

The passage across the Atlantic Ocean was called the **Middle Passage** because it was the middle segment of the triangular trade route and also the longest, taking from six weeks to several months. The number of slaves subjected to this difficult voyage is estimated to be between 9 million and 15 million, reaching a peak between

TRIANGLE TRADE Trade between the North American English colonies, Africa, and the Caribbean islands in which slaves were brought from Africa as laborers and sugar cane was sold to the New England colonies for the manufacture of rum in New England distilleries.

MIDDLE PASSAGE The passage across the Atlantic Ocean on slave ships.

the years of 1700 and 1800, when 60,000 to 70,000 slaves were transported each year. It is thought that 3 million to 5 million did not survive the voyage due to malnutrition, starvation, or a variety of diseases caused from unsanitary conditions aboard the ships. Those who did survive the trip were sold to individuals, companies, or religious institutions. In the British colonies the condition of slavery was usually permanent, though in Spanish colonies, slaves could purchase their freedom and participate in society. Most Africans brought to the colonies as part of the slave trade were men; the most desirable were healthy and young and able to withstand the heat of the southern colonies. Dark-skinned people were preferred as well, because it was more difficult for them to escape and blend into the Native population.

Growth of the Southern Economy

The economy of the southern colonies grew because of cash crops, the availability of slave labor, and inexpensive land. Rice was a cash crop for South Carolina. Tobacco benefitted the Chesapeake plantation owners, and cotton became an important crop for Georgia. The South depended upon transatlantic trade for much of its income; they produced crops that could not be grown in England or elsewhere.

England began restricting the shipments of southern products when Parliament enacted the Navigation Acts in 1651. The acts required the colonists to use only British ships to import or export goods, prohibited the colonists from trading with people who were not British citizens, and stated that the colonists could export products that were grown or produced in the colonies, such as sugar, cotton, and tobacco, only to British ports.

MERCANTILISM An economic doctrine that says government control of foreign trade is of central importance.

The Navigation Acts were the result of England's desire to enforce **mercantilism**. Mercantilism is an economic doctrine that says government control of foreign trade is of central importance. Mercantilism held that the mother country should have a trading monopoly with the colony, giving the mother country a favorable balance of trade and prohibiting the colonies from trading with other nations. Colonists resented the acts because they limited their trade with England when they believed they could obtain higher prices for their products in other countries.

Native Americans Enslaved

Before the Europeans arrived in North America, Native Americans enslaved war captives for labor or, possibly, sacrifice. After the Europeans established colonies they purchased war captives from the Native Americans to cultivate crops that were grown on the large plantations of the South and in the British sugar plantations in the Caribbean.

The British, French, and Spanish each sought to establish trading relations with Native American tribes to gain an advantage over the other nations by having captured slaves available to them. Some Europeans considered Native American slaves more profitable than African slaves in certain situations. The cost of obtaining and transporting Africans was greater than obtaining Native American slaves, and many traders preferred Native American women and children as household servants and laborers.

British owners of plantations in the southern colonies preferred African slaves for several reasons. They feared that Native American slaves would run away, disappear into the wilderness, and be assisted in escape by other Native Americans. The plantation owners were aware of the fact that friendly relations with Native Americans were not constant, and feared that the Native Americans might not always be willing to supply the needed quantity of laborers. Finally, the British landowners' demand for slave labor was greater than the Native Americans could provide. By the 1680s African slaves were the primary source of labor on the plantations in the South. The need for more laborers continued to increase and, as land became scarce, colonists moved into less populated areas. Native American slaves were not used in large numbers after 1730.

MID-CHAPTER QUESTIONS

1. Compare and contrast the groups that are identified as Eastern Woodlands Native Americans. Your answer should include a discussion of the geographic location where each group lived, common traits and practices, and differences.

2. Discuss the Age of Exploration. Identify explorers who discovered new areas and discuss the countries that supported their explorations and the purposes of their explorations. Describe the problems they encountered in their journeys and the significance of their discoveries.

3. Compare and contrast the religious groups that established colonies in New England and the Mid-Atlantic. Identify the countries from which they departed, the reasons they came to the New World, their accomplishments in the New World, and the problems they encountered in establishing colonies.

4. Compare and contrast colonies in New England, the Mid-Atlantic, and the South. Explain similarities and differences in lifestyle, methods of adapting to the environment of the New World, and attempts to develop their economies.

FORMULATING AN AMERICAN IDENTITY

Immigration, the expansion into new frontiers, and slavery were three driving forces behind the development of the colonies. The budding identity of the colonies was not one of homogeneity. The continual quest for new lands and the frictions between differing cultures gave rise to conflict while an increasing reliance on slavery shaped the new world's commerce.

Immigration

Many colonial era immigrants arrived from the British Isles and other areas in Europe. Some came to find their fortune; some came because they were religiously or politically oppressed; some came because they were poor and were looking for a new start. Some immigrants came as **indentured servants**, agreeing to work for a specified number of years to repay the cost of their passage that had been paid for by a landowner or businessman. Many indentured servants worked in the Chesapeake area and the Carolinas.

The Scotch-Irish immigrants were Scots who had lived in Northern Ireland. Most were educated and skilled in trades. Some settled in New England before being

INDENTURED SERVANT
A person whose passage to the North American colonies was paid for in exchange for a specified number of years of work for the person purchasing passage.

HISTORY COMES ALIVE: WESTWARD EXPANSION

Two unrelated events helped shaped the westward expansion movement. The abolishment of primogeniture and Bacon's Rebellion provided impetus for settlers to move west into the frontier areas of the nation.

The English practiced the law of primogeniture, which is the right of a first-born son to inherit all real estate owned by his father if the father dies without a will. By the time the American Revolution ended, all colonies had abolished the law of primogeniture. As a result, all children could inherit real estate.

Bacon's Rebellion set the stage for westward expansion because Bacon's attacks on Native Americans in the interior of Virginia proved that all society's classes—rich or poor—could fight a common enemy. As frontiers opened, settlers worked together to accomplish common goals and protect themselves from common enemies.

attracted to the middle colonies, especially Pennsylvania and west to present-day Pittsburgh. They also settled in the Carolinas, where they often became frontiersmen and clashed with Native Americans.

German immigrants arrived in Pennsylvania in the 1680s and settled near Philadelphia. By the beginning of the American Revolution, nearly one-third of Pennsylvania's population was German. Germans from the Rhineland fled persecution in the early 1700s and settled the Hudson River valley area.

Smaller groups of immigrants also found places to settle. Swedes settled in the Delaware Valley, the Swiss established Beaufort, South Carolina, and the French Huguenots (Protestants) settled areas of South Carolina and southern Virginia.

Frontier Settlement and Social Conflict

FRONTIER Land at the edge of a country or settlement.

A **frontier** is the land at the edge of a country or settlement. America's first frontier was the Atlantic seaboard, the areas around Jamestown, Plymouth, and Massachusetts Bay Colony. As the colonists formed communities in those areas, they drove away game, used available lands for houses and churches, and exhausted the land that was available for agricultural use. Colonists who desired isolation, wanted to obtain fertile land, sought the opportunity to establish a new community, or dreamed of a life of adventure moved away from European settlements and on to lands to the West.

The second colonial frontier for British colonists was in western New England, the Piedmont of Virginia, western areas of Pennsylvania, and the back country of the Carolinas. As lands in the Mid-Atlantic and South became home to European colonists, communities developed and game vanished. Then the colonists explored and settled new frontiers farther to the west. When they crossed the Allegheny Mountains and entered the Ohio River and the Mississippi River valleys, they encroached on lands that were part of New France. This area was inhabited by French fur trappers and traders who wanted to maintain the region's forests in order to protect the wealth of the pelt and fur industry.

The French, who had come into the Great Lakes region from Canada to develop the fur trade and to hunt, lived in small villages that did not damage the forest. In order to continue to dominate their fur trading areas, the French aligned themselves with Native Americans. They established trade relations, intermarried, and created alliances with Native American groups such as the Algonquians and Hurons, who were fierce enemies of the British. In contrast, the British colonists who went into the frontier were settlers and entrepreneurs, eager to expand British territory by establishing homes and communities.

The British colonists' use of the land led to conflicts with the Native Americans and the French. The British aligned themselves with the Iroquois, which blunted the impact of the alignment the French had with other Native American tribes. The conflicts with the French were not resolved until the conclusion of the French and Indian War in 1763.

Slave Society

Slavery existed in every colony, north and south. Initially, New England was the center of the colonial slave trade and provided African slaves to the southern colonies. In the late 1600s and 1700s, most slaves were brought into the British colonies through Savannah and Charleston. In 1641, Massachusetts was the first colony to recognize the legality of slavery, and by the early 1700s there were approximately 1,000 slaves in New England. By mid-century, New England's slave population was approximately 13,000.

In northern colonies, slaves were utilized primarily for urban purposes and employed as domestic, or household, servants. Slaves were frequently admitted into family circles and were taught religious and moral principles because many believed it was the duty of the white person to teach the Africans Christianity. Discipline of household slaves was milder than discipline of field hands working on southern plantations. In New England, social class and economic standing often depended upon the number of slaves in a household, but most slave-holding families owned only a few slaves.

Urban slaves in northern and southern colonies were generally fed and clothed better than plantation slaves. They usually lived in their owners' homes—often in a back room or attic—or in a separate building if the owners were wealthy enough to provide separate accommodations. Urban slaves worked in shipyards and warehouses for their owners. Some were skilled masons and carpenters while others were apprentices in various trades.

Most slaves brought into the colonies were used as laborers on the large farms and plantations in the Chesapeake region growing cash crops. Slavery became the foundation of southern agriculture, and whether a slave was tending livestock or working with crop production, the life of a slave was demanding. The hours of daylight or the tasks to be accomplished dictated the work of a slave, and the treatment of slaves depended upon their masters and overseers. An owner, or master, had a monetary interest in his property and tended to treat slaves better than overseers, whose only goal was to maximize crop production.

Field slaves worked long hours—sometimes up to sixteen hours a day during harvest and often ten or more hours during the remainder of the year. They worked in groups of twenty or more, called *gangs*.

Overseers punished slaves who completed tasks poorly or slowly by whipping them, requiring extra work, or withholding food. Field slaves were usually given at least a half day of non-working time on Sundays.

Plantation slaves lived in family units, but the cabins were simple one- or two-room buildings that had dirt floors, were sparsely furnished, and were hot in the summer and cold in the winter. More than one family commonly lived in a single cabin.

Slaves received food rations on a weekly basis. Owners provided corn meal and flour, lard, and some meat, which provided the bulk of the slaves' meals. Some greens and a few vegetables were also included. Some plantation owners permitted the slaves to grow their own vegetables to add to the rations they provided. A slave's day began at daybreak with a breakfast prepared in a central location. A pot of vegetables cooked as a soup or stew usually constituted a noontime meal, which the slaves ate when they were brought from the fields for a break from work. A family member—usually a woman—prepared evening meals from the week's rations. Diets usually contained enough calories but often lacked essential nutrients.

Owners provided clothing for their slaves or the fabric from which clothing could be made. Slaves received clothes once or twice a year and shoes once a year. Sometimes the owners provided clothing near Christmas. Young children did not usually wear clothes, and the elderly were provided with less clothing than field workers, who needed more clothing during the colder months. Slaves who worked as domestic help were sometimes provided with clothing their owners no longer wanted.

SLAVE SOCIETY An economic and social system built on slavery.

Some owners tolerated marriage in **slave society** in part because they believed slaves would be less likely to run away if married. When they occurred, weddings sometimes included traditional African ceremonies. However, marriages between slaves were not legally recognized. Because of this, owners could—and did—sell family members, including children, at the local slave auction or to other plantation owners, regularly breaking up family units.

Religion was part of the slave society. Planters encouraged slaves to participate in religion because it was believed slaves were easier to control if they held religious beliefs. The owners controlled the sermons and the texts in the churches built for the slaves. There slaves were told to be honest, to obey, and not to steal.

Many slaves practiced their own religions, which had foundations in African beliefs and practices. Slave services not sanctioned by the owners focused on freedom and on hope for the future. Slaves gathered in their cabins or nearby wooded areas, where they had privacy from their owners. These religious gatherings included sermons, prayers, and singing. The Negro spiritual was an important part of the slaves' religion and the lyrics described their difficult lives and their hopes for the future.

ECONOMIC DEVELOPMENT

America's colonial economy was export driven because it was based upon mercantilism. Fishing, lumbering, tobacco, cotton, and shipbuilding formed the foundation of New England's economy. Rum, iron, furs, and the products of small manufacturing businesses were also important. The Mid-Atlantic economy was dependent upon the wheat, flour, bread, and other products emerging from the fertile farmlands of Pennsylvania, Delaware, New York, and New Jersey and the furs obtained on the frontier. The southern economy was based on fishing and cash crops such as tobacco, rice, and indigo. The South also produced forest products such as tar and pitch, furniture, and fruit.

Seaports

As seaport communities increased in population, a definite social structure developed. At the top of the **social hierarchy** in seaports was the merchant class, who built elegant homes designed in the style of expensive English homes. They wore clothes imported from London and furnished their homes with expensive European furniture. Specialized professionals, shopkeepers, and skilled artisans were important to the growth of seaports. These

workers and artisans such as barrel makers (coopers) and carpenters were important members of the middle class and were often employed in the construction of ships and shipping containers. Blacksmiths made nails and fittings for the ships. Shopkeepers sold imported goods obtained from the merchants to other residents.

Seaport communities were dependent on the lowest class of the social hierarchy. Laborers loaded ships with export products and unloaded the exotic spices, household furnishings, elegant fabrics, and specialty items from around the world that were desired by the wealthy plantation owners, merchants, and upper classes. Sailors and slaves were necessary for the survival of the seaport economy. Slaves worked as day laborers on the docks in Charleston, loading and unloading cargo. Sailors took cargo from England to America, and from America to England.

Boston, New York, Philadelphia, Baltimore, and Charleston were coastal communities that grew into important seaports and export centers during the colonial era. The smallest seaport during the colonial era was Baltimore. The city developed as a result of its deep natural harbor, its proximity to the rivers upon which water-driven mills were located, and the sandy plains areas near the Chesapeake Bay where the tobacco industry developed. Baltimore, which grew to approximately 7,000 residents before the American Revolution, became a shipbuilding center. By the mid-1700s tobacco was shipped to Europe regularly from the port and flour and grain were shipped to British colonies in the Caribbean.

Charleston, a Carolina seaport of approximately 11,000 residents by the 1770s, was the southernmost English city on the Atlantic coast. Shipments of rice, indigo, and forest products were sent from the port to Europe and to British islands in the Caribbean.

By the 1770s, Boston and New York had populations of approximately 15,000 each and had become important seaports. Boston was part of the triangle trade, receiving shipments of molasses and exporting rum. Boston's harbor became a center for colonial resistance when England imposed duties on tea. In the 1640, the Dutch leader, Peter Stuyvesant, ordered that a wharf be built in New York harbor. The wharf, which was completed in 1648, was followed by others, enabling New York to become a major shipping center in the 1700s. Philadelphia was the largest seaport in the colonies. The natural harbor, abundance of merchants, and population of 25,000 made the city an important export center for wheat and other grains grown in the Mid-Atlantic colonies.

SOCIAL DEVELOPMENT AND CONFLICT
Salem Witch Trials

Events occurring during the mid- to late-1600s affected the social conscience of the colonists and led to conflict with England. Salem, Massachusetts, a Puritan colony, was thriving. However, several farming families who wanted to separate from the

SOCIAL HIERARCHY
The arrangement of society in differing classes of wealth.

town quarreled with Puritan leaders. The leaders believed that any argument was the result of the devil's influence, and accused these individuals of being witches and working with the devil to harm the community. Trials were held, and hearsay evidence was admitted to convict the accused of witchcraft. Twenty people were hung as a result of the **Salem witch trials**.

Metacom's War

As New England colonies expanded, they encroached on Native American lands. Metacom, a Wampanoag chief, organized a number of Native American tribes to resist European incursions that threatened their land and game. Metacom was defeated and killed in 1676.

At the time of **Metacom's war**, the colonists were trading with England and adopting more aspects of British culture, customs, and manners. Following the war, England revoked the Massachusetts Bay Colony charter and established the Anglican Church in New England. Both of these actions caused resentments and tensions that simmered for years.

The Middle Colonies

The Quakers were a source of tension in the Middle Colonies. The British considered Quakers troublemakers because they condemned slavery, treated Native Americans fairly, and believed authorities should not interfere with their lives.

The Dutch were another source of tension. The Dutch held claim to a territory called New Netherland, which contained parts of present-day New York. The main city on the island of Manhattan, called New Amsterdam, threatened British control of the colonies. In 1664, King Charles II ordered several British frigates to sail into New Netherland; the colony surrendered without a fight. However, skirmishing between English and Dutch continued in the region for another ten years until New Netherland was officially ceded to England in 1674.

THE ALBANY CONGRESS

In June 1754, representatives from seven colonies, leaders of the Iroquois, and colonial officials met in Albany, New York, to devise a plan of union that would provide a common defense against France in the frontier war the colonists believed was inevitable. The plan had two purposes—to secure the support of the Iroquois in the fight against the French and to form a colonial alliance.

The Iroquois had been aligned with the French but were trading with the British in the Ohio Valley at the time of the congress. The Native Americans wanted to align themselves with the eventual winner. However, they agreed to support the British colonists after they were promised weapons and supplies.

Benjamin Franklin, a Pennsylvania representative to the Albany Congress, drafted the **Albany Plan of Union**. The plan provided for one general government for all colonies that would resolve issues relating to the frontier, war, and relationships with nations. A President-General would be appointed by England, and the colonial assemblies would appoint members of a Grand Council. If the President-General

DID YOU KNOW?

The principle of freedom of the press was affirmed in a 1735 case involving libel. John Peter Zenger, a German immigrant, had served as an apprentice to a newspaper owner before becoming the publisher of the *New York Weekly Journal*. Articles appeared in Zenger's paper that condemned the royal governor of New York. The governor had Zenger arrested and charged with seditious libel.

Andrew Hamilton represented Zenger at trial and argued that truth was an absolute defense to libel. A jury agreed with Hamilton's arguments and found Zenger not guilty. The verdict affirmed the principle of freedom of the press in colonial America.

were to die, the Speaker of the Grand Council would be the successor. Members of the Grand Council were to be chosen for three-year terms. After the first term, representation would be determined by the financial contribution of the colonies. The president was authorized to make treaties with the advice of the Council, and the Council had the authority to make laws for levying duties, regulating Indian affairs, and regulating new settlements.

The plan was unanimously approved but no colonial legislature ratified the plan. Since the plan was not ratified, it was not sent to England for approval. However, the Albany Plan of Union was significant in that it drew the colonies closer together. It was an important precedent in the coming decades when the colonies began thinking about independence.

THE ENLIGHTENMENT

The **Enlightenment** in Europe was a period when thinkers applied scientific reasoning to human nature and discussed liberty, democracy, and religious tolerance. Enlightenment philosophers challenged the role of religion and the theory of the divine right of kings. They promoted the idea of natural rights.

John Locke, Jean-Jacques Rousseau, and Baron de Montesquieu were European philosophers who were influential in the colonies. Locke and Montesquieu believed in the separation of powers within the government. Locke and Rousseau believed that government was based on a social contract. They argued that the government drew its power from the governed, who agreed to let the government infringe their personal liberty for the good of all. Thus, government was based on mutual consent.

These European concepts of how government should work provided the philosophical basis of the American Revolution, the Declaration of Independence, and the Constitution of the United States.

The Great Awakening

The **Great Awakening** was a religious revival in the American colonies that took place in the mid-1700s. The Great Awakening had its roots in England when George Whitefield and John and Charles Wesley began to object to the lack of emotion in religion. The coldness and stiffness of English religion encouraged Whitefield to establish a new style of preaching where he attempted to draw crowds by preaching sermons in non-traditional settings outside and while riding on horseback. The religious revival was characterized by "fire and brimstone" preaching and by outward displays of powerful emotion.

The Great Awakening had the most followers in New England and the Mid-Atlantic colonies. George Whitefield introduced his novel style of preaching to Boston in 1740. He also argued that slaves should be freed. Jonathan Edwards, a colonial preacher, delivered sermons that stressed introspection and questioning the authority of church leaders. He urged his followers to realize that they, not the clergy, had the power for spiritual renewal.

The Great Awakening formed important connections between the colonies as itinerant preachers moved throughout the region and used the press to secure donations. Although the movement formed connections, it also created theological and social conflict as centralized church authority came under attack.

ENLIGHTENMENT An intellectual movement in the 1700s in Europe and North America in which philosophers developed theories of natural rights and promoted scientific reasoning.

GREAT AWAKENING A religious revival in the colonies during the mid-1700s that had its roots in England.

END OF CHAPTER TAKE-AWAYS

■ Native Americans of the Eastern Woodlands: They were hunters, fishers, and gatherers living from Maine to Florida and from the Atlantic coast to the Mississippi River.

■ Early Explorers: In the New World, European nations sought wealth and passages to the West.

■ The Colonial Experiments: Spanish explorers and missionaries explored the south in search of gold. The French found profitable fur and pelt trade in Canada and the Mississippi and Ohio River valleys.

■ The Puritans of New England: Plymouth and Massachusetts Bay Colony were Puritan settlements.

■ The Quakers of the Mid-Atlantic Peace-loving and opposed to war, the Quakers settled in Pennsylvania.

■ English in the Chesapeake: Tobacco became a cash crop for plantation owners in the Chesapeake region.

■ The Slave Trade: Rum was exported to Africa where shipments of slaves were gathered to sell to southern plantations.

■ Economic Development: Seaport communities had a social hierarchy involved in exporting and importing products that benefitted economic growth.

■ Social Development and Conflict: England's attitude toward colonists led to dissension.

■ The Albany Congress: A union plan adopted by the Albany Congress served as a basis for plans for the new American government.

■ The Enlightenment: Concepts of government from European philosophers served as the philosophical basis for the Declaration of Independence and the U.S. Constitution.

RESOURCES

Anti-Slavery International, Recovered Histories. (n.d.). The middle passage. Retrieved from http://www.recoveredhistories.org/storiesmiddle.php#reading

Campbell, Donna M. (2010, March 21). Puritanism in New England. Retrieved from http://public.wsu.edu/~campbelld/amlit/purdef.htm

Chaney, T., Cohen, K., & Cotton, L. P. (2002, July 15). Jamestown: The Virginia Company of London. Retrieved from http://www.nps.gov/jame/historyculture/the-virginia-company-of-london.htm

Constitution Society. (n.d.). Albany Plan of Union (1754). Retrieved from http://www.constitution.org/bcp/albany.htm

Eastern Woodlands Indians. (n.d.). Retrieved from http://portfolio.educ.kent.edu/mcclellandr/zackthezipper/easternwoodland.htm

Grymes, C. A. (n.d.). Bacon's rebellion. Retrieved from http://virginiaplaces.org/military/bacon.html

Mayflower Compact. (2008). Retrieved from the Lillian Goldman Law Library, Avalon Project website: http://avalon.law.yale.edu/17th_century/mayflower.asp (Original work published 1620)

Miller, H. (n.d.). The lure of sotweed: Tobacco and Maryland history. Retrieved from http://www.stmaryscity.org/History/The%20Lure%20of%20Sotweed.html

National Humanities Institute. (1998). Jonathan Edwards: On the great awakening. Retrieved from http://www.nhinet.org/ccs/docs/awaken.htm

United Nations Educational, Scientific, and Cultural Organization. (n.d.). Cahokia Mounds state historic site. Retrieved from http://whc.unesco.org/en/list/198

Section 2
Becoming a Nation: 1754–1865

The French– Indian War

The United States has engaged in foreign wars throughout its history. Most recently, in the 2000s, the United States became involved in conflicts in Iraq and Afghanistan, two countries halfway around the world. These wars were enabled in part by advanced technology. Transport ships could carry troops across oceans. Fighter planes could fly great distances. Radios and computers allowed commanders to keep in touch with and control the movements of soldiers thousands of miles away.

You might think that fighting distant wars requires this advanced technology. But that is not the case. Nations have been fighting wars overseas for centuries. The French and Indian war of the mid-1700s was one such conflict. With no advanced communications, and with only wooden sailing ships for transportation, Great Britain and France engaged in a conflict extending to virtually every part of the globe. In fact, the battle between France and Great Britain was much more extensive than U.S. wars in Afghanistan and Iraq. The European powers fought each other not only in Europe, but also in Central America, West Africa, India, and the Philippines. They also clashed in North America. You will read about that North American conflict, called the French and Indian War, in this chapter.

BEGINNINGS

FRENCH AND INDIAN WAR The war between Great Britain and France in North America from 1754–1763. Various Native American nations, including the Iroquois Confederacy, also took sides. The war was part of a worldwide contest between Great Britain and France.

SEVEN YEARS' WAR A global war between Great Britain, France, and their allies between 1756 and 1763. The French and Indian War was part of this wider conflict.

The **French and Indian War** of 1754–1763 was one in a long series of conflicts between England and France that began in 1689 and extended through 1815. Before 1754, conflicts between France and England in North America were primarily fought in New England and Canada, sometimes involved Native Americans, and did not result in boundaries being changed. The French and Indian war escalated the conflict. It was the last war fought on the North American continent between England and France and the Native American allies of both—and was fought to gain control of North America. The war spread to Europe and was referred to as the **Seven Years' War**.

The conflict between Britain and France in North America involved both land and trade. France had explored and settled the areas along the St. Lawrence River in

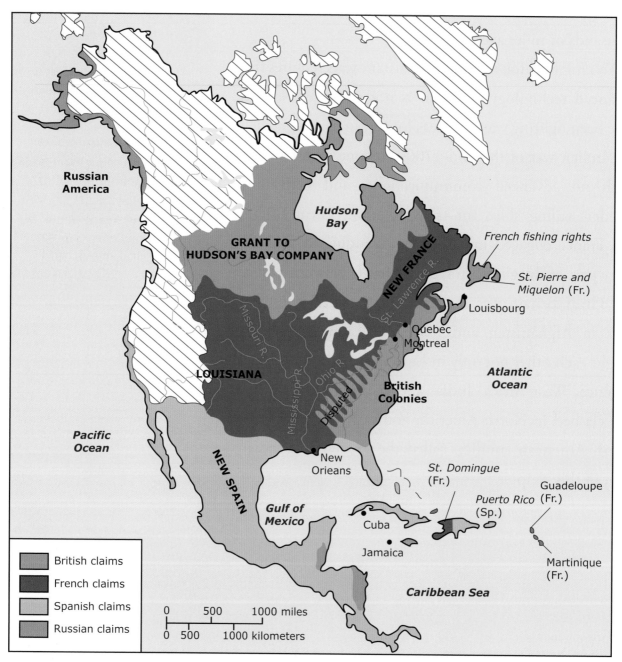

North America, 1750

Canada and had expanded its claims into the Mississippi River and Ohio River valleys. The French who moved into those areas were primarily traders and trappers, and they established small settlements and trading posts along the rivers and streams. They found that the fur trade was lucrative and that people living in Europe desired the quality beaver and other fur pelts that they obtained in the river valley areas under French control. The French traded with the Native Americans, married them, and established harmonious working relationships.

British colonists, in contrast, tended to establish permanent settlements—first along the Atlantic seaboard and then in the colonies' interior, referred to as "the frontier." As British colonists expanded their search for land and new settlements, they came into conflict with Native Americans and the French who claimed the land as theirs.

The Iroquois, a group of Native Americans living in the New York area, had formed a confederacy with several tribal groups. The **Iroquois Confederacy** traded with the British and Dutch colonists, destroyed settlements belonging to the Algonquians and Hurons who were allies of the French, and did not align with either the British or the French.

As British settlers moved into the lands of New France, they began trading with former French allies and with Native American tribes that had been under Iroquois control. In addition, a company formed for land speculation—the Ohio Company—was given a grant of 500,000 acres in the interior by the British king for the purpose of moving traders and settlers into the area.

Early in 1754, the governor of Virginia, a member of the **Ohio Company**, sent a 21-year-old surveyor, future President George Washington, to the interior to tell the French they should leave the area. In April of that year, Washington began construction of a fort where the Ohio, Monongahela, and Allegheny Rivers met, near present-day Pittsburgh, Pennsylvania. The fort, which had been a small British trading post established in the 1740s, was not completed before the French seized it and forced Washington and his men to retreat. The French completed the fort, naming it Fort Duquesne in honor of the French governor-general in North America.

Violence in the fur-rich area continued. Washington and his men built **Fort Necessity**. The French attacked and Washington surrendered. Washington and his troops were given permission to return to Virginia, unharmed, with the promise that the British would not construct any forts in the Ohio Valley for a one-year period. The British had expected an escalation of French military actions and urged the colonial leaders to establish an alliance with the Iroquois Confederacy, which by then had six member nations and was sometimes called the Six Nations. The meeting resulted in an adoption of the **Albany Plan of Union**, but the plan was not ratified by the colonial legislatures or Great Britain.

MANY DEFEATS

Washington's surrender of Fort Necessity in 1754 was the first major defeat of the war for the British colonists. England responded by sending **Edward Braddock** to command North American forces. Braddock's first goal was to capture **Fort Duquesne**, but he planned to surprise the French by attacking multiple French forts simultaneously.

In 1755, Braddock, accompanied by his aide George Washington, and more than 2,000 soldiers set out for Fort Duquesne. They travelled on the road Washington

IROQUOIS CONFEDERACY A confederacy among several Native American groups in the New York and upper North American colonial regions.

OHIO COMPANY A company formed for land speculation and settlement. It was granted land in the Ohio area by the British king.

FORT NECESSITY A fort built by George Washington that the French captured in an early defeat in the war for the British colonists.

ALBANY PLAN OF UNION An attempt to provide a more centralized government that represented both the colonies and Great Britain.

EDWARD BRADDOCK The English commander for Britain's North American forces after Washington surrendered Fort Necessity.

FORT DUQUESNE A French fort in present-day Pennsylvania. Braddock led the attack on Fort Duquesne personally.

HISTORY COMES ALIVE

In 1754, the Governor of Virginia sent George Washington and a group of Virginians to build a road from Virginia to the Monongahela River in Pennsylvania and to defend the newly constructed English fort there. When Washington arrived he learned the French were in control of the fort, named Fort Duquense.

Washington and his men made camp at Great Meadows, an area a few miles from the French fort, and attempted to contact a nearby encampment of French soldiers. A skirmish ensued, and Washington's men captured and killed most of the French. Washington then constructed a palisaded, circular fort at Great Meadows that he called Fort Necessity. In response, French soldiers marched to Fort Necessity and defeated Washington's troops in one of the first battles of the French and Indian War. Washington retreated, and the French burned Fort Necessity.

MONONGAHELA RIVER The river that joins with the Ohio River and Allegheny River near present-day Pittsburgh, Pennsylvania.

LOUIS-JOSEPH DE MONTCALM The French leader who fought against the British in the Battle of Quebec.

FORT WILLIAM HENRY A fort built on the northern shore of Lake Champlain by the British to counter the effects of Fort Carillon.

had cut through the wilderness the year before but widened it to accommodate the large equipment and greater number of soldiers they were moving to the fort. When Braddock and his men reached the **Monongahela River**, they were ambushed by the French, and Braddock was seriously injured. The British once again retreated. Braddock died a few days later near Fort Necessity.

The French continued their military successes. In 1756, under the leadership of **Marquis de Montcalm,** they attacked the northern New York area and captured a number of English trading posts and the English Fort Oswego. From Oswego, the French moved to Fort William Henry, located on Lake George in the present-day state of New York.

Fort William Henry had been built by the British to counter the effects of Fort Carillon—later named Ticonderoga—to the north on the shore of Lake Champlain. In March 1757, the French had attempted to take Fort William Henry, but had failed. In August, Montcalm and several thousand soldiers and Native American allies returned to the fort. The French contingency assaulted the fort, the British garrison surrendered, and the French agreed that those within the fort would march out with war honors, be safeguarded, and moved to another fort. Although Montcalm asked the Indians to honor the terms of surrender, they were eager to plunder, since this was their only form of payment for fighting. The Native Americans began murdering and plundering, ultimately killing between 100 and 200 people as the British attempted to leave the fort. Some of the British escaped, others were rescued by the French, and many were taken captive by the Native Americans. Many Native Americans died as a result of their actions because smallpox had been widespread within the fort at the time of surrender, and they became infected. The French victory at Fort William Henry was tarnished because of the massacre, and Montcalm later tore down and burned the wooden fort.

POLICY SHIFT

WILLIAM PITT England's prime minister in 1757 who provided more funds and military personnel to fight the French in the French and Indian War.

The British suffered devastating losses during the early years of the French and Indian War, but the tide of the war changed when **William Pitt** became England's prime minister in 1757. Pitt believed that additional funds and manpower were needed to defeat the French in Europe and North America. He also implemented a policy of not treating colonial officers as inferior to British officers and urged cooperation between British and provincial military. The cooperative endeavor

Fort Louisbourg on Cape Breton, Nova Scotia.

boosted the morale of the colonials and resulted in an increase in military enlistments in the colonies.

In 1758, Pitt sent a fleet to capture the **Fortress of Louisbourg**, a French stronghold on Cape Breton Island in Nova Scotia. The British troops were under a new command, and after a several-weeks battle, they captured the fort and its outposts. The victory at Fort Louisbourg was the first important victory for the British in the war.

Later in the year the British returned to **Fort Carrillon** near the present-day New York and Vermont border. The fort was strategic because it was located on a trade route on the southern shore of Lake Champlain near a portage between that lake and Lake George. Montcalm and his French troops prevailed against the British on their first attempt to capture the fort. The British retreated, regrouped, attacked the fort a second time, and captured it in 1759. The fort was renamed "**Ticonderoga**," an Iroquois name meaning "junction of two waterways."

In August 1758, British troops crossed Lake Ontario to attack Fort Frontenac at the lake's northwestern end, where the present-day city of Toronto is located. The fort was an important communication and supply link to New York, Quebec, and the Ohio Valley. It was captured easily.

The British still needed to capture Fort Duquesne in order to control the river access to the Ohio Valley. In September 1758, they attacked the fort but were repulsed by the French. Facing the prospect of the impending harsh winter weather, the British considered the option of waiting to attack the fort until spring. When they received information that the French holding the fort were in a weakened position, the British decided to continue their attack, and the French abandoned the fort in late November. The British rebuilt the fort, naming it in honor of William Pitt.

The devastating losses suffered by the British in the early stages of the war had been stemmed, and the tide of war changed in favor of the British during the battles in 1758.

FORTRESS OF LOUISBOURG
A French stronghold on Cape Breton Island in Nova Scotia that was captured by the British. The victory was the first important victory for the British in the war.

FORT CARRILLON A French fort near the present-day New York and Vermont border and on the southern shore of Lake Champlain.

FORT TICONDEROGA The former French Fort Carrillon.

MID-CHAPTER QUESTIONS

1. Describe the events leading up to the French and Indian War. Include in your discussion the events occurring in Europe and North America that caused the outbreak of hostilities. Identify involvement of the colonists in the war and explain why the war was one in a series of wars being fought by the British.

2. Discuss the early campaigns of the French and Indian War. Identify the problems encountered by the British and the reasons for their defeats. Explain the significance of the British losses and the French victories.

3. Explain how governmental policy shifts affected the approach to war. Describe the changes Pitt made and the reasons for the changes. Discuss the British campaign in North America after the changes in policy. Identify important British victories in 1758 and 1759; explain their significance; and describe how the victories affected the remainder of the war.

VICTORY

During the last phase of the French and Indian War, the British defeated the French at Forts Niagara, Quebec, and Montreal to gain control of the lands that France controlled in North America. **Fort Niagara**, located on Lake Ontario at the mouth of the Niagara River, was an important entry for fur trading in the Ohio Valley. The fort had been constructed by the French in the early 1700s. It had been enlarged after the initial battles in the French and Indian War, and had become one of the strongest fortifications in North America. In 1759 the British attacked the fort and the French surrendered, giving control of Lake Ontario to the British and limiting access to the forts in Quebec and Montreal.

Quebec was situated on the north side of the St. Lawrence River at the top of steep cliffs. The French general, Montcalm, expected the British to attack Quebec but believed the attack would come from Lake Ontario in the west or Lake Champlain in the south. Instead, the British general, General **James Wolfe**, who had been one of the commanders at Fort Louisbourg, brought his army down the St. Lawrence River. To gain access to the city, the British scaled the cliffs and brought several thousand soldiers onto the **Plains of Abraham**, a flat area outside the city walls, where the two nations met in battle. The British attack in the summer of 1759 was successful, and the French retreated approximately one hour after the battle had begun. Both Montcalm and Wolfe died as a result of wounds they suffered in the battle.

Montreal was the last important French stronghold in North America. The city, situated on a high point of an island in the St. Lawrence River, was surrounded by British forces in September 1760. With the city's supply lines cut, the French surrendered without fighting.

The European campaigns also ended in 1760. In that year **George III** was crowned king of England, and he began directing his focus toward the American colonies rather than toward a war on the European continent.

The war, however, continued on for more than two years in India and the West Indies in the Caribbean. Spain entered the war in 1762, and the British responded by attacking Spanish possessions, including Manila in the Philippines and Havana, Cuba. Negotiations to conclude the war began late in 1762 and were finalized in 1763 with the signing of the **Treaty of Paris**.

POSTWAR ISSUES

The Treaty of Paris awarded England Canada, several Caribbean sugar islands, and all territory east of the Mississippi River, other than the city of New Orleans. It also guaranteed England navigation of the entire Mississippi. In exchange for Cuba and the Philippines, Spain ceded Florida to England, ending territorial conflict between Georgia and Florida. France was awarded Louisiana.

The French and Indian War caused further tension with Native Americans, many of whom believed (with good reason) that the English colonists wanted their land. After learning that the British would not give them annual gifts as the French had, **Pontiac**, an Ottawa chief, formed alliances with other Native American tribes

FORT NIAGARA A fort located on Lake Ontario at the mouth of the Niagara River that was an important entry for fur trading in the Ohio Valley.

QUEBEC The location of a Canadian battle where British general James Wolfe defeated Montcalm.

JAMES WOLFE The British commander who defeated the French at Quebec.

PLAINS OF ABRAHAM The location of the Battle of Quebec.

MONTREAL The last important French stronghold in North America. It surrendered to British forces 1760.

GEORGE III The king of England during the American colonial period.

TREATY OF PARIS The treaty concluding the Seven Years' War, also known as the French and Indian War.

PONTIAC An Ottawa chief who formed alliances with other Native American tribes to strike British forts, causing havoc and unrest in the Ohio Valley.

to strike British forts, causing havoc and unrest in the Ohio Valley. In response, the British government passed the Proclamation of 1763, which closed lands west of the Appalachian Mountains to settlement.

The colonists were outraged by the Proclamation of 1763. With the French gone, the colonists wanted the freedom to expand across the continent. Instead, England was deliberately limiting them while continuing to quarter troops in colonial homes.

In addition, the French and Indian War had left England with a massive debt. Since the war had been fought for North America, England thought it fair to pay for it by raising taxes on North American imports and exports. These taxes, along with the Proclamation of 1763, angered colonists and helped lead to the Revolutionary War.

END OF CHAPTER TAKE-AWAYS

■ Beginnings: The war was called the Seven Years' War in Europe and was one of a series of wars between England and France. The war in North America erupted because of the desire for land in the Mississippi and Ohio River valleys. The French wanted the land for fur trading and trapping. The English wanted the land for settlement and expansion of the colonies. The Native Americans wanted to retain the land as their own.

■ Many Defeats: The first years of the war saw defeats for the British. Battles at Forts Duquesne, Necessity, Oswego, and William Henry were won by the French.

■ Policy Shift: William Pitt became prime minister and allotted more funds and troops for the war effort in North America. Victories at Forts Louisbourg, Carrillon, and Duquesne in 1758 were significant victories for the British.

■ Victory: Victories at Fort Niagara, Quebec, and Montreal provided the British with dominance in North America. The Treaty of Paris was signed in 1763.

■ Postwar Issues: Native American unrest about the possibility of future settlement in the lands east of the Mississippi River led to the passage of the Proclamation of 1763 and England's rising debt led to new taxes for the colonists..

REFERENCES

Anderson, F. (2006). *The war that made America: A short history of the French and Indian War*. New York, NY: Penguin.

Blum, J., McFeely, W., Morgan, E., Schelsinger, A., & Stampp, K. (1993). *The national experience: A history of the United States*. (8th ed.) Boston: Wadsworth.

Borneman, W. R. (2007). *The French and Indian War: Deciding the fate of North America*. New York, NY: Harper.

National Park Service. (n.d.). Fort Necessity National Battlefield: The Braddock campaign. Retrieved from http://www.nps.gov/fone/braddock.htm

Ohio History Central. (2005, July 1). Fort Duquesne. Retrieved from http://www.ohiohistorycentral.org/entry.php?rec=705

Ohio History Central. (2005, July 1). French and Indian War. Retrieved from http://www.ohiohistorycentral.org/entry.php?rec=498

Ohio History Central. (2005, July 1). Proclamation of 1763. Retrieved from http://www.ohiohistorycentral.org/entry.php?rec=1443

DID YOU KNOW?

The origins of the tune *Yankee Doodle* are unknown but the tune is believed to have been written by a British surgeon during the French and Indian War to ridicule the New Englander soldiers, whose appearance was in stark contrast to the British. The word "Yankee" referred to the colonists, and "doodle" defined a fool or simpleton. Feathers were worn by women in high European society, and it was believed that colonists, wearing their homespun clothing, wanted to appear elegant by sticking a feather in their tricorne or coonskin hats. The colonists adopted the song and sang it with pride when they defeated the British in the American Revolution.

STUDY ALERT

The Treaty of Paris gave England the area of Canada, territory east of the Mississippi River, except the city of New Orleans, and several French sugar islands in the Caribbean. England was guaranteed navigation of the Mississippi River. Spain ceded Florida in exchange for the return of Cuba and the Philippines. France was awarded Louisiana.

Toward the War for U.S. Independence

Across the globe and throughout history people have participated in revolutions to resist or overturn the rulers of the day. This is exactly how the United States gained its independence at the end of the eighteenth century, and it is how nations even today oust corrupt or oppressive leaders. In 2011, people in Libya, a country in North Africa, revolted against their leader, Muammar Qaddafi, and his corrupt policies.

The underlying causes for each of history's revolutions are unique, but one cause is universal: people feel as though they are not being governed justly and that they have little say in the decisions of their government.

In the 1700s the North American British colonists began to experience just these feelings. The discontent mounted as George Grenville, Britain's prime minister, introduced a series of provocative laws that created economic hardships for the colonists. One of these was the Sugar Act, passed in 1764, which limited colonial trade markets and reduced colonial income. These conditions led colonists to feel that they did not have a just influence on the legislation that was governing their way of life.

COLONIAL RESISTANCE

By the mid- to late 1700s, the French and Indian War and funding for European allies left Britain in great debt. Britain sought to obtain repayment for these debts in part by increasing taxes on the colonists, which created undue financial hardships and demonstrated how powerless the colonists were in controlling their own fate.

Repeal of the Stamp Act

Two years after the conclusion of the French and Indian War, the British Parliament imposed a tax on the American colonies that required payment for the use of legal documents, diplomas, newspapers, and even playing cards. Every piece of printed paper was required to have a stamp on it, showing that tax was paid. The purpose of the **Stamp Act** was to help pay for the British troops who were stationed in the colonies for their defense. Those not paying the tax for the stamps were subject to prosecution. Although the tax was relatively small, colonists became enraged over the idea that Parliament believed it had the authority to directly tax them without their permission or approval, and the colonists were concerned that Parliament would continue to impose similar taxes in the future.

Resistance to the Stamp Act took various forms. Virginia's assembly, the House of Burgesses, enacted the Stamp Act Resolves, proposed by Patrick Henry. The Resolves stated that American colonists had the right to be taxed only by their representatives and that colonists living in Virginia should only pay taxes imposed by their legislature, the House of Burgesses. Virginia's governor vetoed the Resolves and dissolved the legislature. In Massachusetts, John Adams, a lawyer, wrote resolutions protesting Parliament's actions and several Massachusetts communities did the same. James Otis, a Boston lawyer, wrote a pamphlet that discussed reasons why the Stamp Act should be repealed. At the request of Otis, the Massachusetts legislature invited colonies to send delegates to New York City to discuss the taxes imposed by Parliament.

In October 1765, six months after the passage of the Stamp Act, delegates from nine colonies met to discuss their opposition to the tax at the **Stamp Act Congress**. The delegates submitted to the king and Parliament a declaration of rights that reaffirmed their loyalty to England, stated their opposition to being taxed by Parliament, stated their belief that the duties would be burdensome and impossible to pay, and requested the repeal of the duties.

Colonial merchants and traders responded by signing non-importation agreements. The Boston agreement of 1768 provided they would not send for or import any goods or merchandise from Great Britain for a one-year period except salt, coal, fish hooks and lines, wool-cards, duck, and hemp. The agreement also provided that they would not purchase common imports such as tea, glass, paper, or other goods.

Some colonies created committees, called **Committees of Correspondence** that actively provided opposition responses to Parliament after the passage of the Stamp Act. Riots and demonstrations by patriotic mobs provided the most dramatic impact. Once Parliament realized that the colonists' resistance to the Stamp Act could produce consequences that were detrimental to the commercial interests of Great Britain, it repealed the Stamp Act in 1766. While Britain repealed the Stamp Act, however, the **Declaratory Act** was passed, stating that Parliament could make future laws for the colonies as it saw fit. Many colonists viewed the repeal of the Stamp Act as a victory but also realized that the Declaratory Act signaled that future taxes were inevitable.

STAMP ACT An act of the British Parliament that taxed all legal documents, diplomas, newspapers, and playing cards and required a stamp placed on them to show that the tax had been paid.

STAMP ACT CONGRESS A colonial congress held in October 1765, at which delegates from nine colonies met to discuss their opposition to the Stamp Act.

COMMITTEES OF CORRESPONDENCE Committees established within the colonies to discuss the ramifications of the Sugar Act.

DECLARATORY ACT An act of Parliament that declared Parliament had authority to make laws for the colonies in all matters.

STUDY ALERT

The Stamp Act was a direct tax imposed on the colonies to raise money. The tax was relatively small but colonists became enraged over the idea that Parliament believed it had the authority to tax them without their permission, and the colonists were concerned that Parliament would continue to impose taxes.

Townshend Acts

In 1767, Parliament passed another revenue tax that would raise money to support Great Britain's defense and protection of the colonies. The act was named for Charles Townshend, Chancellor of the Exchequer, who proposed the acts after submitting a budget to Parliament, showing the need for new duties. The act placed duties on lead, glass, paper, and tea—products that the colonies imported—and controlled the finances of the colonies. The acts also provided that customs officials would be paid from the funds and by the British government, not the colonies.

Opposition to the **Townshend Acts** was not instantaneous, as opposition to the Stamp Act had been, but it was eventually widespread. John Dickinson, a Pennsylvania lawyer and member of the colonial legislature, wrote a series of anonymous essays entitled *Letters from a Farmer in Pennsylvania* in which he objected to the taxes and argued the taxes were illegal. The letters circulated throughout the colonies, gaining support for opposition to the Townshend Acts. The Massachusetts legislature sent a petition to Parliament, requesting a repeal. Other colonial legislatures also requested relief, but Parliament refused to consider the petitions, even dissolving the Massachusetts legislature because of its request. Colonial opposition became widespread, and in the fall of 1768, British troops began arriving in Boston.

Charles Townshend died in September 1767, and Lord North became Great Britain's minister of finance. British manufacturers were feeling the effects of the non-importation agreements and the resulting decline in trade with the colonists. In 1770, Parliament acquiesced to the demands of the manufacturers and repealed all of the Townshend Acts except the tax on tea.

International Sons of Liberty

The **Sons of Liberty** were societies formed in the colonies during the summer of 1765 after the passage of the Stamp Act to resist Parliament's actions regulating colonial affairs. These patriotic groups conducted demonstrations and led rebellious activities, such as tarring and feathering public officials. Their riots led to the eventual repeal of the Stamp Act. There were many groups in almost every colony that collectively referred to themselves as the Sons of Liberty. The term became a general term for a variety of public demonstrations, both organized and impromptu. One key element of the efforts of these groups was the use of the press. Many members of the Sons of Liberty were publishers and used pamphlets to distribute their agendas.

Although membership in the Sons of Liberty was considered secret, a list has been compiled that identifies numerous members. The list includes many colonial leaders, some who would eventually become the founding fathers of the United States. John Adams, Paul Revere, John Hancock, Patrick Henry, and Samuel Adams are believed to have been members.

The Boston Massacre

British troops arrived in Boston in 1768 to enforce the Townshend Acts. Tension between the troops and colonists rose to the point that a street fight erupted in 1770 in which a patriot mob began throwing snowballs, sticks, stones, and other

TOWNSHEND ACTS Parliamentary acts named for Charles Townshend, Chancellor of the Exchequer, that placed duties on lead, glass, paper, and tea—products that the colonies imported—and controlled the finances of the colonies.

SONS OF LIBERTY Societies formed in the colonies during the summer of 1765 after the passage of the Stamp Act to resist Parliament's actions that regulated colonial affairs.

items at the British troops. The British troops fired into the crowd and five colonists were killed. Two soldiers were found guilty of manslaughter but the captain was acquitted.

A newspaper account of the incident portrayed the young colonists as "unarmed boys" and "lads" and described the soldiers as having clubs and bayonets. The newspaper article described the deaths of the five men in detail and identified those who were wounded. One of the dead was Crispus Attucks, a black man, who became the first victim of the American Revolution. The **Boston Massacre** occurred on the day Parliament was asked to repeal the Townshend Acts.

Following the tragedy, the fervor of colonial discontent continued to rise. In some colonies individual colonists and patriotic groups tarred and feathered British officials. They hung and burned effigies of unpopular British officials in protest. One protest that took place in Boston in 1773 is remembered as the **Boston Tea Party** because colonists disguised themselves as Native Americans, boarded a ship, and dumped its cargo of tea into the harbor after Parliament enacted a bill to charge a tax on all tea brought into the colonies. The Sons of Liberty played a key role in this event.

BOSTON MASSACRE A confrontation between colonists and British troops who were stationed in Boston for the purpose of enforcing the Townshend Acts.

BOSTON TEA PARTY A protest by colonists who disguised themselves as Native Americans, boarded a ship, and dumped its cargo of tea into the harbor after Parliament had enacted a bill to charge a tax on all tea brought into the colonies.

Crispus Attucks at the Boston Massacre

HISTORY COMES ALIVE

Tarring and feathering was a form of medieval brutality dating from the time of the Crusades that patriot mobs used, or threatened to use, in the American colonies against **Loyalists**. British officials identified colonists who supported the king rather than the independence movement as *Loyalists*. The colonists referred to individuals who supported the English as **Tories**. Tarring and feathering was a popular method of showing opposition to the Stamp Act and the officials who had been sent to the colonies to enforce it. It was first used in colonial seaports in the 1760s. After the Townshend Acts were passed, the practice increased, and was used again when the colonists expressed opposition to the Tea Act and the tax on tea. Tar, which needed to be very hot when it was applied, was available from shipyards. Feathers, which were thrown onto the tar, could easily be found in pillows in any colonial home.

LOYALISTS British name for those who supported the British against the colonists. The colonists referred to the Loyalists as Tories.

TORIES Colonial name for those who supported the British against the colonists. Tories were identified as Loyalists by the British.

1. How did the colonists respond to the Stamp Act? In your answer, consider the actions of the British and the effects that these actions had on the colonies. Why was this new legislation so provocative in the colonies?

2. What were the Townshend Acts? Explain the purposes of the acts and describe the results of the passage of the acts.

3. What were the events surrounding the Boston Massacre and why did it play such a significant role in the build-up toward the American Revolution?

4. Why did the demonstrations of the Sons of Liberty and acts such as the Boston Tea Party become increasingly confrontational and sometimes violent?

THE FIRST CONTINENTAL CONGRESS

After the Boston Tea Party, Great Britain demanded payment for the tea spilled into the harbor—the Bostonians refused. To punish the colonists, Parliament passed a series of acts. One prohibited British officials from being tried in colonial courts for crimes occurring in the colonies. Another act ended self-government in Boston and gave the British governor authority over all Boston town meetings. The Quebec Act of 1774 extended Canadian borders, cutting the boundaries of Connecticut, Massachusetts, and Virginia and allowing Canadians to remain Catholic. Protestant colonists feared the act would allow French Canadians to extend their religion into colonial areas. Before the Tea Party, Parliament enacted the Quartering Act, which required Bostonians to quarter British troops.

After the Tea Party, Parliament also enacted the Boston Port Act, closing Boston's port to all ships except British. English troops were sent to Boston to block the harbor from incoming goods. The acts were referred to as the **Intolerable Acts** by the colonists and Coercive Acts by the British and were the basis of correspondence among the colonies by Committees of Correspondence that urged the colonists to stop trading with England.

Colonies sent delegates to meet in a continental congress to discuss trade boycotts. In September 1774, all colonies except Georgia sent delegates to Philadelphia for the **First Continental Congress**. John and Samuel Adams from Massachusetts, Joseph Galloway and John Dickinson from Pennsylvania, and Richard Henry Lee, George Washington, Patrick Henry, and Benjamin Harrison from Virginia were among the delegates.

Delegates did not advocate independence. They wanted instead to have the king and Parliament correct the wrongs committed against the colonies. Joseph Galloway presented a Plan

INTOLERABLE ACTS Parliamentary acts that required Bostonians to quarter British troops, closed the port of Boston to all ships except British, and sent English troops to Boston to block the harbor from incoming goods. The acts were referred to as the Intolerable Acts by the colonists and Coercive Acts by the British.

FIRST CONTINENTAL CONGRESS Colonial meeting in 1774 to discuss trade boycotts.

of Union in which a Grand Council would represent colonial views. Galloway's plan also provided for a president general who would be appointed by the King to represent English authority in the colonies. The plan was introduced in a conciliatory manner, stating to the King that the colonists were asking for a redress of grievances and assuring the King that the colonists were faithful servants. **Galloway's Plan of Union** also signaled that the colonists wanted a political union with England.

Although the Galloway Plan was well-received by many delegates, it was unacceptable to the majority of the colonies. Representatives of the colonies passed resolutions against the plan at meetings in and around the city of Boston and in Suffolk County, Massachusetts. These resolutions, which were sent to the First Continental Congress, became known as the Suffolk Resolves.

The **Suffolk Resolves** declared the Intolerable Acts unconstitutional and requested officials implementing the acts to resign. The Resolves suggested that Massachusetts become a free state until the repeal of the acts and recommended the Massachusetts government keep tax collections rather than giving them to British officials. The Suffolk Resolves urged the colonists to **boycott** English goods, establish a militia, and begin preparing for war. One of the strongest resolutions passed unanimously by the Suffolk delegates was the statement that a king's subjects no longer owe loyalty to a king who violates their rights.

The Galloway Plan was not adopted, and the Suffolk Resolves were debated by the delegates at the First Continental Congress. Although some delegates believed the ideas set forth in the Resolves were radical and had the possibility of resulting in a war between the colonies and Great Britain, the delegates adopted the Resolves. Because the delegates had agreed to boycott trade with England, they established the Continental Association to enforce the boycott. The boycott included non-importation of English goods, non-exportation of goods to England, and the non-consumption or use of English goods.

The delegates prepared a **Declaration of Rights and Grievances** to send to King George III. The declaration objected to the taxes imposed on the colonies by Parliament, the unconstitutional powers of commissioners, the requirement that some trials of colonists take place in England, the closing of Boston's harbor, the passage of the Quebec Act, the dissolving of legislatures, and the limitations placed on Massachusetts government. The Declaration of Rights and Grievances identified the rights the colonists believed they were entitled to. Among the rights listed were the entitlement of life, liberty, and property; all of the rights and liberties of their ancestors who were born in or had emigrated to the colonies; the right to participate in government and be properly represented in Parliament; their right to benefit from the privileges of the common law and British statutory law in effect at the time of North American colonization; the right to peaceably assemble; and the right not to have a British standing army in the colonies. The declaration asked for the restoration of the colonists' inalienable rights and that the infringements and violations of rights be repealed to restore harmony between the colonists and the British government.

The congress agreed to meet again in the spring of 1775 if their grievances had not been properly addressed.

GALLOWAY'S PLAN OF UNION A plan presented to the British to create a North American colonial government in which the colonists would have more of a voice in the government while continuing a political union with Britain.

SUFFOLK RESOLVES Declaration that the Intolerable Acts were unconstitutional and that officials who were implementing the acts resign from office.

BOYCOTT The refusal to buy, sell, or use British products.

DECLARATION OF RIGHTS AND GRIEVANCES A declaration sent to King George III by the delegates to the First Continental Congress objecting to the taxes imposed on the colonies by Parliament, the unconstitutional powers of commissioners, the requirement that some trials of colonists take place in England, the closing of Boston's harbor, the passage of the Quebec Act, the dissolving of legislatures, and the limitations placed on Massachusetts government.

END OF CHAPTER TAKE-AWAYS

■ **Colonial Resistance:** Resistance to Parliament's actions began after the passage of the Stamp Act, in various forms. Some colonies passed resolutions stating the belief that the colonists could only be taxed by their representatives. Colonial leaders wrote pamphlets about the unconstitutionality of the taxes, and some colonists rioted. Merchants decided to boycott English trade, and delegates from several colonies met in congress to urge the repeal of the act. As more restrictions were placed on the colonists in the form of the Townshend Acts, colonial resistance became stronger. Secret societies, called the Sons of Liberty, were formed and protests became an important form of resistance. One protest was the Boston Tea Party, a protest on the tea tax. Tension in Boston continued, and in 1770 five colonists were killed in the Boston Massacre.

■ **The First Continental Congress:** Delegates from all colonies except Georgia met to discuss grievances and create a plan to work in cooperation with England. After the Suffolk Resolves were received by the congress, the delegates compiled a list of grievances and rights to send to the English king, and they agreed to meet later if there was no response.

DID YOU KNOW?

Thomas Paine wrote, "These are the times that try men's souls" in *The Crisis,* a series of essays published in the *Pennsylvania Journal* during the American Revolution. Paine emigrated to the American colonies from England in 1774 with the help of Benjamin Franklin. *The Crisis* explained why the American colonies should be independent and inspired the colonial troops. As a journalist, Paine aroused emotions in his famous works—*Common Sense, The Age of Reason,* and *The Rights of Man.* However, his religious views led him to a lonely life steeped in poverty and he was plagued by debt collectors.

REFERENCES

Allison, R. (2011). *The American Revolution: A concise history.* New York, NY: Oxford University Press.

Massachusetts Historical Society. (2001). The Sons of Liberty. Retrieved from http://www.masshist.org/objects/cabinet/august2001/august2001.html

Raphael, R. (2002). *A people's history of the American Revolution: How common people shaped the fight for independence.* New York, NY: Harper Perennial.

The Sugar Act of 1764. (2008). Retrieved from http://ahp.gatech.edu/sugar_act_bp_1764.html

Warren, J. (2009). *The Suffolk resolves.* Retrieved from http://ahp.gatech.edu/suffolk_resolves_1774.html (Original work published 1774)

Wood, G. (2003). *The American Revolution: A history.* New York, NY: Modern Library.

The way people share information is constantly changing. Cable news networks broadcast throughout the day, journalists spread stories through Twitter, and people share information on social networks with their friends. All of these methods of communication make geographical distance no obstacle for keeping up-to-date with the rest of the world.

This was not always the case, however. In earlier times, information travelled slowly; the speed with which people could transmit information represented power. During the American Revolution, colonists relied on newspapers that were delivered on horseback to spread information throughout the colonies. The information in these newspapers allowed groups to come together in their strategy to resist the British. These groups, called committees of correspondence, were set up by local governments to exchange ideas for defending their rights as colonists. This network of communication helped the colonists mount an effective resistance against the British army.

TWO ARMIES AND THEIR STRATEGIES

The American Revolution was the longest war ever fought on American soil. Since it involved the rebellion of British subjects, it was in some respects a civil war. The war was sustained by a uniquely democratic and popular movement, fostered by the free press and the committees of correspondence. Approximately 20 percent of the North American colonists were loyal to the British, but most colonists made efforts to remain neutral. Although some Loyalists shifted allegiances, only about 60 percent of the Loyalists were firm supporters of the revolution. Throughout the war, the British made strategic use of Loyalist support in the colonies.

At the beginning of the revolution, the colonies did not consider themselves an independent country. Many patriots did not consider their fighting of stationed troops to constitute a rebellion against the crown, and large numbers of colonists believed some of the battles were simply overzealous flare-ups of minority factions.

The British goal throughout the revolution was to terminate the colonists' thrust for independence. The colonists' goal was to force the British to withdraw from the colonies.

At the beginning of the war, the ragtag colonist army was hardly comparable to the British Redcoats. The British were professional soldiers—well dressed and well trained. Britain also had a well-equipped and powerful navy. Colonial soldiers, in contrast, were mostly farmers, tradesmen, and other citizens, not trained fighters. Each of the colonies formed a militia, and together the colonies created the **Continental Army**, under the leadership of George Washington. Colonial soldiers used the terrain to their advantage during battles, but the British had better weapons and fought with precision. Colonial soldiers lacked training and discipline and used American hunting rifles that were not designed for warfare. However, the Americans sometimes used their lack of formal military training to their advantage by employing guerrilla tactics, such as fighting small skirmishes and quickly escaping into the woods.

The British increased their advantages by hiring professional German soldiers as mercenaries. Nearly 30,000 German soldiers, called **Hessians** after the name of their German home state, fought alonside the British.

The Continental Army also received German support, however, due to a relationship between colonist Benjamin Franklin and Prussian officer **Baron von Steuben**. During the harsh winter of 1777–1778, when the Continental Army was encamped at **Valley Forge**, near Philadelphia, von Steuben introduced the soldiers to Prussian tactics and military organization. Von Steuben helped create a more organized army, developed a training program for the soldiers, and established a program for camp sanitation. As the war progressed, the Continental Army became a more efficient and more European-like military, partly as the result of Von Steuben's efforts.

After several major battles, colonial leaders also enlisted the support of the French. The French and British had long been military enemies in Europe, and the French saw the American Revolutionary War as a way to challenge British forces. The French provided money and most of the European muskets, bayonets, and cannons that were used by Washington's army. A wealthy young marquis who was a member of the French Royal Army learned of the colonial struggle for independence

CONTINENTAL ARMY The colonial army commanded by George Washington.

HESSIANS German soldiers who were paid to fight for the British.

VON STEUBEN A Prussian army officer who helped create a more organized army, developed a training program for the soldiers, and established a program for camp sanitation.

VALLEY FORGE Winter camp for the Continental Army in 1777–1778.

and decided to volunteer on their side. The Marquis de Lafayette and other French officers sailed to the colonies, arriving in the summer of 1777. The Continental Congress commissioned Lafayette a major general. In 1780, Lafayette convinced the French government to send French troops and supplies to help Washington's army.

The Press and Women

Two other significant forces in the Revolutionary War were women and the press. Newspapers, printed on hand-operated presses, provided news about the war to all thirteen colonies. Dispatchers on horseback distributed the papers. The printers who received copies of newspapers then reprinted the news to share with colonists in that specific geographic area. This helped unify the colonial forces and kept the colonies apprised of the events of the Revolution.

Colonial women helped the war effort by producing goods for the soldiers, acting as spies, fighting in the war, and helping cook and clean in the soldiers' camps. Catherine Moore Barry, a South Carolinian, assisted the Continental Army by contacting men to join in battle and lay a trap for British general Cornwallis and his troops. Barry's actions helped the Continental Army force Cornwallis to retreat. Margaret Corbin followed her husband into battle in New York, and was seriously injured in the battle in which her husband was killed. Women in Philadelphia formed an association and made warm shirts for the colonial soldiers.

Early Skirmishes

The first phase of the American Revolution began in April 1775 in Massachusetts, before the colonists had officially declared independence. The British viewed the early confrontations as acts of insurgency rather than war, and they attempted to suppress the rebellious colonists. The colonial militia, outnumbered by the British, adopted a strategy that was primarily defensive. Early on, the British attempted to subdue the colonists near Concord because they believed colonial leaders were located there and that the Massachusetts militia was storing arms in the area. The British marched into Lexington and exchanged shots with the colonists on the village green. Colonial soldiers retreated and the British marched on to Concord, where they encountered more Massachusetts militia. The British did not find the colonial leaders because the leaders had been warned of the pending British attack and had left before they arrived.

After the battle at Concord, colonial soldiers returned to Boston and began a yearlong siege of the city to remove it from British control. In order to obtain military equipment for the Boston siege, in May 1775, Ethan Allen, the commander of the Vermont Green Mountain Boys, and **Benedict Arnold**, the future American traitor, attacked and captured cannons at Fort Ticonderoga, located on Lake Champlain. A month later, the first major battle of the American Revolution took place in Boston. The battle is called the battle of **Bunker Hill**.

The colonials believed that the British were going to occupy the Charlestown Peninsula, and on the night of June 16, 1775, Colonel William Prescott and a group of Massachusetts militia began fortifying one of the hills on the peninsula. The next morning, the British, under the command of **General William Howe**, began a drive to capture the hill. Twice the colonial soldiers repulsed the British, but on

CHARLES, LORD CORNWALLIS The British commander who was eventually defeated at Yorktown.

BENEDICT ARNOLD Commander at West Point and effective colonial leader who eventually defected and became a British spy.

BUNKER HILL The first major battle in the American Revolution.

WILLIAM HOWE The British general who commanded the king's troops for the first part of the Revolutionary War, including the attack on New York City.

the third attempt, the British captured the hill. Although the colonials lost control of the hill, they gained confidence in their ability to fight and defeat the British. Prescott lost few men. The British, although victorious, sustained heavy losses. More than 200 British soldiers were killed and more than 800 were wounded. In March 1776, the colonists captured the area overlooking Boston Harbor and the British evacuated the city.

THE SECOND CONTINENTAL CONGRESS

The month following the battles of Lexington and Concord, the Second Continental Congress convened in Philadelphia. While the First Continental Congress had gathered to discuss grievances with Britain, the Second Continental Congress met to decide how to deal with the British actions toward the colonies. The Second Continental Congress acted as government for the colonies—raising armies and making treaties. Thomas Jefferson, a Virginia planter and lawyer; Benjamin Franklin, a Pennsylvanian; and John Hancock, a delegate from Massachusetts, were among the 65 delegates attending the Second Continental Congress.

Most delegates were not in favor of independence and the congress sent a direct appeal to King George III to resolve the situation peacefully. The **Olive Branch Petition**, in addition to requesting a peaceful resolution, declared the loyalty of the colonists to Britain. The king, however, refused the petition.

The congress agreed to establish a continental army to defend against the British threat, and in June 1776 they commissioned George Washington, a Virginian, commander of the forces. To pay for the military supplies, the congress voted to authorize the printing of money. As hostilities with British soldiers escalated, the call for independence started to crescendo. Not all delegates, however, were authorized to vote for independence without first obtaining the approval from their colonies. In early June, **Richard Henry Lee**, a Virginia delegate, presented a resolution to declare independence from Great Britain and to plan a confederation.

A committee began working on a draft of the document in which the congress would declare the colonies' independence from Great Britain. Members of the committee included Thomas Jefferson, Benjamin Franklin, Roger Sherman of Connecticut, Robert Livingston of New York, and John Adams of Massachusetts.

OLIVE BRANCH PETITION An appeal sent from the delegates of the Second Continental Congress to King George III to end the differences between the colonies and the mother country peacefully.

RICHARD HENRY LEE A Virginia delegate to the Second Continental Congress who proposed the colonists become independent from Great Britain.

The Declaration

The drafters of the **Declaration of Independence** explained in the preamble of the document that decency required an explanation why it was necessary to dissolve political ties. Before listing the reasons, the drafters explained why they believed the long list of abuses and patient suffering of the colonists needed to result in the altering or abolishing the British-led government and the establishment of a new government. The colonists claimed that governments are created to protect the rights of individuals and that the current government in the colonies—the British king—failed to protect the colonists' rights to life, liberty, and the pursuit of happiness. The drafters of the Declaration of Independence went on to identify the specific grievances they had with the British monarch, George III.

DECLARATION OF INDEPENDENCE The colonists' declaration that they intended to be free and independent from Great Britain.

- Colonial governors could not pass laws for the benefit of the colonies without the approval of the king.
- Laws that affected the colonists were made far from the colonies and colonial records.

- The colonial legislatures had been dissolved.
- The British government kept standing armies in the colonies during peace without the consent of the colonial legislatures.
- Colonists were required to house British troops.
- The British government had shut off trade between the colonies and other countries.
- Parliament imposed taxes on the colonists without the colonists' consent.
- The colonists were deprived of the right to trial by jury.

At the end of the Declaration, the colonists reiterated that they believed they had asked Britain to resolve these and other grievances but that their requests had been denied. They stated that even more unacceptable practices had been put into place by the British government. The drafters referred to the king as a *tyrant* and charged that this type of person was not a suitable ruler.

With this document, the colonists declared independence from Britain, which the colonists knew was going to anger the British king. The Declaration ends with a commitment to pledge life, fortune, and sacred honor to protect the values described in the document.

The delegates then faced the problem of creating a government for the newly formed union. They adopted the Articles of Confederation, which served as the new nation's first constitution. Because of their fear of an overpowering government similar to the one from which they had just dissolved ties, the Articles of Confederation gave most power to the states. This document served as the nation's constitution until 1789, when the US Constitution replaced it.

FIGHTING IN THE NORTH

The second phase of the Revolution lasted from summer 1776 to October 1777. After retreating from Massachusetts, British commander Howe arrived in New York harbor with soldiers, sailors, battleships, supply ships, and cannons to invade New York. They quickly defeated the colonial army and gained control of the city and port. At the end of August, General Washington's soldiers were badly defeated by the British at the Battle of Long Island. The British pressed Washington's troops through New Jersey, substantially damaging his forces along the way. During the winter months, major fighting slowed and Washington decided to retreat to set up a winter headquarters at Morristown, New Jersey. Charles, Lord Cornwallis, commander of British troops, continued the pursuit.

Reversing the strategy of retreat, George Washington advanced his troops toward Trenton, New Jersey in the early hours of December 26, 1776. The colonial army surprised the Hessians stationed there, and Washington's troops took control of Trenton. They moved on to Princeton, and by January 3, 1777, the British had, for the most part, been driven from New Jersey. The Americans were encouraged, and morale improved. About this time the French began providing war supplies for the Americans.

Philadelphia

After the success in New York, General Howe prepared to capture Philadelphia, the capital of the newly declared independent United States. In the summer of 1777, he left New York and sailed toward the Chesapeake Bay. Washington was

Valley Forge.

prepared for the attack and had several thousand men positioned to defend the capital. On September 11, 1777, Washington's troops met Howe's troops west of Philadelphia on the shores of the Brandywine River.

The British and Americans faced each other from across the river, but Howe waited to attack until some of his troops forded the river upstream and flanked Washington's troops. The tactic worked, and Washington's forces were defeated. It was not a rout, however; Howe failed to deliver a fatal blow.

Fortunately, the colonial government had time to move to York, Pennsylvania, before the British arrived. The colonists moved military supplies from the city as well, and when Lord Cornwallis and the British soldiers arrived in Philadelphia on September 26, 1777, they found a peaceful city with little sign of the colonial government or army.

Washington was eager to retake Philadelphia and engaged in battle with the British at Germantown, five miles north of Philadelphia. He hoped to surprise the British and Hessians, as his troops had done at Trenton, by attacking unexpectedly at dawn, but the troops were not close enough to their targets early in the morning to benefit from the element of surprise, and a thick, heavy fog covered the battlefield during the day.

The Loyalist support of Howe and the British was starting to wane at this point. Colonists with money resented having to house British soldiers and those without money were forced to compete over reduced supplies of goods. These inconveniences made more and more colonists support independence.

After the American defeat in Philadelphia in the Battle of Brandywine, Washington moved his troops to **Valley Forge**, 20 miles northwest of Philadelphia, for the winter. Washington's army spent the harsh winter of 1778 there and endured the winter of 1779 in New Jersey. In 1780, Benedict Arnold was appointed commander at West Point, but it was later discovered he intended to surrender West Point to the British. Arnold fled, became a member of the British army, and was named brigadier general.

Saratoga

Approximately one week after the Battle of Brandywine, British commander John Burgoyne led troops south from Canada to engage the Continentals with an entire army.

The two sides met near Saratoga, New York. On September 19, 1777, Burgoyne's forces clashed with large numbers of New England militiamen led by Horatio Gates. The British prevailed, but each army lost between 500 and 600 men. Despite the losses, the Americans' spirits were buoyed because they had not been routed. During the next few weeks, some of Burgoyne's soldiers deserted while American troops were replenished.

Thaddeus Kosciusko, a Polish engineer who had been commissioned by the Continental Congress to fortify American battle sites, planned the

HISTORY COMES ALIVE

Colonists used many flags before and during the American Revolution to show patriotism and strength. For example, militias used flags to identify their group or regiment. Early in the revolution, Boston patriots hung a red and white striped flag over the Liberty Tree and called it the *liberty flag*. The South Carolina navy's flag contained a yellow field with a rattlesnake coiled, poised to strike, with a motto that read, "Don't tread on me." This was either a symbol of vigilance or a warning. Rhode Island's flag had white stars in a field of blue, and some consider this flag's design the basis for the country's first flag. The Continental Army used more than one flag, preferring regimental flags to a single army flag, but it did use a flag with stars and stripes that contained a circle of thirteen stars on a field of blue.

defense for the battle of Saratoga. The Americans captured military supplies and sent troops to the Hudson River to prevent the British from retreating across the river. Burgoyne began retreating but eventually decided to discuss surrender. He and Gates agreed that Burgoyne's men would be taken to Boston and permitted to return to Britain if they agreed not to fight again in North America.

The victory for the Americans at **Saratoga** was a major turning point in the American Revolution. After Burgoyne's surrender, France decided to provide military assistance and enter the war as an ally of the Americans. Americans' hopes for independence grew, and the French assistance helped stem the British drive at Yorktown.

SARATOGA A battle that was the turning point of the American Revolution.

MID-CHAPTER QUESTIONS

1. The two sides of the Revolutionary War were different in many ways. What were the principal differences between the British and the American sides? How did these differences lead to unique advantages and disadvantages during the fighting?

2. While the Revolutionary War was principally fought between the British and the colonists, what other world powers were involved? How did this global involvement affect the outcome of the war?

3. What was the intention behind the Declaration of Independence? What were the major reasons the colonists felt the need to separate themselves from the British king?

4. How were women involved in the war? How did newspapers affect the outcome of the fighting?

THE WAR IN THE SOUTH

The British changed tack and decided that it made more sense for them to win the South and work their way north from there. The South was closer to other British colonies in the Caribbean and it also supplied valuable resources. British

Loyalists living in the North Carolina in 1776 attempted to stamp out the rebellion in the South and secure the area for England. They began a march to the sea to join with the British naval forces but they met, and were defeated by, the Continental Army before they reached the sea. When the British navy reached Charleston, they also encountered resistance and were defeated.

After the two battles in the Carolinas, the British moved north. On May 1, 1778, Henry Clinton became commander of the British forces, replacing Howe. King George III ordered Clinton to hold New York and to encourage Native American attacks in frontier areas. Clinton moved troops from Philadelphia and marched them toward New York in June. At Monmouth Court House, in New Jersey, Washington's army attacked Clinton's troops. Both sides claimed victory, but the battle showed American troops had benefitted from their training during their winter encampment at Valley Forge.

After Clinton and his troops arrived in New York City, he began planning for an invasion of the south. Loyalists living in the southern colonies provided support for the British, and Clinton's goal was to capture Charleston, South Carolina. Before approaching Charleston, Clinton first attacked Savannah, Georgia, which he captured without suffering major losses.

Charleston

CHARLESTON South Carolina's largest seaport and city where a large loyalist population lived.

In December 1779, Clinton sailed from New York to Charleston with more than 100 ships, carrying more than 10,000 soldiers and sailors. **Charleston** was important to the British because it was the South's largest city and most important seaport. Additionally, it had a large population of Loyalists. In April, Clinton's ships blockaded the harbor while the British soldiers entered the city from several miles south. The Americans surrendered in May; the surrender gave the British control of South Carolina and Georgia. Clinton turned the British command over to Lord Cornwallis and returned to New York. In response to the defeat at Charleston, the Americans sent more soldiers south. The Americans were severely defeated by the British at the battle of Camden, near Charleston, in late summer 1780.

Fighting continued in the Carolinas, and the Americans scored decisive victories at the Battle of King's Mountain and Cowpens. Cornwallis and his troops moved north into North Carolina, and ultimately, Virginia, believing that the British troops remaining in South Carolina would be adequate to combat the attacks of the American soldiers. He was wrong. The Americans, under the direction of Nathaniel Green, attacked British outposts in the Carolinas and forced the Redcoats to return to Charleston and Savannah, where the Americans contained them.

Saratoga had been a turning point for the Americans in the north, and American victories in the south at King's Mountain and Cowpens turned the course of the war away from the British.

Weather conditions in the South aided the rebel cause. The British army's equipment was not suited for the warmer southern weather. Nor was the army prepared to deal with the mosquitoes and the spread of diseases, including malaria, that wreaked havoc on British resolve.

African-Americans in the War

African-American slaves made up a significant part of the Southern population. Both the British and colonists considered how this could influence the dynamics and outcome of the war. The slaves themselves saw the Revolutionary War as an opportunity to secure freedom.

When Washington became commander of the Continental Army in 1775, he barred further recruitment of African-Americans to fight in the war for independence but permitted the blacks who had fought at Lexington, Concord, or Bunker Hill to reenlist. The colonists feared the British might purposefully recruit black Southerners to rebel against colonial landowners, but Washington and Congress were wary of having slaves among their troops. The British, however, had to weigh the advantage of having slaves aid their cause against angering Loyalist slave owners in the South. For this reason, they initially vacillated on the idea of encouraging a slave rebellion.

At the time Washington was barring the recruitment of African-Americans, Lord Dunmore, the royal governor of Virginia, was asking them to join a regiment of soldiers that would be known as the Ethiopian Regiment. In an official proclamation issued in 1775, Dunmore promised freedom to any slaves who would joined the regiment. Dunmore's offer was in part retaliation against Virginians who protested after he seized their militia armory in Williamsburg. The confiscation of one of Virginia's major defenses against a slave revolt, and the threat to offer freedom to runaway slaves, incensed white Virginians and was a major catalyst to that state's support of the Revolution.

After Clinton took Charleston he offered a deal to the slaves that echoed Dunmore's deal. Over 10,000 blacks in the South took up the offers of Dunmore and Clinton.

Eventually, as circumstances became more dire, the Continental Army also admitted more slaves into its ranks. During the harsh winter of 1777–1778, many soldiers in the Continental Army became ill and died. As a result, Washington approved a Rhode Island proposal to establish a Rhode Island regiment of free and slave African-Americans. The Rhode Island legislature agreed to provide compensation to slave owners, and if the slaves that were purchased by the state were found to be acceptable for service, they would be freed. The regiment was never totally composed of African-Americans but fought in several battles, including Yorktown. Other African-Americans served as the result of a lottery-based draft because states were unable to fill their quotas with volunteers. All states except the Carolinas and Georgia eventually accepted blacks into state regiments. As many as 5,000 fought alongside the rebels, hoping the outcome of the war would secure their liberty.

Not all of the African-Americans who served in the Revolution remained free. The provisional peace treaty, the Treaty of Paris of 1782, provided for the return of runaway slaves, and after the battle of Yorktown, Americans made efforts to return the surviving African-Americans to their former owners for re-enslavement. The British prevented many of the African-Americans fighting for them from leaving the United States, and some of the African-Americans were enslaved in the Caribbean.

STUDY ALERT

George Rogers Clark led American soldiers into the west to capture French and English settlements, gain access to lands north of the Ohio River, and open up the Mississippi River to maintain the free passage of goods from the Spanish living in New Orleans.

THE WAR IN THE WEST

The fighting in the West did not significantly affect the outcome of the Revolutionary War. A young Virginia militiaman, George Rogers Clark, devised a plan to protect the western settlements, gain access to lands north of the Ohio River, and open the Mississippi River to maintain the free passage of goods from the Spanish living in New Orleans. His plan was to capture the French villages and English forts in the Ohio River valley to neutralize the British control of the area. He succeeded in this mission by taking the outposts Kaskaskia on July 4, 1778, and Vincennes not long after.

Native American tribes once again found themselves affected by the quibbles between European powers and colonists. The following is from a speech made at the Second Continental Congress to the Iroquois confederacy in 1775.

Brothers and friends… this is a family quarrel between us and Old England. You Indians are not concerned in it. We don't wish you to take up the hatchet against the king's troops. We desire you to remain at home, and not join on either side, but keep the hatchet buried deep… Brothers! we live upon the same ground with you… We desire to sit down under the same tree of peace with you: let us water its roots and cherish its growth, till the large leaves and flourishing branches shall extend to the setting sun, and reach the skies.

Some Native tribes attempted to remain neutral to the fighting, most sided with the British, others fought for the colonists, and some remained loyal to the French and Spanish. The war even caused the powerful Iroquois confederacy of six nations to split. As with black slaves, the British saw potential in encouraging Native American fighters to turn against the colonists who were encroaching on their native lands. Approximately 13,000 Native Americans fought for the British cause. Of them, the Mohawk leader Joseph Brant caused the most trouble for the colonists.

The American Revolution had devastating effects on the Native American population, especially for those who sided with the British. Even more devastating for Native tribes was the smallpox pandemic that escalated in the wake of the battles. The war also precipitated the frontier wars that continued for years after the fighting of the American Revolution had ended.

SURRENDER AT YORKTOWN

Lord Cornwallis and his troops marched into Virginia after his attempts to secure the southern states for the British. The Marquis de Lafayette and French troops followed Cornwallis north from Virginia. The British camped at Yorktown, a tobacco port on the York River, expecting General Clinton to bring supplies and ammunition from New York.

In 1781, the French landed approximately 6,000 troops in Rhode Island. Their commander, Comte Rochambeau, met with General Washington to devise a plan of attack against the British. Washington believed an attack on New York City should be the goal, but Rochambeau persuaded Washington to march the troops south. Washington, in an effort to fool the British, sent false dispatches indicating the French and American troops were headed to New York City.

DID YOU KNOW?

When Lord Cornwallis surrendered to the Americans at Yorktown, the British regimental band played a tune made famous in the 1600s, entitled "A World Turned Upside Down." The words of the tune stated the world would be upside down if buttercups buzzed after bees, boats were on land and churches were on the sea, ponies rode men, and grass ate cows. The tune symbolized the idea of the world turning upside down, because the British, despite having a professional army, were unable to put down a rebellion of colonists.

The British fleet sailed into Chesapeake Bay to deliver supplies to Cornwallis, but the French fleet was waiting. Admiral Comte de Grasse, the French naval leader, defeated the British, preventing them from delivering the supplies. On land, the French and Americans shelled the British troops, and in October Cornwallis surrendered. Yorktown was the last major battle of the American Revolution, and the defeat of the British there caused the British government to begin negotiations to end the conflict. The conclusion was formalized with the signing of the Treaty of Paris in 1783.

Treaty of Paris 1783
US Bicentennial 20 cents

END OF CHAPTER TAKE-AWAYS

■ **The Two Armies and Their Strategies:** The British soldiers were professionals and well trained. They used German mercenaries and relied on traditional techniques of warfare. The colonial side included local militias who fought battles and then returned home, and the Continental Army led by George Washington.

■ **The Second Continental Congress:** This acting governing body convened to decide how to deal with the British actions toward the colonies. It ultimately issued the Declaration of Independence.

■ **Fighting in the North:** After the British prevailed at Brandywine, they captured Philadelphia, which had been the seat of the newly formed government. At Saratoga, the tides of the war turned in the favor of the colonists.

■ **Fighting in the South:** Charleston, South Carolina, was a Loyalist stronghold and major seaport. The city played a key role in British strategy.

■ **The War in the West:** Native Americans fought for both the British and the Americans in the American Revolution. When George Rogers Clark captured French settlements, the Ohio Valley was no longer under British control.

■ **Surrender at Yorktown:** The French helped the Americans at Yorktown beat Lord Cornwallis, ending the American Revolution.

REFERENCES

Appleby, J. O., Brinkley, A., McPherson, J. M., & National Geographic Society. (1998). *The American journey*. New York, NY: Glencoe/McGraw-Hill.

The Avalon Project: Yale Law School. (2008). Journals of the Continental Congress—Speech to the Six Nations; July 13, 1775. Retrieved from http://avalon.law.yale.edu/18th_century/contcong_07-13-75.asp

Berkin, C. (2005). *Revolutionary mothers: Women in the struggle for America's independence*. New York, NY: Knopf.

Countryman, E., & Foner, E. (1985). *The American Revolution*. New York, NY: Hill and Wang.

Finkelman, P., & Lesh, B. A. (2008). *Milestone documents in American history: Exploring the primary sources that shaped America*. Dallas, TX: Schlager Group.

McCullough, D. G. (2005). *1776*. New York, NY: Simon & Schuster.

Nash, G. B. (2005). *The unknown American Revolution: The unruly birth of democracy and the struggle to create America*. New York, NY: Penguin Books.

Wood, G. S. (2002). *The American Revolution: A history*. New York, NY: Modern Library.

CHAPTER 5

Founding a Republic, 1781–1796

The purpose of the United States Constitution is to ensure liberties for the country's citizens. This makes the nation's founding document something of a paradox: in order to guarantee liberties, the founding fathers adopted certain restrictive laws. The debate that started with the drafting of the Constitution about the restrictiveness of these laws has continued throughout US history. Some believe the laws are not restrictive enough, while others contend they are in fact too restrictive.

To many people today, a written constitution seems like the most obvious, sensible basis for a new government. But in the late 18th century, the idea was innovative and daring. Early Americans had to craft a document that would balance many sets of competing interests. Through the debates that raged in closed committee meetings, newspaper columns, and tavern halls, a central question emerged: What sort of government would be strong enough to govern a nation stretching half a continent, but weak enough to ensure the freedoms of all its diverse peoples?

STATE CONSTITUTIONS

As early as 1776, the Continental Congress had invited states to draft their own constitutions. Before the war, the states had been governed by colonial charters, the royal orders that determined how each colony would be ruled. Most colonies had enjoyed some degree of local representation, usually in the form of an elected assembly that worked with a royal governor appointed by the king of England. Now with many of the old colonies almost like independent nations, determining new local governments was a challenging proposition.

Americans' experience with the written rules of colonial charters was likely a major inspiration for the drafting of written state constitutions. The British constitution was an unwritten set of traditions and legal rulings that guaranteed its subjects a number of rights, but after seeing many of those rights denied in the lead up to the revolution, most Americans wanted to make sure their constitution was written. As a result most state constitutions had some declaration of natural rights, individual rights Americans believed all people to have naturally by virtue of being human. Many of the natural rights came from old British guarantees, such as protections from illegal searches and the right to trial by jury.

The state constitutions also grappled with the problem of representation. In Britain, the Parliament consisted of two houses, the elected House of Commons and the House of Lords, made up of only noblemen. British philosophers believed these two houses balanced the interests of aristocrats and commoners and prevented an abuse of power by either the rich or the poor. Americans debated how to achieve a similar balance without promoting the sort of aristocracy many thought out of place in a free nation. This was important, as few thinkers of the time supported direct democracies. Looking at examples from ancient Greece, they believed that democracies often allowed the majority to abuse the minority, and might even degenerate into mob rule. Instead the ideal government was a republic, such as the imagined one of early Rome, where virtuous and outstanding leaders would be elected as representatives who would temper the passions of the larger public. Some states, including Pennsylvania and Georgia, approved unicameral, or single-house, legislatures elected by the people, making their governments much more directly democratic. But most chose bicameral, or two-house, legislatures, usually a lower house chosen by the people and a higher house chosen by the lower house. Also, remembering the oppressive interference of the royal colonial governors on the eve of the American Revolution, most states had a weak executive office; Pennsylvania chose not to have a governor at all.

Despite being one of the last written, the Massachusetts state constitution became highly influential. When voters rejected the first two attempts, John Adams, a lawyer and revolutionary leader, suggested a special convention specifically to draft a new version. To better balance the power of its two-house legislature, the convention in Massachusetts established a strong governor elected by the people. The governor was given a fixed salary so as not to

The ancient Greek philosopher, Plato.

be financially dependent to state representatives, and the right to veto legislation. Seeing the wisdom of such checks and balances, other states soon added strong executives as well.

CONGRESS

Although the Continental Congress had managed the war effort for nearly two years, once delegates signed the Declaration of Independence in 1776, the United States needed more formal arrangements for its new government. The congress formed a committee with John Dickinson as its chair, and the group put forward a plan for a strong central government. This plan allowed for the control of western territories, equal representation for each state, and the power to tax states in proportion to their population. Busy fighting a revolution against a strong British authority, most delegates opposed Dickinson's plan, instead envisioning an arrangement where states held the most power.

The Continental Congress approved the **Articles of Confederation**, arguably closer to an alliance of independent states than a plan for a central government. Under the Articles, states could vote on national issues in a single national legislature, where each state was to have one vote. The decisions of the vote were final, as there was no executive such as a president or prime minister. The most important powers the Articles gave the central government were for situations that individual states likely would not want to handle on their own. These included the powers to conduct wars, to negotiate treaties, to appropriate funds for legislation, and to handle relations with western tribes of Native Americans.

Such a list of powers still did not guarantee a strong central government. For every important responsibility given to the US government under the Articles, there was a limitation that severely inhibited action. While the confederation could declare a war, it could not draft troops to fight. The government could pay for projects with borrowed money, but could not tax the states to pay its bills. It was also able to sign treaties and conduct diplomacy, but without the power to regulate state commerce, such as imports and exports. And how was the government to negotiate with Native Americans, when under the articles it did not even own the unsettled western territories?

Perhaps most important, the legislature of the confederation was designed to be naturally conservative. Because any amendments to the Articles needed to be unanimous, there was little chance that the government could adapt to meet new challenges and circumstances. With opinions on many issues—ranging from commerce to finance to slavery to individual rights—the chance of all thirteen colonies agreeing on much of anything was slim. Nevertheless, the complete Articles were sent to the individual state legislatures for ratification in 1777; Virginia was the first to sign. By 1781, with Maryland's approval, each of the original colonies had now joined together in a government of confederated states.

ARTICLES OF CONFEDERATION The first constitution of the United States.

CONFEDERATION

The end of the Revolutionary War brought no end to the challenges facing the fledgling United States, and the chief among them was the economy. As colonies, the states had been part of a huge British commercial empire, and they lost a number of economic benefits with independence. As the states began again to buy manufactured British goods, hard gold and silver currency flowed out from America, but no longer back in from Britain. As a result, many of the new states printed their own currency, often driving up inflation.

The weakness of the Articles of Confederation was behind many of these problems. Congress had debts to creditors at home and abroad. It could not pay back the war bonds many soldiers and other Americans had bought to support the Revolution, leaving these people without cash to spend and depressing the economy further. The states had their own debts, but Congress could neither force the states to pay nor tax them to deal with its own bills. Some colonial legislators pushed for a stronger central government, including New York's Alexander Hamilton and Virginia's James Madison, but when they proposed a 5 percent tax on imports to give Congress a modest regular income, Rhode Island vetoed the proposal.

There were other signs that the Americans lacked enthusiasm for the current union. In 1783 a group of disgruntled revolutionary officers considered an armed protest against overdue payments from Congress, and it took a personal visit from George Washington to calm the so-called Newburgh Conspiracy. At times important matters for Congress were postponed for a lack of **quorum**, the minimum number of state representatives necessary to proceed with discussing business. Americans could not even rely on the location of the nation's capital, which jumped between Philadelphia, Annapolis, and New York, among other locations.

Through these difficulties American thinkers wrestled with how they might create a stronger union without undermining the liberty of the states. Some agreed with the French writer Baron de Montesquieu that a virtuous republic would be impossible over long distances because the peoples' representatives would be easily corrupted serving so far away from home. In the approach to the Revolution many Americans had complained of just this problem in the British Parliament, where they believed new ministers quickly fell into the deal-making of London's bureaucracy and forgot about common people. Others, including Madison, believed a strong republic might help prevent corruption in a geographically large nation. Like another philosopher, David Hume, they believed that bringing together representatives from the distant states would help cancel out the selfish interests of each region and help the country make wise decisions.

STATE DISPUTES

Having been given so many powers under the Articles of Confederation, the new states often argued as if they were independent nations, mostly over land and taxes. The source of land disputes were the valuable western territories between the Appalachian mountains and the Mississippi River that the Americans had won from the British. Contested claims arose because many colonial charters had vaguely granted all the lands to "the south seas," allowing certain states to claim everything from the Atlantic Ocean to the Mississippi itself. Often through creative legal reasoning, states such as New York, Pennsylvania, and Connecticut bickered over the lands that would become Ohio, Kentucky, and other future states. Meanwhile, Delaware, Rhode Island, and other states with firm western boundaries felt cheated in the rush of land speculation.

Further complicating western land claims were the conflicting results of treaties with Native Americans. United States officials had pressured Native Americans into a number of land treaties following the Revolution, but often negotiators had dealt with only one of many tribes who claimed a given territory. When different tribes sold or ceded the same lands to multiple states, land disputes became even messier.

The immense value of the western lands made compromises all the more difficult, especially since states were looking for sources of income to combat the bad economy. Because speculators had made illegal land sales before the Revolution, lobbyists were pressuring states to endorse these purchases. Although disagreements continued for years, some relief came when Virginia agreed to give up its claim to all lands north of the Ohio river, allowing Congress to take control of what would be called the Northwest Territory and to invalidate previous claims there by private speculators.

Disputes also arose when states tried to boost incomes by taxing one another. Because the Articles left Congress no power to regulate trade, states could levy taxes on the use of waterways and on imports and exports. With international trade already suffering following the settlement with Britain, disagreements over internal commerce only served to make the new union that much more uneasy.

SECTIONALISM

In the years immediately following the Revolution, Americans were still determining exactly how the liberty they had won would look. All the impassioned talk of freedom had called many old practices and habits into question. Most agreed that even hints of a formal aristocracy had no place in a true republic, and observers noticed how Americans began to abandon certain polite titles and gestures of respect. State legislatures also struck blows for greater freedoms, changing laws that gave eldest sons preference in inheritances and lowering the amount of property a person needed to own in order to be allowed vote. Still, these reforms chiefly helped white male citizens. For the women, Native Americans, and African-Americans who together formed the majority of those living in the new United States, many questions of freedom had yet to be answered.

Different groups of states often had their own answers for who was to enjoy the new liberties of the United States. These local differences in public opinion and policies resulted in **sectionalism**, a strong commitment to the special interests of a given region. As Americans considered more and more what changes might be needed to strengthen the union, sectional issues often presented the most difficult challenges to reform.

SECTIONALISM Political views dominated by the interests of a certain region of the country.

The North

The northern states had a diverse mix of small and large populations, with varied industries such as farming, fishing, and logging, and a mix of religious sects including Quakers, Presbyterians, and Episcopalians. They were also more urban, with a denser population and three of the largest port cities in the country. But perhaps most significant, these states lacked a major cash crop like tobacco or rice, and thus were less reliant on slave labor, leaving many Northerners to consider what freedoms African-Americans deserved.

Benjamin Franklin.

A number of Revolutionary leaders, including Ben Franklin and Alexander Hamilton, had abolitionist sympathies, and activists such as Quaker John Woolman helped Pennsylvania outlaw slavery entirely, a move echoed in the state constitution of Vermont a few years later. The performance of free blacks in the workplace impressed some Northerners. The African-American scientist Benjamin Banneker and the former slave turned poet Phyllis Wheately became minor celebrities. By no means were all Northerners in favor of abolition; in fact New York kept a sizeable slave population until the 1830s. But through the work of charities such as the Manumission Society and the Society for the Relief of Free Negroes, free blacks and concerned whites caused some to doubt the place of slavery in a democratic republic.

Many Northerners also reconsidered the political contributions of women. They thought that if the country was to depend on virtuous leaders, the role of mothers and wives in raising honorable children and families had a political significance. Some states went even further, with New Jersey granting property-owning women the right to vote for almost two decades following independence.

The South

In the southern states, slavery remained a major factor in nearly every aspect of local politics. When other states hoped to regulate Britain's commerce with America, Southerners worried their slave-grown tobacco and rice crops might suffer as a result. And though some, including Virginia governor Thomas Jefferson, expressed their distaste for slavery, few Southerners were motivated to give up their pool of free labor. Although George Washington and some other planters inspired by the Revolution eventually freed their slaves, Jefferson, despite his misgivings, famously would not. Even those who thought slavery a moral ill could often see no way to end it. How could hundreds of thousands of slaves, whom many whites still thought inferior, be integrated into society? Slavery grew more entrenched in the South, especially after the 1793 invention of the cotton gin, which made cotton fabulously profitable and pushed the demand for slaves even higher.

The southern state of Virginia did make a major contribution to religious freedom in America. The South had never seen the close ties between church and state

HISTORY COMES ALIVE

Benjamin Franklin is the only American to sign all four of the most important documents in the founding of the United States. These include the 1776 Declaration of Independence, the 1778 Treaty of Alliance with France, the 1783 Treaty of Paris, and the 1787 Constitution of the United States. This unrivaled range of experience seems fitting for a man who served so many roles in the colonies and the new independent nation. Over the years Franklin served as a writer, printer, scientist, musician, philosopher, statesman, ambassador, and even the country's first postmaster general. Over the years he invented the lightning rod and bifocal glasses, and was responsible for the first public library and the first fire department in the city of Philadelphia.

that had been common in the colonies of New England, so when Jefferson helped introduce the Virginia Statute for Religious Freedom in 1777, it passed into law. The document stopped the state from supporting the Church of England or any other sect, and guaranteed free religious practice and protection from religious discrimination to all Virginians. The statute later became part of the state constitution and was influential in other states.

The West

As the western populations grew following the Revolution, many state governments became more democratic. Most western and more rural settlers were poorer and younger than the established gentry of eastern counties, and as western representatives were elected to state legislatures, wider classes of Americans gained a voice in lawmaking. Some state capitals even moved to more central locations where they would be more convenient for western visitors.

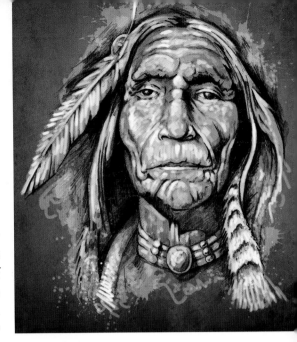

The continued settlement of western lands also created regular conflicts with the Native Americans already living there. The new Congress signed a series of treaties in the 1780s with tribes including the Cherokee, the Choctaw, the Chickasaw, and the Iroquois in an attempt to sort out western ownership. However, these treaties did not always produce lasting agreements, as controversies arose over the authority and rights of the native negotiators who had signed the accords.

Foreign Influence

Even after the 1783 Treaty of Paris, the United States continued to clash with Great Britain and other European powers. A number of prickly disagreements with the British persisted, beginning with trade. While Britain agreed to sell its goods to the United States, it restricted other commerce, and closed off its colonies in the West Indies to American shipping. Southerners were incensed about Britain's failure to compensate American planters for the slaves who had escaped or been freed by the British during the Revolution. There were also disagreements about the northern and southern boundaries of the United States' western territories, and the most troubling issue was Britain's refusal to evacuate a number of forts around the Great Lakes. For years after the official end of the war, Britain still had hundreds of troops stationed in the American West, often working to undermine US diplomacy with Native Americans in those regions.

Despite its alliance with France during the Revolution, the new United States also had trouble gaining respect in Europe as a world nation. When the United States sent John Adams to Britain in 1784 as a diplomatic minister, he worked for months on American grievances but accomplished very little. Meanwhile the British failed to even send a single envoy to serve in the new American capital, more evidence that despite winning independence, the United States was nowhere near equal standing with its European rivals.

Jay-Gardoqui Treaty

The United States even saw tension with Spain, which had been a late ally against Britain during the Revolution. Unhappy with the southern borders of American territory drawn at the Treaty of Paris, Spain closed the Mississippi River at Port Orleans to American shipping in 1784, making it much more difficult and expensive for western farmers to get their goods to market. The United States sent New York Congressman John Jay to negotiate the issue with Spanish official Don Diego Gardoqui, but the deliberations stalled. Jay offered not to tax Spanish imports in exchange for Spain opening ports for US trade in Europe and the Caribbean. Incensed by what they saw as a handout to the Spanish in exchange for shipping rights that would mostly benefit the North, southern politicians led Congress in rejecting the **Jay-Gardoqui Treaty** and leaving the issue of Mississippi unresolved.

MID-CHAPTER QUESTIONS

1. How did colonial experience affect the drafting of state constitutions? Where did states concentrate power? How did the Massachusetts state constitution differ from those written earlier?

2. Describe the organization of the US government under the Articles of Confederation. What were the weaknesses of the Articles? How did they help contribute to a weak economy and difficulties with diplomacy?

3. How did political life change for poor white men, women, slaves, free African-Americans, and native tribes following the Revolutionary War? Or did it change at all? How did slavery affect the political cultures of the northern and southern states?

4. What issues made the settlement of the western territories difficult? What steps did Congress take to make the process of settlement more orderly?

THE NORTHWEST TERRITORY

Despite the arguments over the Northwest Territory, Congress could not keep settlers from streaming into the available western lands. Congress needed to act quickly, and its eventual solution for managing the territory was arguably the most impressive political accomplishment of the confederated era.

As early as 1784 Thomas Jefferson had proposed dividing the Northwest Territory into ten new states, each of which could apply for statehood once they reached the same population as the smallest state in the union. Congress then passed the Land Ordinance of 1785, which divided the available lands into townships with 36 equal square-mile plots. To promote orderly community development, the law also reserved four plots in each township for the US government, including one that would be made available for a public school.

Congress intended the Land Ordinance not only to guide settlement, but also to create revenue. Initially the smallest section of land available was one of the square-mile plots, and buyers had to pay with cash, restricting land sales to the very wealthy and encouraging some poorer Americans to simply continue squatting on the land. Congress had also given prominent groups of speculators, such as the Ohio Company, the first choice of lands for sale. Later Congress allowed citizens to make purchases by trading in war bonds from the Revolutionary era, but the price of purchasing western lands remained a barrier for many. The continued growth of illegal settlement, and in some cases the lack of reliable law and order, finally moved Congress to pass a more definitive plan for western settlement.

The Ordinance of 1787, now known as the **Northwest Ordinance,** proved an extremely significant event in the growth of the American nation. The law called for dividing the Northwest Territory into eight units with each new territory under the control of a governor, secretary, and three judges that Congress would appoint. White male residents of the new territories who owned property could participate in the government. When a territory's population surpassed 5,000, the voters could elect a legislature, and when there were over 6,000 residents, they could apply for statehood, after drafting a state constitution. The territorial governments also gave the governor the power to veto bills, but guaranteed the rights of free religious practice and trial by jury.

Most important, the Northwest Ordinance outlawed slavery in the new territories. This meant that as the eventual states of Ohio, Indiana, Illinois, Wisconsin, and Michigan joined the union, the senators they sent to Congress would have little motivation to preserve the institution of slavery. For more than half a century forward, the question of slavery dominated each new state's entry into the union, as abolitionist activists and southern farmers clashed over the number of potential proslavery votes in Congress, an intense debate that would contribute to the coming of the Civil War.

NORTHWEST ORDINANCE Congressional legislation that provided the method for developing the Northwest Territory into states.

CONSTITUTIONS

As the Articles of Confederation strained the union of the United States with each passing month, fervent supporters of a stronger republic, including Jefferson and Madison, called a formal conference in 1786 to consider possible changes. When delegates met in Annapolis, Maryland, they found that only five states were in attendance, but the discussion nevertheless soon moved to consider a full convention to write a new constitution for the United States. Congress called for the convention to meet the following year in Philadelphia. There delegates would try to define a system of government worthy of the ideals of the Revolution.

Shays' Rebellion

A dramatic conflict that began in Massachusetts later that year further illustrated the need to rework the governance of the United States. The trouble began with the difficult economic circumstances facing a number of poor farmers in New England, many who were veterans of the Revolutionary War. As they struggled to pay their war debts, many states raised taxes on working people, causing farmers and laborers to take on higher debts of their own. Perhaps most frustrating, many Americans had lost large investments when they sold their war bonds to speculators for a fraction of their list value, believing even a tenth of their original investment would be better than never receiving payment from the state governments. When the state governments who had helped make life so difficult on ordinary people began overseeing home foreclosures and prison terms for debtors, popular anger reached a tipping point.

Following the lead of farmer and war veteran Daniel Shays, many New Englanders began armed protests and other forms of civil disobedience. Shays led his followers to force the closure of a county courthouse in 1786, preventing the court from authorizing foreclosures and ruling on other lawsuits for unpaid debts. But when the insurgents looked to seize the arsenal in Springfield that produced and stored the US military's firearms, the movement flirted with a full rebellion, and thus it is often called **Shays' Rebellion**. It was only stopped when the same wealthy Bostonians who held many of the debts in question helped raise a militia to disperse Shays and his men. The dire effects of the unregulated economy on poor working people, and the inability of Congress to command forces against a near insurrection, further demonstrated the pressing need for a stronger central government. A few months later, delegates gathered in Philadelphia to look for new solutions.

The Framers of the Federal Constitution

While many historical leaders from this period are given the modern title of "Founding Fathers," perhaps no group better deserves such recognition than the delegates to the Constitutional Convention of 1787. The states had elected the men who gathered in Philadelphia that summer in much the same way as they had formed committees of correspondence and the Continental Congress during the Revolution. A number of the fifty-five delegates had served in those bodies as well, and they represented a wide cross section of talented American citizens. Most were relatively young for leaders, in their thirties and forties, and ranged in profession from farmers to lawyers to merchants. They came from every state except for Rhode Island, which refused to participate, and of course, because they were drawn from the pool of citizens, there were no women or people of native or African descent.

The figures in attendance included future presidents George Washington, Thomas Jefferson, and James Madison, scientist and diplomat Ben Franklin, future treasury secretary Alexander Hamilton, and a number of other important leaders, including George Mason, Robert Morris, and John Dickinson. Once the debates began, important proposals were decided only by a majority vote, and the proceedings of each day were kept secret from the public, to prevent sensational rumors from spreading until the delegates were ready to present their formal plan to the American public.

The Virginia and New Jersey Plans

The first framework the delegates worked with came largely from Madison's ideas and became known as the **Virginia Plan**. It called for a bicameral legislature consisting of a lower house elected directly by the people and an upper house elected by the lower house. The number of representatives per state would be determined by population. The Virginia plan also gave veto powers to an executive elected by Congress; the executive would not be allowed to otherwise participate in lawmaking. Most smaller states thought the proportional representation gave unfair advantages to larger states, and they put forward an alternative.

What became known as the **New Jersey Plan** had instead a unicameral legislature with one vote per state, similar to the current Congress under the Articles. However, to strengthen the central government, the New Jersey Plan gave Congress the power to tax and regulate trade. Favoring smaller states and resembling the current Articles, the New Jersey plan attracted few supporters; only New Jersey,

SHAYS' REBELLION An armed rebellion of farmers in postwar Massachusetts protesting mortgage foreclosures and high debt.

STUDY ALERT

At the Constitutional Convention delegates from twelve states determined a new system of government for the United States. After considering the Virginia and New Jersey plans, the delegates reached important compromises to balance the representation of large and small states.

VIRGINIA PLAN A plan for a bicameral legislature with the number of each state's representatives based on a state's population.

NEW JERSEY PLAN A plan of government that provided for a unicameral legislature with equal voting power by each state.

New York, and Delaware voted in favor. In response, the convention appointed a special committee with one representative from each state to hash out the difficult question of Congressional representation.

Led by Roger Sherman of Connecticut, the delegates agreed on a clever solution. In what would become known as the **Great Compromise**, the new Congress would have a bicameral legislature consisting of a lower house, eventually called the House of Representatives, with members determined by a state's population, and an upper house called the Senate comprised of two legislators from each state. Popular vote would elect representatives to the House, while state legislatures would appoint those serving in the Senate. This solution not only provided a balance between the interests of small and large states, but also drew from both democratic and republican philosophies.

Agreeing on one house with proportional representation led to another controversy. How should the hundreds of thousands of slaves, who had no political rights in this government, be counted? While northern delegates thought slaves should be left out of population tallies, southern delegates complained that in some states, such as South Carolina, slaves comprised nearly half the total population. As a compromise, the delegates arrived at an infamous agreement that perfectly illustrated the degrading treatment of African-Americans in the states: Each slave would be counted as three-fifths of a person, as part of the **Three-Fifths Compromise**.

While some northern delegates favored ending slavery, and especially the brutal transatlantic slave trade, the threats of southerners to quit the convention if slavery became an issue made significant reform unrealistic. Antislavery sentiment was only expressed in an agreement that Congress could regulate the slave trade after 1808, if enough support existed.

Ratification

Although some delegates had their complaints about the final product, the delegates signed the Constitution in September, and sent it to the states for ratification. Each state would hold its own convention on whether to ratify, and the Constitution would become law when nine states approved it.

The public debate over ratification was one of the richest political discussions in all of American history. The Constitution's strongest supporters quickly adapted the title of **Federalists,** as they advocated for the document's strong central government. In what became known as the **Federalist Papers**, Madison, Hamilton, and Jay anonymously wrote a series of nearly a hundred essays in American newspapers calling for ratification.

Critics of the Constitution became known as **Antifederalists**. After experiencing the Articles of Confederation, few Antifederalists wanted the central government to stay ineffective, but they also believed that larger governments created more opportunities for corruption. Antifederalists feared that only the rich would have the power and connections necessary to win large-scale elections, effectively creating a new aristocracy. But Federalists countered that the process would in fact elevate the most skilled and talented people, no matter what their social background.

Many of the votes in the state conventions were close, particularly in some of the larger and more influential states. By

George Washington.

GREAT COMPROMISE Plan establishing a bicameral legislature with one house based upon population and the other having equal representation from all states.

THREE-FIFTHS COMPROMISE The agreement of congressional delegates to count slaves as only three-fifths of a person when determining proportional representation.

FEDERALISTS Those favoring ratification of the Constitution and a strong central government.

FEDERALIST PAPERS Essays written by supporters of ratification of the Constitution.

ANTIFEDERALISTS Those opposing ratification of the 1787 Constitution.

DID YOU KNOW?

Scotch-Irish immigrants brought their rye whiskey-making tradition to Pennsylvania. Under Washington's administration, the government offered land in Kentucky to individuals who would settle the area and grow corn. Because corn was perishable, settlers began making whiskey from corn. Kentucky whiskey became known as bourbon, taking its name from the county bordering the Ohio River where it was shipped by river to New Orleans. Tennessee whiskey is also made of corn and could be called bourbon, but distillers prefer their sipping bourbon be called "whiskey."

narrow margins, Massachusetts, Virginia, and New York all approved the Constitution, and all of the remaining states eventually followed. After nearly a year of planning and debate, Americans had redefined the very nature of their government.

Even when the new Congress first met a year later, there were more major changes in store for the young United States. A lingering concern with many Americans was the Constitution's lack of a written **Bill of Rights** to place explicit limits on how the government could govern its citizens. Under the leadership of Madison, and with the rights guaranteed by the state constitutions in mind, Congress drafted 10 amendments guaranteeing freedom of religion, freedom of the press, the right to assemble, the right to jury trials, and other important freedoms that many Americans cherish to this day. The drafting and ratification of the Constitution and the Bill of Rights were monumental achievements that have inspired democracies all over the world.

When it came time to select the first president to lead the young nation in its new government, the people chose the strong and steady former general George Washington, who took office in 1789. He proved to be successful as America's first president, but often as much for the things he did not do as for those he did. Like many of the other men who had labored to write the Constitution, he understood that an effective democratic system required both powers and restraints.

BILL OF RIGHTS The first ten amendments to the Constitution.

END OF CHAPTER TAKE-AWAYS

- **State Constitutions:** As early as 1776, states started drafting their own constitutions, relying on models from successful democracies in history for guidance. The ideas in these documents influenced the federal constitution.
- **Congress:** A newly convened congress passed the Articles of Confederation, which defined a loosely unified group of independent states as opposed to a centrally governed republic.
- **Confederation:** The weaknesses of the Articles of Confederation and the challenges of finding success as a new nation posed economic problems. These problems forced the states to consider better forms of government.
- **State Disputes:** Since each state enjoyed so much independent power under the Articles, many conflicts arose among them, especially over land and tax issues.
- **Sectionalism:** As the states considered a better form of government, the central challenge was addressing the regional concerns of the states.
- **The Northwest Territory:** Two ordinances from Congress attempted to govern the settling of land west of the Appalachian Mountains and north of the Ohio River.
- **Constitution:** At the Constitutional Convention in Philadelphia in 1787, the framers wrote the Constitution that is still in use today. Hamilton and others wrote essays encouraging states to ratify the document.

REFERENCES

Bowen, C. D. (1966). *Miracle at Philadelphia: The story of the Constitutional Convention, May to September 1787*. Boston, MA: Little, Brown.

Kurland, P. B., & Lerner, R. (1987). *The Founders' Constitution*. Chicago, IL: University of Chicago Press.

Rakove, J. N., & Handlin, O. (1990). *James Madison and the creation of the American Republic*. Glenview, IL: Scott Foresman/Little Brown Higher Education.

Morris, R. B. (1985). *Witnesses at the creation: Hamilton, Madison, Jay, and the Constitution*. New York, NY: Holt, Rinehart, and Winston.

Faber, D., & Faber, H. (1987). *We the people: The story of the United States Constitution since 1787*. New York, NY: Scribner's.

Founding a Republic, 1796–1824

Mosque in Algeria Square, Tripoli, Libya.

In February 2011, many residents of Libya revolted against the leadership that had been in place since 1969. By October 23, 2011, Libya was "liberated" from the rule of Muammar Qaddafi. During the period of civil war, the rebels created their own governing body, the National Transitional Council.

The struggle faced by the Libyans is not the first example in history of a country reborn. The United States, too, went through a period of revolt and transition during and after the Revolutionary War. From 1796 to 1824, the United States began to put into practice the principles of its newly ratified constitution. This would not be without difficulties, as competing agendas emerged as the nation grew.

When the first president, George Washington, finished his second term and the first contested presidential election in American history took place, the United States faced threats from hostile imperial powers and from Native tribes. At the same time, the new government, with a constitution of yet-untested political ideals, grappled with questions regarding the extent of federal power. Two political parties emerged during this period. Under this "First Party System," the United States experienced internal political pressures that tested the new constitution.

THE CONSTITUTION AND COMMERCE

The Constitution, the most fundamental source of law in the United States, was instrumental in determining how the new government would operate. Article I of the Constitution establishes Congress, the most representative branch of government and the regulator of the nation's commerce. Specifically, Congress's "enumerated powers" include the power to:

1. Collect taxes to pay the nation's debt and defense costs.
2. Borrow money on credit.
3. Regulate commerce with foreign nations, Indian tribes, and among the states.
4. Coin and regulate money, including punishing counterfeiting

While these powers were specifically listed in the Constitution, the extent of the federal government's power over commerce and finance soon came into question.

The first major controversy arose when Alexander Hamilton, secretary of the treasury under Washington, proposed the creation of a national bank. Hamilton believed the bank, modeled after the Bank of England, was necessary to collect taxes and make loans. However, the Constitution did not expressly give Congress this power.

Hamilton argued that the Constitution had an **elastic clause**, meaning Congress had the right to create a national bank because the Constitution granted to the federal government (in this case, Congress) the authority to take any action "necessary and proper" to fulfill its Constitutional function. Hamilton argued that certain federal powers are implied if they are not strictly forbidden. This view became known as the **implied power doctrine**, and was held by those with a **broad constructionist** view of the Constitution. Those holding the broad constructionist view believe it is appropriate to interpret the Constitution's meaning rather than simply following the letter of its words.

On the other hand, Thomas Jefferson, secretary of state, and James Madison, a congressman from Virginia, asserted that Congress had no power to create a national bank because the Constitution did not expressly provide this power. Jefferson and Madison believed the Constitution should be interpreted exactly as written, a position known as **strict constructionism**.

While Hamilton's view prevailed when Washington signed the Bank Bill of 1791, creating the National Bank, the argument over the extent of federal power in the area of commerce continued.

In 1824, a case known as *Gibbons v. Ogden* significantly expanded federal power based on the Supreme Court's interpretation of the Commerce Clause. The Commerce Clause, Article I Section 8, gives Congress the authority to "regulate commerce with foreign nations, and among the several States, and with the Indian tribes."

ELASTIC CLAUSE A view that government has the authority to exercise powers that are "necessary and proper" to fulfill its Constitutional function.

IMPLIED POWER DOCTRINE A view that government has the authority to exercise powers outside of the express written law if they are not forbidden.

BROAD CONSTRUCTIONISM A belief that the Constitution can be interpreted for meaning outside of the strict wording.

STRICT CONSTRUCTIONISM A belief that the Constitution should be interpreted exactly as written.

In *Gibbons v. Ogden*, New York granted Ogden exclusive rights to use the navigable waterways in the state of New York. However, Gibbons began operating a competing steamboat service after Congress issued him a license. Gibbons's lawyer argued that Congress had *exclusive* power to regulate "interstate" commerce (commerce among the several states) based on the Commerce Clause. The New York courts disagreed. Gibbons appealed to the Supreme Court after New York told him to stop operating his boat.

The court held that commerce under the Commerce Clause was more than just trade among the states. The Commerce Clause gave Congress power over *all* aspects of commerce between states, including commerce related to U.S. waterways. Any law passed by Congress designed to regulate commerce would take precedence over and supersede conflicting state laws. Some limitations existed, including a clear rule that Congress could not regulate goods exclusively made, moved, and sold within one state.

Strict constructionists generally believed this ruling did not expand Congressional power, but merely clarified it. Meanwhile broad constructionists argued the ruling amounted to an appropriate expansion of federal power.

Gibbons v. Ogden gave the federal government almost exclusive power to regulate many aspects of commerce and trade. Congress would use that power to make significant changes during the development of the new republic.

WASHINGTON'S NEW GOVERNMENT

EXCISE TAX A tax imposed on businesses on goods sold.

George Washington ran unopposed for both of his terms as president of the new United States. With the exception of a rebellion by farmers in 1794 due to an **excise tax** on whiskey (a tax on the amount of whiskey sold), Washington was considered a hero and was widely respected by most Americans during the first six years of his two-term presidency.

Toward the end of his second term, Washington faced mounting challenges, including the threat of war with Britain and France and the struggle to define the role that the federal government would play in America's economy. The division over the role of the federal government in commerce was one driving force in the creation of separate political parties during this era. Washington was deeply troubled by the dissension during his second term in office, and warned against the development of opposing political parties during his farewell address.

Much of the political upheaval during Washington's presidency can be traced back to the policies of Alexander Hamilton, President Washington's treasury secretary.

Hamilton's Financial Program

Alexander Hamilton, an attorney who played a major role in the Constitutional Convention, served as treasury secretary under Washington. In that role, Hamilton grappled with critical economic challenges facing the fledgling nation.

Hamilton sought to break the British hold on the American economy and to encourage the United States to develop its

George Washington.

own industries. The United States had long been dependent upon British goods paid for using money earned from agricultural exports. Hamilton believed this limited the growth of the economy, especially when compared with other industrialized nations. Hamilton accomplished his aim of reducing dependence on foreign industry by providing government aid, or subsidies, to encourage new business growth. Hamilton also helped fund an improved system of transportation in the United States that made transporting goods easier.

One of the most difficult challenges Hamilton faced, however, was the $54 million debt acquired by the federal government and the $25 million debt acquired by the states during the Revolutionary War. Some new states were not repaying their debt quickly. As a result, the United States had difficulty obtaining foreign credit, as lending to the government was seen as risky business.

To tackle this problem, Hamilton introduced a "redemption plan" to redeem, at face value, the securities issued by the Constitutional Congress during the Revolutionary War. He also introduced his "assumption plan," suggesting the federal government take responsibility for repaying state debt. The government would then refinance the debt by borrowing money at a lower interest rate. The United States would get this money by issuing new government securities bonds.

Hamilton's proposals were met with great resistance from states that had already repaid their debt. These states, including Maryland, Pennsylvania, North Carolina, and Virginia, did not wish to be taxed to repay the debts of the other states. Critics, like Jefferson and Madison, also expressed concern that war speculators would be made rich by Hamilton's actions, as they had purchased war bonds for pennies on the dollar.

After a six-month battle, Jefferson and Madison arranged a compromise with Hamilton. Hamilton got the votes for his redemption and assumption plans in exchange for agreeing to relocate the nation's new capital from New York City to Philadelphia and then ultimately to a federal district on the border between Maryland and Virginia. The new capital—Washington, D.C.—would sit on the bank of the Potomac River near Virginia.

While Hamilton's plans continued to worry some Americans, they did improve U.S. creditworthiness abroad. Hamilton paid for some of his redemption and assumption plans by raising tariffs on imports, and suggested the increased revenue be used to help pay the interest on the nation's debt. Hamilton's tariffs were also controversial, as they were seen as expanding Congressional power further. Many felt the tariffs also would lead back to the crushing taxation that had led the colonists, at least in part, to revolt against Great Britain.

Hamilton also faced considerable opposition for another plan: his effort to create a national bank. Hamilton believed the creation of the bank was necessary to collect tax revenue, hold federal funds, and issue loans to the government and other borrowers. He also believed the new central bank would allow for the establishment of a more stable paper currency.

In 1791, Congress created a national bank with a 20-year charter. While the creation of the First Bank of the United States was a victory for Hamilton, the decision deeply divided the administration of Washington's second presidential term. Washington himself was reluctant, but signed the bank into law because he believed it was necessary to secure the nation's financial well being. The issue became so divisive that Thomas Jefferson resigned his post as secretary of state to organize the mounting opposition to Hamilton's economic policies.

Jefferson and his supporters had several objections to the bank. They objected to creating a centralized financial power; they feared it would lead to corruption

Alexander Hamilton.

and increased speculation; they feared the bank would fall under the control of wealthy overseas interests or northeasterners; and they argued that the federal government did not have the power to create a national bank because the authority to do so was not enumerated in the Constitution.

Hamilton's financial program was largely successful despite stiff opposition. Nevertheless, his policies were seen as elitist and too similar to the British model of economic development. Many also felt his policies vested too much power in a large federal government. It was the intense opposition to many of Hamilton's policies that led to the creation of the first political parties in the United States.

POLITICAL PARTIES EMERGE

Hamilton's economic vision was founded upon a capitalistic, industrial, and mercantile system. His policies favored taxation, a national bank, and the fostering of manufacturing and industry.

On the other hand, Thomas Jefferson, a founding father and the secretary of state under George Washington, believed that manufacturing was a threat to the American agrarian lifestyle. Jefferson was also opposed to large cities, indicating in his Notes of the State of Virginia in 1787 that areas where large populations collected were likely to be meccas of corruption, disease, and poverty. Instead of manufacturing and large cities, Jefferson envisioned a country of independent farmers who maintained their personal freedoms through their ownership and cultivation of the land. Jefferson's vision was appealing to farmers, as well as to small business owners.

The division between Hamilton and Jefferson ultimately resulted in the development of the nation's first political parties. Supporters of Hamilton and his policies soon became members of the **Federalist Party**. Jefferson and his supporters became the **Democratic-Republican Party**, or simply the Republican Party.

Political disagreements had persisted among leaders for much of Washington's second term in office, but it was not until Jefferson resigned from Washington's cabinet in 1793 that he officially formed the Republican Party. The party was formed first in Congress and then within each of the states. The party opposed the actions of the Federalists and fielded an alternative candidate when Federalist John Adams ran for president in 1796.

Political parties, such as the Federalists and Republicans, are not mentioned in the Constitution of the United States and were a source of much concern for President Washington as he left office. Washington feared that partisanship would threaten the unity of his beloved America, and lead once again to war.

FEDERALIST PARTY An early political party in the United States that believed in implied powers, broad constructionism, and a strong central government.

DEMOCRATIC-REPUBLICAN PARTY Also known as the Republican Party, this early U.S. political party believed in a strict constructionist view and states' rights.

Federalists

Led by Alexander Hamilton and Vice President John Adams, the Federalist Party drew its support primarily from eastern port cities and New England. Party members believed in Hamilton's doctrine of implied powers and were broad constructionists, arguing that the Constitution should be loosely interpreted. Their aim was to create a stable, secure republic that would allow businesses to prosper and that would be safe for men of property.

Ideology

The Federalists generally favored corporate and commercial interests. They advocated for a strong centralized federal government, a national bank, and the imposition of import tariffs to protect industry.

Many Federalists believed that the masses (the public) were prone to unchecked passions and social disorders. They felt a strong central government was needed to impose rule and restrain a tendency toward anarchistic behavior. Strongly opposed to mob rule, the Federalists believed that political leaders should not be criticized once they had been elected.

Republicans

The Democratic Republicans, the other political party to emerge during the early national period, were led by Thomas Jefferson and James Madison. Known as Republicans, their primary supporters came from the South or farmers on the frontier.

Ideology

The Republicans heavily favored agricultural interests over industry. They were also supported by craftsman and recent immigrants to the United States.

Republicans were strict constructionists, believing that the Constitution should be interpreted strictly and that the federal government's power existed only in those powers specifically enumerated in the Constitution. The party also opposed a strong central government, the creation of a national bank, and imposition of protective tariffs. Instead of a strong federal government, the party believed in states' rights and feared that the Federalists favored a monarchy instead of a democracy. The Republicans also believed that the Federalists were an elitist "pro-business" party that would enrich the wealthy at the expense of the poor.

While the name might be confusing to some, the Republican Party of the 1790s and 1800s was the forerunner to today's Democratic Party.

The French Revolution, which was underway during this formative time in American history, divided the Federalists and Republicans even further. The French Revolution was caused by high taxes and resentment of the aristocracy, and eventually led to a war between Great Britain and France when Great Britain intervened. Federalists supported Great Britain, believing that the British system was the best system of government in the world. The Federalists opposed the French and their revolution because they believed the revolution would result in mob rule and the destruction of private property rights. The Democratic-Republicans, on the other hand, sympathized with the French and supported their revolution because of the democratic ideals it represented.

The lines between these two parties were clearly drawn by the end of George Washington's second term in office. When it became clear that Washington did not intend to remain in office, Americans prepared for their first-ever contested, two-party presidential election. President Washington strongly urged Americans not to divide into what he deemed divisive political parties, but his warnings went unheeded as Americans entered into the election of 1796.

STUDY ALERT

The Federalists: The political party led by Alexander Hamilton favored a strong centralized federal government, corporate and commercial interests, a national bank, and the imposition of import tariffs to protect industry. Many Federalists believed in Hamilton's doctrine of implied powers and were broad constructionists, arguing that the Constitution should be loosely interpreted.

STUDY ALERT

The Republicans: The political party led by Thomas Jefferson opposed a strong central government, the creation of a national bank, and imposition of protective tariffs. The party instead believed in states' rights and feared that the Federalists favored a monarchy. Republicans were strict constructionists, believing that the Constitution should be interpreted exactly as written.

THE ELECTION OF 1796

In the election of 1796, opposing parties fought for the presidency for the first time. Federalist party leaders nominated John Adams and Thomas Pinckney, and Republican party leaders nominated Thomas Jefferson and Aaron Burr. Leaders engaged in ten weeks of furious campaigning, including the distribution of hand-bills and leaflets. Extensive press coverage reported the candidates' mudslinging, such as Jefferson being called a "mean-spirited, low-lived fellow, the son of a half-breed squaw, sired by a Virginia mulatto father."

During the campaign, the Republicans painted Adams as a monarchist and were highly critical of Washington's acceptance of Hamilton's financial plans. Meanwhile, the Federalists portrayed Jefferson as an atheist and a supporter of the French who would lead the United States into war with Britain.

Except for Aaron Burr, who visited each New England state, the nominees *themselves* did little personal campaigning. Adams did not believe in campaigning, remaining at home in Massachusetts until after the vote. Jefferson also did not campaign in a traditional sense, although he did not rebuff the Republican's efforts.

Seventy votes were required to win the presidency, and Adams earned 71 electoral votes. Under the rules at the time, Jefferson, who finished second, became the vice president. (The Twelfth Amendment, passed in 1804, established a separate ballot for vice president and president.)

PRESIDENT JOHN ADAMS

John Adams's transition to power went smoothly, but his presidency was rife with political turmoil. Adams frequently disagreed with both political parties; he made his own decisions despite opposition even from his own cabinet. Adams also struggled for control of the War Department, which was loyal to Hamilton.

Adams also inherited considerable tensions with France when he took office, tensions that many, including Alexander Hamilton, hoped would bring the United States into war with France. The French were involved in a conflict with Britain at the time, and because France considered the United States to be a British ally, the French had plundered approximately 300 U.S. merchant ships. Tensions mounted even further after the XYZ Affair, which involved three French agents demanding bribes and a loan from the United States in order to continue diplomatic relations with the United States.

To respond to French provocations, Adams made several important decisions. He strengthened the Army and the Navy during his term. To pay for the bolster-ing of defense, Adams levied new taxes, including a direct tax on property in 1798. This angered taxpayers, leading to a bloodless uprising by German-speaking farmers known as the Fries Rebellion.

Adams angered more of the public, as well as Jefferson and Madison, with the passage of the Alien and Sedition Acts in 1798. The Alien and Sedition Acts were designed to quash the political voice of pro-French immigrants in the United States by authorizing the deportation of foreigners and increasing the residency require-ment from five to fourteen years. Opponents, including Jefferson and Madison, argued that these acts were unconstitutional, and issued resolutions on behalf of the states of Kentucky and Virginia that argued that the federal government was a compact of states and thus the states themselves should be allowed to determine the constitutionality of federal actions.

Adams also supported cutting off trade with France, and allowed Americans to seize French ships. As a result, the Americans became unofficial allies of Great Britain between 1798 and 1800. Adams soon became convinced that France was intending to tone down its anti-American rhetoric and discontinue its seizure of American ships. Thus, Adams sought to avoid a full-fledged war with France. In 1799, he sent diplomat William Vans Murray to France to try to negotiate peace. France, under the rule of Napoleon Bonaparte, realized that fighting with the United States was not advantageous. Adams was so proud of his efforts to avoid war and secure peace with France that he had this accomplishment mentioned on his epitaph.

The Jefferson Memorial.

THE ELECTION OF 1800

The election of 1800 came during much public displeasure with the Adams Administration. The election was a rematch of the 1796 election, with John Adams and Charles Pickney the Federalist Party nominees and Aaron Burr and Thomas Jefferson the Democratic-Republican candidates.

The campaign, often referred to as the Revolution of 1800, was bitter, with slanderous accusations from both sides. For example, Adams warned that if Jefferson was elected, Christianity would be destroyed and prostitutes would "preside in the sanctuaries now devoted to the worship of the Most High."

The Federalists asserted the Republican support of the French Revolution proved them radicals who would destroy the country, while Republicans accused the Federalists of being pro-British, pro-centralization, and pro-monarchy.

John Adams lost the election, due in part to heavy opposition within his own party. The Republicans were also aided by the larger number of delegates in their stronghold, the southern states, due to the Constitution's Three-Fifths Compromise, which counted a slave as a partial person when determining a state's number of electoral votes.

Burr and Jefferson tied, so the House of Representatives decided the outcome. Under pressure from Alexander Hamilton to block Burr, the House selected Jefferson. Despite the political infighting and partisanship, power changed hands peacefully after the election. This sent an important precedent for the new republic.

PRESIDENT THOMAS JEFFERSON

Hailed as the People's President, President Thomas Jefferson was sworn in on March 4, 1801. In his first inaugural address, Jefferson outlined what he believed to be the essential principles of government. He played down the deep partisanship that had marked the election of 1800, redirecting Americans towards their common purpose and voice in a representative government.

Thomas Jefferson and Alexander Hamilton had long been seen as representing two starkly different ends of the political spectrum, and during his presidency Jefferson sought to undo many of the pro-government policies of his Federalist predecessors. In what become known as the Jeffersonian Democracy, Jefferson sought to reduce taxes that had been raised by Hamilton and Adams and to lower the national debt. He was a proponent of states' rights and sought to minimize what he saw as an alarming expansion of federal powers, as seen in the creation of a national bank and growing military.

The most significant achievement of Jefferson's first term in office was the Louisiana Purchase of 1803. This purchase, which will be explored in further detail later in this chapter, involved the acquisition of an enormous amount of land between the Mississippi River and the Rocky Mountains, which currently is home to fifteen U.S. states and parts of two Canadian provinces. Jefferson agreed to pay a total of $15 million in cash and canceled French debt in exchange for the land. While Jefferson was a strict constructionist and struggled with the constitutionality of the purchase, he understood its importance to the future of the growing nation.

During his first term, Jefferson also faced challenges from pirates and navigated the country through the Barbary War, which will be explored later in this chapter.

Thomas Jefferson was reelected in 1804, defeating Federalist Charles Pinkney. Jefferson's second term in office was wrought with considerably more conflict than his first. During this term, Jefferson faced mounting threats from the French. He also outlawed the importation of African slaves in 1806.

Finally, Jefferson passed the Embargo Act, restricting American ships from trading with Great Britain and France from 1807 to 1812. The Act was designed to protect U.S. interests and neutrality, but it failed to do that and instead helped to contribute to the War of 1812.

JOHN MARSHALL AND THE SUPREME COURT

John Marshall was chief justice of the Supreme Court during Jefferson's presidency and was instrumental in shaping the role of the judicial branch. The Federalists appointed Marshall to the Supreme Court after their defeat in the 1800 election, as part of the Midnight Judges Act. Passed because the Federalists knew they had lost control of both the executive and legislative branches, the Midnight Judges Act changed the number of justices on the Supreme Court from six to five, so Jefferson could only appoint a judge if two judges stepped down during his term.

HISTORY COMES ALIVE

Supreme Court Chief Justice John Marshall and President Thomas Jefferson were enemies, but did you know they were also relatives? Marshall was related to Jefferson on his mother's side, and both Marshall and Jefferson were descendants of Virginia Colonist William Randolph.

Despite their familial connection, John Marshall and Thomas Jefferson were bitter political enemies. John Marshall was a Federalist and espoused the expansion of federal powers, especially the power of the Supreme Court. Marshall developed the principle of judicial review, where he argued that the Supreme Court has the task of determining the constitutionality of any act of the other two branches of government.

Thomas Jefferson, a Republican, wanted to minimize the power of the central government, and believed that Marshall went too far in expanding the power of the Supreme Court.

Prior to this appointment, John Marshall served as the secretary of state during Adams' presidency and had been a long-time Federalist leader. In his role as chief justice he made a number of important rulings, using Federalist principles to build a strong central government over Democratic-Republican objections. The court, for example, repeatedly interpreted the enumerated powers of Congress broadly to offer more authority and typically confirmed that federal law had supremacy over state law.

Marshall also changed the way opinions were issued. The prior procedure had each justice writing his own opinion, but under Marshall's authority, the Supreme Court began to hand down a single opinion so that the Court's rule could be clearer. This was important because the decisions of the Supreme Court became binding **precedents,** meaning the rulings became the guiding principle applied in all subsequent cases.

Perhaps Marshall's most important and lasting contribution, however, was the ruling in *Marbury v. Madison* in 1803. In *Marbury*, the court struck down an act of Congress, declaring it unconstitutional. Essentially, this ruling established the power of **judicial review**, the court's power to determine whether a law is constitutional. This right is not expressly granted in the Constitution, but Marshall believed that the court had to "expound and interpret" laws as part of its obligations.

Marshall and his court believed that, because the Constitution is the supreme law of the country, it must necessarily take precedence over any conflicting laws. The court, therefore, must strike down laws that are in violation of the Constitution. Unless the court had the power to do this, the Constitution would, in effect, be nullified and cease to be enforceable.

Marshall's principle of judicial review increased the Supreme Court's importance in government, making the court the final decision maker on matters of constitutionality. This decision put Marshall at odds with Thomas Jefferson, who believed that judicial review made the courts more powerful than the executive branch. Despite Jefferson's strong objections, the doctrine of judicial review remains in force to this day.

PRECEDENT A legal decision handed down by a court that serves as the law in subsequent cases.

JUDICIAL REVIEW The court's power to determine if a law is constitutional.

MID-CHAPTER QUESTIONS

1. What branch of government is responsible for regulating commerce and which article of the U.S. Constitution enumerates those responsibilities? What court case further detailed the role of this branch of government in commerce? What were some of Alexander Hamilton's strategies in the area of commerce and why were they controversial?

2. Explain some of the fundamental differences between the Federalist Party and the Republican Party. Who were some of the notable leaders within each party?

3. Explain some of President John Adams's strategies for dealing with the mounting pressure from France. Why were these policies controversial and how did they ultimately affect his bid for presidential reelection?

THE WEST

From the earliest years of its existence, the United States was expanding, and during Jefferson's presidency, the landmass of the United States doubled in size with the Louisiana Purchase. This opened the door for further westward expansion, which was later known as "manifest destiny," the idea that the United States was *supposed* to expand, by divine destiny, to new territories and areas. The lands acquired by the Louisiana Purchase became known as the American West and symbolized the essence of American identity and rugged individualism.

White and Indian Relations

At the start of the 1800s, relations between Indians and whites were, with some exceptions, largely peaceful, after a series of ugly battles during the 1790s. In 1796, the Government Trading Act had established government trading houses to regulate trade with the Indians. While fraud was rampant because trade was hard to control, trade had also become common and allowed for frequent interaction between whites and Indians. This trade began to break down cultural stereotypes. Many whites, for example, no longer viewed Indians as a threat but instead began to consider them as their "red children" and sought to improve their way of life through education. For instance, in March 1819, the Civilization Fund Act was enacted to provide funding for and encourage the white settlers to provide schools for the Indians.

The Indians, meanwhile, embraced new tools and technology. New agricultural methods, hunting rifles, and even household cooking utensils and colorful fabrics were incorporated into the Indian way of life, and many tribes, including the Cherokees and Seminole Creek Indians, largely assimilated to the European lifestyle. The schools contributed to the assimilation, and a new and more peaceful era of Indian–White relations began.

With the War of 1812, government trading houses began to suffer financially and private traders sought to do away with them. An act of Congress abolished private trading houses in May 1822 and private traders' fraudulent dealings with Native Americans spun out of control.

In 1823, Marshall and his court ruled in *Johnson v. M'Intosh* that private parties could not purchase land from Native Americans. In this decision, Marshall established the **discovery doctrine**. This doctrine held that tribes residing on discovered land did not hold the title to the land, nor were they sovereign. Rather, these tribes merely had the right to occupy the land. The land on which they resided could not be purchased by private individuals, but only by the discovering government.

DISCOVERY DOCTRINE A court ruling that determined that Native American tribes residing in discovered land did not hold the title to the land, nor were they sovereign.

While the decision helped prevent the defrauding of Native Americans by private individuals, it was an important step in the government's claims on Native American lands, claims that would culminate in future showdowns between government forces and Native Americans.

Nevertheless, during this era Jefferson sought peaceful means to establish U.S. sovereignty over the Indian nations inhabiting the land newly acquired through the Louisiana Purchase. The U.S. Mint had prepared special Indian Peace Medals, which were symbols of friendship towards the Indians. Frontiersmen also offered flags, gifts, and medicine to Native Americans they came to know as they headed west. Some tribes were wary at first of the peace medals, with one chief returning his because "he was afraid of the medal or any thing that white people gave to them." The medals eventually became prized by Native people and were used by future presidents in negotiating with tribes.

The Louisiana Purchase

The Louisiana Purchase is often considered one of the most important real estate ventures in U.S. history and was a major contribution to America's westward expansion.

In 1803, Napoleon, the well-known French emperor, retained control of what was known as the Louisiana Territories. The Louisiana Territories consisted of over 600 million acres of land between and including what are now the states of Montana and Louisiana. France was at war at the time and Napoleon was threatening to cut the United States off from the port of New Orleans, which would result in a huge loss of trade between the United States and its western settlements. President Thomas Jefferson was so threatened by the prospect that he considered entering into an allegiance with England to combat the French.

Jefferson sent ministers Robert Livingston and James Monroe to France to explore political options, attempt to purchase New Orleans and Florida, or enter into an alliance with the British against the French. To the Americans' surprise, Napoleon offered much more to the diplomats.

Napoleon's war against Britain was draining his finances and military resources, necessitating a new source of income. He offered to sell the Louisiana Territories to

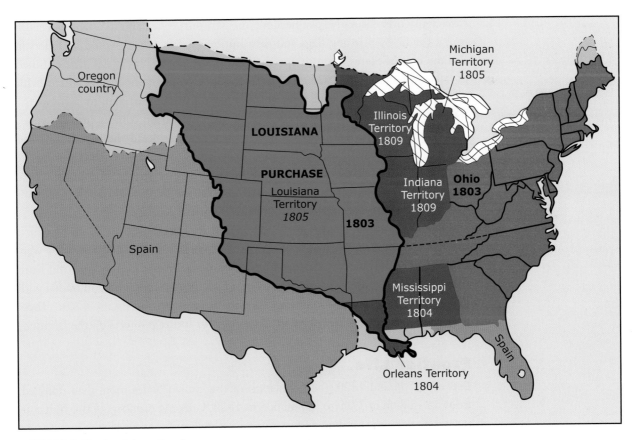

FIGURE 6.1 The Louisiana Purchase.

the United States for $15 million dollars, which came to less than 4 cents per acre of land. The United States would pay $11.25 million directly to France and would forgive $3.75 million of France's debt. The United States accepted and, after a year of negotiations and conventions, signed the Louisiana Purchase Treaty on April 30, 1803.

Jefferson's decision to move forward with the Louisiana Purchase was daring. In doing so, he had disregarded his promise to reduce the national budget. Perhaps more importantly, the Constitution made no mention of a presidential authority to acquire new territories. Jefferson's decision was, however, motivated by a number of important goals supported by his political party, including the vision of an agrarian-based society.

While the purchase caused controversy and unrest in parts of the original colonies, mostly due to the reduction of their political power in the aftermath of the purchase, the advantage and opportunity it afforded the United States far outweighed the political unrest it caused.

The Louisiana Purchase not only allowed for the continued use of established trade routes, it also opened up a huge portion of the West and gave the United States control over the majority of the continent. The expanding population also had room to grow on the new frontier; this growth began after the expeditions of Lewis and Clark.

Lewis and Clark

In 1804, Jefferson ordered the exploration and documentation of the land purchased from France in the Louisiana Purchase. The expedition was to catalog the new resources available to the country in this largely unexplored land. The exploration was also meant to identify the native tribes in the West, to establish U.S. sovereignty over the native people along the Missouri River, and to establish a claim to the Pacific by planting flags and distributing medals, which would let Jefferson and the United States claim title to the land under the discovery doctrine outlined in *Johnson*. Jefferson also wished to learn about the topography and weather of this new territory. The main goal, however, was to find an efficient path to facilitate the trade with Asia and to help stop the British fur traders from coming into Oregon.

Jefferson named Army captain Meriwether Lewis to head the expedition, and Lewis chose William Clark as his leader. They would spend two years exploring the new territory, from 1804 to 1806, making the first ever trip cross country to the Pacific Coast. Their trip would have a strong historic impact, although it was not widely noticed until around the turn of the twentieth century.

On their journey, Lewis and Clark produced around 140 maps, all of which covered the yet-uncharted area of the Pacific Northwest. Natural resources were also identified. While they did not find a commercial route to Asia, they did learn that Native Americans along the Mississippi had already dealt with and traded with European settlers and that there was a way to travel to the Pacific Coast. These discoveries were enormously beneficial to trade for future pioneers on the frontier.

Frontier Life

Between 1796 and 1820, the population of the United States more than doubled, from 3.9 million in 1789 to 9.6 million in 1820. Growing numbers of this burgeoning population were heading west, with nearly 2 million Americans living in nine new states and territories west of the Appalachians. Composed of young couples, poor farmers, and others who sought their own lands and opportunities in the West, frontiersmen came to embody the American spirit of adventure and ruggedness. The lure of free or inexpensive land drew millions of Americans over the Appalachian Mountains westward, into the Ohio River Valley and beyond.

Pioneers frequently travelled west in covered wagons, on horseback, and on foot. Pioneers on the frontier frequently chose wooded areas to build their homes, where lumber was in ample supply. Thus, the log cabin and covered wagon became symbols of the American frontier and westward expansion.

While frontier life was marked with excitement and opportunity, it presented countless difficulties. Unfamiliar with the geography and weather of these regions, pioneers often had trouble transporting their goods and families and faced disease and death. Pioneers also faced attacks from Native American tribes seeking to protect their lands from western encroachment. Years later, in his 1893 thesis, Frederick Jackson Turner described the significance of the frontier on American life as "the meeting point between savagery and civilization."

Frontier life is perhaps best illustrated by the life of the legendary Daniel Boone. Boone lived from 1734 to 1820, and established one of the first English-speaking settlements west of the Appalachians, in what is now Kentucky. His adventures, both real and mythical, captured America's fascination with the frontier.

THE WAR OF 1812

As more and more Americans headed west, tensions continued to mount between the United States and Great Britain. Between 1802 and 1815, England was engaged in the Napoleonic Wars against France. During this period, British naval ships seized American ships, seamen, and cargoes, culminating in the British warship *Leopard's* opening fire on the *U.S.S. Chesapeake* in 1807. The British were forcing American sailors into the British Navy and were attempting to hinder American trade, resulting in a unique challenge for Jefferson.

The Barbary Pirates

For generations, pirates from the Barbary Coast of Africa, including the North African regions of Tripoli, Tunis, Morocco, and Algiers, ruled the Mediterranean, capturing European ships and crews for ransom. During the colonial period, Americans did not need to fear these pirates, as the British Royal Fleet protected colonial maritime interests. After the Revolutionary War, the United States agreed to pay $80,000 in tribute to the Barbary pirates, considering such tribute the cost of doing business

The National Road, now U.S. Route 40, was built to connect Cumberland, MD to St. Louis, MO and was one of the longest, most elaborate routes built during the early 19th century. While the road was originally to be built in the early 1800s, the War of 1812 prevented construction until 1815. The first portion of the road connected Cumberland with Wheeling, WV, and then beyond through Ohio upon the insistence of Henry Clay. This was also one of the first routes in the country to collect tolls to assist in the cost of repairs and maintenance.

with the East. Thomas Jefferson strongly opposed the payment of such bribes, arguing that such tributes only opened the door for further Barbary demands.

When Jefferson became president, he rejected Tripoli's demands for a $225,000 bribe and an annual tribute of $25,000. When the leaders in Tripoli declared war, President Jefferson sent naval vessels toward the Barbary Coast, beginning the First Barbary War. The show of force threatened the Barbary Alliance between Tripoli, Tunis, Morocco, and Algiers, but Tripoli still managed to destroy an American vessel and capture her crew. Despite the embarrassment that the ship's capture caused, Jefferson continued his naval action, and by 1805 a treaty brought the crisis to a close. While considered a victory for Jefferson, the treaty involved the United States still paying a ransom of $60,000 for each American sailor that had been captured. The war that had been started to prevent the payment of tributes essentially ended with the payment of tributes.

The Embargo

Jefferson was loathe to enter into war with Great Britain, and sought to act with equal caution and wisdom in dealing with the British after the incident with the *U.S.S. Chesapeake* as he had done with the Barbary Pirates. Along with Secretary of State James Madison, Jefferson introduced a new policy of *peaceful coercion*. This policy assumed that Europe depended heavily on American goods. To take advantage of that assumption, Jefferson signed the Embargo Act of 1807, which sought to keep American ships from taking cargo to any nation until England and France lifted their restrictions on American trade.

The embargo did not work the way Jefferson and Madison had hoped. The French and British did not depend on American imports as much as the Americans had thought, and Federalist merchants sought to thwart the embargo by continuing to trade with Europe. Great Britain continued its blockade, stopping American ships from reaching or delivering cargo into Europe. Similarly, Napoleon continued his Continental System, whereby he blocked British ships or ships that had been at British ports from entering French ports. As a result, despite Jefferson's efforts, Americans continued to be trapped. If they stopped at British ports, they faced French seizure, and if they did not carry British goods, they faced seizure by the Royal Navy.

While the embargo did not have a crushing effect on Europe, it did begin to cripple the American economy. American exports plummeted from $108 million in 1806 to $22 million in 1808. Jefferson, Madison, and other Republicans were accused of crushing the American economy in an effort to avoid war with Great Britain.

James Madison and the Young Republicans

Despite discontent over the embargo, James Madison was elected president in 1808. While considered by many to be a weak statesman, Madison was a respected philosopher, congressmen, and founding father.

Even though he faced mounting tensions with Great Britain in various naval disputes, Madison was leery of entering into war with Great Britain and preferred diplomatic methods of solving the problems between the United States and Great Britain. Continuing his predecessor's commitment to peaceful coercion, he repealed the ineffective embargo in 1809 and signed the Non-Intercourse Act. This act allowed the United States to trade with all nations except England and France; this was Madison's attempt at lifting the harmful effects of the embargo while continuing its embargo against the

Fort McHenry, Baltimore, Maryland. Francis Scott Key composed "The Star Spangled Banner" here during the War of 1812.

French and English. When this attempt at peaceful coercion failed, Madison made another effort, this time with a measure called Macon's Bill No. 2. This bill reopened trade with Britain and France, but allowed the president to call for new sanctions if any nation meddled with American commerce.

Napoleon only paid lip service to this act, and both the French and the British largely ignored its principles. As a result, Madison came under intense pressure to pursue non-peaceful options against Great Britain. Many Americans believed that Great Britain was assisting in the Native American revolts, led by Tecumseh and the Western Indian Confederation. Others argued that the United States should annex Florida from Spain, one of England's European allies.

A group called the Young Republicans, nicknamed "War Hawks," agreed with these sentiments and exerted intense pressure on the president to declare war upon Great Britain. Led by Henry Clay of Kentucky and John C. Calhoun of South Carolina, the Young Republicans pushed Madison to ask Congress to declare war on Great Britain in June 1812. Madison complied. In declaring war, he demanded that the United States have territorial control within its own borders, and that it enjoy neutrality and free trade on the Atlantic. The War of 1812 was underway.

There were several reasons for the War of 1812. British naval advances, blockades, and policies were seen as hurting American commerce and agriculture. Many Americans wanted to annex Florida from Spain and wanted to defeat the Indians, who were supported by the British in the West. Furthermore, many Americans believed war was the only way to preserve America's honor with the British.

The British Invasion

After months of battles in the Atlantic, in 1813 the British Royal Fleet began consistently harassing American ships up and down the Atlantic Coast. In 1814 the British sailed up Chesapeake Bay and invaded the American mainland, burning government buildings in the District of Columbia, including the White House, and advancing on Baltimore. There, they met organized American forces at Fort McHenry, which inspired Francis Scott Key to compose "The Star Spangled Banner." For the next several months, Americans once again found themselves battling the British on American land, and were largely on the defensive.

Meanwhile, the war raged in the West. The United States was unable to take advantage of its geographical advantage because of difficulties in transportation and resupply. The Americans invaded western Canada in the summer of 1812 but had to retreat because of the lack of adequate supplies.

Hartford Convention

The economic hardships of the War of 1812 were perhaps nowhere worse than in New England, which depended largely on the shipping industry. As a result, New Englanders opposed the war from the start, and continued to express their dissatisfaction throughout the war.

In 1814, representatives from Massachusetts, Connecticut, Rhode Island, New Hampshire, and Vermont met at what became known as the Hartford Convention.

Led by congressmen Daniel Webster, some of these representatives suggested that New England secede from the Union, while the majority voted for revisions to the Constitution. In an effort to end the so-called "Virginia dynasty" of presidents, these New England delegates voted that the presidency be limited to one four-year term and that the office had to be held by representatives from different states. Others suggested additional amendments to further regulate trade and commerce.

By late 1814, the nation faced internal threats of secession and external threats, including the invasion by Great Britain. Fortunately, that year England finally defeated Napoleon in Europe, and sought to end its battles in the United States. On Christmas Eve 1814, the Americans and British signed the Treaty of Ghent, which required both nations to give up their territorial gains and determine a border between the United States and Canada.

PRESIDENT JAMES MONROE

With support from President Madison, James Monroe was elected president in 1816, and reelected in 1820. He was the fifth president of the United States, and the last of the Virginia dynasty of presidents. He also represented the last of a breed of Republicans in the tradition of Jefferson.

James Monroe's presidency was initially marked as the "Era of Good Feelings," a period that involved little political strife. Later in his first term, the United States faced a depression that became known as the Panic of 1819. This depression lifted in part when Great Britain slowly increased its imports of American goods.

Monroe also engaged the nation in a fervent debate over how the Missouri Territory would be admitted into the Union—as a slave or a free state. The Missouri Territory applied to enter the union as a slave state in 1819, and this application failed. Congress continued to debate the elimination of slavery in Missouri until the Missouri Compromise was passed in 1820. This compromise allowed Missouri to enter as a slave state, while Maine entered as a free state. The compromise also barred slavery north of the latitude 36° 30' N. This compromise was later overturned in 1857 when the Supreme Court declared it unconstitutional in the Dred Scott case.

Monroe also faced criticism for his handling of relations with Native Americans. In 1817 he sent General Andrew Jackson to subdue the Seminole Indians in Florida and to punish Spain, whom Monroe believed was supporting the Native Americans in Florida. In what became known as the First Seminole War, Jackson's actions became the subject of much Congressional scrutiny and debate, but later Jackson was cleared of all suggestions of misconduct, aided by the largely expansionist sentiments in Congress.

Monroe Doctrine

James Monroe's greatest contribution as president was a policy that later became known as the "Monroe Doctrine." In this new foreign policy, which he outlined in his annual address to Congress in 1823, Monroe declared that the United States would not entangle itself in the internal affairs or external disputes of European nations. More important, Monroe declared that the Americas were to be no longer "subject for further colonization" by those same European nations. At the time he delivered the speech, Monroe, along with Secretary of State John Quincy Adams, intended the policy to serve as a warning to Spain not to try to reconquer Latin American lands that fought hard for independence from Spain during the Napoleonic Wars. Monroe also intended to prevent Russia from continuing to influence Alaska and the Pacific Coast of the United States.

END OF CHAPTER TAKE-AWAYS

■ **The Constitution and Commerce** – Article 1 of the U.S Constitution established Congress, giving it the responsibility to regulate commerce.

■ **Washington's New Government** – George Washington, the first president of the United States, was elected, unopposed, for two terms. As secretary of the treasury, Alexander Hamilton's controversial financial program levied taxes and created a national bank.

■ **Political Parties** – The Federalist Party believed in a loose interpretation of the Constitution and supported a strong central government. The Republicans had a strict constructionist position and favored states rights.

■ **President John Adams** – In the election of 1796, Federalist John Adams defeated Republican Thomas Jefferson, who then became vice president under Adams. As a result of disagreements with France, President Adams expanded the Army and Navy by raising taxes and passed the Alien and Sedition Acts of 1798.

■ **President Thomas Jefferson** – In 1800, Republican Thomas Jefferson defeated John Adams' in his bid for reelection. Jefferson oversaw the Louisiana Purchase, which more than doubled the size of the nation in 1803.

■ **John Marshall** – Chief Justice Marshall expanded the scope and power of the court with judicial review.

■ **The West** – With the purchase of the Louisiana Territory, more Americans headed west of the Appalachian Mountains. The land was surveyed by the historic expedition of Lewis and Clark.

■ **The War of 1812** – The United States went to war with Great Britain as a result of ongoing tensions over ships and cargo in the Atlantic and England's support of Native American uprisings.

■ **President James Monroe** – Monroe introduced the Monroe Doctrine, stating that the United States would not meddle in the affairs of Europe and European nations could no longer colonize or meddle in the Americas.

REFERENCES

Gawalt, G. W. (n.d.). America and the Barbary pirates: An international battle against an unconventional foe. Retrieved from the Library of Congress website: http://memory.loc.gov/ammem/collections/jefferson_papers/mtjprece.html

Henretta, J. A., Brownlee, W. E., Brody, D., & Ware, S. (1987). *America's history to 1877*. Chicago, IL: Dorsey Press.

Holt, M. (2008). *By one vote: The disputed presidential election of 1876*. Lawrence, KS. University Press of Kansas.

James Madison Museum. (n.d.). James Madison. Retrieved from http://jamesmadisonmuseum.vabion.com/?page_id=56

Graff, H. F. (Ed.). (2002). John Adams: The retreat from war. In *Profiles of U.S. presidents* (3rd ed.). Retrieved from http://www.presidentprofiles.com/Washington-Johnson/John-Adams-The-retreat-from-war.html

Library of Congress. (2010, October 28). Alien and Sedition Acts. Retrieved from http://www.loc.gov/rr/program/bib/ourdocs/Alien.html

Stites, F. N. (1997). *John Marshall: Defender of the Constitution*. New York, NY: Longman Press.

University of Virginia, Miller Center. (2012). American president: A reference resource. Retrieved from http://millercenter.org/president/adams/essays/biography/3

The White House. (n.d.). Thomas Jefferson, 1801–1809. Retrieved from http://www.whitehouse.gov/about/presidents/thomasjefferson

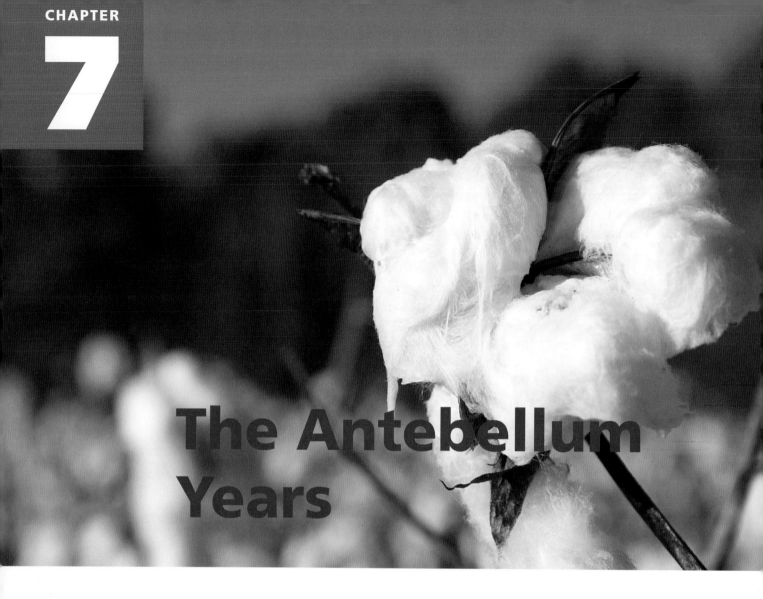

The Antebellum Years

There is not a single item in our homes today, from kitchen tables to running shoes, that cannot be traced back to the production processes developed during the antebellum era. The creation of the cotton gin and the mass production of furniture, clothing, and shoes in factories that relied on interchangeable parts all took place during this time, called the Industrial Revolution. The antebellum age also saw the rise of the class to which many Americans belong today—the middle class. This class was able to earn wages for work and could own land or property without having to belong to the American elite.

The antebellum era also involved historical events that continue to affect our modern age. Driving through urban areas today, one sees the results of the influx of residents to cities that occurred during this period. Without a doubt, the antebellum years were some of the most formative in American history. In this era, the nation turned away from its years of revolutionary struggle toward industrial advancement, and then ultimately back to struggle, but this time toward the Civil War.

NATIONALISM AND MARKET SOCIETY

The pre-Civil War era was marked by a growing sense of American nationalism following the War of 1812. During this period, Americans enjoyed pride in their nation. President James Monroe was elected in 1816, a time with relatively few tensions among parties and a growing sense of unity across the new nation.

In this period, many Americans believed they had a responsibility to spread their democratic form of government and Christianity from the East Coast to the Midwest and beyond, all the way to the Pacific Coast.

Called the American **Manifest Destiny** by newspaper editor John L. O'Sullivan in the 1845 issue of the *United States Magazine and Democratic Review*, the nationalistic principle of Manifest Destiny was used by President Polk's administration to encourage American expansion west. Travelling difficult westward routes, millions of Americans followed this Manifest Destiny, creating an unprecedented demand for improved transportation and spreading industrial and agricultural workers throughout the nation.

By the end of the antebellum area, U.S. nationalism was at an all-time high. While expansionists pushed west, anti-expansionists held more firmly to their position that Americans should focus on strengthening the American economy rather than on expanding its borders. Anti-expansionists included notable figures, including Abraham Lincoln, who expressed this position first as a lawyer and then as a congressman after 1833.

Furthermore, specific and distinct nationalistic identities formed in the North and South. The North began to expand its urban, immigrant, and highly industrialized identity. Many in the North also wanted a strong, centralized government and believed that the U.S. federal government held ultimate authority over individual states. Meanwhile the South had a more agricultural identity, where slavery played a critical role in the economy of Southern plantations and influenced the lives of nearly every citizen in some way. Many Southerners believed firmly in **states' rights**, the idea that each state had the right to determine what was unconstitutional on the federal level because the states had originally formed the Constitution. A primary proponent of this states' rights position was John C. Calhoun, who expressed it in his essay "South Carolina Exposition and Protest."

The strong American national identity, in its Northern, Southern, expansionist, or non-expansionist elements, was not the only remarkable component of the antebellum era. The decades leading up to the Civil War also involved the expansion of the U.S. market economy. During these years, the U.S. economy in the North shifted largely from a farming economy to a market economy. A **market economy** is defined by the demand for goods and services. Employees earn wages in a market economy. The shift to a market economy took hold most significantly in the northern and western portions of the nation, where technological advances, immigration, and transportation improvements made the shift from agriculture to industry easy. These changes would become critical underlying factors of the Civil War.

MANIFEST DESTINY The widely held belief that it was inevitable for the United States to spread westward and claim all of the lands to the Pacific Ocean.

STATES' RIGHTS Rights reserved for state governments or issues that the federal government does not have authority to control in the individual states.

MARKET ECONOMY An economy driven by the forces of supply and demand and based on the exchange of money for goods and services.

TRANSPORTATION

The antebellum period was marked by a redistribution of where Americans lived. They moved from farms to cities during this time—a process known as **urbanization**—and from the eastern part of the country to the western. Those who came to reside in cities included millions of immigrants who sought work in industry. Each of these trends required dramatic advances in the nation's transportation technology.

URBANIZATION The development of population centers or cities and the social, industrial, and governmental organizations that help them function.

Canals

The construction of canals was one of the most important developments of the transportation revolution. Unlike roads, which were expensive to maintain and made for rough wagon travel, canals allowed travel by boat that was relatively fast and easy. Canals made it possible for people and goods from inland areas to move to coastal areas. The most successful canal built during this era was the Erie Canal, which was officially completed in 1825. It made it possible for farmers and manufacturers in the Great Lakes region to easily transport their products to the East Coast.

The overwhelming success of the Erie Canal paved the way for dozens of other canals, all designed with the goal of improving trade with the West. While building the canals involved considerable amounts of capital and labor, they were soon seen as a way to keep the market economy thriving and people moving.

Steamboats

Closely related to the success of canals was the advancement of boating transportation. Robert Fulton had invented the steamboat in 1807, but it had been too large and

required too much wood and coal to operate efficiently. Furthermore, the steamboats had difficulty navigating the shallow waters of many newly constructed canals. Growing demand to move people and goods put engineers to work to design models that did not have these limitations. By the early 1820s steamboat improvements had cut the cost of traveling by rivers in half, and by the 1830s steamboats were the primary means of transportation on U.S. rivers and lakes. By 1840 an elaborate, well-organized system of water travel, which involved canals and steamboats, was well underway.

Railroads

Interest in railroads also began to grow during this period. Around 1830, the Baltimore and Ohio Railroad began operating, and by the early 1850s, railroads began to expand their tracks quickly, making travel between New York, Pennsylvania, and Chicago easier than it had ever been.

Railroad expansion during the antebellum era also lowered the cost of moving farming equipment, supplies, and farmers west, making it easier for pioneers to farm new lands. Railroads also made it much easier for Americans to buy and sell goods throughout areas connected by the railroads.

By the end of the antebellum era, railroads had begun to replace steamboats and were already carrying more freight. Railroads were able to travel uphill and far inland, beyond the reach of water travel. Railroads were also built at a fraction of the cost of canals and were becoming more reliable and faster than any other means of land travel. Railroad technology continued to improve, and soon it was affordable and practical to move from one part of the country to another. The majority of this development of the rail system occurred in the northern parts of the country; disputes between states in the South significantly slowed the development of rail travel there.

AGRICULTURE

In the years before the Civil War, agriculture still dominated in the South. With the development of Cyrus McCormick's automatic power-reaper, grain production improved throughout the nation, especially in the West. Another important crop was tobacco. While tobacco production had slowed during the Revolutionary War, it had returned to its pre-War levels by the 1820s.

Cotton and the Cotton Gin

Even with slave labor, cotton farming during the colonial era was notoriously costly and time-consuming. As a result, cotton farming was not as lucrative as some other crops, such as tobacco and rice.

In 1793, however, Eli Whitney invented the **cotton gin**. This machine separated cotton fibers and seeds automatically, enabling a slave to process over 50 pounds of cotton in one day. Because of patent issues, Whitney was unable to cash in on the development of his invention and cotton gins proliferated throughout the nation, with farmers and inventors creating countless models and adaptations.

The development of the cotton gin revolutionized American agriculture and culture. Southern farms rapidly expanded. Sprawling Southern plantations, which depended primarily on slaves for farming, became the driving force behind agriculture, economics, and even politics in the South. To increase cotton production on their plantations, Southern landowners purchased a growing number of slaves from Africa and the West Indies before the importation of slaves was banned by Congress in 1808. With large, fertile plots of land, cotton gins, and plentiful slave labor, cotton production in the South became hugely profitable. When slave importation from foreign lands ended, many slave owners began to trade in slaves themselves, selling the children of their existing slaves to meet the increased demand.

The development of the cotton gin and the expansive growth of cotton did not only affect the South. In the North, business owners created factories to spin and process the cotton into fabric, which was then turned into a variety of textiles that merchants could sell to growing markets that were newly accessible due to advances in transportation. English textile mills were also major purchasers of Southern cotton.

FACTORIES

The cotton gin was not the only advancement in the area of factory production during the antebellum period. In what became known as the **Industrial Revolution**, which occurred from the 1820s to the 1890s, machines and organized workers replaced hand production in nearly every area of industry.

COTTON GIN A tool that separates cotton fibers from the seeds of the cotton plant; this machine allowed laborers to process cotton much faster than doing it by hand.

INDUSTRIAL REVOLUTION A dramatic change in technology that streamlined manufacturing, communication, transportation, and production processes.

STUDY ALERT

Invented by Eli Whitney, the cotton gin (short for *engine*) mechanically separated raw cotton fibers from seeds. This process used to be notoriously labor-intensive. This invention prompted cotton farming to explode in the South, and for clothing and textile production to expand in the North.

Cotton Gin.

Technology

In addition to the cotton gin, Eli Whitney's other great contribution to manufacturing was the development of interchangeable parts, which allowed workers to easily replace broken pieces of machinery. This development reduced the cost and increased the speed of factory work.

Factory owners improved on Whitney's inventions, creating other beneficial technologies and multiplying productivity. For example, textile mill inventor Richard Garsed made improvements to textile processes that doubled the speed of his factory operations. In 1842 he invented the "cam and harness," which made it possible for elaborate fabrics to be created by machine more quickly and efficiently than making them by hand.

Another industrial step forward at this time was the use of water power in mills. Flour mills featured machines that moved grain, cleaned it, ground it to flour, moved the flour, and cooled it, all with the power of water. One inventor, John Sellars, and his family, used water power to develop products such as wire sieves, fire hoses, paper, and more.

In 1824, inventors and many others joined forces to create the Franklin Institute of Philadelphia, one of the first formal associations of mechanics in the nation. The institute recognized and celebrated mechanics for their accomplishments and disseminated information about the development and use of industrial technological advances. By 1840, such advances affected every industry, from steel and iron products to food, weapons, and textiles.

Textiles

Many of the most important advances in industry during the antebellum era came in the area of textiles. As mentioned previously, the cotton gin made growing and processing cotton more affordable, and gave rise to the boom of textiles in the North.

An ever-growing demand for textiles drove innovation in their production methods. Textile innovators used Whitney's concept of interchangeable parts and devised new machines such as lathes and planers, which enabled them to compete effectively with British manufacturers in terms speed and quality for the first time. American textile factories also created fabrics with unique and elaborate patterns, which were in much demand at the time and which had previously been produced mostly by Europeans.

Shoes

In the early years of the nation, most shoes were produced in Massachusetts, and many were assembled in a town called Lynn. Local capitalists gave shoe-making supplies to women and children who lived on farms, and they stitched together sections of shoes. Merchants then collected these and took them back to Lynn, where they were assembled and sent to markets throughout the nation.

As manufacturing technologies improved, so did the production of shoes. Buckles replaced ribbon for lacing, and soon could be mass produced, and machines crafted leather compounds into soles. In 1846 the sewing machine was invented and replaced hand-stitching in shoes. With these advancements, shoemaking slowly moved from home-based operations to factory production.

The Labor Movement

The advances in industry also translated into unprecedented strides in the American workforce. For the first time in history, work began to be organized with the express purpose of increasing productivity.

People who grew up working on farms were now being pulled from outdoor work, or *outwork*, to work instead in workshops. Age was not a factor during this labor movement—men, women, and children alike found work in industry. In some areas, children under the age of 16 made up nearly half of the workforce, often working grueling 12- to 14-hour days and abandoning their formal educations.

Additionally, for the first time in history, workers began to perform their duties in assembly lines. In pork-packing plants in Cincinnati, for example, workers stayed in stations and were assigned specific tasks, such as weighing or tagging the slaughtered pigs, which came through on overheard rails operated by water power. While the technology was simple, the organization of workers into an assembly line highly improved the productivity of the plants.

Advances in labor also involved how workers were remunerated and cared for during their employment. The textile industry in the United States faced stiff competition from British manufacturers, in part because of cheap labor in Great Britain. To remain competitive, American textile manufactures began relocating and housing workers in towns near their plants. In a unique approach, the Boston Manufacturing Company recruited many young, single women to work in its textile plants. These women were paid more than they could earn for outwork, were offered housing through the company, and were provided access to cultural events and outings. This concept of providing for workers became known as the Waltham Plan, and soon was adopted by other textile mills, which came to hire nearly 40,000 female workers by the early 1830s.

In addition to employing female workers, some textile plants hired entire families. Textile plants in Rhode Island found great success hiring families in what became known as the Fall River Plan. The Waltham and Fall River Plans helped New England textile manufacturers gain advantages over other American factories, but it took further labor and technological improvements before they could compete with British producers. By the late 1820s, American plants were gaining the competitive edge over their British competitors.

Despite advances in some areas of labor, many workers lived and worked under deplorable conditions, and collective bargaining was illegal at the time. However, soon strikes began to occur, during which workers demanded better conditions. In 1834 the National Trades Union was formed, one of the first unions in the nation. A group of women workers organized and came to be known as the *Lowell Girls*. The Lowell Girls adopted revolutionary rhymes for the cause of labor, including the following song lyrics sung by workers who were protesting:

Oh! isn't it a pity, such a pretty girl as I
Should be sent to the factory to pine away and die?
Oh! I cannot be a slave, I will not be a slave,
For I'm so fond of liberty,
That I cannot be a slave

Later the government began to protect laborers. President Martin Van Buren developed a 10-hour workday for federal employees in 1840, and in 1842 the Massachusetts Supreme Court legalized the work of trade unions.

COMMUNICATION

Along with advancements in industry, the country made important strides in communications during the antebellum era. Inventor Samuel Morse built on new discoveries about electromagnetism to help invent the telegraph. Morse showed that communications could be sent over many miles using a series of dots and dashes that became known as Morse Code. By the mid-1800s, Morse Code was being used to dispatch trains and was helping spread news throughout the nation.

U.S. Postal System

The U.S. Postal Service used advancements in transportation and communication during this era to improve its services. The first big improvement was the use of steamboats to carry mail between the 1820s and 1850s. Mail speed improved again in the mid-1800s when rail transport replaced the use of steamboats. Rail was so important to the Postal Service that postal workers sorted mail on train cars.

POPULATION GROWTH

During the decades leading up to the Civil War, the United States saw unprecedented population growth. The population of the United States in 1820 was 10 million, in 1830 it was 13 million, and by 1840 it was nearly 17 million. By the start of the Civil War era, the population of the United States had exploded to over 31 million people. This population growth exceeded that of Great Britain, France, and Germany at the time.

During this period, the white population grew faster than the black population. The ban on the slave trade in 1808 had largely succeeded in stopping the sale of new slaves into the United States, with the exception of some pirating of slaves from Africa during this period. The growth of the black population was also limited by disease and the conditions in which many were forced to live. While slave mothers gave birth to large numbers of children, many died in infancy, and those who did survive had a much shorter life expectancy than whites. By the mid-1800s, there was one black slave in the United States to every five white citizens.

Over the same period, white infant mortality improved as medicine improved. While still subject to diseases and epidemics, whites overall were living longer, which helps explain the consistent growth of the white population during the antebellum period. Furthermore, immigration began to grow during this period. Between 1830 and 1831, over 14,000 immigrants came to the United States, and between 1832 and 1846 nearly 72,000 immigrants came. This number nearly quintupled between 1847 and 1854, when almost 335,000 immigrants entered the country. Many of these immigrants came from Ireland, Germany, and other parts of Europe.

HISTORY COMES ALIVE

Mark Twain, born Samuel Langhorne Clemens, was perhaps America's best known and most beloved novelist and humorist. Born in 1835 in Hannibal, Missouri, he began working as a newspaper printer and typesetter at a young age. There he published his first stories and became a steamboat pilot along the Mississippi River, a river he adored with passion that was evident in his writings. The most famous of these writings were two novels, *The Adventures of Tom Sawyer* (1876), and its sequel, *Adventures of Huckleberry Finn* (1885). These two novels are considered classics in American literature, and Huck Finn has been called the Great American Novel. In his book *Roughing It*, Mark Twain paints a caricature of frontier life, which involved American movement west of the Mississippi River to the Pacific Coast. In this work, characters like Sugarfoot Mike, Pock Marked Jake, and others epitomize stereotypes of the wild, rough ways of western pioneers.

Federal Land Rush

As the American population grew, so did the geographic expansion of the nation. More and more Americans followed the idea of Manifest Destiny and moved west. The federal government aided the pace of this expansion by passing the **Preemption Act of 1841**. In this act, Congress formally acknowledged that people often lived on public land before they formally purchased it from the government. To keep the land from speculators, Congress made it easier for settlers to purchase 160 acres of land from the government if they agreed to build homes and otherwise improve the land. The **Graduation Act of 1854** made it even cheaper for settlers to purchase land, in some cases at less than $1.25 per acre. Each of these acts, in addition to the proliferation of rail and steamboat travel, made it possible for more Americans to head west in search of a better life.

PREEMPTION ACT OF 1841
A law passed by Congress to prevent speculators from claiming areas of open land that made it easier for settlers to purchase 160 acres of land from the government.

GRADUATION ACT OF 1854 Another act passed by Congress that reduced the price of purchasing land and thereby encouraged Americans to move west.

Urbanization

In addition to moving west, more Americans began to move into towns and cities during the antebellum era. As industry grew and jobs were created, more and more families moved from farms to cities to find work. Similarly, immigrants were attracted to cities in order to work. The populations of New York, Philadelphia, Pittsburgh, Baltimore, Boston, and other cities grew radiply from 1820 to 1860. In some cases, these cities quadrupled in size during the years leading up to the Civil War. Many Irish immigrants, who tended to be less wealthy than German immigrants, remained in large cities where work could be found, and *Irish quarters* soon developed in every major Northeast city.

NEW SOCIAL STRUCTURES

In the years leading up to the Civil War, new social structures began to develop in the United States. As a result of the labor movement and improvements in technology and productivity, Americans had access to more goods and could make more money than ever before. As a result, a distinct middle class developed in the North.

The Middle Class

As Northern cities were flooded with workers from farms and from abroad, a wage labor system developed. This means people were paid an hourly wage for work.

The growth of industry and commerce in combination with this new system allowed workers to make more money. This payment system in turn enabled the development of America's first middle class—workers whose financial welfare came from the wages they earned. The middle class included engineers, mechanics, craftsmen, and others who owned homes and small areas of land. Many farmers also entered this middle class, capitalizing on growing demand for the meat, produce, and agricultural products necessary for a thriving industrial economy.

This middle class was behind many of the era's social reforms. Members of the middle class worked to eliminate prostitution, alcohol, and other social activities they deemed dubious. They also sought to improve the American education, prison, and mental health systems, and were the primary abolitionists in the nation.

This middle class also spread further west, as farmers and settlers pursued opportunities in new lands. Settler-friendly federal land laws made it easier for those moving west to build middle-class lives on new land.

The middle class was seen less in the South, where factory workers, lawyers, doctors, ministers, and merchants were a smaller proportion of the population than in the North. Classes in the South divided more along the lines of planters. Large plantation owners with many slaves were one class, owners with smaller plots and fewer or no slaves made up another class, and the slaves themselves were a third class. The Southern middle class saw less growth and reform than its Northern counterpart since its members often found themselves linked to the planter class.

Distribution of Wealth

Wealth was not evenly distributed during the antebellum period. After the Revolutionary War, the wealthiest 10 percent of the nation owned from one-third to one-half of the nation's wealth. During the Industrial Revolution, this changed considerably, so that by the start of the Civil War, the wealthiest 10 percent owned more than two-thirds of the nation's wealth.

Social Mobility

Despite the development of the middle class during this period, there was still little upward mobility for those at the bottom of the social structure. This was best seen on May Day in New York City, when residents of the city would move into new homes. Prior to the Industrial Revolution, such moves were relatively simple, as residents had few goods to move from place to place. By the 1820s New York's more affluent residents began to own more and more things, making May Day moves a complicated juggling of carpets, paintings, and other possessions.

In contrast, poorer New Yorkers had very few items for their May Day moves. Many of these workers suffered from high rents, periods of unemployment, poor pay, and injuries associated with working in difficult industry conditions. And there was little opportunity for these poorer Americans to move up into the more affluent

1. What was " Manifest Destiny," and how did it affect the geography and population of the United States during the antebellum era? How did the development of improved methods of transportation affect the pursuit of Manifest Destiny?

2. What was the Industrial Revolution? How did the growth change the way many Americans lived and worked in the antebellum era?

3. How did the U.S. population change in the years leading up to the Civil War? What were some of the causes of population growth? Did slave populations grow at the same rate as white populations? Why or why not?

portions of society. While all classes saw increases in income during the Industrial Revolution, there was little movement from lower classes to the middle class during this period.

POLITICAL CULTURE

By the early 1820s, wealth requirements on voting had been lifted, making it possible for all free white males to vote and prompting many more Americans to participate in political parties. In the North, some free black men were also able to vote. While slaves and women were still barred from the political process, voting had become more inclusive, and hence the 1820s became known as the age of the common man.

While the early years of antebellum saw the predominance of a one-party system centered around the Democratic-Republican Party, disagreements shortly led to a division into two distinct main political parties: the Democratic-Republicans, commonly known as Republicans, and the National-Republicans, later called the Whigs.

The Republicans believed strongly in states' rights and opposed central banking. They supported agrarian ways of life, aggressive westward expansion, and slave ownership. The Whigs believed in centralized power and banks, reform for schools and prisons, less-aggressive expansion, industrialization, and urbanization.

THE ELECTION OF 1824

The election of 1824 involved four main candidates, all of whom were Republicans, but who represented the different factions within the splintering party. The candidates were William Crawford, the secretary of treasury; John Q. Adams, son of John Adams and secretary of state under James Monroe; Henry Clay, who was Speaker of the House; and General Andrew Jackson, who became famous for his role in the Battle of New Orleans during the War of 1812. None of the candidates received the majority of the

popular or electoral votes. Jackson received the most, with 99 electoral votes and 151,363 popular votes. Adams had 84 electoral votes and 113,142 popular votes. Crawford came in third and Clay fourth.

According to the 12th Amendment of the Constitution, the House was to vote for the president under these circumstances. Each state had one vote and the top three candidates—Jackson, Adams, and Crawford—could be considered. Clay could not compete and cast his support behind Adams, whom he believed was most suited for the presidency. Adams was indeed elected president, and later named Clay to be his secretary of state, in an arrangement that many, especially in Jackson's camp, later referred to as the "corrupt bargain."

PRESIDENT JOHN QUINCY ADAMS

During the election of 1824, Henry Clay built the New England–Ohio Valley Coalition, which supported further industrialization and the rights of business owners. As president, John Quincy Adams set out to put into practice the plans of this coalition. Adams's plan was to promote "the improvement of agriculture, commerce, and manufactures, the cultivation of the mechanic and of the elegant arts, the advancement of literature and the progress of the sciences, ornamental and profound." To that end, Adams sought to further American exploration of the Far West and to create a national university and an observatory. Adams and Clay also developed economic policies known as the **American System**, which included tariffs to protect and grow American markets for agriculture and manufacturing, as well as subsidies to improve commerce.

These plans appeared to benefit the wealthiest businessmen in the nation, and did not endear Adams to many Americans, which in turn helped Jackson's ever-mounting popularity increase. Adams faced monumental opposition in Congress, and as a result was not able to accomplish many of the plans of his American System. Nevertheless, with the support of representatives from certain industries, Congress agreed to raise tariffs on various raw materials, including iron, molasses, wool, and more. This legislation came to be known as the tariff of abominations, as it raised the cost of living for many, especially in the South, where British goods were heavily imported.

Further damaging his image in the South and in the expanding West was Adams's support for the rights of Native Americans. Adams believed that Georgia had fraudulently gained the 1825 treaty against the Creek nation in which they ceded their once-protected land to the government of Georgia. The result was a face-off between the governor of Georgia and Adams over the rights of Native Americans. This confrontation lent ever more to the popularity of Andrew Jackson, who vigorously supported the rights of landowners in the South and West.

As president, John Quincy Adams was seen as an aristocrat, and was believed to be arrogant and aloof. In fact, Adams did not work to inspire or organize his own party. Adams even refused to campaign for reelection in 1828, saying, "If my country wants my services, she must ask for them."

AMERICAN SYSTEM The economic policy of President John Q. Adams that added tariffs with the hope of protecting American markets. It resulted in an increase in the cost of living, particularly in the South, and the policy became known popularly as the *Tariff of Abominations.*

PRESIDENT ANDREW JACKSON

As a result of Adams's political troubles, Andrew Jackson was confident of a win in the election of 1828, and he mounted a strong, strategic campaign. He appealed to voters throughout the nation and from every class and region. He made vague campaign promises about lowering tariffs and supporting westward expansion, giving few specifics in an effort not to alienate any voters. During his campaign, Jackson and his supporters came out against the special privileges of the aristocracy and fostered an ideal of democracy for all Americans. Jackson was seen as a candidate for the common man and an advocate for states' rights.

Jackson's party, which had once been known as the Democratic Republicans or Republicans, soon became known simply as Democrats, while Adams's camp was known as the National Republicans. Jackson's sway at the time was such that the party was referred to simply as the Jacksonians.

Jackson's primary opposition came from New England, where Adams-supporting business owners distrusted his vague promises and gruff approach. Nevertheless, Jackson was resoundingly elected in 1828, with farmers, labor unions, skilled workers, and western expansionists all offering support.

As president, Jackson announced sweeping reforms in the way public offices were held in Washington. He announced that high-level federal officials would serve for only four years, introducing a rotation of federal officers that enabled him to reward campaign supporters. While he chose cabinet members, he rarely relied on his official cabinet. Instead, Jackson had an informal group of advisors, his **kitchen cabinet**, which included several newspaper editors from the South.

> **KITCHEN CABINET** An informal group of advisors to the president.

Jackson believed it was his duty to destroy obstacles to everyday people achieving the American dream. He strongly opposed tariffs, the rebellious state of South Carolina, Native Americans, and especially the Second Bank of the United States. While Adams sought to strengthen this bank, Jackson saw it as a representation of "special privilege" and wanted its charter revoked.

Racial Tensions

Jackson saw Native Americans as obstacles to white expansion west; his convictions on this issue predated his election as president. He wrote to President Monroe in 1817, "I have long viewed treaties with the Indians an absurdity not to be reconciled with the principles of our government." He turned his back on his former allies, the Cherokee, and convinced them to sell millions of acres of their land for cents on the dollar.

Now with the power of the presidency and the support of white westerners from all classes and occupations, Jackson pursued his goal to remove all Indian tribes to lands west of the Mississippi River. He did not believe that Native Americans could be upstanding citizens because he saw them as barbaric, and he did not attempt to bring them into the political process.

Indian Relocation and the Trail of Tears

In his effort to relocate Native Americans to lands west of the Mississippi River, Jackson pursued multiple strategies. First he withdrew troops who were deployed to protect tribal lands in the Southeast. Southeast states wanted these Indian lands because they were rich for cotton growing and lay in the path of white settlement. Jackson's withdrawal of troops left the

> ## STUDY ALERT
>
> **Trail of Tears: Cherokee Indians in Georgia were forced to leave their lands and travel west of the Mississippi to a territory in modern-day Oklahoma. Forced to leave in winter, nearly 5,000 Cherokee died on this long, treacherous journey known as the Trail of Tears.**

Five Tribes of the Southeast—the Chickasaw and Chocktaw in Mississippi, Alabama, and Tennessee, the Seminole in Florida, and the Cherokee and Creek of Georgia and Alabama—subject to the state laws that were stacked against Native Americans.

The Cherokee in Georgia, for example, were forced to cede lands in 1825 and again in 1827. Then in 1828, Georgia declared that the Cherokee were not a protected Indian nation, and were *tenants* on the state's land. Other southeast states followed suit, making it possible for more whites to take Native American land.

INDIAN REMOVAL ACT OF 1830 A plan to relocate the Indian nations from the Southeast to areas west of the Mississippi River. What was initially described as a voluntary process quickly became one of force.

Also in an effort to move Indians, Jackson spearheaded the **Indian Removal Act of 1830**, which traded Native American land in the Southeast with land west of the Mississippi. Jackson had federal negotiators convince the tribes that the land west of the Mississippi was not owned and that they could live on it freely and indefinitely. Knowing that if they did not agree, tribes would be forcibly removed, Indian leaders reluctantly signed hundreds of agreements to move west.

If tribes did not agree to move west, per the Indian Removal Act, Jackson waged war against them. General Winfield Scott and an army of 7,000 men forced the tribes out. By 1837 all Indians were gone from much of the Southeast, except for the Cherokee in Georgia and a portion of Florida's Seminole. The Seminole, joined by runaway slaves who had married into the tribe, waged a guerrilla war against Jackson's troops and state militias. The Seminole Wars continued even after Jackson's presidency and reached farther north than Florida.

TRAIL OF TEARS A name given to the relocation of Cherokee Indians who were forced to move from their native lands to areas west of the Mississippi River. The tragic consequences of this federal policy included the deaths of thousands of Native Americans.

In 1836 a treaty was signed with the Cherokee, giving them two years to leave their lands and head west. In 1838, only 2,000 Cherokee of the original 18,000 tribal members had left their land. In the summer of 1838, President Martin Van Buren had General Scott round up most of the remaining Cherokee and place them in concentration camps. In the winter of that year, the Cherokee were forced to begin the treacherous and long march from their lands in Georgia to the new Indian Territory in present-day Oklahoma. Nearly 5,000 Cherokee died on the **Trail of Tears** and some 11,000 survived.

DID YOU KNOW?

The Civil War has been given many names over the past 150 years. Among many others, these names include *Mr. Lincoln's War,* the *Southern Rebellion,* and the *War for States' Rights.* Many Southerners still refer to the Civil War as the *War of Northern Aggression.* This is partly because of a nostalgic view on states' rights but also because of the obliteration that the Southern economy suffered during the war.

Free Blacks in the North

During Jackson's presidency, many blacks in the North may have been free, but they did not enjoy the same privileges and protection as whites. While Jackson fostered the age of the common man, opening electoral doors for even uneducated white males of all walks of life, free blacks in the North did not enjoy those rights. In fact, many free blacks, Native Americans, and all women were excluded from the electoral process. Blacks were segregated from whites throughout the North and were often the victims of various forms of racial prejudice.

The situation for free blacks was even more precarious in the Northwest, where they often had to show proof that they were free. In most of these states, including Ohio, blacks were not permitted to own property or to vote. They also frequently were the victims of assault, rape, and murder at the hands of whites. Many free blacks created their own schools, clinics, and orphanages.

The Nullification Crisis

South Carolina was a unique slaveholding state during Jackson's presidency. In 1830, 56 percent of South Carolina's population was comprised of slaves, and as a result, the state's wealthy landowners constantly worried about slave rebellions and the movement to abolish slavery. Meanwhile, South Carolina strongly opposed Adams's tariff of abominations. South Carolina's state convention adopted an **ordinance of nullification**, which declared null and void the tariff acts of 1828 and 1832. This bold step essentially said that states, such as South Carolina, had the right to declare the constitutionality of federal laws. South Carolina did this based largely on ideas presented by John C. Calhoun in his piece in the South Carolina Exposition in 1828. Even though Calhoun was now Jackson's vice president, Jackson and pro-slavery landowners in South Carolina strongly distrusted his position, and Calhoun resigned as vice president in 1832. Martin Van Buren, who pushed for the resignation to consolidate his own power, succeeded him to the vice presidency in 1833.

> **ORDINANCE OF NULLIFICATION** A law passed by the state of South Carolina that voided the federal tariff acts of 1828 and 1832 and directly challenged federal authority over states' rights.

Meanwhile, Calhoun was elected a U.S. senator from South Carolina and continued to lead the nullification movement. No other states joined the movement, and many Southern states still strongly supported Jackson. Jackson argued that nullification was unconstitutional, and he reinforced forts in the area and sent warships to South Carolina, sending a strong message to those supporting nullification. He made it clear that the government would act forcibly against any acts of treason and seccession, and pushed for the **Force Bill**, which allowed him to use force to enforce acts of Congress, such as the tariffs in question.

> **FORCE BILL** A bill passed under Jackson's administration that allowed the federal government to use force to make states comply with laws passed by Congress; the bill was passed in response to the Nullification Crisis in South Carolina.

Because Calhoun had not gained the support of others in the South, he worked out a compromise with Henry Clay, whereby tariffs in South Carolina were reduced over time. The Tariff Reduction Bill and the Force Bill were both passed. The Nullification Crisis ended with the demonstration that no state in the United States could nullify a federal law. The only option for states like South Carolina was secession, which foreshadowed ominous events to come.

The Bank War

Jackson also vigorously pursued the dissolution of the Second Bank of the United States during his presidency. The role of the bank was to stabilize the nation's supply of money. Jackson opposed the bank, and many in Congress disagreed with him. His primary opponents in Congress, Henry Clay and Daniel Webster, tried to stop Jackson by pushing for a recharter of the bank before the 1832 elections, which they knew Jackson would veto. Jackson did veto the bill, but in doing so, he argued that the Second Bank advanced the interests of the wealthy over everyday Americans. Jackson then pursued the destruction of the Second Bank prior to its charter's expiration in 1836 by engaging in a *bank war*. He removed the secretary of the treasury, replacing him with Roger B. Taney. Taney withdrew the government's money from the Second Bank and deposited those

Andrew Jackson statue at the St. Louis Cathedral.

funds into state banks. More and more Americans became divided over the issue, which gave rise to the formation of the Whig Party and the official reemergence of a two-party system in America.

Jacksonian Democracy

The Jacksonian Democracy refers to democratic spirit and the two-party system that emerged during the mid-1830s and continued to the mid-1850s. Andrew Jackson fought against the special privilege of elites in government, in contrast to the previous Jeffersonian Democracy, which, while frowning upon aristocracy, favored educated elites. The Jacksonians put little emphasis on education but sought to expand the access of all white men, even uneducated ones, to the electoral process.

Jacksonian democracy sought to strengthen centralized power by expanding the power of the executive branch over Congress. Jacksonians pursued the nation's Manifest Destiny of westward expansion. The Whig Party, which took on much of the Jeffersonian Democracy's ideals, placed strong emphasis on the role of schools and universities, and sought to place more power in the hands of Congress and individual states. The two-party system of the Jacksonian democracy was prevalent until the eve of the Civil War, when the politics of slavery became predominant.

PRESIDENT MARTIN VAN BUREN

Martin Van Buren, Jackson's vice president since 1833, ran for president in 1836. He ran largely on Jackson's record and victories in the Nullification Crisis and the bank war; he defeated three Whig opponents. His election was based largely on this record and the support he had in the populous states of New York, Pennsylvania, and Virginia.

Van Buren proved to be an uninspiring, if not an unpopular president. He was not one of the Founding Fathers and had few ties to them. He also was not a successful war hero, as Jackson had been. Additionally, Americans experienced a painful economic depression during his presidency. The end of the Second Bank in 1836 had resulted in high inflation, followed by a deflationary effect caused by banks only accepting gold and silver for payments. As a result, the United States fell into the Panic of 1837 and a depression that lasted for years afterward. Americans experienced severe levels of unemployment and bank failures. Many blamed Van Buren for this depression, particularly because he opposed the federal government's involvement in alleviating these financial woes. He further maintained an elegant style and appeared as though he cared little for the plights of many Americans. It was during this period that Van Buren began to be called *Martin Van Ruin* by his opponents.

Compounding Van Buren's lack of popularity was his oversight of the Trail of Tears. Van Buren also continued his predecessor's wars against Native Americans, and engaged federal forces in the Second Seminole War to secure Florida from Native guerrilla fighters. In free states, Van Buren's involvement in this costly war was particularly unpopular because it was seen as an effort to expand slaveholding in the South. During this period, Van Buren also refused to come to the aid of Mormons who had been forced out of their homes in Missouri, for fear of losing voter support in Missouri.

Despite the depression, the Trail of Tears, the Indian Wars, and his failure to lead during the Mormon War, Van Buren still managed to keep his Democratic party behind him and win the nomination for president. But he was defeated by Whig candidate William Henry Harrison in 1840.

END OF CHAPTER TAKE-AWAYS

■ **Market Society:** The U.S. economy moved away from a farming economy to an economy based on providing goods and services and workers making wages. Markets expanded during this time because the nation became more accessible due to the development of canals, steamboats, and railroads.

■ **Industrialization:** The United States underwent an Industrial Revolution, in which technology and organized labor made it possible to produce goods more quickly and affordably. The telegraph and the postal system revolutionized communication and Eli Whitney's cotton gin revolutionized textile commerce.

■ **New Social Structures:** This era saw the rise of a new middle class, which included factory workers and farmers who earned enough money to own homes and/or land. The distribution of American wealth remained predominantly with the rich, however, and the poor enjoyed little social mobility.

■ **President John Quincy Adams:** John Quincy Adams sought to promote agriculture and manufacturing by raising tariffs on imported goods. His "American System" soon became unpopular, however, especially in the South, which depended on foreign goods.

■ **President Andrew Jackson:** Andrew Jackson strongly supported the Manifest Destiny of Americans to move west and sought to relocate Native Americans to lands west of the Mississippi River. He faced challenges from South Carolina in the Nullification Crisis, and from supporters of the Second Bank of the United States.

REFERENCES

Henretta, J. A., Edwards, R., & Self, R. O. (1987). *America's history to 1877*. Chicago, IL: Dorsey Press.

Howe, D. W. (2009). *What hath God wrought: The transformation of America, 1815–1848*. New York, NY: Oxford University Press.

Johnson, W. (2001). *Soul by soul: Life inside the antebellum slave market*. Cambridge, MA: Harvard University Press.

Potter, D. (1977). *The impending crisis: America before the Civil War; 1848–1861*. New York, NY: Harper Perennial.

Wilentz, S. (2005). *Andrew Jackson*. New York, NY: Times Books.

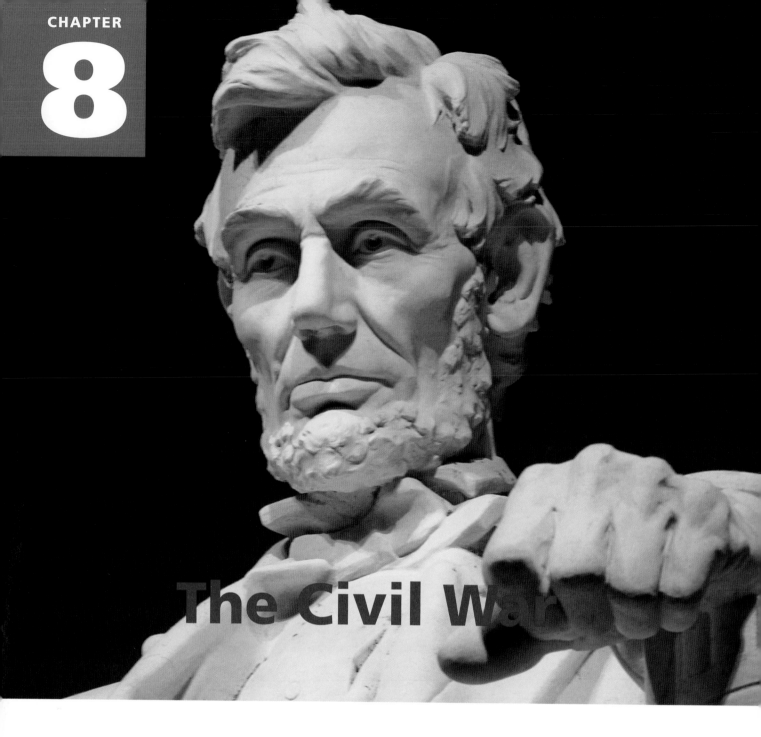

The Civil War

While the United States today is truly one united nation with no serious threat of any state seceding from the union, there are still some significant political divides in the country. Voters in a group of Southern states, for example, predominantly vote for Republican presidential candidates and, in 2000, the presidential candidate for the Democratic Party, Al Gore, received no electoral votes from Southern states—not even from his home state of Tennessee.

The overwhelmingly and uniformly Republican South is a rather new phenomenon, as there was a large block of Southern states that voted for Democratic candidates all the way through to 1964 because of lingering animosity toward Republicans for their progressive views on slavery. What is not new, however, is the fact that eleven states of the old Confederacy as well as Kentucky, Oklahoma, and West Virginia generally vote together. These states, in fact, were known for a long time as the "Solid South" because of their political uniformity, which dates all the way back to the time of the American Civil War.

THE INSTITUTION OF SLAVERY

Southern landowners depended on slaves to help keep production costs for cotton down; however, there is some disagreement among experts on whether slave labor was actually less costly than wage labor. Southern landowners at the time had much of their wealth tied up in slaves and in land, so losing that source of labor was a cause of concern. Also of concern to many Southerners was the question of what would happen once large slave populations were suddenly liberated.

Slaves were first brought to the United States with the earliest settlers, and slave populations continued to expand even after the importation of slaves became illegal in 1808 with the passage of the Act Prohibiting the Importation of Slaves. In the decades leading up to the Civil War, planters sought to expand slavery throughout the Southwest. As a result, slave populations in Alabama, Mississippi, Louisiana, Arkansas, and Texas grew from nearly 500,000 in 1840 to over 1.5 million in 1860.

Slave Culture

The slave culture in the South centered predominantly on work. Some slaves worked within the households as servants, while others were drivers, blacksmiths, and carpenters. However, most slaves worked in the fields, gathering and processing cotton, tobacco, and other crops. On smaller farms, slaves would work side by side with their masters, while on larger plantations, slaves worked in the fields for hours in the gang system, whereby one or two slaves set the pace and all worked in unison.

The quality of a slave's life varied largely, depending upon the temperament of their owners and, in some cases, depending on the farm on which they worked. On wealthier plantations with kinder owners, for example, slaves might be better clothed and fed than some poor whites, both in the North and the South. Despite this, slaves were well aware that their treatment depended entirely on the will of their masters, and that they were cared for not as humans, but as property. In fact, a justice of North Carolina's Supreme Court, Thomas Ruffin, said, "The power of the master must be absolute to render the submission of the slave perfect."

The submission of blacks was based largely upon racist ideology. Many in the South held to the belief that blacks were inferior to whites, and therefore should never be free, because, the belief held, blacks would not know what to do with their freedom. Such ideology also held that by enslaving the black man, the white man did not have to perform tasks and duties that were "beneath" him, lending to the argument that slavery essentially helped whites be "more free." Southern politician William Yancey once said it most succinctly to a group of Northern whites, "Your fathers and my fathers built this government on two ideas; the first is that the white race is the citizen and master race, and the white man is the equal of every other white man. The second is that the Negro is the inferior race."

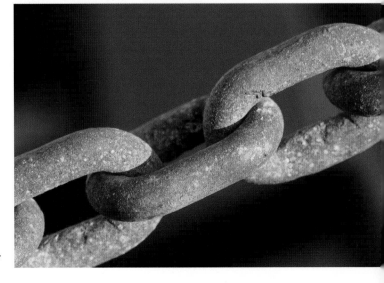

Such racist ideology had a tremendous impact on slave culture. Slaves endured unspeakable atrocities at the hands of some masters, being exploited, beaten, raped, and otherwise mistreated, as the "inferior" race and as the white man's "property." The law not only permitted abuses of slaves, but the racism was institutionalized in the laws of the time. For instance, the laws stipulated harsh penalties for slaves who tried to leave or disobeyed their masters. The laws also forbade the education of slaves. Such racism perpetuated the idea of black inferiority by ensuring that blacks would not be educated or offered the same opportunities as whites received.

Under such oppression, slave culture developed around religion and mutual suffering. Slaves were often Christians, and strongly identified with themes of the Israelites' bondage in Egypt and their ultimate deliverance to the Promised Land. Current suffering and future emancipation became the themes of Negro spirituals, worship services, and life itself.

The Slave Family

As a result of the harsh conditions and racism they faced, slaves held strongly to their family relationships. Marriage was common among slaves, although slaves were not permitted to enter into contracts so their marriages were not matters of law.

Often slaves married each other and lived as nuclear families, but sometimes circumstances broke up families. The domestic slave trade, which involved the sale of slaves "down river," (to states farther South where punishments were typically harsher and life harder) threatened the nuclear slave family, often dividing husbands and wives, children and parents. Masters often traded slaves to make money, but they also did it to discipline slaves by dissolving their families. Such separations became so common that by the end of the Civil War, nearly one quarter of all slave men over the age of forty had at one point been separated from their wives.

The integrity of slave families was threatened not only by the domestic slave trade, but also by the behaviors of Southern planters. It was common for white men to rape slave women, a practice that was even extolled in some white circles as preventing Southern prostitution and allowing for more virtue among white women. As a result of this, a mixed race grew, with slave mothers giving birth to their mas-

ters' children. The existence of these children served as a reminder of the vulnerability of female slaves, who were exploited not only by slave owners but also by their male relatives and teenage sons.

Despite such divisions to the slave family, slaves still developed elaborate familial relationships, which became a source of comfort and survival. Slave fathers raised children to live in such a way that they might be spared discipline from their masters. Mothers worked in fields, but also took care of domestic duties such as cooking, cleaning, gardening, and raising children. It was not uncommon for slave mothers to nurse infants while toiling in the fields. In many cases, these slaves were not able to raise their own children due to their work obligations, however, so their children were often raised by elderly members of the community.

The roles of husbands and wives were unique within slave families. Because marriages were not a matter of contracts, slave husbands did not have a legal superiority over their wives, as white husbands had over their wives. Slave marriages were often more balanced than white marriages, in which wives were considered largely subservient to husbands. Furthermore, husbands were more likely to be sold "down river," and were more often away visiting other families or farms. As a result, slave families frequently saw the mothers as the heads of often single-parent households.

Children in slave families often enjoyed more freedom than did their parents. While their parents and older siblings labored, younger children spent their days playing with each other and with white children. Former slave Frederick Douglass captured the life of a slave boy this way,

> The first seven or eight years of a slave-boy's life are about as full of sweet content as those of the most favored and petted white children of the slaveholder … He literally runs wild, a spirited, joyous, uproarious, and happy boy, upon whom troubles fall only like water on a duck's back.

By the age of eight, however, many slave children began to learn their role in the field, while some others were taught how to serve as domestic slaves and to perform light household duties. As they grew older, children came to understand more of the reality of their lives as slaves, usually as a result of experiencing a whipping, hearing comments from masters and other whites, or enduring the sale of loved ones to other plantations.

Beyond the immediate families of mothers, fathers, and children, slaves developed elaborate networks of extended family members. Elderly slaves would serve in patriarchal or matriarchal roles, helping to guide the affairs of younger slaves and the discipline of children. Young slaves grew up calling relatives and non-relatives "Aunt" and "Uncle," making it possible for a child to continue to have parental figures even if his actual parents were sold to other plantations. The slave family was a large one, bonded together by hardship but also mutual respect and a common goal—survival.

Southern Society in a Slave Economy

Southern whites were generally prosperous. In fact, in 1860, only people living in areas of the Northeast, Great Britain, and Australia boasted higher incomes than whites in the South. Such prosperity depended on the export of agricultural products produced predominantly in the South—tobacco, sugar, rice, and most important, cotton. By 1860, Southern exports of cotton to Europe accounted for nearly two-thirds of the entire nation's export trade. By selling enormous quantities of cotton to European markets, where demand for textiles was great, the South made a fortune on the backs of slaves.

While the economy in the North depended largely on Americans purchasing Northern goods and upon technological advances to improve productivity, the South's success hinged largely on foreign markets, new land, and slavery. European demand continued to grow, but cotton crops tended to destroy land more quickly than other crops did, so Southern farmers were always seeking more land. As a result, the future of the West, and whether it would be a slaveholding frontier, became a critical issue leading up to the Civil War. By 1860, slaveholding had spread from the Southeast coastal states throughout the Mississippi River Valley and farther west.

The Southern economy was inextricably linked to the expansive institution of slavery. While few slaves came into the country from Africa after 1808, slave populations continued to climb through high birthrates among slave families. The ever-expanding population of slaves in the South gave Southern planters

a growing pool of low-cost laborers. Without such expansive and affordable slave labor, the South could not have continued to produce cotton inexpensively and could not have remained competitive in international markets.

Southern plantation owners created an elaborate system of work for slaves, which was similar in many ways to factory lines, but was much more difficult and punishing for the worker. Slaveholders required that their slaves have specific tasks and that they be highly organized. On large plantations, slaves were organized into **gangs**, which often specialized in areas of picking, plowing, hoeing, and other tasks. Such gangs were overseen by drivers, who were often slaves themselves, as well as overseers, who were white. Such task specification made the work of these farms more lucrative.

As a result of the effective gang system and tremendous demand for cotton, Southern planters saw unprecedented wealth. Nearly all planters in the South made on average 10 percent profit on their investments in slave purchases in the 1840s and '50s. Even the most established textile firms in the Northeast did not make such profits.

With this growth came two problems. First, as Southerners expanded their investments in slaves and land, they did not invest in manufacturing. As a result, a growing number of whites moved to towns and cities in the North, where work in manufacturing was amply available. This caused the South to lose skilled workers and voting populations to the North. The second problem stemmed from a negligence to invest in education and training for its workforce. With many skilled workers moving North, and no new, educated workers to replace them, the South was losing the skill-sets necessary for future economic development.

Furthermore, in the North, factory owners were able to use a variety of methods to keep their employees working hard, such as the threat of firing, economic rewards, and appeals to Christian values. Conversely, Southerners used severe forms of coercion and oppression to maintain their economic upper hand. To continue these methods, the South had to isolate itself from the North. Furthermore, because the South exported its goods and materials extensively to Europe, it enjoyed a high level of cultural and economic independence from the rest of the United States. It was this slave-dependent, isolated Southern economy that soon clashed with the North.

WESTERN EXPANSION AND MANIFEST DESTINY

While the South's slave economy and the North's manufacturing economies grew, another form of growth was underway in the United States during the Civil War era—populations of Western areas. As has been shown, many Americans believed it was their right and duty to expand the nation and its ideals from "sea to shining sea." This westward expansion was coined **Manifest Destiny** by John L. O'Sullivan, a newspaper editor. Americans followed various, often treacherous, routes as they headed west, including the Oregon Trail.

At the time, railroads were still extending westward, but none led all the way to the Pacific. As a result, many who traversed these trails did so in covered wagons, on horses, or even on foot. The trails were rough, so traveling with people and possessions was demanding, especially in rain and snow. The pioneers also faced disease and injury with little medical assistance; childbirth along the trails posed

SLAVE GANGS A method that Southern slave-owners used to organize their slave labor—it was known as much for its brutality as its efficiency.

MANIFEST DESTINY The widely held belief that it was inevitable for the United States to spread westward and claim all of the lands to the Pacific Ocean.

significant risks. As a result, many people died along these routes. Furthermore, bandits and other criminals plagued the routes, making travel west all the more treacherous.

The were many reasons for migrating west. Some sought fortune, especially when gold was discovered in the Sacramento Valley in 1848. In 1849 alone, over 80,000 migrants arrived in what was then the Territory of California, seeking their fortunes. Other Americans sought religious autonomy, including Mormons who took the Mormon Trail into Utah. Still others sought to acquire land, which was available at low or no cost. And still others were convicted of crimes or faced warrants for arrest, and headed west to flee the law. Between growing criminal populations and a lack of established governments, a pervading lawlessness took over in areas of the West.

The growth of populations in the West prompted the question of whether slavery should be allowed in these territories. Different Americans had different—and often diametrically opposed—approaches to this divisive question.

During the Mexican War, when the United States annexed Texas, New Mexico, and California in exchange for $15 million, one approach to slavery, called the Wilmot Proviso, became popular. Proposed by David Wilmot of Pennsylvania, it declared that the United States government should prohibit slavery in any area acquired from Mexico. This proviso was largely based upon a free-soil ideology, which held firmly to the position that no slavery should be permitted in western territories. Composed of anti-slavery members from both Whig and Democratic Parties, a Free Soil Party arose in the late 1840s and existed into the 1850s, and attempted to lead the charge in preventing the expansion of slavery in the West.

In contrast, John C. Calhoun, a South Carolina politician, voiced the view of the Deep South and the slave states. According to his position, the U.S. Congress had no constitutional right to prevent slavery in the territories. Calhoun argued that citizens had the right to take all of their property, including slaves, with them as they moved. A less extreme version of this position, held by other Southerners, was that Southerners had the right to hold slaves within at least some territories in the West.

In yet another position on slavery in the West, some leaders suggested a **popular sovereignty** position. Led by Democrat Lewis Cass, those who held the popular sovereignty position believed that the decision on whether or not to allow slavery in western territories should be up to the governments of those territories. The idea of popular sovereignty found favor with many because it shifted responsibility for slavery in the territories from Congress to the local territorial legislatures. While this ideology had some ambiguities, it was considered one of the primary ways to maintain unity in the expanding nation as it grappled with the divisive question of slavery.

The issue of slavery in the West came sharply into view by the 1850s. After the **forty-niners** flocked to California to search for gold, President Zachary Taylor advised California settlers to apply for statehood quickly. Because few southerners had gone to California in search of gold, there was not a strong movement in support of slavery in California. As a result, California and New Mexico were admitted into the Union as free states in December 1849.

Southern congressmen were alarmed by the lack of support for slavery in these Western territories and fought Taylor over the future of slavery, not only in the West but also throughout the nation. Southerners like Calhoun feared that popular

POPULAR SOVEREIGNTY The belief that territories should have the right to decide whether to allow slavery, rather than the federal government.

FORTY-NINERS A nickname for pioneers who moved to California in 1849 in search of gold.

sovereignty would not adequately protect the rights of slaveholders, and feared that admitting California into the Union as a free state would forever alter the balance in favor of anti-slavery forces in Congress. Arguments flared for months in the early 1850s over the future of slavery, with Calhoun predicting possible civil war over the issue.

The result of the debates was the **Compromise of 1850**, a series of laws that were written by Whigs Henry Clay and Daniel Webster and Democrat Stephen A. Douglas. This compromise sought to placate Southerners who feared that Western states would become a safe haven for runaway slaves, and to address concerns of the Northern residents, who wanted popular sovereignty to take hold in former Mexican lands. According to the compromise:

COMPROMISE OF 1850 A series of laws that attempted to address the concerns of both Northerners and Southerners regarding the slave policy of new Western territories.

1. California was admitted into the Union as a free state.
2. New Mexico became a territory under the principle of popular sovereignty, leaving the ultimate decision about slavery up to the territorial government.
3. Utah also became a territory under popular sovereignty.
4. The trading of slaves was abolished in the District of Columbia, though slavery itself was not abolished in that region.
5. A fugitive slave law was put in place. This law severely punished anyone who sought to keep slaveholders from recovering their runaway slaves in any state or territory.

The Compromise of 1850 succeeded in averting the threat of Southern secession—but only temporarily.

CHANGES IN AMERICAN SOCIETY

America saw tremendous changes in the early Civil War era. With the expansion of the West and the development of new technologies, the United States saw many advancements in transportation and industry. Factories grew and modernized, increasing demand for skilled laborers throughout the Northeast. Furthermore, during this period more immigrants were entering the United States than ever before, forever changing the cultural landscape of a nation.

Growth of Railroads

While canals continued to carry more than railroads in the early 1850s, railroads were undergoing considerable advancements during this period. Railroad companies laid much more track than before, building lines to connect New York and Pennsylvania to Chicago. By building these westward tracks and lowering their fares, railroad companies made it easier for people and property to head farther west, and also for manufacturing to continue to grow in western cities, such as Chicago. By the end of the decade, railroads had exceeded the capacity of canals, and had lowered the cost of farming and industry in the West. Because of railroads, more farmers could move themselves and their equipment to areas that canals could not reach. As a result of the railroad expansion, more farmers settled on lands in the West and began producing crops that could be exported to the East.

In addition to expanding agriculture in the West, railroads expanded urbanization in the West. By moving goods west, railroads increased demand for grain storage facilities, warehouses, flour mills, and factories that produced farming equipment. Cyrus McCormick moved his company's operations from western Virginia to Chicago, to create reapers and other machines closer to areas where farmers were producing grain.

Western cities such as St. Louis and Chicago soon surpassed Boston and Baltimore in size. Railroad growth was concentrated in the North and Midwest. Complex lines were developed throughout the area, stimulating economic and industrial growth. Meanwhile, rail lines into the South were far simpler. Some lines were poorly connected and unnecessarily convoluted, due to competition among railway companies and conflicts between states, which made using railroads in the South unduly expensive. This became increasingly problematic for the South during the Civil War, because the movement of arms and provisions into the South was difficult and financially prohibitive.

Because railroads were made of high-grade iron, the American iron industry expanded and modernized to keep up with the demand for rails. To build train cars, tracks, and engines, more factories popped up throughout the Northeast. Railroads not only moved skilled workers and machines, but also led to the growth in number of these workers and the development of more machines.

Growth of Industrialization

Industry grew in the North and the Northwest during the 1850s. By 1860, manufacturing in the North was only exceeded by industry in Great Britain and France.

The factories built during this period relied heavily on technological advances and large numbers of skilled workers. Manufacturers used power-driven machinery and elaborate production lines to develop products like agricultural machines, sewing machines, guns, watches, and more.

Innovator Cyrus McCormick used power-driven conveyor belts to help workers on assembly lines. Manufacturer Samuel Colt built his factory in Hartford, Connecticut in the 1850s. It used technological advances to manufacture the pistol Colt had designed. With more and more Americans demanding such weapons, Colt's factories began producing tens of thousands of Colt revolvers every year.

During this period there was also a major change in how power was provided to factories. Simple waterpower was no longer sufficient for the demands of growing industries; steam power stepped up to meet the demand. The stationary steam engine was refined and brought into widespread use in the several years leading up to and during the Civil War.

The growing use of the stationary steam engine shifted the manufacturing base from small U.S. cities to large cities and seaports. The use of steam directly expanded the size and importance of large cities along the Great Lakes and the Atlantic seaboard. By the late 1850s, cities in the West, such as Chicago, had broken smaller Eastern cities' monopoly on industry.

The growing demand for the manufacturing of machines advanced industrialization in the United States. In the 1850s, the same factories and machines that created parts for guns also made parts for sewing machines, clocks, and other devices. Products produced during this era of industrial growth became household names, including Singer sewing machines, Yale locks, Colt revolvers, Remington rifles, and McCormick reapers.

Immigration

In addition to the growth of railroads and industry, the United States experienced large growth in immigrant populations. In 1860, more than one-fourth of the free white adult men in the United States were immigrants, and many of those lived in the North. By 1860, over 1.5 million Germans, 2 million Irish, and 750,000 British immigrants had entered the United States. At the time, there was no federal legislation limiting immigration.

Coming to the United States to escape religious persecution, famine, or disease in Europe or to pursue greater opportunities in America, these immigrants were largely unskilled workers, farmers, and peasants. They were so eager to earn a better wage and create a better life that they were willing to work longer, harder hours for less pay than many American-born workers. As a result, immigrants made up a large proportion of the unskilled labor force in the United States during this period.

In particular, Irish immigrants flooded into the United States, settling largely in areas of New England. By 1850, Irish immigrants accounted for more than a third of Boston's workforce. Because they worked longer hours for less pay, Irish immigrants made it possible for Boston's factory owners to compete for the first time with smaller, more efficient manufacturing outfits in other parts of New England.

The living and working conditions of European immigrants were poor. Immigrants, while largely eating better than they had in their famine-ravaged homelands, often lacked enough money to buy land or build homes. The long difficult workdays and meager income took a toll on their health. For example, immigrants experienced more miscarriages and deaths from disease than other segments of the population. As a result of poor sanitation, epidemics spread quickly among immigrant communities. In 1849 alone, over 5,000 people, many of whom were immigrants, died in a cholera epidemic in New York. While wealthier whites left the cities during these epidemics, immigrants were largely unable to leave. As a result, by 1860, the annual death rate from disease in New York, Philadelphia, and Boston was 34 of every 1,000, compared to only 15 per 1,000 in less urbanized areas.

POLITICS IN THE 1850S

The advancements in technology and industry, and the expansion of Western, urban, and immigrant populations, helped make the United States a political hotbed. The future of slavery in the West, and in the nation as a whole, became the focal political issue of the day.

During the 1850s, the United States experienced its first actual battles over the issue of slavery. In what became known as **Bleeding Kansas**, a guerrilla war ensued in 1854 between supporters and opponents of slavery. In 1859, John Brown, who was involved in Bleeding Kansas, captured an arsenal in Harpers Ferry, Virginia with the hopes of sparking a slave revolt to end slavery.

With such battles as a backdrop, political lines over slavery began to be clearly drawn. Many Southern politicians pledged their allegiances to the institution of slavery over the union of the United States. Meanwhile, Northern politicians began to take a firmer anti-slavery stance.

Kansas-Nebraska Act

Much of the political debate of the mid-1850s stemmed from the Kansas-Nebraska Act. A senator from Illinois, Stephen A. Douglas, was a staunch advocate of Western expansion, and wanted his own Chicago to be the eastern terminal for a transcontinental railroad, rather than a Southern city such as New Orleans, Memphis, or St. Louis. To that end, in 1854 he introduced the **Kansas-Nebraska Act**. This act established Nebraska as a free territory, and Kansas, which had entered the Union as a free state, as a slaveholding territory.

To garner Southern support of his bill, Douglas conceded that the popular sovereignty provision of the Compromise of 1850 voided the prohibition of slavery in the northern portion of the Louisiana Territory. In other words, slavery could be permitted within lands of the Louisiana Purchase, should the people within those territories allow it. With these concessions, the bill passed with much support from the South; throughout the North, anger raged over the act. Northerners rallied behind a new party, the Republican Party, which was based largely upon absolute opposition to slavery in the Western territories.

Collapse of the Second American Party System

The issue of slavery destroyed the Second American Party System. The Whig party was deeply divided over the Fugitive Slave Act of the Compromise of 1850, which gave the federal government the responsibility to capture and return runaway slaves who had made it to free soil. The Whig Party was so divided that it lost badly to the Democrats with the election of President Pierce in 1852. This was the last campaign the Whigs would participate in as a formal American political party.

The job of unifying the nation fell to the Democrats. The Democratic Party largely supported the principle of popular sovereignty, which gave authority to the respective territories to make their own decisions about the matter. The Democratic Party found support in the growing immigrant populations in the North, as well as those throughout the nation who felt maintaining unity was more important than fighting over slavery.

Nevertheless, the Democrats had a growing number of detractors. In the South, many did not like the policy of popular sovereignty, and

BLEEDING KANSAS A series of violent incidents that took place in the 1850s along the Kansas-Missouri border over whether Kansas should be admitted as a free state or a slave state.

KANSAS-NEBRASKA ACT An 1854 law that created the territories of Kansas and Nebraska.

demanded that slaveholding be a protected right throughout the nation. In the North, more and more became disillusioned with the Democrats, believing them too weak on the question of slavery. These detractors demanded instead that slavery be abolished throughout the United States, not only in the Western territories. Furthermore, many in the North, especially among the business class, distrusted the Democratic Party's vision for limited government. These voters wanted the government to promote economic growth, and they increasingly became a part of a new, growing Republican Party.

The Know-Nothings

The fledgling Republican Party found great support from a group called the Know-Nothings. This group was primarily composed of Protestant males in the North, many of British descent, who strongly feared and opposed the growing presence of Roman Catholic immigrants from Ireland. The Know-Nothings sought to minimize immigration and naturalization, in large part due to their distrust of immigrants' allegiance to the Pope in Rome. The group got its name because when asked about the nature of the group's activities, members were to answer, "I know nothing."

The Republicans and the Know-Nothings made great strides in the Congressional elections of 1854, winning the majority of seats in the House of Representatives that year. A strong opposition to the Democrats was mounting.

DID YOU KNOW?

The phrase "John Brown Eyes" comes from an important abolitionist, John Brown, who participated in the guerrilla warfare known as "Bleeding Kansas" in 1854, and who later captured an arsenal in Harpers Ferry, VA. John Brown's goal at Harpers Ferry was to bring about a black state and to tackle the question of slavery by force. John Brown's efforts were considered a failure, and he was hung for his participation. Nevertheless, Brown's stand brought the issue of slavery to the forefront, rejuvenating abolitionists' efforts and eliciting considerable fear among Southerners, who worried about slave rebellions and violence.

The Election of 1856

The Republican Party had a clear ideology. Its members believed slavery would create two classes of people: masters and slaves. Masters would be above the law while slaves and poor whites would suffer their injustices. Republicans argued masters and slaves should not exist in a free society, that all men should be free, independent, and able to pursue the American dream. Southern Democratic ideology, conversely, held that blacks were an inferior race and should never become free citizens.

Violence continued to grow over this issue. A gang that supported slavery destroyed portions of Lawrence, Kansas. Then, in what became known as the Pottawatomie Massacre, New York abolitionist John Brown, along with his sons and helpers, murdered five settlers in Kansas who supported slavery.

The events that earned the name Bleeding Kansas provided the backdrop for the election of 1856, which pitted Republicans against Democrats for the first time. The Democrats named James Buchanan as their candidate, and their primary issue was to uphold the Kansas-Nebraska Act. The Republicans named Army explorer John C. Fremont as their candidate. The Republicans argued that Democrats wanted to expand slavery throughout the nation; this argument won them the support of at least one famous former Democrat, poet Walt Whitman. Meanwhile, Southern Democrats said they would support secession if Fremont won the election. Buchanan won the election of 1856 over Fremont by gaining more electoral votes, even though Fremont carried eleven states over Buchanan's five. Immediate dissolution of the union over the subject of slavery was once more averted, albeit narrowly.

1. What was slave culture like in the South? Describe aspects of slave families and threats to those families. Also describe the importance of the institution of slavery to the economy of the South.

2. What role did the West play in the battle between abolitionists and slaveholders? Describe each side's position.

3. What role did railroads play in the years leading up to and during the Civil War? How did industrial advancements affect the United States during this period? What roles did immigrants take on in the urban North?

4. How did America's Second Party System cease to exist? What two parties emerged from this era? Describe the election of 1856 and how party politics played a crucial role in that election.

LEADING TO WAR

The election of 1856, while temporarily avoiding Civil War, brought the nation one step closer to irreparable division over the issue of slavery. Blood had already begun to be spilt in Kansas and elsewhere, and the debate raged over whether or not popular sovereignty was the best solution to the question of slavery in the Western territories.

Dred Scott Decision

In 1856, slave **Dred Scott** sued for his freedom. Scott lived with his master, an Army surgeon, in states where slavery was prohibited. In his lawsuit, Dred Scott argued that his residence in the slave-free states of Illinois and Wisconsin made him free. In *Dred Scott v. Sanford*, the Supreme Court was faced with the same issue that was deeply dividing Congress and the nation as a whole.

The Supreme Court included five Southern Democrats, each of whom wrote an opinion in the case, but Chief Justice Roger Taney summarized the Court's opinion in March 1857. He ruled that blacks, whether slaves or free, could not be citizens of the United States, and as such, Dred Scott did not even have the right to sue in federal court for his freedom.

Beyond that, the Court ruled that because the Fifth Amendment of the Constitution prohibited the taking of property without due process of law, Congress could not pass laws that deprived individuals of their "slave property." Thus, the Missouri Compromise, which prohibited slavery in the Louisiana Territories, was unconstitutional and Scott's living in free territory could not have freed him.

Furthermore, the Court found that Congress could not extend to territorial governments any powers that itself did not possess. In other words, if Congress had no power to prohibit slavery in the territory, the territorial government also could not pass such a law. In this way, the Supreme Court argued that the only time a territory could prohibit slavery was at its point of admission to the union as a state, not before.

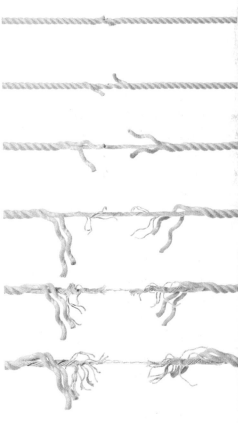

DRED SCOTT A slave who attempted to sue for his freedom. The result was a decision from the Supreme Court that stated slaves were property, not people.

While President Buchanan and Southern Democrats hoped that Republicans, in deference to the Court, would accept this decision, *Dred Scott* essentially declared the Republican platform unconstitutional. Republicans argued that the Court was part of a "slave power" conspiracy. The decision also undercut the position of Northern Democrats, such as Stephen A. Douglas, who supported popular sovereignty. The country was all the more deeply divided and on the brink of fighting about these deep-seated issues.

Panic of 1857

As the North continued to expand its manufacturing production during this period, factory owners were largely unable to gauge demand for products. As a result, they often overproduced materials and subsequently had to lay off factory workers. Unemployment grew and eventually fueled what became known as the Panic of 1857.

During the 1850s, Europe experienced an economic depression, which lowered the demand for goods from the United States Additionally, westward expansion in the 1850s meant that many banks were giving railroad companies large loans to expand their tracks. But soon the value of western land dropped and railroads slowed their expansion. The railroad companies defaulted on their large loans, which in turn caused commercial credit to dry up. Many railroad workers lost their jobs or sustained pay cuts.

PANIC OF 1857 An economic downturn that demonstrated the growing interconnectedness of world markets and the perils of overproduction.

In what became known as the first worldwide economic depression, the **Panic of 1857** reached its height when a large lender, Ohio Life Insurance and Trust Company, failed. Ohio Life's management was involved in fraudulent activities and as a result, there was a threatened run on the banks in 1857.

The failure of banks, European markets, and railroad companies and resulting large-scale unemployment affected the American economy for years. Many economists believe the Panic of 1857 continued until the Civil War.

Lincoln-Douglas Debates

When Stephen A. Douglas sought reelection as senator from Illinois, he faced stiff opposition from a political figure with growing popularity, Abraham Lincoln. Lincoln was as a gifted attorney, speaker, and politician, and was now Illinois's strongest Republican.

Lincoln challenged Douglas to a series of seven debates. During these Lincoln-Douglas debates, Lincoln ferociously attacked the institution of slavery, arguing that blacks should receive "all the natural rights enumerated in the Declaration of Independence." While not supporting full equality for blacks, Lincoln argued that "in the right to eat the bread, without leave of anybody else, which his own hand earns," the black man "was the equal of every other living man."

From Lincoln's perspective, a plan was underway to expand slavery. Using the *Dred Scott* decision and the Kansas-Nebraska Act as evidence, Lincoln argued that the South sought to expand slavery not only into the West, but throughout the United States. He pressed Douglas hard, asking him how he could accept the *Scott* decision, which ruled against popular sovereignty, and still support popular sovereignty publically.

In response, Douglas took a new approach to popular sovereignty in a debate in Freeport, Illinois. In what has become known as the Freeport Doctrine, Douglas argued that settlers in new territories could stop slavery in practice (although not legally) by simply refusing to adopt local legislation designed to protect it. Douglas's Freeport doctrine helped him win the election, by a narrow margin, as many in Illinois sought a way to address the question of slavery in the West without dissolving the union.

Secession

Leading up to the election of 1860, the nation was more deeply divided than ever on the issue of slavery. Southern Democrats, led by Senator Jefferson Davis, argued that the Republicans were dead-set on destroying slavery in the South. The fears of Southern Democrats were furthered by John Brown's rebellion at Harpers Ferry, when he led eighteen armed followers in a rebellion with the purpose of creating a black state within the South. Brown was captured and later hung, but was nonetheless extolled as a hero by abolitionists in the North.

Fearing slave rebellions as a result of John Brown's raids, Democrats of the North and the South split in the election of 1860. Southern Democrats endorsed Buchanan's vice president, John Breckinridge, for president and Northern Democrats nominated Douglas. Meanwhile the Republicans named Lincoln their candidate. Lincoln won a resounding victory, appealing to Northern abolitionists and Western settlers, arguing that the South did not have the right to secede from the Union.

For many in the South, Lincoln's election made secession immediately necessary. Throughout the campaign, violence spread over the issue of slavery. Many Southerners felt Lincoln would foment slave rebellions, and that their very lives, not just their way of life, were at stake.

FORT SUMTER An Army fort in South Carolina, and the location for the first shots of the American Civil War.

Within weeks of Lincoln's election, South Carolina seceded from the Union. Mississippi, Florida, Alabama, Georgia, Louisiana, and Texas soon also seceded. These states formed the Confederate States of America, created a constitution, and were led by Jefferson Davis as president. James Buchanan was still in office when the states seceded and began provoking the North. In one instance, South Carolinians fired upon an unarmed merchant ship as it entered Charleston harbor. Buchanan sought to avoid full-fledged war by backing down, and did not send in the Navy to protect the vessel. He had, however, reinforced federal troops at Fort Sumter. Tensions were at a boiling point even before Lincoln officially took office.

Border states, including Delaware, Maryland, Kentucky, Tennessee, North Carolina, and Virginia, did not immediately join the Confederate states, but nonetheless defended the right of any state to secede.

In his inaugural address on March 4, 1861, Lincoln said he would welcome back the seceded states into the union, but he was not going to offer them concessions for doing so. He said that secession was illegal and that violent acts in support of secession amounted to revolution. He gave the South a choice—rejoin the union or go to war.

The South did not consider Lincoln's offer, and demanded the surrender of **Fort Sumter**, an Army post. When the Union forces there refused to surrender, the Confederates opened fire. On April 14, 1861 Fort Sumter surrendered to the Confederates, and in response, Lincoln

CONSCRIPTION The practice of requiring members of the population who meet certain qualifications to serve in the armed forces.

sent 75,000 federal troops to put down the insurrection. The American Civil War was underway.

The Confederate attack on Fort Sumter became symbolic for the North, which rallied around its commander, Major Robert Anderson, and around Lincoln, who called for more troops. Lincoln's appeals for unity kept Maryland, Delaware, Kentucky, and Missouri in the union, as well as the western portion of Virginia, which became the state of West Virginia in 1863. This was a critical victory for Lincoln during the crisis of secession, because it meant the capital of the nation in the District of Columbia would not be surrounded by enemy land.

POLITICAL LEADERSHIP IN THE CIVIL WAR

Within a week of the surrender of Fort Sumter, Lincoln ordered General Winfield Scott to arrest anyone suspected of subversive acts or speech. By doing so, Lincoln was suspending the writ of habeas corpus in the Constitution, which protected citizens from being imprisoned indefinitely without charges being filed. Initially the suspension applied only in Maryland, which was a critical state near the capital and which was deemed a threat to join the Confederacy, but by 1862, Lincoln expanded the suspension of habeas corpus nationwide. Lincoln also strengthened and consolidated his political power by declaring martial law, by introducing **conscription**, and by taxing the North at unprecedented levels in order to pay for the war.

Meanwhile, in the South, Confederates accepted the leadership of President Jefferson Davis, but refused to create a strong centralized government such as the one they had left. This made it difficult to develop firm laws on economic matters, martial law, and conscription, which would have helped the Confederates organize their efforts.

Instead of strong political leadership, Confederate leadership depended largely on a unifying racial identity. Davis argued that the South was fighting for its right to expand West in order to prevent the advance of the black man on their land, and to secure the rights of freedom for whites. Another political leader of the Confederacy, Alexander Stephens, concurred, saying the Southern government's "cornerstone rests upon the great truth that the Negro is not equal to the white man, that slavery—subordination to the superior race—is his natural or normal condition."

Despite these proclamations, the Confederacy faced political challenges from within, particularly from poor Southern whites. Food became a problem, with armies forcing farmers to give up more and more food as the war progressed. As such, poor whites called the war "a rich man's war and a poor man's fight." Many refused conscription, and with a weak government, enforcement was almost impossible. As a result, the Confederacy considered arming its slaves.

Under the leadership of General Robert E. Lee and President Davis, the Confederates voted to enlist black soldiers, saying that black soldiers fighting for the Confederacy would win their freedom. The war ended before Davis's efforts to enlist blacks could be measured.

HISTORY COMES ALIVE

West Virginia and Nevada both became states during the Civil War. Nevada's statehood was hurried on by Union sympathizers, who wanted Nevada entered into the Union prior to Lincoln's reelection bid in 1864. Nevada is commonly referred to as the Battle Born state because of its entry into the Union during the Civil War. Popular rumors abound that Nevada was only ushered into the Union because Lincoln needed its vast silver mines to help fund the Civil War. While not considered an official barrier to statehood, Nevada only had 400,000 citizens when it was entered into the Union, far fewer than any other state upon entrance to the Union. This fact helps further the thought that Lincoln ushered Nevada into the Union to help pro-Union causes, especially the passage of the Thirteenth Amendment, which banned slavery in 1865.

EMANCIPATION

For Lincoln and his military generals, the Civil War was not just about reuniting the nation. It was also about the abolition of slavery and the **emancipation** of slaves. Many argued that abolition was not just a moral matter, but a military one, because slavery made it possible for the Confederates to feed and supply their troops.

EMANCIPATION The liberation of slaves.

The first instances of emancipation took place on the battlefield, where Union commanders freed slaves who had escaped into Union territory. Union Army General Benjamin Butler described freed slaves as "contraband of war," arguing that Union forces would not return them to slavery. Lincoln later signed a law stating that the seizure of all property, including slaves, was lawful, and began the process of freeing slaves behind Union lines.

The overall issue of emancipation divided Republicans into three groups. The smallest group, the conservatives, wanted slavery ended ultimately, but held that the government's role was exclusively to stop its expansion in the Western territories. These Republicans believed emancipation within existing states would be up to those respective states. Radical Republicans conversely held that the federal government should immediately end slavery everywhere. The moderates, the largest group, wanted to emancipate the slaves, but did not want to lose the support of border states by rushing the process.

As the war continued and losses mounted, the emancipation movement gathered strength. Abolitionists wanted Southerners to pay for the war by losing their slaves. This growing movement, led by Congressmen Charles Sumner and Thaddeus Stevens, began the process of emancipation faster than conservative elements of the movement thought possible.

First, Congress abolished slavery in the District of Columbia in 1862, promising compensation to former slaveholders in order to keep them loyal to the Union. Then in June 1862, Congress abolished slavery in all territories of the Union, reaffirming the Wilmot Proviso and fulfilling the aspirations of the Free Soil Party.

Lincoln waited for tides to turn on the battlefield to declare his next step in the emancipation process.

That opportunity came after the Battle of Antietam, which, while deemed a Union victory, involved the worst single day in U.S. military history, with 4,800 dead and 18,500 wounded. Shortly after, on September 23, 1862, President Lincoln issued his famous Emancipation Proclamation.

The Emancipation Proclamation

In the proclamation, President Lincoln declared that on January 1, 1863, all slaves in all states would be free. He had given slave states 100 days to return to the Union and keep slavery intact, and none agreed to do so.

The Emancipation Proclamation did not have an immediate effect on any slave. Lincoln left slavery untouched in border states, because he wanted to keep their allegiance, and he did not free slaves in areas occupied at the time by Union armies—Tennessee, western Virginia, and southern Louisiana—because he wanted those areas to align more fully with the Union.

As the Union armies continued to advance, however, the Emancipation Proclamation freed more and more slaves in Union-occupied battlefields. The Proclamation also largely changed the meaning of the war—emboldening the resolve and the cause of warriors and families throughout the North. Even before the end of the war, two states, Maryland and Missouri, freed their slaves, and three occupied states, Tennessee, Louisiana, and Arkansas, soon did the same. The proclamation had another unexpected effect: more and more freed slaves began to join the Union Army. By the end of the war, nearly 200,000 freed slaves were fighting with Northern soldiers.

On January 31, 1865, Congress completed the legal work of emancipation by approving the Thirteenth Amendment to the U.S. Constitution.

THE CONFEDERATE HOME FRONT

Life in the South became difficult during the Civil War. The armies fought most of the battles near the border and on Southern land. As a result, Southern households had to provide provisions, either willingly or by force, to both Confederate and Union forces.

Food was in little supply in the South during the Civil War. With many males away fighting in the war, farms that were once prosperous produced far less than they did before. On plantations with slaves, fear of slave rebellion, escape, and, in Union-occupied regions, the gradual emancipation of slaves all lowered productivity. Even more, farms were ravaged by the war; many were burned or otherwise destroyed in battle. Food shortages were further exacerbated by interruptions to the rail system that made it nearly impossible for food and other supplies to be transported to communities in need.

New Economic Opportunities

Despite these hardships, the Civil War introduced new economic opportunities for the South. During the early days of the war, Southern industry began to grow in order to keep up with demand for weapons, uniforms, and other military supplies. While the Confederacy did not support a strong, centralized government, the government did need to oversee these growing economic sectors. For example, they needed to regulate the output of workers who spun cloth for uniforms and those who forged iron cannons in their large Richmond factories.

The growth of Southern economic sectors, such as manufacturing, was overseen by the Confederacy's Ordnance Bureau, led by a former Northerner, General

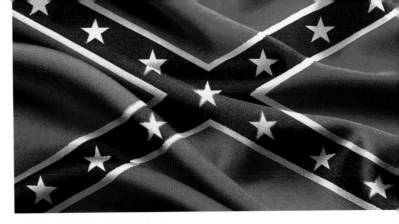

Josiah Gorgas. Gorgas oversaw the development of arsenals and mills, and he also encouraged entrepreneurs to invest in the manufacturing of weapons.

The efforts of Gorgas and others to build up the economy of the South during the Civil War did not go without notice, especially within Europe, which the Confederacy hoped would join their cause. William E. Gladstone of Britain wrote,

> There is no doubt that Jefferson Davis and the other leaders of the South have made an army; they are making, it appears, a navy; and they have made what is more than either—they have made a nation. We may anticipate with certainty the success of the Southern states.

While Gladstone would be wrong, and while Europe would not join the Confederate cause, there was no doubt that the South was making economic strides to support its war.

Women

In the years leading up to the war, wealthy Southern women played an important part in secession, often spurring men on to support secession as part of their patriotic and familial duty. During the Civil War, women assumed new roles to support their families and the South. In addition to raising children and tending to homes, women also farmed the land, nursed the sick, and housed soldiers. Women also took jobs in local industries and used their earnings to help support their families and clothe their soldiers. Women coordinated and ran fundraising events, including dances and bazaars, to help raise funds and support for their troops.

The situation for poorer women in the South was different. Food shortages more directly affected many of them. These hardships sometimes forced women to take desperate measures to provide food for their families. In one instance, women armed themselves with knives and pistols and looted stores in search of food. Indeed, the situation for poor white women in the South was far different than that of their wealthy neighbors.

THE UNION HOME FRONT

The 22 million white Northerners greatly outnumbered the 9 million white Southerners. As a result, not all Northern men needed to fight in the Civil War, which was not the case in Dixie. During the fighting's early months, lif-e in the North went on largely as usual. Men who were not enlisted worked in factories and on farms, and women went about many domestic duties as usual.

As the war progressed, though, changes in Union life developed, from how the federal government collected money to the roles of women, and more. For example, Lincoln faced challenges in keeping the army manned, so he instituted conscription in 1862. Using the Militia Act of 1862, the federal government imposed a draft on all states that failed to meet their recruiting quotas. With more and more men entering the war, the home front within the Union began to change.

Finances and the Economy

Another large change came in the form of a new tax. To raise funds for the war, the Union instituted the first ever **income tax**. Congress also developed an elaborate national banking system and began to print the first national currency, known as **greenbacks**. As the war progressed, more taxes were added, including excises taxes on most goods, license taxes on many activities and most professions except the ministry, taxes on corporations, stamp taxes on certain documents, and inheritance taxes. These taxes financed nearly 20 percent of the war effort. By the end of 1862, the Union effort was costing the American taxpayers nearly $2.5 million per day.

Meanwhile, the federal government gave more public land to pioneers and to railroad companies seeking to lay track for the transcontinental railroad. They also passed the **Morrill Act**, which gave states federal lands on which to build colleges and universities, and to protect much land from further development.

Women

In the early months of the Civil War, women's lives were not largely changed, because not all Northern men needed to fight in the war. These women continued tending to their homes and their children, and would mend and sew soldier's uniforms and repair other equipment in their free time.

As the war progressed, more and more women, especially young, unmarried, or widowed women, joined the workforce to support the war effort. Women worked in factories, post offices, and especially in hospitals. In fact, most of the nurses and workers involved in the Sanitary Commission, which provided health services to the Union during the war, were women. Under the leadership of Dorothea Dix, the first woman to receive a major federal position, thousands of female nurses joined the Union war effort. Overcoming years of prejudice and taboos over treating the bodies of men, these nurses played a critical role in minimizing Union deaths. They also opened an important door for women to hold jobs outside their homes.

Civil Liberties

In addition to opening doors for women in the workplace, the Civil War led to an initial expansion of the civil liberties of free black men in the North. Free blacks joined the Union war effort, and the soldiers of the 107th U.S. Colored Infantry Division were responsible for one of the decisive victories for the Union at Fort Fisher.

Nevertheless, President Lincoln came under harsh criticism for limiting American civil liberties when he suspended the writ of habeas corpus during the war. By allowing citizens to be held without hearing or trial, Lincoln limited American civil rights, arguing that such a bold step was necessary to help preserve the unity of the nation.

UNION TRIUMPH

Between 1861 and 1864, the Union rallied and organized its war machine. Funds were effectively raised through a variety of taxes and borrowing, and government and industry in the North worked closely to keep forces supplied and operative. Manufacturers were building more weapons and delivering them quickly to forces on the front line. Even heavy causalities did not dissuade Northerners from their cause, instead reaffirming their resolve against slavery and its supporters. More and more women joined the Union teams to help injured soldiers and to keep supplies produced and flowing to those soldiers still in battle.

By 1864, it was a different story in the South, which had strained its resources, its people, its infrastructure, and its supplies. The South was only able to stand as long as the resolve of its people held firm. The two fundamental beliefs of the Southerners—that the war could be won and that it was a just war whose burden fell on the poor and rich alike—were challenged by the larger and better organized North and its economic advantages.

Following some Confederate victories at Fredericksburg and Chancellorsville, Robert E. Lee took the bold step to invade the North at the Battle of Gettysburg in 1863. In this move, Lee hoped to threaten the North, convince Europe that the South could win the war, and strengthen the resolve of the Democrats that the South could not be defeated. After two days of considerable losses, Lee sent 13,000 men, under the command of General George E. Pickett, to take Cemetery Hill at Gettysburg. There, Confederate armies were crushed. Having lost over 23,000 men in three days of fighting, Lee retreated and would never again attempt to invade the North. The Battle of Gettysburg was one of the crucial turning points in the war and marked a shift in the Union's favor.

In November, a few months after the Battle of Gettysburg, President Lincoln delivered his Gettysburg Address. In the address, Lincoln articulated clearly why the Union was fighting the war, and attested to the fact that the causalities sustained in Gettysburg would not be in vain. His address further rallied the Union behind the fight.

As a result of Gettysburg, financial and military support for the Confederate cause began to dry up. Even rich Southern planters became leery of investing in the war. Furthermore, the South's efforts to resupply and provide medical services to their front lines were highly disorganized, exacerbated by the fact that no reliable, consistent rail system existed in the Southern states. With depleted supplies, troops, financing, and morale, the Southern armies entered into the final phases of the Civil War.

The presidential election of 1864 came in the midst of these closing Civil War maneuvers. During the election, Lincoln defended his pursuit of war vehemently and advocated his plans for emancipation. To underscore the need for unity, Lincoln's Republicans temporarily renamed themselves the National Union Party and nominated Andrew Johnson, a Democrat from Tennessee, to serve as vice president.

Lincoln won the election against General George McClellan. Lincoln's opposition remained strongest in border states and among the naturalized immigrant populations of large cities. Lincoln received overwhelming support from the troops, who wanted the war to continue until the demands for emancipation had been met.

Also in 1864, Union forces under General Ulysses S. Grant mounted offensives that would amount to the closing moves of the war. Grant led his forces into Virginia, where, despite suffering great losses to own forces, he eroded Lee's Army. In a long closing battle, Grant forced Lee to a showdown by cutting off Confederate supply lines. Lee was forced to surrender in defeat at the **Appomattox** Courthouse in Virginia on April 9, 1865.

In a second important offensive, Grant sent General William Tecumseh Sherman into Georgia to capture Atlanta. The goal was not so much to defeat Lee's armies, but to take the fight to the people of the South in such a way that they would no longer want to support the war. With little difficulty, Sherman captured Atlanta and then, along with his troops, pursued his "march to the sea," where he set out across Georgia and ultimately captured Savannah, Georgia.

In this process, Sherman employed Grant's idea of **total war**, whereby the battle is not only fought militarily, but economically and psychologically. Sherman destroyed the Confederates' property, railroads, and supply stations across Georgia and South Carolina. This exacted a severe psychological toll on the Confederacy, proving to them that they could not protect their own homes from the advancing might of the Union's armies. Southern families wrote in terror to their loved ones on the front lines, and those Confederate soldiers often deserted and rushed home to protect their families from the Union onslaught.

Key Confederate forces surrendered to Sherman in North Carolina, and other Confederate forces followed suit soon after. While Grant and Sherman's total war brought about the South's surrender, its long-term success was ambiguous. During the four years of the Civil War, the Union prevented the South from seceding, but also destroyed its economy and its productive capacity. Southern factories, railroads, storehouses, and farms lay in ashes. Nearly one in every three Confederate soldiers had lost his life, amounting to over 260,000 dead. Furthermore, with the end of slavery came the end of the economics of the South as a whole.

The Civil War answered some questions for the maturing United States. Slavery would no longer exist in the Western territories, in the South, or anywhere in the United States, for example. The new order, however, brought many other questions forward: What would happen to the new South now that it was bereft of its agricultural supremacy and productive means? What would become of the freed slaves and how would they find education and work in a newly constructed union? And in the North, how would future governments of the United States help meld peace on such a scarred landscape? Lincoln alluded to the challenges of answering these questions in his Gettysburg Address, describing the "great task remaining before us." This task would play out over the years of American Reconstruction.

APPOMATTOX The location of the surrender of General Robert E. Lee of the Confederate Army on April 9, 1865.

TOTAL WAR A practice of war that shows no regard for the distinction between the military and general population.

END OF CHAPTER TAKE-AWAYS

■ The Institution of Slavery: Slaveholding was a core part of Southern culture, where blacks were thought to be inherently inferior to whites.

■ Western Expansion and Manifest Destiny: Americans moved West, forcing the nation to decide whether these new territories should permit slavery.

■ Changes in American Society: Transportation and industry developed while millions of immigrants entered the nation.

■ Politics in the 1850s: The new Republican Party sought to end the expansion of slavery.

■ Leading to War: The Supreme Court's *Dred Scott* decision, along with debates about admitting new states, led the nation toward the brink of war.

■ Emancipation: Freeing the slaves became a moral and tactical goal for the Union, and emancipation came in degrees over the course of the war.

■ The Confederate Home Front: The South suffered greatly during the Civil War, being the battleground for many battles.

■ The Union Home Front: Enjoying a larger population, the North was not as immediately affected by the war as the South.

■ The Union Victory: In 1865, Confederate forces under the leadership of Robert E. Lee surrendered officially at Appomattox.

REFERENCES

Faust, D. G. (2008). *This republic of suffering: Death and the American Civil War*. New York, NY: Alfred A. Knopf.

Foner, E. (2010). *The fiery trial: Abraham Lincoln and American slavery*. New York, NY: W. W. Norton and Company.

Foote, S. (1963). *The Civil War: A narrative*. New York, NY: Random House.

Goodwin, D. K. (2005). *Team of rivals: The political genius of Abraham Lincoln*. New York, NY: Simon and Schuster.

Henretta, J. A., Brownlee, W. E., Brody, D., & Ware, S. (1987). *America's history to 1877*. Chicago, IL: Dorsey Press.

Kolchin, P. (1993). *American slavery: 1619–1877*. New York, NY: Hill and Wang.

McFeely, M. D. (Ed.). (1990). *Ulysses S. Grant: Selected letters and memoirs*. New York, NY: Literary Classics of the United States.

Royster, C. (1991). *The destructive war*. New York, NY: Alfred A. Knopf.

Sears, S. W. (1983). *Landscape turned red: The battle of Antietam*. New Haven, CT: Ticknor and Fields.

Ward, G. (1990). *The Civil War*. New York, NY: Vintage Books.

Woodward, C. V. (Ed.). (1981). *Mary Chestnut's Civil War*. New Haven, CT: Yale University Press.

Section 3
Forging a National Identity: 1865–1945

CHAPTER 9

Reconstruction

The United States has come a long way in its effort to ensure all citizens have equal rights. But few would claim today that every US citizen is in fact equal. For example, only 8 percent of children who grow up in impoverished communities graduate from college by the age of 24. This statistic is much higher in middle-class and affluent communities. This achievement gap is just one of many examples that demonstrate that the United States has yet more human rights battles to win before all citizens truly enjoy the same opportunities.

Real progress in civil rights takes time. Laws may change overnight, but the internal beliefs and behaviors of people take generations to evolve. During the era of Reconstruction following the Civil War, the federal government amended the Constitution and passed legislation to expand the rights of citizens and promote equality. The principle of equal protection under the law that was established in the 1870s was the foundation for other civil rights struggles in the late twentieth and early twenty-first centuries, notably in the movements for women's rights, equal employment, and educational opportunities.

Efforts during Reconstruction proved that the government alone could not end racial inequality. It would take many more years of individual activism and social movements to change the way Americans treat one another in society and in the law.

LINCOLN'S TEN-PERCENT PLAN

The Confederacy surrendered on April 9, 1865, ending the Civil War. The Union was victorious and the United States ended some 200 years of slavery. Less than a week later, on the night of April 14, 1865, President Abraham Lincoln was assassinated, and the question of how to rebuild the broken nation after four years of war was left to Congress and a new president.

Under **Presidential Reconstruction**, first Lincoln, and then his successor, Andrew Johnson, focused on securing loyalty from white Southerners and reintegrating Southern states into the Union. There was less concern at that juncture for African-American civil or political rights. President Lincoln began making plans for Reconstruction even before the end of the war. He wanted to make it easy for the Southern states to be readmitted to the United States and rebuild their state governments. Lincoln's **Ten-Percent Plan** would allow the re-entry of Southern states if a minimum of 10 percent of eligible white voters took a loyalty oath of allegiance to the United States. In addition, the new state government had to acknowledge the end of slavery. In 1864, before the Civil War even ended, Tennessee, Arkansas, and Louisiana were readmitted under these terms.

But **Radical Republicans** in Congress were not happy with Lincoln's plan. Congress did not want to acknowledge representatives from former Confederate states and wanted to make it much more difficult for former Confederates to regain political rights. Republicans in Congress also wanted to make sure that African-Americans gained not only freedom, but civil and political rights. They also wanted stricter federal control over the establishment of new state governments.

The **Wade-Davis Bill**—proposed by two Radical Republican Congressmen, Benjamin F. Wade (Ohio) and Henry Winter Davis (Maryland), in July 1864—would have required a *majority* of Southern white men (eligible voters) to take a loyalty oath. It was unlikely such a majority could be achieved in many states, so the Wade-Davis Bill would have effectively meant federal (and therefore Republican) control over Southern states. President Lincoln vetoed the Wade-Davis Bill in 1864 because he was more interested in putting the Union back together than in controlling the Southern states. By the spring of 1865, however, Lincoln was taking a more radical position, realizing the need for federal oversight, especially if black civil and political rights were to be achieved. Lincoln's assassination ended any changes that might have been made to his Reconstruction plan.

JOHNSON'S RECONSTRUCTION PLANS

Abraham Lincoln was succeeded in office by his vice president, **Andrew Johnson**, a former farmer from Tennessee who was resentful of the power of Southern plantation owners. Johnson had risen in state politics as an advocate for the common man and remained loyal to the Union when the Civil War broke out. Lincoln appointed Johnson vice president in 1864 to reward this loyalty and to balance his candidacy with a moderate border-state choice. Though Johnson had supported emancipation

PRESIDENTIAL RECON-STRUCTION The first phase of Reconstruction, between 1865 and 1867, during which presidents Lincoln and then Johnson put forth lenient plans for readmitting the former Confederate states into the Union, centering on securing loyalty oaths and issuing pardons to former Confederate leaders.

TEN-PERCENT PLAN Lincoln's wartime plan for readmitting former Confederate states into the Union if 10 percent of a state's eligible voters swore an oath of allegiance to the United States.

RADICAL REPUBLICANS The radical wing of the Republican Party, which dominated Reconstruction policy and advocated civil rights for African-Americans and strict oversight of the Southern states after the Civil War.

WADE-DAVIS BILL A bill proposed by two Radical Republican Congressmen in 1864, but vetoed by President Lincoln, that would have required a majority of a former Confederate state's eligible voters to take a loyalty oath before being readmitted to the Union.

ANDREW JOHNSON The new Republican vice president who became president after Abraham Lincoln was assassinated; he presided over federal Reconstruction efforts between 1865 and 1868.

and supported the enlistment of blacks as Union soldiers during the war, he was ultimately no champion of the rights of the freedpeople and no friend of Radical Republicans in Congress.

Under Andrew Johnson's phase of Presidential Reconstruction, between April and December 1865, the federal government dealt primarily with the status of individual white Southerners. Whereas during the war Johnson had spoken in harsh terms against traitors to the Union, after the war he advocated for "leniency, reconciliation, and amnesty." Though Johnson denied the property rights of the wealthiest planters and the political rights of former rebel leaders, he angered his fellow Republicans in Congress by pardoning many individual former Confederates and returning confiscated lands to white yeomen farmers. Johnson appointed temporary state governors, but under the principle of states' rights he allowed Southern states to re-elect their own representatives to Congress. Johnson envisioned a new South in which the planter class would be ousted from power and the government would instead be ruled by small landowners and farmers, but under his plan many Southern elites were able to resume their former economic and political positions.

With the **Thirteenth Amendment** to the US Constitution abolishing slavery in 1865, President Johnson considered the work of Reconstruction finished. Johnson required all states to ratify the Thirteenth Amendment in order to re-enter the union, but radicals in Congress wanted to go further and make sure black political and civil rights were guaranteed under new state governments. Fearing that without federal enforcement white rule would return to the post-slavery South, during the period of **Congressional Reconstruction** after 1865 lawmakers focused on issues related to the freedpeople and citizenship rights. Congress was able to pass landmark civil rights legislation, address issues of employment and education through the **Freedmen's Bureau**, and secure ratification of two additional Constitutional amendments: the **Fourteenth Amendment** establishing national citizenship for the former slaves, and the **Fifteenth Amendment** granting voting rights to black men.

Beginning in early 1866, the Radical Republican Congress expanded the work of the Freedmen's Bureau and passed civil rights legislation to counter the **Black Codes** set in place by Southern state legislatures to control the black population. Almost all of the new state governments established under President Johnson's Reconstruction plan enacted Black Codes, or laws restricting the economic and civil rights of newly freed African-Americans. These laws, which varied by state and locality, denied blacks the right to own land, required them to sign work contracts with white employers or face vagrancy charges, prohibited their freedom to move to another area, denied them the right to bear arms, forced black children away from their parents and into apprenticeships with white employers, and in other ways allowed whites to continue to control the economic lives of African-Americans.

Congress sought to prohibit such actions through federal legislation, but President Johnson vetoed their first efforts in early 1866. Johnson believed that such national civil rights legislation violated the principle of states' rights by imposing a federal definition of equality. Congress overrode Johnson's veto, however, and passed the first Civil Rights Act in 1866, establishing African-Americans as national citizens with the same rights as white citizens, a principle that was subsequently written into the US Constitution in the Fourteenth Amendment, which was ratified in 1868.

THIRTEENTH AMENDMENT One of three Reconstruction-era amendments to the US Constitution proposed by the Radical Republicans, the Thirteenth Amendment was ratified in 1865 and ended slavery in the United States.

CONGRESSIONAL RECONSTRUCTION The period between 1866 and 1877 during which the Radical Republicans in Congress controlled federal Reconstruction policy and focused on securing civil and political rights for African-Americans.

FREEDMEN'S BUREAU A federal agency established by Radical Republicans in Congress in 1865; it distributed aid and provided legal and educational services to former slaves.

FOURTEENTH AMENDMENT One of three Reconstruction-era amendments to the US Constitution proposed by Radical Republicans, the Fourteenth Amendment was ratified in 1868 and granted national citizenship and equal protection under the law to African-Americans for the first time.

FIFTEENTH AMENDMENT One of three Reconstruction-era amendments to the US Constitution proposed by Radical Republicans, the Fifteenth Amendment was ratified in 1870 and granted all men the right to vote regardless of "race, color, or previous condition of servitude."

BLACK CODES Laws passed in various Southern states that restricted the economic opportunities and civil rights of newly freed African-Americans.

General Grant.

President Johnson continued to reject the goals and proposals of Congress; for example, he would not renew funding for the Freedmen's Bureau and reversed early efforts to redistribute land to the former slaves. In these actions he increasingly aligned himself with white Democrats in the South and, by the end of 1866, Radical Republicans in Congress sought not only to pursue their Reconstruction agenda without Johnson's support, but to impeach him. In spring 1867, Congress passed the Tenure of Office Act, which stated that a president could not dismiss high-level officials appointed by a previous president without Senate approval. This was a direct attempt to prevent Johnson from removing President Lincoln's popular secretary of war, Edwin M. Stanton, who supported the radicals' positions. Johnson had suspended Stanton and attempted to replace him with General **Ulysses S. Grant**. On this charge of violating the Tenure of Office Act, Congress began impeachment proceedings against Johnson in early 1868. He was acquitted, but only by one vote. He served out his term for the remainder of that year, granting unconditional amnesty to all former Confederates as one of his last acts in office.

THE FOURTEENTH AMENDMENT

Bypassing both the president and state leadership, in December 1865 Congress established a joint committee on Reconstruction to determine conditions for readmitting the remaining states to the union. The states would be required not only to abolish slavery, but also to ratify the Fourteenth Amendment, which defined national citizenship to include all blacks, including former slaves. Although the Civil Rights Act passed

ULYSSES S. GRANT The celebrated Union Army general and Republican who was elected president in 1868 and went on to promote civil rights legislation during the Reconstruction Era.

HISTORY COMES ALIVE

The earliest and some of the strictest Black Codes were passed in Mississippi immediately after the war. The "vagrancy" sections sought to limit the freedom and mobility of African-Americans:

> Section 2. *Be it further enacted,* that all freedmen, free Negroes, and mulattoes in this state over the age of eighteen years found on the second Monday in January 1866, or thereafter, with no lawful employment or business, or found unlawfully assembling themselves together either in the day or nighttime, and all white persons so assembling with freedmen, free Negroes, or mulattoes, or usually associating with freedmen, free Negroes, or mulattoes on terms of equality, or living in adultery or fornication with a freedwoman, free Negro, or mulatto, shall be deemed vagrants; and, on conviction thereof, shall be fined in the sum of not exceeding, in the case of a freedman, free Negro, or mulatto, $150, and a white man, $200, and imprisoned at the discretion of the court, the free Negro not exceeding ten days, and the white man not exceeding six months.

Source: *Laws of the State of Mississippi, Passed at a Regular Session of the Mississippi Legislature, held in Jackson, October, November and December, 1865* (Jackson, 1866).

in 1865 and vetoed by President Jackson had already granted rights of citizenship to African-Americans (the bill passed as the Civil Rights Act of 1866 the following year), Congress knew that only a Constitutional Amendment would fully protect blacks from state and local governments attempting to deny those rights.

The Fourteenth Amendment granted citizenship to "all persons born or naturalized in the United States." It overruled the main clause of the 1857 US Supreme Court decision *Dred Scott v. Sandford*, which stated that African-Americans were not citizens. The Fourteenth Amendment also declared that the rights of US citizens—including due process and equal protection—could not be denied by the individual states.

During the Reconstruction Era, the Fourteenth Amendment also prevented former Confederate leaders from holding political or military office, but it offered a compromise on the issue of the political representation of the Southern states. Before the Civil War, the US Constitution counted only three-fifths of the enslaved population for purposes of representation. With the Fourteenth Amendment, African-Americans counted as full citizens, increasing the number of representatives from Southern states. The Fourteenth Amendment required Southern states to acknowledge black male voting rights or potentially lose part of their representation.

The government never enforced the section of the Fourteenth Amendment dealing with representation and voting rights, however, and replaced it just two years later by the ratification of the Fifteenth Amendment, which stated,

> The right of citizens of the United States to vote shall not be denied or abridged by the United States or by any State on account of race, color, or previous condition of servitude.

Even with the passage of the Fifteenth Amendment, however, Southern states and localities instituted a variety of ways—from literacy tests and poll taxes to violence and intimidation—to prevent blacks from fully exercising their right to vote and to restore white Democratic political control.

RECONSTRUCTION IN THE SOUTH

The Reconstruction Era was a time for transformation in the South. Slavery—one of the central institutions of its earlier social, cultural, and economic systems—was over. This meant large changes for the people who were used to relying on the labor of slaves and, more significantly, to the newly freed people themselves.

African-Americans

For the former slaves, freedom meant, first of all, basic human rights, such as the freedom to have a family, to worship, and to pursue an education. One of the main issues in the transition from freedom to slavery, however, was the question of work. The Southern economy was destroyed by the war. The labor of the former slaves was needed in order to rebuild that

STUDY ALERT

There are three Reconstruction Era Amendments to the US Constitution. These are the Thirteenth, Fourteenth, and Fifteenth Amendments, which abolished slavery and granted basic citizenship and voting rights to black men. The Equal Protection Clause of the Fourteenth Amendment was an important legal foundation for later cases challenging race and sex discrimination.

SHARECROPPING A contract labor arrangement that replaced plantation slavery in the South, in which tenant farmers leased farm land and then shared crop proceeds with the landowner.

economy, but without owning their own land, how would the freedpeople survive in an agricultural economy?

One freedman described the end of the Civil War with these words, captured in the book *Remembering Slavery*,

> [Master] come home and told us the War was over and we was all free. The negroes didn't know what to make of it, and didn't know where to go, so he told all that wanted to stay on that they could just go on like they had been and pay him shares ... about half went on off and tried to do better somewheres else.

Working Conditions

One early experiment for putting freedpeople to work as paid labor and maintaining agricultural production during the war was the Banks Plan, which required former slaves to sign one-year contracts to stay and work on former plantations in exchange for food, housing, and payment in the form of a small percentage of the crop proceeds or a monthly salary. Such plans were used to model the **sharecropping** arrangements set up after the war.

Land ownership was a goal for many former slaves, but most of those who remained in the rural South after the Civil War ended up in share-cropping contracts. Sharecropping involved renting small farm plots to tenant farmers, who then paid their rent with the crops—in some cases, as much as 50 percent went to the landlord. Black sharecroppers also rented or purchased seeds and equipment on credit, so many former slaves began their free lives in a perpetual cycle of debt. As most former slaves had little or no cash, they had no choice but to use credit to purchase goods sold at inflated prices.

To pay off debts, the sharecroppers had to produce the highest-value crops—cotton, corn, or sugar—rather than engage in diversified farming to support their own families. At the same time, their crops were often undervalued due to racism. Consequently few black sharecroppers ever got out of debt and moved off the rented land. Under this system, the white landowners remained in control of and were the financial beneficiaries of the agricultural economy in a feudal-type arrangement.

Still, many African-Americans preferred sharecropping to wage labor. The former slaves were primarily skilled in agriculture, and sharecropping allowed them some control over their daily work and family lives. They were able to maintain their own homes at a distance from the white landowners, did not work directly under white control on a daily basis, and could use the land for a small family garden or do other work for cash if they had extra time. Many poor whites also worked as sharecroppers.

While many former slaves worked in the fields, others had no choice but to work for wages in the cities. Until at least the 1880s, African-Americans were routinely kept out of white unions. They also lacked the training and education necessary for higher paying jobs. African-American men in Southern towns and cities were relegated to unskilled factory work and unregulated day labor, while often the only option for black women was to work as domestic servants—laundresses, cooks, and nannies—for white families.

One of the main civil rights issues of the immediate post-Civil War era was racial discrimination in employment. Through the 1870s, Republicans in

Congress and in new state governments worked to prevent discrimination not only in public facilities such as railroads and schools, but also in private businesses. Radical Republicans also worked to overturn the Black Codes that imposed vagrancy fines on unemployed or underemployed blacks or that forced individuals into contracts or apprenticeships. Republican Reconstruction Era efforts focused on protecting the rights of workers in economic contracts and disputes, rather than favoring the plantation and business owners. After the end of Reconstruction, black laborers and the black community continued to struggle to attain education, job training, and union membership, as well as to fight racial discrimination in hiring and wage practices.

Freedmen's Bureau

Radical Republicans were right to fear that many Southern whites would attempt to regain control over the black population after the Civil War. As soon as former Confederates were returned to power under Presidential Reconstruction, state legislatures of 1865 and 1866 enacted Black Codes in an attempt to re-institutionalize white supremacy and limit the freedoms of the former slaves.

As a response to these political and legal problems, and under the aegis of the Republican Party, in March 1865 Congress created the Bureau of Refugees, Freedmen and Abandoned Lands, which operated under the Department of War between 1865 and 1871. Commonly known as the *Freedmen's Bureau*, the agency assisted the freedpeople, heard grievances, and provided resources and information to Southern blacks and poor whites.

As the war came to an end in 1865, the main role of the Freedmen's Bureau was to provide food, shelter, and medical care to the former slaves. The Bureau quickly broadened its role, however, to provide legal and social services to the freedpeople, such as assistance in reuniting families, formalizing marriages that were not officially recognized in the era of slavery, and negotiating labor contracts. Former slaves felt these issues defined freedom and control over their own lives. These issues could not be entrusted to local governments, which either lacked the money or manpower to deal with them or were run by resentful former Confederates who sought to limit the rights of the freedpeople.

Before the war even ended, many former slaves, as well as reformers, believed that the federal government should redistribute parcels of land confiscated from or abandoned by former Confederates. The idea of "40 acres and a mule" was ultimately only a suggestion, however, for although there were some early small-scale experiments to establish former slaves as free farmers, there was never a widespread policy or commitment from the federal government. African-Americans themselves felt they had earned the right to the land they had worked as slaves, but the Freedmen's Bureau only arranged for freedpeople to rent the land as sharecroppers and encouraged them to save money to buy their own land in the future. The Freedmen's Bureau also helped negotiate sharecropping and wage labor contracts.

In 1866, President Johnson vetoed further funding for the Freedmen's Bureau on the argument that it provided resources to blacks that were not available to whites. This was not entirely accurate, as many poor Southern whites also used the services of the Freedman's Bureau. Congress overrode the president's

veto and voted to maintain a commitment to Reconstruction by keeping the agency running.

By 1870 the main focus of the agency—and what became the primary legacy of the Freedmen's Bureau—was creating educational opportunities. Working with missionaries and reformers, the Freedmen's Bureau established hundreds of schools for former slaves throughout the South. These schools were staffed by teachers, both black and white, from the North and from local Southern communities. In addition to primary schools—which were attended by children as well as by some adults who had previously been denied even basic literacy—the Bureau and its allies also helped establish a system of colleges and teacher-training schools for African-Americans. Some of these historically black colleges are still in existence, including Fisk University in Tennessee, Hampton University in Virginia, and Howard University in Washington, D.C. The federal government funded these schools, as it did agricultural schools in the West, with land grants and other resources.

While the Freedmen's Bureau helped slaves immediately after the war, it also created resentment among white Southerners and lacked political support in the North. By the early 1870s, the nation was ready to move on from the expense and heartache of the Civil War and the Freedmen's Bureau seemed to remind people that the North and the South still could not resolve their differences. President Ulysses S. Grant canceled it fully in 1872.

White Republicans

Under Presidential Reconstruction, many white Democrats were able to reclaim political offices in the newly re-admitted states. After 1866, under Congressional Reconstruction, Republicans, both black and white, took control of the remaining Southern states, filling local and state offices and sending representatives and senators to Congress.

Southern Democrats called some white Southerners who joined the Republican Party **scalawags** and accused them of betraying the Southern cause by supporting Reconstruction. Others were small, independent farmers who resented the pre–Civil War political and economic control of the planter aristocracy and sought to oust them from power. Some white Southerners who joined the Republican Party had, in fact, opposed secession and had supported the Union during the war. Regardless of their reasons, the primary concern of white Southern Republicans was the economic rebuilding of the South. Eventually, those who were unwilling to support the more radical racial equality proposals of the Republican Party moved into the Southern Democratic Party of white supremacy.

Another group many Southerners resented were **carpetbaggers**, or Northerners who came to the South during the Reconstruction years purely for financial or political opportunity. Symbolized by their carpeted travel bags, they were seen as temporary intruders who did not have the true interests of the South at heart. This term was applied to entrepreneurs looking to buy up businesses or land, and to Republican politicians taking over local and state

SCALAWAGS Derogatory name for white Southerners who were accused of betraying the Confederacy by joining the Republican Party and voting for Republican candidates during the Reconstruction era.

CARPETBAGGERS A derogatory name for Northerners who came to the South during the Reconstruction years purely for financial or political opportunity.

governments. It was also used to describe Northern reformers and even teachers—many of whom were former abolitionists—who came to the South to promote racial equality.

Ultimately, Republicans in the South—whether black or white—were driven out by the violence and intimidation of groups such as the **Ku Klux Klan** (KKK) and by the reconstituted Democratic Party itself, which, by 1877, had managed to take back control of local and state governments. By that time, even many Northern Republicans had lost political interest in Reconstruction, black Republicans had been voted or intimidated out of office, and the Republican Party had become a minority power in the South.

KU KLUX KLAN A white supremacy organization formed by former Confederates in Tennessee in 1865 that engaged in violence throughout the postbellum South as a reaction against black political empowerment.

New State Governments

For a brief time in the 1870s, Radical Republicans took control of many Southern state governments and elected an unprecedented number of black men to political office at both state and national levels. Some of these new black officeholders were educated free men from the North, coming to serve and represent Southern states. Others were Southern-born and even former slaves. Altogether there were some twenty African-Americans elected to the US House of Representatives between 1870 and the 1890s, and two black Reconstruction-era Senators, both from Mississippi: Hiram Revels was elected in 1870 and Blanche K. Bruce, a former slave, was elected in 1875.

By 1877, most Southern state governments were "redeemed" by the Democratic Party and the Republican Party no longer controlled Southern politics. In his book *Forever Free*, historian Eric Foner documented the description from one former slave who said, "The whole South—every State in the South—had got into the hands of the very men who held us as slaves." White Democratic state governments effectively disenfranchised the black population and wrote racial segregation into law. After Blanche Bruce's term ended in 1881, there would not be another African-American elected to the US Senate until 1967.

Economic Issues

At the end of the Civil War, four million freedpeople needed work. To complicate matters, the white planter class had lost much of its wealth and was not in a position to spur the rebuilding process. Furthermore, the financial panic of 1873 affected the ability of businesses and individuals to borrow and save money, start new businesses, or pay fair wages.

Another major economic dilemma was how to rebuild the Southern infrastructure after four years of war. The war had not only affected the lands, crops, and animals in the South, but the Union Army had also destroyed many factories, railroads, and bridges. Rebuilding the railroads alone was a major and controversial focus of Reconstruction politics and government funding.

Even before the Civil War, the North had a more diversified and urban industrial economy than the plantation economy of the South. Northern markets were rapidly spreading westward due to immigration, migration, and the railroads. After the Civil War, it was difficult for the South to catch up to the rest of country. The Southern economy was still important, however, for growing the crops that supported the national economy, especially cotton.

The post-slavery Southern economy was also held back for many decades by continued racism. Black Codes restricted the economic options of African-Americans and most were unable to attain adequate education or property ownership. By the 1880s, large numbers of blacks were migrating to Northern cities. Even though racism in the North still relegated most blacks to low-paying and low-status jobs, they were escaping agricultural work and the blatant segregationist policies and increasing violence in the South.

The South recovered as a major cotton producer under the sharecropping system, and also built an industrial economy with textile mills. But the former slaves, as well as many white farmers and workers, still barely survived in a cycle of poverty, debt, and low wages.

MID-CHAPTER QUESTIONS

1. What were the main goals and criticisms of Presidential Reconstruction under President Abraham Lincoln and then under President Andrew Johnson?

2. After President Lincoln was assassinated, Radical Republicans in Congress took the opportunity to advance their own vision for Reconstruction. Explain the main goals and accomplishments of Congressional Reconstruction.

3. What three amendments to the US Constitution were made during the Reconstruction era and what did each accomplish?

4. Congress established the Freedmen's Bureau to assist the Southern people and economy in the transition from slavery to freedom. What were the main goals and activities of the Freedmen's Bureau?

PRESIDENT GRANT

According to Radical Republicans, President Andrew Johnson had been too lenient on former Confederates and had ignored the status of the former slaves. In 1868 the Republican Party nominated for president the celebrated general, Ulysses S. Grant, who had brought the Union Army to victory in the Civil War.

The Election of 1868

Grant had shown concern for the economic status of African-Americans during the war—putting contraband and fugitive slaves to work for wages—and had enforced a continued military presence in the South after the war. President Johnson had previously attempted to install Grant as his new secretary of war, replacing Lincoln's appointment, Edwin Stanton, an action that had led to impeachment proceedings against Johnson. Grant had gained friends in the Republican Party by supporting Congress rather than the president and conceding Stanton's position back to him.

In 1868, the Democrats nominated Horatio Seymour, a former governor of New York who advocated limited federal government. Seymour rejected Congress's civil rights agenda and rejected the legality of the Republican Reconstruction governments that had been established in Southern states. In many areas of the South, black voters were prevented from casting their legal ballots in the presidential election. This, along with the increasing violence of the KKK, was proof for many Northern whites of what a Democratic victory in 1868 would bring.

The popular vote in the presidential election of 1868 was closely split. Seymour commanded 47 percent of the popular vote, though Grant overwhelmingly won the electoral vote and the election. Radical Republicans in Congress were able to continue their Reconstruction agenda with President Grant's support, including securing passage in 1870 of the Fifteenth Amendment, granting suffrage to black men.

President Ulysses S. Grant.

President Grant's campaign slogan had been "Let Us Have Peace," and he worked to limit military engagements with Native Americans in the West as well to stabilize the status of freedpeople and race relations in the South. In 1870, Grant created the Department of Justice, and in 1871, he passed the Ku Klux Klan Act in an attempt to stop racial violence in the South. In addition to placing on trial and imprisoning some leaders of the KKK, Grant increased the number of federal troops in the South to prevent race-based violence and protect black voting rights. By enforcing the Fifteenth Amendment in the South, Grant helped many black Republicans win elections to office as well. Grant was re-elected in 1872. By this time the Union had readmitted all former Confederate states and had granted a general amnesty to former Confederate military and political leaders.

Northern Disillusionment

Although President Grant promoted the Radical Republican Reconstruction plan, and was proactive in securing and enforcing black civil rights, scandal marred his presidency and the era. Widespread patronage and political corruption, embezzlement, and bribery came to light, in some instances involving close members of Grant's administration. In 1875, for example, the Whiskey Ring scandal revealed that corrupt government officials had stolen millions of dollars collected as taxes on liquor and had received bribes from distillers in several major cities. Such scandals, though not directly involving the president, diminished Grant's popularity and ultimately marred his legacy. Additionally, by the mid-1870s, the nation as a whole was losing interest in Reconstruction efforts and wanted to put the war behind them and focus on other issues. For better or worse, the Democratic Party had rebuilt itself and was presiding over stable state governments, and many moderate Republicans wanted to let the South work out its own problems and stop devoting federal funds and troops to enforcing the law.

Ulysses S. Grant was elected for a second term in 1872 despite political corruption and despite the fact that a

Liberal Republican movement had broken off in opposition to Grant and the Radical Reconstruction policies. The Liberal Republican candidate in 1872 was newspaperman Horace Greeley, whom Grant defeated by a landslide. Other Liberal Republicans, who supported black civil rights but called for an end to federal Reconstruction policies and for returning power to the states, moved into the Democratic Party after the election of 1872.

Grant's re-election effort also overcame the fact that many of the Southern states were being run by Democratic office holders. The Democrats had also succeeded in sending many representatives to Congress; in fact, by 1874 Democrats controlled the House of Representatives.

Despite Grant's success in prosecuting members of the KKK, vigilante justice and lynching continued to spread throughout the South. White supremacist groups continued to target and intimidate Republican Party members and sympathizers, both black and white. Grant and the Republicans in Congress responded one last time with the Civil Rights Act of 1875, which included a landmark effort to integrate schools and establish equality in other "public accommodations." However, the version of the law that finally passed was less radical than early versions and provisions of the act were not enforced.

The financial panic of 1873, caused in part by over-speculation in the postwar railroad boom, also weakened support for the Republicans—and for Grant. The financial panic led to bank failures, a stock market crash, and high unemployment that plunged the nation into a depression for several years, all of which only weakened support for Reconstruction spending and for the Republicans. In 1876 Grant did not receive his party's nomination for re-election. Instead, the Republican Party chose moderate **Rutherford B. Hayes**, a former general in the Union Army and governor of Ohio. Hayes ran against Democrat Samuel J. Tilden, governor of New York. Hayes won a remarkably tight election, but his presidency signaled the end of Reconstruction and returned power or "home rule" to white Democrats in the South.

RUTHERFORD B. HAYES The Republican nominee for president in the controversial election of 1876, which resulted in Hayes's victory and the conclusion of federal Reconstruction efforts.

THE ELECTION OF 1876

In the 1876 US presidential election, Republican Rutherford B. Hayes ran a close race against Democrat Samuel J. Tilden. Both candidates sought to distance themselves from the scandals of the Grant administration. Tilden ran on the Democratic platform of governmental and financial reform, including ending Reconstruction. The Republicans chose a moderate candidate in Hayes, but the party platform called for a continued need for Reconstruction in the South in order to protect black civil rights. Tilden won 51 percent of the popular vote, but electoral votes from the Southern states of Florida, Louisiana, and South Carolina were left uncounted and in question due to accusations of fraud. Without those states, Tilden held 184 electoral votes to Hayes's 165. The fact that the election was so close, and that a Democrat had won the popular vote, reflected the mood of the nation and the rebuilt power of the Democratic Party. The remaining 20 electoral votes, however, were ultimately awarded to Hayes by an emergency Electoral Commission, making Hayes the winner by just one electoral vote and without winning the popular vote.

STUDY ALERT

While President Grant made progress in civil rights for blacks and prosecuted the KKK, his presidency was marred by scandal and racial injustice continued. In fact, with each year Democrats gained a stronger and stronger influence in the state governments of the South and began to again assert their control in the federal government.

The election outcome was approved by a Republican-dominated Congress and by President Grant, but it was widely believed that Hayes had made an informal concession to Democrats in Congress in exchange for their support. In what became known as the **Compromise of 1877**—or by critics as the Corrupt Bargain—Democrats agreed to accept the Electoral Commission's decision and the Republicans agreed to remove federal troops from the South and support federal funding for railroads and infrastructure in the South. This was never a formal agreement, but was believed to be part of the Congressional conversation behind settling the disputed election and, in fact, Hayes's election ended the era of federal Reconstruction efforts.

COMPROMISE OF 1877 An informal agreement between Republicans and Democrats in Congress in the wake of the contested presidential election. It resulted in the end of federal Reconstruction policy in exchange for Republican Rutherford B. Hayes taking the presidency.

THE END OF RECONSTRUCTION

Beyond formally ending slavery in the United States, Reconstruction meant different things for different groups. Was the goal of Reconstruction to secure black civil and political rights? Political reintegration of Southern states and former Confederate rebels? Redevelopment of the Southern economy and infrastructure?

Reconstruction encompassed all of these goals, and the end of Reconstruction came to different states at different times. As individual states re-entered the union by normalizing their election procedures and electing members to state and national office, so black civil and political rights were written into law and enforced by a federal military presence. As this process was under way in some states under Republican control, other states were being "redeemed" by Democrat-run governments that sought to undo much of that effort and re-institutionalize white supremacy.

The US Supreme Court also had a role in bringing about the end of federal Reconstruction in a series of cases beginning in 1873. The "Slaughterhouse Cases" (so named because they involved the claims of several New Orleans slaughterhouses) were not specifically related to race relations, but ultimately undermined the force of the Fourteenth Amendment when the Court argued that the Equal Protection Clause protected national rights of citizens, but that the federal government was not obligated to protect state-granted rights.

Another case dealing with the Fourteenth Amendment, however, was specific to race relations and black civil rights. In the 1876 case *United States v. Cruikshank*, the Court ruled that the federal government could not prosecute crimes of the KKK; the Court said such cases fell under the jurisdiction of the states. Many Southern states, of course, did nothing to stop or prosecute such crimes—indeed, it was well known throughout the South that political leaders and local law enforcement condoned mob violence and sometimes directly participated in it. By 1877, the North was losing interest in the plight of the freedpeople and social problems of the South, and Democratic state governments had ensured that racial hostility and segregation were rewritten into law or allowed to exist beyond the law.

If the Supreme Court chipped away at the radical intentions behind the Fourteenth Amendment, the results of the 1876 election led to the true end of Reconstruction. Formal Reconstruction ended in 1877 when the federal government, under newly elected President Hayes, ended its programs and military presence in the South. In March 1877, soon after his inauguration, Hayes removed troops from the last two Reconstruction states, handing Louisiana and South Carolina over to Democratic control.

Perhaps the greatest lesson of Reconstruction was that the effects of 200 years of slavery—racism, discrimination, and violence—could not easily or quickly be remedied through the law. Segregation, lynching, and white supremacy defined the "new South" for many more decades and the end of Reconstruction was only the beginning of a long new phase of the civil rights struggle for African-American citizens.

END OF CHAPTER TAKE-AWAYS

- **Lincoln's Ten-Percent Plan:** President Lincoln's goal was to rebuild the nation as quickly as possible after the Civil War, so he made it relatively easy for rebel states and former Confederates to rejoin the union.
- **Johnson's Reconstruction Plans:** President Johnson focused on rebuilding state governments, but his efforts were deemed too lenient by radical reformers in Congress.
- **The Fourteenth Amendment:** The Radical Republicans in Congress wanted to make sure that newly freed people were granted the full rights of US citizenship.
- **Reconstruction in the South:** Between 1865 and 1877, the federal government created agencies, legislation, and funding to rebuild the Southern agricultural economy and secure the civil, legal, and political rights of 4 million former slaves.
- **President Grant:** President Grant advanced radical Reconstruction goals to protect African-Americans, passing landmark civil rights legislation and prosecuting violent white supremacists.
- **The Election of 1876:** The contested election of 1876 resulted in a Republican victory in the White House with Hayes as president, but signaled the end of federal Reconstruction efforts.
- **The End of Reconstruction:** Democratic office holders and the Supreme Court began to weaken some of the most progressive achievements of Reconstruction and a new era of civil rights struggles for African-Americans began.

REFERENCES

Berlin, I., Favreau, M., & Miller, S. F. (Eds.). (1998). *Remembering slavery: African Americans talk about their personal experiences of slavery and emancipation.* New York, NY: The New Press.

DuBois, W. E. B. (1977). *Black Reconstruction in America: An essay toward a history of the part which black folk played in the attempt to reconstruct democracy in America, 1860–1880.* New York, NY: Atheneum. (Original work published 1935)

Edwards, L. (1997). *Gendered strife and confusion: The political culture of Reconstruction.* Urbana, IL: University of Illinois Press.

Faulkner, C. (2003). *Women's radical Reconstruction: The freedmen's aid movement.* Philadelphia, PA: University of Pennsylvania Press.

Foner, E. (2005). *Forever free: The story of emancipation & Reconstruction.* New York, NY: Vintage Books.

Foner, E. (2002). *Reconstruction: America's unfinished revolution, 1863–1877.* New York, NY: Harper Collins.

Franklin, J. H. (1994). *Reconstruction after the Civil War* (2nd ed.). Chicago, IL: University of Chicago Press.

Litwack, L. (1979). *Been in the storm so long: The aftermath of slavery.* New York, NY: Knopf.

McPherson, J., & Hogue, J. (2009). *Ordeal by fire: The Civil War and Reconstruction* (4th ed.). New York, NY: McGraw-Hill.

Westward Expansion

Today, some of the poorest counties in the nation are found on Indian reservations. The poverty rate on Indian reservations is often more than double the national rate and unemployment in some communities is as high as 80 percent. How did these circumstances come about?

From the earliest days of the United States, the nation attempted to avoid or eliminate native peoples. This policy began to shift, however, during the nineteenth century. Instead of exterminating Native Americans, the government attempted to exterminate Native American culture. Indians were prohibited from speaking their own languages, children were swept away from their families and taken to boarding schools, and families were no longer allowed to rely on their honored traditions. In short, the Native way of life was gone and Indians were forced to adapt to life on reservation lands without their ancient cultural traditions.

Long after the West was "won" by the United States, problems persist for American Indian communities, both on and off the reservation, including poverty, unemployment, lack of adequate healthcare and education, high suicide rates, alcoholism, and environmental destruction. These problems are a constant reminder of the hardships Native people have faced since the spread of white settlement first threatened the Indian way of life in the North America.

GOLD AND SILVER RUSH

For many white Americans of the mid-nineteenth century, the West promised adventure, freedom, and new opportunities. Before 1850, however, the western frontier of settlement reached to Kentucky, Ohio, or Kansas; the expanse of land west to the Pacific coast drew primarily explorers, hunters, trappers, traders, and missionaries. The number of permanent white American settlers in the far western territories was small until the discovery of gold and silver in the hills and riverbeds of the newly acquired territories of Utah, Nevada, Oregon, and California.

California was part of the larger southwestern territory acquired by the United States in 1848 with the Treaty of Guadalupe Hidalgo, which ended the Mexican-American War. That same year, gold flakes were discovered in northern California, at Sutter's Mill. The mill owners tried to keep the discovery secret, but within a few months the news had spread. The first hopeful migrants came from Oregon in the north and Latin America in the south; after 1849, these were followed by an international gold rush bringing profit-seeking "forty-niners"—miners, prospectors, bankers, suppliers, and their families—from the eastern United States and abroad from Europe and Asia. Only a few thousand American citizens lived in the territory before 1848, but more than 300,000 new migrants had arrived in California by the mid-1850s.

The California gold rush lasted only a few years, with most of the major wealth-creating discoveries made by 1850. At first it was easy to pan for gold. It required no special skills or equipment, and a few big fortunes were made. This inspired the rush of other fortune-seekers. However, eventually it became difficult for individual prospectors to find and collect enough gold to make the effort worthwhile. Soon only big businesses with the right technology and the ability to hire laborers continued to profit.

In the process, however, the entire California economy expanded and the diverse population was there to stay. The small village of San Francisco had become a major boom town and international port. Within a few years, the transcontinental railroad connected the West to eastern markets. California ultimately offered much more than gold in its fertile lands and natural resources, and settlers found success in farming and ranching. California was quickly admitted to the union as a free (non-slave) state in 1850, sparking one of the great controversies leading to the Civil War a decade later.

By the time the California gold rush was coming to an end, a new opportunity for fortune arose in the West: silver was discovered in western Nevada in 1858. The discovery of the **Comstock Lode**, a major vein of silver ore in the hillside under what is now Virginia City, shifted the focus of migration and mining from California to Nevada. More than 30,000 people descended upon the region, and they extracted millions of dollars worth of silver with the help of new mining technologies and the railroads. The Nevada silver rush—which also included new discoveries of gold in the region—lasted into the 1870s, longer than the California gold rush.

The nineteenth century ended with one last major gold rush on the final frontier of US western territory. The United States had purchased the Alaska territory from Russia in 1867, but paid little attention to the region until the news that gold had been discovered there in 1896. The Alaskan, or Klondike, gold rush drew some 100,000 prospectors and settlers from the United States and Canada in the late

COMSTOCK LODE A major vein of silver ore discovered in Virginia City, Nevada in 1858, resulting in a silver rush of migration and mining in the region.

1890s. Small towns grew from a few hundred residents to tens of thousands and were characterized by a Wild West atmosphere of drinking, gambling, and dancehalls. Unlike California or Nevada, however, life and farming in the Alaskan climate and environment were too difficult to attract many permanent settlers after the gold rush ended.

HOMESTEAD ACT

Explorers, trappers, and miners were drawn to the West for new and profitable resources, but they were soon followed by settlers seeking land for farms and ranches. While gold and silver had drawn hundreds of thousands of migrants across the continent in search of fortunes, the federal government stepped in to encourage millions more Americans and new European immigrants to settle permanently in the West. Under the **Homestead Act** of 1862, the US government granted land claims of 160 acres to heads of households, who received full ownership and title after settling and working to improve the land for five years.

The timing of the Homestead Act was no accident. The Republicans in Congress used their political power during the Civil War to encourage settlement of the free west, and to prevent the spread of southern slavery and the power of slaveholding Democrats—in fact, freed slaves could also apply for homesteads. The Homestead Act of 1862 advanced Republican political and economic goals: promoting not only a free, non-slaveholding, society, but also the spread of agriculture to support the increasingly industrialized and overpopulated east. The development of the agricultural West strengthened the United States' role as a food supplier for both domestic and international markets.

The Homestead Act ushered in a new pioneer movement. It was not, however, small farmers who could grow surplus crops for the growing markets, especially on small plots in the arid West. Instead, it was big agricultural business interests, private land speculators, and the railroad companies that profited from the government-sponsored homesteading era. In addition to populating the West by distributing lands, the federal government forced Indians off their lands and onto reservations, created new territorial and state boundaries and governments, and made land and cash grants to railroad companies. All of these government actions profited private business as well as individual farmers.

HOMESTEAD ACT An act of Congress passed in 1862 that encouraged westward settlement by granting claims of up to 160 acres of land to families willing to settle and improve the land.

LAND GRANTS

The federal government promoted western settlement and the spread of industry and agriculture through millions of acres of land grants, not only for individuals, but for public colleges and private railroad companies. Two other major land acts were passed by Congress the same year: the **Morrill Land-Grant Colleges Act** and the **Pacific Railway Acts**.

The Morrill Act promoted the growth of agricultural knowledge and technology by providing land for public colleges. States could either build a school on the land or sell the land and use the proceeds to build elsewhere or expand an existing program. Under the Morrill Act, the federal government gave away claims to more than 17 million acres in the late nineteenth century, building national economic strength with the new towns that were created around these schools and the railroad lines that connected them. The earliest schools established under the act were in the Northeast and Midwest, places such as New York, Iowa, and Illinois, as the act specifically excluded southern states that had rebelled against the union during the Civil War. Land-grant colleges were eventually funded in every state and the renewal of the Morrill Act in 1890 included the South, creating many of the historically black colleges still in existence today.

Land-grant colleges and universities provided some of the first higher education and teaching opportunities for African-Americans and women. The land-grant schools had a special mission to teach agricultural sciences, animal husbandry, nutrition, home economics, and the industrial and mechanical arts, and provided a more systematic scientific and technological education than was offered at that time in the private liberal arts schools in the east.

As Western settlement expanded, the railroads continued to develop along sectional lines. By 1860, approximately two-thirds of all railroad lines built were in the North. The limited number of routes and areas served by rail in the Southern states posed a military disadvantage for the Confederacy, who had difficulty moving troops and supplies. After the Civil War there was a national commitment to increase lines between towns and complete the transcontinental railroad. The South continued to be at an economic disadvantage, however, as more Northern land was developed, more grant money was extended there, and more railroad lines were built there, connecting major Northern industrial cities and markets to new agricultural hubs in the West and Midwest.

It was in the economic and military interest of the federal government to have a national transcontinental railroad, and under the Pacific Railway Acts of the 1860s, two private companies—the Union Pacific Railroad and the Central Pacific Railroad—were given access to millions of acres of land and government loans to build their lines. The Central Pacific line would run east from California to Utah and the Union Pacific would go west from Iowa. Together they laid more than 1,700 miles of track. The two lines officially met at Promontory Point, Utah on May 10, 1869.

A partnership between government and private business, the Pacific Railway Acts granted access to millions of acres of valuable land to private railroad companies, who often sold off the surrounding lands after a section of track was completed, using the profits to build more lines. The land grant bills led to the completion of the transcontinental railroad, but after it was completed it was politically unpopular to continue to give away so much land and money to private companies. Because the railroad boom was stalled by the Civil War and then by Reconstruction efforts, the South was largely left out of the economic advantages.

The federal land grant and railroad building programs promoted further immigration from Europe and Asia. The completion of the transcontinental railroad and other lines depended on large numbers of Chinese laborers immigrating to California. From the other direction, European immigrants pushed westward for farmlands, escaping over-crowded eastern cities and low-wage factory work. Germans, Swedes, Norwegians, and other groups filled Midwestern agricultural process-ing cities such as Chicago, Milwaukee, and Cincinnati.

After Native Americans were pushed off their lands, the US govern-ment sponsored a series of land runs in the 1890s, offering free or low cost lands in former Indian territories to the public for farming and settlement. One of the most famous of these land runs, or land rushes, was the Oklahoma Land Run of April 22, 1889, which resulted in some 50,000 people showing up on a single day to stake land claims.

MORMONS

Mormonism (or the teachings of the Church of Jesus Christ of Latter Day Saints) was founded in the 1820s by Joseph Smith of western New York. Smith experienced a series of religious visions, including what he described as a visitation by an angel. According to Smith, the angel alerted him to the location of golden tablets buried near his home, upon which were engraved the foundations of a new American religion. Smith pub-lished his translation of the tablets as the *Book of Mormon* in 1830, and soon set out with his followers to establish the one true church in America. The group migrated from Ohio to Missouri—where Smith believed their new city would be built, until they were attacked and driven out by other settlers in 1838—and then into Illinois. By the mid-1840s, nearly 12,000 Mormons lived in Nauvoo, Illinois. The Mormons were constantly harassed by outsiders who were threatened by the potential economic and political power of this group—who lived communally and expected a divine right to the land—and by their unorthodox practice of polygamy, or having multiple spouses. Non-Mormons were also threatened by the leadership of Joseph Smith, who in 1844 announced he would run for president of the United States.

Smith was murdered in Illinois that same year and the new Mormon leader, **Brigham Young**, and his followers headed farther west in search of land to establish their community. They finally settled in the Utah territory, founding Salt Lake City in 1847. The Mormon pioneers traveled along a 1,000-mile route from Illinois to Utah known as the Mormon Trail. This emigration lasted over twenty years, from 1846 until the completion of the transcontinental railroad in 1869 limited the numbers of overland settlers traveling by horse and foot.

From the settlement of Salt Lake City in 1847 to Utah's admission as a state in 1896, Mormons were involved in conflicts with other settlers, Native Americans, and the federal government. Mormons planned not only to build their own community, but to convert Indians and teach them how to farm and raise livestock. But the desert and mountainous land in the Great Basin of the Utah and Nevada territory were not ideal for agriculture, and groups such as the Utes, Shoshones, and Paiutes had survived in the area not as farmers, but as nomadic gatherers and hunters of small game. Large numbers of Mormon settlers descended on the region within a short period of time, increasing the demand on the already limited natural resources

BRIGHAM YOUNG The Mor-mon leader who led his followers on a migration from Illinois in search of land to establish their new community, Young helped found Salt Lake City in 1847 and became the first governor of the Utah territory.

Brigham Young.

in the area. The settlers also faced drought and diseases that made it difficult to grow their first crops and feed their livestock, all of which made conflict with local Native Americans inevitable.

Chief Walkara (or Chief Walker) of the Timpanogos band of Ute Indians in the Great Basin was among those who intially established friendly trade relations with the Mormon settlers, helping one missionizing group through a difficult winter and measles epidemic. Walkara spoke English and even converted to Mormonism in 1850. But the continued and rapid growth of white settlement in the region, combined with inter-Indian conflicts and pressure on Indians from the US government, led to conflict. In 1853, the Walker War, a brief conflict between Indians and Mormon settlers, resulted in deaths on both sides.

The early Mormon settlers were also in conflict with the federal government over the issue of the church's political power in the territory and over plural marriages, practiced by many within the Mormon religion at that time, but illegal under US law. In 1857, just a few years after the Walker War, there was an armed confrontation between Mormon settlers and US military forces sent to put down an alleged Mormon rebellion. The conflict created tension and hysteria between Mormon and non-Mormon settlers; in the bloodiest confrontation of the Utah War, a group of armed Mormon miltiamen attacked a peaceful group of overland emigrants on their way to Califronia in September 1857, killing 120 men, women, and children in what came to be known as the Mountain Meadows massacre. The stand-off with US troops ended in an agreement that pardoned the Mormons involved in the massacre in exchange for Brigham Young stepping down as governor of the Utah territory. The issue of plural marriage was not officially banned by the church until 1890; a ban on polygamy was made a condition of Utah statehood in 1896.

MANIFEST DESTINY

MANIFEST DESTINY A term used beginning in the 1840s to justify the idea that the United States had a historical and even God-given destiny to expand westward and inhabit the continent from coast to coast.

The term **manifest destiny** was used beginning in the 1840s to refer to the idea that the United States had a historical and even God-given destiny to expand westward and inhabit the continent from coast to coast. Journalist John L. O'Sullivan coined the term in the 1840s, writing in his New York newspaper articles justification for the annexation of Texas and for US claims on the Oregon territory. O'Sullivan wrote in 1845 that these territorial claims were justified

> … by the right of our manifest destiny to overspread and to possess the whole of the continent which Providence has given us for the development of the great experiment of liberty and federated self-government entrusted to us.

From the early colonial settlements of the 1600s until the time of the American Revolution, the European and African-American population of the United States was concentrated along the eastern seaboard, with only scattered settlement beyond the Appalachian Mountains. Thomas Jefferson—who served as president from 1800 to 1808—did more than any previous leader to focus on the West as the source of American growth and character. The West was necessary for Jefferson's vision of the United States not only as a nation of self-sufficient farmers able to feed itself, but also as a world military power controlling a great expanse of the North American continent.

The Louisiana Purchase of 1803 more than doubled the geographical size of the United States and opened up a new era of western land speculation. With the discovery of gold in California and the building of the railroads, in just a few short decades references to the West went from meaning the frontiers of Ohio or Kentucky to meaning the Pacific coast, as far west as settlement could go. Combined with an aggressive policy of removal or extermination of the native peoples who already lived on that land, by the 1840s Jefferson's vision had become the manifest destiny of the United States as a whole—of a people with a God-given right or mission to inhabit the entire continent.

The US Pacific coast.

Manifest destiny was therefore both an ideology of the progressive march of civilization and a justification for specific policies that promoted a rapid period of exploration, territorial acquisition, and westward settlement in the mid-nineteenth century. The expansion of western settlement was central to the spread of both the Northern industrial and Southern agricultural economies. Land was necessary in order to fulfill the democratic promise of the United States as a land of opportunity, and the West lured pioneers from the East as well as immigrants from abroad. Westward expansion was therefore not only economically and politically motivated, but also the fulfillment of a philosophical or spiritual destiny.

INDIAN WARS

I was born upon the prairie, where the wind blew free and there was nothing to break the light of the sun. I was born where there were no enclosures and where everything drew a free breath. I want to die there and not within walls. I know every stream and every wood between the Rio Grande and the Arkansas. I have hunted and lived over that country. I lived like my fathers before me, and, like them, I lived happily—Ten Bears, Yamparika Comanche, 1867, quoted in *Bury My Heart at Wounded Knee*

HISTORY COMES ALIVE

Many stories of the pioneer days focus on the sense of adventure, but the journey itself was often one of hardship and death. In 1852, Lydia Rudd traveled for five months by wagon train from Missouri to the Oregon territory, recording the difficult lives of the pioneers in her diary. This diary is collected in *Women's Diaries of the Westward Journey* edited by Lillian Schlissel.

> *May 9: We passed a new made grave today … a man from Ohio. We also met a man that was going back. He had buried his Wife this morning …*
>
> *May 11: Our men are not any of them very well this morning. We passed another grave to day which was made this morning … He was from Indiana. We met several that had taken the back track for the states [returning to the east], homesick I presume …*
>
> *June 12: Passed five graves this morning …*
>
> *June 23: Sickness and death in the states [back east] is hard but it is nothing to be compared with it on the plains …*

They held a paper for me to sign, and that is all I got for my lands…Look at me. I am poor and naked. I do not want war with my Government. The railroad is passing through my country now; I have received no pay for the land …
—Red Cloud, Oglala Sioux, 1870, quoted in *Our Hearts Fell to the Ground*

Native Americans paid the price for the idea that the West was a land of unlimited opportunity and expansion for the United States. From the first English settlements in the 1600s, through the European wars for empire in the 1700s, to the opening and then closing of the frontier in the 1800s, there was not a time when there was *not* some conflict or battle or treaty or negotiation with Native Americans in the area that is now the United States.

In the years between 1860 and 1890, the United States made a final push for expansion and growth across the continent, and Native Americans engaged in the final battle for their lands and, in many cases, their cultures. Western settlement was spurred in this time period by factors such as the discovery of gold in California and the availability of lands for settlement through government Indian policy and through passage of the Homestead Act and the completion of the transcontinental railroad.

By the time of the Civil War, the majority of the Indian population in the United States was already living west of the Mississippi River. They were pushed even farther after the territorial acquisitions of the Mexican-American War and the California gold rush brought a steady flow of white settlers and soldiers westward in the 1850s and 1860s. By 1860, the overall US population had reached 30 million, but the Native American population had dwindled to just 300,000. This population was now trapped between the crowded eastern US cities and farms, the new settlements and boom towns of the Midwest, and the new states and territories of the Far West.

As it had been throughout the history of white–Indian relations, by the late nineteenth century different tribes had different interactions and experiences with white settlers and with the US government. Some had adapted to agricultural and farming lifestyles and some had even made alliances with whites against other tribes. Many had local treaties or informal agreements leading to years of peaceful relations with white settlers. When it came to signing treaties, however, some native groups were highly organized and able to negotiate the interests of large numbers of peoples; others were dispersed, small in numbers, or leaderless, which made them vulnerable to white efforts at assimilating them or removing them.

After the 1850s, the primary Indian policy of the federal government was to move them onto reservation lands. Many conflicts of the late nineteenth century involved the forced relocation of native peoples off of their lands, attempts to keep them on the designated reservation lands, and, eventually, Indian rebellion against difficult conditions—hunger, weather, lack of suitable farmland—on some of the reservations. There was also the problem of corrupt military and government officials in charge of the reservation system, who profited by selling supplies to or withholding resources from the Indians.

After 1850, there were hundreds of simultaneous conflicts and encounters, battles, and relocations across the Southwest,

Canyon de Chelly, Arizona.

Northwest, and Great Plains regions. White settlers and prospectors flooded into Arizona and New Mexico, where local conflicts over land led to a shift in US policy toward Southwestern groups, such as the Apache and Navajo (which included numerous individual groups). With the end of the Mexican-American War in 1848, the United States acquired the territory of New Mexico and the federal government switched allegiance to the Mexicans in the region, who were declared US citizens, away from their long-standing allies, the Apache and the Navajo.

Military efforts to push the Apaches and Navajos onto reservations and to capture their leaders began during the Civil War. In the winter of 1863–1864, Union army colonel and former Indian agent Kit Carson led hundreds of US soldiers in an attack on Navajo villages in the Canyon de Chelly in northern New Mexico. Rather than engage in direct battle, Carson's goal was to force the Navajo to surrender to the United States. He led a brutal campaign against the native people that included burning their crops and supplies, stealing or killing horses, and taking groups of starving and cold people as prisoners. The relentless pursuit continued several more years, culminating in what is known as the Long Walk a relocation of more than 8,000 Navajo to the Bosque Redondo reservation by 1866.

Over the next decade, the Apache faced a similar fate, as lands promised by official treaties were denied and the people were forced onto reservations far from their original homelands. In 1881, the Apache warrior **Geronimo** led a group of followers off of the San Carlos Reservation in Arizona, where they had endured hunger, disease, and lack of supplies. Geronimo and his followers fled to Mexico where they planned to fend for themselves in the wilderness. Over the next several years, Geronimo was recaptured and escaped several times until, in 1886, more than 5,000 US troops were sent to capture a small group of about 25 Apache individuals, forcing Geronimo himself to finally surrender.

GERONIMO Apache warrior who surrendered in 1886 after leading a group of followers fleeing a reservation in Arizona.

In the Northwest, the Nez Perce, Paiute, Bannock, and Modoc were among those pushed by white settlers backed up by federal troops trying to secure new boundaries of US-claimed territory between the 1850s and 1870s. In 1877, **Chief Joseph** led a large group of some 800 Nez Perce, mostly families, women, and children, on a trek longer than 1,000 miles through parts of Idaho and Montana, toward Canada. The group was pursued by the US Army for several months and never made it to the Canadian border. Many died on the journey, but the remaining Nez Perce were captured in a final conflict in October 1877 and removed from the Northwest entirely, relocated to Indian territory in Kansas.

CHIEF JOSEPH Leader of the Nez Perce who in 1877 led a large group of followers on a difficult and ultimately unsuccessful trek to Canada to avoid relocation onto the reservation.

The largest and final battles for the West occurred during the Plains Wars of the 1870s and 1880s. In these conflicts the Comanche, Ute , Cheyenne, Arapaho, and Sioux were forced off their lands and saw their cultural traditions and livelihoods destroyed. When the federal government was not involved in direct military engagement against Native Americans, the army and civilians pursued a direct but unofficial policy of extermination of the American buffalo.

The buffalo were central to many aspects of Plains Indians life and culture. For centuries Native Americans had hunted the buffalo in sustainable numbers, though by the late eighteenth century they had developed more effective large-scale hunting with the use of horses and guns, methods that threatened the North American buffalo supply. White hunters greatly increased the slaughter. While some buffalo were killed by white settlers and hunters for meat or hides, many more

were slaughtered to meet demands for fur and leather in international and industrial markets. The decimation of entire herds was made possible by new technologies, such as the railroad and telescopic rifles. Where Indians killed thousands of buffalo per year, white Americans killed millions. Within just twenty years after the end of the Civil War, American buffalo were brought near extinction, their numbers dwindling from as many as 30 million in the mid-1800s to just a few hundred by the 1880s.

It did not escape US leaders that the slaughter of the buffalo also helped advance their military and political goals. The rapid decline of the buffalo herds threatened Indian independence by reducing their food and hide supplies, and weakened their cultural traditions. In the 1970 book *Bury My Heart at Wounded Knee*, author Dee Brown quoted United States Army General Philip Sheridan stating, "Let them kill, skin, and sell until the buffalo is exterminated, as it is the only way to bring lasting peace and allow civilization to advance."

Throughout the last decades of the nineteenth century, the primary US Indian policy was to force the native people of the Great Plains onto reservations. Two major treaties toward this goal were signed immediately after the Civil War. The Medicine Lodge Treaty of 1867 arranged for the Cheyenne and Arapaho to be resettled on reservations in the Oklahoma territory, and the Fort Laramie Treaty of 1868 established reservation land and hunting rights for the Sioux nations. Although the Indian leaders who negotiated and signed the treaties honored the agreements, many white settlers and emigrants traveling through the region on their way to Oregon and California did not. Civilians expected the US military to protect them and their interests in the land, and to exterminate Indians if conflicts arose.

For example, soon after the Medicine Lodge Treaty was signed, several white settlements were caught between warring bands. After white settlers were killed in Kansas and other southern plains areas, US cavalry troops led by **George Armstrong Custer** retaliated in an attack on a Cheyenne camp in the fall of 1868. At the Battle of Washita, Custer's troops killed men, women, and children, including the respected leader, Black Kettle, who had led the people through the Sand Creek Massacre in Colorado just a few years earlier, in which a peaceful encampment of Cheyenne and Arapaho were attacked by white militia. The Washita attack was denounced by many US citizens and by the local federal Indian agent as a massacre, but it was only the beginning of Custer's career in the war against Indians.

Unlike Lakota Sioux leader Red Cloud, who agreed to work with the United States under the terms of the Fort Laramie Treaty, **Sitting Bull** rejected relocation to the Great Sioux Reservation created in South Dakota. By 1876, Sitting Bull had thousands of followers, and US army troops were sent to enforce military control on the reservation. One of the greatest battles of the Plains Wars took place in the Montana territory in June 1876. Colonel Custer was among the more than 200 US soldiers killed at the Battle of Little Bighorn, in what was a swift and decisive victory for the Sioux under the leadership of Sitting Bull and Crazy Horse.

GEORGE ARMSTRONG CUSTER US cavalry officer who fought for the Union Army during the Civil War and went on to lead troops against the Plains Indians. Custer was killed in a conflict with the Sioux at the Battle of Little Bighorn (Custer's Last Stand) in 1876.

SITTING BULL Leader of the Sioux who led a large group of followers who rejected the reservation and confronted US soldiers in major battles at Little Bighorn in 1876 and later, in 1890, at Wounded Knee, where Sitting Bull was killed.

Grave markers at Wounded Knee, South Dakota.

The Battle of Little Bighorn—also known as Custer's Last Stand—was only a temporary victory for the Sioux, however, and certainly not the end of conflict with the United States. Indeed, even more US troops were sent to the region in an effort to keep Sioux and other Indians on the reservation and to capture their leaders. Crazy Horse surrendered a few months after the battle and was arrested and killed in 1877. Sitting Bull temporarily escaped to Canada but later returned and surrendered to the United States, only to reappear a few years later in the final conflict at **Wounded Knee**, South Dakota in 1890.

Big Foot, leader of the Sioux, lies on the ground after being captured at the Battle of Wounded Knee.

The Battle of Little Bighorn ended one phase of the Sioux War, but was only the beginning of the final pursuit of the Plains Indians. The conflict ended at Wounded Knee, South Dakota, a few years later. In 1889–1890, Sioux Indians gathered at the Pine Ridge Reservation to practice the **Ghost Dance**, and US troops were sent in to put a stop to the ceremony and to prevent Sitting Bull from attempting to flee the reservation again. Sitting Bull was arrested and killed on December 15, 1890, along with several other men in a preliminary confrontation. Two weeks later, on December 29, 1890, US soldiers attempted to confiscate weapons at the Indian camp at Wounded Knee on the reservation. By most accounts, events escalated after a shot was fired in a minor scuffle. US soldiers ultimately pursued and killed 150 Indians and wounded many others, including women, children, and the elderly.

The battle at Wounded Knee was the symbolic end to the Indian Wars of the nineteenth century. For most native groups, the war had already been lost in the relocations, mistreatment, and tribe-by-tribe decimation over the previous decades, even centuries, before 1890. The many battles between 1860 and 1890 were just the most accelerated and coordinated campaign by the United States to finalize what had begun centuries earlier. From the point of view of white Americans, the West was a land of opportunity and freedom, of cowboys and gold and the pioneer spirit. From the point of view of Native Americans, however, Wounded Knee was merely the culmination of more than 300 years of European-American attempts to dominate the land, resources, and culture of the continent. As Black Elk, an Oglala Sioux leader, later reflected on the massacre at Wounded Knee: "A people's dream died there. It was a beautiful dream."

Ghost Dance

The Ghost Dance was part of a religious movement practiced by many western Indian groups in the late nineteenth century as a strategy against white encroachments on their land. The Ghost Dance was introduced in 1870 among the Paiutes, but resurfaced in 1890 among the Sioux and other Plains groups. The US government's attempt to stop the Ghost Dance movement led to the Battle of Wounded Knee in 1890.

The Ghost Dance was introduced among the Paiutes by Wovoka, also known as Jack Wilson, who had a vision in 1888–1889 of the end of the world, the return of the dead ancestors, and a peaceful future. Wovoka taught that Native Americans should return to their traditional ways, reject

WOUNDED KNEE The final and symbolic end to the Plains Indian Wars of the nineteenth century, the battle at Wounded Knee, South Dakota in 1890, resulted in the deaths of many Sioux men, women, and children, including the death of leader Sitting Bull.

GHOST DANCE A religious movement practiced by many western Indian groups in the late nineteenth century that emphasized the need to return to traditional ways and honor their ancestors in the hopes of a future return to their homelands.

the culture of whites, pray, and practice the Ghost Dance ceremony. If they did so, Wovoka believed, their lands, hunting grounds, and wild game would someday be returned to them.

This message of action and hope quickly spread among many western Indians, who were defeated in spirit by years of relocation, hardship, and conflict with whites. While Wovoka preached a nonviolent message of cultural and spiritual renewal, a few groups, especially among the Sioux, adopted a more militant version of the Ghost Dance religion that emphasized removal of whites from the land. Some Sioux even wore Ghost Dance shirts that they said protected them from bullets. For these reasons, white officials became increasingly concerned about large numbers of Native Americans gathering to practice the Ghost Dance. In 1890, US troops were sent to the Sioux reservation in South Dakota, where a US agent said the dancers were becoming wild. White officials banned the ceremony and attempted to disarm the Indians, resulting in a confrontation that led to the massacre of Sioux at Wounded Knee in December 1890.

MID-CHAPTER QUESTIONS

1. What was *manifest destiny* and how did it influence government policy and the settlement of the West?

2. What factors explain the accelerated push for westward expansion and settlement after 1850?

3. White settlers and Native American nations signed many treaties throughout the country's growth toward the Pacific. Why did western Indian reservation policy and treaties fail?

4. In what ways were Native American communities and cultures dismantled in order to make way for white settlement? Why were the Native American populations treated in the way that they were?

ALLOTMENT/DAWES ACT

Some whites were sympathetic to the plight of Native Americans during the last decades of the nineteenth century. White reformers decried the treatment of Indians by the federal government—the broken treaties, the forced relocations, and the terrible conditions on some reservations. One of the most noted white reformers was Helen Hunt Jackson, who wrote the book *A Century of Dishonor* in 1881. Still, most reformers sought, at best, to assimilate Native Americans into white society. That included converting them to Christianity, educating Indian children in white schools, and establishing Native Americans as family farmers and owners of private property.

DAWES SEVERALTY ACT An 1887 Act of Congress that broke up the reservation system and allocated individual farming plots to Native Americans.

These efforts led to the passage of the **Dawes Severalty Act** of 1887, which broke up the reservation system and allocated individual farming plots of up to 160 acres to Native American heads of household. Those who farmed the land and gave up tribal membership were eventually also granted US citizenship. But farming the land was often difficult for Native Americans, many of whom lacked the culture or tools for settled agriculture. In addition, the allotted lands were often in desert-like or mountainous regions especially poor for farming. Over the years, many Indians were forced by poverty to sell their lands and, therefore, much of the land promised to Indians either through reservations or allotments was ultimately settled by whites.

Intended to help Native Americans toward individual self-sufficiency, the Dawes Act was a final attack on communal identity. It placed Native Americans under the direct oversight of the federal government--through the Bureau of Indian Affairs and through US citizenship—undermining tribal authority and leaving only a few scattered reservations in the United States.

FREDERICK JACKSON TURNER FRONTIER THESIS

Frederick Jackson Turner was an American historian at the turn of the twentieth century. In 1893, Turner published a paper titled "The Significance of the Frontier in American History," in which he explained that the existence and promise of a frontier had greatly influenced American history and culture. Turner defined the "frontier" as the furthest outpost of settlement, "the meeting point between savagery and civilization." The distance from "civilization" influenced the character of those exploring or settling the frontier, as they had to rebuild social institutions such as government, churches, and towns. Turner argued that the frontier was the basic model for American democracy, for on the frontier the individual was more important than the group, and the realities of frontier life promoted equality among individuals.

In 1890, the United States Census Bureau declared that the western frontier was "closed." The Pacific coast had been reached by settlers and all land in between had been claimed, with American cities, industries, and people now spread across the continent. Frederick Jackson Turner was responding to what this closing or end of the frontier might mean for the next phase of American identity. Turner's thesis was based on an evolutionary understanding of human society as a process from wilderness to civilization, from simple to complex. Beginning with the colonies and through to the settling of the Far West, the United States was propelled forward by the idea of breaking free from old forms of society to create new communities and economies. Without a west toward which to constantly look and aspire, what would be the new basis of American identity? Would democracy survive as American society became more complex? These were the questions asked by Turner and others who were influenced by his writings.

> **FREDERICK JACKSON TURNER** Historian whose influential 1893 paper on "The Significance of the Frontier in American History" explained the impact of the frontier on American democratic culture and identity.

Turner's thesis influenced the next generation of historians and scholars as a way to understand the American character and political development. Problems with Turner's thesis included, first of all, the idea that the frontier was closed at all, as there were still large amounts of land to be settled and territory to be organized. Second, he assumed that the West was all wilderness and savagery, ignoring the complexity of Native American societies and history. Last, as influential as Turner's concept was as it applied to the continental West, twentieth-century thinkers, such as President Theodore Roosevelt, sought the opening of new frontiers in global expansion and imperialism, spreading American influence further abroad.

SPANISH-AMERICAN WAR

With the winning or closing of the American West at the end of the nineteenth century, the United States had entered a new era of conquering lands, resources, and native peoples abroad. The late 1800s saw American expansion and growth in population (immigration) and industrialization, and the country began looking abroad for new materials and markets. By the 1890s, the United States was poised to become a global power—building trade relations, encouraging missionaries, and justifying military intervention to secure and protect new economic and political interests. In particular, the period was characterized by a desire for imperial control of Latin American resources and by competition with Europe for new Pacific and Asian markets, especially in China.

In the late 1860s, the United States watched as Cuban revolutionaries began fighting to gain their independence from Spain, the European power that had controlled the region and its valuable sugar plantations for some 400 years. By the 1890s, the Cuban independence struggle had escalated and the Spanish had retaliated with the destruction of crops and infrastructure and violence against the rebels and the Cuban people. Nearly 100,000 Cubans, including women and children, were killed, and reports in US newspapers raised fears that Americans living in Cuba were in danger. The United States was already keen on removing Spanish interests in the western hemisphere, so the Cuban problem compelled the Americans to intervene.

In 1897 President William McKinley called upon Spain to grant independence to Cuba and prepared to send military protection for American interests in Cuba. In January 1898, the *USS Maine* battleship entered Havana Harbor where, a few weeks later, an explosion on the ship killed more than 250 crewmembers. Although later reports indicated the explosion was an accidental detonation onboard the ship, the United States treated the tragedy as a hostile attack and soon declared war on the Spanish.

SPANISH-AMERICAN WAR An 1898 conflict between Spain and the United States over the issue of Cuban independence and Spanish imperial claims in the Caribbean and the Pacific, which resulted in US control of Cuba, Puerto Rico, and Guam and led to the Philippine-American War.

The **Spanish-American War** lasted only a few months and was fought not only in Cuba but also in the Pacific islands of the Philippines. It was primarily a war at sea, and the superior US navy sunk nearly the entire Spanish fleet in the battles of Manila Bay in the Philippines and the Bay of Santiago de Cuba. Theodore Roosevelt, formerly assistant secretary of the Navy, made a name for himself as leader of the Rough Riders, a volunteer regiment that helped capture Santiago.

The Spanish-American War ended in December 1898 with the Treaty of Paris, an agreement that resulted in Spain losing its colonies in the Caribbean and the Pacific. The United States gained temporary control of Cuba, and military authority over Puerto Rico, Guam, and various other islands. The United States previously had no claim or interest in the heavily populated islands of the Philippines, which were far removed from the continental United States, but the country was increasingly interested in Pacific naval bases, especially between the United States and China. As the Spanish-American War drew to a close, however, the United States was also concerned about European nations dividing up the Philippine islands.

As in Cuba, however, there was a growing independence movement in the Philippines. Spain sold the territory to the United States while it still could, for $20 million. Between 1899 and 1902, US troops engaged in a full-scale war against Filipino rebels. Thousands of Americans died in the Philippine-American War—in battle and from disease—and possibly as many as 1 million Filipino civilians were killed in brutal guerrilla warfare. Many American citizens back home were horrified by reports of atrocities against Americans, but also by reports of American soldiers involved in the killing, torture, and imprisonment of civilians, including children. American citizens back home began to question the justification for the war and the costs of imperialism. The Anti-Imperialist League was created in 1898 and was critical of US annexation of the Philippines and of American imperialism in general. The United States spent the next several decades slowly handing over control to an independent Filipino government.

Colonies (Puerto Rico)

Besides acquiring military control over Cuba and the Philippines, in the 1890s the United States annexed other regions in the Caribbean (Puerto Rico) and in the Pacific (Hawaii and Guam). With sugar plantation business interests in mind and a desire for a Pacific naval base, in 1893 the United States annexed Hawaii. Puerto Rico was another important sugar economy, and was also important to US military and economic plans to control the Caribbean and build a Central American canal between Atlantic and Pacific ports. Like Cuba, Puerto Rico had been controlled by the Spanish since exploration in the 1500s. The Treaty of Paris ceded the island to the United States.

END OF CHAPTER TAKE-AWAYS

■ **Gold and Silver Rush:** The discovery of gold in California and silver in Nevada spurred a new era of Western settlement.

■ **Homestead Act:** The federal government granted millions of acres of free land to settlers.

■ **Land Grants:** The US government promoted western expansion through land grants—much of it former Indian lands—not only for individual settlers, but for public colleges and for creation of the transatlantic railroad as well.

■ **Mormons:** Early Mormons were compelled by their religious beliefs to move westward and build a new settlement of believers, a trek that brought them to the Utah territory.

■ **Manifest Destiny:** The idea that the United States had a historical and even God-given destiny to inhabit the continent from coast to coast.

■ **Indian Wars:** The United States engaged in a series of wars with Native Americans across the Plains and Far West.

■ **Allotment/Dawes Act:** Legislation that broke up the reservation system and allocated individual farming plots to Native American individuals and families.

■ **Frederick Jackson Turner Frontier Thesis:** Historian Frederick Jackson Turner examined the influence of a perpetual frontier on American democratic identity and culture and considered the effect of the closing of the frontier.

■ **Spanish–American War:** In 1898 the United States entered into a war with Spain that resulted in US annexation of Cuba, Puerto Rico, and Guam, and the beginning of the Philippine-American War.

REFERENCES

Brown, D. (1971). *Bury my heart at Wounded Knee: An Indian history of the American West.* New York, NY: Henry Holt.

Calloway, C. G. (1996). *Our hearts fell to the ground: Plains Indian views of how the West was lost.* Boston. MA: Bedford/St. Martin's.

Hine, R. V., & Faragher, J. M. (2007). *Frontiers: A short history of the American West.* New Haven, CT: Yale University Press.

Isenberg, A. C. (2000). *The destruction of the bison: An environmental history, 1750–1920.* New York, NY: Cambridge University Press.

Paul, R. W. (1988). *The Far West and the Great Plains in transition, 1859–1900.* New York, NY: Harper & Row.

Waldman, C. (2000). *Atlas of the North American Indian* (Rev. ed.). New York, NY: Facts on File.

White, R. (1991). *"It's your misfortune and none of my own": A history of the American West.* Norman, OK: University of Oklahoma Press.

White, R. (2011). *Railroaded: The transcontinentals and the making of modern America.* New York, NY: W.W. Norton.

Where do you shop when you need to buy a new light bulb? How about when you want to buy a new book by your favorite author? The chances are that you buy many of your goods and services from large national or multinational corporations. You might look for hardware in your local Home Depot store, for example, or you might order your books online from Amazon.com. The business world is increasingly dominated by large corporations that continue to acquire smaller companies. This improves their competitive edge in the marketplace.

When did this trend start? Following the Civil War, Reconstruction, and continued expansion west, the United States experienced a season of unparalleled economic growth as it approached the turn of the nineteenth century. During this era, the country saw the explosion of large corporations, many having over one thousand employees. America's most prominent business moguls, such as Andrew Carnegie and John Rockefeller, emerged during this era. These business tycoons accumulated unprecedented wealth and established a model for the large corporations of the future.

RECESSIONS

Between the years of 1879 and 1882, the United States enjoyed a boom in railroad construction, as lines and companies sprang up throughout the nation, increasing demand for steel production and improving transportation of goods, services, and skilled laborers throughout the nation. However, prior to this boom, the United States experienced a severe recession. In the years following the Civil War, Europe's economy contracted, triggering a full-fledged economic panic in the United States by 1873. During this Panic of 1873, the largest bank in America, Jay Cooke & Company, failed, and owner Jay Cooke, who was a primary financier during the Civil War, was forced to declare bankruptcy.

Railroads in the North suffered greatly as a result of the Panic of 1873, and began to cut the wages of railroad workers regularly. The Pennsylvania Railroad cut wages by 10 percent, and then again by another 10 percent a few months later. Furthermore, workers were required to work longer shifts and lines, without additional pay or days off. As a result, many workers went on strike, some seizing trains and refusing to move them. Other railroad workers joined them, causing what was later called the **Great Railroad Strike** of 1877. The strikes soon became violent, with protestors setting fire to trains and personal property. Governors in several states sent in armed militias and National Guardsmen to restore order.

The Great Railroad Strike was part of what came to be known as the Long Depression, which lasted from October 1873 to March 1879. Thus the Long Depression lasted even longer than the Great Depression, which is marked by 43 months of contraction. Some economists even consider this period of economic contraction to have lasted far longer, from 1873 through 1896, with brief economic upswings during that period.

The railroad boom, which started approximately between 1879 and 1882, did not protect the United States from further severe economic downturns. By 1893, the railroads were overbuilt, and some railroad companies became involved in dangerous speculation and unwise takeovers of competitors, all of which affected the stability of some of the largest rail lines in the nation.

In 1893, the Philadelphia and Reading Railroad Company failed. Thousands of railroad workers lost their jobs. Shortly after that, thousands of Americans, fearing for the security of their bank deposits, rushed to withdraw their money from the banks. Soon credit dried up, and nearly 500 banks failed. Thousands of other companies, including the Union Pacific Railroad and the Northwest Pacific Railway, also failed over the next several months.

The effects of the Panic of 1893 and the resulting recession were felt most distinctly in industrialized parts of the country, where factories struggled to keep their doors open when credit was drying up and demand for products plummeted. Farmers also suffered as a result of dropping demand for crops and agricultural products throughout the nation. Mines in the West closed, and unemployment skyrocketed.

GREAT RAILROAD STRIKE Workers whose wages were drastically cut during the economic downturn during the 1870s waged a violent protest that was eventually suppressed by local, state, and federal forces.

Even for those who maintained their employment, life remained uncertain. The recession led thousands of unemployed laborers to strike, with some heading to Washington to express their concerns directly. One such group was known as Coxey's Army. In the first "march on Washington," Coxey's Army, led by populist Jacob Coxey, demanded that the government address the concerns of unemployed American laborers. Workers wanted Washington to create jobs and public works projects to help improve their lot during the second year of this four-year recession.

Several other labor actions throughout the nation threatened the well-being of many Americans and the US transportation system. Coal miners went on strike in Pennsylvania in that same year, 1894, and later railroad workers went on strike in Chicago, stalling rail lines into one of the largest and most influential cities in the nation.

During this period, more and more silver mines opened throughout various parts of the country, which meant that silver began to flood the market. The influx of silver supply lowered the cost of the shiny commodity, which had a broad, depressing effect on the US economy. In an effort to address the deflation of silver, Congress passed the **Sherman Silver Purchase Act**, which required the government to purchase silver at market prices. While mine owners approved, the act resulted in a drain on the gold reserves of the federal government. To stop the drain, President Grover Cleveland convened a special session of Congress to repeal the Sherman Act. President Cleveland also borrowed $65 million from mogul J.P. Morgan to stop the drain on American gold reserves.

SHERMAN SILVER PURCHASE ACT Legislation intended to reverse deflation that required the federal government to increase the amount of silver it purchased.

Interest in silver mining declined sharply, and many silver mines closed and never reopened. The economic pressures framed the 1896 presidential election, and pro-gold Republican William McKinley soundly defeated pro-silver candidate William Jennings Bryan. By 1897, the recession began to lift. One precipitating factor in the improvement was the Klondike Gold Rush, which began in that year and helped restore American economic confidence.

ROBBER BARONS: THE RISE OF MONOPOLIES

As seen in the case of President Cleveland borrowing money from Morgan, wealthy American business owners were a signature feature of the decades following the Civil War. The era is commonly referred to as that of the **robber barons**, men who accumulated tremendous wealth, often under dubious circumstances.

ROBBER BARONS Men who accumulated tremendous wealth, often under dubious circumstance.

The term *robber barons* was first commonly used to refer to German aristocrats who charged ships exorbitant sums to travel along the Rhine, without adding any value to their journey. Both in Germany and in the United States at the turn of the century, the robber barons were deemed greedy, selfish, and cutthroat. In 1934, political commentator Matthew Josephson applied the term *robber baron* to the wealthy elites of this era.

The rise of robber barons between 1870 and 1920 was made possible by the industrialization of the nation between those years. For example, as oil refineries grew and became more productive, their owners and operators became exceedingly wealthy. Wealth became highly concentrated during this period, much of it in the hands of robber barons.

By 1900, twenty-two men in America were billionaires and appeared to live up to the name *robber baron*. Of these billionaires, nine made their money in railroads. They built the companies that laid 200,000 miles of railroad track in the United States during the decades following the Civil War.

Three of the robber barons of this era had inherited their fortunes, and five were financiers. Of those five financiers, most made their fortune in the financing of railroads.

These twenty-two robber barons included Jay Cooke and J.P. Morgan. The group also included Andrew Mellon, Charles M. Schwab, Leland Stanford, Andrew Carnegie, John D. Rockefeller, and John Jacob Astor.

These robber barons came from a variety of backgrounds and had numerous accomplishments. For example, Leland Stanford was an attorney, business owner, governor and senator in California, and the founder of Stanford University.

Two railroad financiers, Jim Fisk and Jay Gould, epitomized the moniker and the stereotypes surrounding the robber barons. Jim Fisk was a stockbroker and Jay Gould was a railroad developer. Fisk and Gould were engaged in an epic showdown with Cornelius Vanderbilt over who would control the Erie Railroad. Prior to the showdown, Vanderbilt had amassed a tremendous fortune in various areas of transportation, including steamships and railroads.

In what became known as the Erie War, Fisk and Gould joined forces with Daniel Drew, the treasurer of the Erie Railroad, to take over the railroad by any means possible. Founded in 1833, the Erie Railroad connected Lake Erie to New York, opening the door to relatively easy travel between Chicago and New York. While the government had limited the number of shares of stock a company could sell, Fisk, Drew, and Gould conspired to issue too much stock in the Erie Railroad, thus watering down the stock and making it largely worthless.

Vanderbilt bought too much of this stock, losing nearly $7 million. He gave control of the railroad over to Fisk, Drew, and Gould. While Gould later returned much of this money, Vanderbilt lost control of the railroad and was embarrassed by the exchange.

Fisk and Gould later named Boss Tweed director of the Erie Railroad. Tweed was the director of Tammany Hall, the Democratic Party's political machine in New York City and state. He was also a New York state senator, and in exchange for the title of director of the railroad, Tweed arranged favorable legislation for Fisk and Gould.

In 1877, Tweed was convicted of embezzlement, fraud, and political corruption. Ironically, when he was held on bail, Gould was the primary bondholder.

The Erie War and the scandals surrounding Boss Tweed epitomize the stereotypical dealings of these robber barons, many of whom often resorted to bribery, illegal accounting, and other spurious financial practices to gain primary control over US big business.

Robber Baron or Market Entrepreneur?

While some historians consider all of the millionaires of the early twentieth century robber barons, some of these captains of industry made their money honorably. For example, J.P. Morgan held to a firm moral code, one based on something he once described to Congress in this way: "character determines credit." Morgan lived by that standard, and became an adept financier and dealmaker, a market entrepreneur who did use the government to do his bidding. As historian Paul Johnson writes of Morgan, "He was in no sense a Robber Baron. His riches were based on standard, respectable margins and incremental accumulation."

Similarly, another wealthy entrepreneur of the era, James J. Hill, built the Great Northern Railroad without government subsidies, insisting on paying for massive land and material purchases in cash rather than accepting government loans. Hill came from humble beginnings and built his fortune by working hard and saving his earnings. Hill insisted on building his railroads with the highest quality materials, unlike some railroad owners who received government subsidies. The latter were paid by the mile, and often used cheap materials and built unnecessarily long routes to earn larger government paychecks.

Monopolies

Whether they are considered heroes or villains, the robber barons became synonymous with railroad and other monopolies, which became commonplace toward the turn of the nineteenth century. **Monopolies**, like the Great Northern or Erie Railroad Companies, occur when a business maintains predominant control over a market. In the case of the robber barons, wealthy moguls such as Fisk and Gould sought to control profitable railroad lines and the accompanying government subsidies. Once they controlled segments of transportation, these robber barons attempted to control the businesses connected by these railroads, including factories, steel mills, grain elevators, refineries, and other areas of the US economy.

A good example of the rise of monopolies during this period is the work of John D. Rockefeller and Standard Oil. Like Hill, Rockefeller had humble beginnings and his father was a peddler. Rockefeller worked hard and saved nearly everything he earned, and invested his first $4,000 in an oil refinery in Cleveland, Ohio.

Rockefeller strived to improve and expand his business. For example, he introduced **vertical integration**, whereby his company made the materials internally that it used to produce its products, or purchased the companies that provided these materials, in order to save time and money. Rockefeller also studied how to turn oil byproducts into valuable products, such as lubricants, gasoline, petroleum jelly, paint, varnish, and much more—Rockefeller even turned waste products into profits.

In addition to growing his businesses, Rockefeller acquired many others. He eventually assembled them all into Standard Oil.

Meanwhile, he cut costs by cutting waste. Standard Oil became so efficient the company was able to offer refined petroleum at a much lower cost than that of his competitors. As a result, Standard Oil's market share rose from 25 percent in 1870 to 85 percent by 1880.

The oil industry appeared to lend itself to such monopolies, given the limited locations of oil reserves and high cost of developing refineries. Rockefeller's monopoly was a **trust**, an organization that combines several businesses under a centralized board of trustees.

MONOPOLY An economic condition that exists when one company or trust has such a significant influence in one area of industry that it can single-handedly influence prices and undermine competitive markets.

VERTICAL INTEGRATION A practice whereby companies internally make the supply materials they use to produce their products, or purchase the companies that provide these materials, in order to save time and money.

TRUST An organization that combines several businesses under a centralized board of trustees.

SHERMAN ANTITRUST ACT Legislation that requires the federal government to investigate trusts and prevent them from reducing competition in the marketplace.

John Jacob Astor created the first trust in the United States. A fur trader, real estate owner, and patron of the arts, Astor created the American Fur Company, which was a trust over a number of fur companies, including Pacific Fur and Southwest Fur.

Such trusts grew at an astounding rate in the late 1800s and early 1900s. In 1899, more than 1,200 companies had been absorbed by such trusts. More and more monopolies held the power to control the entire US economy. For example, in 1901, J.P. Morgan's United States Steel Corporation controlled over 80 percent of the nation's steel production.

Antitrust Legislation

The federal government had few options when it came to controlling or limiting the power of such trusts. In 1890, Congress passed the **Sherman Antitrust Act**, which sought to ban trusts and monopolies that hindered interstate trade. Senator John Sherman wrote the act and explained why it was necessary, saying, "They had monopolies…of old, but never before such giants as in our day. You must heed their appeal or be ready for the socialist, the communist, and the nihilist. Society is now disturbed by forces never felt before." With the Sherman Antitrust Act, the government hoped to gain the power to dissolve behemoth organizations that wielded too much power over the US economy.

The logic behind antitrust laws, such as the Sherman Act, was that monopolies and trusts held too much unregulated power of the US economy and the American consumer. If a monopoly owned all of the businesses in a certain area, it could conceivably charge consumers any price for that product. When it came to essential products and services, such as transportation and energy, monopolistic pricing could damage the US economy.

The Sherman Antitrust Act failed to adequately define trusts, and was challenged by the Supreme Court in 1895. In *U.S. v. E.C. Knight*, the Supreme Court considered a case brought against the American Sugar Refining Company, which, by 1895, controlled 98 percent of the market of sugar production in the United States. In the decision, the court, which opted for a laissez-faire approach to business affairs, said that Sherman applied only to commerce, not manufacturing or production, and thus stripped the act of any real power over the nation's largest monopolies.

The Court's ruling did not prevent government officials from continuing to try to use Sherman to limit the power of the robber barons and divide large monopolies into smaller organizations. For example, President Roosevelt made a point of using Sherman to control expansion of one particular company: J.P. Morgan's Northern Securities Company. With this company, Morgan sought to combine two railroad lines, which would have given him monopoly control over transportation from Chicago to the Pacific. The economic stability of the entire nation rested on the transportation industry at the time, with farmers, manufacturers, mill

The US Supreme Court.

operators, miners, merchants, and consumers all heavily dependent on these rail lines. Roosevelt considered it too much power for the monopoly, and successfully used Sherman to stop the merger in 1904.

A few years later, in 1911, it was Standard Oil's turn to face federal antitrust prosecution. For years the argument had been waged that Standard Oil would engage in predatory pricing, whereby it would price petroleum products so low that it would drive all of its competitors from the market. Critics feared that Standard Oil would then sharply raise its prices, because it was no longer checked by competition.

Rockefeller had fought off the argument for years, but he was beginning to lose the battle. At its zenith, Standard Oil owned 88 percent of the market, but by 1911, Rockefeller's market share had dropped to 64 percent. In that year, the Supreme Court ruled that Standard Oil was a large, dangerous monopoly and needed to be broken into smaller firms.

In an effort to further its authority over such monopolies, Congress later introduced the Clayton Act of 1914. The Clayton Act was designed to give the Sherman Antitrust Act more power by clearly defining what business practices might lessen competition in the marketplace.

High Finance: J.P. Morgan

Morgan, unlike some robber barons, was born into a relatively affluent family. The son of a banker, Morgan was well educated and served as an apprentice at a financial firm when he was twenty-two years old. At the age of twenty-four in 1961, Morgan began his own financial firm, J.P. Morgan and Company. The Civil War began that year, and Morgan, like many other wealthy men in the North, paid someone $300 to take his place in the Union Army. Within the next several years, Morgan became the nation's prime financier and essentially changed the U.S. economy with his purchases, efficiencies, and acquisitions.

In 1869, Morgan defeated the stereotypical robber barons Jim Fisk and Jay Gould at their own game when he took control of the Albany and Susquehanna Railroad in what was dubbed the Susquehanna War.

Morgan refinanced and reorganized several other railroads throughout the country, including the New York, West Shore, and Buffalo Railway; the Philadelphia and Reading; and the Chesapeake and Ohio. Along with Jim Hill, Morgan was instrumental in financing and organizing the Great Northern Railway.

In addition to personally financing and organizing countless corporations, Morgan also sought to organize and gather individual business owners together, in order to improve their profitability. In 1889 and 1890, Morgan brought the presidents of various railroads together in an effort to stabilize railroad fares and quality, even though he did not own the other railroads. These were the first such conferences of their kind, and they helped mark Morgan's hand not just in a few railroad companies, but in the entire railroad industry of his time.

Meanwhile, Morgan purchased countless small steel production firms, until he was seen as a possible competitor to the great steel producer Andrew Carnegie. Carnegie and Morgan met and decided to merge their firms. The result was the creation of U.S. Steel in 1901, the largest and most powerful manufacturing firm of its time.

Morgan was also instrumental in averting the Panic of 1907, which threatened to cripple the US economy. Several New York banks were on the brink of bankruptcy. Morgan worked with bank executives to secure international lines of

Steel mill.

credit and purchased stock in hurting companies in an effort to forestall the financial crisis. Morgan also leveraged his power and position in U.S. Steel to buy shares in Tennessee Coal and Iron, which played an important role in preventing the deepening of the recession. Morgan financially benefited from the deal, though, and refused to make his earning public, which earned him the dubious title robber baron.

Steel

The U.S. Steel Company was one of the largest, most powerful manufacturing companies of the period. But it did not begin that way. Rather, U.S. Steel began with a hard-working immigrant named Andrew Carnegie.

Carnegie was born in Scotland in 1835, the son of a handloom weaver. In 1848, the Carnegies moved to the United States, where Andrew worked as a bobbin boy in a Pennsylvania textile mill. He later worked as a telegraph messenger and operator. While he did not have a formal education, Carnegie learned bookkeeping in night school and became an avid reader and student of the arts. In 1853, he began working for the Pennsylvania Railroad Company, where he learned much about cost cutting and the growing value of an important material, steel.

Carnegie made several important investments during this period, and ultimately formed the Keystone Bridge Company. Using his previous connections with the Pennsylvania Railroad, Carnegie produced the steel used by this and several other railroad lines, and began to focus his attention on the nation's growing demand for steel.

Carnegie used the Bessemer process for producing steel. In this process, raw iron could be fired in a controlled way, producing valuable steel more safely, inexpensively, and efficiently than other methods. Like Rockefeller, Carnegie also made vertical integration a regular practice, whereby he bought and operated the suppliers of various raw materials. Carnegie Steel was largely responsible for producing the elevated railways and the materials for skyscrapers that were much in demand at the time. Carnegie employed highly skilled workers and continually sought new efficiencies in his production, and as a result the company continued to turn enormous profits despite the economic downturns of the late 1800s. Steel was so much in demand, and Carnegie such a major player in the industry, that Carnegie Steel's annual profits were $40 million, an enormous sum at the time.

Morgan took notice of Carnegie's successes, and sought to create a merger of Carnegie Steel and several of its competitors. In 1901, Morgan and Carnegie, along with Charles M. Schwab, the president of Carnegie Steel, created the United States Steel Company. U.S. Steel merged Carnegie's Steel Company, the Federal Steel Company owned by Elbert Gary, and the National Steel Company, owned by Judge Moore. This merger created a $1 billion trust that dominated the market for steel production in the world. U.S. Steel ultimately controlled the pricing of steel and limited competition through its monopolistic hold over the industry.

STUDY ALERT

Bessemer Process: A method by which raw iron could be fired in a controlled way, producing valuable steel more safely, inexpensively, and efficiently. Andrew Carnegie employed this method effectively at the Carnegie Steel Company.

Railroads

Railroads were the single most important industry and mode of transportation in the late 1800s and the early 1900s. Railroads had played an important role throughout the Northeast and Midwest, and by the 1860s, the US government had decided to build a transcontinental railroad, connecting the Atlantic and Pacific coasts.

The Union Pacific railroad began laying track in a westward direction near Omaha, Nebraska, while the Central Pacific Railroad laid track in an eastward direction from Sacramento, California. Both railroads were given huge plots of government land and millions of dollars in federal loans to accomplish the work. Central Pacific hired thousands of immigrants from China to help lay its lines through the Rockies and other difficult places. Meanwhile, Union Pacific hired thousands of European immigrants to do similar work. In 1869, the two railroads met in Promontory, Utah, officially making North America the first continent to have a railroad that traveled from coast to coast.

Over the next several years, railroad mileage continued to soar. The United States had 35,000 miles of railroad track in 1865; by 1890, that amount was nearly 163,000 miles. All of this and subsequent construction required huge sums of money, and opened the door for robber barons to make significant investments in railroads. For example, Thomas Clark Durant and the Ames brothers of Boston made millions building the Union Pacific Railroad. Meanwhile, tycoons Leland Stanford, Collis Potter Huntington, Mark Hopkins, and Charles Crocker formed the Pacific Quartet and made millions building the Central Pacific Railroad. The Pacific Quartet largely monopolized travel in California during this period, and made incredible fortunes as a result.

Another such robber baron, Cornelius Vanderbilt, had made his fortune previously in steamships, but after the Civil War he turned his attention to railroads. Vanderbilt quickly acquired several rail lines, including the New York & Harlem Line, the Hudson River Line, and the New York Central railroad. With stunning skill, Vanderbilt consolidated these lines into a connected system, enabling people and goods to travel more easily from New York City all the way to Buffalo, about 300 miles. He later purchased the Lake Shore & Michigan Southern Railroads, extending the reach of his line all the way to Chicago. In the process, Vanderbilt amassed an incredible fortune, some $105 million at the time. He was the richest man in America when he died in 1877.

In addition to Vanderbilt, countless other tycoons participated in the railroad boom. One was Russell Sage, a railroad executive and millionaire from New York who worked closely with Jay Gould and others. Edward Henry Harriman became the director of the Union Pacific Railroad and exerted significant control over that important line. Henry Bradley Plant, another wealthy businessman of this era, saw a tremendous opportunity in the bankrupt rail lines of the South after the Civil War. Plant invested in the Atlantic and Gulf Railroad and the Charleston and Savannah Railway, and expanded his holdings to include steamships and hotels. As such, Plant created a transportation and service conglomerate that was instrumental in rebuilding portions of the South after the war.

HISTORY COMES ALIVE

The Pacific Quartet, also known as the Big Four, was composed of Leland Stanford, Collis Potter Huntington, Mark Hopkins, and Charles Crocker, who were largely responsible for building the Central Pacific Railroad. Stanford was a grocer and future governor of California. Huntington was a hardware merchant and Hopkins was his business partner. Crocker was a merchant of dry goods who later became heavily involved in banking. These men made millions of dollars building the Central Pacific, in part through their relationship with the federal government. Congress had passed the Pacific Railway Act of 1862, granting loans and land to help the Big Four build these important and lucrative transcontinental rail lines. Leland Stanford used his fortune to begin Stanford University in California. However, when Congress opened up a formal inquiry into the use of these federal lands and loans, the records of the other members disappeared in a suspicious fire.

Other tycoons, including Jim Fisk and Gould, turned to questionable tactics and blatant speculation to increase their share of the railroad market. Fisk, Gould, and others became notorious for engaging in corrupt practices and bribing government officials to obtain lucrative railroad contracts and secure favorable legislation. They sought to create a nationwide railroad monopoly; they never fully achieved that.

MID-CHAPTER QUESTIONS

1. Explain the Panic of 1873 and the Long Depression of 1873–1879. What were some of the causes of this period of economic recession, and how was the labor workforce affected?

2. Define the stereotype of the robber baron. Use specific examples from some wealthy individuals during the era. Also define a monopoly and a trust, and the laws that the federal government used to help control such monopolies.

3. What were some of the achievements of John D. Rockefeller, Andrew Carnegie, and J.P. Morgan in the areas of oil, steel, and high finance? Explain their legacies with specific examples.

4. Explain how railroads helped shape American entrepreneurship in the Gilded Age. In other words, how did their creation and expansion translate into some men making millions?

Oil

In addition to the tremendous power of railroad executives and financiers, several other robber barons had enormous influence over the US economy during the turn of the century. In particular, tycoons made millions in the oil industry during this period.

John D. Rockefeller revolutionized the refining and profitability of the oil industry. Based in Ohio, which was one of five main oil-producing centers in the United States, Rockefeller was adept at absorbing his competitors. He focused fully on improving his operations, lowering the costs of transporting oil, lowering his prices so as to beat back his competitors, and then ultimately buying those competitors out of the oil market. In 1872, during a four-month stretch that came to be known as the Cleveland Conquest, Rockefeller's Standard Oil purchased 22 of its 26 rivals in the Cleveland area.

Soon Standard Oil became the Standard Oil Trust, a conglomerate of 41 companies run by Rockefeller and his board. The Trust was essentially a monopoly that ran nearly all of the oil refining and sales within the United States. Standard Oil was a vast, powerful, and often hated organization that controlled 4,000 miles of oil pipelines, 5,000 oil transport vehicles, 20,000 wells within the United States, and over 100,000 employees.

Eventually the media, public interest groups, and the federal government became leery of Standard Oil's omnipotence, and a strong antitrust movement emerged. Leading the charge was a **muckraker**, an investigative journalist who writes articles on topics of public interest with the hope of bringing about reform, named Ida Tarbell, who in 1904 published *The History of the Standard Oil Company*, wherein she detailed the monopolistic and aggressive pursuits of the company and its founder. Tarbell accused Rockefeller of predatory pricing, an accusation that raged throughout the public and at various levels of government.

MUCKRAKERS Investigative journalists who sought to publish articles on a variety of topics of public interest with the hope of bringing about reform.

The Ohio state government pursued antitrust statutes against Standard Oil. Other states followed suit, culminating in a showdown in New Jersey. Then, in 1911, the US Supreme Court found that Standard Oil had violated the Sherman Antitrust Act, and ordered that it be separated into 34 different companies.

Nevertheless, the impact of Standard Oil and Rockefeller remained. He had developed business models, innovations, and unique financing, including the first oil futures market. The impact that Rockefeller had on the oil industry and financial markets remains today.

THE GILDED AGE

The era of robber barons, industrial growth, railroad expansion, high finance, and glittering wealth became known as the Gilded Age. During this period in U.S. history, every man saw an opportunity to achieve incredible wealth, and rags-to-riches stories of people like Andrew Carnegie captured the national imagination.

Lifestyle

The **Gilded Age** refers to the period in U.S. history from the end of the Civil War through the turn of the twentieth century. The term was coined by Mark Twain, who wanted to draw a distinction between a Golden Age—one that was entirely good—and a Gilded Age—one that only appeared to be good as a result of a thin

GILDED AGE An era dating from the end of the Civil War through the turn of the twentieth century characterized by increasing wealth, industry, and corruption on one hand, and poverty and helplessness on the other.

veneer of gold. In an ironic depiction of the era, Twain wrote, "What is the chief end of man?—to get rich. In what way?—dishonestly if we can; honestly if we must."

As such, the Gilded Age was marked by lavish living for the rich. High society dinners, evenings at the opera, and million-dollar investments in the fine arts marked the lives of the wealthy. New York City became the center for much high-society living, where, for example, Sherry's Restaurant held dinners on horseback for members of the elite New York Riding Club. In yet another example of the excess of the ruling classes during the Gilded Age, one high society woman held a dinner party in the honor of her dog, which came to the gala wearing a $15,000 collar made of real diamonds.

According to Andrew Carnegie's treatise on wealth, called the *Gospel of Wealth*, it was the rich's responsibility to provide for the poor, but not necessarily with government as the conduit for such giving. Rather, the robber barons gave millions to charities, colleges, museums, schools, libraries, opera houses, hospitals, and much more. In fact, Rockefeller gave over $500 million, nearly half of his entire net worth, to philanthropic causes.

While the wealthy gave to these causes and enjoyed elegant dining cars on railroad lines, phonographs, and even electric lights, life was exceedingly difficult for the poor in America. By 1890, 11 million of America's 12 million families earned less than $1,200 per year, an alarming figure in light of the socialite's $15,000 pet collar! Of those 11 million families, many lived with an average annual income of $380.

As a result, many poor lived in miserable conditions, often crowding into dirty and violent tenement housing. Public outcry against the robber barons and their tremendous wealth began to grow, with the nation's poor looking to the government and the media for redress of their concerns.

In New York, Boss Tweed's Tammany Hall may have met the needs of more poor New Yorkers than the government before it, but it was marred by corruption, and Boss Tweed lined his own pockets at the expense of those he vowed to serve. Such corruption was believed to be rampant in government.

To the outside world, Americans may have amassed tremendous wealth, but they were considered unsophisticated and insensitive to the needs of their own poor.

THE RISE OF MEDIA

In addition to an explosion of industry, the Gilded Age saw a surge in media communications. More news was gathered and transmitted through the media during this period of history than ever before.

In 1901, an important stride was made in the sharing of information when Guglielmo Marconi and others worked together to send the first wireless radio signal to Europe from the United States. Continued advancements in the area of radio broadcasting made it possible for information to be spread throughout the world quickly, and also made it possible for public opinion to change much more quickly.

Hearst castle, the California estate built by William Randolph Hearst.

Furthermore, as seen in the muckraking journalism of Ida Tarbell and her quest against Standard Oil, the media were playing a prominent role in keeping business owners and government officials accountable to the people, but with only varying degrees of success. Other popular muckrakers from this era, including Upton Sinclair and Lincoln Steffens, sought to keep the spotlight on the meatpacking industry and the slums of Chicago, respectively. Their investigative reports energized a dogged labor force, and were designed to help regulate big businesses at a time when the government had yet to do so.

Hearst

Two formidable newspapermen, William Randolph Hearst and Joseph Pulitzer, emerged as media powerhouses during this period. Hearst started the *New York Journal* in 1883, and Pulitzer began the New York World in 1896.

Hearst and Pulitzer were infamous for running public-interest and sensational stories. This penchant earned their work the name **yellow journalism**, which refers to journalists' efforts to use catchy headlines and dubious tactics to sell more newspapers.

Hearst created a newspaper and magazine empire, much like Rockefeller did with oil and Morgan did with financial institutions. He owned papers on the West Coast, and engaged in a bitter circulation battle with Pulitzer. Hearst owned 40 newspapers and magazine companies at the height of his career.

Hearst was frequently accused of distorting the news, running fake photographs, sensationalizing stories, and even accepting bribes in order to run slanted pieces. Many believe that Hearst and the sensational pieces in the *New York Journal* led the United States into its war with Spain in 1898. Because of such yellow journalism, Hearst himself became the object of muckrakers. Upton Sinclair, an American author who was once a candidate for governor in California, criticized Hearst for whipping up popular support for war in 1898 in the book *The Brass Check: A Study of American Journalism*, published in 1919.

Ironically, Hearst's legacy from this period is largely shaped by another form of media, in this case, film. In 1941, Orson Welles released his film *Citizen Kane*, based largely on the life and exploits of William Randolph Hearst, who is depicted in a less than complimentary light. While Hearst fought the release of the film, it has been named one of the best films of all time, and continues to shape Hearst's memory.

YELLOW JOURNALISM Refers to journalists' efforts to use catchy headlines and dubious tactics to sell more newspapers.

STUDY ALERT

Yellow Journalism: The effort of journalists to use catchy headlines and dubious tactics, rather than solid research and facts, to sell more newspapers. William Randolph Hearst was accused of using these practices to wage a circulation war with Joseph Pulitzer.

END OF CHAPTER TAKE-AWAYS

■ **Recessions:** Despite tremendous growth in the years following the Civil War and Reconstruction, the United States experienced two serious recessions during the Gilded Age, marked by bank failures and high unemployment.

■ **Robber Barons:** The robber barons were wealthy American moguls who were believed to have amassed their fortunes by cheating the common man, by employing corrupt methods, and by being ruthless. The robber barons included figures such as John D. Rockefeller, Andrew Carnegie, J.P. Morgan, and Jim Fisk.

■ **The Gilded Age:** An era marked by extraordinary growth and a glittering upper class. Wealthy Americans threw lavish balls, lived in high style, supported the arts, and frequented the opera, even as millions of Americans lived below the poverty line.

■ **The Rise of the Media:** The American media grew during this era, with muckrakers and newspapermen, such as William Randolph Hearst, possessing extraordinary power and influence over public opinion. Radio communications also began during these years, and enabled the spread of information faster than ever before.

REFERENCES

Johnson, P. (1997). *A history of the American people.* New York, NY: Harper Collins.

Lord, W. (1960). *The good years.* New York, NY: Harper Brothers.

Maddow, B. (1979). *A Sunday between wars.* New York, NY: W.W. Norton.

Rather, D. (1996). *Our times.* New York, NY: Scribner.

Traxel, D. (1998). *1898.* New York, NY: Alfred Knopf.

Traxel, D. (2006). *Crusader nation.* New York, NY: Alfred Knopf.

Weinstein, A. (2002). *The story of America.* New York, NY: Agincourt Press.

The Progressives

n 2011, protestors flocked to Wall Street. Angry at financial inequality, widespread unemployment, underemployment, and foreclosures across the United States, protestors sought to expose the uneven distribution of wealth and to demand government regulation of corporate profits. The protestors exposed stories of CEOs who made millions of dollars in bonuses while laying off employees and emphasized the contrast between the wealth of the richest 1 percent of Americans and the rest of the population, many of whom were suffering from financial hardship.

This was not the first time in U.S. history that citizens' concerns about economic inequality and corporate power led to protests and efforts for reform. The years between 1900 and World War I are called the Progressive Era. The United States was once a country of small farmers, but the industrial revolution transformed the nation. By the early twentieth century, many Americans lived in cities where they did repetitive work in factories, risking injury for low wages. At the same time, unregulated corporations created a small group of very wealthy Americans and an expanding middle class. Industrial advances and legal developments that protected big business had created vast differences between the rich and the poor.

During the Progressive Era, many Americans shared a belief that things could be better. Progressives looked to the government to help create a safer, fairer society through increased regulation of industry, labor, and other areas.

SOCIAL REFORMS

One of the hallmarks of the Progressive Era was a collective emphasis on reform. Local campaigns often achieved national prominence. During the Progressive Era, many reformers looked to the government to protect the nation's best interests. Reformers, however, were the ones who defined those interests—sometimes to the detriment of those they were trying to assist.

Even in the Progressive Era, not all Americans were reformers, and many opposed Progressive ideals. The campaigns to prohibit alcohol and to grant women the right to vote, each of which led to the passage of a new Constitutional amendment, succeeded only after many years of tireless activism. Reformers' efforts to establish safer workplaces, labor laws, and government protection for the poor and disenfranchised faced strong opposition and remain controversial today.

Prohibition

In the late nineteenth century, saloons and taverns existed all over the United States. These establishments offered men a place to fraternize, participate in union and local politics, and enjoy their leisure time—and have a few drinks. Saloons were especially important to poorer men and immigrants, as they offered the men warmth, shelter, and a place to connect to their community. The popularity of saloons caused their numbers to increase quickly. By 1900, there were 10,000 saloons in New York City alone; in San Francisco, there was one for every 215 citizens. However, many people, especially women, felt that saloon life adversely affected a man's ability to work, save money, and participate in family life. Women across the country began to speak out publicly against drinking and saloon culture. This push to curtail alcohol consumption was called the **temperance movement.**

In 1873, a group of Protestant anti-alcohol activists met in Cleveland, Ohio, to form the Women's Christian Temperance Union (WCTU). Frances Willard, elected president of the WCTU in 1879, led the group to become the biggest women's organization in the United States. Under Willard's leadership, the organization sponsored educational campaigns warning of the dangers of alcohol, lobbied for laws to ban the sale of alcohol, and supported candidates for political office who supported the organization's goals. In an 1883 letter to the magazine the *Century*, Willard described the WCTU's organization and goals:

> The evolution of our activities has been from the individual to the home, thence to society, and finally to the Government itself.

> The W.C.T.U. stands as the exponent, not alone of that return to physical sanity which will follow the downfall of the drink habit, but also of the reign of a religion of the body ....

Although temperance remained the group's main goal, Willard advocated a "Do-Everything Policy" for the WCTU. Accordingly, the WCTU took on many additional causes, including voting rights for women, prison reform, and care of orphans.

TEMPERANCE MOVEMENT
The late nineteenth- and early twentieth-century effort to decrease or ban the production, sale, and consumption of alcohol.

Following the Progressive ideal of federal regulation, the WCTU and many other temperance reformers in the late nineteenth and early twentieth centuries advocated **prohibition**, a complete national ban on alcohol. Some temperance reformers were industrial leaders, such as Henry Ford, concerned that alcohol made their workers less efficient. Others were rural Protestants who hoped to preserve their small-town way of life from the corrupting influence of city living and immigrant culture. In 1895, the Anti-Saloon League was formed under the leadership of the Reverend Howard Hyde Russell. Unlike the WCTU, the Anti-Saloon League focused solely on temperance. The League's strategy was to apply pressure to lawmakers of both political parties to support this single issue. Although many states already had laws against alcohol, the Anti-Saloon League and other prohibitionists at the beginning of the twentieth century lobbied the federal government for a national response. In 1913, Congress passed an amendment to the Constitution to ban alcoholic drinks entirely. However, the amendment still had to be ratified by the states, where it faced stiff opposition.

Urbanites and urban areas with their large population of working-class and immigrant constituents generally opposed prohibition. Many resented the possibility of government intrusion in their personal lives. Laborers and politicians often used bars as important venues for conducting business and community building. Moreover, alcohol played an important part in many immigrant cultures. However, urban opposition to prohibition was unable to overcome the three-quarters of the country that already lived in dry counties or states and wanted to extend the ban on alcohol. Anti-immigrant sentiment also helped the amendment gain support. During World War I, patriotic citizens became suspicious of German-sounding breweries. Wartime shortages also prompted Congress to outlaw the use of barley and hops for liquor. In 1919, Nebraska became the thirty-sixth and final state needed to ratify the amendment. On January 16, 1920, the Eighteenth Amendment made it illegal to make, sell, or transport intoxicating liquors. Prohibition remained in effect until the amendment was repealed in 1933.

PROHIBITION A complete ban on alcohol.

Suffrage

Prohibition was not the only effect of the temperance movement. Women's involvement in organizations such as the WCTU helped spur a lively political culture for women. The organization's Do-Everything Policy inspired thousands of women across the country, in both urban and rural environments, to pursue activism for various causes outside of the home. Such activism provided experience in reform activities and organizational participation. Frances Willard also argued that women had the right—indeed, the duty—to protect the moral health of the family and the country. She and many other women in the WCTU believed that women needed **suffrage**, or the right to vote, to achieve these goals.

Although the question of women's suffrage had been raised periodically since U.S. independence, the suffrage movement began in earnest during the antebellum period, when questions of citizenship and slavery occupied American political discourse. After the Civil War, the Fifteenth Amendment protected the right of freed

SUFFRAGE The right to vote.

Suffragettes.

slave men to vote, and suffragists wanted this political power to extend to them as well. A few states agreed. In 1869, Wyoming became the first state to grant women the right to vote.

Nationally, however, resistance remained strong. This stemmed largely from long-cherished American ideals about gender. Women were expected to tend to the home and the family's moral rectitude, whereas men were expected to work in the world outside the home, a world often portrayed as too dangerous and corrupting for women.

In the face of such strong resistance, the suffrage movement lost steam in the late nineteenth century, but the Progressive spirit revived it. The idea that the federal government could right previous wrongs appealed strongly to Progressive suffragists. Dynamic leaders such as Carrie Chapman Catt and Alice Paul used the new faith in governmental reform to create a widespread and vocal national movement. The National American Woman Suffrage Association (NAWSA), led by Catt, rallied hard for a Constitutional amendment, using moderate, respectable methods such as orderly parades. The National Woman's Party, led by Alice Paul, was more radical. Paul and other members of the party staged hunger strikes and highly public protests, often faced arrest, and drew attention as victims of an oppressive system. With help from these two groups, public support for women's suffrage swelled during the late 1910s. Campaigning for reelection in 1916, President Woodrow Wilson publicly supported a Constitutional amendment to establish women's suffrage.

Still, the battle was not yet over. Catt had instituted the "Winning Plan": a finely-tuned strategy that carefully directed suffrage activism at the state and national level. In states where women could already vote, suffragists tried to gain support for the Constitutional amendment. In states where women could not vote, suffragists began by fighting for limited women's suffrage—for example, in presidential primaries. Suffragists also fought to elect congressmen who agreed to support suffrage at the national level. Because resistance to women's suffrage was strongest in the South and East, Catt worked especially hard to win support in at least one state in each region. As a result of these efforts, the Woman Suffrage Party of Greater New York gained more than 60,000 new participants in ten months. In 1917, Arkansas and New York offered their support for the amendment. The Constitutional amendment was passed by the House of Representatives in 1918 and the Senate in 1919. In 1920, Tennessee became the last state vote needed for ratification. The Nineteenth Amendment to the Constitution federally protected women's right to vote. It was one of the lasting victories of the Progressive Era.

Plessy v. Ferguson

Progressivism was largely a white, middle-class movement. As such, it did not always represent the best interests of all Americans. The African-American community, for example, had reason to reject white Americans' faith in the protective possibilities of the government. After the Civil War, Reconstruction-era politicians instituted a slew of reforms aimed at achieving some degree of racial equality. However, by the turn of the century, much of their work had been undone. Rather than continuing the Reconstruction project of increasing African-Americans' civil rights and economic opportunities, white communities in the South instituted "Jim Crow" policies that stripped blacks of their political power, their economic potential, and their civil rights.

These Jim Crow laws segregated blacks from whites in many areas of their lives. Jim Crow laws determined where blacks could work and live, which public institutions welcomed them, and which schools they could attend. Even the right to vote, guaranteed to African-American men by the Fifteenth Amendment, was denied to many blacks through evasive measures such as poll taxes and property requirements. Jim Crow laws developed at the state and local level. However, the federal government, far from condemning these developments, upheld segregation in a pivotal Supreme Court Case in 1896.

Although Southern states had been pursuing segregationist policies since the end of Reconstruction, the question of these policies' constitutionality was only addressed in 1896, by the Supreme Court case of *Plessy v. Ferguson*. The case concerned a Louisiana state law that segregated train cars. Homer Plessy, who was one-eighth black, challenged the law by sitting in a white railroad car. When he refused to leave, he was arrested. The case, addressing whether state and local governments had the right to institute segregationist policy, came before the Supreme Court after a series of appeals. The Court determined that segregation was legal, based on the idea that "separate" did not necessarily mean "unequal." Therefore, these segregationist laws did not violate the equal protection under the law that had been granted to African-Americans after the Civil War by the Fourteenth Amendment.

The Supreme Court's decision left the question of segregation up to the states, and Southern states continued their segregationist policies. The ruling that legally sanctioned segregation lasted for more than 50 years, until it was overturned in *Brown v. Board of Education* in 1954. In this pivotal decision, the Court ruled that segregation did not allow for equal protection under the law and, therefore, did violate the protections granted by the Fourteenth Amendment.

The Great Migration

With Jim Crow laws firmly in place, African-Americans experienced restrictions in almost every aspect of their lives. Though the institution of slavery had ended, many white Americans sought to ensure that African-Americans remained limited in their political, legal, and financial rights. The phenomenon of **lynching** also exploded in the late nineteenth century. Many white southerners felt that Reconstruction had undermined the white establishment's economic, cultural, and political power. Some white Americans used lynching, a kind of mob hanging or execution, as a tool of political repression and vigilante justice to reassert control over African-Americans. Victims of lynching were sometimes, but not always, accused of criminal behavior, sexual misconduct, political resistance, or transgressing racial divides. In the last decade of the nineteenth century, there were an average of 187 lynchings each year. The unpredictability and brutality of lynching made it especially terrifying.

Another way that southern whites intimidated and tried to assert control over African-Americans was through the **Ku Klux Klan**, founded in the South in the years directly following the Civil War. The Klan started out as groups of former

LYNCHING A hanging or other public killing by a mob, rather than legal authorities. Most victims of lynching in the United States were African-Americans.

KU KLUX KLAN An organization that favored repression of African-Americans, Jews, Catholics, and immigrants and often committed acts of violence to intimidate these groups.

Confederate soldiers who beat and murdered African-Americans and Republican politicians in an effort to win back political power and white supremacy. Klan members terrorized black families and Republican politicians, and destroyed blacks' property, schools, and churches. Propelled by suspicion of Catholics, Jews, and immigrants, as well as by long-standing racial tensions, the Klan experienced a resurgence during the 1910s. By 1925, it had become a strong political force, with more than 3 million members.

The Ku Klux Klan on parade down Pennsylvania Avenue, 1928.

For African-Americans, who had little political power and limited financial means, living in Klan territory meant living in near-constant fear of violence and intimidation. African-Americans in the South were often prevented from voting. In addition, African-Americans, already financially disadvantaged from centuries of slavery, often found it impossible to buy land in the largely agricultural South. Because the South had not kept up with the industrializing north, other job opportunities were limited. Men who could not buy their own land were limited to low-paying work as **sharecroppers** or tenant farmers on land owned by whites. African-American women worked as agricultural laborers, domestic servants, and washer women for white families. Such arrangements offered little potential for economic success and, in many ways, mimicked the power relations and racial dynamics of slavery.

SHARECROPPERS Farmers who do not own their own land but pay a portion of their harvest to the land's owner in exchange for being allowed to farm there.

Unlike the South, the North had developed rapidly in the late nineteenth and early twentieth centuries. The North boasted large cities with industrialized factory jobs and higher wages. When the United States entered World War I in 1917, many men joined the military, causing widespread labor shortages. Business representatives from the North travelled south in search of labor. Huge numbers of African-Americans left their homes to seek new opportunities in Northern cities. This period, when more than 400,000 Southern blacks moved north, is known as the **Great Migration**.

GREAT MIGRATION The period from 1916 through the 1930s when more than 400,000 African-Americans moved from the South to Northern cities.

Although the North lacked the legally instituted segregationist policies found in the South, it was no sanctuary from racial tension and violence. Many white laborers in the North, especially immigrants, felt threatened by and hostile toward the new population of African-Americans, whom the white laborers saw as competitors for jobs. Making matters worse, Northern cities were often divided into ethnic enclaves, and the presence of newcomers in these neighborhoods often led to conflict. In the late 1910s and early 1920s, race riots broke out in more than twenty-five Northern cities. In East St. Louis, Illinois, more than forty blacks and nine whites died in a 1917 fight over jobs. In Chicago, thirteen days of racial conflict in 1919 left thirty-eight people dead and more than 500 injured, and the homes of about 1,000 African-American families were destroyed. Despite job competition and outright violence, the Great Migration continued through the 1930s, and African-Americans became a major presence in Northern cities.

Immigration and the Progressive Era

African-Americans were not the only group to face discrimination in the Progressive Era. Industrialization and expansionism in the nineteenth century had turned the United States into a world power, offering the promise of jobs, wealth, and political sanctuary to people from across the globe. Like Southern blacks, immigrants were often pushed out of their homelands by political or economic factors in many parts of Europe and pulled to the United States by the lure of a better life.

In the mid-nineteenth century, large numbers of Irish and German immigrants came to the United States. However, starting in the 1870s, increasing numbers of Southern and Eastern Europeans made the journey to American soil. By 1890, the overwhelming majority of immigrants were from these areas in Europe, and more continued to flood into the United States. By the turn of the century, immigrants made up almost 30 percent of the population in the major U.S. cities.

Gates to America

In order to handle the massive tide of immigrants, the United States built a processing facility for newly-arrived immigrants on Ellis Island near Manhattan, with a clear view of the Statue of Liberty. From the time the facility opened in 1892, immigrants at Ellis Island were subject to bureaucratic wranglings and invasive medical inspections before they could be granted their papers. In addition, inspectors peppered immigrants with questions about their political beliefs in an effort to identify radicals and criminals. Serious medical issues, criminality, and radical political beliefs were all grounds to turn immigrants away. Approximately 2 percent of applicants were refused entry. These disappointed people faced a long, hard journey home.

Ellis Island.

The West Coast equivalent of Ellis Island, Angel Island, opened off the coast of San Francisco in 1910. In 1882, following anti-immigrant furor against Chinese laborers whom white workers saw as competitors for jobs, Congress passed the Chinese Exclusion Act in an effort to limit the number of Chinese workers. One of the main tasks of Angel Island was to enforce the policy of Chinese exclusion. Under the policy, Chinese immigrants who met certain requirements, such as having a relative in the United States or a profession that was deemed desirable, were still allowed into the country. However, 30 percent of applicants were turned away from Angel Island.

Melting Pot?

Irish and German immigrants had faced prejudice in the mid-nineteenth century, but the overwhelming numbers of immigrants who brought unfamiliar cultures to the United States in the late nineteenth and early twentieth centuries ignited even more widespread fear and hostility. The majority of these immigrants came from countries in Southern and Eastern Europe such as Italy, Poland, Russia, and Bohemia. They spoke unfamiliar languages, and they increased the country's Catholic and Jewish populations. Some espoused radical political traditions, such as socialism and anarchism.

Ethnic enclaves where immigrants could converse in their own language and practice their religion sprang up in many major cities. These enclaves retained a separate cultural identity that Americans often found foreign. As automobiles made commuting more convenient, many long-time residents of these neighborhoods moved out to escape the areas' rapidly changing demographics. When wealthier residents moved away, immigrant neighborhoods often became impoverished.

Cultural identity often determined not only where immigrants lived, but also their jobs. Certain industries became dominated by particular ethnicities. For example, Russian and Polish Jews tended to work in the needle trades in New York, whereas Slavs and Poles found work in steel mills. **Nativists**—mostly white Protestant laborers and union members who opposed immigration and immigrants—resented the intrusion of these new people from cultures they found strange, who seemed to isolate themselves rather than assimilate to "American" ideals and culture. In addition, nativists believed that immigrants stole American jobs and accepted substandard wages, driving down pay for all workers.

NATIVISTS Americans who opposed immigration and immigrants.

Changes in Immigration Policy

The influence of nativists was soon felt in U.S. immigration policy. Although Chinese immigrants had been instrumental in building railroads and mining resources in the West for decades, the workers' willingness to work for lower wages, as well as their cultural differences, raised the suspicions of many native-born Americans. In 1882, Congress passed the Chinese Exclusion Act, barring almost all Chinese immigrants from entering the United States. No other group of immigrants was legally excluded based on national origin. This law lasted in some form until 1943.

Although the Chinese were subject to the most restrictive immigration policy, nativist sentiment led the U.S. government to limit immigration from other countries as well. With support from Massachusetts Senator Henry Cabot Lodge, Congress passed a bill requiring adult immigrants to pass a literacy test in order to be admitted to the country. The bill also banned immigration from all Asian countries except Japan and the Philippines. Presidents Grover Cleveland, William Howard Taft, and Woodrow Wilson all vetoed the bill. Finally, in 1917, Congress overrode the presidential veto, and the bill became law. Further limits on immigration soon followed.

In 1919, following World War I, concern over communist and anarchist activity—including attacks on government officials, industrial leaders, and the public—set off a Red Scare, or period of anti-Communist fervor. Attorney General A. Mitchell Palmer led the federal government to arrest and deport thousands of radicals, many of them non-citizens. The Red Scare increased Americans' suspicion of immigrants. In an effort to control the country's cultural makeup, lawmakers created an immigration policy based on **quotas**, which limited the numbers of people from certain groups allowed into the country. In 1921, Congress passed an emergency immigration bill. Under this bill, a total of no more than 350,000 immigrants would be granted visas to enter the country. Furthermore, each year, the United States would allow in only the number of immigrants from a country equal to no more than 3 percent of the population of that nationality in the United States in 1910. In 1924, a new version of the law called the National Origins Act further restricted immigration by limiting the number of immigrants to 2 percent of each nationality's population in the 1890 census—which reflected far fewer Southern and Eastern Europeans than the 1910 census. In approving this law, President Calvin Coolidge stated, "America must be kept American." In 1927, Congress reduced the total number of immigrants to 150,000 and the number allowed from each country to 2 percent of that nationality's population in the United States in 1920. However, Congress permitted free and open immigration from any nation in the Western Hemisphere, a decision that would hugely increase the numbers of Latin American immigrants. The quota system continued to define American immigration policy until 1965, when the Immigration Act was passed. In the effort

QUOTAS A fixed number of people from certain groups, used historically in immigration systems.

to end the discrimination against Asians and Southern Europeans, this act ended the quota system. Instead, it favored a more equal number of immigrants from all countries.

ACTIVISTS AND INNOVATORS

By the turn of the twentieth century, the United States was a country in flux. The Industrial Revolution, the Civil War, and huge waves of immigration had caused changes that led to problems such as urban poverty and labor unrest. Racial and ethnic tensions continued to plague the nation as well. In the Progressive Era, not only broad movements, but also influential reformers and political activists worked to help solve these problems. Each individual in this section played a major role in changing American culture. Together, their work embodies the spirit of innovative reform that characterized the Progressive Era.

Booker T. Washington

African-American leader Booker T. Washington recognized that, even after the abolition of slavery, black men and women continued to suffer financial degradation, physical danger, and political disenfranchisement. Washington was born in 1856 to a slave mother and a white father. As a young man after the Civil War ended slavery, he worked in mines and as a janitor while pursuing higher education. After attending the Hampton Institute, Washington became an important educator and thinker in the black community.

Unlike earlier anti-slavery activists such as Frederick Douglass, who advocated full civil and political equality, Washington believed that the best strategy for black Americans was to work toward economic progress. Rather than attacking and reviling whites for centuries of racial abuses, Washington suggested that African-Americans take advantage of the white need for competent laborers. The South, ravaged by the Civil War and lagging behind the industrialized North, required a large agricultural labor force. Therefore, Washington believed that African-Americans needed schooling that would teach them how to be better farmhands and tradesmen. In 1881 he founded the Tuskegee Institute to provide this kind of education.

ATLANTA COMPROMISE
Booker T. Washington's strategy to racial progress, which accepted segregation and urged blacks and whites to work together for the benefit of both groups.

Washington hoped that, by proving themselves economically useful to white people, African-Americans could start to achieve greater economic power and property ownership. Though Washington worked privately against the legal structures that limited the options of Southern blacks, he publicly promoted a more moderate approach. Rather than aiming his critiques at whites and their policies, Washington put the burden for racial progress on the backs of African-Americans, asking them to accept their current status as laborers in the hopes of rising up financially as a community. In 1895, Washington articulated this platform in a speech given in Atlanta, so his vision of racial progress came to be called the **Atlanta Compromise**. In this speech, Washington seemed to accept the system of segregation but urged blacks and whites to work together toward "mutual progress." His Atlanta Compromise garnered him both friends and enemies. Many whites—including members of the Southern elite—believed his ideas to be sound, wise, and pleasingly moderate. However, many in the black community, such as W.E.B. DuBois and Ida B. Wells, disapproved of his willingness to concede to whites on issues such as segregation.

W.E.B. DuBois

W.E.B. DuBois, another pivotal figure in the African-American community, was Washington's most vocal critic. DuBois was born in Massachusetts in 1868 and later became the first African-American to earn a doctorate at Harvard University. Whereas Washington advocated industrial and agricultural education for a wide range of African-Americans, DuBois advocated for community investment in the "talented tenth," the brightest African-Americans in the country. DuBois believed that these people—educated, competent, articulate— should represent the needs of the African-American community and lead the way out of racial oppression. Indeed, he argued, if this group were to follow Washington's plan, the potential of these talented individuals would be crushed by the utilitarian, manual-labor education they would receive.

DuBois' classic work, *The Souls of Black Folk,* published in 1903, detailed the power and potential of the black community. Rather than concede to the economic needs of whites, DuBois called for full civil, economic, and political equality for African-Americans. Based on this idea, in 1906, he cofounded the Niagara Movement, which asked African-Americans to be proud of their race and their heritage and not to submit to any racial oppression whatsoever. The Niagara Movement and DuBois's call for racial parity led him to help found the National Association for the Advancement of Colored People (NAACP) in 1909. In alignment with Progressive ideals, this national organization aimed at governmental change and social justice. The membership included both blacks and whites, with whites making up the lion's share of the national leaders. However, DuBois himself edited the NAACP's influential journal, *The Crisis*. The NAACP remains a leading organization in race relations today.

Unlike Washington, DuBois was prepared to directly attack the structural and economic systems that were implicated in racial injustice. As the world entered World War I, DuBois offered a scathing critique of capitalism and the global economy in the popular magazine the *Atlantic Monthly.* The war, he noted, was merely a continuation of the exploitation of disadvantaged people, including Africans, Asians, and other nations made up of people of color. He claimed that the United States, far from living up to its democratic values, relied on the oppression of other, poorer nations and peoples to maintain its world supremacy.

Ida B. Wells

W.E.B. DuBois was certainly not alone is his radical perspective on racial justice. Ida B. Wells, another contemporary civil rights activist, was born a slave in Mississippi in 1862. Her parents and younger brother were both killed by yellow fever in 1878, leaving her in charge of her family. She moved her family to Memphis, where she worked as a teacher and cared for her younger siblings.

Even as a very young woman, Wells refused to ignore discriminatory policies. In 1882, she pressed charges after being removed from a whites-only car on a segregated train. A brief local victory was quickly denied by the state supreme court. Angered by segregation and the courts that upheld it, Wells turned her sharp intellect to journalism. She became the editor of Memphis's black newspaper, a surprising accomplishment for a woman—particularly a black woman—in that era.

Wells's anger found its specific, lifelong target in 1892, when a local lynch mob murdered three of her friends. From that point on, Wells embarked on an unending crusade against lynching. Her outspoken articles on the subject incited white mobs to target black places of business, and Wells herself received death threats. Unwilling to stay in such a precarious situation, Wells moved to New York and then to Chicago. In each city, she continued to speak out against racial prejudice and lynching.

Well's harsh condemnation of racial injustice stood in stark contrast to Booker T. Washington's accomodationist views. In fact, Wells openly advocated armed resistance to white violence. She did not believe in provoking violence but asserted that every black house should include a gun for self-protection. Because the law offered little protection against lynch mobs, she argued that it was up to individual black families to protect themselves.

Wells assisted in the creation of the NAACP and petitioned the federal government to assist with her anti-lynching campaign. In addition to combating race discrimination, Wells helped develop black women's clubs in Chicago and advocated for women's suffrage during the 1910s. In an era when women—especially black women—had little access to economic, social, and political power, Ida B. Wells refused to be silenced.

Sinclair Lewis

Like Ida B. Wells, the writer Sinclair Lewis used words to call attention to problems in American society. His novel *Main Street,* published in 1920, critiqued the provincialism and ignorance of rural America. His tone came as a shock to a nation that had long defined itself by the heart and strength of character of its rural folk. Lewis's vision of rural America exemplified a debate about American culture in the early twentieth century. Although farming and westward expansion had defined the nation since its inception, by the early twentieth century, the country's growing cities were creating a new and influential urban culture marked by diversity, poverty, artistic expression, and labor unrest. Rural Americans came to see cities as centers of vice and immorality. Many urban dwellers, like Lewis, mocked the stagnant insularity of small towns.

Lewis also satirized the credulity of middle-class Americans and their susceptibility to the influences of advertising and consumerism. His novel *Babbitt* focuses on a middle-class American businessman and exposes how thoroughly Americans used products to define themselves and their status. The book warned that an America defined by prosperity and access to consumer goods was a shallow society indeed.

Jane Addams and Hull House

Jane Addams was another important reformer during the Progressive Era. She was born in Cedarville, Illinois, in 1860 to a well-to-do family. Although she received a college education, women like Addams had limited career choices. Uninterested in marriage, teaching school, or caring for relatives, Addams turned her attention to the world around her, a world filled with poverty and suffering. On a trip to London, Addams visited Toynbee Hall, one of the first **settlement houses**—community centers that offered education, recreation, and other services in poor neighborhoods—in the world. Inspired by what she saw, Addams moved to

SETTLEMENT HOUSES
Community centers that offered education, recreation, and other services to poor city-dwellers.

Chicago with her close friend Ellen Gates Starr, bought a large home on the outskirts of downtown, and started a settlement house. Addams and Starr called the settlement house Hull House. The residents of the impoverished neighborhood around Hull House were primarily Southern and Eastern European immigrants. Addams and Starr slowly built Hull House into a true community center for these immigrants, providing meals, lectures, and a gathering spot for sports, games, and camaraderie.

Hull House attracted scores of young, college-educated white women as volunteers and residents. These women, like Addams, were driven by the Progressive spirit of reform and a Christian imperative to help the less fortunate. This female-run institution enabled young women to engage with politics, to live autonomously and with a sense of purpose, and to work closely with other women. As the Progressive Era went on, settlement houses sprang up in most major U.S. cities. Most were established by women.

Addams also used Hull House as a starting point for advocating for the poor on a national level. She and her peers lobbied for protective legislation for women and children, better working conditions, and women's suffrage. The public stance that women at Hull House and other settlement houses took on issues such as poverty, consumer protection, and labor conditions helped women activists gain critical experience in political engagement. Suffragists used such examples to argue that women were culturally suited to taking care of the health and well-being not only of their families, but of their communities and the nation as well.

Addams, like Ida B. Wells, remained engaged in social activism for the rest of her life. During World War I, Addams was instrumental in founding the Women's Peace Party in 1915. At first this organization had much support, but once America entered the war, pacifism quickly became unpopular. Suffragists who had previously supported the party distanced themselves, fearing that its unpopularity would reflect poorly on the suffrage movement. Despite suspicions raised by her wartime pacifism, Jane Addams remained respected for her settlement house work. In 1931, she became one of the few women to be honored with the Nobel Peace Prize.

LABOR

At time of the American Revolution, most Americans worked the land. By the Progressive Era, the United States had become a much more mechanized, industrialized, urbanized nation. Many of the poorest Americans still worked as sharecroppers or agricultural day-laborers, often with limited access to modern farming equipment. However, especially in cities, more and more Americans were working for set wages, rather than selling goods that they had grown or made themselves. These changes raised many new issues for laborers and labor reformers.

Child Labor

Throughout much of U.S. history, work was a family affair. In the early days of the nation, families relied on every member to help with farm life. Children started out with small tasks and gained more responsibility in accordance with their increasing age and ability. In keeping with this trend, as mills and factories developed, whole families often hoped to be hired together. Many employers were happy to hire young workers. In fact, younger workers were often particularly desirable because their age (and skill level) meant they could be paid less than their adult counterparts. In the 1880s, 25 percent of all workers in the Southern textile industry were under fifteen.

Many families relied on their children's earnings. For these children, school was an unaffordable luxury. Many Progressive reformers aimed to make education mandatory for all American children. This goal soon brought them into conflict with the practice of child labor.

Progressives' interest in universal childhood education was based partly on changing ideas about children and childhood that had begun to take hold in the nineteenth century. Middle-class families stopped believing their children should work and act like adults. Childhood was starting to be sentimentalized as an ideal time of innocence, freedom, and play. Adults increasingly saw children as innocents in need of education and protection.

Progressives also saw education as a way to help immigrants and the working classes. Reformers such as John Dewey promoted public education as the route to a free, equal, and harmonious society. Others supported free public education as a way to help Americanize immigrants from foreign cultures. Many Americans were suspicious of Catholic immigrants and the parochial schools these immigrants often attended, sometimes with funding from local governments. Politicians hoped that mandating free public education would promote Protestant, American values in these immigrant children.

In the opinion of Progressive reformers, children should go to school and should not be subjected to the cruelty of the unhealthy, corrupting world of work. However, the actual experience of many children was far from this ideal. Employers benefited from the cheap wages they could pay children, as well as from the young workers' stamina and nimbleness. Child laborers endured long hours and brutal, unhealthy conditions in dirty factories and sooty coal mines. In addition, children were far more likely to be involved in labor accidents than were adults. Progressives lobbied for increased governmental regulation to help solve the problems of child labor.

In 1903, labor activist Mary "Mother" Jones organized a two-month march of child workers, many of them physically disabled from industrial accidents and unsafe labor conditions. They walked from Philadelphia, Pennsylvania, to the

summer home of President Teddy Roosevelt on Long Island, New York. The president refused to acknowledge the marchers when they arrived, but the public spectacle nevertheless proved effective. Pennsylvania soon changed its state laws to require all workers to be over fourteen. In 1904, activists established the National Child Labor Committee and began a nationwide campaign for states to reform their labor laws. By the mid 1910s, almost every state had made it illegal to hire young children, and working hours for older children were curtailed as well.

Progressive pressure also led to new regulation of women's working conditions. Most middle- and upper-class married women did not work outside the home, but poor women did grueling work for low pay as domestic servants, as washerwomen, or in factories. Educated single women worked mainly as teachers or nurses. Because women were perceived as frail, and because of their role in childbearing, reformers felt that protective legislation should apply to women as it did to children. Although these laws did improve working conditions, they also emphasized women's dependency and frailness, an outlook that helped limit women's opportunities throughout the twentieth century.

Organized Labor

Although men earned more than women or children, they too often worked under uncomfortable and dangerous conditions for inadequate pay. Employers generally want to maximize the business's profit, sometimes at the expense of their employees. During the late nineteenth and early twentieth centuries, some employers tried to make more money by not maintaining safe work environments, paying workers very little, cutting workers' wages, and unjustly firing workers. In response, workers began to organize groups called **labor unions** to work together to improve conditions and raise wages.

LABOR UNIONS Groups of workers organized to improve working conditions and wages.

Labor unions faced powerful obstacles. Workers could lose their jobs just for joining a union, even if they did not commit any public acts of resistance against their employers. Union participation also meant that an individual's personal needs were less important than the good of the group. Otherwise, union activities could not succeed. For example, if a union voted to strike, all of its members had to go along with the decision, or the strike could be less effective. However, strikes often caused hardships for individuals. Workers on strike received no pay and could be fired from their jobs. In addition, American workers were a diverse group. It was a challenge to bring together workers who spoke different languages, came from different racial and religious backgrounds, and had different skill levels. That unions developed at all, against these odds, is proof of how necessary workers found the protections that unions could offer.

The labor movement began in earnest in the 1870s. In 1877, after a series of wage cuts, railroad workers across the country went on strike. Public reaction to these strikes, which were often accompanied by violence, was mixed. Some Americans

HISTORY COMES ALIVE

Before the Progressive Era, individual states were responsible for laws regarding issues such as education and women's suffrage. The first state to allow women the right to vote was Wyoming, in 1869—fifty years before a Constitutional amendment granted this right. States such as Tennessee began building public schools by the middle of the nineteenth century. To a large extent, the Progressive Era was responsible for making these issues important to the national culture. Public schooling was perceived as a way to integrate and assimilate immigrant children into American culture and to educate the future labor force. Many reformers saw a link between women's activism on behalf of Progressive causes and their right to vote. What do you think are the pros and cons of state versus federal legislation? Were the Progressives right to see education and women's suffrage as national issues? Are there any state issues today that you think the federal government should control, or vice versa?

blamed foreigners for inciting the violent strikes. State and local governments sent troops to disperse strikers and rioters, and more than a hundred people were killed in Baltimore, Pittsburgh, and other cities. Despite this unfortunate beginning, more Americans joined unions as the century wore on. By 1886, the Knights of Labor, founded by Uriah S. Stephens in 1869, had more than 700,000 members. The Knights of Labor called for many labor reforms, including equal pay for men and women who did equal work. The American Federation of Labor (AFL), formed in 1886 and led by Samuel Gompers, was a conglomeration of many skilled craft unions that maintained independence but helped support the other unions in the federation. By 1920, the AFL had more than 4 million members.

Labor unions used a variety of strategies to achieve their aims. When labor abuses occurred, unions might boycott an employer, go on strike, form picket lines, or enter into negotiations with employers. For example, Gompers preferred to negotiate agreements with management to protect union workers, although he supported striking when necessary. Another important strategy that helped unions succeed was to invoke solidarity in workers across state lines. Workers did not only support their own friends, colleagues, and communities. Rather, national unions prompted workers to protest with workers in other towns and industries. Well into the twentieth century, unions remained important mechanisms for workers to combat economic exploitation and unsafe working conditions.

Many employers and industrialists found unions threatening. They used a variety of tactics to try to lessen unions' influence. Some employers tried to avoid hiring union members. During strikes or protests, employers fired union agitators. Some companies also tried to hire non-union workers to replace the strikers.

Both sides also turned to violence. In 1886, a bomb went off at a protest in Haymarket Square in Chicago, killing seven police officers and four additional people. Despite a lack of evidence, eight immigrants were convicted of the crime. In 1892, a private army hired by company management attacked striking workers at the Carnegie Steel Mill, in Homestead, Pennsylvania. After a fierce battle, nine workers and three soldiers were dead. State troops later broke up the strike, and more than 160 strikers were accused of crimes.

Despite violent responses to strikes, support for unions and labor protests became so strong by the turn of the twentieth century that socialists and labor leaders in the United States tried to form a worldwide labor union, which they called the International Workers of the World (IWW) and which was nicknamed the Wobblies. The Wobblies hoped for an international Marxist revolution that would put laborers in charge of production. Though they never attracted widespread support, the Wobblies helped to bring the ideas of class struggle, capitalist exploitation, and radical labor politics into the American parlance.

During and after World War I, however, the Russian Revolution and increased suspicion of foreigners caused many Americans to become suspicious of socialism and communism. This suspicion extended to labor unions and the immigrant workers who belonged to many unions. In addition, immigration and the Great Migration were making American cities increasingly diverse.

Racial and ethnic tensions—and the riots that resulted from competition over jobs—further undermined worker solidarity. By the 1920s, unions remained a force in American labor, but their power had diminished from its turn-of-the-century peak.

Upton Sinclair and *The Jungle*

Union activity helped draw attention to the precarious lives of American laborers. The urban poor, especially immigrant workers who did not speak English, were often at particular risk of being exploited. Unable to negotiate effectively, many skilled immigrant workers were shunted into the worst jobs that America offered, such as working in slaughterhouses to process meat. By the early twentieth century, slaughterhouses and packinghouse in the Midwest were supplying meat to people around the country. Most Americans had not given much thought to the new process of industrialized meat production, which was beginning to replace local butchers. Consumers knew little about the working conditions of slaughterhouse workers and meatpackers.

Then, in 1906, the socialist writer Upton Sinclair published a book that aimed a spotlight at the meatpacking industry. *The Jungle* is a fictional account of a Lithuanian immigrant family living in the slums of Chicago. The book describes, in nauseating detail, the toxic environment at the meatpacking factory where the main character, an honorable but luckless man named Jurgis Rudkis, works. Sinclair describes the suffering of the miserable and diseased animals that were slaughtered there. He explains how the meat was processed with little regard for sanitation and ground up into meat products along with rats, rat feces, and even human body parts. Although the book is a novel, Sinclair based his descriptions of the meatpacking plant on diligent research. The book was a sensation. Americans looked at their sausages suspiciously and cried out for reform.

President Theodore Roosevelt, outraged by the allegations in *The Jungle*, insisted that the Chicago packinghouses be inspected. The inspection showed that Sinclair's descriptions were accurate. In a change from the government's nineteenth-century practice of trying to limit its regulation of industry, Roosevelt backed two pieces of federal legislation: the Meat Inspection Act and the Pure Food and Drug Act, both of which became law in 1906. The Meat Inspection Act made meat inspection a federal right and duty and allowed the federal government to create standards for cleanliness and hygiene. The Pure Food and Drug Act required food, drugs, and alcohol to be properly labeled and sold as labeled, without harmful additives or fillers. The law placed patent medicines and other kinds of peddled consumables under the purview of the federal government. Roosevelt also created the Food and Drug Administration (FDA), a federal agency to regulate and inspect consumable products in the United States. In the Progressive Era, unlike in the conflicts of the nineteenth century—when the battle between states' rights and federal power tore the country apart—the federal government acted decisively to promote reform.

Sinclair's book prompted a major change in U.S. policy on what was acceptable to eat and sell as food. The irony of the story is that Sinclair had hoped that his story would call attention to the plight of immigrants and workers. Ending the book with an impassioned defense of socialism, Sinclair seemed more interested in inspiring a radical call to arms for workers across the country than in prompting federal regulation of food production. Rather than rioting in the streets in support of labor, however, Americans expressed their faith in federal protection by supporting the president and his new regulations. Sinclair said in disappointment, "I aimed at the public's heart, and by accident I hit it in the stomach."

Muckrakers

The Jungle was instrumental in the passage of some far-reaching Progressive legislation. However, Sinclair was not a lone voice in the wilderness. To the contrary, starting in the late nineteenth century, a new breed of investigative journalist took to the streets, looking to expose urban poverty and corruption. These journalists, known as muckrakers, a term coined by President Theodore Roosevelt, approached their subject matter with the specific goal of sparking reform. Muckrakers hoped that, when their writing exposed the darkest aspects of American existence to public scrutiny, readers would demand change.

During the Progressive Era, Americans were so entranced by this kind of journalism that many muckrakers became household names. Muckrakers often published articles in magazines and journals, some of which had national distribution. Some turned their reports into popular books. One of the first and most influential muckrakers was Jacob Riis. In 1890, Riis published *How the Other Half Lives*, a book that included photographs of the squalor of the urban slums. *How the Other Half Lives* gave middle-class Americans a rare glimpse into a world of deprivation that was invisible to many. Ida Tarbell, another well-known muckraker, wrote about corruption within Standard Oil and the moral failings of its leader, John D. Rockefeller. Her allegations horrified the public, and popular opinion turned against this important American businessman.

Ironically, the Progressive ideal that governmental regulation could help to solve social, cultural, and economic problems often ran up against the unpleasant reality that the government itself was hardly free of corruption. Muckrakers frequently turned their attention to a world of politics dominated by urban machines and by politicians corrupted by the promise of power and money. For example, Henry Demarest Lloyd wrote about the influence monopolies held over government. Lincoln Steffens revealed corruption at the local level in his book *The Shame of Cities*.

Muckrakers' popular exposés helped unify American public opinion on a wide variety of issues. When they learned about the seedy underbelly of American politics, industry, and cities, many Americans responded—as muckrakers had hoped—by demanding change in the form of government regulation.

MID-CHAPTER QUESTIONS

1. Progressive reformers worked to fix a variety of societal problems. What are some of the problems they addressed? What were some of the solutions they proposed and enacted? In your opinion, were these solutions successful?

2. Many Progressives believed that they needed to right the wrongs of previous eras. What nineteenth-century forces helped create the problems that Americans addressed during the Progressive Era?

3. What Progressive Era ideas, solutions, and debates are similar to those in today's society and political culture? Which are different?

4. How did different groups of Americans experience the Progressive Era differently? Who benefited from Progressive reforms? Who did not?

MECHANIZATION

Progressives favored orderly, scientific approaches to improving daily life and eliminating societal troubles. Progressive innovators saw efficiency and orderliness as key attributes of progress. Incorporating these values in factories also helped cut costs and increase output. As a result, many industries during the Progressive Era changed their business models to enable large-scale growth and increase profits.

Assembly Lines

One of the most important business innovations during the Progressive Era was the assembly line. An assembly line is a way of putting together a product in which each worker does one task. The underpinnings of the assembly line were developed by engineer Frederick W. Taylor. In the late nineteenth century, Taylor pioneered the principles of **scientific management**—the practice of analyzing a work process to break it down into parts and maximize efficiency. Taylor believed that individual laborers should not have autonomy over their labor. Rather, to improve efficiency, managers should keep track of the bigger picture. These managers would analyze the skills and methods of each worker and make all the decisions about the work process—decisions previously left to skilled craftsman. Workflow would be timed with a stopwatch to find the quickest, fastest, and most profitable way to carry out each step. Workers would be held to the efficiency standards established by these studies. Because assembly lines broke down complicated processes into simple tasks, unskilled workers could take over jobs previously done only by skilled workers.

Many Progressive Era industries adopted Taylor's ideas and built their own assembly lines. The benefits to companies quickly became obvious. For example, Henry Ford, the founder of the Ford Motor Company, instituted a moving assembly line at his automobile company in 1913. Before Ford started using the assembly line, cars took twelve and a half hours to build. With the new assembly line, workers could build a car in ninety-three minutes. As a result, Ford could produce more cars at lower costs. Ford passed along some of the savings to customers, making cars, which had been prohibitively expensive for most Americans, affordable to the middle class. Ford also used financing options to help to make cars more affordable. By the 1920s Ford was selling so many cars that Americans owned 80 percent of the cars in the world. American car culture exploded in the 1920s, as people used their new vehicles for commuting, vacations, status, and even dating.

Although businesses and customers benefited, assembly lines had some drawbacks for laborers. Previously, American industrialized laborers carried out a slightly varied set of tasks. By contrast, the assembly line required workers to weld a single spot, operate a lever, or carry out another simple, repetitive task over and over for the entire workday. In the name of efficiency, industrial work became so

SCIENTIFIC MANAGEMENT
The practice of analyzing a work process to break it down into parts and maximize efficiency.

STUDY ALERT

In the workplace, the Progressive values of orderliness, mechanization, and scientific progress had benefits and drawbacks. Assembly lines increased production, lowered the prices of goods, and created jobs for unskilled laborers. However, these jobs were often simple, repetitive, and tedious, and they did not provide workers with a sense of pride or accomplishment.

segmented that jobs often required little skill. Many workers were no longer able to feel pride in their craftsmanship or autonomy on the job.

Slaughterhouses

Slaughterhouses across the country were transformed by the assembly-line model. For much of American history, highly skilled workers would slaughter one animal at a time and butcher it into its many parts. However, industry leaders saw the potential to increase profits by industrializing this process. By the Progressive Era, slaughterhouses around the country had mechanized the killing and butchering process into a massively efficient, modern meatpacking industry.

During the nineteenth century, the Midwest supplied the majority of the cattle for the country's meat. However, transporting live cattle was expensive and logistically difficult. Meat seller Gustavus Swift came up with a solution: a refrigerated railway car that would keep meat cold as it was shipped across the country. As a result of Swift's innovation, cattle could be slaughtered closer to where they were raised, and slaughterhouses sprang up in locations such as Chicago, Illinois; Fort Worth, Texas; and Kansas City, Missouri. Swift's additional innovations helped transform the meat industry into a multistep, totalizing process. Rather than focusing solely on livestock transport or refrigerated cars, Swift built a **vertically integrated** firm, meaning that the company handled the entire process from start to finish. This slaughterhouse empire comprised all parts of the industry, from transporting livestock to slaughtering and butchering animals to shipping packaged meat. Many other companies followed Swift's lead. Chicago soon became a mecca of slaughterhouses and meatpacking plants. By 1900, the city produced 82 percent of the meat eaten by Americans.

VERTICALLY INTEGRATED
A way of running a company so that it handles all steps of a process in its industry.

Not surprisingly, slaughterhouses did not make pleasant workplaces. On the assembly lines, workers would repeat the same action throughout the day, be it killing the animals, eviscerating them, or packing the meat. Conditions in the slaughterhouses were hot, smelly, and bloody. In his novel *The Jungle*, which chronicled the abuses of the meat-packing industry, Upton Sinclair provided many Americans their first, horrifying glimpse into the industry.

From the automobile factory to the slaughterhouse, the assembly-line model played an important role in America's labor history. The predictability of the assembly line work eased language barriers and allowed unskilled immigrants entry into wage work. Assembly lines increased efficiency, helping industry thrive and making goods and consumables more affordable. Workers, however, often found assembly line work tedious and wearisome.

POLITICAL REFORM

The nineteenth century was marked by a laissez-faire attitude toward politics and the economy—that is, a belief that the worlds of politics and economics should be left alone, free from government intervention. However, by the Progressive Era, corruption and scandal had become widespread, and many people looked to the government to reform and regulate itself and commerce. Progressive politicians enthusiastically took on the task.

The Pendleton Act

Ever since the presidency of Andrew Jackson, the distribution of federal government jobs had been based on a spoils system, under which newly elected politicians installed their own friends, supporters, and relatives in government jobs, regardless of qualifications or merit. In 1881, President James A. Garfield was assassinated by Charles Guiteau, a mentally disturbed man who was upset at having been denied a civil service job in the federal government. Guiteau's extreme act raised the issue of civil service reform.

As popular support for reform grew, Ohio Senator George Pendleton sponsored a bill in Congress to make civil service jobs more accessible to well-qualified candidates based on merit. At first, the bill was defeated. However, after President Chester Arthur stepped in to support it, the Pendleton Act was passed in 1883. The Act established an independent, nonpartisan Civil Service Commission. The Commission's task was to ensure that a percentage of government jobs was reserved for those passing a written test. Reformers hoped that the change would help the government hire more competent workers and that deserving applicants outside the spoils system could be hired for civil service jobs—at least 10 percent of civil service jobs.

Tammany Hall

In the late nineteenth and early twentieth centuries, many large cities were run by **political machines**, parties run by "bosses" who supervised a network of neighborhood representatives and local politicians such as aldermen. By providing jobs, housing, and other assistance to city residents, especially immigrants, machines built a loyal following of voters and were able to remain in power for long periods of time. In exchange for the services machine politicians provided, they often asked constituents for money or votes.

In New York City, the political machine Tammany Hall ruled city politics for decades. Residents of the city lived in wards represented by aldermen, many of whom were part of the machine. As a result, the machine, rather than the city, took control of local services such as garbage disposal, sewer systems, and plumbing. The machine also provided services such as assisting families in the midst of emergencies and helping local businesses acquire liquor licenses. The need for votes kept machine politicians invested in the wards they represented.

However, the system also provided many opportunities for corruption. Before an alderman would provide desired city services, the machine often required favors—sometimes, outright bribery and kickbacks—as the price of its assistance. Machine politicians also demanded constituents' votes as repayment for any assistance or services provided.

Williams Marcy "Boss" Tweed, an early leader of Tammany Hall, set the tone for the organization. Tweed was arrested in 1871 for masterminding the theft of millions of dollars from the city in connection with the building of City Hall. His conviction did not end Tammany Hall's hold on New York City, however. George Plunkitt, an Irish Tammany Hall leader at the turn of the century, bragged that he did not need bribes, preferring "honest graft": the preferential treatment and economic favor that came with political power. Machines ruled major American cities throughout the Progressive Era. In fact, Tammany Hall remained a strong force in New York politics until the 1930s.

Grant's Scandals

Since the Civil War, political corruption had become an important national issue. In the 1870s, the presidential administration of the beloved Civil

POLITICAL MACHINES
Political parties run by "bosses" who provided jobs, housing, and other assistance to city residents, especially immigrants, in exchange for money, loyalty, and votes.

STUDY ALERT

The Persistence of Corruption: Public disgust with government corruption did not prevent ongoing political scandals and corruption from marring the optimism of the Progressive Era. Despite reformers' best efforts to expose and end political corruption and exploitation, such deeply ingrained practices often proved difficult to uproot.

War hero Ulysses S. Grant came to be associated with ineffectual leadership and corruption. In 1875, a major scandal erupted around a group of alcohol manufacturers and federal employees called the Whiskey Ring, who had cheated the government out of millions of dollars. The main offender was Grant's own private secretary, and others involved in the scandal also had ties to Grant. In addition, a major economic depression that began during Grant's administration seemed to be linked directly to his party's involvement with a major railroad mogul.

As a result of the ongoing scandals, several factions broke off from the Republican Party after Grant's administration ended in 1877. The Stalwarts believed that the main focus of the government should be unresolved problems from the Civil War. The Halfbreeds were focused on reforming government itself. The Mugwumps, disgusted by political machines, focused their reform efforts specifically on city politics. The Mugwumps were interested in limiting machine power not from concern for social justice or poverty, but because they favored less government in general. Regardless of the group's motives, the Mugwumps' push for good government became part of the Progressive Era's broader movement for government reform.

The Teapot Dome Scandal

Despite reformers' efforts, machine politics and government scandals continued to occur—and to draw national attention—throughout the Progressive Era. In fact, the governmental philosophy of the time posited that the governments and corporations should work together to ensure that corporations were operating legally and to help spur economic growth. In theory, the government could both overrule corporations that grew too large and powerful and step in to assist companies that needed support.

In practice, the line between assistance and corruption could be fuzzy. In 1922, a major scandal emerged that became known as the Teapot Dome Scandal. The secretary of the interior had offered the rights to two major oil reserves to oil companies without going through the standard practice of accepting bids. The secretary was ultimately sentenced to prison for accepting hundreds of thousands of dollars in bribes in exchange for the use of the oil reserves. Although President Warren G. Harding was not personally implicated in the scandal, it nonetheless tainted his presidency.

The Federal Income Tax

Not all the political changes during the Progressive Era involved corruption. One important innovation of the period was the institution of a federal income tax. Although individual states had, at times, levied income taxes, the federal government did not gain this power until the presidency of William Howard Taft. The Supreme Court had overturned an earlier attempt to pass a federal income tax law in 1895. The change in policy therefore required a change to the Constitution. With Taft's support, the Sixteenth Amendment allowing the federal government to collect income tax passed in 1913.

At first, the federal government levied a tax of 1 percent on incomes of more than $3,000 and 6 percent on earnings of more than $500,000. As the United States prepared to enter World War I, the

federal government looked for new ways to increase revenue. In 1916, the government raised the general income tax from 1 to 2 percent. Taxes for those earning higher incomes and for corporations increased as well. Income taxes soon became one of the most important sources of revenue for the federal government.

TEDDY ROOSEVELT

Theodore, or Teddy, Roosevelt occupies a unique place in American history. Roosevelt was an exuberant embodiment of the Progressive spirit who made it his personal mission to take on many of the nation's residual problems from the nineteenth century. As president from 1901 to 1909, he helped to set the tone of the new century.

Roosevelt came from a wealthy New York family, but he built an image based on strength, masculinity, and hard work. His hobbies included boxing, hunting, and hiking. After the untimely death of his mother and wife, he went west and lived a rough life on the dangerous frontier. After returning to New York City, his achievements as a police officer earned Roosevelt an appointment, in 1897, to assistant secretary of the Navy. In the next few years, his achievements grew rapidly: he led the elite Rough Riders cavalry troop in the Spanish-American War, served as New York's governor, and was elected vice president of the United States under President William McKinley. After McKinley was assassinated by anarchist Leon Czolgosz in 1901, Roosevelt became president.

As president, Roosevelt did not hesitate to exert his considerable influence in matters both domestic and foreign. For example, he tweaked the time-honored Monroe Doctrine, which stated that Europe was not to intervene in the Western Hemisphere, adding the "corollary" that the United States had the right to operate as the world's police in the Western Hemisphere. This bold policy change set the stage for a vastly increased U.S. presence in Latin America. Roosevelt's bravado in both international and domestic issues was part of his appeal. After a string of ineffectual presidents and decades of laissez-faire policy, many Americans approved of Roosevelt's readiness for action.

Preservation and the Department of the Interior

One of Roosevelt's pet projects was the conservation of America's natural beauty. In addition to his own enthusiasm for outdoor activity, Roosevelt was influenced by the conservation movement, which aimed to conserve, or protect, the natural wonders of the United States from the belching smoke stacks and sooty urban jungles associated with the spread of industry. Although Roosevelt was not the first person to take on this task, as president, he expanded the government's mandate, adding protection of public land to the list of responsibilities of the federal government. He also hugely expanded the system of national parks, added many millions of acres to the national forest system, and began the process of declaring national monuments. Roosevelt's protection of the land did not please many industry leaders, who had

hoped to have less restricted access to the land. Despite their objections, Roosevelt's deep love of nature and outdoor activities and his stubborn determination carried the day. Later administrations also helped keep national parks a part of our country's heritage. In 1916, the administration of President Woodrow Wilson established the National Parks Service under the jurisdiction of the Department of the Interior. Today, many Americans still use and enjoy the National Parks.

Trust Busting

Another one of Roosevelt's major legacies comes from his treatment of big business. Before his presidency, the U.S. government had placed few regulations on businesses, and many industries had formed huge **trusts**, or groups of companies that work together to limit competition and corner the entire market on a product. By joining together with their competitors to form trusts, companies created monopolies that could set high prices without fear of being underbid.

When Roosevelt became president, some antitrust laws did exist, but lax enforcement had left them largely ineffectual. When Roosevelt attempted to enforce these laws to regulate industry, he faced opposition from Congress. Instead of fighting to have Congress pass new legislation, Roosevelt used his executive privilege to combat trusts, relying on prior legislation to combat trusts that were involved in interstate trade. Roosevelt's strategy of using previously existing antitrust laws to circumvent the House and the Senate was effective. Over the course of his presidency, his administration began antitrust lawsuits against 45 companies under the Sherman Antitrust Act. For example, as a result of a lawsuit that Roosevelt brought against the Northern Securities Company, a trust that had combined railroad companies, the Supreme Court ordered the company to disband.

In addition to basic enforcement, Roosevelt and his administration found ways to broaden the reach of federal antitrust laws. The Constitution grants the federal government jurisdiction to regulate only interstate trade and commerce; trade within a state remained under the purview of the state. The Roosevelt administration appealed to the Supreme Court to expand the understanding of interstate commerce. Roosevelt won a significant victory in 1905, when the Court defined meatpacking as an example of interstate commerce and therefore subject to federal regulation, because both the animals and the meat travelled across state lines. Though the manufacturing itself happened in one state, the trade undeniably crossed over state lines and could be regulated by the federal government. This decision not only forced the Swift meatpacking trust, which included a number of meatpacking competitors, to dissolve but also paved the way for increased federal government control of many other industries.

Roosevelt's struggles to limit the power of big business extended beyond the courts. In 1902, a major coal strike threatened the national coal supply. Roosevelt called union leaders and industry leaders to the White House to negotiate. When they failed to reach an agreement, Roosevelt threatened to use the U.S. military to take over the mines. Although this action would have exceeded his presidential powers, his impetuous declaration made the mine owners reconsider. The strike finally ended with an agreement brokered by Roosevelt's handpicked arbitration committee. Publicity surrounding the incident helped to increase public support for

TRUSTS Groups of companies that work together to limit competition and corner the market on a product.

DID YOU KNOW?

Booker T. Washington was the first black man to be invited to eat with the president of the United States. Theodore Roosevelt, the 26th president, extended the invitation because he admired Washington's rags-to-riches story and regarded him as an impressively dedicated character. The other reason was that after the Civil War, most African-Americans supported the Republican Party. Roosevelt hoped that his invitation would curry favor with black party delegates. However, the event outraged some whites, particularly in the South. In fact, one Senator from South Carolina publicly proposed killing one thousand African-Americans in response. Following this backlash, Roosevelt became more reserved in his public praise of Washington.

unions and organized labor. Roosevelt's popular trust-busting activity also helped him win election to a second term.

During Roosevelt's second term, he expanded the federal government even more. He put more industries under the control of the Interstate Commerce Commission. In response to the public outcry about the meatpacking industry inspired by Upton Sinclair's muckraking novel *The Jungle*, Roosevelt extended the influence of the federal government to make sure the country's food supply was edible, nutritious, and properly labeled. The Pure Food and Drug Act and the Meat Inspection Act were two more victories in Roosevelt's quest to regulate industry in ways that would protect American consumers.

THE POPULIST MOVEMENT

Despite rapidly increasing industrialization and urbanization, much of the U.S. population in the Progressive Era still lived as farmers in rural areas. Starting in the late 1800s, many farmers and rural folk began to join together to work for common causes. This Populist Movement was defined by its commitment to causes such as bettering the lot of agricultural workers, promoting economic fairness, and putting more money in circulation. By the 1890s, the movement had become so strong that it created an influential political party.

Farm Workers

Though much of the country was blessed with fertile soil, many farmers in the late 1800s struggled. Farming was a high-risk enterprise highly dependent on weather and other factors outside of small farmers' control. As Americans moved west to build homesteads, farms, and ranches, the climate of the Great Plains presented a particular challenge. Variations in weather patterns and droughts made yearly outputs highly variable. In addition, because much of the area did not have enough water for large-scale crop production, farmers needed to use specialized techniques to succeed. Weather and climate were not the only challenges farmers faced. Railroad companies charged exorbitant prices to ship farm products to distant markets. High tariffs allowed American manufacturers, protected from the threat of foreign competition, to charge high prices for farm equipment.

The need for expensive equipment and plenty of land often led farmers to borrow money from banks. Many of these banks charged very high interest rates on farmers' mortgages and loans. In addition, a decline in the amount of currency in circulation at the time adversely affected those in debt. A string of economic depressions during the late 1800s aggravated small farmers' precarious position. Those who were unable to repay their debts lost their land, and many were forced to become tenant farmers or sharecroppers.

Farm Reform

Individually, small farmers lacked the economic and political force to combat the power of large banks, railroad companies,

Cheap land and rich, plentiful mineral resources drew many Americans to the West throughout the nineteenth century. Sometimes this movement brought settlers into conflict with local Native Americans. In the decade preceding the Civil War, more than 150,000 settlers ignored U.S. treaty agreements and moved to Sioux land. Native Americans often resisted such incursions, leading to a series of wars and skirmishes from the 1860s into the 1880s. However, this resistance proved ineffective, and many Native American groups were confined to reservations or forcibly relocated to make room for settlers. After the Civil War, these settlers included many African-Americans who left the South for the promise of economic prosperity and freedom in the West. By 1880, 40,000 African-Americans lived in Kansas, more than anywhere else in the West. A new wave of westward migration began in the late 1880s, when drought struck the Midwest. Untenable agricultural conditions led 50,000 people to leave the upper Midwest between 1885 and 1890 in search of arable land and a more agreeable climate. Beginning in the 1880s, the discovery of widespread mineral deposits in the far West and the Pacific Northwest attracted so many settlers that the area's population grew from 100,000 to 750,000 in twenty years.

and equipment sellers. However, coming together to take action would be no easy task. The rural farming population was spread across the country. Deep-set racial divisions also made many poor white farmers reluctant to see common cause with their African-American counterparts. Despite these limitations, many farmers across the country did join forces to promote the cause of farm reform.

The farm reform movement began after the Civil War, when local farmers banded together to join the Grange. At first, the Grange was intended to be an organization to help combat the isolation of small farmers. It was organized as a national movement with local chapters. However, as the Grange's popularity grew in the 1870s, farmers used the organization not only to plan social activities, but also to form cooperatives to increase their economic power. Soon, the Grange blossomed into a political movement with the aim of influencing states to pass legislation limiting the power of railroads and storage facilities.

Farm Unions

In the 1870s, as the Grange's popularity waned, the national movement gave way to a new form of agricultural organization called the Farmers' Alliance. The Alliance began as a local movement in Texas during the depression of 1877 but spread across the country in the 1880s. Like the Grange, the Farmers' Alliance formed local cooperatives in an attempt to fight high costs and falling crop prices. However, these efforts often proved ineffective. For example, in Texas, the Alliance tried to form one big state cooperative to sell all the farmers' cotton at once. However, in order to establish the collective, organizers needed money. The farmers could not raise enough, and banks refused to grant loans to help start the cooperative. In the face of such obstacles, the Alliance began to support political goals such as giving the government ownership of transportation and communication technology and companies, having the government provide farmers with low-interest loans, and allowing voters to elect their U.S. senators directly.

The Farmers' Alliance was made up mainly of poor white farmers, especially in the South and Midwest. In 1886, a white man founded a separate organization for African-American farmers called the Colored Alliance. Most of its members were agricultural workers such as cotton pickers who did not own their own land. However, it never became as popular as the all-white Farmers' Alliance. Members of the two organizations also did not always share the same goals. In 1891, the Colored Alliance declared a cotton pickers' strike in Arkansas.

The strike was led by a black agricultural worker named Ben Patterson. White farm owners objected violently to the strike and to the idea of paying higher wages to black workers. In the end, fifteen strikers, including Patterson, were killed by local authorities and a mob of angry white farmers.

The Populist Party

In 1890, the concerns raised by the Farmers' Alliance led to the formation of a new political party. The Populist Party—or the People's Party, as it was also called—grew rapidly in the next few years. Populist candidates won a majority of seats in the state legislatures in South Dakota and Minnesota. Some states even elected Populist candidates to the U.S. Senate.

To achieve any kind of national prominence, the Populist Party needed to mobilize a huge number of people. Racial tensions threatened the party's success. The Democrats, still a predominantly Southern party, played on Southern whites' mistrust of African-Americans to draw white farmers away from the People's Party. However, by the early 1890s, the Populists had enough support to put forth national candidates. The Populist platform promised to put more money in circulation, based on the belief that the **gold standard**—the practice of making money equivalent to a set amount of gold—had limited the supply of available currency, to the benefit only of banks and industry. Populists also demanded strict regulations on corporate interests and a nationalized railroad system to protect American farmers from private railroad companies seeking to maximize profits. Populists also supported limiting the number of immigrants who could enter the country, in an effort to curry favor with the labor movement.

GOLD STANDARD The practice of making money equivalent to a set amount of gold.

James Weaver, the Populist presidential candidate in the election of 1892, did surprisingly well, winning 10 percent of the popular vote. The party continued to grow throughout the 1890s. After a major depression in 1893 severely affected both farmers and the urban poor, Populist leader Jacob Coxey led hundreds of unemployed men to Washington, D.C. in 1894 to demand that the government create jobs to alleviate the unemployment crisis. "Coxey's Army" failed to bring about any concrete change, but the protest received national attention and helped spur Populist energy across the country.

In the election of 1896, discontent with the gold standard took center stage. Backing currency with a fixed amount of gold limited the amount of currency in circulation, a limit that unduly burdened poorer Americans. Populist leaders decided to abandon their diverse platform in favor of a single-issue approach: changing the gold standard to a less restrictive silver standard. However, the Democrats endorsed the same platform. The Populists had to choose whether to back the Democrats or split the vote and hand the election to the Republicans. Although most Populists chose to support the Democrats, Democratic candidate Williams Jennings Bryan lost the election. Following this defeat, the Populists' direct influence faded. However, many of their ideas were adopted

STUDY ALERT

The Labor Movement and Farm Reform: The labor movement and farm reformers shared many key ideas, including a faith in the power of collective action. Unions, the Farmers' Alliance, and the Populist Party all relied on the idea that, together, individuals could combat the powerful forces of banks and industry.

by the two major parties during the Progressive Era. In many ways, the farmers' movement of the late nineteenth century had set the stage for Progressive Era regulation and reform.

Tenant Farmers and Sharecroppers

Many members of the Grange, Farmers' Alliance, and Populist Party were struggling, but most owned their own farms. The very poorest farmers did not even own their own land. Tenant farmers and sharecroppers rented plots of land from wealthier farmers. In return for the use of the land, they had to give a portion of their crop to their landlord. Tenant farmers might have some of the equipment they needed and were thus entitled to keep more of their crop. Sharecroppers, however, had no equipment and were entirely dependent on farm owners for supplies. This dependence made it easy for farm owners to exploit sharecroppers, who often found it nearly impossible to escape their situation.

Poor whites had worked as sharecroppers in the South before the Civil War, but sharecropping expanded rapidly in the postwar years. After the war, sharecropping was one of the only work options open to freed slaves. Although some of the earliest, most radical Reconstruction reformers had attempted to procure land for former slaves, this program largely failed. Thus, former slaves were left with no land and, after centuries of working for no pay, had no money to invest. Economically impoverished freedpeople had few options. Many were forced to work for the same people from whom they had just been emancipated. Rather than pay wages, these cash-strapped former owners lent their tenants a share of their property and the use of their equipment. In exchange for the use of the land and equipment, tenant farmers and sharecroppers paid the farm owners a share of the harvest.

Sharecropping had some advantages over migrant agricultural work. Sharecroppers could maintain family homes and ties to their local community. For former slaves, the ability to keep their families together represented a significant improvement over the days when slave families were routinely broken up. Still, life was not easy for sharecroppers and tenant farmers. Because money came only at harvest time, they were financially strapped for much of the year. Local stores—sometimes run by the same people who owned the land—lent supplies on credit, based on the tenant farmers' and sharecroppers anticipated earnings once the harvest came in. Many local merchants charged excessive prices and interest, keeping sharecroppers in an ongoing cycle of debt.

END OF CHAPTER TAKE-AWAYS

- **Social Reforms:** Progressive reformers were responsible for establishing prohibition and women's suffrage. At the same time, the Supreme Court ruled that racial segregation was Constitutional. Discriminatory Jim Crow laws in the South pushed many African-Americans to northern cities for jobs and greater equality.

- **Activists and Innovators:** Progressive Era reformers addressed race relations, embarked on anti-lynching campaigns, took steps to alleviate urban poverty, worked to improve labor conditions, and critiqued the American consumerist ethos.

- **Labor:** Workers formed labor unions to improve working conditions. Reformers also worked to end the practice of child labor and expand access to education.

- **Mechanization:** Assembly lines increased efficiency, sped up production, lowered operating costs, and created jobs for unskilled workers. The meat industry was industrialized, and large companies took full control of production and distribution.

- **Political Reform:** Although Progressive reformers exposed and fought government corruption, scandals and corruption continued into the twentieth century.

- **Teddy Roosevelt:** President Theodore Roosevelt expanded the power of the federal government and sought to tame the power of trusts and corporate interests.

- **The Populist Movement:** Small farmers across the nation joined together to improve their economic situation—at first through cooperatives, and later through political action.

REFERENCES

Chicago Historical Society. (2001). Slaughterhouse to the world. Retrieved from http://www.chicagohs.org/history/stockyard/stock4.html and http://www.chicagohs.org/history/stockyard/stock2.html

Evans, S. M. (1989). *Born for liberty: A history of women in America*. New York, NY: The Free Press.

Fink, L., & Paterson, T. (2000). *Major problems in the gilded age and the progressive era: Documents and essays*. Boston, MA: Wadsworth.

Henretta, J. A., Brody, D., & Dumenil, L. (2006). *America: A concise history, Vol. 2: Since 1865* (3rd ed.). Boston, MA: Bedford/St. Martin's.

McGerr, M. (2005). *A fierce discontent: The rise and fall of the progressive movement in America, 1870–1920*. New York, NY: Oxford University Press.

Tindall, G. B., & Shi, D. E. (2004). *America: A narrative history* (6th ed., Vol. 2). New York, NY: W.W. Norton & Company, Inc.

Zinn, H. (1995). *The people's history of the United States: 1492–present*. New York, NY: HarperPerennial.

The U.S. Role
in the Great War

A soldier returns home from war. The battlefield took one of his legs, but it also left incurable psychological wounds. He has seen how modern technology can damage and destroy a human body, and he cannot forget what he saw. The images are tattooed in his mind. The deafening thunder of machine guns and explosives fill his dreams. When he closes his eyes, he sees blood—some of it his own, but most of it his buddies'. He cannot forget his comrades who died in battle, and he feels guilty that he survived. Loud noises make him jump. Fireworks sound like bombs. Camera flashes remind him of tracer fire. His family knows something is wrong, but he cannot tell them what it is. This is his burden to carry, and they would not understand anyway.

This soldier's experience is not unusual, nor is it new. Many who experienced combat, whether in the mountains of Afghanistan in 2011 or the trenches of northern Europe in 1915, suffered similar symptoms. Today, the condition is called post-traumatic stress disorder. In the era of World War I, it was called shell shock.

THE WILSON YEARS

Woodrow Wilson's election as president in 1912 did not come from a sweeping victory. He won only 42 percent of the popular vote, and his victory was largely credited to a split in the opposing Republican Party. Wilson had a platform, but no popular mandate.

Still, Wilson's presidency brought great changes to the United States. During his first term (1913–1917), he spearheaded a series of reforms as part of his New Freedom program. New Freedom reforms lowered the tariff, or tax, on imported goods, which helped to lower the prices of those goods. Other reforms included revising the U.S. banking system, prohibiting unfair business practices, and outlawing child labor. Wilson's first term also saw the ratification of two Constitutional amendments: the Sixteenth, which gave Congress the power to authorize the collection of income tax, and the Seventeenth, which provided for the direct election of senators. Two more amendments were ratified during Wilson's second term in office (1917–1921). The Eighteenth Amendment banned alcoholic beverages, ushering in the era of Prohibition. The Nineteenth Amendment gave women the right to vote. Yet, for all these achievements, a single event defines Wilson's presidency: World War I, or the Great War, as it was then called.

ALLIED POWERS During World War I, Britain, France, Russia, and eventually, the United States.

CENTRAL POWERS During World War I, Germany, Austria-Hungary, Bulgaria, and the Ottoman Empire.

The Hesitation

By 1914 Europe had become entangled in a web of alliances. Nationalism made European countries eager to prove their superiority. Minority groups within the Austro-Hungarian Empire sought independence. These factors made Europe a keg of gunpowder waiting to explode. The assassination of the crown prince of Austria-Hungary provided the spark.

When war erupted in 1914, President Wilson pledged a path of neutrality for the United States. Personally, having experienced the Civil War as a child, he wanted to spare the nation the carnage and heartache of another war. Politically, he feared that war would not only derail his program of reforms but also splinter the country. As Wilson noted in his August 1914 Declaration of Neutrality, "the people of the United States are drawn from many nations, and chiefly from the nations now at war." Those nations included Great Britain, France, and Russia as the **Allied Powers** and Germany and Austria-Hungary as the **Central Powers**. Wilson feared that sympathy for these mother countries would create conflict within the population of the United States. Therefore, Wilson concluded,

> The United States must be neutral in fact, as well as in name, during these days that are to try men's souls. We must be impartial in thought, as well as in action, must put a curb upon our sentiments, as well as upon every transaction that might be construed as a preference of one party to the struggle before another.

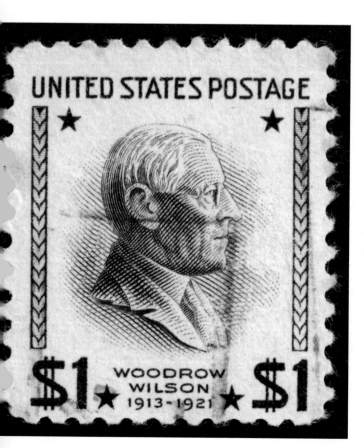

UNITED STATES POSTAGE

$1 WOODROW WILSON 1913-1921 $1

This was easier said than done. The economy of the United States depended on trade with the belligerents, especially Great Britain and France. As the combatants on both sides ran low on cash, the United States loaned them money—though it loaned almost ten times more to the Allies than to the Central Powers.

The greatest test of American neutrality came on May 7, 1915, with the sinking of the *Lusitania*. A British passenger ship, the *Lusitania* had almost completed its journey from New York to England when a German U-boat (submarine) attacked and sunk it. Almost 1,200 people died, including more than 120 Americans. The deaths provoked an outcry in the United States, including calls for retaliation. Wilson, still determined to spare the country the trauma of war, responded with written protests to Germany and demands for an apology. Eager to keep the United States out of the war, Germany agreed to restrict its use of submarine warfare. From that point forward, German U-boats no longer sank ships in the war zone on sight. Instead, ships flying neutral flags—such as the flag of the United States—would be warned and crews and passengers would be given time to board lifeboats. Former President Theodore Roosevelt and Republican Congressman Henry Cabot Lodge attacked Wilson for being weak and cowardly, but the president stayed the course and kept the United States out of the conflict, temporarily.

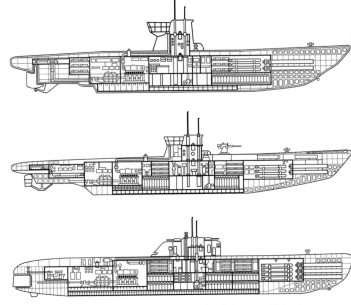

Three kinds of German U-boats.

Broken Promises

Wilson's decision served him well in the short term. He won re-election in 1916 with the slogan "He kept us out of war." In his second inaugural address, Wilson swore that "we stand firm in armed neutrality since it seems that in no other way we can demonstrate what it is we insist upon and cannot forget." Still, he warned, the United States might be forced "to a more active assertion of our rights as we see them and a more immediate association with the great struggle itself." Less than a month later, on April 2, 1917, Wilson stood before Congress asking for a declaration of war against Germany. U.S. involvement in the war, Wilson said, was necessary to "make the world safe for democracy."

What changed his mind? A believer in peace and international cooperation, Wilson had offered to mediate the conflict. In January 1917, both sides rejected his offer. In addition to this rejection, the course of the war changed.

By 1917, the war had been locked in a stalemate for three years. Both sides were exhausted. A British naval blockade had pushed Germany to the brink of collapse. German leaders decided lifting the restrictions on submarine warfare was their only chance to break the blockade. On January 31, 1917, they announced that unrestricted submarine warfare—sinking ships on sight, without warning—would resume the next day. On February 3, Wilson cut U.S. diplomatic ties with Germany.

The final straw came a few weeks later, when the British turned over a German message they had intercepted and decoded. The message, meant for the German ambassador in Mexico, proposed that Mexico enter the war on the side of the Central Powers and attack the United States. In return, when the Central Powers won the war, Mexico would receive Texas, New Mexico, and Arizona. The

TOTAL WAR A war that involves all aspects of society, both civilian and military.

PROPAGANDA The spread of deceptive or distorted information in order to promote a cause.

Zimmermann Telegram, as the message was named, reached Wilson on February 24, 1917. A week later, American newspapers printed it. The telegram turned the tide of public opinion against Germany. Americans demanded the United States go to war. Congress acquiesced, declaring war on April 6.

America at War

Under Wilson's leadership, the nation mobilized. The war was a **total war**, involving or affecting every citizen in the country. Millions of American men volunteered for the armed forces. Millions more were drafted. Women went to work in factories to produce the supplies needed for the war effort. Even those who did not work in factories were expected to contribute to the war effort, by buying Liberty Bonds to help fund the war or by growing food in "victory gardens."

The first American troops reached France in June 1918 under the command of General John J. Pershing. The American Expeditionary Force, as it was called, turned the tide of the war. Providing much-needed boosts of morale, manpower, and supplies to the Allied Powers, the American forces helped break the stalemate.

Back home, still haunted by the bloodshed of the Civil War, President Wilson worried about the country's reaction to the deaths of American soldiers in an overseas war. He feared the rising number of American casualties would turn public opinion against the war effort. To encourage public support for the war, he created the Committee on Public Information (CPI). The CPI, led by George Creel, hired thousands of "Four-Minute Men" to give pro-war speeches at movies theaters and other public meeting places. The Committee also used **propaganda,** or information meant to further a specific agenda. Propaganda promoted enlistment in the armed forces, conservation of food, and the sale of Liberty Bonds. Some propaganda posters, such as the Uncle Sam "I Want You" poster, played on people's sense of patriotism. Others played on fear, including one poster that showed the Statue of Liberty in flames.

The Wilson Administration also made it illegal to speak out against the war. In June 1917, Congress enacted the Espionage Act. The act made it illegal to encourage disloyalty or interfere with the draft. It granted the postal service the right to refuse

HISTORY COMES ALIVE: WESTWARD EXPANSION

World War I was the first mechanized war. It harnessed the power of the Industrial Revolution to change the way battles were fought. While soldiers still fought hand to hand, new inventions, such as the tank, the machine gun, poison gas, the submarine, and the airplane, allowed combatants to kill more soldiers from greater distances. One soldier, upon seeing tanks on the battlefield for the first time, described them as "huge mechanical monsters" that made "strange throbbing noises." In a poem titled "Anthem for a Doomed Youth," British soldier Wilfred Owen described "the monstrous anger of the guns … the stuttering rifles' rapid rattle … [and] the shrill, demented choirs of wailing shells." Often, the sounds of the guns would echo long after the machine guns had stopped firing.

delivery of any material that violated the act. The next year, Congress passed the Sedition Act, which made it a federal offense to "utter, print, write, or publish any disloyal, profane, scurrilous, or abusive language" about the U.S. government, the Constitution, or the armed forces. The Sedition Act also outlawed the display of flags of the Central Powers. When the war ended, much of this legislation remained on the books.

Coalition Building

The "War to End All Wars" finally ended at 11 a.m. on November 11, 1918, and the fighting moved off the battlefield and into the halls of diplomacy. Negotiating the peace was to be an exercise in **conference diplomacy**. The Allies would meet in Paris and negotiate acceptable terms among themselves. Once they had agreed on a set of terms, they would present their terms to the defeated Central Powers.

As early as 1917, before the United States entered the war, Woodrow Wilson had laid out his vision for a "Peace Without Victory." In Wilson's words,

> Victory would mean peace forced upon the loser, a victor's terms imposed upon the vanquished. It would be accepted in humiliation, under duress, at an intolerable sacrifice, and would a leave a sting, a resentment, a bitter memory upon which terms of peace would rest, not permanently, but only as upon quicksand.

Therefore, Wilson concluded, the best possible peace would be a peace between equals that respected each nation's rights and sovereignty.

After the United States entered the war, Wilson turned his vision of peace without victory into what he saw as a practical plan for world peace. His **Fourteen Points** called for arms reduction, freedom of the seas, free trade, self-determination, an adjustment in colonial claims, a multi-national peacekeeping organization, and an end to secret treaties. When Wilson presented the plan to Congress in January 1918, Congress and representatives of the other Allied nations called it a "landmark of enlightenment in international relations." Germany agreed to the November 11 armistice, or cease-fire, on the condition that the peace treaty be based on the Fourteen Points.

England: Building a Bridge

Woodrow Wilson arrived at the Paris Peace Conference hailed by the European people as a hero, but viewed with suspicion by his European counterparts. The president considered his Fourteen Points practical and necessary. European leaders saw them as too idealistic. The European combatants had no interest in "peace without victory." France, especially, wanted someone punished for the death and destruction the war had wreaked across Europe. Georges Clemenceau, France's representative at the peace conference, had little interest in Wilson's Fourteen Points. He wanted Germany to pay.

It fell to the British prime minister, David Lloyd George, to balance Wilson's idealism and Clemenceau's blood thirst. His efforts did much to shape the final treaty. However, Lloyd George, like Clemenceau, felt pressure at

CONFERENCE DIPLOMACY
Type of diplomacy in which representatives of different countries meet to discuss common problems.

FOURTEEN POINTS Woodrow Wilson's peace plan, which called for arms reduction, freedom of the seas, free trade, self-determination, an adjustment in colonial claims, the creation of the League of Nations, and an end to secret treaties.

On October 2, 1919, while touring the country to garner support for the Treaty of Versailles, Woodrow Wilson suffered a massive stroke. He had experienced minor strokes before, but this one completely debilitated him. The stroke paralyzed the left side of the president's body. He could not speak, write, or walk. The White House kept his condition secret from the country, with Wilson's wife controlling access to the president during his recovery. Although he did regain some of his abilities, Wilson never fully recovered from his stroke. He completed his presidency a frail man.

TREATY OF VERSAILLES
Treaty with Germany that concluded World War I and punished Germany for the war.

REPARATIONS Compensation for war damages.

LEAGUE OF NATIONS A multinational peacekeeping organization established after World War I.

home to punish Germany for the war. The result was the peace built on quicksand that Wilson feared.

Versailles

The **Treaty of Versailles**, presented to Germany in May 1919, spelled out the peace terms with Germany. While Wilson considered it the best possible treaty under the circumstances, it fell far from the "peace without victory" he had imagined in 1917. Peace was, in fact, forced upon the loser, and the victor's terms imposed upon the vanquished.

The Versailles treaty took away approximately 10 percent of Germany's land and all of its overseas colonies. It limited the size of the German army and navy and forbid the existence of a German air force. The Rhineland region along the French border became a demilitarized zone. Most humiliating for Germany, the treaty placed full blame for the war on Germany's shoulders. In the so-called War Guilt Clause, the treaty forced Germany to take full responsibility for the war and reimburse the Allies for the costs of the war. The **reparations** payments totaled billions of dollars and contributed significantly to the economic chaos that led to Hitler's rise to power. It took until October 2010 for Germany to pay off its reparations debt.

German leaders felt angry and betrayed. They had been promised a treaty based on the Fourteen Points and that promise had been broken. Still, they had no choice. Germany, like the other nations of Europe, was in no position to resume the fighting. On June 28, 1919, German leaders signed the treaty.

League of Nations

Woodrow Wilson walked away from the Paris Peace Conference with one victory: the creation of the **League of Nations**. Wilson envisioned the League of Nations as an organization that would negotiate peaceful solutions to future conflicts, a diplomatic alternative to the battlefield. The last of the Fourteen Points, it was the only point that the Allied Powers agreed to fulfill—but only after serious and painful wrangling on Wilson's part.

Wilson returned to the United States a shadow of his former self. The strain of the Paris Peace Conference had made him ill, and his illness had impaired his political skills. He was unprepared for the battle that lay in front of him.

The 1918 elections had changed the balance of power in Congress. No longer did Wilson's Democrats have control. The Republicans, led by Henry Cabot Lodge, held the Senate majority. Lodge had become Wilson's mortal enemy, made angry by Wilson's defeat of Theodore Roosevelt in the presidential elections and delay in declaring war in Germany. Instead of working with the Republican majority, Wilson alienated them by refusing to include any Republicans among the U.S. representatives to the Paris Peace Conference.

Wilson presented the Versailles treaty to the Senate for approval in on July 10, 1919, but his earlier slight had not been forgotten. Two different groups in the Senate opposed the treaty. The "Irreconcilables," unequivocally opposed to the League of Nations, refused to sign the treaty under any circumstances. The "Reservationists," led by Henry Cabot Lodge, felt the treaty compromised U.S. interests. They would ratify the document if certain amendments were made. Wilson refused. The treaty, he said, must be accepted as written.

Wanting to show the Senate that the American people were on his side, Wilson set off on a speaking tour of the country. He warned that without the League, another world war loomed on the horizon. The tour took its toll, however. Wilson collapsed after giving a speech in Colorado. A week later, he suffered a massive stroke.

In November 1919, the Senate Foreign Relations Committee, led by Henry Cabot Lodge, presented the Treaty of Versailles to the full Senate for a vote. The Senate voted against it. For the first time in history, the U.S. Senate rejected a peace treaty. The League of Nations was established, but the United States played no part in it. Without the involvement of the United States, the League proved to be incapable of stopping the later aggression that led to World War II.

The international community, however, recognized Wilson's role in ending the war and establishing the League. In 1920, President Woodrow Wilson was awarded the Nobel Peace Prize.

STUDY ALERT

The treatment of Germany in the Treaty of Versailles and the weakness of the League of Nations become important in the years after the war. They created circumstances that led to Adolf Hitler's rise to power in Germany and the outbreak of World War II.

MID-CHAPTER QUESTIONS

1. The United States attempted to stay out of the Great War initially. Why did President Wilson break his promise of neutrality in the world war?

2. While the young men went off to Europe to fight, many changes developed at home. How did involvement in the war affect life in the United States?

3. Why might the Treaty of Versailles be considered the "peace upon quicksand" that Wilson warned against?

4. Why did the U.S. Senate reject the Treaty of Versailles?

ISOLATIONISM

After the war, the United States turned inward. Instead of assuming a position of global leadership as President Wilson had hoped, the country pursued a policy of **isolationism**, or staying separate from the world. The focus turned from fighting enemies abroad to rooting them out at home.

ISOLATIONISM A policy of staying out of, or separate from, international affairs.

Anti-German Sentiment

The war stirred up strong anti-German feelings. Once Congress declared war on Germany, a war on German culture followed. State governments and local citizens sought to remove any hint of German influence in their jurisdictions. Across the United States, communities took similar actions. They banned works by German composers, such as Beethoven and Bach, and works of literature by German authors. They shut down German-language newspapers. They forbid the teaching of the German language in public schools. They even changed the names of German foods. Sauerkraut, for example, became "liberty cabbage."

Propaganda posters demonized Germany. The posters called Germans "Huns" and depicted them as monsters who committed acts of unspeakable inhumanity. One poster showed a German soldier leading a young girl away from a burning village, insinuating an act of child rape. By association, German Americans were also viewed with suspicion, as if their heritage automatically made them traitors. Some German Americans tried to disguise their background by changing the names of their businesses or their own names. In a few instances, German Americans were attacked and beaten. More often, homes and businesses belonging to German Americans were vandalized.

When the war ended, the anti-German sentiment did not disappear, but it was soon overshadowed by fear of a different group: communists.

Red Scare

In 1917, Russia experienced two revolutions and the start of a civil war. World War I strained Russia's resources to the breaking point, and the government's seeming inability to solve the crisis caused the Russian public to lose confidence in it. The first revolution occurred in March 1917. Russia's czar, or emperor, was overthrown and replaced with a democratic provisional government. A few months later, in October 1917, communist revolutionaries called Bolsheviks overthrew the provisional government. The second revolution sparked a civil war, between the Bolsheviks, also called the Reds, and their opposition. The civil war ended with a Bolshevik victory in 1922, at which time Russia became the Soviet Union, a totalitarian communist regime.

RED SCARE Campaign after World War I and the Russian Revolutions to root out suspected communists in the United States.

The instability forced Russia to withdraw from the world war early and sent shockwaves through the international community. Russia was the first nation in the world to experience a communist revolution. Other governments feared the spread of the Red Menace, as communism was called, to their countries. That fear infected the United States. From 1919 to 1920, the United States experienced a **Red Scare** in which the government investigated suspected communists, conducted mass arrests and deportations of foreigners, and tightened immigration legislation.

Other unrest that followed the war compounded that fear. Workers went on strike, demanding higher pay, better working conditions, and collective bargaining rights. Labor unions, especially those that represented immigrant workers, became viewed as hotbeds of anti-government activity.

A union called the Industrial Workers of the World, or the IWW, drew the most suspicion. Nicknamed the Wobblies, the IWW was openly socialist and often participated in large labor strikes. The public often interpreted IWW strikes as unpatriotic, and viewed the Wobblies' socialist beliefs as a grave threat to the United States' security.

The government feared not only communists but also anarchists, those who believed in the abolition of all governments. Anyone who had opposed U.S. involvement in the war topped the list of suspected anarchists. Immigrants did not fall far behind.

Political Cartoons

Just as World War I propaganda posters fed a campaign of anti-German sentiment, political cartoons fed the hysteria of the Red Scare. These cartoons appeared in newspapers across the country; even though the images varied, the messages offered the same theme: the United States is in immediate danger. Cartoons often depicted the enemy as a bearded Eastern European immigrant. The cartoons often made no distinction between Bolshevism (communism) and anarchy, or they depicted the two philosophies in conspiracy against the United States.

One cartoon, which appeared in the *Philadelphia Inquirer*, showed a long-bearded man crawling out from under an American flag, as if he was sneaking into the United States. He carried a knife labeled Bolshevism in one hand and a torch labeled anarchy in the other. The caption read, "Put Them Out and Keep Them Out."

A cartoon in the New York *Evening World* showed a bearded man holding an American flag that had been cut. Only the red stripes remained. According to the caption, the red stripes are "All They Want In Our Flag."

Another cartoon showed an anarchist placing a bomb at the Statue of Liberty. Many anarchist movements used bombs as political statements, and it was a series of bombings that brought the Red Scare to its climax.

The Palmer Raids

In 1919, anarchists mailed bombs to a number of influential Americans, from business tycoons J.P. Morgan and John D. Rockefeller to Supreme Court Justice Oliver Wendell Holmes. In June, a bomb exploded at the home of U.S. Attorney General Mitchell Palmer.

Palmer sprang into action. In an essay titled "The Case Against the 'Reds'," Palmer warned that "Like a prairie fire, the blaze of revolution was sweeping over every American institution of law and order…crawling into the sacred corners of American homes." Therefore, Palmer concluded, all Reds must be purged from American society. Palmer made no distinction between the anarchists and the Reds.

The U.S. Department of Justice created a special task force. The task force, under Palmer's leadership, raided suspected communist and anarchist organizations and gathering places, including offices of the IWW. Palmer conducted the raids without search warrants and denied legal counsel to the thousands who were arrested. Hundreds of immigrants were deported.

Palmer claimed that the raids uncovered proof of terrorist plots against state and federal governments. None of the suspected attacks ever occurred. Palmer quickly lost credibility. In addition to his failed predictions, Palmer had also offended Congress and many Americans with his disregard for Constitutional rights.

Sacco and Vanzetti

Fears of anarchists and immigrants culminated in the trial of two Italian immigrants, Nicola Sacco and Bartolomeo Vanzetti. The two men were arrested and tried for murder in 1920. Historians today still debate the men's guilt, but not the unfairness of their trial.

On April 15, 1920, a payroll clerk and a security guard at a factory near Boston were killed and robbed of thousands of dollars in cash. According to eyewitnesses, two men committed the crimes and then drove off in a car with two or three other men. Several weeks later, police arrested Sacco and Vanzetti.

Neither Sacco nor Vanzetti had a criminal record, but each men owned a gun. One bullet from the crime scene seemed to match Sacco's gun. None of the stolen money was ever found, nor was any of the money ever connected to the two men. No other suspects were ever arrested.

The case went to trial in 1921. Most of the prosecution's evidence focused on Sacco and Vanzetti's immigrant backgrounds and anarchist beliefs. Both men were convicted.

Believing they had been tried unfairly, the defendants petitioned for a new trial. The petitions, which were reviewed by the judge in the original trial, were denied. The law at the time forbid any other appeals or any further review of the evidence. On August 23, 1927, Sacco and Vanzetti were executed.

Closing Borders

The conviction of Sacco and Vanzetti illustrated the growing nativist sentiment in the United States. **Nativism** is the belief that native-born Americans are superior to immigrants, especially if those immigrants came from southern or eastern Europe. This nativism expressed itself not only in the association of immigrants with communism and anarchy, but also in the growth of the Ku Klux Klan. The Klan's resurgence in the 1920s resulted in part from the success of the film *Birth of a Nation*. The film, directed by D.W. Griffith, depicted the founding of the Klan in the late 1800s. Controversial because of its use of racial stereotypes, the film became a recruiting tool for the new Klan. This new Klan not only targeted African-Americans but also Catholics and Jews, because Catholics from southern Europe and Jews from eastern Europe were among the largest immigrant groups of the era.

Both the war and the Red Scare contributed to growing immigration restrictions. The first restriction came in 1917, when Congress implemented a literacy test for new immigrants over the age of 16. To pass the test, immigrants had to demonstrate reading comprehension in any language. The 1917 Act also increased the tax that new immigrants were required to pay when they arrived in the country and established an Asiatic Barred Zone, which banned entry for immigrants from most of Asia.

Immigration Quotas

In 1922, Congress established quotas to further restrict the flow of new immigrants into the country. The quotas limited the annual number of immigrants from any nation to 3 percent of the total foreign-born population from that nation in the United States as calculated in the 1910 census. For example, if the 1910 census counted 100 immigrants from Spain, the new law allowed only three Spanish immigrants into the United States each year. The quotas, in effect, limited the total number of new immigrants to 350,000 per year.

Congress adjusted the quotas with the Johnson-Reed Act. Also known as the Immigration Act of 1924, the Johnson-Reed legislation tightened the quotas that had been established in 1922 and changed the way the quotas were calculated. The new act reduced the quota percentage from 3 percent to 2 percent and changed the census year used for the calculations from 1910 to 1890. In addition, Johnson-Reed stated that quota calculations would be based on the ethnic origins of the entire American population, rather than just on the number of foreign-born Americans. As a result the quota for immigrants from the United Kingdom and western Europe increased and immigration from southern and eastern Europe became even more limited. The 1924 Act also banned all Asians from immigrating to the United States.

The severe restrictions established by U.S. immigration law, as well as the deportations associated with the Red Scare, could have created tension between the United States and other countries. Such tensions did not occur, however, possibly because of the onset of a greater crisis. Five years after the passage of the Johnson-Reed Act, the world was plunged into the vast economic crisis of the Great Depression.

END OF CHAPTER TAKE-AWAYS

■ **The Wilson Years:** The United States had been reluctant to enter World War I, but it eventually helped the Allied Powers achieve victory. The Treaty of Versailles punished Germany for the war and established the League of Nations. The United States Senate rejected the treaty and the United States did not join the League.

■ **Isolationism:** After the war, the United States turned inward. It pursued campaigns against suspected communists and anarchists and limited immigration into the country.

REFERENCES

Library of Congress. (n.d.). U.S. participation in the Great War (World War One). Retrieved from http://www.loc.gov/teachers/classroommaterials/presentationsandactivities/presentations/timeline/progress/wwone/

Library of Congress, American Memory. (n.d.). Immigrants, nativism, and Americanization. Retrieved from http://lcweb2.loc.gov:8081/ammem/amrlhtml/dtimmig.html

Library of Congress, American Memory. (n.d.). The increasing power of destruction: Military technology in World War I. *Newspaper Pictorials: World War I Rotogravures*. Retrieved from http://memory.loc.gov/ammem/collections/rotogravures/rotomil.html

Massachusetts Judicial Branch, Supreme Judicial Court. (2010). Sacco & Vanzetti exhibit. Retrieved from http://www.mass.gov/courts/sjc/sacco-vanzetti.html

Meyer, G. J. (2007). *A world undone: The story of the Great War, 1914 to 1918*. New York, NY: Delacourte Press.

Our Documents: 100 Milestone Documents from the National Archives. (n.d.). President Woodrow Wilson's 14 points (1918). Retrieved from http://www.ourdocuments.gov/doc.php?doc=62

Our Documents: 100 Milestone Documents from the National Archives. (n.d.). Zimmermann telegram (1917). Retrieved from http://www.ourdocuments.gov/doc.php??doc=60

Smithsonian National Museum of American History. (n.d.). The price of freedom: Americans at war: World War I. Retrieved from http://americanhistory.si.edu/militaryhistory/printable/section.asp?id=8

Tuchman, B. W. (2004). *The guns of August*. New York, NY: Presidio Press. (Original work published 1962)

U.S. Senate website. (n.d.). Woodrow Wilson addresses the Senate. Retrieved from http://www.senate.gov/artandhistory/history/minute/Woodrow_Wilson_Addresses_the_Senate.htm

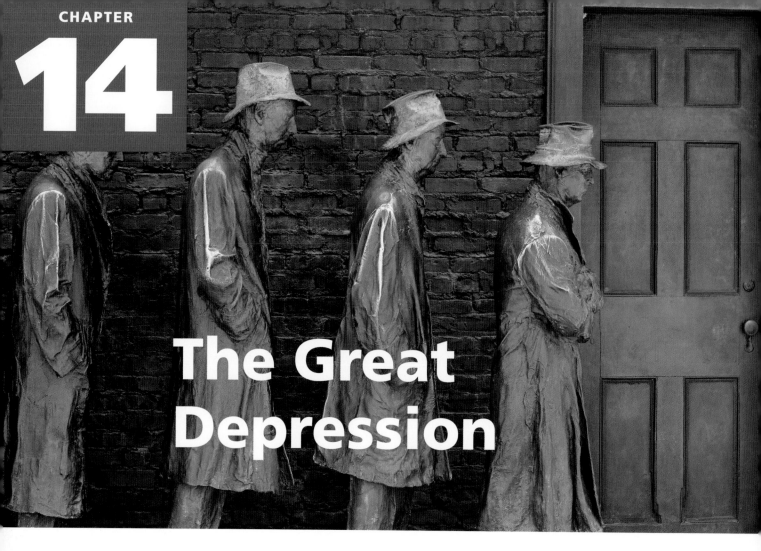

The Great Depression

The Great Depression was the worst economic slump of the twentieth century. In 1933, nearly one out of every four workers could not find a job. Farmers were hit especially hard as crop prices fell to half their previous level. All economic indicators pointed to prolonged hardship. Indeed, this hardship lasted for well over a decade.

In an effort to prevent the devastation that resulted from this economic malaise from happening again, the country enacted new economic legislation. The nation still experienced occasional economic downturns, but nothing on the magnitude that occurred during the 1930s.

Several decades later, the government started to repeal some of the Depression-era laws that regulated bankers and investors. Many scholars believe that it was the repeal of these banking protections that allowed for the 2008 financial crisis, which would come to be known as the Great Recession.

Both the Great Depression and the Great Recession had tragic effects on the welfare of the nation. The tragedy of the Great Depression, however, was far greater. The Depression's cost could be measured in lives as well as dollars. It led to a vast and widespread uncertainty throughout the entire nation.

HOUSING MARKET

Following the end of World War I, the construction of private homes boomed in the United States. In the early 1920s, the price of land and homes began to soar, and construction was the landmark of nearly every state in the nation, with housing accounting for nearly 62 percent of the nation's gross domestic investment during that period. This boom meant that banks were lending, and more and more Americans were taking on mortgages to own homes. As such, residential mortgage debt, on properties other than farms, grew from $9.4 billion in 1920 to $18.4 billion in 1925 to $30.2 billion in 1930. More and more Americans were becoming homeowners, and were doing so by borrowing money in the form of mortgages.

Meanwhile, federal policies assisted in this boom. The Federal Reserve kept mortgage interest rates at an unprecedentedly low level, which in turn kept banks lending, individuals borrowing, property values growing, and speculators flooding the American housing market. These speculators bought land at low prices and sold it for remarkable profits throughout the 1920s, especially in Florida, where more and more Americans were moving and purchasing homes to enjoy warmer climates. With the boom came increased demand for construction supplies and other materials, which were largely brought into Florida by train. Soon these trains were unable to keep up with the demand, and were altogether unable to bring in construction materials into the state, resulting in railroad failures. Meanwhile, those who lived in Florida were faced with increased cost of living, and were soon unable to live there. As a result, a housing slump started in the mid-1920s in Florida, followed by a nationwide housing slump a few years later.

During this period, four primary financial organizations were lending money to individuals, in the form of mortgages, to purchases homes. These groups included mutual savings banks, life insurance companies, commercial banks, and savings and loan groups, or thrifts. These companies offered many **balloon loans**, which offered individuals extremely low payments but at interest rates and payments that ballooned over time. The idea was that many Americans preferred low initial payments and assumed that they could always refinance the loan before the balloon payments came due. This thought was based on the faulty assumption that homes would continue to grow in value, and that credit would continue to be amply available. Furthermore, more and more banks were allowing higher loan-to-value ratios on their loans, which meant that individuals were allowed to borrow 50 percent or more of a home's value, which increased the risk not only to homeowners, but also to banks.

As more and more Americans began to lose their jobs, they were no longer able to pay their mortgages, even at low initial payment rates. Homes went into foreclosure at unprecedented levels, and the prices of homes dropped significantly. Between 1928 and 1933, home prices plummeted by over 30 percent, making it impossible for many homeowners to refinance their loans. Straddled with ballooning home payments and dropping income, millions of Americans defaulted on their mortgage loans, resulting in the national mortgage crisis of the 1930s. Many banks that had made loans during the housing boom of the 1920s failed as a result of thousands of mortgagees defaulting on their loans. Even after taking back homes in foreclosure, banks were unable to recover their investments. In fact, many savings and loan

BALLOON LOANS Loans offered by banks to individuals that started with a low interest rate but escalated over time.

institutions failed completely, while other institutions, such as commercial banks, struggled to stay afloat.

The mortgage crisis meant that thousands of Americans lost their homes and became homeless. These homeless Americans crowded into the homes of other family members, resulting in overcrowding and the spread of disease. Many who did not move in with relatives moved to impoverished sections of their cities and built shacks out of flattened tin cans, crates, and cardboard. These shantytowns sprang up throughout the country and became known as **Hoovervilles**, a name given by Americans who were deeply disappointed in President Herbert Hoover's inability to end the Depression.

HOOVERVILLES Shanty-towns that served as makeshift dwellings for many who became unemployed during the Great Depression.

BLACK MONDAY

The American economy expanded significantly from the end of World War I through the 1920s, giving rise to the term the **Roaring Twenties**. Between 1927 and 1929, industrial output grew by over 25 percent, with more and more Americans taking advantage of electricity and purchasing electric products. More Americans also were purchasing cars, which were produced less expensively thanks to Ford's development of the assembly line. Growth in the economy also meant considerable growth in the stock market. Stock indices boomed nearly 400 percent between 1926 and 1929, and many Americans believed that the stock market was a consistent, sure-fire way to make money.

ROARING TWENTIES An era of general prosperity and speculation that drove the stock market up.

Much of the high experienced by Americans during the 1920s, such as the housing and automotive booms, came to a halt on Monday, October 28, 1929. On that day, known as **Black Monday**, shares on the New York Stock Exchange plummeted to an all-time low. Starting on Black Thursday, October 24, 1929, stocks had become exceedingly volatile. Thousands of investors who had put all of their money, as well as borrowed sums, into the stock market lost enormous amounts of money. Corporate shares fell nearly 80 percent by Black Tuesday, October 29, 1929.

BLACK MONDAY October 28, 1929: the date on which the Roaring Twenties came to an end in a crash on Wall Street.

STOCK MARKET

Throughout the Roaring Twenties, consumer goods were in high demand. Americans purchased electronic appliances, homes, cars, and much more. As a result, factories were operating at high capacity, unemployment was low, and national sentiment was positive. Americans felt they had more wealth, and as a result, were investing more and more in the stock market. Many chose to put their entire life savings into the stock market, and throughout the nation, many boasted that the stock market was a permanent way to make lasting money. Even one economist, Irving Fisher, boasted, "Stock prices have reached what looks like a permanently high plateau."

During this period, many Americans made purchases based upon installment contracts, which is much like a layaway system. Items were paid for in installments on credit, and ownership was official when the last payment on an item was made. This type of purchasing involved risk, and risk-taking appeared to be the norm during this era. More and more people were speculating on the stock market, meaning that they would buy many seemingly affordable shares in companies with the hopes of making enormous profits. Many times, investors borrowed the money that they used to speculate on the stock market, creating an enormous bubble of

STUDY ALERT

Hoovervilles were poor shantytowns constructed by Americans left otherwise homeless during the Great Depression. These shantytowns had crude homes made of cardboard and tin, and were named in derision of President Herbert Hoover, who many Americans felt did not do enough to alleviate suffering during the Depression.

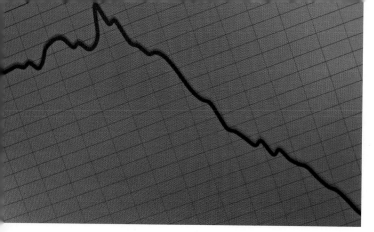

risky borrowing and speculative spending. Shares in company stock became abnormally inflated, much as the prices of homes and land had become during the housing boom of this time period. In an effort to slow this speculation, the Federal Reserve raised interest rates, which made it harder for speculators to borrow money to play on the stock market. These increased rates meant that there was less borrowing, which in turn decreased consumer spending and construction throughout the nation.

Stock market speculation came to a head in late October 1929. On Thursday, October 24, 1929, known as Black Thursday, the stock market experienced a steep decline in share prices, followed by a leveling off on prices on Friday and Saturday. Then, on Black Monday, October 28, 1929, share prices plummeted again, with the market dropping by another 13 percent. By Tuesday, October 29, shareholders entered into a panic, selling off 16,410,030 shares. Thousands lost nearly everything they had during the plummet.

Over the next three years, stock prices continued to fluctuate drastically, but with a general downward trend. Given the severe stock market losses, American sentiment changed drastically. Americans stopped purchasing consumer goods, and many were soon unable to pay for items purchased with installment contracts. As a result, overall consumer spending and manufacturing output plummeted. With less buying and manufacturing, more and more Americans lost their jobs, deepening the depression and resulting in the failure of more businesses and banks. Millions of people sought to get their money out of banks, because they believed their money was unsafe there. Between January of 1930 and March of 1933, over 9,000 banks closed their doors.

Meanwhile, the Federal Reserve's hike in interest rates, which was designed to slow market speculation, had an unintended, devastating consequence. In order to maintain an equal exchange rate with the United States, other nations throughout the world had to raise their interest rates as well. This not only translated to depressions in other countries, but lowered the demand for American exports. This furthered the deepening of the depression in the United States, with more manufacturers failing and more Americans losing their jobs.

EFFICIENCY MOVEMENT A movement to rid the government and the economy of waste and inefficient systems and practices.

HOOVER'S PLAN

Herbert Hoover became president in 1929, and faced the stock market crash only 8 months after he took office. Hoover, a Republican, believed that if business was left to itself, without much government interference, it could correct the economic woes facing the nation. Hoover himself was a staunch proponent of the **Efficiency Movement** in the United States, believing that the economy could improve if inefficiencies were eliminated. As such, Hoover rejected many bills aimed at directly involving the federal government in the economy. He felt that such efforts would give the federal government too much power. Hoover also believed that if the government were to begin doling out welfare checks to the poor and sick, such payments would become addictive. Americans would lose their will to work hard and nationwide dependence on the federal government would ultimately hurt the economy.

Instead, Hoover sought to encourage volunteerism, whereby the government would work with public organizations to foster the greater good of Americans. In one such effort of volunteerism, Hoover encouraged major American banks to join the National Credit Consortium (NCC), a conglomerate of large banks that were exhorted to loan money to smaller banks, to prevent more financial institutions from failing. Many large banks were reluctant to make such risky loans, and the NCC was largely unproductive.

Smoot-Hawley Tariff Act

To address the deepening economic downturn, Hoover asked local and state governments to help provide for the needs of those left destitute at the start of the Depression, but many of these local governments lacked the funds necessary to do so. To help remedy this problem, Hoover took several steps. One such effort was the **Smoot-Hawley Tariff Act** of 1930.

The Smoot-Hawley Act raised tariffs, or taxes, on goods imported into the United States. Smoot-Hawley raised taxes on over 20,000 imported agricultural and industrial goods, in an effort to discourage imports and encourage the purchase of American-made products. The hope was that by making imports less desirable, demand for American goods would grow, increasing productivity and fostering job creation.

Senator Reed Smoot and Representative Willis C. Hawley sponsored the law, which President Hoover signed on June 17, 1930. The bill raised tariffs to the second highest level ever in the United States, second only to a similar tariff passed in 1928.

Within weeks of its passing, other nations retaliated by increasing tariffs on American goods. This further weakened American exports. Overall, international trade plummeted by nearly 60 percent between 1929 and 1934, and many economists consider this tariff act one of the most significant precipitating factors of the Great Depression. In fact, some pundits blame the stock market crash of 1929 in large part on discussions about raising tariffs.

In addition to signing the controversial tariff act into law, President Hoover made other attempts to mitigate the effects of the economic downturn. In one of his last efforts to combat the Depression, Hoover passed the Emergency Relief and Construction Act, which opened the door for the government to spend tax money on public works programs directly, to put more Americans to work. The Emergency Relief and Construction Act formed the **Reconstruction Finance Corporation** (RFC), which gave local governments money to put more Americans to work on public roads and other projects. This government agency, formed in 1932, also helped relieve the effects of the Great Depression by lending money to railroads, banks, businesses, and other institutions whose failure would have deepened the nation's economic woes. While the RFC got off to a bumpy start, President Franklin D. Roosevelt later reorganized and continued the work of the RFC as part of his New Deal. Later, many loans made by the RFC were ultimately repaid. The RFC is commonly considered Hoover's greatest contribution to combating the Great Depression, though many Americans felt that it was too little too late.

DID YOU KNOW?

During periods of recession, those with resources and capital often end up with considerably more assets by the end of the recessionary period. One example of this phenomenon is the investment success of John Paul Getty. During the Roaring Twenties, Getty had amassed a considerable fortune in the oil industry, in excess of $3 million. During the Great Depression, Getty used his fortune to purchase distressed oil properties, undervalued stock, and the Pacific Oil Company. He emerged from the Great Depression far richer than he was before. This practice is a common one—occurring even in present-day recessions.

SMOOT-HAWLEY TARIFF ACT A law that raised taxes on imported goods. The law accelerated the effects of the Great Depression.

RECONSTRUCTION FINANCE CORPORATION A federal relief agency formed in 1932 under Hoover that sought to give local governments money to put more Americans to work on public roads and other projects.

MID-CHAPTER QUESTIONS

1. Describe the housing market in the years leading up to the Great Depression. In particular, what was the housing market like in Florida? How did speculation become a problem in Florida? What organizations were lending money to Americans during this period to build and buy homes? How did the Federal Reserve assist in this housing boom?

2. Describe the events leading up to and on Black Monday.

3. Explain the Stock Market Crash of 1929. Who were speculators and what role did they play in the crash? What impact did the crash have on other areas of the American economy, especially banks?

4. How did President Herbert Hoover attempt to address the Great Depression? What parts, if any, of his plan worked? What was the Smoot-Hawley Act, and did it help alleviate the Depression? If not, why not?

FIRST AND SECOND NEW DEALS

By 1932, the Great Depression had worsened. Twelve to 15 million Americans had lost their jobs, meaning one of four workers was unemployed. Businesses, banks, manufacturers, and other companies continued to fail regularly. Most Americans felt that Hoover's Administration had not done enough to relieve their suffering. His commitment to rugged individualism, volunteerism, and improved efficiency failed to meet the immediate needs of millions of Americans, who were unemployed, hungry, and increasingly homeless.

As a result, in 1932, Franklin Delano Roosevelt was elected president in a resounding defeat of incumbent Hoover. Unlike his predecessor, Roosevelt believed firmly that the government held the primary responsibility for leading the nation out of the Great Depression. During his inaugural address, Roosevelt sought to encourage the American people and renew their hope in the economy and the government. It was in this speech that he spoke the famous words, "The only thing we have to fear is fear itself."

Immediately upon taking office, Roosevelt called Congress into a special session to enact laws designed to relieve the Depression. This session led to dozens of laws and anti-depressive measures that Roosevelt called the **New Deal**.

The term "new deal" was first coined by Roosevelt when he accepted the Democratic Party's nomination for president. In that speech, he said, "I pledge you, I pledge myself, to a new deal for the American people." The New Deal is frequently divided as the

NEW DEAL A series of programs established under Roosevelt's administration that sought to bring relief, recovery, and reform to the many suffering through the Great Depression.

First New Deal, referring to Roosevelt's work and Congressional legislation between 1933 and 1934, and the Second New Deal, spanning from 1935 to 1938.

The principles that comprised the New Deal came from a variety of sources. Roosevelt authored some of the ideas, and others were conceived by members of his Brain Trust, a group of advisors who helped create several New Deal programs. Elements of the New Deal also came from Congressional leaders, prominent Democrats, and others.

The New Deal had primarily three purposes. First, Roosevelt sought to immediately provide relief for poor and indigent Americans, those left living in Hoovervilles who had lost their jobs, homes, and possessions in the Depression. Second, the New Deal aimed to foster business and thus create jobs. Third, the New Deal wanted to reform government agencies and aspects of business to prevent the United States from ever experiencing another Depression of this scope and magnitude.

These three goals of the New Deal are commonly referred to as the three Rs—relief, recovery, and reform. First, the New Deal sought to give Americans some immediate relief, to make sure they had enough money to make ends meet. The Hoover administration had largely failed to provide such relief, and paid the price at the polls. In contrast, Roosevelt's New Dealers made immediate relief a primary goal of the new administration's first hundred days, and garnered much popularity as a result.

In the area of recovery, the New Dealers sought to create long-lived infrastructure. As a proponent of Keynesian economics, Roosevelt believed government investment in public works projects meant long-term economic improvement. Many of the agencies created by the New Deal not only provided immediate relief by giving Americans jobs, but also lent to recovery efforts by creating infrastructure such as roads, dams, parks, schools, and more.

In the area of reform, Roosevelt's administration sought to put policies and agencies in place to help prevent the repeat of such a catastrophic economic downturn. Roosevelt wanted to reform both the banking industry and the U.S. stock market, so Americans would once again confidently invest and secure their income.

As a result, one of the first acts of the First New Deal involved saving the nation's embattled banking industry. Countless banks had failed prior to 1933, and in February 1933, so many banks had failed that a rush on the banks ensued. To help mitigate the nation's fears, Roosevelt declared a bank holiday on March 6, 1933, closing all banks indefinitely. On March 9 at Roosevelt's prompting, Congress passed the Emergency Banking Act, which gave the government the right to closely examine the financial records of U.S. banks. The government was also given the right to only reopen those banks in a strong financial position.

Later that week, half of the banks in the country reopened their doors, and those banks held nearly all of the nation's deposits. Within his first few weeks in office, Roosevelt had managed to quell the nation's fears in the banking system for the first time in nearly four years.

A few months later, Roosevelt signed the **Glass-Steagall Banking Act** into law, giving the Federal Reserve more control over banks. This law also created the Federal Deposit Insurance Corporation (FDIC), which insured deposits up to $2,500, and then later up to $5,000. This again helped build American confidence in their government, their banks, and ultimately the U.S. economy.

GLASS-STEAGALL BANKING ACT A law that established mechanisms for the federal government to monitor the practices and welfare of banks more closely.

In 1933, Congress also passed the Securities Act. This law required companies selling stock to give potential investors full and accurate information about the stock. As a follow up to that, Congress also created the Securities and Exchange Commission (SEC) in 1934 to oversee the sale of securities and to protect investors and others from speculation and the other practices that led to the stock market crash of 1929.

As seen with the Emergency Banking Act, the Glass-Steagall Banking Act, the Securities Act, and the creation of the Securities and Exchange Commission, the New Deal was largely about rebuilding American confidence. While many do not believe the New Deal actually ended the Great Depression, it helped Americans cope with the effects of the Depression and allowed them to hope that the nation's economic power could be restored.

Acts and Plans

The First New Deal was replete with what has become known as Roosevelt's alphabet soup, with many new agencies and pieces of legislation. One of the most important of these new acts was the National Industrial Recovery Act of 1933. This act created the National Recovery Administration (NRA), which in turn created codes of conduct for various industries and businesses. The codes were written by representatives of the industries, and defined minimum wages workers were expected to receive and maximum hours they were expected to work. The NRA ultimately set the lowest possible prices that businesses could charge for their goods and services, thus reducing some price competition. The NRA also hoped to limit the production of some goods, so that over time prices on consumer goods would go up, increasing business profits. Another goal of the NRA was to bring businesses, government, and individuals together to make the best decisions for the future of the economy. The NRA was declared unconstitutional by the U.S. Supreme Court in 1935 in the *Schechter v. United States* case. In that case, the NRA was deemed a violation of the separation of powers.

In its efforts to meet the immediate needs of the poor, the New Deal sought to put young men to work. Through the Civilian Conservation Corps (CCC), young men were employed by the government in various conservation efforts. They worked as landscapers, helped build dams, repaired historic areas and roadways, created trails and parks, and more. In another, similarly direct plan to help relieve unemployment, the Civil Works Administration (CWA) sought to help some Americans land high-paying jobs in construction, but this program was discontinued in 1934 due to its high cost.

Similarly, the Public Works Administration (PWA) created thousands of jobs. People were hired to build various public buildings and sites, including courthouses, roads, dams, schools, and more. The PWA continued its efforts throughout the First and Second New Deals, and only came to an end as the United States ramped up its production in preparation for World War II.

In another effort to combat unemployment, the Tennessee Valley Authority (TVA) used public funds to hire locals to build several dams throughout the Tennessee River Valley, which was particularly hard-hit during the Depression. As a result, not only were people hired, but floods were also controlled and electricity was provided to residents of the valley. The TVA continues today as a publically owned corporation that still is the primary supplier of electricity to the region.

Meanwhile, the Federal Emergency Relief Administration sought to better address the problems faced by local governments, which did not have enough money to help meet the needs of their impoverished citizens. To assist those who could no longer pay their mortgages, and to avoid growing the problem of homelessness, the Home Owners Loan Corporation (HOLC) was instructed to lend money, at low interest rates, to those who were struggling to pay their mortgages. By refinancing these mortgages, the government hoped to prevent further foreclosures. In fact, between 1933 and 1935, nearly one million people refinanced their loans through HOLC, and avoided foreclosure. In another effort to shore up the housing market, which had played such a crucial role at the outset of the Great Depression, Roosevelt created the Federal Housing Administration (FHA) in 1934. The FHA insured the loans that banks and other lenders gave to individuals who wanted to build and purchase homes. FHA remains an active program today, offering first-time homebuyers and others significant incentives to purchase homes.

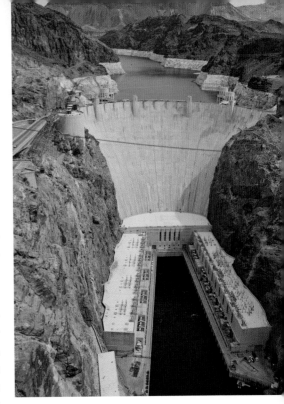

Hoover Dam.

In a concerted effort to help farmers, who struggled significantly during the Depression, the Roosevelt Administration began the Agricultural Adjustment Administration (AAA) in 1933. In an effort to raise prices for farming products, and thus increase income for farmers, the AAA sought ways to limit agricultural production of products such as corn, wheat, milk, cotton, and livestock. Less supply would increase the price of these farm products. A tax was levied on those who processed agricultural products, and that income was used to pay farmers not to produce as many products as they had done previously.

The work of the AAA was controversial. While it did increase farming income, it lowered the production of food items and cotton when many in the nation needed food and clothing. In 1935, the Supreme Court declared the AAA unconstitutional. In response, the government paid farmers not to decrease production, but rather to leave some land vacant.

In another effort to help farmers, the Farm Credit Administration (FCA) was established in 1933. The FCA sought to help farmers continue to operate, and not shut down their farms and their productivity, by making long- and short-term loans available.

The emphasis of the New Deal was not so much on ending the Depression as it was on helping Americans with their immediate needs. But with each of these plans and agencies came a great deal of controversy, such as the AAA controversy mentioned above.

Furthermore, many detractors of the New Deal feared that the government was becoming socialist. For example, in the case of the TVA, some argued that the government's ownership of such a company was verging on blatant socialism, and that the government could leverage its size, position, and capital to undercut several privately-owned energy suppliers in the region. Much of the spending associated with the First New Deal came from cuts Roosevelt achieved in the military and other areas. Unlike the First New Deal, the Second New Deal, from 1935 to 1938, involved considerably more federal deficit spending. Roosevelt found it necessary to continue such spending during this period, given the continuing economic hardships faced by millions of Americans.

During the Second New Deal, Roosevelt launched yet another program designed to address unemployment: the Works Progress Administration (WPA). Much like the CCC, CWA, PWA, and the TVA before it, the WPA, started in 1935, provided jobs to those in need of work. In 1939 it was renamed the Works Projects Administration, and it operated until 1943. WPA workers built national parks, roadways, bridges, dams, and other projects. The WPA also created work for writers, actors, musicians, and other artists, who had been hit particularly hard during the Depression. In all, the WPA accounted for the employment of over 8.5 million Americans.

Another important piece of legislation in the Second New Deal was the passage of the **Social Security Act** in 1935. With little or no income, poor housing, and few ways to care for themselves, the elderly were suffering in the bleak economy. To address the needs of the elderly, the Social Security Act gave income to retired workers. The money for Social Security came from a double tax on the income of wage earners. The Social Security Act also created an unemployment insurance program, which provided temporary income to those who were out of work. Social security and unemployment payments continue to be some of the most popular federal spending programs in the United States.

Social Security was a popular program from its inception. It made workers feel that they were saving retirement money, and in fact it was billed as a retirement savings plan, even though funds collected were redistributed immediately to the elderly. Americans were beginning to again have hope in the future. Social Security also provided financially for members of American society who were indigent or had disabilities.

Nevertheless, Social Security had its opponents. On the one hand, conservatives feared the involvement of the government in the lives and finances of individuals, and the power granted to the government through Social Security. Social security also resulted in a large amount of money being removed from the private sector and being controlled by the government instead of being deposited into private bank accounts or investment accounts. On the other hand, Social Security did not do enough to protect the most vulnerable members of American society, including African-Americans and impoverished women.

Roosevelt's Second New Deal had many of the same detractors as the First New Deal. Conservatives, business owners, and even conservative Democrats feared that Roosevelt was instituting socialism in the United States. Many argued that Roosevelt was creating a nation of handout-seekers, people who would forever become dependent on the government for a free paycheck. Many also feared the enormous amount of power that his New Deal gave the president, fearing that there would be a permanent imbalance of power in favor of the executive branch.

One such detractor who was particularly vocal was a Roman Catholic priest, Father Charles Coughlin. Coughlin blamed the Great Depression on crooked bankers, Wall Street executives, and Jews. Coughlin had a regular radio program, whereby he frequently and publically criticized Roosevelt and his New Deal. At the height of his program, Coughlin had 40 million listeners.

Surprisingly, the Second New Deal also garnered an unexpected set of detractors on the far left of Roosevelt. Led by Congressmen Huey Long, these New Deal opponents believed that Roosevelt was not doing enough to combat the effects of the Great Depression. Long believed that the Depression was caused by income

SOCIAL SECURITY ACT A law that established the Social Security system, which distributes federal assistance to retirees and the unemployed.

inequalities, and demanded that the rich in America "share the wealth" with the poor. Long suggested that the rich pay exorbitant taxes so that every American family could at least have an annual income of $5,000 per year.

Many argue that Roosevelt's WPA came largely in response to Long and other leftist critics. Through the WPA, the federal government hired over 10 million Americans to work on various public works projects, spending nearly $10 billion in the process.

In addition to continuing efforts to help the unemployed and the poor, the Second New Deal also continued its efforts to provide aid to beleaguered famers and homeowners. As has been shown, the AAA had already been found unconstitutional by the Supreme Court. In reaction to this decision, Roosevelt signed the Soil Conservation and Domestic Allotment Act in 1936. Much like AAA, the Soil Conservation and Domestic Allotment Act offered public subsidies to farmers to slow down the production of food items. The act also offered subsidies to farmers who planted crops that enriched the soil, unlike wheat, which tended to deplete the nutrients in soil. Two years later, in 1938, Democrats in Congress passed the Second Agricultural Adjustment Administration, which came at the problem of agricultural pricing by limiting the amount of land farmers were permitted to use. By reducing cropped land, the administration again sought to increase the price farmers would earn for their products.

Meanwhile, the Second New Deal also addressed concerns of those who lived in urban areas. In 1937, Congress passed the United States Housing Act, creating the United States Housing Authority (USHA). USHA assisted the American urban poor through new federal public housing projects. USHA helped build new housing for over 500,000 Americans in need.

In addition to addressing the needs of American farmers and city-dwellers, Roosevelt sought to help Native Americans during the Second New Deal. During Roosevelt's first term, Congress had passed the Indian Reorganization Act (IRA) to help various Indian tribes organize their governments, and to formally recognize these tribal governments on a national level.

The IRA also sought to further help Native Americans by reversing the Dawes Severalty Act of 1887. The Dawes Act had weakened tribal governance by stating that only individual Native Americans, not tribal councils, could own land. The IRA sought to help Native American tribes own land.

The IRA had only limited success in alleviating the needs of Native Americans, in large part due to the response of the Native American tribes themselves. Some, like the Navajo in southwestern regions of the United States, summarily rejected the IRA, in a general distrust of the American government. Other tribes had difficulty understanding the terms of the IRA, and what it meant for their particular needs. Many struggling Native Americans found more immediate relief through other New Deal programs, such as the PWA, the CCC, and the WPA. These programs accounted for nearly 100,000 Native American young men finding work.

Roosevelt's New Deal also addressed the needs of millions of employed workers in the United States, primarily by giving them the right to organize into powerful unions. In 1935, Congress passed the National Labor Relations Act, which essentially enabled unions to organize strikes, express their demands, and perform other functions without experiencing harsh responses from business owners. This bill, also known as the Wagner Act, opened the door for even small labor unions to have a

STUDY ALERT

The New Deal was authored and directed by President Franklin D. Roosevelt, Democratic leaders, and Congress in the 1930s in an effort to mitigate the effects of the Great Depression. The New Deal involved a series of legislative acts and government agencies that sought to provide relief, recovery, and reform.

significant impact on the everyday lives of workers in the manufacturing industry. By 1937, General Motors had recognized the workers' right to organize into unions, and those unions had coordinated sit-down strikes whereby workers sat at their stations and did not leave until GM agreed not hire non-union workers to do union work.

As a result of the National Labor Relations Act, two important unions in particular, the American Federation of Labor (AFL) and the Congress of Industrial Organizations (CIO), came to hold considerable power and influence the lives of millions of American workers.

In another important piece of labor legislation in the Second New Deal, Congress passed the Fair Labor Standards Act in 1938. This act set the minimum wage for workers at 25 cents per hour. The act also capped the maximum workweek at 44 hours, requiring that employers pay employees' overtime, or extra pay, for hours worked beyond 44 hours. The Fair Labor Standards Act also banned children under the age of 16 from working in manufacturing plants or during school hours.

During this period, Roosevelt proposed the addition of more justices to the Supreme Court, in the hopes of preventing more of his New Deal plans from being found unconstitutional. In so doing, Roosevelt lost some traction, even among his own party, some of who were concerned by his efforts to expand his power and pack the Supreme Court with justices who favored his New Deal.

As has been shown, the New Deal brought considerable and immediate relief to millions of Americans. Many who had been unemployed found jobs, those who couldn't afford food found some relief in the prices of particular foods, and many who had lacked housing secured homes. Nevertheless, the New Deal failed to meet all of the goals that it set out to accomplish. By 1940, still eight million Americans were out of work.

In addition to failing to meet some of its goals, the New Deal cost Americans billions of dollars. Roosevelt and New Deal Democrats aimed to spend in order to help America regain its economic strength, and in the process, spent much more money than was collected in taxes. Such exorbitant federal spending programs meant that the government ran some of the greatest deficits in its history. The federal deficit nearly doubled as a result of New Deal spending, growing from $22.5 billion in 1933 to $40.5 billion in 1939.

Most historians and economists agree that the true catalyst for the nation's recovery from the Great Depression was not the First and Second New Deals, but

Franklin Delano Roosevelt Memorial.

rather the onset of World War II. Military spending, growth in manufacturing of weapons and other war materials, as well as the employing of more workers to serve in the military and in manufacturing offered Americans true, lasting recovery from the Great Depression. America also benefitted from the war being fought on distant soil; the country did not have to rebuild from wartime destruction.

Nevertheless, the New Deal brought about lasting change through many of its pieces of legislation, particularly in the area of labor and social security. With these acts the government became and remains a primary player in the economy of the United States. The government also became the primary provider of welfare programs, and a supporter of powerful labor movements.

The New Deal also meant tremendous growth in the power and influence of the Democratic Party. Democrats were the majority party during the Civil War, but became major power players as a result of Roosevelt's successes and the New Deal. The Democratic Party also become less of a party for those in the rural South; it began appealing to workers, immigrants, union members, and elite reformers in the North.

DUST BOWL

Furthering the effects of the Depression, particularly in the West, was the **Dust Bowl**, a period of serve dust storms that nearly crippled the prairie and surrounding regions. The severe storms plagued the prairies of the United States and Canada from 1930 to 1936, and were caused by severe droughts and over-farming.

During the Roaring Twenties, farmers in the West farmed extensively, and enjoyed a long stretch of wet weather and ample rains. During this period, farmers worked the land without allowing it to lie fallow, without rotating crops, without planting crops that restored nutrients to the soil, and without employing other methods to prevent erosion and land damage. The grasses of the plains, which had held down the soil for millenia, were replaced by food crops. When dry weather hit, these crops were wiped away, leaving the soil to dry, turn to dust, and be carried off by high winds.

The Dust Bowl blew dust from the Midwest toward the East and South. The dust created large black clouds, blackening cities as far as the East Coast, including Washington, D.C., and New York City. After crippling these cities, the dust clouds blew out to the Atlantic Ocean, where they were ultimately deposited. These dark black storms were called Black Rollers and Black Blizzards, and made visibility nearly impossible. In fact, many Americans reported that they could not see more than a few feet within one of these Black Blizzards. The storms crippled work, transportation, and daily life in a nation already plagued by economic catastrophe.

The Dust Bowl was concentrated in New Mexico, Colorado, Kansas, and the Texas and Oklahoma panhandles, affecting nearly 100 million acres of land. Many farms in the region simply could not produce crops. The Dust Bowl compounded the effects of the Great Depression, causing even more Americans to be out of work.

The Dust Bowl left over 500,000 Americans homeless. In addition, thousands of Dust Bowl residents contracted dust pneumonia and other diseases; many died. Thousands of others left their farms and homes and headed east or far west in search of homes and work. Many of these people came to be known as Okies, since many came from Oklahoma, and settled in California and other states where the living was better than on farms destroyed by the Dust Bowl. These Okies frequently worked as migrant workers, which means they moved from field to field in search of work. John Steinbeck—and other authors—wrote about their plight in celebrated works such as *The Grapes of Wrath* and *Of Mice and Men*.

DUST BOWL A period of serve dust storms that nearly crippled the prairie and surrounding regions.

STUDY ALERT

The Dust Bowl refers to a series of severe dust storms that crippled the American Plains during the Great Depression. The Dust Bowl resulted from severe drought and over-farming, and caused thousands of Americans to lose their homes, move to other states, and fall ill.

HISTORY COMES TO LIFE

Steinbeck's Grapes of Wrath includes this conversation between a tenant farmer and a tractor driver who has been instructed to bulldoze straight lines in a field, even if it means driving over homes.

"And that reminds me," the driver said, "you better get out soon. I'm going through the dooryard after dinner."

"You filled in the well this morning."

"I know. Had to keep the line straight. But I'm going through the dooryard after dinner. Got to keep the lines straight. And—well, you know Joe Davis, my old man, so I'll tell you this. I got orders wherever there's a family not moved out—if I have an accident—you know, get too close and cave the house in a little—well, I might get a couple of dollars. And my youngest kid never had no shoes yet."

END OF CHAPTER TAKE-AWAYS

- **The Great Depression:** A period from 1929 to the late 1930s, marked by the Stock Market Crash of 1929, bank and business failures, high unemployment and inflation, widespread homelessness, and disease.
- **Housing Market:** During the 1920s, home loans were readily available and many people built or bought homes with the expectation of prices continually going up. This boom ended promptly during the beginning of the Great Depression, and millions of Americans lost their homes.
- **Black Monday:** Monday, October 28, 1929, the day shares on the New York Stock Exchange suffered an unprecedented drop in value.
- **Hoover's Plan:** President Herbert Hoover believed that creating efficiencies and removing inefficient government and business practices were sufficient to get the United States out of the Great Depression.
- **First and Second New Deals:** Plans authored and directed by President Franklin D. Roosevelt, Democratic leaders, and Congress in the 1930s in an effort to mitigate the effects of the Great Depression.
- **Dust Bowl:** A series of severe dust storms that crippled the American Plains during the Great Depression. The Dust Bowl came as a result of severe drought and over-farming, and caused thousands of Americans to lose their homes, move to other states, and fall ill.

REFERENCES

Burg, D. F. *The Great Depression*. (1996). New York: Facts on File, Inc.

Kennedy, D. M. (1999). *Freedom from fear: The American people in depression and war 1929–1945*. New York: Oxford University Press.

McElvaine, R. S. (1984). *The Great Depression*. New York: Times Books.

Shlaes, A. (2008). *The forgotten man: A new history of the Great Depression*. New York: Harper Perennial.

Steinbeck, J. (1992). *The grapes of wrath*. New York: Penguin Books.

Watkins, T. H. (1993). *The Great Depression: America in the 1930s*. Boston: Little, Brown.

World War II

World War II was the defining event of the twentieth century. Never before had so many men entered battle at one time. Never before had civilians joined the fray on such a massive scale. Never before had an industrial society been so focused on the destruction of an enemy.

Sixty years after the attack on Pearl Harbor, enemies again attacked the United States on its home soil. The terrorist attacks of September 11, 2001 share many parallels with the tragedy that spurred the United States to join the Second World War in 1941. Both attacks shocked a nation at peace. Both attacks caused the death of thousands. Both attacks provoked the United States to engage in extended and complex wars far away from home. Profound ideological differences also fueled both wars. In 2001, a militant terrorist enemy opposed to democratic ideals challenged the United States. In World War II, the United States found itself in the middle of two extreme political systems: fascism on one extreme, and communism on the other.

APPEASEMENT

For the United States, the two decades between the end of the First World War and the start of the Second were tumultuous. The Great Depression devastated America financially: one in every four workers lost his job, and millions lost their homes or businesses. As the 1930s wore on, Americans were aware of rising tensions in Europe, but they resisted being drawn into far-off disputes. In the minds of many, America's involvement in the First World War had been a mistake. Even though President Wilson had negotiated the Treaty of Versailles and introduced the idea of a League of Nations, Congress later rejected the charter, and the United States never took its seat at the League. As many as 37 million soldiers and civilians died worldwide during World War I, at least 116,000 from the United States. American isolationism reached its height in the late 1930s with the passage of the Neutrality Acts, designed to prevent the United States from choosing sides in what many saw as the inevitable European war to come. In this way, American isolationism effectively appeased aggression rather than standing up to it. The policy of **appeasement** guaranteed that sooner or later war would come.

APPEASEMENT The foreign policy of attempting to pacify expansionist nations by making small concessions instead of openly engaging in war.

Failure of Versailles

The Treaty of Versailles was controversial from its initial signing in 1919. The "Big Four" victorious nations—France, Great Britain, the United States, and Italy—set terms that were extremely harsh on Germany, which lost all of its colonies, the vast majority of its army, and a great deal of territory.

In addition to these losses, Germany was forced to agree to pay massive war reparations. The timetable for these payments stretched decades into the future. In fact, the schedule called for Germany's last reparations to the United States to be paid in 2020. To ensure that the payments were made on time, French troops occupied Germany's industrial heartland, the Ruhr Valley.

The entire German nation despised the terms of the treaty. The mix of military occupation and economic deprivation was doubly humiliating and bred resentment. Much of that anger was aimed at the new German government that the Big Four created to replace the old monarchy. The Weimar Republic—named for the city that became its capital—was tainted from its earliest days with the stigma of signing the treaty. Its leaders, however, had no say in the terms of the treaty because Germany had been so utterly defeated at the end of the war.

The French and British negotiators felt justified imposing difficult terms on Germany, because they had suffered devastating losses of money and men. French leaders were especially embittered toward Germany, as 1.3 million French soldiers had been killed in action during the war. An additional million Frenchmen emerged from the war crippled. Many British referred to the time as a "generation without fathers," because approximately one-third of all British men sent to war did not return due to being killed in battle, being gassed in trenches, or succumbing to disease.

President Woodrow Wilson worried that the treaty demanded too much of Germany, but his main interest in the negotiations lay in the creation of the League of Nations. He allowed France and Britain to set the terms for Germany in exchange for their support in the creation of the world's first permanent international body. Little did he know that Germany's anger would doom the League of Nations and its mission to promote international peace and cooperation. Moreover, the League was undermined at its birth by Wilson's inability to convince the U.S. Congress to ratify its charter, leaving the United States powerless to assert its influence when it might have done the most good. During this time, Wilson suffered a stroke that left him unable to promote the League and barely able to hold onto life.

Rise of Hitler

Adolf Hitler came from a humble background and suffered many setbacks in the course of his early career. During the First World War he served in the trenches as a corporal and was wounded in a mustard gas attack. When peace came in 1918 he was recovering in a hospital. He joined the German Worker's Party within months, however, and was in the streets criticizing the terms of Versailles to all who would listen.

For much of the 1920s, few people listened closely to what Hitler and other extremist politicians had to say. The country turned its attention to rebuilding a society and economy that had been greatly damaged by years of all-out war. The Weimar Republic was the first taste of democracy most Germans had ever experienced, and reactions ranged from exhilaration to disorientation.

Weimar has been criticized as an inherently flawed, unpopular, and weak regime, but it survived some severe challenges Germany faced in the 1920s. Its leaders successfully quelled armed insurrections by extremists on the political left and right. In 1923, the administration also overcame Germany's worst period of **hyperinflation**, when the deutsche mark became practically worthless and families' savings were exhausted by buying necessities. The height of the crisis saw Germans pushing wheelbarrows full of paper money to the bakery to purchase a loaf of bread.

HYPERINFLATION A condition when money becomes increasingly worthless. This occurred in Germany between the First and Second World Wars

What ultimately doomed Weimar and cleared the path for Hitler's Nazi regime was political instability. Many different factions in German society formed small parties, which then had to form coalition (or partnership) governments in order to wield power. These coalitions had a tendency to fall apart as various party leaders vied for power. Nothing seemed to get done in the capital, and most people grew disillusioned with the Weimar Constitution.

In this environment, deeply conservative and nationalist forces associated with the army grew steadily in influence. Many right-wing nationalists had never wanted a democratic system of government in the first place. They did not trust the workers and their unions, nor did they like the socialist and left-wing parties for whom the workers tended to vote. As Weimar floundered, it became easier to portray the government as beholden to radicals and workers' unions. By stressing Weimar's association with the hated Treaty of Versailles, conservative politicians undermined popular support for democracy itself. Everything that had happened after 1918 was tainted by the defeat and humiliation of the army and the nation.

Hitler's National Socialist Party (NSDAP) was only a minor player in German politics for much of the 1920s. While imprisoned in 1924 for leading an unsuccessful uprising, Hitler wrote the first draft of *Mein Kampf* (*My Struggle*). This is both the story of Hitler's early life and the political manifesto that made him a rising political star. By the end of the 1920s, Hitler's rhetorical abilities and ruthless style of leadership brought the Nazis greater and greater power, and in 1932, when the

Weimar Republic was on the brink of falling apart, he convinced the senile and dying President von Hindenburg to appoint him chancellor. A few weeks later there was a fire in parliament (the Reichstag), for which a Dutch communist was tried and sentenced to death. At this point, the Nazis suspended most German civil rights, arrested their political enemies, and seized power for good.

Imperial Japan

Japan was particularly hard-hit by the global depression of the 1930s. The country had seen massive and rapid industrialization in the preceding decades, including a boom in population and a mass migration of farmers into cities to become factory workers. At the same time, however, Japan's ability to trade goods and food was limited by the protectionist policies of Europe and the United States. Every country was trying to protect its own workforce and industries from foreign competition during the economic downturn. The result was that international trade shrank rapidly, as did everyone's gross domestic product (GDP).

The economic crisis rocked Japan's fragile democratic government. Tensions threatened to boil over between the traditional Samurai elite and the newly wealthy industrial class. Traditionalists had a strong grip on Japan's armed forces, while the westernized industrial class congregated in growing urban centers such as Tokyo.

As the 1930s progressed, right-wing militants pressed the emperor and parliament to adopt a more aggressive position in international relations. They raised concerns about the harmful influence westernization was having on Japanese society and urged a greater reverence for the emperor and Japanese tradition.

Japanese militants also believed that their country had been slighted by foreign powers that raised tariffs on Japanese goods and refused to allow immigration from Japan for blatantly racial reasons. Japan needed new sources of raw materials and

cheap food to feed its growth, but most of Asia was already under the control of western imperial powers. To the right-wing, it seemed the deck was stacked against Japan, and nothing short of military action would enable the country to claim its rightful place in the world. As far as they were concerned, that place was as the dominant power in East Asia.

Japan did have a foothold on the Asian mainland, and it was here that it took its first steps of aggressive expansion. With its victory over Russia in the Russo-Japanese War of 1905, Japan had won territory on the Liaotung Peninsula in Manchuria (Northeastern China). In 1919, Japan established the Kwantung Army to protect railway traffic within its Manchurian colony. Acting independently from the Japanese prime minister, the Kwantung Army hatched a plot to take over all of Manchuria. On September 18, 1931, the Kwantung Army alleged that a South Manchurian Railway train under its protection had been attacked by Chinese soldiers. Officers of the Kwantung Army used this phony incident as a justification to capture the city of Mukden.

Once the Japanese authorities discovered what was going on, they tried in vain to reestablish control over the rogue military officers in Mukden. This incident, however, was indicative of larger changes to come. In May 1932, army officers in Tokyo staged a violent rebellion. The prime minister, Inukai Tsuyoshi, was killed. Eventually order was reestablished and the rebel officers were executed, but popular sentiment was shifting away from the weakened civilian authorities toward the increasingly powerful military.

Japan's aggression in Manchuria led to an increase in criticism from the international community. In 1932, for example, the League of Nations demanded that Japan withdraw from Manchuria immediately. Instead, Japan left the League of Nations the following year. Japan pretended to address this criticism by reestablishing former Manchu Emperor Puyi, but in reality Japan retained its domination of the area and even renamed it "Manchukuo."

The events in Manchuria exposed the fundamental weakness of Japan's civilian government, the rising power of the military authorities, and the ambivalent attitude of the Japanese people toward modernization and western influence. The emperor tried to straddle these conflicting forces within Japanese society, but was powerless to prevent the actions that were being taken in his name.

Lend-Lease Act

The rise of Hitler and the changes in imperial Japan had little effect on U.S. policy or action. Revulsion against the bloodbath of the First World War led the western democracies to embrace internationalism and reject the stockpiling of military weapons. In the 1920s, people believed that the harsh lessons of modern warfare had been learned, and that WWI was truly the war to end all wars (in fact, it was called the Great War until hostilities broke out yet again at the opening of World War II). Yet already by 1922 Benito Mussolini had gained control of Italy, becoming the first of Europe's fascist strongmen. Mussolini openly mocked the continent's pacifist tendencies, remilitarizing his country and setting an important example for Hitler in Germany. As the fascists flexed their muscles in Europe and Japanese militarists did the same in Asia, western leaders alternated empty threats with open appeasement. Neither worked.

By the late 1930s it was beginning to dawn on the British, American, and French leaders that the fascists were set on remilitarization, but no one knew what Hitler's ultimate goal actually was. Did he mean to acquire control of neighboring lands for the *lebensraum* (living space) he insisted Germany needed? Or was he bluffing to enhance his prestige and consolidate power at home?

France and Britain struggled to balance a desire to believe that the terms of Versailles made another war unlikely with the need to develop a pragmatic national security strategy. As a result, military spending dried up nearly completely in Great Britain and France during the 1920s. France pinned all its hopes on hundreds of miles of fixed artillery and fortifications called the **Maginot Line**. French military officers expected that if Germany did manage to rearm itself, it would take an invasion route similar to the one it took in World War I. It did not to occur to the French that invading armies could sidestep these batteries and ambush their otherwise defenseless troops, which is what happened once the war began.

Great Britain and the United States were no bet-

LEBENSRAUM a German word meaning *living space*; Hitler claimed the German people needed more room to live and used this idea as a reason for his expansionist goals.

MAGINOT LINE An ineffective line of defense established by the French along its border with Germany.

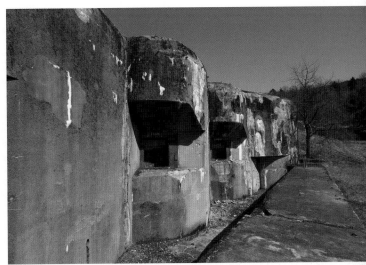

The Maginot Line.

ter prepared for war against Germany and Japan than were the French. They were, however, luckier in terms of geography. While France was exposed to invasion by a long eastern border, Britain was protected by the English Channel and the North Atlantic Sea. The United States felt even more secure, bordered by oceans on either side. This sense of security was unrealistic, however: advances in airplane warfare made the world a much smaller place.

In addition to this false sense of security, there were two other major obstacles that kept democratic leaders from taking action. The first obstacle was a dreadful lack of military power; twenty years of paltry spending and inadequate training had left most nations vulnerable to attack. The second obstacle was the reluctance of the voting public to acknowledge the growing threats to peace. Both the British and American public wished to believe that their leaders could avoid a new war, or at least leave their countries unscathed by one.

While France, Britain, and the United States were busy hoping for war not to happen, Hitler and Mussolini took advantage of the lack of international response. Germany expanded into Austria with little global outrage. In September 1938, British Prime Minister Neville Chamberlain flew to Munich to sign away parts of Czechoslovakia with the hope of guaranteeing "peace for our time." This was the final unsuccessful attempt to appease German expansion.

In September 1939, Germany invaded Poland, which launched the Second World War. Germany had earlier agreed (in a secret non-aggression pact with Soviet Premier Joseph Stalin) to split Poland down the middle, keeping the western half and giving the eastern half to the Soviets. Poland, however, was protected by iron-clad treaties with France and Great Britain, meaning that an invasion of its territory automatically triggered a declaration of war by both major powers.

Hitler believed that France and Britain would abandon its promises to Poland, as they had with Austria and Czechoslovakia, but he was wrong. In Great Britain, Chamberlain recognized what a mistake he had made in trusting Hitler's promises, while French Prime Minister Édouard Daladier knew this was the allies' final chance to halt German aggression. Still, even with the backing of France and Great Britain, Poland quickly succumbed to Germany's *blitzkrieg* (lightning war) tactics.

It fell to a new Prime Minister, Winston Churchill, and to his staunch ally, U.S. President Franklin D. Roosevelt, to convince their respective constituents that war was necessary. Unlike totalitarian states seen as Nazi Germany or Stalinist Russia, democracies rely on the support of citizens, soldiers, and manufacturers to convert to a war-footing. The process could not be rushed.

While this process took place, much of continental Europe fell to the Germans. Over the eight months after invading Poland, they cleared a path through Scandinavia, conquered Belgium and the Netherlands, and arrived on France's doorstep. In May 1940, German tanks and troops sidestepped the Maginot Line by plowing through the Ardennes Forest, splitting the allied forces in two. More than 300,000 Allied troops were rescued from German capture by an extraordinary flotilla consisting of everything

BLITZKRIEG A method of warfare perfected by Hitler's forces that shocked enemies with its speed and power.

from naval vessels to private yachts and fishing dinghies that sailed from Dunkirk on the French coast to England in late May and early June.

Europe was left reeling from the devastatingly effective German tactics. France was conquered, and only a daring ragtag expedition had prevented Britain from being taken out of the war as well. For the next year, Great Britain fought on completely alone.

One of the most trying times of the war for Britain occurred from May through October 1940. The **Battle of Britain** was waged almost entirely over the skies of Great Britain. At its outset, most believed that Germany would prevail, but Britain had several key strengths that permitted it to survive the assault that had knocked out nine other European powers. Foremost among these was a highly sophisticated air defense infrastructure called the *Dowding System*. The aircraft of the Royal Air Force (RAF) also had some advantages over the German air force, called the *Luftwaffe*. Over the course of the battle, German strategy evolved. At first the attacks concentrated on coastal airfields and command centers; by late summer, however, German bombers focused their raids on London and other urban centers in an effort to demoralize the civilian population and force Britain to surrender. Although these bombing raids killed more than 30,000 civilians, British morale was bolstered by the sight of King George and Queen Elizabeth in Buckingham Palace and by Churchill's stirring speeches in which he assured his people that this was "their finest hour." By thwarting the Luftwaffe's attack, the British prevented an invasion of their homeland and gave future allies such as the United States time to prepare.

In Washington, D.C., President Roosevelt looked on in horror and frustration. He was prevented from lending much more than moral support to Great Britain by a series of laws passed by Congress in the 1920s that aimed to keep the United States out of foreign entanglements by making it illegal to sell arms to any party engaged in military conflict. The 1920s and '30s were a time of extreme isolationism in the United States. Politicians from both parties shunned the internationalism that had inspired Woodrow Wilson to commit American troops to World War I. This was part of the reason the U.S. legislature never ratified the charter of the League of Nations and generally remained leery of taking sides in any European conflict.

As Roosevelt came to understand Britain's position in the war, he stressed repeatedly in speeches to Congress and the American public the dangers posed by German (and Japanese) aggression. He warned that if Britain fell, no allies would remain capable of fighting alongside American troops. The United States would be alone and extremely vulnerable to militarists with global ambitions.

In 1939, the president persuaded Congress to repeal the law against selling weapons to nations at war. This permitted the United States to sell arms to Great Britain, but only as long as they had sufficient cash to afford them. By the end of 1940, that cash was gone. So Roosevelt and his aides came up with a plan that allowed the United States to lend over $50 billion worth of arms to the Allied countries with no cash expected up-front. Known as the **Lend-Lease Plan,** this strategy kept the Allies supplied long enough for the American public to recognize that it had little choice but to join the war.

BATTLE OF BRITAIN Britain's defense of Germany's costly attempt to defeat Churchill by bombing British civilian centers such as London.

LEND-LEASE PLAN President Roosevelt's strategy for aiding Allied forces by supplying them with much-needed supplies.

DID YOU KNOW?

When they were debating the issue of providing arms to Great Britain (and if so, on what terms?) many American politicians raised the poor record of its World War I allies in repaying their loans as an example of the unreliability of such arrangements. In point of fact, the only country to repay its World War I loans to the United States was Finland, and they only completed their payments in 1976! Clearly, lending allies money with which to buy weapons was not a very good investment, which is why Roosevelt pressed the idea of common history and democratic ideals over financial gain.

PEARL HARBOR

In the decade that followed Japan's takeover of Manchuria in 1931, the United States watched with apprehension as Japan become increasingly aggressive toward its Asian neighbors. American diplomats and politicians attempted to curb Japanese militarism through harsh trade sanctions during the 1930s, to no effect. In fact, they inadvertently strengthened the hand of Japanese militarists, who argued that the United States was an unreliable trading partner whose treatment of Japan was tinged by a feeling of racial superiority.

Another event to increase the strain on the diplomatic relations between Imperial Japan and the United States occurred in 1937, when a Japanese air attack sank a U.S. gun boat patrolling the Yangtze River in China. While Japanese forces claimed not to have known that the vessel belonged to the Americans and also paid reparations for the damages, the sinking of the *USS Panay* made U.S. political leaders more skeptical of Japanese intentions.

By 1941 America's political leaders knew that Japan was interested in staging an attack on U.S. interests, because its spies had successfully deciphered the secret code Japan used to send diplomatic and military cables around the world. It was for this reason that the U.S. military had moved its entire Pacific Fleet to the naval base at **Pearl Harbor** in Hawaii. At the time Hawaii was a U.S. territory, not yet a state. Pearl Harbor occupied a key position in the strategically important South Pacific region, halfway between the West Coast and Japan, and it seemed a safe place to maintain a large reserve of warships and aircraft until they were needed. The United States also stopped shipping oil to Japan in an effort to quell its rapidly militarizing government.

That safety was an illusion, however, shattered on the morning of December 7, 1941. Japan launched wave after wave of bombers armed with specially adapted torpedoes to destroy American ships as they lay docked in the harbor. Thousands of sailors were still asleep in their bunks. Well over 2,400 soldiers and sailors were killed and nearly a thousand more were injured. Hundreds of aircraft were destroyed as they sat on the tarmac. The Pacific Fleet was decimated.

A Day of Infamy

The attack on Pearl Harbor destroyed the last vestiges of American isolationism and brought World War II directly to the American people. On December 8, President Franklin Roosevelt addressed Congress to demand they declare war on Japan, which they promptly did. Calling December 7 "a day which will live in infamy," Roosevelt called on the nation to dedicate itself to defeating Japan and avenging the deaths of the more than 2,400 servicemen who died at Pearl Harbor.

Pearl Harbor became a symbol for Americans of the dangers of complacency and isolationism. The size of the United States and the critical role it played in the global economy meant it no longer had the luxury of avoiding foreign entanglements, as it did in its early days. The United States had the option of entering the First World War, and only did so at a late stage, on its own terms. America's entry into World War II, however, was

PEARL HARBOR The location of a naval base in Hawaii, where on December 7, 1941, Japanese bombers destroyed the U.S. Pacific Fleet in a surprise attack; this event directly caused the United States to join the fighting of World War II.

STUDY ALERT

American Isolationism: Before World War II Americans believed that their geography—protected as they are by two oceans—meant that they could stay out of foreign entanglements. Just as western Europeans learned that they could not appease tyrants such as Hitler, the United States learned that it was better to remain engaged in foreign affairs than to wait until war was inevitable.

unavoidable. And thanks to Japan's alliance with the other Axis powers, Germany and Italy, the United States was soon drawn into the European theater of war as well.

Many scholars have drawn parallels between Pearl Harbor and the surprise attacks on the United States launched by *al Qaeda* on September 11, 2001. In both instances, there were certainly warnings of impending trouble, but no specific information as to the time or place of the attacks. The attacks on September 11 resulted in 3,000 deaths. The attacks of September 11 also led the United States into protracted wars, this time in Afghanistan and Iraq.

THE PACIFIC THEATER

Immediately after Pearl Harbor, Japan launched other invasions across Southeast Asia. Japan's goal was to strike swiftly against the Allies before they had a chance to reinforce their defenses, in the same manner as the German *blitzkrieg*. By late spring 1942 they had swept across the Malay Peninsula and taken two significant parts of the British Empire, Hong Kong and Singapore.

The bombing of Pearl Harbor provoked the United States to ramp up its military production on a scale never before seen. Roosevelt vowed to produce 60,000 aircraft and 75,000 thousand tanks, in addition to numerous warships that would replace and expand upon the fleet lost at Pearl Harbor. Of tremendous importance to the Allied war effort was the deciphering of Japan's naval communications code in mid-1942. With this knowledge, the U.S. Navy was able to thwart a Japanese attack on Port Morseby, thereby safeguarding Australia from invasion. Furthermore, in June 1942, U.S. naval forces were waiting near Midway Island in the central Pacific when the Japanese launched a massive attack on the strategically important base. The Battle of Midway became a major turning point in the war: Japan lost four aircraft carriers and hundreds of aircraft. After this battle, Japan never launched another offensive in the Pacific.

The following three years of the war were marked by intense fighting, most of it taking place on small tropical islands. Guadalcanal was one such island, fought over by American and Japanese forces for six months in late 1942 and early 1943. The Allies' hard-fought victory there foreshadowed later campaigns in the Solomon Islands and New Guinea. The most brutal battles, however, came in the final year of the war, when Japanese forces struggled to defend their heavily fortified positions on Iwo Jima and Okinawa. The closer Allied forces came to the Japanese homeland, the more fierce each battle became.

INTERNMENT The detention of Japanese Americans as a part of the U.S. response to the bombing of Pearl Harbor.

Internment

Pearl Harbor also led the U.S. government to round up 120,000 Japanese Americans living on the West Coast and force them to relocate hundreds of miles from the coast to one of ten large **internment** centers. This was all done in the name of protecting the homeland. Two-thirds

Japanese-American internment camp wall.

Race and the War in the Pacific: There is no doubt that racial tensions contributed to the deterioration of U.S.–Japanese relations in the decades before World War II. After the attack on Pearl Harbor, however, mistrust of Japanese Americans became so strong that the government forced approximately 120,000 of them into internment camps for the rest of the war. It is also true that Japanese treatment of American prisoners of war was brutal, and the refusal of Japan to surrender even after its leaders knew it could not win reinforced American stereotypes about Japanese fanaticism.

VJ DAY The name given to the day of Japanese surrender, which can refer to August 14, 1945 (the initial day of surrender) or September 2, 1945 (the day on which the official surrender document was signed).

DOUGLAS MacARTHUR

of those interned were U.S. citizens, and the rest were resident aliens or illegal immigrants. None were ever charged with a crime. Yet they spent the entire war living in primitive barracks surrounded by barbed wire and guard towers.

Dr. Seuss

You may be surprised to learn that Dr. Seuss was a political cartoonist in the early 1940s. While some of his cartoons criticized the racist aspects of contemporary society, he defended the U.S. internment of Japanese Americans.

The Intensity of the Japanese Fighters

War in the Pacific was marked by a degree of intensity and raw brutality that differentiated it somewhat from the battlefield in Europe. Japanese soldiers were responsible for horrific atrocities against civilian and military targets alike. One of the most infamous episodes was the Rape of Nanjing in 1937–38, when more than 250,000 Chinese civilians were abused and murdered over a four-month period.

Another instance occurred in April 1942, when a large contingent of U.S. and Filipino soldiers surrendered to Japanese forces on the Bataan Peninsula in the Philippines and they were forced to march at bayonet-point without food or water through sixty miles of jungle. This tragedy marked the largest surrender of U.S.-led military forces in the nation's history. A thousand men died on the side of the road during the Bataan Death March, and thousands more perished in the malarial prison camps to which they were consigned.

The fighting style exhibited by the Japanese in the Pacific inspired a visceral hatred on the part of those forced to fight them. A marine who fought on the island of Peleliu described seeing the mutilated corpse of a fellow American and his emotional response, "From that moment on I never felt the least pity or compassion for them no matter what the circumstances." That marine, E.B. Sledge, later wrote and taught about his wartime experiences. He claimed that this hatred burned in the heart of every marine, and that it allowed him to survive and fight on under appalling conditions.

VJ Day

Under the leadership of General Douglas MacArthur, the U.S. forces conducted a strategy of island hopping, taking on the entrenched Japanese forces one island at a time, en route to Japan. Each island posed its own set of problems for the Americans and none was easily taken. The end of the war came suddenly when the Americans deployed the newly engineered atomic bomb, destroying the cities of Hiroshima and Nagasaki on August 6 and August 9, respectively. On August 14, 1945 news spread of Japan's initial surrender. Though the official surrender ceremony would occur later, this day, known as **VJ Day** (Victory over Japan), effectively marked the end of the Pacific war. While there is debate among contemporary historians about the necessity and morality of dropping the atomic bombs, doing so unquestionably saved the Allied troops from having to invade mainland Japan. The invasion of Japan, scheduled for 1946, would have cost the lives of at least a half million Allied soldiers and countless Japanese civilians and military personnel.

MID-CHAPTER QUESTIONS

1. In what ways did the failures of the Treaty of Versailles set the stage for the rise of Hitler and World War II? Discuss what the winners hoped the treaty would accomplish, and why the Germans hated it so much.

2. What similarities do you see between the Japanese attack on Pearl Harbor in 1941 and the September 11, 2011 attacks by al Qaeda? What inspired each? How did the United States respond to the attacks? Were those responses justified?

3. What was going on in Japan and the world during the 1930s that contributed to the rise of militarism there? How did the Depression affect Japan? What did Japan hope to gain through its aggression?

MacArthur

General MacArthur was the U.S. figure most closely associated with the war effort in the Pacific. He was a brash but brilliant military leader. Before the war, MacArthur had been stationed in the Philippines. He was a natural-born showman who was a favorite of the wartime press. Photos of him with his trademark corn-cob pipe and dark sunglasses made him enormously popular with the American public, but his relations with his military commanders and civilian strategists were notoriously rocky. He was seen as a loose cannon who could not always be relied upon to follow orders.

On September 2, 1945, MacArthur presided over the official Japanese surrender ceremony on behalf of all the Allies. Shortly thereafter he became the supreme commander of the Allied powers in Japan. Although the nominal head of state was the emperor, in reality MacArthur had almost complete control over the reconstruction of Japan. He oversaw the writing of a new constitution, the creation of a new educational system, and the enactment of major social reforms.

THE EUROPEAN THEATER

On the other side of the globe, the European theater was divided between the Eastern and Western fronts. In the early stages of the war, Hitler was successful in his intention to open only one front at a time. He managed this through the negotiation of canny alliances. The most important of these was the non-aggression pact with Stalin, which allowed Germany free reign in Poland and Central Europe. Hitler then turned his attention to countries to the north and west of Germany, swiftly conquering them or establishing docile regimes.

However, by the end of 1940 Hitler had grown irritated by the two remaining independent European powers: Great Britain and the Soviet Union. He could not convince the British to make peace, despite the massive bombing raids of the Battle of Britain and submarine attacks on British supply ships that left the country short of food and war materials. So he instructed his generals to plan an invasion of the Soviet Union, hoping that by eliminating his last potential rival on the continent he could consolidate his gains and force Britain to succumb. Hitler's plan to invade the Soviet Union was called *Operation Barbarossa*. It became the largest organized military invasion in history—as well as one of the bloodiest--and it failed to achieve Hitler's aims. Germany's losses in the Battle of Stalingrad and the eventual failure of the entire operation paralleled the failure of Napoleon to overtake the same lands some 130 years before and also marked a decisive turning point in the progression of the war. It is nearly impossible to overstate the extent of the losses to both sides during this phase of the war; the casualties were well into the millions and entire areas along the Eastern Front were annihilated.

Holocaust

While Hitler's generals were pursuing the enemy abroad, his agents inside Germany and occupied Europe were moving against the minority groups that Hitler had long identified as the enemy within. At the top of the list were Europe's Jews, but Hitler also despised the Roma (Gypsies), homosexuals, the mentally ill, and communists. These groups were identified and persecuted, stripped of their legal rights and possessions, and finally sent to concentration camps where they were used as slave labor, continually abused, and in many cases, eventually killed.

Starting in 1942, Heinrich Himmler began implementation of the "final solution," the systematic execution of millions of Jews and other minorities. Himmler was the head of the SS, which had evolved from a paramilitary organization in the early days of the Nazi Party into an elite, separate branch of the armed services. The final solution resulted in the death of an estimated 6 million European Jews. Hitler's obsession with murdering these civilians ultimately interfered with his efforts to take over all of Europe. In the later stages of the war, when things were starting to go badly for the German army, trains (and the scarce fuel to run them) continued to send victims to the death camps at a furious pace. Hitler drove away or alienated many of the people he most needed to make his war machine run, including a number of Jewish scientists who fled the country and helped the Allies defeat him instead (including several key nuclear scientists who worked on the Manhattan Project and developed the first atomic weapons).

HOLOCAUST The Nazi's persecution and execution of millions of Europe's Jews and minorities.

Since the end of the war and the full revelation of the horrors of the **Holocaust**, many have wondered why the United States did not do more to prevent or deter the tragedy. During the 1930s, when it would have been possible to accept more refugees fleeing from Hitler's Europe, the United States barred entry to all but a few, arguing that economic conditions did not permit large-scale immigration. Anti-Semitism played a part in U.S. policy, but isolationism was equally important. During the war, as more information about the death camps leaked out, attempts were made to convince U.S. leaders to bomb the camps or the rail lines that supplied them. Neither suggestion was taken up, though a war factory just outside the

Auschwitz-Birkenau death camp was bombed in mid-1944. Historians continue to debate to what extent Allied leaders were aware of these crimes before the final months of the war, and the sluggishness of U.S. war planners to take action.

D-Day

At the end of 1943, the Big Three (Stalin, Roosevelt, and Churchill) met to discuss Allied strategy in Tehran, Iran. Their most important decision was to begin planning for an all-out invasion of occupied France that spring. Code-named "Operation Overlord," the Americans and British (with input from the leaders of the French Resistance) began sketching the plans for what came to be known as **D-Day**.

The invasion was a massive undertaking, and the outcome of the war hinged upon its success. Secrecy was critical, as was intelligence-gathering by the French Resistance. There were also numerous diversions and distractions involved, designed to confuse the Germans into thinking the Allies were landing in one place (Calais, France) when in fact the landing site was hundreds of miles away (on the beaches of Normandy).

Finally, on June 6, 1944, more than 150,000 men landed on five beaches on the coast of Normandy. The code names of these beaches are immortalized in the history books: Gold, Juno, Sword, Utah, and Omaha. The troops were transported in 10,000 aircraft, 1,500 hundred warships, and over 4,000 landing craft. They were greeted by a frenzy of bullets and mortar shells that claimed thousands of lives before they could even find their bearings. Yet at the end of the day, the Allies had gained a beachhead, and from then on the retreat of German forces from occupied territory gained momentum.

The conditions of Omaha Beach on D-Day are hard to imagine. Here is how Medal of Honor recipient Walther D. Ehlers described his experience there in an interview with Ed Tracy for the Pritzker Military Library:

> Where we landed on Easy Red [Omaha Beach] there were three pill-boxes…and on top of that there was a machine gun nest up there that was killing off our GIs like they were going out of style. [Later] we had a chance to meet that German machine gunner. He did survive the war, and he said he was shooting his machine gun and he was crying at the same time because he was killing so many men…It was kind of revealing to know that they had some feelings too. They were just like us. They were supposed to be fighting for their country. And, of course I talk to little kids…and one time a little girl asks me, "How many people did you kill?" And I said, "Honey I didn't kill any people. I wasn't trained to kill people. I was trained to kill the enemy. And if I hadn't killed them I wouldn't be here talking to you." That's the way it was there.

Though the sacrifices at D-Day were great, it marked a change in the morale of the German high command. Fierce battles remained ahead, yet after D-Day the Allies were generally on the offensive and Germany failed to retake the initiative. Not that they did not try: in the Battle of the Bulge (December 1944–January 1945), Germany made one final attempt to break the Allies' line of attack in the dense Ardennes Forest of Belgium. They nearly succeeded, but ultimately fell back. Through the

spring of 1945 the German troops retreated from the lands they had conquered back to their homeland. On the Western front they were harried by the combined armies of Great Britain, the United States, and Canada; on the Eastern front, the Soviet Union's Red Army swept across Poland and into Germany with 3 million battle-hardened soldiers and tens of thousands of tanks and artillery pieces.

VE Day

By the spring of 1945, the worst predictions of Hitler's generals had come to pass. The remnants of the German army were guarding the capital city, Berlin, where Hitler was holed up in a fortified bunker with a handful of loyalists. All around Berlin, the Soviet troops laid siege to the city, choking off food and fuel supplies. While many residents fled in advance of the dreaded Red Army, hundreds of thousands remained trapped.

On April 30, 1945, Hitler committed suicide in his Berlin bunker. A week later, on May 8, known thereafter as **VE Day** (victory in Europe), Germany surrendered unconditionally to the Allied forces, and the war in Europe was over.

VE DAY The name given to the day of German surrender on May 8, 1945.

Hitler was preceded in death by President Roosevelt, just two weeks earlier. He died with the knowledge that victory in Europe was close, but he also had come to the realization that he had placed too much trust in Stalin's promises, and that postwar Europe would be menaced by an emboldened Soviet Union. In fact, whatever territory the Soviet Army liberated in Central Europe or the Far East automatically fell under the Iron Curtain of Russian domination. In this way, the seeds of the Cold War grew out of the concluding events of the Second World War.

Eisenhower

General Dwight D. Eisenhower was the supreme Allied commander in Europe. From his headquarters in England, he oversaw the planning of the invasion of North Africa and later for the invasion of Western Europe (D-Day). "Ike," as he was popularly known, took a tremendous chance in authorizing the invasion on June 6, 1944. Publicly, Eisenhower never wavered in his determination once a decision was made, but privately he was tormented by doubts because he felt a tremendous sense of responsibility for the lives of his men. After giving the order to proceed with D-Day, he spent the evening visiting some of the troops who would carry out

HISTORY COMES ALIVE

World War II was enormously expensive. One of the ways the U.S. government paid the bills was to sell war bonds. Americans would buy the bonds for less than face value, but they could not cash them in for ten years. As the war dragged on the government had to get creative in selling these bonds. Celebrities were used to bring in crowds, who were then persuaded to buy them. One of the biggest draws after 1942 was an enormous pig from southern Illinois called King Neptune. King Neptune weighed over 700 pounds. For years he would be auctioned off, piece by piece to the highest bidder. But King Neptune never went to slaughter. Winning bidders accepted war bonds in place of bacon. In this way, $19 million in war bonds were sold to benefit the Navy's construction of the battleship Illinois, and King Neptune became a legend.

the mission the next day. While he sought to bolster their spirits, one officer later reported that Eisenhower seemed to need the morale boost more than the men did.

He guided the Allied troops through intense fighting, not simply on the battlefield, but among rival officers under his command. For example, tensions frequently flared between the British General Bernard Montgomery and the American General George Patton. Eisenhower needed to be as much diplomat as military strategist, and it was a role for which he was eminently suited. As the *New York Times* noted in his 1969 obituary: "what counted most in his generalship also impressed the voters most: an ability to harmonize diverse groups and disparate personalities into a smoothly functioning coalition."

ON THE U.S. HOME FRONT

In an age of total warfare, it was not possible to separate civilians from the battlefield, nor could any power hope to survive unless every resource at its disposal was thrown into the war effort. For U.S. civilians, this meant that every aspect of their lives changed. Food and fuel were rationed throughout the war, and the government set prices on important commodities and goods. Recycling materials such as rubber and aluminum was important, because imports were severely limited and war production took priority over all other uses.

With most young men away at the front, it was critical that women step in to take their place in the civilian work force. The cultural icon **Rosie the Riveter**, who was depicted on posters flexing her arm beneath the caption "We Can Do It!" was a mainstay of American propaganda, but women really did become a critical pool for industrial labor, along with other groups that had been excluded from these relatively high-paying jobs before the war. Women felt a sense of pride in their elevated status, and knew their efforts were essential. Each military branch also had a special auxiliary for these hardworking, brave women.

ROSIE THE RIVETER A cultural symbol that came to represent the idea that women were capable of doing work traditionally assigned to men who were away fighting in Europe and the Pacific.

President Roosevelt told the American people: "We are all in it together—all the way. Every single man, woman, and child is a partner in the most tremendous undertaking of our American history." Even children were assigned duties, whether watching younger siblings while their mother worked, tending the victory gardens that provided up to a third of the nation's vegetables, or keeping an eye out for subversives.

STUDY ALERT

Technology and War: The progress of the Manhattan Project is an example of a technological breakthrough that was accelerated by the pressures of war. Scientists from around the world had to collaborate with each other and with military and government officials.

MANHATTAN PROJECT A collaborative undertaking organized by the U.S. government that involved scientists and military engineers to develop the world's first atomic weapons.

HANFORD, WASHINGTON The location of the first large-scale nuclear reactor, which played an integral role in the creation of the first atomic bomb.

The Manhattan Project

One especially significant element of the home front was the **Manhattan Project**. In 1939 a group of prominent physicists sent President Roosevelt a letter in which they expressed their belief that recent discoveries in the field of particle physics might enable the creation of a uniquely powerful bomb.

At first Roosevelt hesitated to even discuss such an undertaking, as it seemed both implausible and ruinously expensive. However, the mostly European scientists behind the letter had taken care to recruit the famous German émigré Albert Einstein as a supporter, and a letter signed by Einstein was not easily dismissed.

By the end of the year, Roosevelt had informed Einstein that a committee had been set up to explore the possibility of using nuclear fission to create a uranium-fueled bomb. The committee was made up of scientists and representatives from the Army and Navy, as any weapon that was developed needed to be capable of being deployed to the field of battle.

Over the next five years, scientists from around the world raced to create the first atomic weapon. Although its code name was "Manhattan," the creation of the atomic bomb did not take place in New York. The most important sites for the project were Oak Ridge, Tennessee, and the University of Chicago, where much of the laboratory research took place; Los Alamos, New Mexico, where tests were conducted; and **Hanford, Washington** where the first large-scale nuclear reactor was built.

Hanford Resources

Between 1942, when the first of its reactors went online, and 1971, when its last one was shut down, Hanford produced nearly all the plutonium that America needed for its vast nuclear weapons arsenal. In the process, Hanford became one of the most highly toxic sites in the country, if not the world. Plutonium can pollute ground water, and its radioactivity takes centuries to break down. One particle of plutonium the size of a peppercorn could kill someone almost instantly through intense radioactivity, and 100 metric tons were produced during the Cold War. The Soviets had similar facilities that made far more plutonium and had fewer environmental safeguards.

Within a short time, 51,000 people were at work at the Hanford site. Some people who worked in Hanford did not even know what they were working on until after the first bombs had exploded. Anyone who talked about what went on there was fired and forced to move away. They lived in tents and army barracks until housing could be constructed for them.

Einstein on the Power of the Atom

Not long after the United States ended the war with Japan by dropping nuclear bombs on Hiroshima and Nagasaki, Einstein wrote a telegram that was printed in the *New York Times*. He observed that "the unleashed power of the atom has changed everything save our modes of thinking and we thus drift toward unparalleled catastrophe." It was an ominous statement from a scientist who had, after all, urged President Roosevelt to pursue such weapons.

Many of the scientists who participated in the Manhattan Project did so reluctantly, knowing that the product of their work—if they succeeded—might be used to kill large numbers of people. One reason these scientists participated, however, was that they knew that German scientists were racing them to produce an atomic weapon of their own. They knew that if Hitler were to obtain such a weapon first, he would not hesitate to use it.

Truman's Choices and the Japanese Reaction

After President Roosevelt's death on April 12, 1945, Vice President Harry S. Truman was immediately sworn in. Only then did he learn about the existence of the Manhattan Project, which was close to achieving its goal. Truman was told that the atomic bomb would be complete and ready for testing sometime that summer.

While awaiting the test, Truman convened a committee of civilian and military authorities to debate the issue of what to do with such a weapon. Above all, he needed to know whether the war in Japan could be ended without using it. Would the Japanese surrender, now that it was clear they could not prevail? Or would they fight to the bitter end, defending the Japanese homeland as they had the other islands of the Pacific?

Truman had only three options in front of him regarding Japan. One option was to invade the home islands. His military leaders estimated that such an invasion would result in hundreds of thousands of American deaths and as many as 2 million Japanese deaths. Indeed, the fire-bombing of Japanese cities that began in March had already killed an estimated 80,000 civilians and left upward of a million homeless. Alternatively, Truman could induce the Japanese to surrender, by offering terms they found acceptable. In that spirit Truman reached out to the Japanese within a day of Germany's surrender on May 8, 1945. He prom-ised that the Japanese people would be free "to return to their families, their farms, their jobs." Yet the militants who remained in control of the Japanese government rebuffed the American offer as "propaganda."

Truman's third option was to shock the Japanese into giving up. In the quest to push an incredibly stubborn opponent into surrendering, the atomic weapon seemed a viable choice. That was the conclusion of Truman's expert panel, which met on May 31 and June 1, and it was officially supported two weeks later by a panel of scientists from the Manhattan Project.

On July 26, the Big Three (Truman, Churchill, and Stalin) met at Potsdam to

coordinate the Allied strategy for concluding the war with Japan. There, Truman informed Stalin of the new weapon, and Stalin agreed to join the war effort in Japan (in exchange for possession of Manchuria). The leaders issued a warning that the Japanese should surrender immediately or face "prompt and utter destruction." They received no response.

On August 6, 1945, the *Enola Gay* delivered the single bomb it was carrying over the city of Hiroshima. It destroyed the city and burned a zone of 4.4 square miles, killing 70,000 people instantly and 30,000 more over the coming months from radiation sickness. Still, no surrender was forthcoming. Three days later Truman ordered another bombing over the city of Nagasaki at a cost of 39,000 deaths. This time, Emperor Hirohito acted. He convened a meeting of his cabinet and signaled his intention to surrender, provided the Allies agreed to retain the emperor as Japan's head of state. Even then, with the destructive power of the atomic bomb all too evident, the emperor's decision met resistance, and a palace coup had to be put down by force.

END OF CHAPTER TAKE-AWAYS

■ **Appeasement:** The First World War scarred all who took part in it, leading the victors to reject militarism and the losers to nurse their wounds resentfully. When Germany, Italy, and Japan remilitarized in the 1930s, others tried to appease them in a doomed effort to prevent another war.

■ **Pearl Harbor:** President Roosevelt called December 7, 1941 "a date which will live in infamy" because on that day Japan led a surprise attack on the U.S. Pacific Fleet in Hawaii. The United States soon entered the war in both Europe and Asia.

■ **The Pacific Theater:** Japan succeeded initially in taking control of nearly all of Asia. However, it could not match the industrial might of the Allies, especially the United States, which gradually retook all of Japan's conquests.

■ **The European Theater:** Beginning with the 1939 invasion of Poland, Germany took control of nearly all of Western Europe, but Hitler found it impossible to defeat both the Soviet Union and the United States, who partnered with the British and other allies.

■ **The Home Front:** The Allies—especially the United States—could not win on the battlefield alone. Scientific breakthroughs such as the invention of the atomic bomb, and social breakthroughs, such as women entering the workforce, were also key to America's victory. Large-scale mechanization and bustling American factories churned out large numbers of tanks, planes, and ships at a rate far exceeding what Axis forces could produce.

REFERENCES

American Experience. (2009). Timeline of the war in the Pacific. Public Broadcasting Service
. Retrieved from http://www.pbs.org/wgbh/amex/macarthur/timeline/1942.html

Scarred by history: The rape of Nanjing. (2005, April 11). BBC News. Retrieved from http://news
.bbc.co.uk/2/hi/223038.stm

Boyle, D. (1998). World War II: A photographic history. New York, NY: Barnes and Noble.

D'Este, C. (2003). Eisenhower: A soldier's life. New York, NY: Macmillan.

Eistein, Albert 1879–1955. (2012). In The Oxford dictionary of quotations (6th ed.). Retrieved
from http://www.oxfordreference.com/pages/samplep-18.html

Findlay, C., & Rothney, J. (2011). Twentieth century world. Belmont, CA: Wadsworth-Cengage Learning.

Fulbrook, M. (2002). History of Germany, 1918–2000. Malden, MA: Wiley-Blackwell.

Hanson, V. D. (2007, July 25). Introduction to E. B. Sledge's With the old breed. Retrieved from http://victorhanson.com/articles/hanson072507.html

Independent Lens. (2011). The political Dr. Seuss. Public Broadcasting Service, Georgia. Retrieved from http://www.pbs.org/independentlens/politicaldrseuss/seuss_fla.html

Johnson, P. (1995). The myth of American isolationism. Foreign Affairs, 74(3).

Keegan, J. (1989). The Second World War. New York, NY: Penguin Books.

Litoff, J. (1997). American women in a world at war. Lanham, MD: Rowman and Littlefield.

McClelland, J. (2011, July 13). Paying attention to a forgotten navy pig's plaque. National Public Radio. Retrieved from http://www.npr.org/2011/07/13/137791935/paying-attention-to-a-forgotten-navy-pigs-plaque

New York Times on the Web. (2010). On this day: March 29, 1969. Retrieved from http://www.nytimes.com/learning/general/onthisday/bday/1014.html

Paterson, T. G., Clifford, J. G., Hagan, K. J., Kisatsky, D., & Maddock, S. J. (2010). American foreign relations: Vol. 2; Since 1865. Boston, MA: Wadsworth-Cengage.

Tracy, E. (Producer). (2007, December 5). Walter D. Ehlers: Medal of Honor with Ed Tracy [Audio podcast]. Pritzker Military Library. Retrieved from http://itunes.apple.com/us/podcast/medal-of-honor-with-ed-tracy/id118681082

United States Holocaust Memorial Museum. (2012, May 11). Holocaust encyclopedia: The United States and the Holocaust. Retrieved from http://www.ushmm.org/wlc/en/article.php?ModuleId=10005182

U.S. Department of Energy. (2012, January 8). Hanford World War II era. Retrieved from http://www.hanford.gov/page.cfm/WorldWarIIEra

Welch, D. (1998). Hitler. Philadelphia, PA: UCL Press.

World War II. (2011). In Encyclopædia Britannica. Retrieved from http://www.britannica.com/EBchecked/topic/648813/World-War-II

Section 4
The United States
on the World Stage

The Truman Doctrine

The economic system of the United States—capitalism—gives US citizens the right to own private property and to earn a profit from producing and selling goods or services. These fundamental economic values existed in 1800 and still exist today. Many hold that these values are intrinsically linked with freedoms protected in the U.S. Constitution.

The principles of communism, conversely, outline a society that features no classes, no money, no private ownership, and no political states. In short, these principles contradict many values that are central to U.S. democracy. For this reason, the spread of communism, which took root in Eastern Europe immediately following World War II, was seen as a significant threat to the American way of life. Complicating this threat, and making it even more dangerous, was the proliferation of nuclear weapons in communist countries and around the world. The tensions arising between the United States and the Soviet Union, and their respective allies, became known as the Cold War.

To prevent the threats of communism and nuclear war from spreading, after World War II the United States led an international effort to contain communism and limit the proliferation of atomic weapons. The United States formed alliances with other democratic nations and enlisted the authority of the United Nations in this effort. Despite temporary gains in limiting the development of nuclear weapons and stopping the spread of communism, both threats advanced.

KEY TERMS

- Cold War (p. 264)
- containment (p. 267)
- iron curtain (p. 264)
- Marshall Plan (p. 265)
- NATO (p. 265)
- Truman Doctrine (p. 264)

YOU ARE LEAVING THE AMERICAN SECTOR
ВЫ ВЫЕЗЖАЕТЕ ИЗ АМЕРИКАНСКОГО СЕКТОРА
VOUS SORTEZ DU SECTEUR AMÉRICAIN
SIE VERLASSEN DEN AMERIKANISCHEN SEKTOR
US ARMY

TRUMAN DOCTRINE

Harry Truman ascended to the White House at the end of World War II and spent his entire presidency at war, in one form or another. The weapons and strategies he used in World War II and the Korean War influenced American foreign policy for nearly fifty years.

The first battles of the Cold War began before the Second World War ended. Although allied in the fight against Hitler, the United States and the Soviet Union pursued different goals for post-war Europe. The United States and its Western European allies wanted free and fair elections to be held in those countries that had been liberated from Nazi rule. Joseph Stalin, dictator of the Soviet Union, had agreed to the elections but planned instead to impose communism on the countries liberated by the Soviet army. Those countries would serve as a buffer zone protecting Russia from future invasions.

President Truman was unable to stop the establishment of communism in Eastern Europe. He refused, however, to let it spread any further. The first test of his will came in 1947, when Greece and Turkey faced communist threats. The Greek government was fighting a civil war against the Greek Communist Party. Turkey faced potential conflict with the Soviet Union, partly over control of the Dardanelles Strait and the Black Sea. Both Greece and Turkey had been receiving aid from Britain, but in 1947 the British announced that they could no longer afford to provide the aid. Believing that Stalin was behind the events in both Greece and Turkey, Truman and his advisors decided that the United States must pick up where Britain left off.

Truman went before Congress and asked for $400 million in aid for the two countries and permission to send military personnel to the conflict zones. He told Congress, "I believe it must be the policy of the United States to support free peoples who are resisting attempted subjugation by armed minorities or by outside pressures." The message was clear: the United States must fight for freedom with both its checkbook and its armed forces. Congress approved the aid and the use of US military personnel. The **Truman Doctrine** was born.

TRUMAN DOCTRINE U.S. policy to help countries that are fighting against communist influence or takeover.

IRON CURTAIN

The Truman Doctrine reflected the United States' role as an international leader after World War II and the new alignment of nations in the post-war world. In the words of British Prime Minister Winston Churchill, an **iron curtain** divided Eastern and Western Europe, separating communist countries from democratic ones. This division became the focal point of international relations into the 1990s.

Just as the Soviet Union saw its role as the leader of communist Eastern Europe, the United States assumed the role of leader of the democratic world. In part, this resulted from the global economic situation after the war. The countries of Europe verged on bankruptcy. They had neither the will nor the resources to act as global leaders. By contrast, the war had strengthened the United States economy and helped pull it out of the Great Depression. By war's end, the United States was the only country with the resources to pursue a global anti-communist agenda. The world had become polarized, with the United States and the Soviet Union as the two competing superpowers locked in a **Cold War**.

IRON CURTAIN The ideological divide between the communist countries of Eastern Europe and the non-communist countries of Western Europe.

COLD WAR The period of political and military tension between the United States and the Soviet Union that lasted from 1946 to 1989.

The Marshall Plan

Truman and his advisors knew that supporting anti-communist groups in Greece and Turkey was not enough. Western Europe needed to be strengthened too, so that it could stand against communism on its own and become a more equal partner in its dealings with the United States.

U.S. Secretary of State George Marshall proposed a bold plan to finance the rebuilding of Europe, one that would combat "hunger, poverty, desperation and chaos." The 1948 Economic Cooperation Act provided more than $12 billion in aid to the countries of Western Europe. The act provided food, raw materials, equipment, and money to Western Europe to save it from famine and to spur industrialization and economic growth.

The **Marshall Plan**, as the act became more popularly known, set the precedent for U.S. foreign aid programs. In 1953, Marshall was awarded the Nobel Peace Prize for his efforts—the only general so honored.

Crisis in Berlin

During the first conflicts of the Cold War, the United States and the Soviet Union did not engage in any direct conflict. Their militaries did not meet on the battlefield. Instead, they each supported their own allies, as with the Marshall Plan, and sent aid to the other's enemies, as the United States did in Turkey and Greece. That changed with the Berlin Crisis in 1948–1949.

MARSHALL PLAN U.S. aid package to help rebuild Western Europe after World War II.

At the end of the World War II, Germany had been divided into four zones: one for each of the four leading Allied powers: the United States, Great Britain, France, and the Soviet Union. The city of Berlin, Germany's capital, fell in the Soviet zone, but the city was subdivided among the Allies just as the rest of the country had been. In 1948, the United States, France, and Britain announced that they would be combining their zones to create a separate, democratic West Germany. The Soviet Union responded by blockading West Berlin. Stalin hoped to seize control of the entire city and make it part of communist East Germany.

President Truman refused to let Stalin win control of West Berlin. He authorized a massive airlift that brought supplies into West Berlin. American and British planes made over 200,000 flights to Berlin, bringing an average 4,700 tons of necessities each day. After eleven months, the Soviet Union realized the airlift was successfully detouring the blockade, so it was lifted. The United States and its allies had won the first confrontation of the Cold War. Berlin remained a divided city, a symbol of the Cold War itself.

NATO

The Berlin Crisis, along with the civil war in Greece and hostilities in Turkey, drew the United States into European domestic affairs. Instead of intervening in Europe on an as-needed basis, President Truman wanted to establish ground rules for U.S. involvement, perhaps by forming a defensive alliance between the United States and Western Europe.

A few Western European countries had already established their own defensive military alliance in 1948. They welcomed a similar treaty with the United States.

NATO North Atlantic Treaty Organization; defensive alliance established between the United States and Western European countries in 1949.

In 1951, President Truman established the Civil Defense Administration (CDA) to help prepare Americans for the possibility of nuclear war. Among the CDA's productions was a short film titled Duck and Cover. The animated film featured a character named Bert the Turtle, who taught children to duck and cover in the event of an atomic flash. Accompanying Bert was a little song:

There was a turtle by the name of Bert

And Bert the turtle was very alert

When danger threatened him he never got hurt

He knew just what to do

He'd duck! And cover ...

You can watch the video by visiting the following web address: www.archive.org/details/DuckandC1951.

They wanted a guarantee that the United States would intervene automatically in the event of an attack and help rebuild their militaries.

After months of negotiations, the United States, Canada, the United Kingdom, France, Italy, Belgium, Norway, Portugal, Denmark, Iceland, Luxemburg, and the Netherlands signed the North Atlantic Treaty, creating the **North Atlantic Treaty Organization (NATO).** More members were added over time. By 2011, NATO had 28 members. Under the terms of the treaty, member nations consult with each other about threats and national defense and view an attack against any member nation as an attack against all member nations.

NATO's primary goal, at first, was to provide a balance to the alliance of communist nations in Europe and to stop the spread of communism. Over time, NATO's goals have broadened to address more global concerns, such as terrorism.

The Arms Race

In 1949, the year NATO was founded, the Soviet Union successfully tested its first atomic bomb. The nuclear arms race had begun. The United States and the Soviet Union each wanted to keep ahead of the other in this use of technology and science. The United States developed the next generation of bomb—the hydrogen bomb—in 1952. The Soviets developed their H-bomb the next year. As the two countries competed for dominance, their nuclear arsenals grew.

Throughout the 1950s, both the Soviet Union and the United States worked to develop long-range missiles that could carry nuclear payloads. Delivering a nuclear weapon by missile was much safer than dropping it from an airplane. Both nations developed intercontinental ballistic missiles (ICBMs), missiles that can strike a target thousands of miles away. According to reports, the Soviet Union was far ahead of the

HISTORY COMES ALIVE

Shortly after Fidel Castro seized power in Cuba, he imposed a communist government and established political and economic ties with the Soviet Union. In 1962, a U.S. spy plane photographed nuclear missile sites being built in Cuba. U.S. intelligence services determined that the Soviet Union was providing the missiles.

President Kennedy confronted Soviet Premier Nikita Khrushchev and demanded the removal of the missiles from Cuba. He backed up his demands with a naval blockade of the island to prevent any more Soviet weapons or materials from reaching the island. Khrushchev refused. For thirteen days the world stood on the brink of nuclear war.

Finally, the Soviet Union agreed to withdraw its missiles from Cuba. However, it did not stop developing nuclear weapons, nor did the United States. The two countries, however, did sign a limited nuclear test ban treaty the next year.

United States in the development of ICBM technology. This perceived "missile gap" made the United States increase its efforts to develop missiles. The United States began deploying missiles in Europe in the early 1960s. Believing that the Soviet Union had the capability to launch a full-scale ICBM attack, the United States felt this show of strength was essential.

MID-CHAPTER QUESTIONS

1. How did the situation in Europe at the end of World War II lead to the development of the Cold War?

2. In the late 1940s, U.S. foreign policy focused on the idea of containment. What was containment? Give two examples of how it was implemented.

3. How did the United States strengthen its military and economic ties with Western Europe after World War II?

4. Contrast the United States' current foreign policy with its foreign policy under the Truman Doctrine. Would the United States of 2012 have supported the Marshall Plan? Is the United States currently aiding nations in a similar fashion?

CONTAINMENT

President Truman based his foreign policy strategy on the idea of **containment**. First proposed by diplomat George Kennan in 1947, the goal of containment was to stop the spread of Soviet influence outside of Eastern Europe. Kennan recognized that the United States could not free Eastern Europe from Soviet control. It could, however, prevent the establishment of new communist regimes in other regions. Kennan explained his ideas in an anonymous essay published in the journal *Foreign Affairs*. He called for the "adroit and vigilant application of counter-force" in response to Soviet actions.

To Kennan, the application of counter-force meant financial and psychological pursuits, such as the Marshall Plan and the use of propaganda. Others interpreted Kennan's words to mean the use of the military. Under the Truman Administration, all three methods were used.

CONTAINMENT U.S. foreign policy aimed at stopping the spread of communism.

Seeds of the Vietnam Conflict

After the Second World War, European countries lost many of their African and Asian colonies or granted them independence. Other colonies launched wars for independence against their European rulers. Indochina, or Vietnam, for example, began an eight-year struggle for independence against France in 1945. A young communist named Ho Chi Minh led the Vietnamese independence movement.

President Truman worried that the former colonies would become subject to Soviet influence or worse, become communist. His worries deepened when China became

communist in 1949. Ho Chi Minh's commitment to communism in Indochina fed Truman's fears. As part of the policy of containment, Truman decided it was in the United States' best interest to support France in its war in Indochina. In 1950, the United States sent $15 million in aid to the French war effort. The aid included not only financial assistance, but also the assistance of U.S. military personnel.

THE KOREAN WAR

The biggest test, and demonstration, of the policy of containment came in Korea. What began as a civil war became an international conflict that still remains unresolved.

During World War II, Korea had been a Japanese possession. When the war ended, Korea was divided into two zones: the North was placed under Soviet control and the South under American control. The division was intended to be temporary, with reunification to occur when elections were held in 1947. As had happened in Europe, the Soviet Union refused to hold elections in its zone. Instead, it supported the ascension of communist Kim Il Sung as leader of North Korea. South Korea held elections as planned. In 1949, the Soviet Union and the United States withdrew their troops from the Korean Peninsula.

In June 1950, the North Korean army crossed the 38th parallel, which divided the two Koreas, in an effort to unite Korea under communist rule. By September, the North Koreans had conquered almost all of South Korea. The United States saw the attack as proof that communism presented an active threat to global freedom. Truman immediately authorized aid for South Korea in the form of weapons and supplies.

The United States then appealed to the United Nations for an international military action to stop the North Korean advance and protect South Korea. The UN approved the United States' proposal, in large part because the Soviet Union had boycotted the proceedings.

Stalemate

Under the leadership of U.S. General Douglas MacArthur, UN troops quickly pushed North Korean forces back to the 38th parallel. Then MacArthur faced the question, should he keep going? MacArthur and his troops had a chance to unite the Koreas under a non-communist government, if they continued their march north.

China warned that if UN forces continued beyond the 38th parallel, it would intervene on the side of North Korea. Leaders in the United States and the United Nations thought China was bluffing. MacArthur was given permission to cross the parallel.

MacArthur's troops almost reached the Yalu River, the border between China and North Korea, but China retaliated. The UN leadership had grossly underestimated the size, strength, and will of the Chinese military. Chinese forces quickly pushed UN troops south of the 38th parallel once again. UN forces pushed back to the parallel, but no farther. The war reached a stalemate.

At this point, General MacArthur had a public falling out with his commander-in-chief. The general wanted to attack China directly. Truman wanted the war to stay on the Korean Peninsula. MacArthur wanted to use nuclear bombs. Truman thought the situation did not require the use of such a destructive weapon. The war of words forced Truman to fire MacArthur for insubordination. MacArthur, immensely popular in the United States, returned home to a hero's welcome. Truman's popularity, by contrast, plummeted.

A Permanent Divide

Peace talks to end the Korean conflict began in July 1951 and they dragged on for years. When Harry Truman left office in January 1953, peace still had not been concluded.

Finally, in July 1953, the two sides signed an armistice. The ceasefire established a border between North and South Korea at the 38th parallel. A demilitarized zone (DMZ) was created around the border.

The Korean War failed to unify the Koreas, but it was a significant milestone in the Cold War. The conflict turned the cold war "hot." It demonstrated the U.S. commitment to the policy of containment, both financially and militarily. The war also established a precedent for U.S. military involvement in Asia.

THE KITCHEN DEBATE

Dwight D. Eisenhower became president in 1953. He oversaw the Korean peace negotiations and armistice, and he continued to provide aid to France for its Indochina war.

Soon after Eisenhower's inauguration, Soviet leader Joseph Stalin died. His successor, Nikita Khrushchev, seemed to call for a thaw in U.S.-Soviet relations. Like Truman, Eisenhower did not entirely trust Khrushchev, but the two nations did conduct direct negotiations in 1955. The negotiations did not result in any treaty or agreement, but it did demonstrate that tensions between the two countries had eased.

This thaw also included cultural exchanges between the two Cold War rivals. In June 1959, the Soviet Union set up a national exhibition in New York City. The exhibition shared demonstrations of Soviet life, from music and theater to industry and agriculture. It also highlighted *Sputnik*, the Soviet satellite that had orbited the Earth in 1957 and launched the space race.

A War of Words

The next month, the American National Exhibition opened in Moscow. The exhibit represented the typical American lifestyle, with emphasis on the technology found in American homes, from color televisions to washing machines. The exhibition became the site of one of the most famous, and most public, episodes of the Cold War.

As part of the grand opening of the exhibition, U.S. Vice President Richard Nixon toured the exhibits with Soviet Premier Khrushchev. Reporters and cameramen followed the two men and recorded every word they exchanged. The tour turned into a

debate about the benefits of capitalism versus communism, and the debate reached its crescendo in the model kitchen.

As Nixon showed off modern appliance after modern appliance, Khrushchev proclaimed that the Soviet Union had similar devices and that the Soviet people would not be impressed by the demonstration. Nixon responded by saying that the goal of the exhibit was not to impress the Soviets but "to show our right to choose. We do not wish to have decisions made at the top by government officials who say that all homes should be built in the same way."

The two men continued to debate the merits of communism and capitalism in the guise of housing. Khrushchev claimed that American houses were built to last only twenty years so that Americans would be forced to buy new ones. In the Soviet Union, he continued, houses were built to last forever. Nixon replied that American houses did last more than twenty years, but many Americans wanted to update their homes to take advantage of new technology and designs.

Khrushchev went on to point out that freedom in the United States meant the freedom to be homeless. If an American did not have money, he could not live in a house. He would have to live on the pavement. In the Soviet Union, by contrast, housing was a right guaranteed at birth.

The debate turned to international politics. Khrushchev demanded the removal of foreign bases and Nixon accused him of issuing an ultimatum. The topic turned to nuclear weapons and Nixon told Khrushchev that threatening the use of nuclear weapons could lead to war. The Soviet premier suggested that Nixon's words could have "very bad consequences."

Perhaps realizing they had overstepped the bounds of decorum, the two men apologized and laughed off their differences. The world did not shrug off the war of words so easily. The debate made front-page news in the United States.

END OF CHAPTER TAKE-AWAYS

■ **Truman Doctrine:** The Truman Doctrine stated that the United States would assist countries fighting a communist threat.

■ **Iron Curtain:** The Iron Curtain separated communist Eastern Europe from democratic Western Europe.

■ **Post WWII:** The Marshall Plan helped Western Europe rebuild after World War II. The Soviet Union backed down after a standoff over the fate of Berlin. The United States and Western Europe formed a defensive alliance called NATO. The Soviet Union's development of an atomic bomb began an arms race with the United States.

■ **Containment:** U.S. foreign policy was based on the idea of containment, that the spread of communism should be stopped. The United States provided aid to France in its war in Indochina (Vietnam).

■ **The Korean War:** In 1950, North Korea invaded South Korea with the intent of uniting the peninsula under communist rule. UN troops aided the defense of South Korea. Chinese troops aided the defense of North Korea. The war ended in a stalemate, with a border and demilitarized zone established at the 38th parallel.

■ **The Kitchen Debate:** At an exhibition in Moscow about American culture, US Vice President Richard Nixon and Soviet Premier Nikita Khrushchev argued about communism and capitalism and the Cold War.

REFERENCES

Bostdorff, D. M. (2008). *Proclaiming the Truman doctrine: The Cold War call to arms.* College Station, Texas: Texas A&M University Press.

Gaddis, J. L. (2006). *The Cold War: A new history.* New York, NY: Penguin.

Jones, H. (1997). *A new kind of war: America's global strategy and the Truman doctrine in Greece.* New York, NY: Oxford University Press.

McCullough, D. (1993). *Truman.* New York, NY: Simon & Schuster.

Our Documents: 100 Milestone Documents from the National Archives. (n.d.). Truman Doctrine (1947). Retrieved from http://www.ourdocuments.gov/doc.php?doc=81

Salisbury, H. E. (1959, July 24). Nixon and Khrushchev argue in public as U.S. exhibit opens. *New York Times.* Retrieved from http://www.nytimes.com/learning/general/onthisday/big/0724.html

Smithsonian National Museum of American History. (n.d.). The price of freedom: Americans at war: Cold War. Retrieved from http://americanhistory.si.edu/militaryhistory/printable/section.asp?id=11

U.S. Department of State, Office of the Historian. (n.d.). Milestones: 1945–1952. Retrieved November from http://history.state.gov/milestones/1945-1952

The Boom Years

The advertisements are everywhere. Buy a new television, a new phone, or a different laundry detergent and your life will improve dramatically. Want the American dream? Buy a new car or a new house. If advertisers are to be believed, purchases are the answers to all problems. This idea of "keeping up with the Joneses" or "the one who has the most toys wins" is called conspicuous consumption. This notion says that buying the newest goods and latest gadgets will impress others and bring personal happiness. The emphasis on material goods has become an important force in the American economy. When Americans stop spending, the economy slows dramatically.

Where did this reverence of material goods come from? In large part, it was born during the boom years that followed the Second World War, when consumers were desperate for the goods that war had denied them. Advertisers capitalized on this desire, using billboards, radio ads, television commercials, and catchy jingles to persuade average American consumers that the good life was within reach—if only they bought the latest car, television, washing machine, or other domestic appliance. This combination of need, want, and persuasion transformed the United States into a consumer culture.

CONSUMERISM

In the 1950s, after surviving the tense years of the Depression and the Second World War, Americans exhaled, economically speaking. Instead of saving money, they spent it—on houses, cars, refrigerators, televisions, and other domestic goods. American culture became a consumer culture, driven by demand and by advertising that promoted "the good life." Living "the good life" meant having a car, a house in the suburbs, a television, a washing machine, and leisure time to enjoy these luxuries. Success, happiness, and patriotism were defined in economic terms. "Good" Americans purchased the latest, newest, best appliances. Such purchases demonstrated success and brought happiness. **Consumerism**, the belief in the acquisition of material goods, ruled the day.

CONSUMERISM An attitude that values the acquisition of material goods.

During the Depression and World War II, Americans had held on to their money. They saved it and used it to buy essential goods. The war had also limited the goods that citizens could purchase, as the nation's manufacturing centers focused on supporting the war effort and providing for the war's needs.

Once the war ended, though, all that changed. Wartime production had pulled the United States out of the Depression. In the 1950s, the economy continued to expand. Jobs were readily available. Wages increased. Hourly wages in 1950 were more than double—and sometimes more than triple—what they were in 1935. The average pay for a factory worker, for example, rose from 58 cents an hour in 1935 to $1.59 an hour in 1950. Average household income in 1950 exceeded $4,000 a year, marking a 178 percent increase since the mid-1930s. Between 1953 and 1961, income rose by another 45 percent. People were eager to spend their money. People were especially eager to buy consumer goods, which had not been available during the war. After nearly a decade and a half of economic depression and war, demand for consumer goods exploded.

Pent-up Demand

The transition from a wartime economy to peacetime boom was not smooth or rapid. It took time for factories to switch from military production to civilian production. Americans grew frustrated and desperate.

During the war, the government had controlled the prices of many goods. In 1946, the government lifted the wartime price controls and prices soared. The price of meat doubled over a two-week period. The government answered consumer anger by reinstating price controls.

Inflation and high food prices continued to be a problem for the next four years, although never as severe as they had been in 1946. Congress passed economic control measures, but the legislation proved inadequate. The biggest scare came in 1949, when the economy suffered a serious slowdown. During the first half of 1949, both unemployment and inflation rose. People feared the worst. To help spur a recovery, President Truman offered tax breaks to businesses. In 1950, the economy improved. The start of the Korean War and an increase in military production kept unemployment and inflation low. The boom years were finally booming consistently.

Housing

Housing was in great demand after the war. Young soldiers returning home needed places to live. Young couples married and started families at unprecedented rates. Government programs encouraged the construction of affordable housing and made it easier for people, especially veterans, to qualify for low-interest, insured mortgages.

In the years after the war, though, many Americans chose to buy homes in locations other than where they had grown up. More chose to settle not in cities or rural areas, but in newly created and growing communities on the outskirts of cities. These new communities were called **suburbs**.

SUBURB A residential community on the outskirts of a city.

Levittown

In 1946, building company Levitt and Sons began development of a community about twenty-five miles outside of New York City. The community, called **Levittown**, became the representative symbol of suburban life.

Levittown was a planned community. Levitt built 17,000 homes along with parks, stores, and schools. To keep costs low, the houses were produced assembly-line style and with minimal variations. Every Levittown house followed the same floor plan, differing only in paint color, roof line, and window placement. Each house measured 25 feet by 32 feet. The houses had no basements or garages.

Critics disparaged the Levittown houses, saying the buildings were too monotonous and too uniform. The general public, however, did not seem to share the critics' disdain. The homes in Levittown, New York, sold out quickly. Because of high demand, other Levittown communities were built in Pennsylvania and New Jersey. The suburban boom had begun.

LEVITTOWN A prototypical suburb built in the late 1940s and early 1950s on the outskirts of New York City.

The Suburbs

The development of suburban communities began before the 1920s. After being interrupted by the Depression and the war, a boom in construction in the suburbs took off in the late 1940s. Between 1945 and 1950, more than 80 percent of all homes built in the United States were built in the suburbs.

Suburban growth continued well into the early 1960s. Park Forest, Illinois, for example, was established in 1948 about thirty miles outside of Chicago. By 1950, it already had more than 8,000 residents. A decade later its population had reached nearly 30,000.

What drew so many people to the suburbs? Suburban neighborhoods promised a good life with good schools, safe streets, open spaces, and a sense of community. Most suburbanites were young, white, middle-class families. They usually owned a car, sometimes two. The husband used the car to commute to work. In some suburbs, the husbands took public transportation to work so that their wives could use the car during the day. The wives

STUDY ALERT

The growth of the suburbs and the development of a car culture are connected. Having a car made living in the suburbs possible. Workers could live farther from their jobs. Businesses were spread out and public transportation was not as available as in the cities.

generally stayed at home with the children. Some did hold jobs, though, often as clerks, secretaries, nurses, teachers, or telephone operators.

Suburban communities often had strict rules about who could buy or rent homes. In many cases, these rules prohibited African-Americans and other racial minorities from moving in. In Levittown, for example, the rental contract specifically instructed the tenant "not to permit the premises to be used or occupied by any person other than members of the Caucasian race." While some suburbs, such as Park Forest, Illinois, did have a few African-American residents, most remained segregated white communities.

As the population shifted from cities to the suburbs, businesses followed. Business often established themselves on the edges of cities, where they could be accessed by both city-dwellers and suburbanites. The strip mall became a foundation of the suburban economy. Strip malls catered to the car-centric life in the suburbs by providing sufficient parking and retail variety.

Car Culture

During the baby boom years, car ownership rates skyrocketed. In 1940, there were 27.5 million registered vehicles in the United States. By 1950, that number rose to 40 million. By 1960, the number of registered vehicles exceeded 60 million. By 1970, registered vehicles in the country totaled almost 90 million.

The car reshaped American life. The transformation went beyond the strip mall and the growth of suburbia. Cars replaced public transportation as the primary method of travel. Advertisements encouraged Americans to see the country by driving along its highways and byways. More fundamentally, car ownership became a symbol of success and freedom.

During World War II, car production nearly halted and gasoline was rationed. After the war, car production resumed and people were eager to buy. To meet demand, car makers introduced new models and trained their salesmen on each car's special features. Sales teams were given quotas and instructed to be as aggressive as necessary to close the deal.

In their advertisements, manufacturers promoted each model as a reflection of a certain status or self-image. Ads for sports cars and convertibles, for example, targeted the young and single. Movies that featured hot rods and muscle cars supported this image. By contrast, like the houses in Levittown, the station wagon became a symbol of suburban life. Suburban families relied on their car for work and recreation. A station wagon had space to fit a growing family and its household goods. During the 1950s, station wagon production rose almost 14 percent.

Television

Sales of televisions also skyrocketed after the war. The first televisions were created in the late 1920s, but they did not catch the public's interest until the 1939 World's Fair. World War II put that interest on hold. By war's end, only a few thousand homes had television sets. Between 1945 and 1948, though, television sales increased 500 percent. During the 1950s, Americans bought about 5 million televisions each year.

Like the car, television transformed U.S. culture. It quickly replaced radio as the primary source of entertainment. Popular radio programs such the *Jack Benny Show* and *Burns & Allen* were turned into television series. Variety shows such as the *Ed Sullivan Show* became appointment viewing for many suburban families. People turned to television for definitions of *normal* and *the ideal family*—usually white, middle class, with a working husband, a stay-at-home wife, and two children.

Television also changed the advertising game. Radio brought advertising into people's homes, but television commercials proved an even more powerful advertising medium. TV commercials sold the idea that the "good life" was within economic reach. Often, the ads targeted the woman of the house, trying to persuade her that her life would be easier and more fulfilled if she purchased a new Whirlpool or General Electric appliance or stocked her kitchen cabinets with name-brand treats such as Nabisco cereal or Hershey's chocolate. In this way, television advertising reflected women's growing purchasing power.

A Golden Age

The boom years became the golden age of television. Television became a national mass media, and modern television programming was born. Newsmen such as Edward R. Murrow and Walter Cronkite set the standard for television news. Regularly scheduled news programs and the use of live broadcasts made television a more trusted source than newspapers, radio, and movie newsreels. People at home could see events for themselves in a way that had never been possible before. As a result, television quickly became Americans' primary source of information. The 1950s witnessed the invention of the sitcom, today a staple of television programming, and the introduction of classic programs such as *I Love Lucy* (1951) and *The Twilight Zone* (1959). Soap operas such as *Guiding Light* (1952) also took their first steps, as did game shows and sports broadcasts. With such variety, television provided entertainment for every interest.

DID YOU KNOW?

On August 19, 1950, the American Broadcasting Company (ABC) broadcast the first Saturday morning television programs for children. These programs, however, were not cartoons. Instead, they were live action entertainment: Animal Clinic, with live animals, and Acrobat Ranch. Other networks aired children's programming, such as Howdy Doody and Captain Kangaroo, but those shows aired during prime time, not on Saturday mornings. In 1955, CBS aired the first cartoons on The Mighty Mouse Playhouse, but cartoons did not become part of Saturday morning programming until the early 1960s. By the end of the 1960s, though, Saturday morning cartoons were part of the family routine for many.

MID-CHAPTER QUESTIONS

1. The U.S. economy had to undergo massive shifts after the end of World War II. What made the transition from a wartime economy to a peacetime economy so bumpy?

2. The 1950s saw an explosion of production and consumption domestically. How did the United States become a consumer culture?

3. The United States dealt with the Great Depression in the 1930s and the Second World War in the 1940s. In what ways were the developments of the 1950s inspired or affected by those trying eras?

4. What did it mean to have "the good life" during the boom years?

BABY BOOM

The economy was not the only part of American life that boomed in the post-war years. Marriages and births also increased dramatically. During the 1950s, 97 percent of American women between the ages of 18 and 30 and 94 percent of American men in the same age bracket were part of a married couple. Americans also married at younger ages during this time period. In fact, they married younger during these years than during any other time in American history. The average age of women marrying for the first time was 20 years old. The average age of men marrying for the first time was between 22 and 23.

These young, married Americans chose to have their children quickly. They also had more children than the previous generation. The US population rose by more than 18 percent in the 1950s. In 1940, American families averaged 2.6 children per family. By 1950, the average family size had become 3.2 children. During the 1950s, most couples had two or three children each, but some had as many as four or five children. The interval between children was often short. Between 1946 and 1964, approximately 75 million babies were born in the United States. This explosion of the birth rate is known as the **baby boom**.

BABY BOOM The explosion of the birth rate between 1946 and 1964.

The baby boom resulted in part from the economic prosperity of the era. Many young people had delayed getting married during the hard times of the Depression and WWII. They simply could not afford marriage, a home, or a family. The economic growth of the post-war years put those options within reach.

The baby boom had a tremendous impact on society, from driving the economy to shaping arts and politics. It drove the growth of the suburbs. It forced a building boom, by exponentially increasing the demand for housing and schools. In Michigan alone, more than one million houses were built in the second half of the 1950s. The baby boomers, as the children born during this era are called, continued to shape society as they grew. Their music, clothing, and political tastes shaped the 1960s and 1970s. Their spending habits as adults shaped the economy of the 1980s. In the twenty-first century, the size of the baby boomers' retirement needs are causing politicians and citizens to rethink public programs such as Social Security and Medicare.

INFRASTRUCTURE

The birth rate was not the only thing that exploded during the boom years. The infrastructure of the United States, especially highways, also expanded rapidly in the decade and a half after the war. Projects such as the Mackinac Bridge in Michigan, O'Hare Airport in Chicago, and Idlewild Airport (now John F. Kennedy International Airport) in New York City were built during this era. The United States also partnered with Canada to build the St. Lawrence Seaway, a 2,342-mile canal system that connects the St. Lawrence River and the Great Lakes. The greatest infrastructure project of the era, though, was the construction of the U.S. interstate highway system.

Highways

In 1919, Dwight D. Eisenhower (then a lieutenant colonel) participated in a transcontinental Army convoy that travelled from Washington, D.C., to San Francisco, California. At the time, the journey could only be made by traveling on local roads, some unpaved. The country had no highways and no interstates. The journey took 62 days. About 25 years later, during World War II, General Eisenhower experienced firsthand the German superhighway called the *Autobahn*. Eisenhower saw how the highway enabled quick and efficient mobilization and transportation of troops across long distances. The experience convinced him that similar highways were essential to the function and defense of the United States.

In 1956, President Eisenhower persuaded Congress to pass the National Interstate and Defense Highways Act. The act, officially called the Federal-Aid Highway Act of 1956, authorized $25 billion to create 41,000 miles of interstate highways connecting the continental United States. The highway system was intended to connect every American city with a population that exceeded 100,000 people.

The new highways made driving long distances faster and safer, a bonus for America's growing car culture. Suburban families often traveled the highways on family vacations, which took the form of road trips in the family station wagon.

HISTORY COMES ALIVE

Advertisers sometimes used the highway system and celebrity endorsements to entice people to buy cars. For example, Dinah Shore, who had a popular variety show during the late 1950s and early 1960s, became a spokesperson for Chevrolet. In one ad, she sang the praises of driving a Chevrolet across the United States:

> See the USA in your Chevrolet
> America is asking you to call
> Drive your Chevrolet through the USA
> America's the greatest land of all
>
> On a highway, or a road along the levy
> Performance is sweeter
> Nothing can beat her
> Life is completer in a Chevy
>
> So make a date today to see the USA
> And see it in your Chevrolet
>
> Traveling East, Traveling West
> Wherever you go, Chevy service is best
> Southward or North, near place or far
> There's a Chevrolet dealer for your Chevrolet car
>
> So make a date today to see the USA
> And see it in your Chevrolet

The interstate system changed the American landscape, too. The new highways did not follow the contours of the land as earlier roads did. Instead, they cut wide and straight across the countryside. To accomplish this, workers had to blast through or flatten hills and build bridges across valleys and rivers.

The new highways also bypassed city centers and many existing roadside businesses. In doing so, they contributed to the decline of urban centers. Residents and businesses relocated to have better access to the highways. In this way, the interstate system fed suburban growth.

A CHANGING LABOR FORCE

The American labor force also changed during the boom years, in a variety of ways.

The most immediate change after the war concerned organized labor, or labor unions. During the war, labor unions supported the war effort. They did not push for higher wages nor did they go on strike. In August 1945, however, President Truman announced that unions could seek higher wages. A wave of strikes followed, in the steel, coal, car, and railroad industries. The strikes slowed production of the consumer goods that the public was demanding so vociferously.

The strikes were eventually settled, but Congress wanted to prevent another wave of crippling strikes. The result was the Labor-Management Relations Act of 1947, more popularly known as the Taft-Hartley Act. Taft-Hartley allowed the president to block strikes, limited labor union participation in politics, and allowed states to enact "right to work" laws. The overall effect was to limit the power and influence of labor unions.

Eight years later, two of the most powerful labor unions in the United States merged. For more than two decades, the American Federation of Labor (AFL) and the Congress of Industrial Organizations (CIO) had competed for members and power. In 1955, the two unions joined to form the AFL-CIO, which boasted a membership of about 15 million workers.

SERVICE INDUSTRY An industry or group of companies that provide services instead of manufacturing goods. Banking, medicine, and retail are all service industries.

Despite the high demand for consumer goods and military production, the manufacturing sector of the U.S. economy declined during the 1950s and 1960s. The percentage of workers employed as manual laborers and farm workers also declined. The service sector, however, grew. An increasing percentage of workers were employed in white-collar jobs and service industries. A **service industry** is an industry or group of companies that provide services instead of selling goods. Banking, medicine, and retail are all service industries.

The number of women in the workforce also increased during the boom years. During the war, the number of women who worked outside the home had increased dramatically. An estimated 19 million worked outside the home in 1945. When the war ended, however, many women lost their jobs to returning veterans. Still, women remained a significant and growing segment of the American labor force. According to the U.S. Bureau of Labor Statistics, women made up almost 29 percent of the workforce in 1950. By 1969, that figure had increased to 36 percent. More than half of all working women were married.

THE MILITARY-INDUSTRIAL COMPLEX

In the years immediately following World War II, military production in the United States declined significantly, but it never completely vanished. With the start of the Korean War in 1950, military production ramped up again. The Korean War and the Cold War arms race highlighted the need for continued defense spending and military production, even when the United States was not engaged in a direct military conflict. Consequently, the defense industry continued to grow throughout the 1950s.

As a former general, Dwight Eisenhower understood the need for the United States to have a strong military. As president, however, Eisenhower worried that the defense sector would come to dominate American politics and society. He spelled out his worries in his Farewell Address, a ten-minute televised speech in January 1961 that concluded his presidency.

In his speech, Eisenhower noted that the maintenance of a high level of defense spending, a large standing military, and a sizeable arms industry during a time of peace was "new in the American experience." The influence of this phenomenon, he said, could be felt in every segment of American society. He worried that such influence threatened the structure of American democracy. In his words,

> In the councils of government, we must guard against the acquisition of unwarranted influence, whether sought or unsought, by the military-industrial complex. The potential for the disastrous rise of misplaced power exists and will persist. We must never let the weight of this combination endanger our liberties or democratic processes.

What was this military-industrial complex that so worried the outgoing president? Put simply, the **military-industrial complex** was the network of people and companies that produced weapons and military technology, such as the U.S. military, the Department of Defense, and private military contractors. This network maintained strong ties with members of government, largely because they depended on the federal government for their funding. Eisenhower saw the potential for this network and its political allies to pursue policies and agendas that were in their own interest, but not in the country's best interest. To Eisenhower, the country's best interest should always come first.

Eisenhower's successors, he said, faced new kinds of threats and would be presented with all kinds of proposals for meeting these threats. He called on his successors to weigh each proposal that crossed their desks carefully and to seek balance in their decision-making. Eisenhower warned that the government had the "need to maintain balance in and among national programs—balance between the private and the public economy, balance between cost and hoped for advantage—balance between the clearly necessary and the comfortably desirable."

The United States changed drastically during the 1950s. After the nation struggled through the Great Depression and fought through the Second World War, it entered an era of abundant production and newly realized opportunities for leisure. As these changes unfolded, Eisenhower saw the need to counsel steadiness as he left his presidency.

MILITARY-INDUSTRIAL COMPLEX The military and defense industries that influence foreign and economic policy.

END OF CHAPTER TAKE-AWAYS

■ **Consumerism:** At the end of the Second World War, Americans were desperate for consumer goods. The high demand and slow transition to civilian production led to inflation. The years after the war saw the rise of suburbs, such as Levittown, and the car became an integral part of American culture and suburban life. Furthermore, the 1950s saw television production, ownership, and programming explode.

■ **Baby Boom:** Between 1946 and 1964, the birth rate soared. The growth of families helped create a building boom and influenced the growth of the suburbs.

■ **Infrastructure:** U.S. infrastructure grew during the boom years; for example, the interstate highway system was built during this time.

■ **A Changing Labor Force:** During the boom years, the American workforce changed. Women became a larger segment of the workforce and more workers became employed in service industries.

■ **The Military-Industrial Complex:** President Eisenhower warned against letting the military and its private contractors have too much influence over government

REFERENCES

Abramson, A. (2003). *The history of television, 1942 to 2000.* Jefferson, NC: McFarland.

Ambrose, S. E. (1983). *Eisenhower.* New York, NY: Simon and Schuster.

Ledbetter, J. (2011). *Unwarranted influence: Dwight D. Eisenhower and the military-industrial complex.* New Haven, CT: Yale University Press.

Light, P. C. (1988). *Baby boomers.* New York, NY: Norton.

National Museum of History, Smithsonian Institution. (n.d.).America on the move: On the interstate. Retrieved from http://americanhistory.si.edu/onthemove/exhibition/exhibition_16_1.html

Our Documents: 100 Milestone Documents from the National Archives. (n.d.). Joint address to Congress leading to a decalaration of war against Germany (1917). Retrieved from http://www.ourdocuments.gov/doc.php?doc=90

Our Documents: 100 Milestone Documents from the National Archives. (n.d.). National Interstate and Defense Highways Act (1956). Retrieved from http://www.ourdocuments.gov/doc.php?doc=88U.S. Bureau of Labor Statistics. (n.d.). 100 Years of U.S. consumer spending: 1950. Retrieved from http://www.bls.gov/opub/uscs/1950.pdf

Wagner, R. G., & Wagner, A. D. (2010). *Levittown.* Charleston, SC: Arcadia.

CHAPTER 18

A Time of Turmoil

n 2008, Americans elected Barack Obama, an African-American man, to the presidency of the United States. This accomplishment would have been impossible five decades earlier, when African-Americans had little political power and faced open discrimination. In 1952, only 20 percent of African-Americans were even registered to vote. The policy of segregation forced African-Americans in the South to use separate facilities from those reserved for whites. African-Americans who spoke out or tried to exert political power against these systems faced intimidation and violence.

The Jim Crow South still exists in living memory for many Americans today. However, the civil rights movement so thoroughly changed the possibilities for African-Americans in this country that this period often feels distant and foreign. Fifty years ago, many white Americans could not imagine sharing a bus seat or a classroom with an African-American, much less electing an African-American president. The collective action and pivotal legislation of the 1960s prove that major cultural change is possible. Though filled with conflict and turmoil, the 1960s offer a lesson in how to change society.

FEMINISM

During the 1960s, the United States underwent a major cultural transformation. The success of the civil rights movement inspired many groups to question the historical forces that had privileged white men over other groups in almost every area of life. The **feminist movement** aimed to address women's concerns based on the core idea that women should have the same rights, opportunities, and freedoms as men. Feminists not only fought for legal changes to protect women's rights but also sought to change interpersonal interactions and women's self-perception to promote equality between men and women. Beginning in the 1960s and swelling in popularity in the 1970s, feminist groups, large and small, organized across the country to work toward the goal of women's liberation. The feminist movement is one of the most successful protest movements in our nation's history.

The feminist movement in the 1960s and 1970s is often referred to as the second wave of feminist activity. The first wave was the influence of the suffragists during the Progressive Era, who gained women the right to vote. Encouraged by the success of the suffrage amendment in 1919, feminists sought to pass an additional Constitutional amendment to guarantee equal rights to women under the law. The National Woman's Party started a state-by-state effort to garner support for the amendment. Although this "Equal Rights Amendment" (ERA) resurfaced during the second wave feminist movement in the 1970s, it never passed.

FEMINIST MOVEMENT The struggle for women's liberation and equal rights during the 1960s and 1970s.

THE FEMININE MYSTIQUE A book by Betty Friedan about the disadvantages of women's domesticity. This book helped to mobilize the second wave feminist movement.

The Feminine Mystique

In 1963, Betty Friedan, a well-educated housewife, published a book called *The Feminine Mystique*. It quickly became a bestseller, inspiring widespread organized feminist activity across the country and a concerted effort to change laws to guarantee women's rights. In the book, Friedan challenged prevailing notions about women and domesticity. She charged that unpaid housework and child-rearing created "the problem that has no name." This problem was that smart, educated women were consigned to domestic work and were not allowed fair access to worldly success, financial freedom, or the fulfillment that a career can provide. As a result, she charged, many women felt trapped, unfulfilled, and neurotic, as they wondered why their families and homes left them feeling so unsatisfied. At the time, the home was frequently portrayed as the ideal feminine realm, and women were unprepared for the complicated feelings of boredom and dissatisfaction that came with the joys of caring for a family.

Friedan's ideas struck a chord with women across the country, particularly white, middle-class women. The bored, dissatisfied housewife was largely a middle-class phenomenon. Working-class and nonwhite women often did low-wage, menial labor outside the home—out of economic necessity. Not all housewives were dissatisfied with their situation, but many women found that Friedan had defined a problem with which they had long struggled.

Central to the movement was the idea that women's access to work was vital to their liberation. The feminist movement inspired women both to look beyond domesticity for personal fulfillment and to fight for equal rights in the workplace. Without a job, married women were financially dependent on their husbands. Women often could not afford to leave even abusive or violent marriages. To change this situation, feminist groups such as the Women's Equity Action League (WEAL) and the National Organization of Women (NOW) focused on financial parity and fair and equal hiring practices. Friedan herself was instrumental in forming NOW, which remains one of the largest and most active feminist groups today. Feminists also fought for the opportunity to serve in high-power jobs. In 1971, for example, Congresswoman Shirley Chisholm became the first African-American woman to make a legitimate run for a major party's presidential nomination.

By the end of the 1960s, 42.6 percent of women were working outside the home, and many of these women were married. By 1976, more than half of all married women worked outside the home. This huge increase in working women was matched by an increase in women's access to higher education. The feminist movement helped women to see the value in financial independence, and more women pursued careers and higher education than ever before.

The Pill

Another key issue for feminists was women's health, including sexual health. A large part of the feminist movement's focus on women's health involved women's right to sexual pleasure and reproductive freedom. This newfound interest in women's sexual freedom was inspired partly by the development of the birth control pill, or simply **the Pill**. Scientists developed the Pill in the 1950s, with significant funding secured by Margaret Sanger and the Planned Parenthood Foundation. In 1960, the FDA approved the Pill, making it available by prescription and only to married women. Sex was culturally and medically sanctioned only for those who had taken marriage vows. However, by the end of the 1960s, the Pill was widely available and widely used. In 1965, the Supreme Court case *Griswold v. Connecticut* made it legal to sell birth control to married couples in all states. Unmarried people were included in this protection soon after.

THE PILL Hormonal contraception, developed in the 1950s and approved by the FDA in 1960.

The Pill provided women, for the first time in history, with a reliable and highly effective form of birth control. In 1961, 408,000 women were on the Pill. Two years later, more than 2 million women had prescriptions. Over time, the Pill helped lower the birth rate in the United States from 3.6 children per woman in 1960 to fewer than 2 children per woman in recent years. Because many women now had access to a safe form of birth control, they could separate the risk of unwanted pregnancy from sex. This separation helped lead to a revolution in the way women experienced and acknowledged their sexuality, especially outside of marriage.

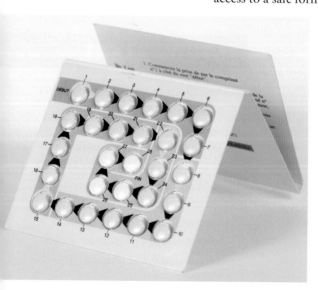

Many feminists were interested in banishing the sexual politics that had long shamed women who enjoyed sex. They encouraged women to experience sex as an act of love and pleasure. They believed that the fear of rape, pregnancy, and sexually transmitted diseases had alienated women from their own sexuality. Besides working to fight sexual coercion and rape, feminists encouraged women to understand and take a positive view of their bodies and their sexual responses. In 1973, the Boston Women's Health Book Collective published a book called *Our Bodies, Ourselves*. In the book, members of the collective shared their personal experiences and medical knowledge in order to help other women better understand their own health issues.

Roe v. Wade

Another of the goals of some of the feminists of the 1960s concerned rights surrounding abortion. Many feminists believed that women were oppressed by being forced to deal with an unwanted pregnancy. Feminists argued that the right to choose when and with whom to bear children was key to women's independence, dignity, and personhood. They saw the ability to end, or abort, an unwanted pregnancy as an important part of this right. Although some states liberalized their abortion laws in the late 1960s and early 1970s, abortions remained illegal in many states unless the mother's life was at risk. Some women without access to legal abortion services resorted to illegal abortions or tried to perform them themselves. Many women died from such unsafe procedures and the resulting injuries and infections.

Feminists fought to make abortion legal. In 1973, the U.S. Supreme Court heard the case *Roe v. Wade*. The Court ruled that state laws restricting abortion during the first three months of pregnancy were unconstitutional. *Roe v. Wade* did not remove all legal restrictions on abortions; it allowed states to limit abortion later in a pregnancy. Still, the ruling guaranteed women access to safe, legal abortions. While *Roe v. Wade* is still in effect well into the twenty-first century, it remains a controversial topic and a focus of modern-day political and cultural debates.

The Feminist Legacy

Besides abortion, many rights we may take for granted today are a direct result of the feminist movement. Before the feminist movement, married women did not have the right to apply for their own credit cards. Many states deemed it legal for a husband to rape his wife. Women who found themselves unhappily pregnant—for any reason—had no legal alternative to having the child. Feminists challenged cultural norms that labeled women as childlike, hysterical, and incapable. They set up rape crisis centers and rallied against domestic violence. They fought for women's reproductive rights, equal pay, and for women to be treated with dignity and respect.

HISTORY COMES ALIVE

In 1968, feminists gathered in Atlantic City to protest the Miss America pageant. Feminists believed that the pageant celebrated women as objects, rather than for their achievements. The protest took place outside the pageant hall. About 200 women gathered with signs and crowned a sheep Miss America to highlight the pageant's absurdity. Feminists discarded what they saw as objects of feminine oppression—makeup, wigs, Cosmopolitan and Playboy, and restrictive undergarments—in a "Freedom Trash Can." Feminists believed that these objects kept women enslaved to a beauty culture that judged women on their appearance, not their character. Although nothing was lit on fire that day, media coverage of the event claimed that women had set fire to their bras. This misconception promoted an image of the protestors as both crazy and dangerous, undermining the seriousness of their work and their perspective. The bra-burning myth clung to feminists for many years.

ASSASSINATIONS

In addition to major changes in the world of social equality, simmering anger and tension also exploded against prominent political leaders during the 1960s. Several shocking assassinations over the course of the decade added to a sense of national unrest.

John F. Kennedy

John F. Kennedy, elected president in 1960, was smart, handsome, and idealistic. His youth and vigor charmed the nation. After the close 1960 presidential race between Nixon and Kennedy, Kennedy's supporters were excited about the new president's innovations, such as the New Frontier, a domestic campaign that aimed to use federal money to increase social services. However, without a Democratic majority in Congress, Kennedy had difficulty getting legislation passed. In addition, he was unable to overcome the foreign policy challenges posed by the tense climate of the Cold War. His attempt to spur a Cuban revolution at the Bay of Pigs failed miserably and publicly. In the **Cuban Missile Crisis**, his initial aggressive response to the placement of Soviet missiles in Cuba helped bring the world to the brink of nuclear war. As the fate of the world hung in the balance, many Americans—aware that the Soviets already had nuclear missiles in Cuba that could travel more than 2,000 miles, which meant they could reach major U.S. cities—prepared for the worst. Fortunately, their fears never came to pass. After a few days of charged diplomatic discussions, both Kennedy and Soviet leader Nikita Khrushchev agreed to back down in order to avoid nuclear war.

CUBAN MISSILE CRISIS A 1962 showdown between the Soviet Union and the United States over the Soviet military presence, especially nuclear weapons, in Cuba.

JOHN F. KENNEDY

13¢ UNITED STATES

Despite Kennedy's mixed political record, few anticipated the events of November 22, 1963. As Kennedy and his wife rode through Dallas in a convertible during a presidential motorcade, waving to adoring fans lining the streets, Kennedy was fatally shot. Police arrested Lee Harvey Oswald, who worked in the building from which the shots apparently had been fired. Oswald had lived in the Soviet Union and had a history of Marxist beliefs, but before he could be interviewed and brought to trial, he too was assassinated by a nightclub owner named Jack Ruby. An official investigation confirmed that Oswald was Kennedy's assassin. However, a robust set of conspiracy theories emerged, claiming that Fidel Castro, the CIA, or the mafia was actually responsible for the assassination. Kennedy's untimely death had a deep emotional resonance for Americans. For many, Kennedy's death marked the end of the innocent hope of the early 1960s and brought the country into a dark and tumultuous era scarred by violence, war, and shattered American values.

Malcolm X

Malcolm X, one of the most strident leaders of the movement for social justice, delivered a message of black radicalism and black pride. He demanded that African-American men and women not bend to the cultural demands of whites. He promoted separatism, black liberation, and violence in the cause of self-defense. Even his name reflected his radical politics: born Malcolm Little, he changed his last name to X to reflect the unknown last name of his African ancestors, who, as slaves, had been forced to take their owners' name. At first, Malcolm X was a member of the militant

Black Muslim sect. However, near the end of his life, he softened his views on separatism and formally split with the Black Muslims to become a Sunni Muslim, a more mainstream denomination. This decision likely led to his assassination. While Malcolm X was speaking to a crowd in Harlem on February 21, 1965, three Black Muslim men shot him to death.

Martin Luther King, Jr.

Martin Luther King, Jr., a leader of the civil rights movement and proponent of nonviolence, was assassinated at his motel on April 4, 1968. King was in Memphis to support a labor strike. When he stepped outside onto the balcony of his room, he was fatally shot. James Earl Ray, a southern white man, was arrested and convicted of King's murder. Although King had spoken out in favor of nonviolence, his death sparked violent rage and led to riots in more than 100 cities across the country.

Robert Kennedy

In the wake of his brother's assassination, Senator Robert F. Kennedy became a national leader. As attorney general in his brother's administration, Robert Kennedy had publicly supported civil rights and integration. When Mississippi's governor refused to let a black man enroll in the University of Mississippi, Kennedy sent federal forces to ensure the student was allowed to register. Elected to the U.S. Senate in 1964, Kennedy took an outspoken position against the escalating war in Vietnam, and he hoped to be nominated as the Democratic presidential candidate in the 1968 election. On June 4, 1968, Kennedy won the California primary against Senator Eugene McCarthy, his fifth primary victory. That night, he was shot and killed in his hotel by a Palestinian man who was angry about Kennedy's position on Israel.

THE ENVIRONMENTAL MOVEMENT

During the 1960s, the modern environmental movement started to take shape. Environmental protection was not a new idea. However, in the 1960s, Americans' awareness of humanity's effects on the environment increased. In 1962, the book *Silent Spring*, by Rachel Carson, brought Americans' attention to the environmental problems caused by the use of chlorinated hydrocarbons. Awareness of such damage inspired many Americans to take action to preserve and protect the country's natural splendor, as well as to undo previous damage from decades of industrial byproducts. In 1970, the budding environmental movement implemented the first Earth Day, a day of recognition of the Earth and the environmental challenges it faces.

Interest in the environment reached the highest political tiers. As a part of his domestic program, the Great Society, President Lyndon B. Johnson urged Congress to pass legislation to help protect the American landscape, aiming to improve air and water quality and to expand the national park system. In 1970, President Richard Nixon created the **Environmental Protection Agency (EPA)**. The EPA became a vital player in environmental reform, overseeing the cleanup of environmental disasters and

ENVIRONMENTAL PROTECTION AGENCY (EPA) The federal agency responsible for creating and enforcing national guidelines for acceptable practices with regard to the environment.

setting standards for acceptable environmental practice in industry and in the production of consumer products. On December 31, 1970, Nixon signed the **Clean Air Act** into law. He declared, "I think that 1970 will be known as the year of the beginning, in which we really began to move on the problems of clean air and clean water and open spaces for the future generations of America."

CLEAN AIR ACT A law, passed in 1970, to decrease air pollution in the United States.

Interest in the environment was not confined to politicians. Many middle-class young people, disillusioned by racism, capitalism, and bourgeois values, "dropped out" of mainstream society and headed for communes or small rural communities. Often, these individuals took a keen interest in preventing environmental destruction and returning to a simpler, purer relationship with the natural world. They believed in the ideals of healthy, unprocessed food; sustainable farming; and self-sufficiency. In a direct rejection of middle-class values, hippies and utopians tried to eke out a life from the land. They hoped that living simply would provide spiritual satisfaction—and an alternative to what they saw as the uptight world of class domination, violence, environmental destruction, and power plays.

Although most of these communities did not last very long, the impulse behind them tells a lot about this era. Both idealistic and radical, many members of the environmental movement in the 1960s truly wanted to rework the way American culture was structured. Many believed that capitalism and greed were directly linked to the destruction of the natural world and that the connections between them were so embedded that the only way to fix society was to leave it and start a new version. The ideas of these early environmentalists continue to influence the environmental movement today.

VIETNAM

One of the greatest crises of the 1960s in the United States was the war in Vietnam. The United States generally supported anti-colonial revolutions, but Cold War politics complicated the situation in Vietnam, a French colony since the late nineteenth century. If the French left, the communist group supported by the United States during Japan's occupation during World War II would likely take over Vietnam's government. During the Cold War, the world divided into two groups: countries that sided with the United States and countries that became communist and allied with the Soviet Union, or USSR. U.S. officials feared that a communist Vietnam would start a domino effect in Southeast Asia and influence other countries in the region, one by one, to turn into communist enemies of the United States.

The Conflict Begins

In 1954, the United States helped to install a pro-American government in southern Vietnam, but the communist government in the north held strong. The brutal tactics of the communists in the north, such as murdering people to take their land, caused many people to flee from the north to the south. The new government in the south had a difficult time dealing with the influx of newcomers. The United States offered to help. However, the leader of South Vietnam, Ngo Dinh Diem, was unpopular.

Diem demanded absolute loyalty, stifled opposition, and favored Roman Catholics over the country's Buddhist majority.

By the time John F. Kennedy became president of the United States in 1961, there was widespread discontent in South Vietnam. The population's rejection of Diem increased support for the North Vietnam-sponsored communist resistance movement, the **Viet Cong**. Diem, concerned about the influence of the communists on his people, moved entire families of South Vietnamese peasants to prison-like compounds to prevent contact with communists and communist supporters. In protest of Diem's oppressive political and economic policies, Buddhist monks set themselves afire. These images made their way to American televisions, shocking many viewers. Although Diem had received financial backing from the United States for years, the new and public abuses led Kennedy to support Diem's removal— but not by the Viet Cong. This situation implicated the United States in the events that followed.

In November 1963, South Vietnamese generals overthrew Diem, but the region failed to stabilize. Then, on November 22, Kennedy was assassinated. By then, 16,000 U.S. troops had been sent to Vietnam, a huge increase from the 700 there in 1960. Even so, Kennedy had always distanced himself from the conflict, noting that it was really a Vietnamese fight, not an American one. Opinions differ on whether Kennedy would have followed the same course of military action as his successors did.

Escalation

After Kennedy's assassination, the new president, Lyndon B. Johnson, faced a difficult situation. Against the backdrop of Cold War tensions, the conflict in Vietnam was growing more heated. The entire world seemed to be splitting into two sides— the United States and its supporters against its communist opponents. The conflict in Vietnam made Southeast Asia a pivotal region in the balance of the Cold War. President Johnson embarked on a path of **escalation**, or increased involvement, in Vietnam.

To gain support at home for American involvement, in 1964 Johnson announced that the North Vietnamese had attacked two American vessels in the Gulf of Tonkin without cause. This was not the whole truth. The American vessels had actually been in the Gulf of Tonkin to help plan raids against the North Vietnamese, and Johnson had no conclusive evidence that the attacks had occurred. Nonetheless, Congress approved the Gulf of Tonkin Resolution, authorizing the United States to use force to prevent further attacks and opening the door for a much larger, more active U.S. military role in the conflict. In early 1965, Johnson began Operation Rolling Thunder, an air bombing campaign against North Vietnam. By 1966, almost 400,000 U.S. soldiers were on the ground in Vietnam. The devastating bombing of North Vietnam barely seemed to affect the Viet Cong and North Vietnamese army, however. Using an extensive network of tunnels and resting places, they continued to send weapons and supplies southward.

Johnson was aware that a massive military maneuver might entice one of the nuclear-armed communist powers, the Soviet Union or China,

VIET CONG The North Vietnam-sponsored communist resistance group that opposed South Vietnam and the United States before and during the Vietnam War.

ESCALATION The policy of increasing the U.S. military presence and involvement in Vietnam during the Vietnam War.

to join the fight. The Cuban Missile Crisis had brought the United States and the Soviet Union to the brink of nuclear war less than a year before Johnson took office. He was determined to avoid repeating that situation. Instead of engaging in direct attacks with large numbers of troops and powerful weapons, he and his strategists decided to focus on wearing down the Viet Cong through sustained small-scale offensives like the use of chemical weapons, such as napalm and Agent Orange. Johnson also sanctioned a near-constant bombing campaign with the aim of preventing the Viet Cong from sending weapons and other supplies to South Vietnam. These protracted tactics had limited effect against the determination of the enemy. Many Americans felt that Vietnam was turning into a war that could not be won.

The Tet Offensive

A pivotal moment for public opinion came in January 1968. The South Vietnamese and the North Vietnamese had instituted a truce to celebrate the holiday of Tet. However, on January 31, the Viet Cong launched a deadly attack on Saigon and other South Vietnamese urban centers, even briefly occupying the U.S. embassy in Saigon. The battle ended in a few days with a victory for the Americans and their South Vietnamese counterparts. However, the strength of the surprise attack made many Americans doubt that the war could be won. General William Westmoreland, the U.S. Army commander in charge of the war, assured Americans that everything was going smoothly, but the presence of Viet Cong fighters in the U.S. embassy seemed to contradict his assurances.

War on TV

The Vietnam War was the first war to be extensively televised, and the televised images had a strong effect on public views of the war. Graphic visuals of the bombing campaigns that hammered Southeast Asia, leveling towns and villages and destroying vegetation, including huge stretches of agricultural land, angered many. News reports on American and Vietnamese casualties shocked and horrified the public. Not all news about the war came from the front lines. Televised hearings of the Senate Foreign Relations Committee, led by antiwar Senator J. William Fulbright, examined U.S. policy and military strategy in Vietnam—and raised questions about the war for many people.

Walter Cronkite

After reporting on the Tet Offensive from Vietnam, the beloved news anchor Walter Cronkite departed from his usual neutral stance to express an opinion on the Vietnam War. On the evening news on February 27, 1968, Cronkite proclaimed,

> It seems now more certain than ever, that the bloody experience of Vietnam is to end in a stalemate …. It is increasingly clear to this reporter that the only rational way out then will be to negotiate, not as victors, but as an honorable people who lived up to their pledge to defend democracy, and did the best they could.

President Johnson understood that Cronkite's statement could have serious repercussions for public support of the war. Cronkite rarely offered political judgments, and Americans had tremendous respect for the newsman and his opinions. "If I've lost Cronkite, I've lost Middle America," Johnson said.

Soon, even the president seemed to agree that the war was futile—and was sapping financial resources from important programs such as the Great Society, Johnson's effort to reduce poverty and expand social programs. Johnson decided not to run for president again. He also initiated diplomatic talks to bring about an end to the war. Even as the bombing continued, Johnson essentially declared that victory was no longer the goal of the war. The new goal was to begin the process of leaving Vietnam with as little additional damage as possible.

Nixon's Legacy in Vietnam

Despite his previous support for the war, Johnson's successor, President Richard M. Nixon, also wanted to see the Vietnam War end. Nixon still hoped to win and planned to further escalate the war to force the North Vietnamese to surrender. However, public opinion opposed escalation, so Nixon instead tried to discuss troop withdraws with the North Vietnamese. At the same time, he initiated a secret bombing campaign in Cambodia, where a large number of North Vietnamese and Viet Cong troops were gathered.

Nixon also introduced a new strategy called **Vietnamization**. Under this plan, American troops withdrew from the region in spurts and planned for South Vietnamese soldiers to take their place. Far from solving the conflict, Nixon's policy kept the war going. Vietnamization did succeed in reducing the number of American soldiers in the conflict, however. By 1973, there were only 10 percent as many U.S. troops in Vietnam as had been there in 1969.

VIETNAMIZATION Richard Nixon's plan to withdraw U.S. troops from Vietnam by supporting South Vietnamese replacement fighters.

In the meantime, new information increased opposition to the war still further. In late 1969, the *New York Times* broke a story that shocked many Americans. The previous year, a platoon of U.S. soldiers had entered the small village of My Lai. There, the platoon leader, following orders from higher-up military officials, ordered his men to slaughter hundreds of innocent Vietnamese villagers. The military tried to keep this incident hidden, but one soldier refused to keep the secret.

This man was not the only soldier who felt ambivalent about his role in the war. Most soldiers were very young, and the vast majority were poor or working class. Many felt no particular commitment to the unpopular war they had been drafted to fight. The fighting was sudden and deadly, the natural environment hostile, and the moral mandate murky. Because North Vietnamese and South Vietnamese looked the same and their language was incomprehensible to most soldiers, the soldiers had a hard time distinguishing between friend and enemy. As victory began to seem hopeless, some soldiers deserted, ignored orders, or injured themselves or others in hopes of getting out of Vietnam alive.

Back in the United States, news of the secret bombing in Cambodia broke in 1970, precipitating more antiwar protests at colleges and universities. Tragically, National Guardsman sent to quell the protests shot and killed several student

Opposition to the Vietnam War was not confined to the civilian population. Many soldiers also protested the war, some by simply deserting. Some disgruntled soldiers carried out "fraggings." They threw grenades or fragmentation bombs at their own officers, either for personal revenge or in hopes of avoiding further combat. In 1970, there were 209 fraggings. Back home, members of Vietnam Veterans Against the War testified in the "Winter Soldier" investigation, revealing the savage brutality they had witnessed in Vietnam. In 1971, about a thousand veterans gathered in Washington, D.C., to denounce the war. As a symbolic rejection of their service, they threw their war medals from Vietnam over the fence of the Capitol building.

protestors at Kent State University in Ohio. In January 1971, the Senate repealed the Gulf of Tonkin resolution and refused to supply funds for the Cambodian incursions. Sadly, not all antiwar protesters distinguished between the leaders behind the war and the individual soldiers, many of whom had little choice about going to Vietnam or simply wanted to serve their country. A total of 58,000 American servicemembers died in the war, and hundreds of thousands more were wounded. Moreover, many who returned safely were censured for their participation. After surviving the brutal war, veterans faced the painful experience of coming home to a critical public.

The End of the War

Throughout the early 1970s, President Nixon engaged in peace talks with the North Vietnamese in the hope of finding a way to extricate the United States from the war. However, the North Vietnamese refused to withdraw their troops from the South. Nixon accepted their terms right before the 1972 presidential election—but the South Vietnamese did not, and the peace talks crumbled once again. Nixon then initiated the biggest bombing campaign of the war. This audacious move infuriated many, but peace talks finally proved successful a few months later. The Paris Peace Accords stated that if the United States withdrew all its troops, American prisoners of war (POWs) would be released. Not long after U.S. troops left Vietnam, the North Vietnamese attacked South Vietnam. The South Vietnamese resisted for nearly two years, but in April 1975, as North Vietnamese tanks overtook Saigon and the American embassy, American television viewers were left with one final image of the Vietnam War: desperate South Vietnamese citizens trying to catch the last helicopters out of the region.

The Vietnam War, deadly and unwinnable, is generally regarded as a low point in U.S. military history and foreign policy. Though the war might have prevented further communist expansion on a global scale, American involvement seemed to have merely prolonged the inevitable communist victory. Many Vietnamese were fighting to protect their homeland from outsiders. The war caused terrible destruction, including the deaths of thousands of American soldiers and Vietnamese fighters and civilians. The Vietnam countryside was ravaged by

chemical weapons, citizens were displaced and became refugees, and many fatherless babies were born to Vietnamese women who had had relations with American soldiers. In the United States, the war polarized the country. In addition, the mishandling of the Vietnam War made Americans less trusting of their elected leaders.

CONSCRIPTION

After World War II, the United States continued to maintain a draft. The draft helped fill positions in the military even during peacetime and gave the armed forces a way to fill their ranks quickly in case the tensions of the Cold War broke into actual war. When male citizens turned eighteen, they had to register with the Selective Service, or the draft. During the 1960s, men were eligible for the draft for seven years, between the ages of nineteen and twenty-six, with the oldest being drafted first. When young men's draft cards were pulled, they had to report for duty and were conscripted into a mandatory term of military service. When the war in Vietnam escalated, the number of men drafted increased steadily.

As news from Vietnam reached the United States, the public learned from disaffected soldiers and media sources that the fight seemed disorganized; was based on corrupt principles; and, eventually, was unwinnable. Such revelations fueled the antiwar movement in the United States—and opposition to the draft. The counterculture, based on the ideals of individual freedom from control and repression, did not accept that the rights of an individual citizen were secondary to the needs of the government. Members of the counterculture felt that the government's ability to insist that young men fight and die for their country, especially in an unjust, unpopular war, was unacceptable.

Antiwar protests often involved young men burning their draft cards in a symbolic display of disdain and disobedience. Some draftees fled the country when their numbers came up or ignored their conscription, actions that put them at risk for legal repercussions. Still others looked for loopholes. College students were exempt from conscription, as were men with certain medical conditions. Some men filed for conscientious objector status, claiming that their religious beliefs forbade them from serving in the military. Other men joined reserve units or the National Guard in the hope of avoiding the brutal and deadly conflict half a world away. These methods allowed many middle-class men to avoid military service. As a result, 80 percent of enlisted soldiers in Vietnam were poor or working class. The wartime draft was so unpopular that President Richard M. Nixon promised not only to withdraw the troops but also to end conscription. Since 1973, the United States has relied on an all-volunteer military. However, young men are still required to register in case of a future draft.

STUDY ALERT

The Vietnam War and the protests against it divided the nation. However, although the majority of Americans opposed the war at some points, many did not appreciate the unrest that the protesters created.

CIVIL RIGHTS

The civil rights movement, which largely took shape in the 1950s, was a sustained national effort to achieve racial equality. After decades of fighting to claim long-denied economic, political, and social rights, African-Americans finally achieved legal protection and cultural influence in the 1950s and '60s. The civil rights movement changed the landscape of American race relations. It proved that public organizing and protest could be powerful tools to help enact social and legislative change, providing inspiration—and practical tactics—to other groups that faced discrimination in the United States and around the world. The women's movement and the movement for gay liberation, for example, based their organizational strategies on ideas and tactics successfully used by the civil rights movement. The idea that all Americans are entitled to civil rights—regardless of their race, gender, ethnicity, sexual orientation, or level of ability—has resonated powerfully in American life.

The civil rights movement succeeded in legally desegregating schools, ending Jim Crow laws, and securing protected rights at the federal level. Although it set a national mandate for equal treatment and equal opportunity, the civil rights movement did not completely wipe out racial discrimination or eliminate prejudice. Even today, African-Americans are, on average, paid less, incarcerated more, and more likely to live in poverty than white Americans.

Desegregation of the Military

African-Americans had been attempting to resist racial discrimination throughout the history of the United States, long before the civil rights movement really came together in the 1950s. However, a variety of social and political developments in the mid-twentieth century helped these efforts succeed more than in the past.

During the Cold War, America's values were projected onto an international screen. The United States set itself up as a nation that opposed communism and stood for freedom, liberty, equality, and fairness. Legal discrimination against people of color in the United States contradicted these values. After World War II, President Harry S. Truman began to pay more attention to race relations, in part because the Soviets were explicitly critiquing the treatment of African-Americans in the United States. Even though the Constitution protected the right of black Americans to vote, in the South they had had been functionally barred from voting through quasi-legal and often violent means. However, the Great Migration had brought many African-Americans to northern cities, where they could vote. These new voters were of interest to Truman's party, the Democrats. To appeal to these voters, Truman commissioned the President's Committee on Civil Rights to carry out a national investigation. The committee's 1947 report argued that the federal government needed to play a far greater role in ending segregation and racial discrimination, especially in the U.S. military. The report echoed the advocacy of civil rights and workers' rights activist A. Phillip Randolph, who had headed the Committee Against Jim Crow in Military Service during World War II.

In 1948, Truman followed the report's advice and desegregated the military. Until then, African-Americans in the military had been segregated at all levels and were often given the worst, most menial tasks. This **desegregation** was an early legislative victory for the civil rights movement, and a sign that—at least at the federal level—things were starting to change. However, Southern congressmen blocked a number of additional proposed federal legislative changes, including laws to protect voting and employment rights and a bill against lynching.

DESEGREGATION The process of ending mandated racial divisions in public spaces or institutions.

Brown v. Board of Education and School Desegregation

In the 1898 case *Plessy v. Ferguson*, the U.S. Supreme Court had ruled that states had the right to segregate the races, as separate did not necessarily mean unequal. However, African-American schools and other facilities remained underfunded and dilapidated in comparison to white institutions. By the 1950s, the idea that segregation in the South was separate but equal had become an obvious untruth. The Supreme Court reopened the issue of segregation in 1954 in the landmark case ***Brown v. Board of Education of Topeka, Kansas***. The Supreme Court ruled unanimously that segregated schools denied African-American children the equal protection under the law granted by the 14th Amendment. This case overturned the *Plessy v. Ferguson* decision and was subsequently used to justify outlawing additional segregationist practices across the South. Courts ruled against segregation in public housing, transportation, and public places such as parks and beaches. The National Association for the Advancement of Colored People (NAACP) was instrumental in pushing many of these cases to the Supreme Court.

BROWN V. BOARD OF EDUCATION OF TOPEKA, KANSAS The landmark civil rights case that ruled that the legal segregation of schools unconstitutional.

Legally outlawing segregation was a major victory, but desegregating the South did not go quickly or smoothly. In 1955, the Supreme Court ruled that schools should be desegregated "with all deliberate speed." However, desegregation met with enormous—and often violent—resistance. Ku Klux Klan membership increased tremendously, and whites across the South formed White Citizens Councils to resist desegregation of schools and public places. Often, desegregation had to be enforced through court orders or the threat of losing federal aid. In Little Rock, Arkansas, a plan to desegregate schools was met by massive resistance from White Citizens Councils and from the governor of Arkansas, Orval Faubus. Faubus even called in the National Guard to ensure that the first wave of integration did not occur. Ordered to let nine black students enter the local high school, Faubus lost the use of the National Guardsmen he had placed there to prevent the students from entering when Eisenhower federalized them. However, the students were met by a mob of furious white citizens, screaming in protest. President Eisenhower ordered the 101st Airborne division to initially protect the black students, and guardsmen remained in the high school for the year. To avoid having to integrate the school system, Faubus then closed all the city's high schools. The schools remained closed until the courts finally insisted that they be reopened in 1959.

The Montgomery Bus Boycott

The victory of *Brown v. Board of Education* encouraged African-Americans to join local, grassroots forms of protest against segregation and discrimination in other areas of their lives. In Montgomery, Alabama, local laws stated that blacks had to give up their seats on buses or trains if asked by a white person. In late 1955, a seamstress named Rosa Parks declined to give up her bus seat to a white man. When Parks was arrested, local African-Americans responded by organizing a massive boycott of Montgomery's bus system. The financial effect on the local bus company was so strong that it agreed to integrate. However, city leaders refused to budge on the law. As a result, the bus boycott lasted almost a year until, well into 1956, the Supreme Court agreed with a lower court that segregation on the buses could not stand. This hard-won local victory was a sign of things to come. The success of nonviolent methods of protest set the stage for the future battles of the civil rights movement. Another important development of the boycott was that it brought the community leadership skills of the Reverend Martin Luther King, Jr., to public prominence.

Civil Rights in the Early 1960s

The successes of the civil rights movement in the 1950s inspired additional protests and action throughout the country. Many of these protests were based on the idea of **non-violent resistance**. The Student Nonviolent Coordinating Committee (SNCC) and the Southern Christian Leadership Conference (SCLC), major civil rights groups formed in the late 1950s and early 1960s, agreed that discrimination was best fought through peaceful means. The Congress of Racial Equality (CORE), an interracial organization that had already been working on civil rights issues for about twenty years, was another major proponent of nonviolence. The Montgomery bus boycott had been both successful and bloodless. Nonviolent protests allowed

NONVIOLENT RESISTANCE
The protest tactic, used by many civil rights activists, of committing peaceful acts of civil disobedience, rather than engaging in violent confrontation.

protesters to remain dignified and receive public sympathy. Angry white mobs and enforcement agents tasked with breaking up the protests seemed by comparison to be brutal, violent, and hysterical.

Different kinds of peaceful protests took place across the South in the early 1960s. One of the first was a "sit-in" at a Woolworths deli counter in Greensboro, North Carolina, on February 1, 1960. African-American protesters in many cities followed the same tactic at white-only spaces such as lunch counters, pools, and churches. As a form of protest, these protesters entered these segregated spaces and simply stayed there. Police and ordinary white citizens retaliated, often violently, against the peaceful protestors. Citizens threw rocks and police beat protestors with clubs, but the protestors' commitment to nonviolence was strong.

In 1961, CORE began organizing "freedom rides" as a new way to fight segregation. Federal legislation had already outlawed segregation on public transportation, but buses and trains in many parts of the South remained segregated. To test the boundaries of this legislation, groups of white and black "freedom riders" climbed on buses and rode together through the South. Their actions infuriated many Southerners. The freedom riders endured attacks and beatings in several cities, and mobs burned one of the riders' buses.

White people who resisted civil rights were the norm in the South, not the exception. The citizens who made up the hysterical white mobs were not merely a lunatic fringe. Elected officials and powerful community leaders often led resistance to desegregation. At the University of Alabama, the state governor used his body to block the entrance of potential black students. He backed down only at the insistence of federal marshals, who had been sent to ensure that desegregation occur peacefully. When African-American student James Meredith attempted to study at the University of Mississippi, or "Ole Miss," the governor of Mississippi refused to let Meredith attend, so federal troops were called in. A mob of furious white citizens resisted the soldiers so fiercely that two people died.

Peaceful protestors faced many instances of violence. In Philadelphia, Mississippi, three civil rights workers—two white men and a black man who had come to register African-American voters—were arrested and beaten to death. In Birmingham, Alabama, Commissioner of Public Safety Eugene "Bull" Connor responded to nonviolent protesters with police dogs, fire hoses, and cattle prods. As Americans viewed television images of this aggressive display of force against peaceful marchers, public support for civil rights swelled across the country.

President John F. Kennedy became one of these new supporters. He went on television to promise a major overhaul of civil rights legislation and federal support for African-American voters and the desegregation process. That same night, Medgar Evers, a civil rights leader and prominent member of the NAACP, was shot to death on his property in Mississippi. This tragedy inspired further national support for the movement.

Martin Luther King, Jr.

At this tumultuous time, Martin Luther King, Jr., stepped into the limelight as one of the most prominent leaders of the civil rights

movement. King, the grandson of a slave, had earned a PhD at Boston University and was working as a minister. At the time of the Montgomery bus boycott, King had only been preaching at a local church for about a year. Still, his effective organization of the bus boycott and his flair for public oration brought him into the national eye, where he would remain until his death. His leadership inspired the nonviolent tactics on which the civil rights movement relied. Having read about civil disobedience from earlier thinkers such as Henry David Thoreau and Ghandi, and using the Bible as inspiration, King was instrumental in bringing this form of protest to civil rights organizers.

After the bus boycott, King and other civil rights leaders formed the Southern Christian Leadership Conference (SCLC), an organization for civil rights that explicitly included the black church in the fight against discrimination. The SCLC helped shape the policy and tactics of the resistance movement and provided an opportunity for devoted churchgoers to join the struggle. This was an especially attractive option for female

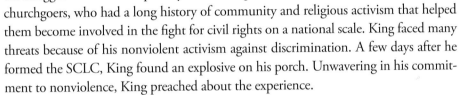

churchgoers, who had a long history of community and religious activism that helped them become involved in the fight for civil rights on a national scale. King faced many threats because of his nonviolent activism against discrimination. A few days after he formed the SCLC, King found an explosive on his porch. Unwavering in his commitment to nonviolence, King preached about the experience.

King was involved in many major civil rights skirmishes and victories. He was arrested after the protests in Birmingham in 1963. While he was in jail, he wrote the classic "Letter from a Birmingham Jail," an eloquent defense of nonviolence as a method of resistance based on love, justice, and hope. Until this point, King had been trying to highlight the injustice of segregation to make it visible to white citizens. After Birmingham, King focused more on getting the federal government to pass far-reaching civil rights legislation. Although King did not necessarily welcome violent responses from those opposed to racial equality, he hoped that that the furious and violent reactions protestors faced would inspire enough public sympathy and support to help pass federal legislation. To encourage further support, in 1963, soon after his arrest in Birmingham, King helped organize a massive march on Washington. The march attracted 250,000 participants and ended with King's famous and rousing "I Have a Dream" speech. His words remained a touchstone for many during the trials to come.

As the 1960s wore on and race riots and demonstrations became more violent, King stayed true to his nonviolent ideals. Even after new black radicals began to call for armed resistance, King refused to advocate violence. In other ways, however, King did become more radical in his ideas. The Vietnam War was escalating, and King highlighted parallels between what he saw as international racial oppression and the domestic variety. By 1966, King had also embarked on a poor people's campaign that directly linked the plight of African-Americans with workers' struggles. Taking on poverty as well as race, King traveled across the country delivering speeches and helping organize marches and protests.

King had little time to focus on his more radical ideas. On April 4, 1968, an assassin ended his life. The career of one of the most beloved and effective leaders of the civil rights movement was over.

Legislative Victories

After the assassination of President Kennedy, President Johnson made good on Kennedy's promise to have the federal government take charge of matters of civil rights. In 1964, he signed the Civil Rights Act, the most expansive civil rights legislation enacted up to that point. The act made racial discrimination illegal in public accommodations such as restaurants and hotels, and it outlawed discrimination in the workplace based on race, religion, national origin, or sex and created the Equal Employment Opportunity Commission (EEOC) to ensure that employers would comply with the laws.

In 1965, King organized a campaign to register black voters, many of whom had been long disenfranchised. Protestors embarked on a long march across Alabama from Selma to Montgomery to promote voting rights. State police met the marchers with armed resistance. President Johnson sent in federal troops, and the marchers continued on to Montgomery. With this spectacle on the national stage, Johnson asked Congress to find a solution. In 1965, Congress passed the Voting Rights Act, which provided federal protection for all voters. In counties where large numbers of voters were unregistered, the act permitted federal examiners to oversee the voter registration process. Local methods of disenfranchisement, such as poll taxes and literacy tests, were banned. In the years following the passage of the Voting Rights Act, a flood of African-Americans registered to vote. In 1960, only 20 percent of black voters had been registered. By 1971, 62 percent were registered.

RACE RIOTS

The 1950s and early 1960s witnessed some major legislative civil rights advances, from the mandate to desegregate schools in 1954 in the Supreme Court's *Brown v. Board of Education* decision to the Civil Rights Act of 1964. However, many civil rights advocates in the 1960s found these policy changes insufficient. For example, although the Supreme Court had ordered schools across the country to integrate "with all deliberate speed," in actuality, desegregation was a slow and often painful process that met with resistance.

Many people in the 1960s were not content to rely on government intervention, which seemed to provide inadequate solutions to poverty and other issues that affected the African-American community. During the 1960s, African-Americans' frustration and anger at centuries of unequal treatment and slow-moving changes led to outbreaks of violence and urban rioting in cities across the country, particularly during the summer months.

These "Long Hot Summers" were largely a reaction to African-Americans' situation in the United States. Centuries of enslavement had kept African-Americans, as a community, from experiencing financial independence or gain. Even after African-Americans gained freedom following the Civil War, discriminatory policies limited their political power, economic earning potential, and educational opportunities. Many civil rights activists in the 1950s and 1960s worked toward specific policy changes, such as ending segregation. In contrast, the **Black Power** movement, which gained prominence in the 1960s, sought to increase black pride, urging African-Americans to resist racism and to rediscover the beauty and dignity of their African heritage. Militant Black Power leaders stoked the simmering fury in the black community about issues such as police brutality. White police officers who beat or killed African-Americans served as a maddening and powerful symbol of white domination and sparked **race riots** across the country.

In New York City in 1964, the police shot a young black man they had arrested. In response, young people in the city rioted for more than a week. In the next few years, riots broke out in cities across the country to protest unfair treatment of African-Americans by police. In Los Angeles in 1965, after a traffic stop led to the beating and arrest of two young black men and their younger brother, a devastating riot broke out in the Watts neighborhood. The Watts Riots lasted nearly a week and resulted in the deaths of thirty-four African-Americans. In 1966, rioting broke out in Chicago, Cleveland, and dozens of other cities. The riots grew more deadly and more widespread each year. Most took place in urban centers in the South, the Northeast, and the Midwest. During the summer of 1967, rioting occurred in more than twenty-two cities. In Detroit, forty-four people died, tanks were called in to subdue the rioters, and millions of dollars of damage marred black urban communities.

RACE RIOTS The violent expression of racial and class inequality that swept through American cities during the 1960s.

Because the riots were largely a reaction to centuries of discriminatory treatment, the government and white Americans bore some responsibility for the situation. In 1967, President Johnson created the Kerner Commission to look into the causes of these race riots. In some ways, the government commission's final conclusion, published in March 1968, echoed the ideas of militant Black Power rhetoric. The report states, "White society is deeply implicated in the ghetto. White institutions created it, white institutions maintain it, and white society condones it."

Acknowledging white society's contribution to the problem did not solve it. A month after the government report came out, Martin Luther King, Jr. was assassinated. His death set off more riots in 125 cities across the country. King, a proponent of nonviolent action, racial integration, and economic equality, was shot dead by a white man. Many felt that King's death exemplified what happened to black men who spoke out publicly for civil rights. In this environment, urban riots acted as a release valve for the powerlessness felt by impoverished African-Americans across the country.

Black Separatism

Even in the wake of legislative victories, many civil rights activists were becoming radicalized. Despite changing laws, many younger radicals noticed that legislation was not exactly changing hearts and minds. Regardless of the laws on the books, Africans Americans and civil rights activists of all races found themselves confronted with widespread resistance to their efforts. Black radicals who believed the true problem to be outside the scope of the government, including some members of the SNCC and CORE, began to distance themselves from more moderate protesters. Stokely Carmichael, the head of the SNCC, turned to the philosophy of black power, which encouraged black separatism from whites. Carmichael even removed white allies from the SNCC in 1966. Black separatists believed that

African-Americans needed to reclaim their own communities, power, heritage, and pride and that whites should play no part in the process. Many younger radicals followed Carmichael away from the nonviolent ideals of the civil rights movement. In later years, the SNCC advocated violent resistance. Meanwhile, on the West Coast, Huey Newton and Bobby Seale created a new organization called the Black Panthers, committed to self-defense and community assistance. Black Panthers in cities across the country armed themselves to defend against police brutality. Many also supported resistance movements in other countries, noting that the struggles of oppressed people exist across national boundaries.

Black pride offered African-Americans the opportunity to examine their history and their roots in Africa. The black power movement sought to celebrate the beauty and dignity of black culture and erase any sense of white superiority. This movement helped change education in the following years, introducing African-American culture and history into classrooms. Colleges added African-American studies departments and classes on black art and literature.

Many white Americans felt threatened by the black pride movement's challenges to white cultural dominance—and by images of armed black men patrolling the cities. The extremism of black separatism turned the tide of popular support. Although Black Power hastened the end of the cohesive civil rights movement, it added to our shared understanding of the value of the black community and black culture. The Black Power movement helped many African-Americans embrace their heritage and question the valuation of white culture and institutions over their own.

Other Communities

The civil rights movement typically refers to African-Americans' sustained fight for rights from the mid-1950s through the 1960s. Although this movement was very public and achieved stunning successes, civil rights do not relate only to African-Americans. Other groups fought for civil rights as well. Many modeled their movements, goals, and tactics on the African-American civil rights movement. For example, the American Indian Movement (AIM) fought to expose the long

history of the nation's prejudices toward American Indians. AIM members engaged in many public acts of resistance, including the occupation of Alcatraz Island from 1969 to 1971. AIM claimed that because Indians "discovered" the island first, it should technically belong to them. This protest sought to empower Indians as a trans-tribal ethnic group and to call attention to the historical displacement of Indians through illegal property deals between Indians and white Americans, including the U.S. government. Many Mexican-Americans, or Chicanos, also became increasingly radicalized at this time. Some demanded university Chicano studies classes and departments. Others focused on the representation of Chicanos in politics. Cesar Chavez, notably, used Chicano identity to stage a successful campaign for the rights of migrant workers.

The gay liberation movement took inspiration from the successes of the civil rights movements as well.

Long subject to police harassment, homosexuals had banded together in small groups and societies but had never been able to engage in large-scale resistance against discrimination. Gay bars were frequent targets of police raids, and gay Americans frequently faced violence and employment discrimination. In 1969, a police raid at a gay bar in New York City led the gay clientele to actively resist the harassment. The ensuing Stonewall Riot spurred a popular and successful movement in which gay people banded together to promote fair treatment, tolerance, and pride.

The civil rights movement has had a longstanding effect on American culture. In addition to expanding the protection of all Americans' civil rights, it proved that groups could use their shared identity to promote political and cultural change. Although discrimination still exists, the strategies and successes of the civil rights movement proved that our country has the potential to progress toward fair treatment, liberty, equality, and equal protection under the law for all.

MID-CHAPTER QUESTIONS

1. What were the major changes that women experienced during the 1960s? How did these changes affect their lives and what evidence do you see in today's world that reflects these changes?

2. Why were so many prominent politicians and cultural leaders assassinated during this time of turmoil?

3. Why did the television coverage of the war in Vietnam affect the social and political unrest of the era? What are the similarities and differences between the way that the U.S. public responded to the conflict in Vietnam and the more recent wars in Afghanistan and Iraq?

4. Why did the condition of black Americans change so drastically during the 1960s? What were the major causes and why were the methods of protest successful or unsuccessful?

THE GREAT SOCIETY

After President Kennedy's assassination in 1963, Vice President Lyndon B. Johnson was sworn into office. A Texas Democrat, Johnson was a political powerhouse. He had worked in Washington for more than two decades, and his trademark tactic was compromise through intimidation. In addition to conducting extensive negotiations, Johnson used both his height and his political influence to sway people to support his legislation. As a congressman, he had proved instrumental in helping to push liberal legislation through Congress. As president, Johnson hoped to follow in the tradition of President Franklin D. Roosevelt. He embarked on a domestic program called the **Great Society**, which included a variety of programs aimed at reducing poverty and racial inequality in the United States.

Following the model of Roosevelt's New Deal, Johnson attempted to relieve economic suffering through the passage of many programs tailored to specific societal ills. The early years of Johnson's presidency were marked by a flurry of legislative victories. In 1964, he both signed into law the Civil Rights Act of 1964 and started a "war on poverty" by having Congress pass the Economic Opportunity

GREAT SOCIETY President Lyndon B. Johnson's set of domestic programs to fight poverty and racial inequality.

Act. This Act created the Office of Economic Opportunity, which administered far-reaching social programs. The Act also allotted money to farmers and small businesses, created work-study jobs for students in higher education, and created the Job Corps, which provided jobs for poor urban young adults. It also created the VISTA program, which mobilized volunteers to assist poor communities in the United States. Although the Great Society ultimately failed to meet its goal of eliminating poverty in the United States, many of its programs had positive and lasting effects.

Head Start

HEAD START A government program, started as part of the Great Society, to provide free or subsidized preschool education to children from poor families.

One enduring program created during Johnson's early presidency was **Head Start**. Johnson, noting the connection between education levels and economic opportunity, focused on education as a way to help prevent poverty. Head Start provided free or subsidized preschool education for impoverished children. In later years, Head Start also provided subsidized preschool for families just above the poverty line. In addition, the federal program provided grants to help cities form their own Head Start centers. The program gave poor families access to federally-provided, free childcare. Head Start was not just a babysitting program, though. Its high-quality preschools helped prepare young children from disadvantaged communities and families to succeed in elementary school. Head Start continues to fund early childhood education centers today.

Johnson also created programs to assist students in other areas of education. He poured money into elementary and high schools through the Elementary and Secondary Education Act in 1965 and created the Higher Education Act, which gave students grants for university study. These programs helped improve education for impoverished and middle-class children and young adults.

Medicare

MEDICARE A government program, started as part of the Great Society, to provide medical insurance to elderly Americans.

MEDICAID A government program, started as part of the Great Society, to provide medical insurance to low-income Americans.

In 1965, Johnson also pushed through legislation to create **Medicare**, a program to provide health insurance for Americans over 65 years of age, and **Medicaid**, a program that insured low-income Americans. These programs represented a compromise. The American Medical Association (AMA) had successfully opposed legislation for a national health insurance system, first proposed by President Harry S. Truman. Insuring limited groups—elderly and impoverished Americans—proved less controversial.

Former President Truman was the first person to sign up for Medicare. By 2011, more than 47 million elderly and disabled Americans relied on Medicare for health insurance. Medicare helps pay for routine doctor visits, hospital care, and preventative health services. Since 2006, Medicare has also helped pay for prescription drugs. Today, Medicare is one of the most popular government programs. The program comes at a price, however. In 2010, Medicare costs were equal to 3.6 percent of the U.S. gross domestic product (GDP). Government officials estimate that, without changes, Medicare spending will reach 5.5. percent of GDP by 2035 and 6.2 percent of GDP by 2085. Over time, the trust fund that has provided much of the funding for Medicare has also become depleted. Government officials predict that it will run out of money completely by 2029. Lawmakers face the challenge of finding ways to continue providing important medical services to elderly Americans while controlling Medicare spending.

The Later Years of the Great Society

The Great Society pumped money into a variety of cultural and social welfare programs besides Head Start, Medicare, and Medicaid. Johnson increased federal funding for public housing, grocery assistance, and rent and mortgage assistance. He founded the National Endowment for the Arts (NEA) and the National Endowment for Humanities (NEH), which provided federal money to promote the arts, artists, and scholars. He also expanded Social Security benefits to include professions that had previously been excluded, such as domestic and agricultural workers.

These programs continued the idealism of the New Deal. Spurred by the idea that the federal government was responsible for the welfare of its people, Johnson—like Franklin Roosevelt—believed that government spending and social programs were the key to ending injustice. At the beginning of Johnson's presidency, this ideal was popular with Americans. In the election of 1964, Johnson won a huge victory against Barry Goldwater, a conservative Republican who spoke vehemently against government spending and social welfare programs.

As Johnson's presidency wore on, however, the public had second thoughts about his agenda. Republicans noted that the cost of Great Society programs was very high. With so many different programs, it was hard to gauge the effectiveness of any individual program. Many of the programs were inexpertly administered, and many Americans felt that the new federal spending had simply created a bloated, ineffectual bureaucracy. Although the poverty level declined throughout American society, especially among African-Americans, the effects did not seem to be substantial enough to justify the huge spending outlays of the Great Society. Moreover, it was unclear what had caused these improvements. Johnson and his supporters credited the Great Society, but his opponents pointed to general increases in national prosperity as the cause of the reduction in poverty. They complained that the president's programs were expensive and ineffectual.

Many of Johnson's former supporters also turned against his policies. Some people were disappointed that the Great Society's reforms had not gone far enough. The escalating war in Vietnam, which was proving costly and increasingly unpopular, further undermined trust in Johnson's leadership. Americans wondered why so much money was being shunted into battles overseas when the money could be used to fight the nation's struggles with domestic problems. In addition, the radical politics of the later 1960s promoted general disenchantment with authorities, including the government. The more radical wings of the civil rights movement, the feminist movement, and other countercultural groups took antigovernment positions. Members of these groups did not believe that government spending was the solution to societal problems.

It proved impossible for the Great Society programs to fulfill all the ambitious, far-reaching goals that Johnson aspired to achieve. Even though public opinion toward the Great

Society as a whole soured, though, some of its programs continue today. Head Start, Medicare, and Medicaid remain important federal programs. The ideas espoused by Johnson and Franklin Delano Roosevelt still form one key element of American political culture. Although federal spending on social programs is often controversial, many Americans agree that the federal government should provide some kind of protection for the poorest and most disadvantaged Americans. What kind of assistance is appropriate and how much money the government should spend, however, remain important topics of debate.

THE YOUTH MOVEMENT

The 1960s were a decade marked by political and social turmoil. Race riots, fury over civil rights abuses, and the escalating war in Vietnam all contributed to an uneasy atmosphere nationwide. To many, it seemed as if the government, economic leaders, and law enforcement officers were leading the country astray.

Protest, Civil and Uncivil

In the face of these problems, many young Americans envisioned a new kind of world without greed, hatred, or injustice. Many members of the youth movement were engaged with political change and proved highly effective at shaping public opinion and legislation. Members of the youth movement fought for civil rights, joined antiwar and anti-authoritarian protests, and worked tirelessly to bring about a cultural shift.

The New Left was one faction of the youth movement of the 1960s. This group of young, middle-class, mostly white people focused their energy on protests. Drawing on the example set by the civil rights movement, members of the New Left organized protests, sit-ins, and occupations across the country. An important group within the New Left was the Students for a Democratic Society (SDS), an organization founded by college students in 1960. Tom Hayden, one of the founders of SDS, wrote their organizing doctrine, the "Port Huron Statement." In it, he explained that the New Left was made up of middle-class youth who were profoundly skeptical of the organizing principles and institutions around them, including corporations, governments, and schools. Hayden called for students to reclaim the world from these larger bureaucratic structures so that they, as individuals, could exert control over their future.

Hayden's ideas inspired student activism and sit-ins across the country, particularly at college campuses. Some protestors focused specifically on injustice within university administrations. At the University of California at Berkeley, students occupied an administration building. In 1968, students at Columbia University in New York occupied administrative offices and buildings and destroyed property. For a week, classes were cancelled. Finally, the city police arrived. Police officers' use of force, which wounded some students, further incensed the student population. Violent clashes between protestors and police took place at other universities as well.

Whereas some students protested the educational system, others focused on the war in Vietnam. Huge antiwar protests took place in colleges and cities across the country. Student protestors also called attention to universities' contributions to the war. For example, government funding paid for university research for the Defense Department, and some universities invited recruiters from weapons and chemical companies to their campuses.

The SDS and the New Left continued their protests through the 1960s. However, the movement soon began to break apart. The Weathermen, an extremist subset of the New Left, used violence and terror to call attention to their agenda. They used handmade explosives to bomb government buildings and university administrative offices, killing a number of people. Like the Black Panthers, who helped turn public opinion against the civil rights movement, the Weathermen soured public opinion on the New Left. Additionally, the FBI and police infiltrated New Left groups and harassed their members, whom the officials saw as a potential threat to the nation. With these pressures, the idealism of the student protest movement waned by the 1970s.

The Counterculture

Another way young people in the 1960s addressed their concerns about the country's direction was by developing a highly visible **counterculture** that came to define the era. Members of the counterculture used music, clothing, lifestyle choices, and political action to differentiate themselves from mainstream America, or "the establishment." These **hippies** were largely young people.

Although communists, leftists, activists, and artists had challenged mainstream American society throughout the twentieth century, the 1960s counterculture was more widespread and vocal than previous movements. Rejecting the worldview that happiness came from economic achievement, many hippies chose instead to experiment with alternate modes of living. Some "dropped out" of society to pursue a hedonistic lifestyle centered on music and drugs. Some tried to reclaim communal living and work by establishing communes and intentional communities. Members of these communities believed that sharing work, land, and, sometimes, sexual partners could liberate people from the cycles of greed and despair that controlled bourgeois Americans. Some young people also found their countercultural home in the protest movement or explored Eastern religions as a way of liberating themselves from Western culture.

In the later 1960s, some hippies identified themselves as politically active Yippies—members of the Youth International Party, a more inflammatory group prone to extremist antics—or as flower children—advocates of peace, love, and beauty. These different groups within the counterculture shared the belief that American culture was based on flawed ideals. Their assessment was based partly on the images they saw on TV and in their communities: vicious attacks on people of color by the police and angry mobs; the horrific deaths of Vietnamese fighters and civilians and American soldiers in Vietnam; and the smug values of older people who seemed indifferent to all the suffering. To members of the youth movement, love, joy, peace, and a shared community were the simple answers to the problems of modern life.

COUNTERCULTURE A movement that used music, clothing, lifestyle choices, and political action to challenge mainstream social and cultural norms during the 1960s.

HIPPIES Members of the counterculture who distinguished themselves by their clothing, music, lifestyle, and politics.

Peace

The war in Vietnam was hugely unpopular among members of the counterculture. The draft threatened the autonomy and self direction of young men and provided a vivid example of the kind of government control that the counterculture opposed. Moreover, war itself represented the opposite of the peaceful utopia promised by the Aquarian Age, an astrological configuration that was supposed to usher in years of peace and contentment. The mandate behind the war also struck many members of the counterculture as morally bankrupt. Mired in Cold War politics and appearing increasingly unwinnable, the Vietnam War seemed to them like a corrupt exercise in global domination.

The New Left focused much of its effort on antiwar protests. Students and other antiwar protestors occupied parks and staged sit-ins and rallies. Young men illegally burned their draft cards in a symbolic act of resistance against the government. One of the most inflammatory antiwar protests happened in Chicago during the 1968 Democratic Convention. Robert Kennedy, the frontrunner for the Democratic nomination for president, had been the favored antiwar candidate. Kennedy had been recently assassinated, however, so many antiwar protesters decided to support George McGovern, another antiwar candidate. Thousands of protesters flocked to the Democratic convention, hoping that the public display of antiwar sentiment would affect the Democratic contenders' position on the war and ensure that the nomination go to an antiwar candidate. This did not happen. The nomination went to Hubert Humphrey, President Johnson's vice president, who seemed to support Johnson's stance on the war.

Mixed in with the legitimate antiwar protesters were Yippies. At this protest, they nominated a pig for president and called for the legalization of marijuana. The media's focus on the Yippies' attention-getting activities made all the protesters seem silly and disruptive.

The disruption upset Richard J. Daley, the mayor of Chicago. He called in police to break up the nonviolent crowds. The resulting mayhem shocked the country. Over the next three days, police beat the peaceful protesters and dispelled them with gas. The effects of this display of power were mixed. The violent actions of the police further alienated members of the New Left from the police and government. However, across the country, most Americans seemed to support the goals, if not the methods, of the police. Many Americans, even those who opposed the war, were growing exhausted by the constant political turmoil and protests. In 1968, Republican Richard Nixon was elected president, in part by mobilizing conservatives, who were especially disgusted by the tumultuous youth movement. Still, in 1969, more than 250,000 people marched on Washington to protest the war. Even as resistance to the war continued to grow throughout the country, so did resistance to the peace movement. This resistance, combined with two tragedies, helped bring the era of campus unrest to a close.

Kent State

In 1970, the media reported on secret American invasions that had been going on in Cambodia. Angered by this escalation, antiwar activists organized protests at campuses around the country. The disorder led many colleges and universities to end classes. At Kent State University in northeastern Ohio, protestors lit bonfires, smashed bottles into police cars, and broke store windows. Fearing that local police would not be able to calm the protests, the governor of Ohio called in the National Guard.

The guardsmen arrived to the sight of the campus ROTC building in flames. When the students started yelling and throwing rocks at the guardsmen, the guardsmen panicked and fired on the crowd, killing two protesters and two students walking past and wounding several others. A famous photograph of a young woman screaming over one of the Kent State murder victims captured the anger and horror of this tumultuous time. A follow-up investigation indicated that the guardsmen at Kent State had been poorly trained and acted indiscriminately. Less than two weeks after the incident at Kent State, National Guardsmen also killed two African-American students at Jackson State College in Mississippi during protests against racial discrimination. Hundreds of colleges and universities closed in solidarity.

These campus shootings helped quiet the antiwar movement. The deaths of these innocent college students showed that the cost of protesting could be painfully high. In addition, Nixon began to promise de-escalation, troop withdrawals, and other concessions that helped satisfy the antiwar protesters. By the early 1970s, protests and public displays of resistance had largely ceased.

Drug Culture

The counterculture was not only about politics and protest. Woven into the 1960s counterculture was also a widespread fascination with drugs. To many young people, mainstream American life seemed unimaginative and dull. Many members of the counterculture saw drugs as one way to follow their interest in expanding limitations. Hippies believed that hallucinogenic drugs such as marijuana and LSD, which altered sensory perceptions, could liberate people from small-minded ideals. Such drugs provided hippies with experiences, or *trips*, that often included the feeling of having spiritual experiences and new ideas about the way the world worked. Using drugs both gave hippies a sense that their minds were being expanded and served to differentiate them from the people hippies saw as uptight members of the establishment who preferred to stay encased in their own limited perceptions.

Music was another important part of the counterculture. Folk music that expressed messages of peace, love, and resistance became central to 1960s protest movements. Often, protestors expressed their unity by joining together to sing simple folk refrains or lyrics from traditional songs. Rock and roll, whose driving beats and racy lyrics had horrified conservative Americans in the 1950s, grew increasingly sexual and political in the 1960s. The music of the 1960s widened the gap between younger and older generations of Americans. However, it also provided a mode of connection for youth across the country. Huge concerts and music festivals, such as Woodstock in 1969, drew thousands of young people. These concerts allowed young people to come together as a generation committed to mind expansion, sensual pleasure, and musical fandom.

Drugs were integral to these celebrations. Drug references were written into song lyrics, and rock concerts became a place to buy, sell, and use drugs. Rock stars such as Jimi Hendrix, the Beatles, and the Grateful Dead created music inspired by the psychedelic drugs they had taken, and their performances often aimed to enhance the psychedelic experiences of audience members. Though history has somewhat idealized the drug and music culture of the late 1960s, the drug culture was not without its victims. Many prominent rock stars and ordinary Americans died from overdoses and overindulgence.

Sexual Revolution

The birth control pill, first introduced to the American public in 1960, had an important effect on the counterculture. By divesting sex from conception, the Pill

allowed women to experience sex without fear of pregnancy. In the past, the cultural stigma of unwed motherhood, among other factors, had steered women away from sex before marriage or with multiple partners. The fear of unwanted pregnancy and social stigma had not completely prevented but did limit premarital sex. When the Pill vastly reduced the risk of pregnancy, it allowed both men and women to enjoy sex recreationally far more than before and helped bring about what historians call the sexual revolution. To illustrate the change, in 1960, only 27 percent of women college students admitted that they were having sexual intercourse. By 1975, that number had nearly doubled to 50 percent. In 1962, at the beginning of this time of change, Helen Gurley Brown published *Sex and the Single Girl*, which detailed the fun sexual adventures of young, single women. This cultural shift toward acceptance of premarital sex represented a major change in both sexual practice and cultural norms.

The counterculture of the 1960s embraced the ideal and practice of sexual freedom. The countercultural critique of mainstream American culture included a condemnation of sexual repression. Many hippies preferred the idea of free love—that is, love that flowed openly and freely and that expressed itself without regard for stuffy social norms and morals. Hippies saw libido as a natural drive that should not be shunted or tamed. They felt that love and sex were inhibited by stale morals and norms. Because the 1960s counterculture was so defined by collective action, there were plenty of opportunities for young people to meet and engage sexually. Concerts, communes, be-ins, and protests all became sites of potential sexual connection.

The sexual revolution, however, was not entirely a time of innocence and play. Though the risk of pregnancy had been reduced, the Pill did not reduce the risk of contracting sexually transmitted diseases. The glorification of free love also presented new difficulties for women. The emphasis on pleasure and spiritual connection did enable women to expect pleasure from sex. However, the fear of pregnancy had long given women a plausible reason to deny unwanted sexual encounters. When use of the Pill became widespread, women could no longer rely on the risk of pregnancy as a reason to decline a sexual invitation. Many men used the countercultural vision of the sex drive as natural, constant, and something that should not be denied to pressure women to have sex. Feminists eventually turned their attention to the issue of consent and sexuality and began to explore the wide-ranging factors that influence a woman's decisions about and her experience of her own sexuality. For example, many feminists started writing about the female orgasm, often in opposition to theorists such as Freud, whom they claimed had long misunderstood the experience. Shulamith Firestone, Kate Millett, and Anne Koedt all wrote pivotal texts on women and sex. Much of their work discredited the idea that the sexual revolution affected the genders equally.

J. EDGAR HOOVER AND THE FBI

J. Edgar Hoover, a young bureaucrat, began his career as the leader of the new intelligence division of the Justice Department in 1919. At the time, the country was in the midst of a Red Scare, or fear of communist activity, and many Americans felt threatened by the strength of the labor movement and the recent Bolshevik Revolution in Russia. The federal government began carrying out raids on suspected radicals in unions and the government. Hoover started keeping files on known radicals and

subversives to help identify potential threats to the country. Some suspected radicals were deported without a trial.

Hoover became the director of the Federal Bureau of Investigation (FBI) in 1924. As the director, Hoover built the agency into a strong, centralized office, creating a national fingerprint directory and keeping extensive files on people he deemed to be subversive. However, Hoover's personal political sympathies often influenced whom he considered subversive. Hoover had always been suspicious of communists, a suspicion shared by many Americans during the Cold War era. In the 1950s and 1960s, Hoover added many new targets to his list. From the mid 1950s to the early 1970s, the FBI carried out a secret program called **COINTELPRO** to track suspicious groups and individuals and render their work ineffective. COINTELPRO often used illegal methods to target civil rights groups, women's groups, and the New Left and their leaders. Fearing Martin Luther King, Jr.'s power and sway, Hoover famously spoke out against King and his civil disobedience. Hoover also illegally wiretapped King's phone and had FBI agents follow, threaten, and blackmail King. A 1969 raid left Black Panther Fred Hampton dead, killed by the FBI as he lay sleeping. The FBI also infiltrated the women's liberation movement, paying informants to join meetings and protests and report any subversive behavior. The public learned about the COINTELPRO in 1971, when it was exposed by media reports. After Hoover's death in 1972, the FBI apologized for the program and promised to prevent such abuses of power in the future.

COINTELPRO An FBI program carried out by J. Edgar Hoover to monitor and control subversive political groups and protest leaders during the 1950s, 1960s, and early 1970s.

END OF CHAPTER TAKE-AWAYS

■ **The Feminist Movement:** Many women joined a sustained fight to achieve equality in economic, cultural, and personal realms.

■ **Riots:** Anger over centuries of racial discrimination and incidents of police brutality sparked riots across the country.

■ **Assassinations:** Several important figures were assassinated during the 1960s, including John F. Kennedy, Robert F. Kennedy, Martin Luther King, Jr., and Malcolm X.

■ **The Environmental Movement:** A movement to protect the environment influenced legislation and cultural activities.

■ **Vietnam:** Cold War politics led the United States to fight a long, hotly contested war in Vietnam. Conscription was used to fill positions in the armed forces.

■ **Civil Rights:** This movement to fight racial discrimination ended legal segregation and influenced several new laws guaranteeing equal treatment to all races.

■ **The Failure of the Great Society:** President Johnson's campaign to end poverty was expensive and mismanaged, leading many to question government spending policies.

■ **The Youth Movement:** In a rebellion against mainstream American society and politics, young people engaged in widespread political protest and a youth culture based on sex, drugs, and rock and roll.

■ **J. Edgar Hoover and the FBI:** J. Edgar Hoover used illegal methods to involve the FBI in a campaign against a variety of suspected 1960s radicals.

REFERENCES

Henretta, J. A., Brody, D., & Dumenil, L. (2006). *America: A concise history, Vol. 2: Since 1865* (3rd ed.). Boston, MA: Bedford/St. Martin's.

Centers for Medicare & Medicaid Services. (n.d.). History. Retrieved from https://www.cms.gov /history/

Rosen, R. (2000). *The world split open: How the modern women's movement changed America.* New York, NY: Penguin Books.

American Experience. (2002). Timeline: The pill. *Public Broadcasting Service.* Retrieved from http:// www.pbs.org/wgbh/amex/pill/timeline/timeline2.html

Tindall, G. B., & Shi, D. E. (2004). *America: A narrative history* (6th ed., Vol. 2). New York, NY: W.W. Norton.

Zinn, H. (1995). *The people's history of the United States: 1492–present.* New York, NY: Harper Perennial.

Nation at a
Crossroads

CORRUPTION
AHEAD

One of the challenges of U.S. foreign policy is to balance the pros and cons of using military force to influence the policies of other nations. Does the United States have a moral responsibility to protect human rights around the world? How can the U.S. government balance the potential costs—including the costs of American and foreign lives—with the potential benefits of promoting ideals such as peace, democracy, and freedom? These questions were hotly debated during the United States' involvement in Vietnam.

United States soldiers were actively involved in conflict in Vietnam for over eight years. It was a drawn-out affair that lacked clearly defined objectives. This made it difficult for policymakers to know how and when to bring the war to a close. Many U.S. citizens vehemently—and sometimes violently—protested the United States' role in the conflict. One reason these protests gained such momentum had to do with the ever-growing place of television in U.S. domestic life. Much of the conflict in Vietnam was broadcast on television stations, enabling people at home to witness the atrocities of war directly from their living rooms. Up until this point in U.S. history, citizens had never been able to see with such clarity the fighting and the costs of war abroad.

NIXON'S VIETNAM

The United States involvement in the Vietnam War started in 1954, nearly a generation before Nixon became involved as president. However, he still played a part in the international politics that shaped the conflict as vice president under President Dwight D. Eisenhower.

In 1954, the United States, the United Kingdom, France, the Soviet Union, and the People's Republic of China met in Geneva with the goal of unifying the Koreas and restoring peace in Indochina (now Vietnam). The assembled nations reached an agreement that split Vietnam in two. A puppet dictator named Ngo Dinh Diem led the South, which was backed by France, while the North, called the Democratic Republic of Vietnam, was led by the Communist Party and backed by the Soviet Union. Nixon watched all of this unfold as vice president and it changed the way he approached international politics.

In spring 1968, with the U.S. presidential elections scheduled for the fall, President Johnson managed to bring North and South Vietnam leaders to the **Paris Peace Negotiations**. Feelings in the U.S. about the war were decidedly mixed, with college protests and sit-ins occurring across the nation. Even the middle class began to speak out against further US involvement and was nicknamed the *silent majority* by the media.

Nixon, however, worried that a successful resolution to the war would hurt his chances of defeating Hubert Humphrey in the presidential election. He sent an envoy, Anna Chennault, to meet with the South Vietnamese president, Nguyen Van Thieu. She told Thieu that Nixon had a plan more favorable to South Vietnam and that he would do his best to implement it if he were elected.

Thieu was aware of Nixon's early involvement with Vietnam as vice president and believed he would do more to push out the communists, leaving Thieu as the victor. He refused to go to the Paris talks; as a result, they collapsed with no resolution. Nixon, along with his advisor, Henry Kissinger, who later became secretary of state, believed that they could reestablish the talks in six months to a year and end the war. By the end of 1968 the U.S. troop levels were at their highest, with over 500,000 troops on the ground. News broadcasts showed images of the war in close to real time and the draft pulled young men into the service.

Nixon and Kissinger's gamble proved to be deadly and long lasting. The war dragged on for five more years as Nixon's administration fought the war with the belief that more weapons and more soldiers had to mean an eventual U.S. victory. For years,

a withdrawal was not even considered plausible because behind North Vietnam were the larger forces of communist China and the Soviet Union. The United States feared that a loss in Vietnam would lead to a spread of communism throughout Asia and throw off the balance of power in the world, leaving the United States open to attacks even closer to home. Vietnam was, in part, a venue to fight out the tensions of the Cold War.

As part of Nixon's efforts to win the war, he began to secretly bomb Cambodia, a country neighboring Vietnam. His goal was to stop China from supplying weapons or troops across the Cambodian border. He did all of this without advising Congress.

PARIS PEACE NEGOTIATIONS
A series of talks in 1968 ahead of the U.S. presidential elections that brought leaders from North and South Vietnam, along with U.S. representatives, to the bargaining table.

When the bombings became public, Nixon at first denied them and then described them as necessary in order to create cover for U.S. troops. The bombings led to more college protests and on May 1, 1970, at a student protest on the campus of Kent State University in Ohio, National Guard troops opened fire on the students, killing four people. Nixon was decisively losing the war on both fronts.

It was not until January 1973 that Nixon finally was able to get the Paris Peace talks underway. An attempt at initiating peace talks in 1972 had been unsuccessful, and Nixon had responded to the communist regime's unwillingness to negotiate with heavy bombings in the big cities of Hanoi and Haiphong, later named the Christmas bombings. These events brought international outrage and forced the Nixon administration to start negotiating.

Nixon's goal became a negotiated peace that could be seen as a win on the world stage. Although a treaty was tentatively signed, the warfare continued until May 1975, when the presidential palace was captured in Saigon and the last Americans were quickly airlifted out, ending the war.

OPENING CHINA FOR TRADE

In 1972, Nixon made a historic visit to the Peoples Republic of China, the first in 25 years by a Western leader to the closed-off communist regime. This visit opened the possibility of trade to China's one billion people. Nixon's diplomacy with China was universally applauded as successful.

The history between the two countries had long been strained. In October 1949, Chairman Mao Tse-tung took over as leader of China. He eventually instituted a system of policies banning most Western literature, education, science, and religion. **Maoism** bore a strong resemblance to basic communist doctrine. In an attempt to remove Western culture's influence, books were burned, religious temples were shut down, and thousands of Chinese citizens were sent to "reeducation" camps to be indoctrinated to the new way of thinking.

Mao closed cultural ties with most of the rest of the world, saying the influence was detrimental, and instituted a series of severe reforms intended to purify the Chinese culture. The United States instituted a trade embargo against China beginning in 1949; it lasted until 1963 and further strained relations.

However, the embargo did help collapse the Sino-Soviet alliance as China increasingly turned to the Soviet Union for assistance to fill the vacuum left by the Western countries. In addition to other disagreements, the U.S.S.R. could not keep up with what China expected and it led to their eventual split.

In Nixon's inaugural address on January 28, 1969, he mentioned the need to normalize relations with China. Mao had the entire transcript translated and printed in the *People's Daily* paper. Then in August 1969, national security advisor Harold Saunders met in secret with Pakistani Ambassador Agha Hilaly to discuss how the United States could assist China in opening up to the rest of the world. Saunders asked Hilaly to, "convey his feelings to the Chinese at the highest level that Asia could not move forward if a nation as large as China remains

MAOISM A series of policies put forth in China by Mao Zedong that highlighted the importance of the peasant worker and maintaining an ongoing revolutionary state.

isolated." Saunders went further and said that the United States would not be a part of any agreement that would advance their isolation, signaling to Mao that America was interested in easing relations and talking about trade.

On October 1, 1970, Mao allowed American journalist Edgar Snow to stand next to him during a parade for photographs that were later published. Mao then met with Snow months later and said he was open to the idea of Nixon visiting China. However, the Nixon administration refused to speak with Snow because he was seen as a leftist. Thus, the administration did not hear of the invitation until months later, when it was published in *Life* magazine.

In April 1971, the US table tennis team visited China as Nixon announced initiatives to open up trade and ease travel restrictions. Over the course of the next year, messages were sent back and forth between Chinese and U.S. diplomats through the Pakistani government. In February 1972, Nixon made his historic visit to China, met with Mao, and played table tennis with Chinese Premier Zhou Enlai. In 2011 the United States had a trade deficit with China of nearly $296 billion—an unthinkable reality before Nixon's presidency.

WATERGATE

President Nixon was looking at a tough reelection campaign in 1972. In 1971, the **Pentagon Papers** were leaked to the *New York Times* by military analyst Daniel Ellsberg.

The lengthy study was a secret compilation of the US involvement in Vietnam commissioned by Secretary of Defense Robert McNamara, who is thought of as the main architect behind the Vietnam War. The papers showed that the federal government had purposely lied about what they were doing in Vietnam, what they had done to cover up those lies, and what their true intentions were when it came to US policy. The Johnson Administration had been reassuring the public that they were not interested in escalating the Vietnam War when all along the plan was already in motion to increase troop numbers. Nixon continued the lies by secretly bombing Cambodia while claiming the United States had not taken any such actions.

Nixon wanted to prevent any future leaks and formed a group of White House staffers called the White House Plumbers. The plumbers' first job was to break into Daniel Ellsberg's office, but they reportedly branched out into investigations of other rivals of Nixon's.

The Nixon administration also began in 1971 to keep a list of enemies, mostly U.S. citizens who they felt were troublesome to the administration. The list included more than fifty people in the news media, ten Democratic senators, all of the House members who were African-American, labor leaders, prominent businessmen, and a number of entertainers.

John Dean, who served as counsel to the president, later testified that several top officials contributed to the changing list and suggested methods of punishing those on the list, such as litigation, withholding of federal grants and contracts, and even prosecution. In a memo dated August 16, 1971 that was entered into the official hearings, Dean wrote, "we can use the available federal machinery to screw our political enemies." The memo was delivered to White House chief of staff H. R. Haldeman, and the list of political enemies was given to another White House counsel, Charles Colson.

G. Gordon Liddy, a former treasury and FBI agent, was part of the Plumbers team and assisted in breaking into Ellsberg's office. He was later recruited by Dean to

PENTAGON PAPERS A classified study by the U.S. Department of Defense about the Vietnam War that was leaked to the New York Times by Daniel Ellsberg in 1971.

help the Committee to Re-elect the President (CRP) and put forth a plan to use burglary, electronic surveillance, kidnapping, and the use of prostitutes to gather information.

John Mitchell, the director of the CRP, rejected Liddy's plan because of its proposed high price tag. Instead, the group made plans to break into the offices of the Democratic National Committee in the expensive **Watergate** Hotel in Washington, D.C. Liddy and Hunt were in charge of the operation.

On their third attempt, the group managed to plant wiretaps on the phones of Democratic National Committee (DNC) Chairman Lawrence O'Brien and Executive Director of Democratic States' Chairman R. Spencer Oliver, Jr. But after listening to some of the tapes, Ehrlichman and CRP's acting chairman Jeb Stuart Magruder decided they needed more.

On June 17, 1972, five men attempted to break into the DNC offices again. This time a security guard named Frank Wills became suspicious when he noticed tape holding a door open. The burglars were caught and arrested. One of them was with the GOP and another claimed to have ties with the CIA. Ehrlichman denied any ties with the burglars, but a cashier's check for $25,000 that was given to the CRP was traced to a bank account belonging to one of the burglars.

Nixon tried to stop the investigations by saying that they would interfere with a CIA operation, and Dean made unsuccessful efforts to get the CIA to go along with the idea. On August 19, Nixon issued a statement through Dean that no one in the White House was involved in the scandal.

But on September 15, all five men, plus Liddy and Nixon campaign aide E. Howard Hunt, were indicted by a grand jury. Eventually the five burglars pleaded guilty, while Liddy and Hunt were found guilty by Judge John Sirica. Liddy received the harshest sentence. Funds used by the burglars were traced back to the CRP, and John Mitchell, who was the former attorney general, was found to have had a secret Republican slush fund that was used for illegal political activity.

Despite all of this evidence, the American public evidently chose to believe that the men surrounding President Nixon had operated without his knowledge or consent. There was still the Vietnam War to contend with and a country that seemed to be pulling itself apart at the seams. Nixon won in a landslide victory in 1972, but two young reporters at the *Washington Post* had more information to reveal.

WATERGATE The scandal surrounding two illegal break-ins to the DNC headquarters in 1972 that were organized by members of the Nixon administration and the Committee to Re-elect the President. Nixon's implication in the crime and the cover up led to his resignation.

The Power of the Press

The political scandal quickly became known as Watergate, and those following the story wanted to know whether the president was directly involved.

As long as no one answered that question, Nixon was safe from prosecution. However, *Washington Post* reporters Bob Woodward and Carl Bernstein were investigating the burglary. The other major U.S. newspapers had let the story go and moved on, but Woodward was approached by a government figure, whom he later nicknamed *Deep Throat*, who fed him inside information in an effort to make the truth public.

Washington Post Publisher Katharine Graham gave the reporters the opportunity to follow every lead. Mark Felt, an FBI official who revealed himself as Deep Throat

in 2005, continued to meet in secret with Woodward and reportedly told him to follow the money trail. Bernstein learned about the $25,000 check that was misappropriated and suddenly the burglary was linked to the Nixon campaign.

Further indiscretions and illegal acts came to light and White House staffers' Haldeman, Ehrlichman, Dean, and attorney general Richard Kleindienst were fired. Nixon's reputation was bruised, but it appeared he was still safe from prosecution or other consequence.

In summer 1973, Special Prosecutor Archibald Cox began one investigation and North Carolina Senator Sam Ervin, later the Senate Watergate Committee's chairman, started another. New Attorney General Elliot Richardson appointed Cox to investigate all illegal activity, including the burglaries that might involve the White House or the CRP.

Senator Ervin was in charge of a seven-member Senate committee to look into the same issues. Early testimony revealed staffer Tom Huston had put forth a proposal to keep track of perceived opponents of the president with the purpose of harassment. The plan was never started but Senator Ervin said it revealed a "Gestapo mentality," similar to the WWII German military police, who kept track of the civilian population and punished those whom they perceived as enemies.

John Dean was called to testify before the Senate Committee and was the first to state for the record that President Nixon was involved and aware of all operations. Nixon denied any involvement.

The Senate Committee and Cox issued subpoenas to Nixon for any related material, but he refused and said he would not appear before the committee. The committee filed suit and Nixon offered a compromise to let Senator John Stennis, who was known to be hard of hearing, listen to the tapes and report back to the committee.

The committee turned down the offer and Nixon told Richardson to fire Cox. Richardson refused and publicly resigned. Acting attorney general Robert Bork fired Cox instead; the events became known as the **Saturday Night Massacre**. Leon Jaworski was appointed the new special prosecutor and the hearing moved forward. John Dean finally outlined in great detail everyone's involvement in the scandal.

In the meantime, Nixon's vice president, Spiro Agnew, was being investigated for criminal activity that took place when he was the Governor of Maryland. On October 10, 1973, Agnew resigned. Congressman Gerald Ford was named the new vice president.

Nixon's personal recorded tapes from conversations he held in the oval office were eventually turned over to the Senate Committee, but there was an unexplained gap in the tape of eighteen and a half minutes.

Nixon appeared on television during a press conference and famously stated, "I am not a crook." As time passed, fewer and fewer Americans believed in his innocence. In July 1974 the House Judiciary Committee adopted articles of impeachment to remove Nixon from the office of the presidency. On August 9, 1974, he resigned.

First President Who Resigned

Nixon's letter of resignation was on official White House stationery and had one sentence, "I hereby resign the Office of President of the United States." The time stamp reads "11:35 AM," initialed by Henry Kissinger, the secretary of state. The resignation was official.

Nixon had insisted in his last days that he had stonewalled efforts to turn over tapes and transcripts because he was protecting the presidency. He said future presidents would have an uncomfortable precedent if he did not refuse. He said that he was ignorant of what the chief members of his staff were doing until 1973, when Watergate came to light. Few believed him.

Finally, in 1974, with a grand jury preparing to indict him, Nixon agreed to turn over 1,200 pages of transcripts of conversations between himself and his aides that revealed profane discussions about potentially illegal activity. By the time Nixon turned over the tapes with the curious gap, no one believed he could remain as president.

There was still the lingering question of whether or not the now-former president would be prosecuted or, at the least, be called to testify. Many wondered about the consequences of compelling a former president to testify under oath.

First Unelected President

Gerald R. Ford, the congressman from Michigan who was appointed vice president in the middle of one of the greatest political scandals in US history, was sworn in as the 38th president of the United States on August 9, 1974, by Chief Justin Warren Burger. To date, he is the only person to serve as president who was not elected to the office.

He said in a speech shortly afterward, "My fellow Americans, our long national nightmare is over. Our Constitution works; our great Republic is a government of laws and not of men. Here the people rule."

The country was still recovering from the Vietnam War and an energy crisis that had triggered a lingering recession. On September 8, 1974, one month after he took office, President Ford gave Nixon an absolute pardon of any and all crimes he may have committed from January 20, 1969, through August 9, 1974.

HISTORY COMES ALIVE

Nixon showed enthusiasm for breaking and entering well before Watergate: While enrolled in law school, he allegedly broke into a dean's office to take an early peek at his grades.

The following is an excerpt from a recorded phone conversation between Nixon and Secretary of State Henry Kissinger in June 1973 about wire-tapping and Nixon's wish to expose the people behind the tapping.

President: Because they have done us in on this thing. Now the biggest tapper was Bobby Kennedy. Now Johnson doesn't appear to be so big but he had the Secret Service do it. And I've ordered Rowley to give me the names of the Secret Service taps and I'm going to put those on it too.

Kissinger: I think…

President: They started it. They wanted to have a gut fight; they're going to get one, Henry, you understand.

Kissinger: I think so.

President: They think they know how to fight but they've never fought anybody before.

Did you know that in 1972, when Nixon said in a recording, "It is not the issue that will harm you; it is the cover up that is damaging," that he was talking about an earlier case, the Alger Hiss trial for espionage in 1948? Nixon admitted that he leaked details of the Hiss case to the press in order to prompt an indictment. The entire quote is, "If you cover up, you're going to get caught. And if you lie you're going to be guilty of perjury, now basically that was the whole story of the Hiss case. It is not the issue that will harm you; it is the cover up that is damaging." Nixon was not expressing regret over what he did; he was simply discussing how leaks work.

The decision was controversial and left many Americans feeling as if they would never have all the answers behind Watergate. Ford said the country had suffered long enough as a result of the Watergate scandal; he said pardoning Nixon would allow the public to let go and move forward.

However, Ford lost to Jimmy Carter in the presidential election of 1976, and many cited Ford's decision to pardon Nixon as a contributing factor to his loss. Ford later stated he had no regrets and many came to see the decision as the right one for the country. The Kennedy Library awarded Ford the John F. Kennedy Profile in Courage award in May 2001 for the unconditional pardon he gave Nixon.

MID-CHAPTER QUESTIONS

1. What did Nixon and Kissinger do to stop the Paris Peace Talks? Were they wrong to do it, if they believed the talks could be reinstated just months after the 1968 election?

2. What did the Committee to Re-elect the President do to try and ensure victory? Given what Nixon did during the Alger Hiss trial, do you believe he knew about the burglaries and other "dirty tricks"?

3. Compare how the public, the press, and the president reacted to the Watergate scandal with how the public, the press, and the politicians of today respond to scandal. What elements are similar and what elements are different?

4. Why was it important for Nixon to open up trade with China? Is the United States better off today because of the country's trade relationship with China, in light of the large trade deficit that exists?

OPEC AND THE OIL SHORTAGES

On October 6, 1973, Egyptian and Syrian military forces led a surprise attack against Israel in the Golan Heights and Sinai area of the Middle East in an attempt to regain territory they lost during the Six-Day War in 1967. The Arab countries attacked on the holiest Jewish holiday, Yom Kippur, and caught Israeli forces off guard. In the first few days of the attack the Egyptian forces were able to gain ground in the Sinai and the Syrians focused their attacks in the Golan Heights. Israel eventually found its footing and counterattacked, regaining the lost ground.

The Nixon administration stepped in to help resupply the Israelis, in part because of the Soviet backing of the Arab countries. Once more, the Cold War played a part in global politics. The Arab states in the Organization of Petroleum Exporting Countries (**OPEC**) established an oil embargo against the United States and other countries that aided Israel.

The oil embargo and the resulting spike in fuel prices appeared to be driving the United States and other Western oil-dependent countries into a recession. Europe and Japan had stockpiled oil and could resist the roller-coaster prices, but only for a

OPEC The Organization of Petroleum Exporting Countries, founded in 1960 to govern the production, price, and export of oil by its members, which include Iran, Iraq, Egypt, Saudi Arabia, and others.

while. They sought to disassociate themselves from the Middle East crisis in an effort to placate OPEC.

When Israel began getting the upper hand in the war, the Soviet Union threatened to step in and defend the Egyptian Third Army. The United States went on nuclear alert. Secretary of State Henry Kissinger, in what was called **shuttle diplomacy**, since he was acting as in intermediary between the two warring parties, talked Israel into pulling back from the Golan Heights and Sinai. OPEC agreed to lift the embargo, but the world had already taken note of how the power was shifting.

ENERGY CRISIS

In March 1973, Nixon placed controls on the price of oil, dictating a ceiling on the price of already-discovered oil. Newly discovered oil could be sold at higher prices. The goal was to create interest in discovering new sources of domestic oil. The United States had been completely energy self-sufficient until the 1950s, but by the 1970s was importing 35 percent of its energy needs, and the figure was rising. Nixon was trying to force U.S. oil companies and the American public into spending the money to open up virgin territories for oil and gas exploration.

However, in October 1973, world politics intervened and Egypt and Syria attacked Israeli forces, starting a war. When the Soviet Union backed Egypt, the Nixon administration felt compelled to assist Israel, angering Arab nations. OPEC responded by imposing an oil embargo and reducing production by 5 percent. Eventually, they would cut back on production by 20 percent at the height of the crisis. Suddenly the U.S. economy was in danger of a deepening recession as a result of the weakened dollar and the rising fuel prices.

Oil prices quickly rose from $3 a barrel to $11.65. Gas went from 30 cents per gallon at the pump to $1.20 and lines snaked around the block.

The U.S. dollar was already trading lower in foreign markets as a result of Nixon's decision in August 1971 to remove the dollar from the gold standard. The International Monetary Fund intervened and established loan practices for smaller countries that needed to import oil but could not afford the quickly rising prices.

The U.S. stock market responded by losing 45 percent of its value from January 1973 to December 1974, one of the worst stock downturns in history.

On November 13, Congress approved the Nixon administration plan to open a trans-Alaskan oil pipeline to supply two million more domestic barrels of oil per day. The massive project was completed in 1977.

Then, on November 27, 1973, Nixon signed the Emergency Petroleum Allocation Act, which placed controls on oil production, marketing, allocation, and price. Nixon asked the American public to turn down thermostats and for corporations to shorten the workday. A speed limit of 55 miles per hour was instituted on the federal highways nationwide. Daylight Savings Time was extended and 90 percent of the country's gas stations stopped selling gas at the pump on Sundays. Sales were limited during the rest of the week to 10 gallons per customer. All of this was in an effort to cut back on foreign-oil

dependence. Oil was diverted from gas production and airlines had their supply cut by 25 percent to ensure there would be enough domestic heating oil for the winter.

Before 1973, people in the United States were under the impression that energy was limitless and cheap. But starting with the OPEC embargo, citizens experienced rising prices for fuel and other consumer goods, as well as "rolling brownouts," which are periods of reduced electric supply. In an embarrassment to Congress, it was discovered that Congressmen had access to a private gas station where prices were below the national average, there was an endless supply, and there were no lines. This information came out just as the details of Watergate began to emerge, further hurting the Republican image. Adding to the national gloom was the realization that new global power players in the Mideast could affect Americans' lives.

Flag of Iran.

HOSTAGES IN IRAN

Ford's presidency ended in 1977 when a Washington outsider from Georgia became president. Jimmy Carter was strong on human rights, but he only served one term as president. His presidency was beleaguered by a stifled economy, continued problems with energy costs, and a hostage situation in the Mideast.

Tension had been mounting between Iran and the United States for several years. The Shah of Iran, a leader supported by the United States, had been ousted and his administration was replaced by a Muslim regime hostile toward the West. On November 4, 1979, the US Embassy in Tehran was overrun by young Islamic militants. They quickly took sixty Americans hostage. The captured Americans were blindfolded and paraded in front of television cameras for a worldwide audience and a stunned United States.

Carter responded on November 11 by instituting an embargo on Iranian oil. That same day, Ruhollah Khomeini, the ruler and religious leader of Iran, announced the release of all female and African-American hostages, because they had already been the victims of "the oppression of American society."

The sanctions did not free the hostages, so on April 11, 1980, Carter initiated a rescue operation. It was aborted when three helicopters malfunctioned in the desert sand. A fourth helicopter crashed during takeoff, killing eight and injuring three others. The next day Iranian TV broadcast footage of the crumpled, smoking helicopter.

The hostage crisis and failed rescue mission damaged Carter's reelection bid and were factors in Ronald Reagan's wide margin of victory. The United States and Iran settled the issue just as Reagan became president on January 20, 1981. All of the remaining hostages were released and Carter greeted them in Germany on their way home. The hostages had been held for 444 days.

STAGFLATION

Stagflation is defined as a slow economy that is simultaneously battling high unemployment and rising prices or inflation. Inflation stood at 12 percent in 1971 when the United States abandoned the gold standard. The situation was exacerbated by the

1973 Arab-Israeli War, during which OPEC imposed an embargo that drastically raised the price of fuel, leading to more inflation and higher unemployment. Unemployment rose to a record 9 percent as the gross domestic product dropped by more than 5 percent.

The United States was also shifting away from a manufacturing economy to a more service-oriented economy, a trend that continues to the present day, leaving some workers without the skills to find employment. The Dow Jones Industrial Average lost almost half of its value over the course of 1973 and 1974, and many investors found other places for their money.

The combination of rising fuel prices, along with record unemployment, a shifting economy, a weak U.S. dollar, an influx of workers, and nervous investors led to a deep recession. This recession lasted well into Reagan's first term and was the background for Reagan's major economic decisions, which shaped the nation's finances for decades to follow.

END OF CHAPTER TAKE-AWAYS

- **Nixon's Vietnam:** Nixon promised to curb Americas's involvement in the war, and he did eventually start withdrawing troops. He also, however, escalated bombing—sometimes covertly—and brought the war into Cambodia.
- **Opening China for Trade:** Nixon visited China and was instrumental in opening friendly diplomatic relations between the Asian giant and the United States.
- **Watergate:** President Nixon and the closest members of his administration planned a break-in at the Democratic National Committee's offices. Nixon and his aides attempted to cover up the scandal, but he eventually resigned over the matter—the first and only sitting president to do so.
- **OPEC and the Oil Shortages:** Nixon and Kissinger aided Israel during the Yom Kippur War and incurred the anger of oil states in the Arab world.
- **Energy Crisis:** Gas prices soared and Nixon's administration introduced policies to curb energy consumption, including price ceilings on oil, which caused long lines at gas stations.
- **Hostages in Iran:** Militant Iranians took hostages at the US embassy in Tehran. It took Carter's administration 444 days to negotiate successfully to bring the hostages home.
- **Stagflation:** A period of high inflation and unemployment persisted throughout Ford's and Carter's administrations.

REFERENCES

Bernstein, C., & Woodward, B. (1974). *All the president's men.* New York, NY: Simon and Schuster.

Carter, J. (2010). *White House diary.* New York, NY: Farrar, Straus and Giroux.

Dallek, R. (2007). *Nixon and Kissinger: Partners in power.* New York, NY: Harper Collins.

Fulsom, D. (2012). *Nixon's darkest secrets: The inside story of America's most troubled president.* New York, NY: Thomas Dunne Books.

Kennerly, D. H., Brokaw, T., Smith, R. N., & University of Texas at Austin. (2007). *Extraordinary circumstances: The presidency of Gerald R. Ford.* Austin, TX: Center for American History, University of Texas at Austin.

Reeves, R. (2001). *President Nixon: Alone in the White House.* New York, NY: Simon & Schuster.

CHAPTER

20

The Reagan Years

During the presidency of Ronald Reagan, television news stations started to broadcast the world's news around the clock. Why was this significant? It marked a dramatic shift in how quickly people could learn about current events. Policy makers and government officials were able to watch unfolding events around the world. This immediacy of knowledge began to inform and change the way the U.S. government responded to crises.

The 24-hour news cycle meant that people watching television in their homes in Omaha, Nebraska, could witness in real time what was happening on the ground in Nicaragua, Somalia, or anywhere else. Regular citizens, in short, could quickly and easily see the effect of US foreign policy in action and decide for themselves whether they supported the governments' actions.

President Reagan himself was also a point of interest for viewers. When President Reagan survived an assassination attempt in 1981, citizens were able to watch the president's near-death experience from their living rooms; Cable News Network covered the story for more than two straight days. Fortunately for the president, his experience as a film actor and his natural charisma meant that he could use this exposure to his advantage.

The United States' cold war with the USSR was still under way, and the economy was still weak, when Reagan ended Carter's reelection hopes in 1980. Reagan, however, exhibited a relaxed but confident persona that reassured U.S. citizens and earned him the nickname the Great Communicator. Reagan was a gifted public speaker and was surrounded by excellent speechwriters such as Peggy Noonan. Reagan's speeches to the public were peppered with personal stories of citizens who had sacrificed everything in wartime or were struggling against great odds with determination and optimism. His vigorous presence did much to sway voters and calm the public.

SUPPLY-SIDE ECONOMICS An economic theory that states the best way to stimulate an economy is to lower taxes and lower the barriers for businesses to produce goods and services by reducing regulation.

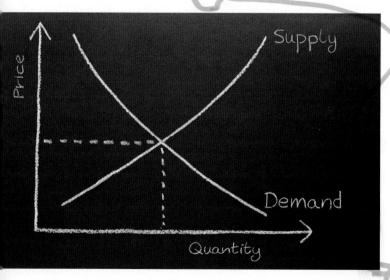

REAGANOMICS

In 1980, the U.S. economy was still recovering from brutal inflation and double-digit lending rates. In an attempt to slow economic growth and slow or reverse inflation, Federal Reserve Chairman Paul Volcker institut-ed a restrictive monetary policy, which slowed spending as expected. The economy continued to slow, however, and moved into another recessionary phase that lasted through 1982.

In response to the decrease in personal spending, Reagan introduced a new economic package that became known as *Reaganomics*. The series of changes that had been initially proposed during Reagan's campaign were a sharp turn in policy from the post-WWII policies of federal spending that emphasized social welfare. Instead, Reagan proposed deep tax cuts for the wealthiest Americans, reduced federal programs, and made the govern-ment smaller.

Trickle Down

The Reagan administration felt that the U.S. tax code had become too long, complicated, and overbearing. Reagan had campaigned on the popu-lar idea of smaller government being an economic solution for the middle class. A smaller government, among other things, would need fewer tax dollars and a simpler tax code. The middle class could keep more of what they earned.

In a televised news conference in July 1981 from his desk in the White House, Reagan referred to the proposal as "a second American Revolution for hope and opportunity" and announced his intention to trim the budget by $41 billion. In order to move the country to prosperity, Reagan pro-posed reducing government spending on social programs, cutting the in-come tax rates, and reducing oversight regulations.

The item that got the most attention was a proposal to cut federal income taxes by 30 percent. These tax breaks applied mostly to the upper income brackets. The em-phasis was put on the reduction in overall taxes for everyone, but the media played up the monetary boost that would be reserved mostly for those already wealthy.

Reagan was advocating **supply-side economics**. Economists who subscribe to this theory believe that the best way to increase prosperity is to make business conditions as favorable as possible for produc-ers or organizations that supply the economy with goods and services. By lowering taxes and making it easier for business to produce goods, people will spend more. More goods will be purchased, which means more goods will need to be manufactured, and more jobs will be cre-ated. In other words, a positive cycle of growth will occur naturally instead of being pushed forward by a large government that takes in more tax dollars to spend on infrastructure and social programs. If the wealthy have large amounts of disposable income, the theory suggests that this income will trickle down through the rest of the economy.

Tax Increases

In 1981 a largely Democratic Congress passed the Reagan administration's new tax policies, instituting an across-the-board tax cut of 25 percent. Reagan's administration also quickly cut more than $30 billion in federal spending and weakened the political clout of organized labor. Reagan's swift changes greatly reduced the burden on suppliers across the nation, and this is largely how his administration is remembered today.

These measures, however, failed to spring the country out of its ongoing recession. They also failed to improve the stock markets, partly due to the escalating federal deficits directly resulting from the changes. The economic data showed clearly that Reagan's policies did not have the effect that he predicted. This startled the president and caused him to scramble to come up with steps to move the country forward. He was still opposed to the idea of raising taxes to generate revenue, but his administration could not ignore the deficit. He turned to what economists refer to as *base broadening*. Rather than directly raising taxes, the government passed the Tax Equity and Fiscal Responsibility Act of 1982, which closed tax loopholes, reduced tax breaks for certain contributions, and restricted benefits in pension plans, among other measures. While this legislation was marketed as a tax reform bill to the public, Reagan's actions amounted to increasing tax revenues. Even though Reagan is often remembered as a champion of reducing taxes, he actually increased taxes in some form for seven of his eight years in office.

As a result, many of the wealthier citizens who benefited from being in a greatly reduced tax bracket were no longer able to shelter funds from taxes, and found themselves paying nearly the same amount that they had been paying. The federal government under Reagan took in an average of 18 percent of the nation's gross domestic product, which was similar to the average under Carter. The economy started to improve. Inflation dipped and the recession ebbed.

Reaganomics had lasting effects on parts of the U.S. economy, however. The growing gulf between rich and poor and a shrinking middle class are often attributed to policy decisions made during the Reagan years. The tax brackets were tied to inflation, but the minimum wage was not, and Reagan left the minimum wage untouched during his entire time in office. Federal funding for states was also slashed from 22 percent of the federal budget in 1980 to 6 percent by the time he left office. In turn, states cut spending on education, sanitation, police and fire departments, and infrastructure, which heavily impacted the middle class.

Under Reaganomics, the wealthy enjoyed a 9 percent increase in income. The middle class saw their income rise just 1 percent, and the poor saw their incomes decline by 8 percent. Single-mother households and African-Americans saw the sharpest decline.

Another bill in 1984 cut income taxes even further, reducing the top income rate from 70 percent to 28 percent. As a result, the budget deficit, which was 2.6 percent during Reagan's first year, fluctuated between 3 and 6 percent during the rest of his first term.

In 1986, with the budget deficit growing larger, Reagan proposed another tax reform bill that would close more loopholes in the tax code. He traveled the country spreading a message of "fairness, growth and simplicity," while Republican supporters argued with his administration to abandon the bill. The Tax Reform Act became law in October 1986. While Reagan's name is widely associated with tax cuts, federal tax receipts grew considerably during his eight years in office.

Social Security Trust Fund

Another piece of legislation Reagan signed in 1983 had to do with the Social Security system. This bill too resulted in an increase in taxes, but again, Reagan did not have to sell it to the public in those terms.

Economists started to worry that the baby boomer generation of people born immediately following the Second World War was going to create a huge burden on the Social Security system when those workers reached retirement age. Since the baby boom generation was much larger than the subsequent one, eventually there could be more people claiming benefits than workers paying Social Security taxes. Alan Greenspan, who would later become the Federal Reserve chairman, headed a committee to examine this problem. He presented a solution that accelerated planned hikes in the Social Security taxes on workers. The act also introduced taxes on high-earning retirees who withdrew money from the fund—no taxes like this had ever existed—and slightly increased the age of retirement.

The idea behind the legislation was to require baby boomers to pay more social security taxes while they were still working in order to make sure the fund was still healthy when it came time for them to retire. Reagan signed the bill in 1983 and the result was an immediate spike in Social Security revenue.

Growth of the Federal Deficit

During Reagan's second term the economy continued upward. The gross domestic product expanded and unemployment went from a high of 7.1 percent in 1985 to 5.2 percent by 1989. The inflation that had stifled the economy during Carter's administration and Reagan's first two years in office dropped to nearly 4 percent. Oil prices also dropped again. Some economists credit the reduction in the marginal

HISTORY COMES ALIVE

The following is an excerpt from President Reagan's First Inaugural Address on Tuesday, January 20, 1981, demonstrating his commitment to reducing the size of the federal government:

In this present crisis, government is not the solution to our problem. From time to time, we have been tempted to believe that society has become too complex to be managed by self-rule, that government by an elite group is superior to government for, by, and of the people. But if no one among us is capable of governing himself, then who among us has the capacity to govern someone else? All of us together, in and out of government, must bear the burden .... Well, this administration's objective will be a healthy, vigorous, growing economy that provides equal opportunity for all Americans, with no barriers born of bigotry or discrimination....With the idealism and fair play which are the core of our system and our strength, we can have a strong and prosperous America at peace with itself and the world.

tax rate from 70 to 28 percent with the rapid growth in the real estate, high-tech, financial, and retail markets during that time. Some attribute it to the larger total tax receipts that Reagan's government collected.

However, all of that was overshadowed by the rising national debt and the widening difference in spending power between the different socioeconomic classes. During the Reagan years the government failed to pass a balanced budget. Reagan never sent Congress a balanced budget to begin with, and Congress padded the budgets he did send with further spending projects. Domestic spending increased during Reagan's second term, with defense spending doubling to more than $330 billion by 1987. According to Congressional Budget Office data, the public debt in 1980 was approximately 26 percent of the gross domestic product—a measure that indicates the total size of the nation's economy—and it had hovered around that level for the ten years prior. After Reagan's eight years in office, public debt had ballooned to 41 percent of the gross domestic product.

Deregulation

Reagan campaigned on the idea of a smaller federal government and took every effort to fulfill that promise by **deregulating**, or removing agencies and laws, especially those that affected private industry. Immediately after coming into office Reagan fulfilled one promise by ending price controls on oil. The cost of oil immediately came down, bringing welcome relief in the middle of a recession. Regulations surrounding corporate mergers were also scaled back, which started a long series of hostile corporate takeovers.

DEREGULATION Reducing or removing government rules or controls over an industry or populace.

Under Reagan attempts were made to reverse rules that protected the environment, such as policies related to hazardous waste, pollution, allowable levels of carcinogens, and the oversight of nuclear power plants. Secretary of the Interior James Watt famously stated, "We will mine more, drill more, cut more timber." He proposed giving individual states the right to regulate the environment.

A special task force set up to look at low-income housing subsidies concluded in 1982 that a deregulated real estate market would better serve the poor. As a result, the federal housing budget was cut by 50 percent to $17.5 billion and federal housing subsidies went from a surplus of 300,000 available rental units in 1970 to a deficit of 3.3 million units by 1985.

The most famous deregulation of Reagan's presidency started with a standoff between Reagan and the Professional Air Traffic Controllers Organization (PATCO), who went on strike. Federal law prohibits strikes by government unions, particularly strikes that would pose a threat to national safety. The union had been negotiating a new contract; it wanted to reduce the controllers' workweek to 32 hours and gain a $10,000 pay increase. Reagan had offered a better pay raise than he was authorized to offer, but it was still short of the desired amount and his offer turned down. The workers went on strike despite Reagan's promise to fire all 11,000 of them.

Reagan made good on his threat. Not only were almost all of the air traffic controllers fired, but they were also banned from ever being hired by the Federal Aviation Administration again. New controllers were hired to replace them. PATCO was decertified and ceased to exist. (President Clinton later removed the ban on rehiring the controllers.)

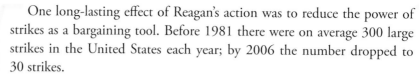

PARTISAN POLITICS Arguing or promoting policy along core political party beliefs; highlighted by an inability to compromise.

One long-lasting effect of Reagan's action was to reduce the power of strikes as a bargaining tool. Before 1981 there were on average 300 large strikes in the United States each year; by 2006 the number dropped to 30 strikes.

Environmental protection fared better than labor bargaining, though, as consumer advocacy groups took the administration to court over Reagan's changes. Judges ruled that many of the regulations had to be reinstated.

PARTISAN POLITICS

The Reagan administration was not the first presidency to stand firmly behind its party's core beliefs and push an agenda that leaned strategically to one side or the other. Reagan's clear stance on issues, however, and what seemed like a lack of willingness to compromise, led to an intensification of **partisan politics**, which refers to politicians voting closely along party lines. The intensity of this pattern continued to escalate during the presidencies following Reagan's, but the trend developed momentum during the 1980s.

Reagan's vehement advocacy for supply-side economics and his administration's firmness, as demonstrated in the firing of the PATCO employees, were partly responsible for this development, but the swing in the economy also contributed.

When the congressional elections of 1982 drew near, the Republicans knew they were in trouble. The economy had failed to recover despite Reagan's new tax cuts and oil deregulation, and the jobless rate climbed to 11 percent. As a result, the Democrats gained 27 seats in the House, giving them a large majority at the expense of many Republicans who had gained their seats on the coattails of Reagan's previous popularity.

However, soon after the midterm election the country moved out of its recession, and Reagan was well positioned for the 1984 presidential election. Industry started to boom and the computer revolution took full flight. Reagan made a political commercial in 1984, called "It's Morning in America Again," that showed the sun rising in small town neighborhoods as people got up to go to work. The narrator talked about American strength and optimism. Reagan drew a direct connection between personal values and political decisions. He highlighted his core beliefs and boasted that he had turned the economy around.

Another factor in the rise of partisan politics was a weakening in the distinction between church and state. Religious issues started to seep into political discussions.

Rise of the Christian Right

The rise of the evangelical voter was well underway by the time Reagan took office. In the 1960s, conservative Senator Barry Goldwater and other outspoken Christian conservatives, such as activist Phyllis Schlafly, paved the way for the masses of the Republican Party to embrace the rising evangelical movement in the country.

The Supreme Court decision in 1962's *Engel v. Vitale* also sparked the rise of the Christian right in politics. The Court's decision made it illegal for public schools to implement a public prayer and recitation. The Court's decision in *Roe v. Wade* (1973), which protected the right of a woman to obtain an abortion, further upset

Christian voters and gave them a cause to rally around. New television programming was also making Christian conservative voters uncomfortable with the direction of the country.

In 1964 Schlafly threw her support behind Goldwater's attempt to gain the Republican nomination. She distributed three million copies of her book, *A Choice Not an Echo*, which argued for stronger ideological values popular in the Midwest and West to become part of the party's core. The book helped Goldwater win the presidential nomination, but moderates in the Republican Party voted in a landslide for Democrat Lyndon B. Johnson. This created a tension between the two sides of the Republican Party.

In 1966, Californian Ronald Reagan saw the support that had carried Goldwater part of the way and jumped into the race for governor against the popular incumbent governor, Edmund Brown. He used Schlafly's ideas to portray Brown as an elitist while describing himself as an ordinary citizen who was trying to make government work for the average person. He won in a landslide. No one made much notice of the fact that Reagan was in fact a twice-married former movie star who had switched parties. He had successfully captured a growing feeling of dissatisfaction among a segment of the United States that felt under-represented: the Christian right. By the time Reagan ran for president in 1980, he had the public support of evangelical ministers Jerry Falwell and Pat Robertson.

The introduction of religion as an acceptable means to determine political value brought with it an element that was difficult to defend or explain and at times find a compromise. Reagan was able to put forth broader themes that appealed to a lot of voters. His ideas lined up with conservative Christian values, but he did not openly declare a religious agenda. However, the door was open for the more conservative wing of the party to emerge.

STAR WARS

By the time Reagan was elected president, the nation had been entrenched in a global cold war with the Soviet Union for more than 35 years. Reagan took a hard-line approach with the Soviet Union. He did not mince words about his stance: On March 8, 1983, Reagan gave a speech to the National Association of Evangelicals in which he called the Soviet Union the **evil empire**.

Two weeks later, he declared the United States was developing a missile defense system that would create a shield that could protect the US population from long-range Soviet missiles.

The United States and the Soviet Union had amassed 60,000 nuclear warheads, despite the 1972 Anti-Ballistic Missile (ABM) Treaty designed to ward off an arms race. An important concept behind the arms race was "mutually assured destruction," which implied that any nuclear attack would be met with an equal attack in response; this theoretically would prevent either the United States or the Soviet Union from starting a war. Reagan was stating the United States was overturning this doctrine by commencing a research and development plan to render Soviet missiles obsolete. The secretary of defense and the secretary of state were brought into the discussion only the day before the speech.

Reagan outlined a plan to create laser and particle-beam weapons that would operate in space with a level of reliability that

EVIL EMPIRE A phrase used by Reagan to describe the Soviet Union to rally support behind his hard-line foreign policy and increased defense spending.

could protect the United States from Soviet missiles. He asked the scientists who had discovered nuclear weapons to "turn their great talents now to the cause of mankind and world peace." Most believed the idea was inconceivable and paid it little attention, until two years later when the administration asked Congress for $26 billion over five years to start the **Strategic Defense Initiative (SDI)**, which became known as Star Wars.

The force field was never developed, though research continued long after it was deemed inpractical. SDI was only one piece of Reagan's military buildup. In total over his eight years, Reagan increased defense spending by 35 percent.

SDI PROGRAM The Strategic Defense Initiative was an idea put forth by Reagan as a defense system against nuclear attacks that would act as a giant umbrella over the United States.

RELATIONS WITH THE U.S.S.R.

In the waning days of the Carter administration, the United States boycotted the 1980 Summer Olympics in Moscow in protest over the Soviet Union's invasion of Afghanistan. One month after Reagan was sworn into office, the young U.S. men's hockey team beat the Soviets, who had dominated the sport for decades, during the medal round of the 1980 Winter Olympics at Lake Placid, New York. The event was called the Miracle on Ice and did more to defeat Soviet morale than the boycott of the summer games. The next year, Reagan began referring to the Soviet Union as the evil empire. In 1983, détente, or peaceable relations, with the Soviet Union seemed far off. This was one reason Reagan increased defense spending so dramatically.

The USSR had failed to match the American military buildup and the Soviets showed signs of dwindling strength. In October 1986 Mikhail Gorbachev, the Soviet leader, agreed to meet with President Reagan in Reykjavik, Iceland, to negotiate an arms agreement. Negotiations appeared to be heading to a successful conclusion at first. An agreement was being reached on reducing the number of intermediate-range missiles in Europe and Asia. The sides also planned to eradicate all nuclear missiles in ten years. This agreement was called the **Intermediate-range Nuclear Forces (INF)** Treaty, which limited either side's INFs to 1,600 delivery vehicles and 6,000 warheads. The talks between the two leaders were described by Vice Admiral John M. Poindexter as a breakthrough.

INF TREATY The Intermediate-range Nuclear Forces Treaty signed in 1987 by the United States and the Soviet Union to reduce weapons stockpiles and move diplomatic relations forward.

Once the subject of the SDI program came up, however, the talks reached a roadblock. The Reagan administration had agreed to delay the use of the missile defense system for ten years, while still conducting research. Gorbachev demanded that implementation be postponed for another decade. Reagan refused; the Soviets refused to agree to anything else without this concession. Both leaders returned to their countries empty handed.

Secretary of State George Schultz continued to pursue diplomacy with Gorbachev, but he found the Soviet leader's attempts to maneuver the United States into removing long-range missiles from Europe unacceptable without comparable concession on the Soviet side.

On February 28, 1987 Gorbachev unexpectedly and suddenly accepted the U.S. proposal of zero-sum, which would have both sides remove all intermediate-range missiles from Europe. Schultz quickly accepted the offer. Gorbachev's advisors had finally convinced him that SDI posed no real threat to the Soviet Union and they should not block efforts to negotiate a reduction in arms.

The INF treaty only reduced arms by 4 percent, but became the first in a series of reductions. This agreement led to a summit in Washington, D.C. between Reagan and Gorbachev. There were many critics of the new treaty, including Nixon and Kissinger, who felt it would weaken the relationship with Europe. Some saw Reagan as bending too far in the Soviets' direction.

Reagan was scheduled to visit Moscow in May 1988, and Republicans asked the Senate to pass the treaty just before he left. A month earlier Gorbachev had reached out to Schultz to complain about Reagan's continued negative rhetoric about the Soviet Union. After that, the tone of Reagan's speeches changed and there was no more mention of an evil empire.

The Moscow summit was considered a media success. Reagan said, "We have decided to speak to each other instead of about each other. It's working just fine." A Soviet reporter asked Reagan about his use of the phrase *evil empire* and Reagan answered, "I was talking about another time, another era."

MID-CHAPTER QUESTIONS

1. Reagan's economic platform relied heavily on the principles of supply-side economics. What are those principles? What are the arguments for and against this type of fiscal and monetary policy?

2. Evaluate Reagan's legacy as a champion of small federal government, cutting federal programs, and deregulating the market. In what ways is this a fair assessment of his presidency? In what ways is this an inaccurate representation of his administration?

3. How would you characterize Reagan's relationship with the Soviet Union? Did his foreign policy toward the Soviets change throughout his time in office?

4. How did Reagan's personality color his time in office? What events during his presidency allowed him to make use of his natural charisma and likeability?

BERLIN WALL, COMMUNISM, AND GLASNOST

In 1986, news broke of a foreign policy scandal that stood to taint Reagan's legacy. His administration oversaw the illegal funding of the Contra rebel group in Nicaragua with money it had raised through the covert sale of arms to Iran. Though an investigation suggested Reagan did not have any direct knowledge of the operation, the Iran-Contra affair caused his popularity to plummet.

His success with the Soviet Union, however, had the opposite effect. Mikhail Gorbachev had used the words *Glasnost*, the Russian word for openness, and *Perestroika*, or restructuring, in a speech just before he became the general secretary. He was laying the groundwork to transition the Soviet Union from an economy completely overseen by the state to a different economic system. In 1985, when

he started using the terms, the Soviet economy was failing and Gorbachev found it necessary to pull financial support from other countries, such as Cuba, which lessened Soviet influence around the globe.

The Berlin Wall that Reagan had famously stood before did not come down until 1989, one year after Reagan left office. But many believe it was his rhetoric, defense spending, and subsequent willingness to negotiate that ultimately led to the destruction of one of the greatest symbols of Soviet dominance. After the Iron Curtain came down, the Soviet Union itself quickly collapsed, the pieces breaking apart into separate countries. Russia took the seat at the UN General Counsel once held by the Soviet Union.

The transition was relatively peaceful and formalized a shift that had been developing for several years--world politics would no longer be dominated by two superpowers arguing over territory and arms.

STUDY ALERT

Reagan was a hard-line negotiator, such as when he fired the striking air traffic controllers. But he also knew when to retreat from a rigid stance, such as when he visited Moscow and changed his rhetoric about the Soviet Union to secure an arms treaty.

ASSASSINATION ATTEMPT

On March 30, 1981, early into Reagan's first term, 25-year-old John Hinckley, Jr., shot him. The attack occurred outside the Hilton Hotel in Washington, D.C., where Hinckley, who was trying to gain the attention of actress Jodie Foster, fired six shots only feet from the president. Secret Service agent Jerry Parr shoved the president into his limousine; at first agents thought Reagan had escaped harm. Parr radioed that Rawhide, the president's Secret Service nickname, was uninjured and that they were headed back to the White House.

Less than a minute later he radioed again--Reagan had begun coughing up blood and they were rushing him to George Washington Hospital. A bullet had missed Reagan's heart by one inch. Parr's fast thinking is credited with saving Reagan's life.

On the operating table Reagan was still able to display his ability to find humor in anything and joked with the doctors, saying, "I hope you all are Republicans." Three others were also wounded in the attack, including press secretary James Brady, who suffered life-altering injuries. Hinckley was declared legally insane and sentenced to life in a mental institution. He occasionally tries to win release.

PROLIFERATION OF THE MEDIA

In 1987, the Federal Communication Commission (FCC) voted to do away with the Fairness Doctrine. The doctrine was created in 1949 to ensure that radio and television broadcasters, and more importantly owners, did not use the stations as platforms for their own agendas. They were required to put the public interest first and present a generally fair presentation of any news story. Over time, the FCC began to allow on-air editorials, but only if opposing viewpoints were given the opportunity for an equal amount of air time.

Also in the 1980s, cable television networks began to emerge without the strict oversight of the FCC. This eventually opened the door for news stations to stray from neutrality in their broadcasts, sometimes with the goal of pandering to a particular audience and boosting viewer ratings. In response, the FCC stopped enforcing the rule on broadcast outlets, as traditional networks looked for ways to compete.

24-Hour News Cycle

The Iran hostage crisis in 1979 inspired businessman Ted Turner to create the Cable News Network (CNN) in 1980. An entire network devoted to **24-hour news** was a revolutionary idea. A typical newscast on a broadcast station was 30 to 60 minutes long. Lighter, hand-held cameras and satellite feeds made it possible to capture more news as it happened. The assassination attempt on Reagan's life, for example, was caught by an ABC cameraman and replayed over and over again on every news station.

The beginning of cable news meant increased competition in the television news industry. During the Carter-Reagan debates, the broadcast news stations decided to exclude independent candidate John Anderson. Turner sought to include him by filming him in an off-site location. After the other two candidates had answered the question, CNN switched to Anderson, who was given the same question to answer. The back and forth between an ongoing live debate and the solitary Anderson meant that CNN had to play catch up, but the idea worked.

24-HOUR NEWS The concept of entire networks devoted only to news and operated 24 hours a day, seven days a week, creating the need for more news items.

STOCK MARKET AND CRASH

Advances in technology were not only changing the way networks broadcast the news. Advances in computer technology also revolutionized the way people and organizations bought and sold stocks.

In the years leading up to autumn 1987, the U.S. stock market was booming, with record numbers of shares trading. Traders began to rely more heavily on computers and the use of automatic buys or sells for larger institutions, which is known as **program trading**. Large funds, such as state pension funds and institutions, put in automatic orders to sell, to ensure they did not suffer losses beyond a certain point. Some of the large funds purchased portfolio insurance, which was essentially a stop order to sell under certain conditions and was carried out by a third party in large, batch orders.

Favorable tax laws related to buyouts, coupled with deregulation of corporate takeovers, increased the number of possible takeover targets and pushed stock prices higher. The other type of program trading at the time was called *index arbitrage.* In this method, traders used computers to detect when the value of a stock was lower than the value of the speculative futures contract. Traders would buy the stock and sell the futures contract in a bid to make money on the difference.

In the months leading up to October 1987, interest rates were rising around the world along with the US trade deficit. In addition, the dollar was becoming weak. Economists were growing wary of a return of inflation.

PROGRAM TRADING Large-volume trades by institutions of stocks and other financial commodities with the use of computer software.

On October 18, investors pulled back just enough to trigger program trades. These sell-offs then triggered recalls of loans made to investors based on the price of their stocks. Borrowing against stock is called "buying on margin" and a recall of the money is known as a "margin call." Waves of margin calls also meant that fewer investors had money available to go back into the stock market and start buying again, which led to heavier losses.

By the end of the day, the S&P 500 stock market index was down by almost 20 percent, an unprecedented amount at the time. After Black Monday, program trading was reined in to ensure the market would not melt down so easily again.

THE GULF WAR

Foreign policy did not become any easier for the United States at the end of the Cold War. With the Soviets no longer presenting an immediate threat to the American way of life, the United States turned its eye to regional conflicts around the world that threatened world peace. One such conflict existed between the Middle East nations of Iraq and Iran.

The two nations fought with one another throughout Reagan's time in office. The United States aided Iraq with weapons and useful information, which eventually enabled Iraq's leader Saddam Hussein to prevail.

After the fighting between the two countries subsided, the United States came to realize it had made a misstep in supporting Iraq's dictator. To help pay for the massive debts he accrued, Hussein invaded his oil-rich neighbor Kuwait.

Reagan's successor, George H. W. Bush, went to war with Iraq over this invasion in 1991. With the aid of allied European nations, Bush forced Hussein to retreat from Kuwait. Bush was content with this outcome and decided not to pursue the capture of the dictator himself, a decision with implications for the future of American foreign conflicts.

END OF CHAPTER TAKE-AWAYS

- **Reaganomics:** Reagan campaigned on a supply-side economics platform to cut government spending and lower taxes. He believed prosperity for wealthy Americans would trickle down to lower socioeconomic classes in the form of jobs. The economy did not recover initially, however, and soaring deficits required Reagan to increase tax receipts throughout most of his presidency.
- **Partisan Politics:** Moral and religious issues started to influence politics during Reagan's administration.
- **Star Wars:** The nickname for Reagan's pet project of building a missile defense shield around the country to protect it from Soviet attacks.
- **Relations with the USSR:** Reagan first took a hard line with the Soviets and ramped up defense spending, but later softened his approach and opened dialogue with Gorbachev.
- **Berlin Wall, Communism, Glasnost:** Cold War tensions finally melted at the end of Reagan's presidency, communism started to wane, and Gorbachev adopted more open diplomatic policies.
- **Assassination Attempt:** Reagan survived a gunshot. He recovered relatively quickly and resumed his duties while his popularity surged.
- **Proliferation of the Media:** Cable networks began reporting news; CNN launched the 24-hour news broadcast.
- **Stock Market and Crash:** Advances in computer technology led to more sophisticated trading mechanisms. Money could be made—and lost—faster than ever.
- **Gulf War:** Iraq's dictator, Saddam Hussein, received U.S. aide in his war with Iran but then invaded Kuwait to pay off debts.

REFERENCES

Alesina, A., & Rosenthal, H. (1995). *Partisan politics, divided government, and the economy.* Cambridge, England: Cambridge University Press.

Atkinson, R. (1993). *Crusade: The untold story of the Persian Gulf War.* Boston, MA: Houghton Mifflin.

Bartlett, B. R. (2009). *The new American economy: The failure of Reaganomics and a new way forward.* New York, NY: Palgrave Macmillan.

Laqueur, W. (1989). *The long road to freedom: Russia and Glasnost.* New York, NY: C. Scribner's.

Niskanen, W. A., & Cato Institute. (1988). *Reaganomics: An insider's account of the policies and the people.* New York, NY: Oxford University Press.

Reagan, R., & Brinkley, D. (2007). *The Reagan diaries.* New York, NY: Harper Collins.

CHAPTER 21

The Bubble Years

On December 5, 1996, the chairman of the Federal Reserve Board gave a speech at a black-tie dinner in Washington, D.C. Alan Greenspan was, at the time, one of the most powerful men in the world. The Fed chairman has the power to control the supply of U.S. dollars and set interest rates for U.S. banks. This gives him unparalleled control over the U.S. and global economy.

Greenspan asked his audience: "But how do we know when irrational exuberance has unduly escalated asset values, which then become subject to unexpected and prolonged contractions as they have in Japan over the past decade?"

Greenspan did not know it at the time, but the phrase "irrational exuberance" would come to define the wild economic boom of the 1990s and early 2000s. Asset bubbles, in which prices rise unsustainably in one or more sectors of the economy, are fairly common in capitalist societies. At the turn of the twenty-first century, the irrational exuberance surrounding the computer technology industry burnt out as the tech bubble burst. Less than a decade later, the collapse of the housing market again caused the economy to recoil and instigated the Great Recession.

CLINTON ECONOMIC POLICY

The United States had fallen into a deep recession during the last two years of George H. W. Bush's presidency. For this reason—and because the collapse of the Soviet Union had eclipsed geopolitics for the time being—the election of 1992 centered mostly on economic issues. As one campaign aide for Democrat Bill Clinton famously put it: "It's the economy, stupid."

Americans were very worried about high unemployment, rising budget deficits, and the specter of global trade shifting more and more jobs overseas. A wealthy businessman named Ross Perot decided to run for the presidency as an independent against the Republican incumbent George H. W. Bush and the Democratic nominee, Bill Clinton. In a hard-fought election, Clinton won a plurality of the votes (more than either of his rivals, but less than half of the total).

President Clinton was an unconventional Democrat, a self-styled "New Democrat." Socially he was liberal, but his economic policies veered away from the pro-union, anti-corporate stance of many in his own party. Clinton's inner circle of advisors included some prominent Hollywood types and a number of business leaders, especially from the high technology hub of Silicon Valley. Clinton immediately clashed with Republicans—and more than a few Democrats—on social policy. But his economic policies were embraced by many of his political opponents. They also proved highly controversial with many traditional Democrats.

Deficit Reduction and World Trade

When Clinton assumed office in January 1993, the federal budget deficit was alarmingly high: for the fiscal year 1992 it amounted to 4.7 percent of GDP. Many economists acknowledged that such deficits were undesirable and a drag on economic growth. But every president from the 1970s through the early 1990s presided over budget shortfalls, often alarmingly large ones. Clinton made it a top priority to balance the budget and reduce the deficit, which was the amount the U.S. government owed its creditors. He succeeded so well in this quest that by the end of his second term it looked as though the country was on the path to paying off its debts entirely.

World trade was a more divisive issue during the Clinton era, and one that left a mixed legacy. Clinton was a strong advocate of **free trade**. Indeed, on this issue he had more in common with many in the Republican Party than he did with members of his own party. Democrats tended to have strong ties to industrial unions, which were especially strong in the "rustbelt" states of the Northeast and Midwest. Unions and their Democratic allies were wary of free trade, as it threatened to undermine U.S. manufacturing jobs.

One of the major developments of Clinton's administration was the North American Free Trade Agreement (NAFTA) between the United States, Canada, and Mexico. Proponents and critics of free trade debate the net effect of joining this trade bloc on American workers. Opponents of free trade believe that NAFTA led to a reduction of domestic manufacturing and other blue-collar jobs, because companies could find cheaper labor beyond U.S. borders. Supporters, however, claim that several economic indicators suggest that companies were more profitable as a result of joining NAFTA on average and were consequently able to hire more workers domestically as well.

FREE TRADE International trade that is not influenced by economic legislation designed to regulate imports and exports.

The Power of the Federal Reserve Bank

People tend to misunderstand the purpose and authority of the **Federal Reserve Bank** (usually called the Fed). It is not, contrary to popular belief, a branch of the U.S. government. It is a private institution, controlled by the largest banks in the country, which nominate the board members responsible for setting the bank's policies. Since Congress authorized its creation in 1911, the Fed has governed the U.S. money supply. It can encourage growth by lowering the cost of borrowing money; or, if inflation is becoming a problem, contract the supply of credit by raising interest rates. As part of its "dual mandate," the Fed is also supposed to encourage full employment, although many critics believe it is not possible to keep inflation low and promote full employment simultaneously.

An extraordinary amount of power is placed in the hands of the chairman of the Federal Reserve Bank. The chairman is appointed by the president but operates independently from executive or congressional oversight. The Fed chairman thus has unparalleled power over the U.S. economy. By contrast, the president's actions are limited by the need to coordinate actions with Congress (and vice versa). No modern Fed chairman has had greater influence—for good and ill—over the U.S. economy than Alan Greenspan.

Greenspan was appointed by the free-market Republican President Reagan, but his tenure continued under the next three administrations, and his relations with President Clinton were remarkably smooth. To his credit, Greenspan's policies revived the U.S. and global economy after more than a decade in the doldrums. However, his fierce opposition to regulating Wall Street meant that reckless and sometimes fraudulent behavior there went unchecked. This anti-regulatory mindset combined with a refusal to raise interest rates paved the way for the massive—and massively destructive—financial and real estate **bubbles** of the early twenty-first century.

FEDERAL RESERVE BANK A private institution that regulates the amount of U.S. money in supply and the costs of borrowing money.

BUBBLE A state of significant economic growth with the potential of a sudden collapse.

Deregulation

For more than twenty years, from the election of President Ronald Reagan to the collapse of the economic bubble in 2008, policymakers viewed government regulation as a detriment to prosperity. There were still regulatory measures in place, but critics of regulation had the upper hand since the days of Reagan. They have portrayed regulators as the enemies of capitalism and economic growth. In many cases, regulatory agencies had leaders who did not believe in the mission of the agency. At other times, the budget or resources of regulatory agencies were slashed, and their freedom of movement curtailed.

Deregulation was the movement to limit government intervention in a wide variety of industries, from energy producers to financial services. Reagan was a key proponent of deregulation, as was his appointed Fed chief, Alan Greenspan. President Clinton was committed to deregulation as well, and some of the most important pieces of legislation associated with the deregulation of banks took place during his administration. Specifically, Congress repealed the Glass-Steagall Act, a Depression-era law that separated investment banks from retail banking and created the Federal Deposit Insurance Corporation. Attempts to regulate the sale and exchange of complex financial assets, such as derivatives, were fought back by Clinton and his Democratic economic advisers.

DEREGULATION A movement to limit government control over business practices.

Tax Increases

In 1993, shortly after taking over as president, Bill Clinton decided to stake his presidency on policy that largely reversed the taxation and spending priorities of his Republican predecessors. Whereas Reagan believed that cutting taxes would boost economic growth, Clinton believed the top priority had to be bringing down the record-high budget deficits. And the only way to do that, he believed, was to increase taxes on high earners and corporations.

The budget for 1994 aggressively cut spending in many areas of the budget. But it also raised taxes on those earning six-figure salaries or above. On the one hand, Clinton's decision was vindicated in the rapidly shrinking budget deficit. However, the tax increases proved very unpopular, especially in conservative-leaning districts, and contributed to a groundswell of opposition to Democratic leadership that would soon result in a historic defeat for the party at the ballot box.

TECH BOOM

By the end of the 1990s the Internet had emerged as a revolutionary force in everything from entertainment to communications to commerce. Indeed, technology promised to usher in a new age not unlike the transformation experienced by the West two centuries earlier in the Industrial Revolution.

The Internet

The Internet is such an important part of our lives today that it is hard to imagine what life was like before it. But it was only in 1990 that the first web page was written. Only slowly did commerce begin to move online, partly because there was little security or trust between buyers and sellers. By the late '90s, however, companies believed they had overcome these obstacles and the Internet was open for business.

Silicon Valley

In earlier decades Silicon Valley, an area near San Francisco, had become the home of numerous technology companies such as Hewlett-Packard that focused on

computer hardware. This area continued to attract innovative technology companies in the '90s, but now most were focused on software and Internet applications. Everyone wanted to establish a foothold in the rapidly expanding market for Internet-based services.

Many Silicon Valley companies were founded and run by young entrepreneurs who had either recently graduated from college or dropped out to pursue their dream. Funding for these startups often came from venture capitalists, who often funded dozens of projects in the hope of striking gold with one or two.

Another way Internet startups raised capital to fund their operations (which were notoriously unprofitable during their early years) was to sell shares on Wall Street through an initial public offering. In the boom years of the late '90s, practically any startup could attract interest from investors eager to own a piece of the next big thing. The problem was that no one could accurately assess the value of these companies, since many produced no revenues and it was unclear when or if they would turn a profit. The price of shares therefore fluctuated wildly. Investors might make a fortune one day, only to have it vanish the next.

When the dot.com bubble finally burst in 2000, it wiped out billions of dollars in investors' portfolios. It was especially damaging to small investors, many of whom traded their tech stocks on the Internet via web-based brokers. Big banks and financial institutions were relatively unscathed, however, and the economy at large, though deflated somewhat, was not severely impacted.

But the popping of the dot.com bubble did have two longer-term impacts on the larger economy. First, it exposed serious conflicts of interest between Wall Street, which made a great deal of money on the IPOs and stock trading of the dot.coms, and individual investors, many of whom ended up on the losing end of the deals. Regulators were slow to intervene on behalf of investors, but eventually both the Securities and Exchange Commission and the attorney general of New York stepped up prosecutions of fraud and financial criminality. Many dot.coms went bankrupt, but so too did some very large, seemingly secure corporations that had hitched a ride on the tech boom. Enron and WorldCom were two such corporations. They were forced to declare bankruptcy, and their executives were prosecuted for fraud and went to jail.

Second, to counteract the steep deflation of the tech sector in 2000, Fed Chairman Alan Greenspan lowered long-term interest rates to help stimulate the economy and encourage investors to return to the stock market. An unforeseen consequence of this action was to inflate a completely new bubble, this time in the real estate sector. This bubble would in turn pop later in the decade, instigating a deep global recession in 2008.

CLINTON'S POLITICAL POLICY

Despite his economically conservative approach to leading the country, Bill Clinton inspired wildly conflicting emotions in the American electorate. This was partly because of his early association with the anti-Vietnam movement and his advocacy of liberal social causes. Clinton was the first baby-boomer president, the first since the Cold War began not to have served in the military, and the first to admit publicly to having experimented with illegal drugs in his youth. From the day he stepped into the Oval Office, Clinton was already inspiring a powerful conservative backlash. It was not long before he found himself fighting for his political life.

Some of the damage was self-inflicted, born of a sense that he needed to accomplish as much as possible in the first year while he still enjoyed political popularity. When he tried to make good on a campaign pledge to allow gays to openly serve in the U.S. military, he found the Pentagon very resistant. In the end, they struck a compromise collectively known as the Don't Ask, Don't Tell policy. Military recruiters would not ask about the sexual orientation of potential servicemembers, and the recruits themselves would say nothing. It was an awkward compromise that remained in place for nearly two decades.

Other political debacles soon followed. The president put his wife, Hillary Clinton, in charge of an ad hoc committee whose goal was to design a more efficient, less costly health care system that would allow all Americans access to medical treatment. But the process was enormously controversial from the beginning. Clinton was criticized for giving the first lady too much authority. Many people thought the government was overstepping its mandate. "Hillary Care," as it came to be known, tarnished the reputation of both the president and the first lady. Health care reform moved to the back of the agenda for more than a decade.

Despite these setbacks, Clinton proved an adept negotiator in Washington with a passion for the details of public policy matched by few other presidents of either party. Important legislation enacted during the Clinton presidency includes the State Children's Health Insurance Program, designed to expand health insurance coverage to children in families who are struggling financially but whose income levels are too high to qualify for Medicaid. He also signed the North American Free Trade Agreement (NAFTA) into law. This agreement expanded trade between Canada, Mexico, and the United States.

Rise of Conservatives

In a very real sense, conservatives never went away, although they did fall back to regroup after Clinton's election. In 1992, after twelve straight years of Republicans in the White House, the party found itself relatively powerless. Democrats controlled both the House of Representatives and the Senate, and now they had the White House as well.

Conservative ideology found its voice in talk radio, especially in the popular nationally syndicated programs of influential commentators such as Rush Limbaugh. Prior to Reagan's presidency, political advocacy on radio and television was regulated by the Federal Communications Commission (FCC). The FCC was guided by the Fairness Doctrine, which held that the nation's broadcasters were limited in number and should therefore reflect the diverse opinions of the people they served. Reagan felt the Fairness Doctrine was a violation of the Constitutional right to free speech, and it was eliminated in the deregulation of the communications industry.

By the early '90s conservative radio and television programs were flourishing nationwide. They tapped into widespread anxiety and anger about the direction the country was taking under Democratic leadership. Concerns about rising crime, high taxes, welfare programs, and a perceived anti-military streak all came to be associated with the current crop of Democratic leaders.

From the outside, the conservative movement appeared to be unified ideologically, but it was actually as fragmented as the American Left. Evangelical Christians were well represented in the coalition. Sometimes referred to as "the silent majority," members of the Religious Right believed that Democratic programs posed a serious threat to the traditional values they espoused. They wanted an end to abortion, publicly funded birth control, and sex education in public school classrooms. They also advocated for prayer in public schools, and a number of other causes that seemed (to their critics) to blur the line between church and state.

Other conservatives were more closely aligned with the libertarian ideology of small government, low taxes, and strong personal freedoms. They were less concerned with questions of morality and values. For some libertarians, the Second Amendment (the right to keep and bear arms) was a pressing concern. Gun rights motivated a large segment of the conservative movement to get involved in politics. The National Rifle Association (NRA) played an important role in mobilizing gun rights activists and opposing any effort in Washington or state capitals to restrict individual access to firearms.

Contract with America

The conservative movement came together in 1994 to achieve a single goal—to take control of Congress back from the Democrats. If they could do that, they believed, they could derail the Clinton White House and open him up for defeat in 2006.

They needed a rallying cry that would nationalize the mid-term elections, which are traditionally about local issues and, to a lesser extent, a referendum on the popularity of the president. In the summer of 1994, a small group of Republican candidates gathered on the steps of the Capitol to sign the **Contract with America**. This contract contained ten proposals or promises to the American people. They shied away from controversial social issues, concentrating instead on lowering taxes, reforming welfare, and reducing regulation.

It was a theatrical but highly effective strategy. While turnout was low—as it frequently is in non-presidential elections—conservative voters flocked to the polls to support the Republican candidates. For the first time in 40 years, Republicans won a majority of the seats in both the House and the Senate.

> **CONTRACT WITH AMERICA**
> The successful political agenda of the Republicans in the 1994 mid-term elections that focused on economic policy.

Republican Control of the House

With the 1994 election, power shifted to a new generation of House Republicans led by Georgian Newt Gingrich. Gingrich was less of an ideological purist than many of the incoming politicians with whom he entered the House. He was able, for instance, to work with Clinton's White House to secure passage of free trade accords such as NAFTA, which many Republicans supported.

On the whole, however, the Republicans were determined to capitalize on their newfound power. The Contract with America laid out a timetable as well as an agenda: they promised to enact all or most of the initial ten legislative items within the first 100 days of the new Congress.

Gridlock on Capitol Hill

In November 1995 the Republican-led Congress sent their budget bill to the White House, and President Clinton promptly vetoed it. The president had warned Congress that if they sent him a budget that included deep spending cuts in entitlement programs

such as Medicare, he would reject it. They sent it anyway, and he kept his promise. The open warfare between the two parties and the branches of government they controlled brought Washington, D.C. to a complete halt. More than 800,000 federal workers were ordered to stay home for 21 days during two separate shutdowns between mid-November and early January of 2006.

The Republicans under Gingrich's leadership had staked their party's future on the standoff with President Clinton. Would the country side with the Republicans, who wanted to slash spending, and force the White House to go along with them? Or would the public agree with the president that the Republicans cared more about scoring political points than they did about the well-being of vulnerable citizens? In the end, public opinion lined up squarely behind Clinton. The public was disgusted by the spectacle of Republicans shutting down the entire government during the busy holiday season. Clinton's poll numbers rose; Congressional Republicans' numbers fell. The Clinton presidency got a much-needed boost.

GROWTH OF CONSERVATISM

Towards the end of the twentieth century, American Conservatism came to be dominated by leaders with a religious or cultural agenda. George W. Bush, the son of President George H.W. Bush, who preceded Clinton, won the 2000 election. W, as he became popularly known, was the first president to hold an MBA (Masters in Business Administration). After something of a wild youth, he had embraced evangelical Christianity, was twice elected governor of Texas, and had the trust of many Republican Party leaders.

Bush ran on a platform that emphasized **compassionate conservatism**. He did not invent the term, but he and his political strategist Karl Rove found it an easily understood way to appeal to moderate **swing voters** (people with no strong loyalty for either party). Bush and Rove worried that such voters were put off by the harsh rhetoric of traditional conservatives. Such conservatives opposed welfare because it wasted resources, or redistributed money from hard-working citizens to

the "undeserving" poor. Compassionate conservatives, by contrast, emphasized the long-term damage to welfare recipients caused by excessive dependency and loss of skills and self-respect.

Compassionate conservatism found its best expression in Bush's commitment to education reform, particularly through the policy known as **No Child Left Behind** (NCLB). Enacted early in Bush's first term, NCLB strengthened the federal government's contribution to public education, which had traditionally been guided by state and local governments. In return for the additional money being offered at the federal level, however, the Department of Education acquired new authority over regulating schools. Standardized tests were to be administered on a yearly basis nationwide. If students did not demonstrate improvement, their schools could be labeled *failing*. Failing schools could be shut down, their administrators and teachers replaced.

NCLB demonstrated the tensions between traditional conservatism and compassionate conservatism. Traditional conservatives railed against the excessive power of Washington over the states and local authorities, who were seen as being more responsive to individual voters. President Bush had to seek support from powerful Democrats, such as Senator Ted Kennedy, to pass the legislation. Bush's appeal to raise the bar for all students—he said he wanted to end "the soft bigotry of low expectations"—resonated with members of both parties. However, the attempt to centralize authority in Washington went against a core value of many conservatives.

On the economic level, the Republican Party under George W. Bush's leadership abandoned conservative principles altogether. The federal budget deficit, which had been whittled down to a manageable size under the Clinton administration, ballooned once again in the first decade of the twenty-first century. This was partially because President Bush won a significant tax cut to address a recession in 2000–2001. It was also related to the exponential growth in military spending after the terrorist attacks on September 11, 2001. But the attitude of the Bush White House to fiscal restraint in general was best summed up by Vice President Richard Cheney, who said that "deficits don't matter."

MID-CHAPTER QUESTIONS

1. What is the purpose of the Federal Reserve Bank and why is its chairman so powerful?

2. What were the major economic achievements of the Clinton administration?

3. How did conservatism become such an important political force in the 1990s and 2000s?

4. What was the long-term impact of the dot.com bubble on the American economy?

UNILATERALISM IN FOREIGN RELATIONS

One of the most common criticisms of the Bush White House is that it alienated the United States from the rest of the world at a time when U.S. influence abroad could have been incredibly strong. In the 1990s, shortly after the collapse of the Soviet Union and the end of the Cold War, America's standing as the world's sole superpower seemed to usher in a new era of peace and prosperity. The North American Treaty Organization (NATO) expanded eastward to the very heart of the region once dominated by the Soviet Union. There was even talk of allowing Russia itself to join NATO, though this was quickly rejected by Russian leaders.

Still, there has always been resistance within America to foreign entanglements. Multilateralism at the end of the twentieth century had many different components: there were military alliances such as NATO, trade agreements such as the WTO and NAFTA, and a strong push to counter

global warming with anti-pollution treaties such as the Kyoto Protocol. Conservatives (and more than a few liberals) were beginning to question how much room the United States still had to maneuver as a global power amidst all these constraints.

Bill Clinton had been enormously popular overseas, and many world leaders had hoped Vice President Al Gore would succeed him. When George W. Bush entered the White House in January 2000, however, he did not have much international experience as either a statesman or a traveler. He earned international enmity several ways, including by deciding not to join worldwide environmental initiatives.

So, when tragedy struck America on the morning of September 11, 2001, it is perhaps not surprising that President Bush's first instinct was not to seek multilateral consensus on possible responses. Once the initial shock of the attack wore off, the Bush White House leapt to action. America's unilateral moment had arrived. Bush sought to wage war against nations that his administration believed harbored terrorists or pursued the development of weapons of mass destruction. In responding to these attacks Bush moved swiftly, without waiting to build international coalitions and support,

TERRORISM

TERRORISM The use of violence to inflict fear and coerce an enemy .

Terrorism is the use of violence to inflict fear and coerce an enemy. While acts of terrorism had affected the United States before the twenty-first century, the events of fall 2001 created a new need to address an escalation of militant radicalism that threatened U.S. law and order at home.

September 11

AL QAEDA A global terrorist organization composed of militant Moslem radicals led by Osama bin Laden.

OSAMA BIN LADEN A Saudi-born terrorist who masterminded the attacks of September 11, 2001 and led the terrorist organization al Qaeda until his death in 2011.

On September 11, 2001, members of the international terrorist group **al Qaeda** hijacked four commercial jet airliners within a few hours of each other. *Al Qaeda* translates from Arabic as *the base*. It was founded in the 1980s by a wealthy Saudi Islamic extremist named **Osama bin Laden**. Bin Laden was a veteran of numerous armed conflicts, including the U.S.-backed war against Soviet forces in Afghanistan between 1979 and 1989, but he became enraged when U.S. troops were stationed in Saudi Arabia during and after the first Gulf War (1990–1991).

On the morning of September 11, nineteen hijackers boarded four planes and took over the controls from the pilots and crewmembers. The hijackers piloted two of the planes into the twin towers of the World Trade Center. Within two hours, both buildings had collapsed. More than 2,000 people were dead, including hundreds of passengers, crewmembers, and the hijackers. The terrorists flew the other two jets toward Washington, DC. One of these struck the Pentagon, the headquarters of all branches of the U.S. armed forces, bursting into flames and killing hundreds. The fourth plane was also headed for Washington, DC, but that plane never reached its destination, because its passengers learned of the fate shared by the other hijacked planes via cell phone, and attempted to take back control of the plane from the terrorists. They succeeded in preventing the plane from reaching Washington, but the hijackers crashed the plane into a field outside Shanksville, Pennnsylvania rather than relinquish control.

America was in a state of shock.

HISTORY COMES ALIVE

The U.S. government conducted a study of the events of September 11, 2001. The findings are summarized in the *9/11 Commission Report.* This report includes the following transcript of a telephone call made by Peter Hanson, a passenger on United 175, the plane that eventually crashed into the South Tower of the World Trade Center. After the plane had been hijacked, he relayed this information to his father:

> *It's getting bad, Dad—A stewardess was stabbed—They seem to have knives and Mace—They said they have a bomb—It's getting very bad on the plane—Passengers are throwing up and getting sick—The plane is making jerky movements—I don't think the pilot is flying the plane—I think we are going down—I think they intend to go to Chicago or someplace and fly into a building—Don't worry, Dad—If it happens, it'll be very fast—My God, my God.*

War on Terror

Al Qaeda had declared war against the United States even before the attacks of September 11. There had been a previous attempt to bomb the World Trade Center in 1993, when a rental truck filled with explosives had detonated in an underground parking garage, killing six people. Additional attacks included the simultaneous bombings of two American embassies in Africa in 1998. A U.S. Navy destroyer, the *USS Cole*, was attacked in October 2000. It suffered extensive damage when a boat laden with explosives rammed it in the Persian Gulf port of Aden, Yemen, killing 17 sailors and injuring dozens of others.

While it was relatively easy for al Qaeda to attack American targets around the globe, the United States had serious trouble striking back at a scattered, nongovernmental organization. Al Qaeda's members came from all over the world—even the United States—but they did not control any government. Attacking al Qaeda was therefore problematic, as it would necessarily entail an attack on a sovereign nation as well. Part of the strategy for the "War on Terror" was to make it clear to states that harbored and protected large numbers of Islamic terrorists (regardless of an affiliation with al Qaeda) that from now on they would be viewed as enemies of the United States.

The United States fought much of the War on Terror in Afghanistan, where al Qaeda had a strong foothold. The fighting there was complicated by severe terrain and profoundly complicated local political and social issues. While the United States and its supporters suffered many losses and faced many challenges in the War on Terror, it did manage to significantly diminish al Qaeda's ability to carry out further terrorist attacks. Perhaps the high point of the War on Terror came on May 2, 2011, when group of Navy SEALS on a mission ordered by President Barack Obama killed bin Laden in his hide-out in Pakistan.

War on Iraq

The War on Iraq became America's most controversial military engagement since the War in Vietnam. More than a decade after it began there is still debate about why the United States took the military action that it did. In the months after 9/11, the Bush White House sought a plan of action that would attack al Qaeda in their own part of the world, both to appease the public's anger and to prevent a future attack that many feared was imminent.

Iraq was under the control of Saddam Hussein, a brutal military dictator who wreaked havoc on his own country through multiple wars with neighboring Iran, an armed invasion of Kuwait, and genocidal attacks on Iraq's minority Kurdish population. Saddam's government had one of the worst human rights records in the Middle East, having used chemical agents to massacre its own Kurdish citizens. It also had a documented record of pursuing nuclear weapons, and throughout the 1990s had been subject to periodic visits by UN-mandated weapons inspectors.

By 2002, Saddam was openly defiant of these inspectors, who as a result became increasingly frustrated and suspicious of Iraqi plans. The United States wanted stronger action to be taken against Iraq by the international community. Secretary of State Colin Powell went to the UN in early 2003 to make the case that Iraq was actively seeking **weapons of mass destruction** (WMD). The UN approved a resolution demanding that Saddam comply with the inspection teams.

The Bush White House was not satisfied with this outcome, however. The United States and its allies began moving troops and war materiel into place to launch an invasion. The invasion of Iraq had as much to with the War on Terror as it did with Saddam Hussein and weapons of mass destruction. It was meant to establish a new right to engage in what Bush called preemptive war.

The events of September 11 had made a profound impact on the Bush administration. In response to this unprecedented attack on American soil, the so-called **Bush Doctrine** was formulated. It held that, in an age of instantaneous communication, when terrorists and hostile states had access to WMDs and the tools to use them, it was no longer possible to await proof of an imminent threat before invoking the right to self defense.

Bush's administration faced criticism from opponents who claimed that this policy set the burden of proof too low for launching a preemptive war. Critics wondered where lines would be drawn to limit the War on Terror, especially when the Bush administration failed to uncover the Iraqi WMDs that made up the major part of the President's case for invading Iraq. His supporters, however, believed that the President's policies were needed to curb terror and protect lives in the modern world.

As for the actual war in Iraq, the allies were initially successful, defeating Saddam's armed forces in a matter of months. But the occupation proved a more difficult task. The transition of Iraq from a dictatorship to a fledgling democracy proved long, bloody, and costly for all involved. In 2005, the fugitive former ruler was captured, put on trial, and executed for his crimes against the Iraqi people. But fighting between Sunni and Shiite Muslims, and between the Arab majority and Kurdish minority, threatened to tear the country to pieces. Only after a fresh infusion of U.S. troops in 2007 did the situation begin to

WEAPONS OF MASS DESTRUCTION Technologically advanced tools designed to kill many people or to destroy large areas.

BUSH DOCTRINE One of the guiding principles of President Bush's foreign policy that called for preemptive warfare in response to modern threats to world peace.

improve. Elections were held in 2005 and 2010 for the Iraqi Parliament, which, while fractious, has produced a constitution, formed working parties and coalitions, and overseen the drawdown of U.S. and allied troops. On October 21, 2011, President Barack Obama announced that the last American troops would exit Iraq on December 31, bringing eight years of warfare and peacekeeping to an end.

END OF CHAPTER TAKE-AWAYS

- **Irrational Exuberance:** Fed Chairman Alan Greenspan served four presidents, during which the economy prospered but dangerous financial bubbles formed.
- **Clinton Economic Policy:** President Clinton defied many within his party to promote free trade, deregulation, and the end of welfare programs. He brought the federal budget deficit under control.
- **Tech Boom:** Investment in technology companies—mainly in Silicon Valley—exploded in the '90s as businesses looked to commercialize the Internet. The bubble popped in 2000, as revenues failed to materialize.
- **Clinton's Political Policy:** Bill Clinton began his presidency with lofty goals, but Democrats lost control of Congress after two years, and he "pivoted" to the center, adopting many of the ideas of his Republican opponents.
- **Growth of Conservatism:** Conservatism changed in the 1990s and early 2000s, spurred by popular radio and TV commentators such as Rush Limbaugh.
- **Unilateralism in Foreign Relations:** After the terrorist attacks of September 11, 2001, President Bush grew impatient of trying to build support internationally for military actions against states he saw as a threat to American security.
- **Terrorism:** After 9/11, the United States embarked on two wars—in Iraq and Afghanistan—while also aggressively targeting perceived threats both at home and abroad.

DID YOU KNOW?

The United States and the United Kingdom are often said to enjoy a "special relationship" based on shared history and a common language. But the personal relationship between leaders can be hit or miss. When George W. Bush replaced Bill Clinton as America's president, few expected the UK's Labour Prime Minister, Tony Blair, to bond with the Texas Republican. Clinton's politics were much closer to his own, but Blair and Bush did become close friends. Both were strong Christians, and each was committed to building a democratic Iraq. But the friendship was mocked in the UK, where Blair became known as "Bush's poodle."

REFERENCES

Aberbach, J., & Peele, G. (2011). *Crisis of conservatism?: The Republican Party, the conservative movement and American politics after Bush*. New York, NY: Oxford University Press.

Critchlow, D., & MacLean, N. (2009). *Debating the American conservative movement: 1945 to the present*. Lanham, MD: Rowman and Littlefield.

Hook, S., & Spanier, J. (2004). *American foreign policy since World War II*. Washington, DC: CQ Press.

McLean, B., & Nocera, J. (2010). *All the devils are here: The hidden history of the financial crisis*. New York, NY: Portfolio/Penguin.

Reinhart, C,. & Rogoff, K. (2009). *This time is different: Eight centuries of financial folly*. Princeton, NJ: Princeton University Press.

Shiller, R. (2005). *Irrational exuberance* (2nd ed.). Princeton, NJ: Princeton University Press.

Zelikow, P. (2011). *The 9/11 commission report: The attack from planning to aftermath*. New York, NY: W.W. Norton.

APA Style

APA style is a set of rules and guidelines for manuscript preparation based on the psychology literature that was developed by the American Psychological Association (APA). APA style is a standard format for academic research writing and is used extensively in the social sciences. The *Publication Manual of the American Psychological Association* (2010) is the style's official guide. The information in this chapter comes from the sixth edition of the *Publication Manual* and its affiliated website.

The *Publication Manual* provides guidelines for formatting a research paper and referencing sources. It provides specific information about organizing the content of the research paper; using effective writing style and avoiding bias in language; employing Standard English grammar and punctuation; and using tables, figures, and graphs to illustrate a research paper. The *Publication Manual* also guides authors through the process of submitting papers for publication. The purpose of this chapter is to focus on the guidelines the *Publication Manual* sets forth for most undergraduate papers.

The *Publication Manual* also includes detailed information about documenting sources—giving credit to the sources that were used to prepare a manuscript. Following these guidelines can help a writer avoid plagiarism. Every type of source used in a research paper must be cited, from journals and books to music and videos. The APA's website (http://apastyle.org) and its accompanying blog (http://blog.apastyle.org) are among the best resources for the most up-to-date information on citing electronic sources.

FORMATTING A PAPER

Each research paper should have four core components:

- Title page
  - Includes the title of the work, running head, and byline
  - May also include school and instructor information
- Abstract
  - Provides a short summary of research and findings
- Body text
  - Includes an introduction with a background of literature consulted, method of research, results, and a discussion of the results
- References
  - Includes all sources referenced in the paper

The following basic guidelines should be used when formatting a paper:

- Use 8½ × 11 in. (22 × 28 cm) paper (standard)
- Use double spacing between lines
- Use a 12-point serif font, such as Times New Roman
- Number each page on the right-hand side at the top of the page
- Use 1-inch margins on each side
- Indent the first line of each paragraph to ½ in. (1.3 cm)
- Align the text to the left, leaving the right margin ragged and unjustified
- Present a title page, abstract, body text, and references, in that order

Some papers may feature other collateral items, such as appendices, author notes, footnotes, tables, figure captions, and figures. They should be placed in this sequence after the references.

Organization is important to help the reader follow the flow of ideas from existing research to original findings. The APA has established common formatting styles to create uniformity in published material that is recognizable to a broad readership. Perhaps most important is that writers remember to not worry about perfectly formatting the paper in APA style until the revision stage. Becoming preoccupied with formatting early on will slow writing progress.

Title Page

The title page includes the title of the paper centered in the upper third of the page. This is followed by a byline, which includes the author's name. In the upper-left corner of the title page, the running head (see the next section for more information) should be identified. Also include a page header that includes the running head to the left and the page number in the upper-right corner.

Running Head

The research paper's title page should include a page header, called a running head, that will appear on each page of the document. Usually a shortened version of the paper's title (two to three words, no more than 50 characters) is used as the running head. For example, if the title of the document is "Everything You Need to Know about APA Citations," an appropriate running header might be "APA CITATIONS." The running head should be flush left in all caps. In the top-left corner of the title page, type "APA CITATIONS" flush left and the page number flush right.

Abstract

An abstract is a summary of the research paper and its findings. It is an extremely important paragraph that allows readers to immediately determine if they are interested in reading the paper. This section begins on page 2 with the header "Abstract" centered on the page with an initial capital A followed by lowercase letters. Abstracts should be brief and usually range between 150 and 250 words. The text should be flush left (without an indention) beneath the title and Arabic numerals should be used for any numbers.

Headings

Using levels of headings provides a hierarchy for the sections in a paper; in effect, they provide the reader with an outline of the paper. Avoid use of only one subsection heading or one subsection within a section. The same level of heading should be given to all topics of equal importance (e.g., Method, Results). At least two subsection headings should be used within a section; otherwise, none should be used. A heading structure for all sections should use the same top-to-bottom progression, regardless of the number of levels of subheading. APA style uses five possible levels of headings, which follow each other sequentially. Thus, if only one level is used, use Level 1; if two are used, use Levels 1 and 2 (the most common combination in most research papers), in that order; if three are used, use Levels 1, 2, and 3, in that order, and so on.

Level 1: Centered, boldface, initial capital letters on important words; on the line above the paragraph

Example:

BASIC FINDINGS

Level 2: Flush left, boldface, initial capital letters on important words; on the line above the paragraph

Example:

Demographic Analysis

Level 3: Indented, boldface, sentence-case heading followed by a period, on the same line of copy as the beginning of the paragraph that follows.

Demographic analysis. The demographic analysis shows that among participating physicians…

Level 4: Indented, boldface, italicized, sentence-case heading followed by a period, on the same line of copy as the beginning of the paragraph that follows.

Demographic analysis. The demographic analysis shows that among participating physicians…

Level 5: Indented, italicized, sentence-case heading followed by a period, on the same line of copy as the beginning of the paragraph that follows.

Demographic analysis. The demographic analysis shows that among participating physicians…

Punctuation and Spacing

Punctuation provides the pace for a sentence and tells the reader where to pause (commas, colons, or semicolons), stop (periods, question marks, or exclamation points), or deviate (parentheses, dashes, or brackets). The different kinds of punctuation in a sentence usually designate different kinds and lengths of pauses. Modern word-processing programs provide the appropriate space for each character, so hit the spacebar only once after commas, colons, and semicolons. Do not add extra spaces around dashes, parentheses, or brackets.

APA style suggests—but does not require—two spaces after punctuation marks at the end of a sentence in draft manuscripts. Because requirements vary across publications, when submitting a manuscript for publication, consult the publication's style guidelines regarding spacing after end punctuation.

Following is a quick guide to some punctuation rules required in APA style.

Period

Periods are used in reference lists after the author's name, the year, the title of a book or article, and the close of the reference; an exception to this close-reference rule is references that end in a website address (electronic references), which do not end with a period.

When in-text citations are used at the end of a sentence, the period should follow the citation. When in-text citations appear at the end of a long, indented quote, periods should not follow the in-text citations. In that case, the period appears at the end of the quote but before the in-text citation. See "Quotations of 40 Words or More," which appears later in this section, for an example.

Colon

Colons appear between the publication location and the publisher listed in individual references. In text, a colon should not be used after an introductory clause that is not a complete sentence. If two independent clauses are separated by a colon, capitalize the word that begins the second clause.

Semicolon

Although semicolons are usually used to separate two independent clauses (complete sentences), a semicolon should also be used to set off items in a series when one or more of these items already includes commas, regardless of whether the items are complete sentences—for example, "The sisters were challenged to ride a bike for two hours; juggle a ball, a book, and a toy car for 10 minutes; and walk on a treadmill for 30 minutes."

Comma

In in-text citations, a comma should be used to set off the year of publication within parentheses. In text, use a comma between all elements in a series of three or more items, including before *and* and *or*.

Quotation Marks

Double quotation marks should be used in the following situations:
- To introduce a word or phrase that is used as slang, a coined expression, or an example of irony
- To identify an article or chapter title in a periodical or book when the title is mentioned in text
- To reproduce or cite material from a published source (only up to 40 words)

Double quotation marks should not enclose quotations of 40 words or more.

Quotations of 40 Words or More

Quotations of 40 words or more should be in a paragraph by themselves, should be indented five spaces without the customary first-line indent, and should not include quotation marks. These block quotations should also be followed by a citation that includes a page number. The citation is presented after the closing punctuation of the block quotation. If the quoted text contains quotation marks, double quotation marks should be used. Note the following example:

> Candy manufactured at the offshore facility was tainted, but testing of product made domestically revealed that it was safe. Representatives

from the manufacturer claimed that the company was unaware of any problems with ingredients or machinery at the offshore plant prior to the discovery of the poisoned product. (Bradenforth, 2007, p. 238)

Italics

Use italics for introduction of a new, technical, or key term (but only on first use of the word; do not italicize the word again if it is used in subsequent sentences). Also use italics in the following instances:

- Letters used as statistical symbols
- Periodical volume numbers in the reference list
- Anchors on a scale (e.g., a survey asks respondents to rate customer service on a scale of *1* to *5*).

Parentheses

Parentheses are used in the following circumstance:

- To set off reference citations in text
- To separate letters that identify terms in a series within a sentence or paragraph
- To enclose the citation or page number of a direct quote
- To introduce an abbreviation
- To enclose numbers that represent formulas, equations, statistical values, or degrees of freedom

Avoid use of back-to-back parenthetical text.

Hyphens

A hyphen should not be used on common fractions used as nouns (e.g., Two thirds of the students missed class); however, a hyphen should be used when the fraction is used as a descriptor (e.g., The student council requires a two-thirds majority to pass a new rule). Hyphens should also be avoided in compounds in which the first word is an adverb (e.g., The nearly vetoed legislation has finally passed) and in situations where there is no possible way a compound term could be misread without it (e.g., The health care industry lobbied Congress for this law). Do not use a space before or after a hyphen.

Dashes

APA distinguishes em dashes (two hyphens placed side by side with no space in between: —) from en dashes (which are slightly longer than a hyphen: –). Note that some word-processing programs include em dash and en dash symbols, often a combination of keystrokes or accessible from the symbols menu. As shown in the examples in the paragraphs that follow, do not add spaces before or after em dashes and en dashes.

An em dash should be used to either highlight a clause or to indicate a diversion from the sentence's primary clause (e.g., The test subjects—who were unaware of the change—disliked the nature of the treatment).

An en dash is used between words of equal weight in a compound adjective (e.g., "medication–nutrient interaction") and between page ranges (e.g., 112–114).

Using Numbers in a Document

Generally, APA style uses numerals to express numbers 10 and larger and words for numbers one through nine. One primary exception to this rule is when a number greater than 10 begins a sentence. In this case, the word should be spelled out (e.g., Forty-eight men were surveyed).

There are several exceptions in which numbers less than 10 are listed in numeric form, generally related to presenting a specific quantity measurement, such as in the following instances:

- When the numbers precede a unit of measurement or a percentage symbol
- When the numbers are used for a mathematical or statistical function
- When used to represent time, dates, ages, scores, or points on a scale
- When placed in a numbered series, parts of book chapters or tables, or in a numbered list of four or more
- When included in a research paper's abstract

If the number of days, months, or years are an approximation, write out the numbers (e.g., The ships takes approximately eight days to reach Portugal). A zero should be written before decimals and numbers that are less than one, except in decimal fractions where the number cannot be greater than one. Plurals of numbers should be written by adding -s or -es, without an apostrophe.

Abbreviations

APA style recommends minimal use of abbreviations, as they can often cause more confusion than clarification and can hinder reader comprehension. Generally, an abbreviation should be used only if (a) it is well known and a reader would be familiar with it, or (b) it saves considerable space and prevents repetition.

A writer must decide whether to spell out an expression or group name every time or spell it out initially and abbreviate it thereafter. If abbreviating, the term must be written out completely the first time, followed by its abbreviation in parentheses. Afterward, the abbreviation can be used without any further explanation.

Do not write out standard abbreviations for units of measurement on first use, but do not use the abbreviation if a specific measurement is not given (e.g., It was 3 cm in length; It was measured in centimeters).

A sentence can begin with an abbreviation or acronym that appears in all capital letters but not if it is all lowercase letters. Some abbreviations are accepted as words in APA style and do not require explanation, including the following well-known terms: IQ, REM, ESP, AIDS, and HIV.

Periods are used with abbreviations for initials of names (e.g., William S. Sanderson), to abbreviate the United States when used as an adjective (e.g., U.S. Navy), in identity-concealing labels for study participants (e.g., participants S. P. and J. M.), and with Latin and reference abbreviations (e.g., i.e., etc.).

Periods should not be used with abbreviations of state names, capital letter acronyms, or metric and nonmetric measurements; one exception is the abbreviation for inch (in.), which includes a period because of the likelihood of its confusion with the word "in."

In general, use Latin abbreviations only in parenthetical material and use the English translations of Latin abbreviations in running text (e.g., use "e.g." in parentheses and use "for example" in text). However, "et al." (and others) and "v." (for versus) should be used for citations, both parenthetical and in text (APA, 2010, pp. 106–111).

Percent and Percentages

The symbol for percent (%) should be used only when it is preceded by a numeral (e.g., 5%). The word "percent" should not be spelled out after a numeral. When a number is not given, the word "percentage" should be used (e.g., a significant percentage of women in the group preferred the reformulated product). In table headings or legends, use a percent symbol in lieu of the word "percentage" to conserve space.

Lists

Elements or ideas in a series can be enumerated to clarify their relationship. This is particularly important when a sequence is lengthy or difficult to understand. Three different forms are possible: a within-sentence list, a numbered list, or a bulleted list. Example of a within-sentence list:

The student's three choices were (a) living in the dorm with a roommate, (b) living alone in the dorm, or (c) living at home.

Listing within a Sentence with Internal Commas

When listing items within a paragraph or sentence with items that include commas, use lowercase letters in parentheses and semicolons, as shown in the following example:

■ The respondents were broken into three groups: (a) high communication apprehension, scoring more than 35; (b) moderate communication apprehension, scoring between 18 and 35; and (c) low communication apprehension, scoring below 18.

Numbered Lists

To list paragraphs in a numbered sequence, such as itemized conclusions or successive steps in a procedure, number each paragraph or sentence with an Arabic numeral followed by a period, as shown in the following example:

1. We divided the study sample into three groups based on income.
2. We further subdivided these three groups into subgroups based on race/ethnicity.
3. We calculated the average monthly income for each of these subgroups.

Bulleted Lists

Numbered lists may imply an unintended and unwanted hierarchy such as chronology or importance. In such cases, a bulleted list, as shown in the following example, is an option:

The physicians were asked questions about the following factors:

■ How long they have been in practice
■ How many patients they see per week on average
■ How many of those patients have private insurance

Each item in the bulleted list should be indented. Items in a bulleted list may be complete sentences or parts of a longer sentence introduced with a colon, but all items in the list should be parallel (e.g., they should all start with the same part of speech or same conjugation, form, or tense of a verb).

REFERENCES AND INTERNAL CITATION STYLE

Proper documentation of sources includes two important steps: creating a reference list and using internal citations. APA guidelines require a structured reference list and parenthetical in-text citations of each source listed in the references. It is critical to carefully follow APA guidelines for placement and style of citations and references. Footnotes and endnotes are occasionally used, but they are secondary to parenthetical citations. Content footnotes are used to clarify or expand on information in the text, and copyright permission footnotes are used to identify the source of quotations. Neither type should be used in place of parenthetical citations in an APA-style research paper.

Citation Style

For parenthetical citations, include author name(s) and year of the publication. If using a direct quotation or paraphrasing a particular passage, the page number must also be included. APA style offers a variety of acceptable citation formats. Example 1 illustrates an effective way to mention the authors in the text of the sentence; it is particularly useful if the writer wishes to describe the cited author in some way. The style of Example 2 results in a complete statement without using the cited author's name in the sentence. Example 3 shows a direct quote from the reference material coupled with mention of the author's name in the sentence. Example 4 combines a direct quote and a complete statement that does not mention the author's name in the sentence.

Example 1:
According to Booth, Colomb, and Williams (2003), you should avoid plagiarism.

Example 2:
You should avoid plagiarism (Booth, Colomb, & Williams, 2003).

Example 3:
According to Booth, Colomb, and Williams (2003), "In all fields, you plagiarize when you use a source's words or ideas without citing that source" (p. 202).

Example 4:
Many authorities have commented on the topic, but this is one of the most effective descriptions: "In all fields, you plagiarize when you use a source's words or ideas without citing that source" (Booth, Colomb, & Williams, 2003, p. 202).

If a source has two to five authors, use all the names of the authors in the first citation, but in later citations, refer to secondary authors with the abbreviation "et al." If a source has six or more authors, in all citations—including the first—list only the first author followed by "et al." and the date (e.g., Smith et al., 2007). Note that if citing the same source more than once in the same paragraph, it is not necessary to include the year in the succeeding citations. See Example 5 for an illustration.

Example 5:

Plagiarism can harm your career (Booth et al., 2003). Several prominent historians have lost credibility because they had plagiarized from the works of others (Weaver et al., 2009). It is best to create your own original content and exercise caution when quoting and summarizing the content of others (Booth et al.).

Some citation styles do not meet the criteria listed previously, including the following:

- Personal communications
- Anonymous works
- Works without publication dates
- Classical works

See Figure 2 for examples of these unusual styles.

REFERENCE TYPE	IN-TEXT CITATION STYLE	REFERENCE STYLE	EXPLANATION
Personal communications that include letters, memos, e-mail, nonarchived discussion groups, personal interviews, and telephone conversations	S. H. Hanson (personal communication, January 1, 2007), or (S. H. Hanson, personal communication, January 1, 2007)	Not included in reference list	Cite personal communication in the text only
No publication date given	(Hamilton, n.d.)	Hamilton, G. (n.d.). *Hope is the verb.* Boston, MA: Cambridge Press.	When no date is given, write n.d. in parentheses for in-text and reference list mentions
A work with no identified author, not designated as anonymous	("College Bound," 2007)	College bound. (2007). *Journal of Teacher Education, 45*(3) 26–31.	In the reference list, alphabetize by title
Works with group authors	(American Psychological Association, 1994)	American Psychological Association. (1994). *The APA manual of style.* Washington, DC: Author.	Alphabetize group authors, such as associations and universities, by the first significant word of the name
A work's author is designated "anonymous"	(Anonymous, 2007)	Anonymous. (2007). *Let's build bridges.* New York, NY: Prentice Hall.	In the reference list, only a work that is explicitly identified as written by "Anonymous" includes the word, which is alphabetized as such.
Classical works	(Plato, trans. 1938), or (Freud, 1931/1997)	Not required	Reference entries are not required for major classical works. That includes ancient Greek and Roman works and the Bible. In cases of the Bible, identify which version was used in the first in-text citation—for example, "(1 Cor. 13:1) [King James Version]."

FIGURE APA.2 APA Citation Style for Unusual References

Reference Style

The APA reference style is preferred for many reasons, but primary among them is that APA style is perhaps the most common form of organizing, citing, structuring, and verifying information in universities today. APA reference style provides all the basic building blocks that make it easier to learn other styles, such as MLA, Turabian, and Chicago style, and underscores the importance of professionalism and rigor in writing. All references should be listed in alphabetical order by the first authors' last name or, if no author is listed, by the title of the source.

Assembling a Reference List

An APA reference list is more than just a simple listing of works cited. Each type of reference—a journal article, a book, a website, or a newspaper article, for example—has its own unique style. The idea behind the reference list is to give readers as much information as possible to seek out the references and gain a deeper understanding of the logic expressed in the paper by reading them. The following are general guidelines for an APA reference list:

- Sources should be arranged alphabetically by the author's last name. If there is no identified author, alphabetize the reference listing by the first main word of the title, excluding "A," "An," or "The."
- Double space or leave one blank line between each line of type in a reference list.
- The first line of a reference is set flush left, but any subsequent lines in the same reference are indented one-half inch (known as the hanging indent).
- Periods separate most parts of a reference, including (a) after the author name(s), (b) after the date, (c) after the closing parenthesis for the date of publication, and (d) at the end of the reference (except for an electronic reference, which requires no period). Periods should also be used after the first and middle initials of each author.
- Commas are used between the author's last name(s) and initials; to separate authors; between the book or periodical title and the volume number; after an issue number and before a page number; and between a volume number and page number. A colon is used to separate the city of publication and the publisher's name.
- The author's names in a reference should be listed as last name first, followed by a comma, and then the first and middle initials, and finished with a period. When there are eight or more authors, list only the first six and abbreviate the remaining authors using ellipsis points ("…"), followed by the final author. If a group or entity is the author, spell out its full name as the author. If a second author of a book or magazine is listed with the word "with," he or she should be listed in the reference in parentheses—for example, "Porter, J. (with Rutter, K. L.)." To reference an edited book, list the editor's name in the author position and follow it with the abbreviation "Ed." or "Eds." in parentheses. If there is no author, the title of the work should be moved to the beginning of the reference.
- The year the work of a reference was copyrighted should follow the authors' names (or title, if there are no authors), appear in parentheses, and have a period at the end outside of the parentheses. For magazines, newspapers, or newsletters, the year, followed by the exact date (month and date) of the publication should be listed in parentheses. If no date is available, "n.d." should be written in parentheses and should be followed by a period.

- The title of an article or chapter comes after the date, followed by the title of the work, periodical, or book. Only the first word of the title and subtitle (if there is one) should be capitalized. The title should not be italicized or have quotation marks around it. All nonweb references should end with a period. Web-based references should include as much of the previously listed information as possible and the digital object identifier (DOI) if available or the web address of the source. If the last item in the reference is a DOI or a website address, it should not end with a period.

- The city of publication follows the title of any book or brochure. Regardless of how well-known a city is, write a comma and the appropriate two-letter abbreviation for the state or territory that is used by the U.S. Postal Service. Spell out country names. A colon should follow the city, state, or country of publication. If the publisher is a university that has the same name as the state or province (e.g., Ohio State), do not repeat the state or province in the publisher location.

- The publisher's name follows the city of publication. The name of the publisher should be as brief as possible, eliminating terms such as "Inc.," or "Co.," but the words "Books" and "Press" should be kept in the reference. If two or more publisher locations are given, give the first listed or the publisher's corporate office, if specified. A period should follow all listings.

- "Page" and "pages" should be cited as "p." and "pp." in instances where book chapters are listed. Periodical page numbers go at the end of the reference, following the title of the journal, and "p." or "pp." is not used. Book page numbers go between the title and the city of publication. All page numbers should include the entire article or chapter, and the beginning and end numbers should be separated by an en dash. Page numbers for entire books are not listed.

- Appropriate abbreviations for use in reference section and in-text citations include the following:
  - chap. = chapter
  - ed. = edition
  - Rev. ed. = revised edition
  - 2nd ed. = second edition
  - Ed. (Eds.) = editor (editors)
  - Trans. = translator(s)
  - n.d. = no date
  - p. (pp.) = page (pages)
  - Vol. = volume (as in Vol. 4)
  - Vols. = volumes (as in four volumes)
  - No. = number
  - Pt. = part
  - Suppl. = supplement
  - Tech. Rep. = technical report

- U.S. states and territories should be indicated with the appropriate two-letter abbreviation used by the U.S. Postal Service. City names and country names should not be abbreviated (APA, 2010, p. 187).

Examples of References

Refer to the *Publication Manual* or its companion website (http://apastyle.org) if citing a resource that is not included among the examples that follow. Different sources have different requirements and rules. Books, journal articles, magazine articles, websites, and other sources each have particular requirements that give proper credit and help readers locate the reference material. If any part of the reference is not included, this amounts to failure to properly credit a source. The following 11 examples illustrate some of the more common reference styles.

Example 1: A book with a single author.

Klein, N. (2000). *No logo*. New York, NY: Picador.

Book author: The author's last name is listed first, followed by the author's first and middle initials (if applicable). The period that follows the initial is also the period that follows the first element (author's name) of the References citation.

Date of publication: The year the book was published is included in parentheses, followed by a period.

Book title: The title is italicized with all words except the first in lowercase. If there is a colon in the title, the first word following the colon is also capitalized. If the book has several editions, the edition of the text goes in parentheses following the title. This element is followed by a period.

Publication information: For all cities, include the state (e.g., Newbury Park, CA), even if the city is well known. A colon is placed after the state and followed by the name of the publisher. Omit superfluous terms such as "Publishers," "Co.," or "Inc.," but keep the words "Books" or "Press."

Example 2: A book with two to seven authors.

Rubin, R. B., Rubin, A. M., & Piele, L. J. (2000). *Communication research: Strategies and sources* (5th ed.). Belmont, CA: Wadsworth.

Book author: The author's last name is listed first, followed by the author's first and middle initials (if applicable). A comma follows the name of the first author, even when there are only two authors to list. Type "&" before the last author is listed. Authors are listed in the order they are listed on the book cover.

Date of publication, book title, and publication information: Follow the format applied in Example 1.

Example 3: A book with eight or more authors.

Brown, L. V., Ecks, T. Z., Walters, F. A., Zim, A., Ricks, J., Bynum, C. T., ... Olsen, L. (2007). *Research methods for undergraduate students*. New York, NY: Text Press.

Book author: The author's last name is listed first, followed by the author's first and middle initials (if applicable). With more than seven authors, list only the first six authors and abbreviate the remaining authors using ellipsis points ("..."), followed by the final author. Do not type "&" before the final author.

Date of publication, book title, and publication information: Follow the format applied in Example 1.

Example 4: An article with only one author in a scholarly journal.

> Kramer, M. W. (2005). Communication in community theatre groups. *Journal of Applied Communication Research, 33,* 159–182.

Article author: The author's last name is listed first, followed by the author's first and middle initials (if applicable).

Date of publication: The year the article was written is included in parentheses, followed by a period.

Article title: The article title is not italicized nor enclosed in quotation marks, and only the first word of the title and the subtitle should be capitalized. The title is followed by a period.

Journal title: The journal title is italicized and all words in the title are capitalized except articles and prepositions ("a," "the," "and," "an," "of").

Publication information: Provide the volume number (in italics) and the page numbers (not italicized) of the article. If the periodical uses successive pagination in its volumes, it is not necessary to include the issue number. If the pagination is not successive, the issue number should be included in parentheses and not italicized—for example, *Consulting Psychology Journal: Practice and Research, 45*(2), 10–36.

Example 5: An article with multiple authors in a scholarly journal.

> Rosenfeld, L. B., Richman, J. M., Bowen, G. L., & Wynns, S. L. (2006). In the face of a dangerous community: The effects of social support and neighborhood danger on high school students' school outcomes. *Southern Communication Journal, 71,* 273–289.

Article author: The author's last name is listed first, followed by the author's first and middle initials (if applicable). Type "&" before the last author is listed. Authors are listed in the order they appear on the article. With more than seven authors, list only the first six authors and abbreviate the remaining authors using ellipsis points ("…"), followed by the final author. Do not type "&" before the final author.

Date of publication, article title, journal title, and publication information: Follow the format applied in Example 4.

Example 6: A magazine article.

> Marano, H. E. (2004, August). Rock around the doc. *Psychology Today, 9,* 47–52.

Article author: The author's last name is listed first, followed by the author's first and middle initials (if applicable).

Date of publication: The year and month the article was written is included in parentheses as "(year, month)."

Article title: The article title is not italicized, and only the first word of the title and subtitle should be capitalized.

Periodical title: The periodical title is italicized, and all words in the title are capitalized except articles and prepositions ("a," "the," "and," "an," "of").

Publication information: Provide the volume number (italics) and the page numbers of the article (not italicized). If the periodical uses successive pagination in its volumes, do not add the issue number. If the pagination is not successive, the issue number should be included in parentheses and not italicized—for example, *Communication Connection*, *2*(2), 3–7.

Example 7: An online magazine or news article.

> Marano, H. E., & Schwartz, B. G. (2004, August). Rock around the doc. *Psychology Today*, *9*, 47–52. Retrieved from http://www.psychologytoday.com

Article author, date of publication, article title, periodical title, and publication information: Follow the format applied in Example 6.

Retrieval information: The rule for electronic resources is to list the information that will help readers find the resource. Do not include the date the document was retrieved unless there is an expectation that the material cited will change over time. Some documents include a digital object identifier (DOI), which is a number that provides a consistent means to find an online document. If the cited publication has a DOI, it is usually prominently displayed at the top of the online document. If the research document includes a DOI, include it at the end of the reference, after the page numbers. For example, Marano, H. E., & Schwartz, B. G. (2004, August). Rock around the doc. *Psychology Today*, *9*, 47–50. doi:10.1187/0142-9052.78.1.298. If no DOI is available, give the home web page for the periodical, not the specific link to the article. Web pages often disappear or change, and this avoids citing expired web addresses.

Example 8: An article from a newspaper database.

> Russell, P. R. (2007, May 11). Saving energy is a hot topic: Energy to develop ways to conserve. *New Orleans Times-Picayune*, p. Money 1. Retrieve0d from www.timespicayune.com

Article author: Follow the format applied in Example 7.

Date of publication: The year, month, and day the article was written are included in parentheses (year, month, day).

Article title, periodical title: Follow the format applied in Example 6.

Publication information: Follow the format applied in Example 7.

Retrieval information: The rule for electronic resources is to list the information that will help the reader find the resource. Do not include the name of the database where the article was found; instead list the newspaper's home web page address. Do not close the web page address with a period.

Example 9: An article from a newspaper with one author and nonconsecutive page numbers.

> McBride, J. (2007, May 30). Pantex crew returns today: Guards union ratifies 5-year pact. *Amarillo Globe-News,* pp. A1, A6.

Article author: Follow the format applied in Example 7.

Date of publication: Follow the format applied in Example 8.

Article title, periodical title: Follow the format applied in Example 6.

Publication information: For newspapers, include the section and page number. Unlike journal citations, newspaper references do require a "p." or "pp." before the section and page number(s). If the pages are not continuous, list the page on which the article begins, insert a comma and a space, and then list the page where the article continues (e.g., pp. A1, A6).

Example 10: An article with no author, from a newspaper.

> Asarco gets approval to auction land in Salt Lake City. (2007, May 30). *Amarillo Globe-News,* p. D6.

Article author: If an article has no author, do not write "Anonymous." The article title is placed first. It is not italicized, and only the first word of the title and subtitle should be capitalized.

Date of publication: Follow the format applied in Example 8.

Article title, periodical title: Follow the format applied in Example 6.

Publication information: Follow the format applied in Example 7.

Example 11: An Internet source.

> How to publish with APA. (n.d.). Retrieved from American Psychological Association website: http://www.apastyle.org

Heading title: Websites and web pages often do not have identified author(s). In such a case, the website section heading is used at the beginning of the reference. It is not italicized, and only the first word of the title and subtitle should be capitalized.

Date of publication: A date is also not often available, so it is acceptable to reference that there is no date identified by typing (n.d.) after the heading title.

Internet site title: Identify the publisher of the resource as part of the retrieval information.

Retrieval information: The rule for electronic resources is to list the information that will help readers find the resource. Only include the complete web page address if the home page of the organization housing the document does not have a search function or if the website is large and hard to navigate, making it unlikely that the reader will be able to find the document from the home address. Do not close the web page address with a period.

Example 12: A picture from a website.

Pollock, J. (1953). *Greyed rainbow* [Painting]. Retrieved from
    http://www.artic.edu/aic/collections/artwork/83642?search_id=1

Artist or photographer: Follow the format applied to authors in Example 6.

Title: The title of the picture is italicized and only the first word of the title should be capitalized. The title is followed by the medium (e.g., painting, photograph, etc.) in brackets.

Retrieval information: Follow the format applied in Example 8.

Example 13: A picture from a book.

Pollock, J. (1953). *Greyed rainbow* [Painting]. In E. G. Landau, *Jackson Pollock*
    (p. 230). New York, NY: Abradale Press.

Artist or photographer: Follow the format applied to authors in Example 6.

Title: Follow the format applied in Example 12.

Book author and title: The word "In" is followed by the author's name. First and middle initials (if applicable) precede the author's last name, which is followed by a comma. The title of the book is italicized and only the first word and any proper nouns are capitalized. The page number(s) or plate number for the artwork is set in parentheses and is not italicized.

Publication information: Follow the format applied in Example 1.

MLA Formatting

Another format used as the standard for research writing at colleges and universities is MLA style, a set of rules and guidelines for manuscript preparation developed by the Modern Language Association of America (MLA). MLA style is a standard of writing used extensively in the humanities. The *MLA Handbook for Writers of Research Papers* and the *MLA Style Manual and Guide to Scholarly Publishing* are the style's official guides. The information in this section comes from the seventh edition of the *MLA Handbook* (2009) and the third edition of the *MLA Style Manual* (2008).

Both books provide guidelines for formatting a research paper and referencing sources. The *MLA Handbook* is geared toward high school and undergraduate students and provides step-by-step advice on all aspects of writing and presenting papers, from choosing a topic and conducting research to devising a thesis statement and creating an outline. The *MLA Style Manual* is tailored to graduate students, scholars, and professional writers. The *Manual* guides authors through the process of writing and submitting papers for publication and explains the peer-review process in detail. The two guides provide specific information about organizing the content of the research paper; using effective writing style and avoiding bias in language; employing standard English grammar and punctuation; and using tables, figures, and graphs to illustrate a research paper. This section will focus on the guidelines the *MLA Handbook* (2009) sets forth for most undergraduate papers.

The *MLA Handbook* and *MLA Style Manual* also include detailed information about documenting sources—giving credit to the sources used to prepare a manuscript. Following these guidelines can help with avoiding plagiarism. Every type of source used in a research paper must be cited, from journals and books to music and videos. Note that this book uses MLA style in its reference lists.

FORMATTING A PAPER USING MLA

Each research paper using MLA style should have three core components:
- A heading and title
- Body text
- A list of works cited

The first page of the research paper begins with the title of the work, the author's name, and the date. The body text is the heart of the paper and should include an introduction and a conclusion. Finally, a works cited section includes all sources in the paper.

The following basic guidelines should be used when formatting a paper:
- Use 8½ × 11 in. (22 × 28 cm) paper (standard)
- Use double spacing between lines
- Use a 12-point serif font, such as Times New Roman
- Number each page on the right-hand side, one-half inch from the top of the page, flush with the right margin
- Use 1-inch margins on each side

- Indent the first line of each paragraph ½ in. (1.3 cm)
- Align the text to the left, leaving the right margin ragged and unjustified
- Include a works cited page

Some papers may feature other collateral items, such as appendixes, author notes, and footnotes. Tables, illustrations, and figures should be placed as close as possible to the related text in the body of the paper.

Organization is important to help the reader follow the flow of ideas from existing research to original findings. The MLA has established common formatting styles to create uniformity in published material that is recognizable to a broad readership. Perhaps most important for writers to remember is that perfecting the paper's MLA formatting is not necessary until the revision stage. If a writer becomes preoccupied with formatting early on, it will slow the writing process. There will be ample time during the revision stage to ensure that the formatting is accurate.

Heading and Title

In MLA style, no separate title page is needed. Instead, at the top of the first page, the writer should type his or her name, the instructor's name, the number of the course, and the date—each on a separate line, double spaced. Next, type the title of the paper on the next line, centered, with headline style capitalization (capitalizing the first letter of main words). Do not italicize, boldface, or underline the title. Double space and begin typing the body of the paper, indenting the first paragraph one-half inch. Spacing after paragraphs should be set to zero.

Header and Page Numbers

Every page of the research paper should have a header that includes the writer's last name and a consecutive page number. The page number should be one-half inch from the top of the page in the upper right-hand corner, flush with the right margin. In the header, type the last name followed by a space before the page number.

Headings

Research papers and scholarly articles in the humanities often do not have formal headings. If a break is needed between ideas, some authors insert an extra blank line between paragraphs. If this method is used, be sure that the extra line does not appear at the bottom or top of a page, where it may be overlooked by the reader. If this occurs, add three asterisks, centered, on the blank line, and use this method consistently throughout the paper, regardless of where in the text the other blank lines appear.

Using levels of heading, however, can provide a transition between unified sections of thought and aid in the flow of a paper. If using headings, do not also use blank lines to signal a break between paragraphs. In MLA style, it is acceptable to use headings labeled with numbers, words, or both. When numbering headings, use consecutive Arabic numerals. If using only numbers, center them on the page. If using only words or a number and words, the heading should be flush left. Do not add extra blank lines above or below a heading.

Punctuation and Spacing

Punctuation provides the pace for a sentence and tells the reader where to pause (commas, colons, or semicolons), stop (periods, question marks, or exclamation points), or deviate (parentheses, dashes, or brackets). The different kinds of punctuation in a sentence usually designate different kinds and lengths of pauses. Modern word-processing programs provide the appropriate space for each character, so type the spacebar only once after commas, colons, and semicolons. Do not include extra spaces around dashes, parentheses, or brackets. Put only one space between sentences. Following is a quick guide to punctuation rules required by MLA format.

Period

Periods are used in reference lists after the author's name, the title of a book or article, the year, the type of medium, and the close of the reference. When in-text citations are used at the end of a sentence, the period should follow the citation. When in-text citations occur at the end of a long, indented quote, periods should not follow the in-text citations. In that case, the period occurs at the end of the quote but before the in-text citation. See "Quotations of More Than Four Lines," which appears later in this section, for an example.

Colon

Colons are used in references between the publication location and the publisher. In the works cited list, use a colon between the title and subtitle of a book or article.

In text, a colon should not be used after an introductory clause that is not a complete sentence. Use a colon to introduce a quotation only if the introductory clause is a complete sentence.

Semicolon

Although semicolons are usually used to separate two independent clauses (complete sentences), a semicolon should also be used to set off items in a series when one or more of these items already includes commas, regardless of whether the items are complete sentences—for example, "The sisters were challenged to ride a bike for two hours; juggle a ball, a book, and a toy car for 10 minutes; and walk on a treadmill for 30 minutes."

Comma

A comma should be used in the works cited list between the publisher and the year. Do not use a comma to set off the page numbers of in-text reference citations. If the title of a work is required in the parenthetical citation, put a comma between the author name and the work title.

In text, use a comma between elements in a series of three or more items, including before *and* and *or*.

Quotation Marks

In addition to use in expressing direct quotations, double quotation marks should be used in the following situations:

- To introduce a word or phrase that is used as slang, a coined expression, or an example of irony

- To identify an article or chapter title in a periodical or book when the title is mentioned in text
- To reproduce or cite material from a published source
- To introduce a translation of a foreign word or phrase

Double quotation marks should not enclose quotations of more than four lines.

Quotations of More Than Four Lines

Quotations that take up more than four lines of text should be in a paragraph by themselves, presented as a block quotation, indented one inch from the left margin without the customary first-line indent. They should be double-spaced and should not include quotation marks. They should also be followed by a citation that includes a page number. The citation is presented after the closing punctuation of the block quotation. If the quoted text contains quotation marks, double quotation marks should be used.

Block quotations are generally introduced by a colon, though some situations may require no punctuation or a different punctuation mark. If the quotation includes more than one paragraph, indent the first line of each paragraph one-half inch.

Example:

Candy manufactured at the offshore facility was tainted, but testing of product made domestically revealed that it was safe. Representatives from the manufacturer claimed that the company was unaware of any problems with ingredients or machinery at the offshore plant prior to the discovery of the poisoned product. (Bradenforth 238)

Italics

Use italics for introduction of a new, technical, or key term (but only on first use of the word; do not italicize the word if again it is used in subsequent sentences). It is acceptable to use italics for emphasis, but do so sparingly, as this can quickly become distracting and ineffective.

Italics are also necessary in the following contexts:

- Letters or words that are referred to as letters or words (e.g., "Some street signs leave off the *e* in *Clairemont.*")
- Foreign words in an English text not typically found in an American dictionary
- The names of books, plays, poems published as books, pamphlets, periodicals, websites, films, TV and radio broadcasts, CDs, dance performances, paintings, ships, aircraft, and spacecraft discussed in the body of the paper

Parentheses

Parentheses are used in the following ways:

- To set off reference citations in text
- To enclose the citation or page number of a direct quote
- To introduce an abbreviation
- To enclose the year of a periodical entry in a works cited list

Hyphens

A hyphen should not be used on common fractions used as nouns (e.g., "Two thirds of the students missed class"); however, a hyphen should be used when the fraction is used as a descriptor (e.g., "The student council requires a two-thirds majority to pass a new rule"). Hyphens should also be avoided in compounds in which the first word is an adverb (e.g., "The nearly vetoed legislation has finally passed") and in situations where there is no possible way a compound term could be misread without it (e.g., "The health care industry lobbied Congress for this law"). Do not use a space before or after a hyphen.

Dashes

In MLA style, type two hyphens to make a dash or use the dash symbol available in most word processing programs' symbol menus. Do not add space before or after the dash. A dash should be used to either highlight a clause or to indicate a diversion from the sentence's primary clause (e.g., "The test subjects—who were unaware of the change—disliked the nature of the treatment").

Using Numbers in a Document

MLA style differentiates between papers that frequently use numbers and ones that seldom use them. Most papers in the humanities, such as those focused on literature, history, or philosophy, use numbers infrequently. For such papers, spell out numbers that are expressed in one or two words; otherwise, use numerals (e.g., two, forty-seven, three hundred, fifty thousand, but $4\frac{3}{4}$; 405; 2,425; 55,000).

For papers that frequently include numbers, such as a technical scientific study that discusses many measurements or one that uses statistical data, use numerals before units of measure (e.g., 4 centimeters, 47 kilowatts) and when numbers are introduced together to refer to related things (e.g., "The membership of the city council rose from 7 to 15 over the last ten years." Notice in this example that "ten" is spelled out because it is not presented with related figures.). In other instances, spell out numbers that are expressed in one or two words.

One primary exception to these rules is when a number expressed in more than two words begins a sentence. In such a case, the words should be spelled out (e.g., "Two hundred and three men were surveyed").

There are several exceptions in which numbers of one or two words would be listed in numeric form, generally related to specific quantity measurements, such as the following:

- To express decimal fractions
- With abbreviations or symbols
- To represent dates, scores, or points on a scale
- With most times of the day, except when time is expressed in quarter-hours or half-hours or in hours followed by "o'clock" (e.g., 4:50, 10:05, half past three, a quarter to nine, two o'clock)
- To show divisions (e.g., page 9; year 4 of the project)

When expressing large numbers, combine words and numerals (e.g., 5.7 billion). In a range of large numbers, give only the last two digits of the second number unless the first digit of the second number is not the same as the first digit of the first number (e.g., 245-57, 1567-91, 295-314, 1989-2004). Write out the century using lowercase letters (e.g., twenty-first century). Plurals of numbers should be written by adding -s or -es, without an apostrophe (MLA 2008, 81–85).

Abbreviations

MLA style recommends minimal use of abbreviations in the body of a paper, as they can often cause more confusion than clarification and can hinder reader comprehension. Generally, an abbreviation should be used only if (a) it is well known and a reader would be familiar with it, or (b) it saves considerable space and prevents repetition.

The writer must decide whether to spell out an expression or group name every time or spell it out initially and abbreviate it thereafter. A term must be written out completely on first use, followed by its abbreviation in parentheses. Afterward, the abbreviation can be used without any further explanation. Generally, MLA requires that abbreviations do not use periods after letters or spaces between letters (e.g., UK, US, CIA, CD, BA, URL). Exceptions to this guideline include the following:

- Use a period and a space after initials used in a person's name (e.g., J. D. Salinger)
- Use a period after most abbreviations that end in lowercase letters (e.g., Czech Rep., dept., govt., misc.)
- Use a period but no space between letters in most abbreviations in which lowercase letters each represent a word (e.g., p.m., i.e., n.p.)

Other guidelines for in-text abbreviations in MLA style include the following:

- Spell out the names of months, but abbreviate them in the works cited list, except May, June, and July
- Most words expressing units of time are spelled out (e.g., second, minute, month, year) with a few exceptions (e.g., a.m., AD, BC)
- Spell out the names of US states and countries, with a few exceptions (e.g., USSR, US, UK)
- Use Latin abbreviations only in parenthetical material. In running text, use the English translations of Latin abbreviations (e.g., use "e.g." in parenthetical text but use "for example" in the text)

Percent, Percentages, and Monetary Figures

Expressing percentages and amounts of money follow a similar format to that of numbers in MLA style. For a paper that uses numbers infrequently, spell out percentages and amounts of money that can be written in three words or fewer (e.g., thirty-four percent, two hundred Euros, four thousand dollars, forty-eight cents).

In papers that frequently use numbers, use numerals with the appropriate symbols (e.g., 28%, 60%, $2.75, ¥5,000, $0.94). The symbols for percent and for various currencies should be used only in combination with a numeral (e.g., "5%, €205"). The word "percent" should not be spelled out after a numeral.

When a number is not given, the word "percentage" should be used (e.g., a significant percentage of women preferred the reformulated product). In table column or row headings or legends, however, use a percent symbol instead of the word "percentage" to conserve space.

REFERENCES AND INTERNAL CITATION STYLE

Proper documentation of sources includes two important steps: creating a works cited list and using internal citations. MLA guidelines require a structured works cited list and parenthetical in-text citations of each source listed in the works cited list. It is critical to carefully follow MLA guidelines for placement and style of citations and references. Footnotes and endnotes are occasionally used, but they are secondary to parenthetical citations. Content footnotes are used to clarify or expand on information in the text, and bibliographic notes are sometimes used to add evaluative comments about sources. Neither type should be used in place of parenthetical citations in an MLA-style research paper.

Citation Style

Parenthetical citations include the author name(s) and usually the page number for the information referenced. When using a direct quotation or paraphrasing a particular passage in a work, include the page number where it appeared in the source document. Do not include a page number when citing an entire work rather than referencing a particular portion of it.

Citations can be formatted in a variety of ways. Example 1 illustrates an effective way to mention the authors in the text of the sentence; it is particularly useful when the aim is to describe the author in some way. The style of Example 2 results in a complete statement without using the author's name. Example 3 shows a direct quote from the reference material coupled with mention of the author's name in the sentence. Example 4 combines a direct quote and a complete statement that does not mention the author's name.

- *Example 1:* According to Colomb, Booth, and Williams, you should avoid plagiarism.
- *Example 2:* You should avoid plagiarism (Colomb, Booth, and Williams).
- *Example 3:* According to Colomb, Booth, and Williams, "In all fields, you plagiarize when you use a source's words or ideas without citing that source" (202).
- *Example 4:* Many authorities have commented on the topic, but this is one of the most effective descriptions. "In all fields, you plagiarize when you use a source's words or ideas without citing that source" (Colomb, Booth, and Williams 202).

If a source has more than three authors, list all the names of the authors in the citations or list only the name of the first author followed by "et al." However, whichever style is used must also be applied to the citation in the works cited list. See Example 5 for an illustration of these citation options.

- *Example 5:* Plagiarism can harm your career (Colomb, Booth, and Williams). It is best to create your own original content and exercise caution when quoting and summarizing the content of others (Sampson et al. 77).

If the works cited list includes more than one work by the same author, add the title of the work—shortened or in full—with a comma after the author name(s) to clarify which of the author's works the citation is referencing.

- *Example 6:* Many authorities have commented on the topic, but this is one of the most effective descriptions: "In all fields, you plagiarize when you use a source's words or ideas without citing that source" (Colomb, Booth, and Williams, *Plagiarism* 202).

Some works have no listed author. In those cases, use an abbreviated version of the article title in the citation.

■ *Example 7:* In 2005, Philadelphia City Schools suspended 215 children because of incidents of plagiarism ("Cheating on the Rise").

Reference Style

The MLA reference style is more accommodating than other styles, including APA, Turabian, and Chicago style. Typically, references are listed in alphabetical order, usually by the authors' last names; if no author is listed, entries are alphabetized by the title of the source. However, MLA offers some flexibility in preparing the list of works cited. If the paper is a historical piece in which the chronology of the sources is important, the writer may decide to arrange the reference list chronologically. Similarly, if, for example, the paper compares various forms of ancient mythology, the writer may choose to group entries by subject matter (e.g., Greek Mythology, Roman Mythology, Norse Mythology).

Entries within the works cited list have similar flexibility. For example, if the paper focuses on a particular music producer, it is acceptable to list associated albums not by artist name, as would be the norm, but by producer name (followed by "prod."). Similarly, if the paper is about a children's book illustrator, the writer can list the associated books' references with the illustrator's name (followed by "illus.") rather than the authors' names.

When creating a list of works cited, think carefully about why the particular sources were chosen and document them in a way that is appropriate for the subject and for the readers' needs.

Assembling a List of Works Cited

An MLA reference list, as the name implies, is a listing of works cited in the text. Each type of reference—a journal article, a book, a website, or a newspaper article, for example—has its own unique style. The idea behind the list of works cited is to give the reader as much information as possible to seek out the references used and gain a deeper understanding of the writer's logic by reading them. Following are general guidelines to the elements included in an MLA works cited list. Note, however, that items included in the citation are ordered and punctuated differently, depending on the type of source:

■ On a new page at the end of the paper, title the references section "Works Cited," centered, an inch from the top of the page.

■ Double-space the entire works cited list, both between and within individual references.

■ The first line of a reference is set flush left, but any subsequent lines in the same reference are indented one-half inch.

■ Entries in the works cited list are usually alphabetized by author's last name (or by article title if no author is given). If the list includes more than one work by the same author, alphabetize these entries by article title. In the first entry, include the author's first name, last name, and middle initial (if applicable). For subsequent entries by the same author, it is acceptable to substitute the author's name with three hyphens followed by a period. Only do so if the author's name is *exactly* the same in each entry. If there are different co-authors, do not abbreviate the entry.

■ Periods separate most parts of a reference. They should be present after the author name(s), after article titles, after publication date, after type of medium, after page numbers of book chapters, and at the end of the reference. Periods should also be used after the middle initials of each author. Commas are used between the author's last and first name(s), to separate authors, and between the book publisher and date. A colon is used to separate the city of publication and the publisher's name.

■ The first author's name in a reference should be listed last name first, followed by the first name and middle initials, and finished with a period. All subsequent author names should appear in typical order (first name, middle initial, last name). When there are more than three authors, list all authors in the order they appear in the original publication or list the name of the first author only followed by "et al." To reference an edited book, insert the editor's name in the author position and follow it with the abbreviation "ed." If there is no author, the title of the work should be listed first.

■ The title of an article or chapter comes after the author name, followed by the title of the work, periodical, or book. Put the article title in double quotation marks, and capitalize all important words in the title and subtitle (if there is one). The title should not be italicized.

■ The city of publication follows the title of any book. The state, province, or country after the name of a city is not required. A colon is placed after the city name.

■ The publisher's name follows the city of publication. Make the publisher's name as short as possible while still ensuring that the reader can identify the publisher. Omit articles (a, an, the) and descriptive words (e.g., "books, publishers, press"). Abbreviate whenever possible (e.g., "Univ., Assn., Acad."). Place a comma after the publisher's name.

■ The year a book was copyrighted should follow the publisher of the book. Place a period after the date. For journals, the date goes inside parentheses after the volume and issue number, followed by a colon. For newspapers, magazines, and online sources, the date goes after the source name (newspaper, magazine, or website name). In these cases, the day, month, and year are included, in that order, if applicable, with no added punctuation. Months—except May, June, and July—are abbreviated. If no date is available, insert "n.d." (for "no date").

■ Include page numbers for periodical articles, book chapters, and online sources, if applicable. Do not use "p." or "pp." before the page numbers and provide only the last two digits of the second number unless the first and last numbers within the range do not start with the same digit (e.g., 197-99 but 197-204). Page numbers for entire books are not listed. If paragraphs are numbered (for example, in an Internet article), use of "par." or "pars." is acceptable.

■ The type of medium is always included in an MLA reference. This indicates the type of source consulted (e.g., Print, CD, Web, LP, Television, Film). The type of medium is always capitalized and is always followed by a period.

■ For Internet sources, always include the retrieval date. List the day, month (abbreviated unless May, June, or July), and year—in that order, without added punctuation (e.g., 5 Feb. 2010)—that the source was last accessed.

■ Appropriate abbreviations for use in the reference section and in-text citations include the following:

– cond. = conductor
– conf. = conference
– illus. = illustrator
– introd. = introduction

- narr. = narrator
- trans. = translator(s)
- n.d. = no date
- n.p. = no place of publication, no publisher
- n. pag. = no pagination
- vol. = volume
- ed. = editor
- par. = paragraph
- pref. = preface
- prod. = producer
- qtd. = quoted
- supp. = supplement
- U = University
- UP = University Press
- writ = written by

Examples of References

If a source does not match any of the examples provided in this section, refer to the *MLA Handbook* (2009) or the *MLA Style Manual* (2008). Both publications offer similar instructions for citing and referencing sources; however, the *MLA Style Manual* provides more detail about types of sources most likely to be used by professors and graduate students.

MLA style imposes different requirements and rules on different types of sources. Books, journal articles, magazine articles, websites, and other sources each have particular requirements that give proper credit and help readers locate the reference material. The following 13 examples illustrate the format for referencing some of the more common types of sources.

Example 1: A book with a single author.

Klein, Nathan. *No Logo*. New York: Picador, 2000. Print.

Book author: The author's last name is listed first, followed by the author's first name and middle initials (if applicable).

Book title: The title is italicized with all important words capitalized. If there is a colon in the title, the first word following the colon is always capitalized.

Publication information: It is not necessary to include a state, province, or country after the name of a city. A colon is inserted after the city and followed by the name of the publisher. Make the publisher's name as short as possible while still ensuring that the reader can identify the publisher. Omit articles (e.g., a, an, the) and descriptive words (e.g., books, publishers, press). Abbreviate whenever possible (e.g., Univ., Assn., Acad.).

Date of publication: The year the book was published follows the publisher's name.

Type of medium: Include, with initial caps, the type of medium of the publication consulted (e.g., Print, Web, CD, Audio Cassette, Microfilm, Performance, Laser Disc).

Example 2: A book with two or three authors.

Rubin, Rhonda B., Alfred K. Rubin, and Lynnette J. Piele. *Communication Research: A Study in Strategies and Sources.* 5th ed. Belmont: Wadsworth, 2000. Print.

Book author: The first author's last name is listed first, followed by the author's first name and middle initials (if applicable). A comma follows the name of the first author, even when there are only two authors to list. All subsequent author names are presented in usual order (first name, middle initial [if applicable], last name). Type "and" before the last author is listed. Authors are listed in the order they appear on the book.

Book title, publication information, date of publication, type of medium: Follow the format applied in Example 1. (Note that edition numbers follow book titles.)

Example 3: A book with more than three authors.

Brown, Lester V. et al. *Research Methods for Undergraduate Students.* New York: Columbia UP, 2007. Print.

Brown, Lester V., Thomas Z. Ecks, Fatima Walters, Adian R. Zim, Akiko Yashimoto, and Jason P. Bynum. *Research Methods for Undergraduate Students.* New York: Columbia UP, 2007. Print.

Book author: The author's last name is listed first, followed by the author's first name and middle initials (if applicable). With more than three authors, it is acceptable to write out the names of all the authors or to list only the first author followed by the abbreviation "et al." Whichever approach is used, the same style must be applied to the in-text parenthetical citations.

Book title, publication information, date of publication, type of medium: Follow the format applied in Example 1.

Example 4: A translated chapter in a multi-author book.

Tocada, Rieko. "Pottery of the Meiji Era." Trans. Ginger Farriday. *The Arts in Japan, 1868–1912.* Ed. Samuel Jensen. London: Wadsworth, 2006. 247-91. Print.

Article author: The author's last name is listed first, followed by the first name and middle initials (if applicable). If applicable, the name of the translator follows the author name.

Article title: The article title is in double quotation marks and is not italicized. Capitalize all important words. If there is a colon in the title, the first word following the colon is always capitalized. A period follows the title, inside the quotation marks.

Book title: Follow the format applied in Example 1.

Book editor: The editor's name is not inverted. If there is more than one editor, use the abbreviation "Eds." (MLA 2009, 157).

Publication information, date of publication: Follow the format applied in Example 1.

Page numbers: After the date, list the page numbers of the chapter. Do not use "p." or "pp." before the page numbers and provide only the last two digits of the second number unless the first digit of both numbers in the range is not the same.

Type of medium: Follow the format applied in Example 1.

Example 5: An article with only one author in a scholarly journal.

Kramer, Micah W. "Communication in Community Theatre Groups." *Journal of Applied Communication Research* 33.2 (2005): 159-82. Print.

Article author: The author's last name is listed first, followed by the author's first name and middle initials (if applicable). For articles with multiple authors, follow the format applied in Examples 2 and 3.

Article title: The article title is in double quotation marks and is not italicized. Capitalize all important words. If there is a colon in the title, the first word following the colon is always capitalized. A period inside the quotation marks follows the title.

Journal title: The journal title is italicized, and all important words in the title are capitalized. If the journal title starts with an article (the, a, an), unless it is a foreign title (e.g., *La Familia*), omit it. No punctuation follows the journal title.

Publication information: Provide the volume number and the issue number (if any) separated by a period, with no intervening spaces. The year the article was written is included in parentheses after the volume and issue number. After the closing parenthesis, add a colon and a space; then include the page numbers of the article. Do not use "p." or "pp." before the page numbers and provide only the last two digits of the second number unless the first digit of both numbers in the range is not the same.

Example 6: A magazine article.

Marin, Helena E. "Proust's Reflective Imagery." *Literary World* 15 June 2004: 47-52. Print.

Article author: The author's last name is listed first, followed by the author's first name and middle initials (if applicable).

Article title: Follow the format applied in Example 5.

Periodical title: The periodical title is italicized, and all important words in the title are capitalized. If the periodical title starts with an article (the, a, an), unless it is a foreign title (e.g., *La Familia*), omit it. No punctuation follows the periodical title.

Date of publication: If applicable, the day, month, and year that the article was published, in that order, follow the periodical title. Put a colon after the year.

Publication information: Do not provide a volume or issue number, even if they are listed. Provide page numbers for the article. If the pagination is not successive, give the first page number and a plus sign.

Example 7: An article from a newspaper.

> McBride, Jenna. "Tornado Rips through City Hall Complex." *Globe News* [Topeka] 30 May 2007: A1+. Print.

Article author, article title: Follow the format applied in Example 6.

Periodical title: The newspaper title is italicized, and all important words in the title are capitalized. If the newspaper title starts with an article (the, a, an), unless it is a foreign title (e.g., *Le Monde*), omit it. If the newspaper name does not include the city of publication (e.g., *Globe News* rather than *Chicago Tribune*), add it in brackets after the name, in roman (not italic). If the newspaper is published nationally (e.g., *USA Today*), no city is needed. Do not include a state name unless it is part of the newspaper's title. No punctuation follows the newspaper title.

Date of publication: Follow the format applied in Example 6.

Publication information: For newspapers, include the section and page number. Do not write "p." or "pp." before the section name (if applicable) and the starting page number. If the article continues past the first page, add a plus sign.

Type of medium: Include the type of medium of the publication consulted (e.g., Print).

Example 8: An article with no listed author, from a newspaper.

> "Asarco Gets Approval to Auction Land in Salt Lake City." *Amarillo Globe-News* 30 May 2007: D6. Print.

Article author: If an article has no listed author, do not insert "Anonymous." The article title is placed first. The article title is in double quotation marks and is not italicized. Capitalize all important words. If there is a colon in the title, the first word following the colon is always capitalized. A period inside the quotation marks follows the title. If the title begins with an article (a, an, the), alphabetize the entry according to the first letter of the first important word.

Article title, date of publication: Follow the format applied in Example 6.

Periodical title, publication information, type of medium: Follow the format applied in Example 7.

Example 9: An online magazine or news article.

> Marano, Hyram E., and Beatrice G. Schwartz. "Proust's Reflective Imagery." *Literary World.com.* U. of Texas, June 2004. Web. 24 Feb. 2008.

Article author: Follow the format applied in Example 6.

Article title: Use double quotation marks around the title if it is part of a larger work. If the article is independent, italicize the title and do not use quotation marks.

Publication information: List the title of the overall website in italics, if it is distinct from the article title. Next include the publisher or sponsor of the website; if none is available, insert "n.p."

Date of publication: If applicable, the day, month, and year that the article was published, in that order, follow the publisher. If no date is available, insert "n.d."

Retrieval information: Insert "Web" as the type of medium. List the day, month, and year of retrieval, in that order.

Example 10: An article from a periodical database.

> Russell, Pierre R. "Saving Energy Is a Hot Topic: Energy to Develop Ways to Conserve." *New Orleans Times-Picayune* 11 May 2007: Money 1. *Lexis-Nexis*. Web. 5 Jan. 2009.

Article author, article title, periodical title, date of publication: Follow the format applied in Example 6.

Publication information: Follow the format applied in Example 7.

Retrieval information: Include in italics the name of the database where the article was found, followed by a period. Next, insert "Web" as the type of medium. List the day, month, and year of retrieval, in that order.

Example 11: An Internet source.

> "Oklahoma Housing Trends, June–Dec. 2009." Chart. *Baystreet Realty.com.* America First Home Loans 2009. Web. 18 Feb. 2010.

Heading title: Websites or web pages often do not have identified author(s). In such a case, the website section heading is listed at the beginning of the reference. The heading is in double quotation marks and is not italicized. Capitalize all important words. If there is a colon in the title, the first word following the colon is always capitalized. A period inside the quotation marks follows the title. If the title begins with an article (a, an, the), alphabetize it by the first letter of the first important word used. If applicable, include a word to describe the type of document (e.g., chart, map, editorial, home page).

Publication information, retrieval information, date of publication: Follow the format applied in Example 9.

Example 12: A film or video recording.

> *Summer Morning.* Dir. Cesar Patino. Perf. John Frisko, Lynn Bosworth, and Tina Dunmore. RKO, 1938. Film.

Film title: Usually the title of the film is listed first in italics. However, if the paper focuses on a particular aspect of the film—such as the prop design, the movie studio, or an actor or director—it is acceptable to insert this information at the beginning of the citation. Think carefully about why the sources were selected and write the entry appropriately for the subject. Include any information that is relevant to the paper.

Director name: Use the abbreviation "Dir." before the director's name. Do not list the last name first.

Performer names: It is acceptable to include the names of the key actors in a film or video recording.

Distributor name: Include the name of the distributor, followed by a comma. Make the distributor's name as short as possible while still ensuring that the reader can identify it.

Year of release: The year the film was released follows the distributor's name.

Type of medium: Include the type of medium (e.g., Film, Video recording, DVD, Laser disc).

Example 13: A personal interview.

Tomlin, Simon. Skype interview. 19 Feb. 2010.

Name of interviewee: In the author position, place the name of the person interviewed, last name followed by a comma then the first name, followed by a period.

Type of interview: Indicate how the interview was conducted (e.g., Telephone interview, Personal interview).

Date of interview: List the day, month, and year of the interview, in that order.

Example 14: A picture from a website.

Pollock, Jackson. *Greyed Rainbow.* 1953. Art Institute of Chicago. *The Art Institute of Chicago.* Web. 6 June 2011.

Artist or photographer: Follow the format applied to authors in Example 1.

Title: Follow the format applied in Example 1.

Date: List the year of completion or n.d. if no date is known.

Collection: List the name of the institution or collection that owns the picture.

Retrieval information: Follow the format applied in Example 9.

Example 15: A picture from a book.

Pollock, Jackson. *Greyed Rainbow.* 1953. Art Institute of Chicago. *Jackson Pollock.* By Ellen G. Landau. New York: Abradale Press, 2010. 230. Print.

Artist or photographer and title: Follow the format applied to authors in Example 14.

Book title: Follow the format applied in Example 1.

Book author: The author of the book appears in standard format of first name followed by last name. The first name is spelled out and middle initials included (if applicable).

Publication information: Follow the format applied in Example 1.

Page or plate number: Following the publication information, list the page or image/plate number for the picture.

Additional Resources

1620	Mayflower Compact	An agreement among the men on the Mayflower to commit themselves to a political body and to establish laws and a constitution for the colony they founded.
1629	Charter of Massachusetts Bay	A charter granted by King Charles I to the Massachusetts Bay Company for a Puritan settlement in New England.
1754	Albany Plan of Union	Proposed by Benjamin Franklin, this was an attempt to provide a more centralized government that represented both the colonies and Great Britain. This document served as a blueprint for the Articles of Confederation.
1763	Treaty of Paris, 1763	The treaty concluding the French and Indian War.
1765	Stamp Act	An act of the British Parliament that taxed all legal documents, diplomas, newspapers, and playing cards and required a stamp placed on them to show that the tax had been paid.
1765	Stamp Act Resolutions	Resolutions that stated that American colonists had the right to be taxed only by their representatives and that colonists living in Virginia should only pay taxes imposed by their legislature, the House of Burgesses.

1767	Townshend Acts	Parliamentary acts named for Charles Townshend, chancellor of the exchequer, that placed duties on lead, glass, paper, and tea—products that the colonies imported—and controlled the finances of the colonies.
1774	Intolerable Acts	Parliamentary acts that required Bostonians to house and quarter British troops, closed the port of Boston to all ships except British, and sent English troops to Boston to block the harbor from incoming goods.
1774	Galloway's Plan of Union	A plan presented to the British to create a North American colonial government in which the colonists would have more of a voice in the government while continuing a political union with Britain.
1774	Suffolk Resolves	Declaration that the Intolerable Acts were unconstitutional and that officials who were implementing the acts resign from office.
1765	Declaration of Rights and Grievances	A declaration sent to King George III by the delegates to the First Continental Congress objecting to the taxes imposed on the colonies by Parliament, the unconstitutional powers of commissioners, the requirement that trials of colonists take place in England, the closing of Boston's harbor, the passage of the Quebec Act, the dissolving of legislatures, and the limitations placed on the Massachusetts government.

1776	Virginia Declaration of Rights	A statement adopted by the Fifth Virginia Convention as a declaration of basic human rights against oppressive government. The Declaration of Independence and Bill of Rights were heavily influenced by this early document.
1776	Declaration of Independence	Declaration adopted by the thirteen colonies at the Continental Congress that established the colonies as independent from Great Britain.
1777	Articles of Confederation	Document, drafted by the Continental Congress, that established the thirteen original colonies as sovereign states organized under a central government.
1783	Treaty of Paris, 1783	Treaty that ended the Revolutionary War and established new territorial boundaries for the United States.
1787	Virginia Plan	A plan for a bicameral legislature with the number of each chamber's delegates based on a state's population. It also gave veto powers to an executive elected by Congress who was not allowed to otherwise participate in lawmaking.
1787	New Jersey Plan	A plan of government that provided for a unicameral legislature with equal voting power by each state. It also provided Congress the power to tax and regulate trade.
1787	United States Constitution	The supreme law of the United States. This document was adopted at the Constitutional Convention in Philadelphia and contains the Bill of Rights as its first ten amendments. It also provides the framework for three branches of government with separate powers.

1783-1788	Federalist Papers	Articles and essays written by Alexander Hamilton, John Jay, and James Madison in support of ratification of the US Constitution.
1789	Jay-Gardoqui Treaty	Treaty with Spain that was rejected by the Confederation Congress because it failed to resolve the issue of US navigation on the Mississippi River.
1791	Bill of Rights	The first ten amendments to the US Constitution, ratified by two-thirds of the states. These amendments protect individual rights and freedoms.
1798	Alien and Sedition Acts	Four bills signed by President John Adams and proposed by the Federalists to guard against anarchy. They were highly controversial and opposed by the Democratic-Republican party.
1803	Louisiana Purchase Treaty	Treaty that led to the US purchase of the Louisiana Territory from France for $15 million, increasing the size of the US territory by 828,000 square miles.
1820	Missouri Compromise	Four bills that established boundaries and the legality of slavery in some territories in the Southwest US acquired after the Mexican-American War.
1823	Monroe Doctrine	Document that established that any interference from European nations in North or South America would be considered an act of aggression.
1854	Kansas-Nebraska Act	A law that created the territories of Kansas and Nebraska under the principle of popular sovereignty.

1857	Dred Scott v. Sanford	A US Supreme Court ruling that determined that African slaves and their descendents are not US citizens or protected by the Constitution.
1862	Homestead Act	Act that provided homesteaders 160 acres of undeveloped land west of the Mississippi River if they agreed to make improvements to the land.
1863	Gettysburg Address	A speech delivered by President Abraham Lincoln during the Civil War at the dedication of the Soldier's National Cemetery. Lincoln inspired the Union to continue to fight by outlining the reasons for war.
1864	Emancipation Proclamation	President Lincoln's executive order that declared free the slaves in the ten states fighting for secession during the Civil War.
1887	Dawes Severalty Act	The act of Congress that broke up the reservation system and allocated individual farming plots to Native Americans.
1930	Smoot-Hawley Tariff Act	A law that raised taxes on imported goods to unprecedented levels. The law accelerated the effects of the Great Depression.
1930s	Neutrality Acts	A series of acts passed to stop US intervention in other countries at a time of turmoil in Europe and Asia; the United States was still recovering from WWI at the time.
1941	Lend-Lease Act	The act that brought an end to the isolationism of the Neutrality Acts by allowing the US government to support activities of other countries through the supply of materials for war.
1941	Atlantic Charter	Document that outlined the doctrine for engagement and post-WWII policy for the Allied countries.

1947	Truman Doctrine	The basis for Cold War policy that allowed for economic or military support for countries threatened by communism.
1948	Marshall Plan	Reconstruction plan that provided economic support to European countries to rebuild after WWII.
1949	North Atlantic Treaty	Treaty that established the North American Treaty Organization (NATO). NATO originally had 12 members and now includes 28. Member nations consult with each other about threats and national defense and view an attack against any member nation as an attack against all member nations.
1954	Brown v. Board of Education	The US Supreme Court decision that declared separate schools for black and white students unconstitutional, making segregation illegal.
1964	Civil Rights Act	Act that made racial discrimination illegal in public accommodations. The law also specifically outlawed discrimination in the workplace based on race, religion, national origin, or sex and created the Equal Employment Opportunity Commission (EEOC) to ensure that employers would comply with the laws.

1965	Voting Rights Act	Law that provided federal protection for all voters, permitting federal examiners to oversee the voter registration process. Local methods of disenfranchisement, such as poll taxes and literacy tests, were banned. In the years following the passage of the Voting Rights Act a flood of African Americans registered to vote.
1973	War Powers Resolution	A joint resolution of Congress that limited the President's ability to declare war without the consent of Congress.

GLOSSARY

A

Age of Exploration A period of competition, conquest, and discovery for European nations lasting from the mid-1400s to the end of the 1500s.

Al Qaeda A global terrorist organization composed of militant Muslim radicals led by Osama bin Laden.

Albany Plan of Union A meeting in 1754 in Albany, New York, in which representatives from the colonies and members of the Iroquois attempted to form an alliance before the French and Indian War.

Albany Plan of Union An attempt to provide a more centralized government that represented both the colonies and Great Britain.

Allied Powers During World War I, Britain, France, Russia, and eventually, the United States.

American System The economic policy of President John Q. Adams that added tariffs with the hope of protecting American markets. It resulted in an increase in the cost of living, particularly in the South, and the policy became known popularly as the Tariff of Abominations.

Andrew Johnson The new Republican vice president who became president after Abraham Lincoln was assassinated; he presided over federal Reconstruction efforts between 1865 and 1868.

Antifederalists Those opposing ratification of the 1787 Constitution.

appeasement The foreign policy of attempting to pacify expansionist nations by making small concessions instead of openly engaging in war.

Appomattox The location of the surrender of General Robert E. Lee of the Confederate Army on April 9, 1865.

Articles of Confederation The first constitution of the United States.

Atlanta Compromise Booker T. Washington's strategy to racial progress, which accepted segregation and urged blacks and whites to work together for the benefit of both groups.

B

Baby Boom The explosion of the birth rate between 1946 and 1964.

Bacon's Rebellion A rebellion in Virginia demanding legislation that would provide financial relief for tobacco planters.

balloon loans Loans offered by banks to individuals that started with a low interest rate but escalated over time.

Battle of Britain Britain's defense of Germany's costly attempt to defeat Churchill by bombing British civilian centers such as London.

Benedict Arnold Commander at West Point and effective colonial leader who eventually defected and became a British spy.

Bill of Rights The first ten amendments to the Constitution.

black codes Laws passed in various Southern states that restricted the economic opportunities and civil rights of newly freed African-Americans.

Black Monday October 28, 1929: the date on which the Roaring Twenties came to an end in a crash on Wall Street.

Black Power A radical political movement that called for an end to racial discrimination, pride in African-American heritage, and the improvement of black communities through separatism.

Bleeding Kansas A series of violent incidents that took place in the 1850s along the Kansas-Missouri border over whether Kansas should be admitted as a free state or a slave state.

Blitzkrieg A method of warfare perfected by Hitler's forces that shocked enemies with its speed and power.

Boston Massacre A confrontation between colonists and British troops who were stationed in Boston for the purpose of enforcing the Townshend Acts.

Boston Tea Party A protest by colonists who disguised themselves as Native Americans, boarded a ship, and dumped its cargo of tea into the harbor after Parliament had enacted a bill to charge a tax on all tea brought into the colonies.

boycott The refusal to buy, sell, or use British products.

Brigham Young The Mormon leader who led his followers on a migration from Illinois in search of land to establish their new community, Young helped found Salt Lake City in 1847 and became the first governor of the Utah territory.

broad constructionism A belief that the Constitution can be interpreted for meaning outside of the strict wording.

Brown v. Board of Education of Topeka, Kansas The landmark civil rights case that ruled that the legal segregation of schools unconstitutional.

bubble A state of significant economic growth with the potential of a sudden collapse.

Bunker Hill The first major battle in the American Revolution.

Bush Doctrine One of the guiding principles of President Bush's foreign policy that called for preemptive warfare in response to modern threats to world peace.

C

Cahokia A man-made earthen city that was the capital of the Mississippian culture.

carpetbaggers A derogatory name for Northerners who came to the South during the Reconstruction years purely for financial or political opportunity.

cash crop A crop that is grown to be sold rather than grown for personal use.

Central Powers During World War I, Germany, Austria-Hungary, Bulgaria, and the Ottoman Empire.

Charles, Lord Cornwallis The British commander who was eventually defeated at Yorktown.

Charleston South Carolina's largest seaport and city where a large loyalist population lived.

Chief Joseph Leader of the Nez Perce who in 1877 led a large group of followers on a difficult and ultimately unsuccessful trek to Canada to avoid relocation onto the reservation.

Clean Air Act A law, passed in 1970, to decrease air pollution in the United States.

COINTELPRO An FBI program carried out by J. Edgar Hoover to monitor and control subversive political groups and protest leaders during the 1950s, 1960s, and early 1970s.

Cold War The period of political and military tension between the United States and the Soviet Union that lasted from 1946 to 1989.

Committees of Correspondence Committees established within the colonies to discuss the ramifications of the Sugar Act.

Compassionate conservatism A political philosophy that suggests general welfare can best be served by adhering to conservative practices.

Compromise of 1850 A series of laws that attempted to address the concerns of both Northerners and Southerners regarding the slave policy of new Western territories.

Compromise of 1877 An informal agreement between Republicans and Democrats in Congress in the wake of the contested presidential election. It resulted in the end of federal Reconstruction policy in exchange for Republican Rutherford B. Hayes taking the presidency.

Comstock Lode A major vein of silver ore discovered in Virginia City, Nevada in 1858, resulting in a silver rush of migration and mining in the region.

conference diplomacy Type of diplomacy in which representatives of different countries meet to discuss common problems.

Congressional Reconstruction The period between 1866 and 1877 during which the Radical Republicans in Congress controlled federal Reconstruction policy and focused on securing civil and political rights for African-Americans.

conscription The practice of requiring members of the population who meet certain qualifications to serve in the armed forces.

consumerism An attitude that values the acquisition of material goods.

containment U.S. foreign policy aimed at stopping the spread of communism.

Continental Army The colonial army commanded by George Washington.

Contract with America The successful political agenda of the Republicans in the 1994 mid-term elections that focused on economic policy.

cotton gin A tool that separates cotton fibers from the seeds of the cotton plant; this machine allowed laborers to process cotton much faster than doing it by hand.

counterculture A movement that used music, clothing, lifestyle choices, and political action to challenge mainstream social and cultural norms during the 1960s.

Cuban Missile Crisis A 1962 showdown between the Soviet Union and the United States over the Soviet military presence, especially nuclear weapons, in Cuba.

D

D-Day The secret and massive Allied invasion of occupied France at the beaches of Normandy on June 6, 1944.

Dawes Severalty Act An 1887 Act of Congress that broke up the reservation system and allocated individual farming plots to Native Americans.

Declaration of Independence The colonists' declaration that they intended to be free and independent from Great Britain.

Declaration of Rights and Grievances A declaration sent to King George III by the delegates to the First Continental Congress objecting to the taxes imposed on the colonies by Parliament, the unconstitutional powers of commissioners, the requirement that some trials of colonists take place in England, the closing of Boston's harbor, the passage of the Quebec Act, the dissolving of legislatures, and the limitations placed on Massachusetts government.

Declaratory Act An act of Parliament that declared Parliament had authority to make laws for the colonies in all matters.

Democratic-Republican Party Also known as the Republican Party, this early U.S. political party believed in a strict constructionist view and states' rights.

deregulation A movement to limit government control over business practices.

desegregation The process of ending mandated racial divisions in public spaces or institutions.

discovery doctrine A court ruling that determined that Native American tribes residing in discovered land did not hold the title to the land, nor were they sovereign.

Dred Scott A slave who attempted to sue for his freedom. The result was a decision from the Supreme Court that stated slaves were property, not people.

Dust Bowl A period of serve dust storms that nearly crippled the prairie and surrounding regions.

E

Eastern Woodlands Native Americans People living in the area east of the Mississippi River at the time the European settlers arrived on the North American shores.

Edward Braddock The English commander for Britain's North American forces after Washington surrendered Fort Necessity.

Efficiency Movement A movement to rid the government and the economy of waste and inefficient systems and practices.

elastic clause A view that government has the authority to exercise powers that are "necessary and proper" to fulfill its Constitutional function.

emancipation The liberation of slaves.

Enlightenment An intellectual movement in the 1700s in Europe and North America in which philosophers developed theories of natural rights and promoted scientific reasoning.

Environmental Protection Agency (EPA) The federal agency responsible for creating and enforcing national guidelines for acceptable practices with regard to the environment.

escalation The policy of increasing the U.S. military presence and involvement in Vietnam during the Vietnam War.

excise tax A tax imposed on businesses on goods sold.

F

Federal Reserve Bank A private institution that regulates the amount of U.S. money in supply and the costs of borrowing money.

Federalist Papers Essays written by supporters of ratification of the Constitution.

Federalist Party An early political party in the United States that believed in implied powers, broad constructionism, and a strong central government.

Federalists Those favoring ratification of the Constitution and a strong central government.

feminist movement The struggle for women's liberation and equal rights during the 1960s and 1970s.

Fifteenth Amendment One of three Reconstruction-era amendments to the U.S. Constitution proposed by Radical Republicans, the Fifteenth Amendment was ratified in 1870 and granted all men the right to vote regardless of "race, color, or previous condition of servitude."

First Continental Congress Colonial meeting in 1774 to discuss trade boycotts.

Force Bill A bill passed under Jackson's administration that allowed the federal government to use force to make states comply with laws passed by Congress; the bill was passed in response to the Nullification Crisis in South Carolina.

Fort Carrillon A French fort near the present-day New York and Vermont border and on the southern shore of Lake Champlain.

Fort Duquesne A French fort in present-day Pennsylvania. Braddock led the attack on Fort Duquesne personally.

Fort Necessity A fort built by George Washington that the French captured in an early defeat in the war for the British colonists.

Fort Niagara A fort located on Lake Ontario at the mouth of the Niagara River that was an important entry for fur trading in the Ohio Valley.

Fort Sumter An Army fort in South Carolina, and the location for the first shots of the American Civil War.

Fort Ticonderoga The former French Fort Carrillon.

Fort William Henry A fort built on the northern shore of Lake Champlain by the British to counter the effects of Fort Carillon.

Fortress of Louisbourg A French stronghold on Cape Breton Island in Nova Scotia that was captured by the British. The victory was the first important victory for the British in the war.

Forty-Niners A nickname for pioneers who moved to California in 1849 in search of gold.

Fourteen Points Woodrow Wilson's peace plan, which called for arms reduction, freedom of the seas, free trade, self-determination, an adjustment in colonial claims, the creation of the League of Nations, and an end to secret treaties.

Fourteenth Amendment One of three Reconstruction-era amendments to the U.S. Constitution proposed by Radical Republicans, the Fourteenth Amendment was ratified in 1868 and granted national citizenship and equal protection under the law to African-Americans for the first time.

Frederick Jackson Turner Historian whose influential 1893 paper "The Significance of the Frontier in American History" explained the impact of the frontier on American democratic culture and identity.

free trade International trade that is not influenced by economic legislation designed to regulate imports and exports.

Freedmen's Bureau A federal agency established by Radical Republicans in Congress in 1865; it distributed aid and provided legal and educational services to former slaves.

French and Indian War The war between Great Britain and France in North America from 1754–1763. Various Native American nations, including the Iroquois Confederacy, also took sides. The war was part of a worldwide contest between Great Britain and France.

frontier Land at the edge of a country or settlement.

G

Galloway's Plan of Union A plan presented to the British to create a North American colonial government in which the colonists would have more of a voice in the government while continuing a political union with Britain.

George Armstrong Custer U.S. cavalry officer who fought for the Union Army during the Civil War and went on to lead troops against the Plains Indians. Custer was killed in a conflict with the Sioux at the Battle of Little Big Horn (Custer's Last Stand) in 1876.

George III The king of England during the American colonial period.

Geronimo Apache warrior who surrendered in 1886 after leading a group of followers fleeing a reservation in Arizona.

Ghost Dance A religious movement practiced by many western Indian groups in the late nineteenth century that emphasized the need to return to traditional ways and honor their ancestors in the hopes of a future return to their homelands.

Gilded Age An era dating from the end of the Civil War through the turn of the twentieth century characterized by increasing wealth, industry, and corruption on one hand, and poverty and helplessness on the other.

Glass-Steagall Banking Act A law that established mechanisms for the federal government to monitor the practices and welfare of banks more closely.

gold standard The practice of making money equivalent to a set amount of gold.

Graduation Act of 1854 Another act passed by Congress that reduced the price of purchasing land and thereby encouraged Americans to move west.

Great Awakening A religious revival in the colonies during the mid-1700s that had its roots in England.

Great Compromise Plan establishing a bicameral legislature with one house based upon population and the other having equal representation from all states.

Great Migration The period from 1916 through the 1930s when more than 400,000 African-Americans moved from the South to Northern cities.

Great Railroad Strike Workers whose wages were drastically cut during the economic downturn during the 1870s waged a violent protest that was eventually suppressed by local, state, and federal forces.

Great Society President Lyndon B. Johnson's set of domestic programs to fight poverty and racial inequality.

greenbacks An early paper currency issued by the U.S. government during the Civil War.

H

Hanford, Washington The location of the first large-scale nuclear reactor, which played an integral role in the creation of the first atomic bombs.

Head Start A government program, started as part of the Great Society, to provide free or subsidized preschool education to children from poor families.

Hessians German soldiers who were paid to fight for the British.

hippies Members of the counterculture who distinguished themselves by their clothing, music, lifestyle, and politics.

Holocaust The Nazis' persecution and execution of millions of Europe's Jews and minorities.

Homestead Act An act of Congress passed in 1862 that encouraged westward settlement by granting claims of up to 160 acres of land to families willing to settle and improve the land.

Hoovervilles Shantytowns that served as makeshift dwellings for many who became unemployed during the Great Depression.

hyperinflation A condition when money becomes increasingly worthless. This occurred in Germany between the First and Second World Wars.

I

implied power doctrine A view that government has the authority to exercise powers outside of the express written law if they are not forbidden.

income tax A policy of requiring citizens to pay a percentage of their earned money to the government.

indentured servant A person whose passage to the North American colonies was paid for in exchange for a specified number of years of work for the person purchasing passage.

Indian Removal Act of 1830 A plan to relocate the Indian nations from the Southeast to areas west of the Mississippi River. What was initially described as a voluntary process quickly became one of force.

Industrial Revolution A dramatic change in technology that streamlined manufacturing, communication, transportation, and production processes.

internment The detention of Japanese Americans as a part of the U.S. response to the bombing of Pearl Harbor

Intolerable Acts Parliamentary acts that required Bostonians to quarter British troops, closed the port of Boston to all ships except British, and sent English troops to Boston to block the harbor from incoming goods. The acts were referred to as the Intolerable Acts by the colonists and Coercive Acts by the British.

Iron Curtain The ideological divide between the communist countries of Eastern Europe and the non-communist countries of Western Europe.

Iroquois Confederacy A confederacy among several Native American groups in the New York and upper North American colonial regions.

isolationism A policy of staying out of, or separate from, international affairs.

J

Jacques Cartier A French explorer who, in the 1500s, sought a northwest passage across present-day Canada to the Pacific Ocean.

James Wolfe The British commander who defeated the French at Quebec.

Jay-Gardoqui Treaty Treaty with Spain that was rejected by the Confederation Congress because it failed to resolve the issue of U.S. navigation on the Mississippi River.

John Winthrop A Puritan lawyer who became governor of Massachusetts Bay Colony.

judicial review The court's power to determine if a law is constitutional.

K

Kansas-Nebraska Act An 1854 law that created the territories of Kansas and Nebraska.

kitchen cabinet An informal group of advisors to the president.

Ku Klux Klan A white supremacy organization formed by former Confederates in Tennessee in 1865 that engaged in violence throughout the postbellum South as a reaction against black political empowerment. The organization favored repression of African- Americans, Jews, Catholics, and immigrants and often committed acts of violence to intimidate these groups.

L

labor unions Groups of workers organized to improve working conditions and wages.

League of Nations A multi-national peacekeeping organization established after World War I.

Lebensraum a German word meaning living space; Hitler claimed the German people needed more room to live and used this idea as a reason for his expansionist goals.

Lend-Lease Plan President Roosevelt's strategy for aiding Allied forces by supplying them with much-needed supplies

Levittown A prototypical suburb built in the late 1940s and early 1950s on the outskirts of New York City.

Line of Demarcation The line dividing Spanish and Portuguese possessions in the New World.

Louis-Joseph de Montcalm The French leader who fought against the British in the Battle of Quebec.

Loyalists British name for those who supported the British against

the colonists. The colonists referred to the Loyalists as Tories.

lynching A hanging or other public killing by a mob, rather than legal authorities. Most victims of lynching in the United States were African-Americans.

M

Maginot Line An ineffective line of defense established by the French along its border with Germany.

Manhattan Project A collaborative undertaking organized by the U.S. government that involved scientists and military engineers to develop the world's first atomic weapons.

Manifest Destiny A term used beginning in the 1840s to justify the idea that the United States had a historical and even God-given destiny to expand westward and inhabit the continent from coast to coast.

Maoism A series of policies put forth in China by Mao Zedong that highlighted the importance of the peasant worker and maintaining an ongoing revolutionary state.

market economy An economy driven by the forces of supply and demand and based on the exchange of money for goods and services.

Marshall Plan U.S. aid package to help rebuild Western Europe after World War II.

Mayflower Compact An agreement among the men on the Mayflower to commit themselves to a political body and to establish laws and a constitution for the colony they founded.

Medicaid A government program, started as part of the Great Society, to provide medical insurance to low-income Americans.

Medicare A government program, started as part of the Great Society, to provide medical insurance to elderly Americans.

mercantilism An economic doctrine that says government control of foreign trade is of central importance.

Metacom's War A war between colonists and Native Americans in New England that helped the colonists become more cohesive in their feelings of resentment of British actions involving the colonists.

Middle Passage The passage across the Atlantic Ocean on slave ships.

military-industrial complex The military and defense industries that influence foreign and economic policy.

Monongahela River The river that joins with the Ohio River and Allegheny River near present-day Pittsburgh, Pennsylvania.

monopoly An economic condition that exists when one company or trust has such a significant influence in one area of industry that it can single-handedly influence prices and undermine competitive markets.

Montreal The last important French stronghold in North America. It surrendered to British forces 1760.

Morrill Act A law that gave states federal lands on which to build colleges.

Morrill Land-Grant Colleges Act (Morrill Act) An Act of Congress first passed in 1862 that promoted the settlement and development of the agricultural West by providing land for public colleges.

mound builders Native Americans who built ceremonial and trading sites, such as Cahokia.

muckrakers Investigative journalists who sought to publish articles on a variety of topics of public interest with the hope of bringing about reform.

N

nativism The belief that native-born Americans were superior to immigrants.

nativists Americans who opposed immigration and immigrants.

NATO North Atlantic Treaty Organization; defensive alliance established between the United States and Western European countries in 1949.

New Deal A series of programs established under Roosevelt's administration that sought to bring relief, recovery, and reform to the many suffering through the Great Depression.

New Jersey Plan A plan of government that provided for a unicameral legislature with equal voting power by each state.

No Child Left Behind The education policy of President Bush that increased the control of the federal

government over school systems and emphasized the importance of standardized testing.

nonviolent resistance The protest tactic, used by many civil rights activists, of committing peaceful acts of civil disobedience, rather than engaging in violent confrontation.

Northwest Ordinance Congressional legislation that provided the method for developing the Northwest Territory into states.

O

Ohio Company A company formed for land speculation and settlement. It was granted land in the Ohio area by the British king.

Olive Branch Petition An appeal sent from the delegates of the Second Continental Congress to King George III to end the differences between the colonies and mother country peacefully.

OPEC The Organization of Petroleum Exporting Countries, founded in 1960 to govern the production, price, and export of oil by its members, which include Iran, Iraq, Egypt, Saudi Arabia, and others.

Ordinance of Nullification A law passed by the state of South Carolina that voided the federal tariff acts of 1828 and 1832 and directly challenged federal authority over states' rights.

Osama bin Laden A Saudi-born terrorist who masterminded the attacks of September 11, 2001 and led the terrorist organization al Qaeda until his death in 2011.

P

Pacific Railway Acts Acts of Congress passed to promote building of a transcontinental railroad, the Pacific Railway Acts of the 1860s granted land and loans to private railroad companies.

Panic of 1857 An economic downturn that demonstrated the growing interconnectedness of world markets and the perils of overproduction.

Paris Peace Negotiations A series of talks in 1968 ahead of the U.S. presidential elections that brought leaders from North and South Vietnam, along with U.S. representatives, to the bargaining table.

Pearl Harbor The location of a naval base in Hawaii, where on December 7, 1941, Japanese bombers destroyed the U.S. Pacific Fleet in a surprise attack; this event directly caused the United States to join the fighting of WWII.

Pentagon Papers A classified study by the U.S. Department of Defense about the Vietnam War that was leaked to the New York Times by Daniel Ellsberg in 1971.

Pilgrims The group of English separatists who settled Plymouth Colony for religious purposes.

Plains of Abraham The location of the Battle of Quebec.

political machines Political parties run by "bosses" who provided jobs, housing, and other assistance to city residents, especially immigrants, in exchange for money, loyalty, and votes.

Ponce de Leon The first Spanish explorer to arrive in Florida and Puerto Rico, where he established the first Spanish settlement.

Pontiac An Ottawa chief who formed alliances with other Native American tribes to strike British forts, causing havoc and unrest in the Ohio Valley.

popular sovereignty The belief that territories should have the right to decide whether to allow slavery, rather than the federal government.

precedent A legal decision handed down by a court that serves as the law in subsequent cases.

Preemption Act of 1841 A law passed by Congress to prevent speculators from claiming areas of open land that made it easier for settlers to purchase 160 acres of land from the government.

Presidential Reconstruction The first phase of Reconstruction, between 1865 and 1867, during which presidents Lincoln and then Johnson put forth lenient plans for readmitting the former Confederate states into the Union, centering on securing loyalty oaths and issuing pardons to former Confederate leaders.

Prohibition A complete ban on alcohol.

propaganda The spread of deceptive or distorted information in order to promote a cause.

Puritans Anglicans who settled Massachusetts Bay Colony in the 1600s.

Q

Quakers Members of the Society of Friends who settled Pennsylvania to escape persecution. They believed in equality for all, pacifism, and personal salvation.

Quebec The location of a Canadian battle where British general James Wolfe defeated Montcalm.

Quorum The minimum number of members necessary to conduct business.

Quotas A fixed number of people from certain groups, used historically in immigration systems.

R

race riots The violent expression of racial and class inequality that swept through American cities during the 1960s.

Radical Republicans The radical wing of the Republican Party, which dominated Reconstruction policy and advocated civil rights for African-Americans and strict oversight of the Southern states after the Civil War.

Reconstruction Finance Corporation A federal relief agency formed in 1932 under Hoover that sought to give local governments money to put more Americans to work on public roads and other projects.

Red Scare Campaign after World War I and the Russian Revolutions to root out suspected communists in the United States.

reparations Compensation for war damages.

Richard Henry Lee A Virginia delegate to the Second Continental Congress who proposed the colonists become independent from Great Britain.

Roaring Twenties An era of general prosperity and speculation that drove the stock market up.

robber barons Men who accumulated tremendous wealth, often under dubious circumstance.

Rosie the Riveter A cultural symbol that came to represent the idea that women were capable of doing work traditionally assigned to men who were away fighting in Europe and the Pacific.

Rutherford B. Hayes The Republican nominee for president in the controversial election of 1876, which resulted in Hayes's victory and the conclusion of federal Reconstruction efforts.

S

Salem witch trials Trials held in Massachusetts for those accused of being witches because they quarreled with the Puritan authorities.

Samuel Champlain A French explorer who founded Quebec in 1608.

Saratoga A battle that was the turning point of the American Revolution.

Saturday Night Massacre The nickname given to the day, October 20, 1973, when special Watergate prosecutor Archibald Cox was fired and Attorney General Elliot

Richardson and Deputy Attorney General William Ruckelshaus resigned.

scalawags Derogatory name for white Southerners who were accused of betraying the Confederacy by joining the Republican Party and voting for Republican candidates during the Reconstruction era.

scientific management The practice of analyzing a work process to break it down into parts and maximize efficiency.

sectionalism Political views dominated by the issues of interests of a certain region of the country.

service industry An industry or group of companies that provide services instead of manufacturing goods. Banking, medicine, and retail are all service industries.

settlement houses Community centers that offered education, recreation, and other services to poor city-dwellers.

Seven Years' War A global war between Great Britain, France, and their allies between 1756 and 1763. The French and Indian War was part of this wider conflict.

sharecroppers Farmers who do not own their own land but pay a portion of their harvest to the land's owner in exchange for being allowed to farm there.

sharecropping A contract labor arrangement that replaced plantation slavery in the South, in which tenant farmers leased farm land and then shared crop proceeds with the landowner.

Shays' Rebellion An armed rebellion of farmers in postwar

Massachusetts protesting mortgage foreclosures and high debt.

Sherman Antitrust Act Legislation that requires the federal government to investigate trusts and prevent them from reducing competition in the marketplace.

Sherman Silver Purchase Act Legislation intended to reverse deflation that required the federal government to increase the amount of silver it purchased.

shuttle diplomacy Secretary of State Henry Kissinger shuttled between Mideast countries in an effort to negotiate an end to the Yom Kippur War.

Sitting Bull Leader of the Sioux who led a large group of followers who rejected the reservation and confronted U.S. soldiers in major battles at Little Bighorn in 1876 and later, in 1890, at Wounded Knee, where Sitting Bull was killed.

slave gangs A method that Southern slave owners used to organized their slave labor—it was known as much for its brutality as its efficiency.

slave society An economic and social system built on slavery.

Smoot-Hawley Tariff Act A law that raised taxes on imported goods. The law accelerated the effects of the Great Depression.

social hierarchy The arrangement of society in differing classes of wealth.

Social Security Act A law that established the Social Security system, which distributes federal assistance to retirees and the unemployed.

Sons of Liberty Societies formed in the colonies during the summer of 1765 after the passage of the Stamp Act to resist Parliament's actions that regulated colonial affairs.

Spanish-American War An 1898 conflict between Spain and the United States over the issue of Cuban independence and Spanish imperial claims in the Caribbean and the Pacific, which resulted in U.S. control of Cuba, Puerto Rico, and Guam and led to the Philippine-American War.

Stamp Act An act of the British Parliament that taxed all legal documents, diplomas, newspapers, and playing cards and required a stamp placed on them to show that the tax had been paid.

Stamp Act Congress A colonial congress held in October 1765, at which delegates from nine colonies met to discuss their opposition to the Stamp Act.

States' Rights Rights reserved for state governments or issues that the federal government does not have authority to control in the individual states.

strict constructionism A belief that the Constitution should be interpreted exactly as written.

suburb A residential community on the outskirts of a city.

Suffolk Resolves Declaration that the Intolerable Acts were unconstitutional and that officials who were implementing the acts resign from office.

suffrage The right to vote.

swing voters Members of the electorate who demonstrate no strong loyalty for either party.

T

Temperance Movement The late nineteenth- and early twentieth-century effort to decrease or ban the production, sale, and consumption of alcohol.

Ten-Percent Plan Lincoln's wartime plan for readmitting former Confederate states into the Union if 10 percent of a state's eligible voters swore an oath of allegiance to the United States.

Terrorism The use of violence to inflict fear and coerce an enemy.

The Feminine Mystique A book by Betty Friedan about the disadvantages of women's domesticity. This book helped to mobilize the second wave feminist movement.

The Pill Hormonal contraception, developed in the 1950s and approved by the FDA in 1960.

Thirteenth Amendment One of three Reconstruction-era amendments to the U.S. Constitution proposed by the Radical Republicans, the Thirteenth Amendment was ratified in 1865 and ended slavery in the United States.

Three-Fifths Compromise The agreement of congressional delegates to count slaves as only three-fifths of a person when determining proportional representation.

Tories Colonial name for those who supported the British against the colonists. Tories were identified as Loyalists by the British.

Total War A practice of war that shows no regard for the distinction between the military and general population.

Townshend Acts Parliamentary acts named for Charles Townshend, Chancellor of the Exchequer, that placed duties on lead, glass, paper, and tea—products that the colonies imported—and controlled the finances of the colonies.

Trail of Tears A name given to the relocation of Cherokee Indians who were forced to move from their native lands to areas west of the Mississippi River. The tragic consequences of this federal policy included the deaths of thousands of Native Americans.

Treaty of Paris The treaty concluding the Seven Years' War, also known as the French and Indian War.

Treaty of Versailles Treaty with Germany that concluded World War I and punished Germany for the war.

triangle trade Trade between the North American English colonies, Africa, and the Caribbean islands in which slaves were brought from Africa as laborers, and sugar cane was sold to the New England colonies for the manufacturer of rum in New England distilleries.

Truman Doctrine U.S. policy to help countries that are fighting against communist influence or takeover.

trust An organization that combines several businesses under a centralized board of trustees.

Trusts Groups of companies that work together to limit competition and corner the market on a product.

U

Ulysses S. Grant The celebrated Union Army general and Republican who was elected president in 1868 and went on to promote civil rights legislation during the Reconstruction Era.

urbanization The development of population centers or cities and the social, industrial, and governmental organizations that help them function.

V

Valley Forge Winter camp for the Continental Army in 1777–1778.

VE Day The name given to the day of German surrender on May 8, 1945.

vertical integration A practice whereby companies internally make the supply materials they use to produce their products, or purchase the companies that provide these materials, in order to save time and money.

vertically integrated A way of running a company so that it handles all steps of a process in its industry.

Viet Cong The North Vietnam–sponsored communist resistance group that opposed South Vietnam and the United States before and during the Vietnam War.

Vietnamization Richard Nixon's plan to withdraw U.S. troops from Vietnam by supporting South Vietnamese replacement fighters.

Virginia Company A joint stock company that was formed to settle the present-day area of Virginia.

Virginia Plan A plan for a bicameral legislature with the number of each state's representatives based on a state's population.

VJ Day The name given to the day of Japanese surrender, which can refer to August 14, 1945 (the initial day of surrender) or September 2, 1945 (the day on which the official surrender document was signed).

Von Steuben A Prussian army officer who helped create a more organized army, developed a training program for the soldiers, and established a program for camp sanitation.

W

Wade-Davis Bill A bill proposed by two Radical Republican Congressmen in 1864, but vetoed by President Lincoln, that would have required a majority of a former Confederate state's eligible voters to take a loyalty oath before being readmitted to the Union.

Watergate The scandal surrounding two illegal break-ins to the DNC headquarters in 1972 that were organized by members of the Nixon administration and the Committee to Re-elect the President. Nixon's implication in the crime and the cover up led to his resignation.

weapons of mass destruction Technologically advanced tools designed to kill many people or to destroy large areas.

William Howe The British general who commanded the king's troops for the first part of the Revolutionary War, including the attack on New York City.

William Penn A Quaker who founded Pennsylvania.

William Pitt England's prime minister in 1757 who provided more funds and military personnel to fight the French in the French and Indian War.

Wounded Knee The final and symbolic end to the Plains Indian Wars of the nineteenth century, the battle at Wounded Knee, South Dakota in 1890, resulted in the deaths of many Sioux men, women, and children, including the death of leader Sitting Bull.

PHOTO CREDITS

Chapter 1 Opener, p. 2: © johnlric (Fotolia); p. 6: © Lars Johansson (Fotolia); p. 7: © Shchipkova Elena (Fotolia); p. 9: © Irochka (Fotolia); p. 10: © Nataliya Hora (Fotolia); p. 11: © AndreasJ (Fotolia); p. 13: © John Tomaselli (Fotolia); p. 14: © PHB.cz (Fotolia); p. 15: © Erica Guilane-Nachez (Fotolia); p. 19: © Andrei Nekrassov (Fotolia); p. 21: © Helder Almeida (Fotolia).

Chapter 2 Opener, p. 26: © James Nicholson (Fotolia); p. 31: © pcphotos (Fotolia); p. 32: © Joy Fera (Fotolia).

Chapter 3 Opener, p. 34: © rook76 (Fotolia); p. 37: © Subbotina Anna (Fotolia); p. 38: © air (Fotolia); p. 39: © Georgios Kollidas (Fotolia); p. 40: © Lambros Kazan (Fotolia).

Chapter 4 Opener, p. 42: © jStock; p. 44: © Mark J. Grenier; p. 45: © rook76; p. 48: © rook76; p. 50: © Mark J. Grenier; p. 51: © Georgios Kollidas; p. 53: © Georgios Kollidas.

Chapter 5 Opener, p. 54: © Kasia Biel (Fotolia); p. 56: © Stefanos Kyriazis (Fotolia); p. 57: © Ben Chams (Fotolia); p. 59: © rook76 (Fotolia); p. 60: © ss-serega (Fotolia); p. 61: © Fernando Cortés (Fotolia); p. 63: © Nejron Photo (Fotolia); p. 65: © nhtg (Fotolia).

Chapter 6 Opener, p. 68: © Dirk Steffen (Fotolia); p. 71: © klikk (Fotolia); p. 72: © Georgios Kollidas (Fotolia); p. 74: © Georgios Kollidas (Fotolia); p. 77: © Celso Diniz (Fotolia); p. 80: © Flavijus Piliponis (Fotolia); p. 83, top-right: © Patricia Hofmeester (Fotolia); p. 83, bottom-left: © FlyFishka (Fotolia); p. 85: © Michael Lijewski (Fotolia).

Chapter 7 Opener p. 88: © Rob Byron (Fotolia); p. 91: © megasquib (Fotolia); p. 92: © D Wetzel (Fotolia); p. 94: © Empath (Fotolia); p. 96, top-left: © Anyka (Fotolia); p. 96, bottom-left: © Kirk Atkinson (Fotolia); p. 98: © Kheng Guan Toh (Fotolia); p. 99: © Vacclav (Fotolia); p. 100: © JcJg Photography (Fotolia); p. 102: © HP_Photo (Fotolia); p. 103: © Gary (Fotolia).

Chapter 8 Opener, p. 106: © Jose Gil (Fotolia); p. 109: © gringo154 (Fotolia); p. 110: © Wild Geese (Fotolia); p. 111: © Mario Savoia (Fotolia); p. 113: © TebNad (Fotolia); p. 114: © Paul Moore (Fotolia); p. 115, top-right: © ollirg (Fotolia); p. 115, bottom-right: © Fotoskat (Fotolia); p. 117: © John Kropewnicki (Fotolia); p. 119: © gemenacom (Fotolia); p. 120: © treenabeena (Fotolia); p. 121: © Gareau Enterprises (Fotolia); p. 122:

© steve estvanik (Fotolia); p. 123: © faberfoto (Fotolia); p. 125: © Xtremer (Fotolia); p. 127: © Rick Sargeant (Fotolia); p. 128: © Joseph Becker (Fotolia).

Chapter 9 Opener, p. 132: © deviantART (Fotolia); p. 134: © Linda McPherson (Fotolia); p. 135: © Christopher Jones (Fotolia); p. 136: © Stocksnapper (Fotolia); p. 137: © Gennady Poddubny (Fotolia); p. 139: © stoonn (Fotolia); p. 140: © Laurin Rinder (Fotolia); p. 141: © Dominique VERNIER (Fotolia); p. 143, top-right: © Dean Moriarty (Fotolia); p. 143, bottom-right: © Christos Georghiou (Fotolia); p. 144: © bradcalkins (Fotolia); p. 145: © kikkerdirk (Fotolia).

Chapter 10 Opener, p. 148: © michael Langley (Fotolia); p. 150: © clearviewstock (Fotolia); p. 151: © clearviewstock (Fotolia); p. 153: © sumnersgraphicsinc (Fotolia); p. 154: © horacio villamonte (Fotolia); p. 155: © Krzysztof Wiktor (Fotolia); p. 156: © laugrim16 (Fotolia); p. 157: © Brian Lasenby (Fotolia); p. 158: © Mary Lane (Fotolia); p. 159: Item from Record Group 111: Records of the Office of the Chief Signal Officer, 1860 – 1985; p. 161: © Marco Regalia (Fotolia); p. 163: © Yevgeniy Zateychuk (Fotolia).

Chapter 11 Opener, p. 166: © Ash Toone (Fotolia); p. 168: © Dragan Boskovic (Fotolia); p. 169: © Georgios Kollidas (Fotolia); p. 171: © Elenathewise (Fotolia); p. 172: © trekandshoot (Fotolia); p. 174: © Zoe (Fotolia); p. 177: © fabioberti.it (Fotolia); p. 178: © Patrikeevna (Fotolia); p. 179: © Brent Reeves (Fotolia).

Chapter 12 Opener, p. 182: © SVLuma (Fotolia); p. 185: © wolf183 (Fotolia); p. 186: © tdoes (Fotolia); p. 188: © alex.pin (Fotolia); p. 190: © vlad_g (Fotolia); p. 193: © Unclesam (Fotolia); p. 196: © Andrei Merkulov (Fotolia); p. 198: © Frog 974 (Fotolia); p. 200: © Franck Boston (Fotolia); p. 201: © Nataliya Hora (Fotolia); p. 204: © JohnKwan (Fotolia); p. 205: © Galyna Andrushko (Fotolia); p. 208: © Jim Parkin (Fotolia); p. 209: © marko04 (Fotolia).

Chapter 13 Opener, p. 212: © onepony (Fotolia); p. 214: © laufer (Fotolia); p. 215: © T shooter (Fotolia); p. 217, top-right: © Stef in BA (Fotolia); p. 217, bottom-right: © Pavel Losevsky (Fotolia); p. 222, top-left: © Corgarashu (Fotolia); p. 222, bottom-left: © Xavier MARCHANT (Fotolia). **Chapter 14** Opener, p. 224: © Pavel Mitov (Fotolia); p. 226: © Cheryl Casey (Fotolia); p. 228, top-left: © maciek905 (Fotolia); p. 228, bottom-left: © laufer (Fotolia); p. 230: © elavuk81 (Fotolia);

REFERENCES

Chapter 1

Anti-Slavery International, Recovered Histories. (n.d.). The middle passage. Retrieved from http://www. recoveredhistories.org/storiesmiddle.php#reading

Campbell, Donna M. (2010, March 21). Puritanism in New England. Retrieved from http://public.wsu .edu/~campbelld/amlit/purdef.htm

Chaney, T., Cohen, K., & Cotton, L. P. (2002, July 15). Jamestown: The Virginia Company of London. Retrieved from http://www.nps.gov/jame/historyculture/the-virginia-company-of-london.htm

Constitution Society. (n.d.). Albany Plan of Union (1754). Retrieved from http://www.constitution.org/bcp/albany.htm

Eastern Woodlands Indians. (n.d.). Retrieved from http://portfolio.educ.kent.edu/mcclellandr/zackthezipper/easternwoodland.htm

Grymes, C. A. (n.d.). Bacon's rebellion. Retrieved from http://virginiaplaces.org/military/bacon.html

Mayflower Compact. (2008). Retrieved from the Lillian Goldman Law Library, Avalon Project website: http://avalon.law.yale.edu/17th_century/mayflower.asp (Original work published 1620)

Miller, H. (n.d.). The lure of sotweed: Tobacco and Maryland history. Retrieved from http://www.stmaryscity.org/History/The%20Lure%20of%20Sotweed.html

National Humanities Institute. (1998). Jonathan Edwards: On the great awakening. Retrieved from http://www.nhinet .org/ccs/docs/awaken.htm

United Nations Educational, Scientific, and Cultural Organization. (n.d.). Cahokia Mounds state historic site. Retrieved from http://whc.unesco.org/en/list/198

Chapter 2

Anderson, F. (2006). The war that made America: A short history of the French and Indian War. New York, NY: Penguin.

Blum, J., McFeely, W., Morgan, E., Schelsinger, A., & Stampp, K. (1993). The national experience: A history of the United States. (8th ed.) Boston: Wadsworth.

Borneman, W. R. (2007). The French and Indian War: Deciding the fate of North America. New York, NY: Harper.

National Park Service. (n.d.). Fort Necessity National Battlefield: The Braddock campaign. Retrieved from http://www.nps.gov/fone/braddock.htm

Ohio History Central. (2005, July 1). Fort Duquesne. Retrieved from http://www.ohiohistorycentral.org/entry.php?rec=705

Ohio History Central. (2005, July 1). French and Indian War. Retrieved from http://www.ohiohistorycentral.org/entry .php?rec=498

Ohio History Central. (2005, July 1). Proclamation of 1763. Retrieved from http://www.ohiohistorycentral.org/entry .php?rec=1443

Chapter 3

Allison, R. (2011). The American Revolution: A concise history. New York, NY: Oxford University Press.

Massachusetts Historical Society. (2001). The Sons of Liberty. Retrieved from http://www.masshist.org/objects/cabinet/august2001/august2001.html

Raphael, R. (2002). A people's history of the American Revolution: How common people shaped the fight for independence. New York, NY: Harper Perennial.

The Sugar Act of 1764. (2008). Retrieved from http://ahp. gatech.edu/sugar_act_bp_1764.html

Warren, J. (2009). The Suffolk resolves. Retrieved from http://ahp.gatech.edu/suffolk_resolves_1774.html (Original work published 1774)

Wood, G. (2003). The American Revolution: A history. New York, NY: Modern Library.

Chapter 4

Appleby, J. O., Brinkley, A., McPherson, J. M., & National Geographic Society. (1998). The American journey. New York, NY: Glencoe/McGraw-Hill.

The Avalon Project: Yale Law School. (2008). Journals of the Continental Congress—Speech to the Six Nations; July 13, 1775. Retrieved from http://avalon.law.yale.edu/18th_century/contcong_07-13-75.asp

Berkin, C. (2005). Revolutionary mothers: Women in the struggle for America's independence. New York, NY: Knopf.

Countryman, E., & Foner, E. (1985). The American Revolution. New York, NY: Hill and Wang.

Finkelman, P., & Lesh, B. A. (2008). Milestone documents in American history: Exploring the primary sources that shaped America. Dallas, TX: Schlager Group.

McCullough, D. G. (2005). 1776. New York, NY: Simon & Schuster.

Nash, G. B. (2005). The unknown American Revolution: The unruly birth of democracy and the struggle to create America. New York, NY: Penguin Books.

Wood, G. S. (2002). The American Revolution: A history. New York, NY: Modern Library.

Chapter 5

Bowen, C. D. (1966). Miracle at Philadelphia: The story of the Constitutional Convention, May to September 1787. Boston, MA: Little, Brown.

Kurland, P. B., & Lerner, R. (1987). The Founders' Constitution. Chicago, IL: University of Chicago Press.

Rakove, J. N., & Handlin, O. (1990). James Madison and the creation of the American Republic. Glenview, IL: Scott Foresman/Little Brown Higher Education.

Morris, R. B. (1985). Witnesses at the creation: Hamilton, Madison, Jay, and the Constitution. New York, NY: Holt, Rinehart, and Winston.

Faber, D., & Faber, H. (1987). *We the people: The story of the United States Constitution since 1787*. New York, NY: Scribner's.

Chapter 6

Gawalt, G. W. (n.d.). America and the Barbary pirates: An international battle against an unconventional foe. Retrieved from the Library of Congress website: http://memory.loc.gov/ammem/collections/jefferson_papers/mtjprece.html

Henretta, J. A., Brownlee, W. E., Brody, D., & Ware, S. (1987). *America's history to 1877*. Chicago, IL: Dorsey Press.

Holt, M. (2008). *By one vote: The disputed presidential election of 1876*. Lawrence, KS. University Press of Kansas.

James Madison Museum. (n.d.). James Madison. Retrieved from http://jamesmadisonmuseum.vabion.com/?page_id=56

Graff, H. F. (Ed.). (2002). John Adams: The retreat from war. In *Profiles of U.S. presidents* (3rd ed.). Retrieved from http://www.presidentprofiles.com/Washington-Johnson/John-Adams-The-retreat-from-war.html

Library of Congress. (2010, October 28). Alien and Sedition Acts. Retrieved from http://www.loc.gov/rr/program/bib/ourdocs/Alien.html

Stites, F. N. (1997). *John Marshall: Defender of the Constitution*. New York, NY: Longman Press.

University of Virginia, Miller Center. (2012). American president: A reference resource. Retrieved from http://millercenter.org/president/adams/essays/biography/3

The White House. (n.d.). Thomas Jefferson, 1801–1809. Retrieved from http://www.whitehouse.gov/about/presidents/thomasjefferson

Chapter 7

Henretta, J. A., Edwards, R., & Self, R. O. (1987). *America's history to 1877*. Chicago, IL: Dorsey Press.

Howe, D. W. (2009). *What hath God wrought: The transformation of America, 1815–1848*. New York, NY: Oxford University Press.

Johnson, W. (2001). *Soul by soul: Life inside the antebellum slave market*. Cambridge, MA: Harvard University Press.

Potter, D. (1977). *The impending crisis: America before the Civil War; 1848–1861*. New York, NY: Harper Perennial.

Wilentz, S. (2005). *Andrew Jackson*. New York, NY: Times Books.

Chapter 8

Faust, D. G. (2008). *This republic of suffering: Death and the American Civil War*. New York, NY: Alfred A. Knopf.

Foner, E. (2010). *The fiery trial: Abraham Lincoln and American slavery*. New York, NY: W. W. Norton and Company.

Foote, S. (1963). *The Civil War: A narrative*. New York, NY: Random House.

Goodwin, D. K. (2005). *Team of rivals: The political genius of Abraham Lincoln*. New York, NY: Simon and Schuster.

Henretta, J. A., Brownlee, W. E., Brody, D., & Ware, S. (1987). *America's history to 1877*. Chicago, IL: Dorsey Press.

Kolchin, P. (1993). *American slavery: 1619–1877*. New York, NY: Hill and Wang.

McFeely, M. D. (Ed.). (1990). *Ulysses S. Grant: Selected letters and memoirs*. New York, NY: Literary Classics of the United States.

Royster, C. (1991). *The destructive war*. New York, NY: Alfred A. Knopf.

Sears, S. W. (1983). *Landscape turned red: The battle of Antietam*. New Haven, CT: Ticknor and Fields.

Ward, G. (1990). *The Civil War*. New York, NY: Vintage Books.

Woodward, C. V. (Ed.). (1981). *Mary Chestnut's Civil War*. New Haven, CT: Yale University Press.

Chapter 9

Berlin, I., Favreau, M., & Miller, S. F. (Eds.). (1998). *Remembering slavery: African Americans talk about their personal experiences of slavery and emancipation*. New York, NY: The New Press.

DuBois, W. E. B. (1977). *Black Reconstruction in America: An essay toward a history of the part which black folk played in the attempt to reconstruct democracy in America, 1860–1880*. New York, NY: Atheneum. (Original work published 1935)

Edwards, L. (1997). *Gendered strife and confusion: The political culture of Reconstruction*. Urbana, IL: University of Illinois Press.

Faulkner, C. (2003). *Women's radical Reconstruction: The freedmen's aid movement*. Philadelphia, PA: University of Pennsylvania Press.

Foner, E. (2005). *Forever free: The story of emancipation & Reconstruction*. New York, NY: Vintage Books.

Foner, E. (2002). *Reconstruction: America's unfinished revolution, 1863–1877*. New York, NY: Harper Collins.

Franklin, J. H. (1994). *Reconstruction after the Civil War* (2nd ed.). Chicago, IL: University of Chicago Press.

Litwack, L. (1979). *Been in the storm so long: The aftermath of slavery*. New York, NY: Knopf.

McPherson, J., & Hogue, J. (2009). *Ordeal by fire: The Civil War and Reconstruction* (4th ed.). New York, NY: McGraw-Hill.

Chapter 10

Brown, D. (1971). *Bury my heart at Wounded Knee: An Indian history of the American West*. New York, NY: Henry Holt.

Calloway, C. G. (1996). *Our hearts fell to the ground: Plains Indian views of how the West was lost.* Boston. MA: Bedford/St. Martin's.

Hine, R. V., & Faragher, J. M. (2007). *Frontiers: A short history of the American West.* New Haven, CT: Yale University Press.

Isenberg, A. C. (2000). *The destruction of the bison: An environmental history, 1750–1920.* New York, NY: Cambridge University Press.

Paul, R. W. (1988). *The Far West and the Great Plains in transition, 1859–1900.* New York, NY: Harper & Row.

Waldman, C. (2000). *Atlas of the North American Indian* (Rev. ed.). New York, NY: Facts on File.

White, R. (1991). *"It's your misfortune and none of my own": A history of the American West.* Norman, OK: University of Oklahoma Press.

White, R. (2011). *Railroaded: The transcontinentals and the making of modern America.* New York, NY: W.W. Norton.

Chapter 11

Johnson, P. (1997). *A history of the American people.* New York, NY: Harper Collins.

Lord, W. (1960). *The good years.* New York, NY: Harper Brothers.

Maddow, B. (1979). *A Sunday between wars.* New York, NY: W.W. Norton.

Rather, D. (1996). *Our times.* New York, NY: Scribner.

Traxel, D. (1998). *1898.* New York, NY: Alfred Knopf.

Traxel, D. (2006). *Crusader nation.* New York, NY: Alfred Knopf.

Weinstein, A. (2002). *The story of America.* New York, NY: Agincourt Press.

Chapter 12

Chicago Historical Society. (2001). Slaughterhouse to the world. Retrieved from http://www.chicagohs.org/history/stockyard/stock4.html and http://www.chicagohs.org/history/stockyard/stock2.html

Evans, S. M. (1989). *Born for liberty: A history of women in America.* New York, NY: The Free Press.

Fink, L., & Paterson, T. (2000). *Major problems in the gilded age and the progressive era: Documents and essays.* Boston, MA: Wadsworth.

Henretta, J. A., Brody, D., & Dumenil, L. (2006). *America: A concise history, Vol. 2: Since 1865* (3rd ed.). Boston, MA: Bedford/St. Martin's.

McGerr, M. (2005). *A fierce discontent: The rise and fall of the progressive movement in America, 1870 –1920.* New York, NY: Oxford University Press.

Tindall, G. B., & Shi, D. E. (2004). *America: A narrative history* (6th ed., Vol. 2). New York, NY: W.W. Norton & Company, Inc.

Zinn, H. (1995). *The people's history of the United States: 1492–present.* New York, NY: HarperPerennial.

Chapter 13

Library of Congress. (n.d.). U.S. participation in the Great War (World War One). Retrieved from http://www.loc.gov/teachers/classroommaterials/presentationsandactivities/presentations/timeline/progress/wwone/

Library of Congress, American Memory. (n.d.). Immigrants, nativism, and Americanization. Retrieved from http://lcweb2.loc.gov:8081/ammem/amrlhtml/dtimmig.html

Library of Congress, American Memory. (n.d.). The increasing power of destruction: Military technology in World War I. *Newspaper Pictorials: World War I Rotogravures.* Retrieved from http://memory.loc.gov/ammem/collections/rotogravures/rotomil.html

Massachusetts Judicial Branch, Supreme Judicial Court. (2010). Sacco & Vanzetti exhibit. Retrieved from http://www.mass.gov/courts/sjc/sacco-vanzetti.html

Meyer, G. J. (2007). *A world undone: The story of the Great War, 1914 to 1918.* New York, NY: Delacourte Press.

Our Documents: 100 Milestone Documents from the National Archives. (n.d.). President Woodrow Wilson's 14 points (1918). Retrieved from http://www.ourdocuments.gov/doc.php?doc=62

Our Documents: 100 Milestone Documents from the National Archives. (n.d.). Zimmermann telegram (1917). Retrieved from http://www.ourdocuments.gov/doc.php??doc=60

Smithsonian National Museum of American History. (n.d.). The price of freedom: Americans at war: World War I. Retrieved from http://americanhistory.si.edu/militaryhistory/printable/section.asp?id=8

Tuchman, B. W. (2004). *The guns of August.* New York, NY: Presidio Press. (Original work published 1962)

U.S. Senate website. (n.d.). Woodrow Wilson addresses the Senate. Retrieved from http://www.senate.gov/artandhistory/history/minute/Woodrow_Wilson_Addresses_the_Senate.htm

Chapter 14

Burg, D. F. *The Great Depression.* (1996). New York: Facts on File, Inc.

Kennedy, D. M. (1999). *Freedom from fear: The American people in depression and war 1929–1945.* New York: Oxford University Press.

McElvaine, R. S. (1984). *The Great Depression.* New York: Times Books.

Shlaes, A. (2008). *The forgotten man: A new history of the Great Depression.* New York: Harper Perennial.

Steinbeck, J. (1992). *The grapes of wrath.* New York: Penguin Books.

Watkins, T. H. (1993). *The Great Depression: America in the 1930s.* Boston: Little, Brown.

Chapter 15

American Experience. (2009). Timeline of the war in the Pacific. Public Broadcasting Service. Retrieved from http://www.pbs.org/wgbh/amex/macarthur/timeline/1942.html

Scarred by history: The rape of Nanjing. (2005, April 11). BBC News. Retrieved from http://news.bbc.co.uk/2/hi/223038.stm

Boyle, D. (1998). World War II: A photographic history. New York, NY: Barnes and Noble.

D'Este, C. (2003). Eisenhower: A soldier's life. New York, NY: Macmillan.

Eistein, Albert 1879–1955. (2012). In The Oxford dictionary of quotations (6th ed.). Retrieved from http://www.oxfordreference.com/pages/samplep-18.html

Findlay, C., & Rothney, J. (2011). Twentieth century world. Belmont, CA: Wadsworth-Cengage Learning.

Fulbrook, M. (2002). History of Germany, 1918–2000. Malden, MA: Wiley-Blackwell.

Hanson, V. D. (2007, July 25). Introduction to E. B. Sledge's With the old breed. Retrieved from http://victorhanson.com/articles/hanson072507.html

Independent Lens. (2011). The political Dr. Seuss. Public Broadcasting Service, Georgia. Retrieved from http://www.pbs.org/independentlens/politicaldrseuss/seuss_fla.html

Johnson, P. (1995). The myth of American isolationism. Foreign Affairs, 74(3).

Keegan, J. (1989). The Second World War. New York, NY: Penguin Books.

Litoff, J. (1997). American women in a world at war. Lanham, MD: Rowman and Littlefield.

McClelland, J. (2011, July 13). Paying attention to a forgotten navy pig's plaque. National Public Radio. Retrieved from http://www.npr.org/2011/07/13/137791935/paying-attention-to-a-forgotten-navy-pigs-plaque

New York Times on the Web. (2010). On this day: March 29, 1969. Retrieved from http://www.nytimes.com/learning/general/onthisday/bday/1014.html

Paterson, T. G., Clifford, J. G., Hagan, K. J., Kisatsky, D., & Maddock, S. J. (2010). American foreign relations: Vol. 2; Since 1865. Boston, MA: Wadsworth-Cengage.

Tracy, E. (Producer). (2007, December 5). Walter D. Ehlers: Medal of Honor with Ed Tracy [Audio podcast]. Pritzker Military Library. Retrieved from http://itunes.apple.com/us/podcast/medal-of-honor-with-ed-tracy/id118681082

United States Holocaust Memorial Museum. (2012, May 11). Holocaust encyclopedia: The United States and the Holocaust. Retrieved from http://www.ushmm.org/wlc/en/article.php?ModuleId=10005182

U.S. Department of Energy. (2012, January 8). Hanford World War II era. Retrieved from http://www.hanford.gov/page.cfm/WorldWarIIEra

Welch, D. (1998). Hitler. Philadelphia, PA: UCL Press.

World War II. (2011). In Encyclopædia Britannica. Retrieved from http://www.britannica.com/EBchecked/topic/648813/World-War-II

Chapter 16

Bostdorff, D. M. (2008). Proclaiming the Truman doctrine: The Cold War call to arms. College Station, Texas: Texas A&M University Press.

Gaddis, J. L. (2006). The Cold War: A new history. New York, NY: Penguin.

Jones, H. (1997). A new kind of war:" America's global strategy and the Truman doctrine in Greece. New York, NY: Oxford University Press.

McCullough, D. (1993). Truman. New York, NY: Simon & Schuster.

Our Documents: 100 Milestone Documents from the National Archives. (n.d.). Truman Doctrine (1947). Retrieved from http://www.ourdocuments.gov/doc.php?doc=81

Salisbury, H. E. (1959, July 24). Nixon and Khrushchev argue in public as U.S. exhibit opens. New York Times. Retrieved from http://www.nytimes.com/learning/general/onthisday/big/0724.html

Smithsonian National Museum of American History. (n.d.). The price of freedom: Americans at war: Cold War. Retrieved from http://americanhistory.si.edu/militaryhistory/printable/section.asp?id=11

U.S. Department of State, Office of the Historian. (n.d.). Milestones: 1945–1952. Retrieved November from http://history.state.gov/milestones/1945-1952

Chapter 17

Abramson, A. (2003). The history of television, 1942 to 2000. Jefferson, NC: McFarland.

Ambrose, S. E. (1983). Eisenhower. New York, NY: Simon and Schuster.

Ledbetter, J. (2011). Unwarranted influence: Dwight D. Eisenhower and the military-industrial complex. New Haven, CT: Yale University Press.

Light, P. C. (1988). Baby boomers. New York, NY: Norton.

National Museum of History, Smithsonian Institution. (n.d.).America on the move: On the interstate. Retrieved from http://americanhistory.si.edu/onthemove/exhibition/exhibition_16_1.html

Our Documents: 100 Milestone Documents from the National Archives. (n.d.). Joint address to Congress leading to a decalaration of war against Germany (1917). Retrieved from http://www.ourdocuments.gov/doc.php?doc=90

Our Documents: 100 Milestone Documents from the National Archives. (n.d.). National Interstate and Defense Highways Act (1956). Retrieved from http://www.ourdocuments.gov/doc.php?doc=88U.S. Bureau of Labor Statistics. (n.d.). 100 Years of U.S. consumer spending: 1950. Retrieved from http://www.bls.gov/opub/uscs/1950.pdf

Wagner, R. G., & Wagner, A. D. (2010). Levittown. Charleston, SC: Arcadia.

Chapter 18

Henretta, J. A., Brody, D., & Dumenil, L. (2006). America: A concise history, Vol. 2: Since 1865 (3rd ed.). Boston, MA: Bedford/St. Martin's.

Centers for Medicare & Medicaid Services. (n.d.). History. Retrieved from https://www.cms.gov/history/

Rosen, R. (2000). The world split open: How the modern women's movement changed America. New York, NY: Penguin Books.

American Experience. (2002). Timeline: The pill. Public Broadcasting Service. Retrieved from http://www.pbs.org/wgbh/amex/pill/timeline/timeline2.html

Tindall, G. B., & Shi, D. E. (2004). *America: A narrative history* (6th ed., Vol. 2). New York, NY: W.W. Norton.

Zinn, H. (1995). *The people's history of the United States: 1492–present.* New York, NY: Harper Perennial.

Chapter 19

Bernstein, C., & Woodward, B. (1974). *All the president's men.* New York, NY: Simon and Schuster.

Carter, J. (2010). *White House diary.* New York, NY: Farrar, Straus and Giroux.

Dallek, R. (2007). *Nixon and Kissinger: Partners in power.* New York, NY: Harper Collins.

Fulsom, D. (2012). *Nixon's darkest secrets: The inside story of America's most troubled president.* New York, NY: Thomas Dunne Books.

Kennerly, D. H., Brokaw, T., Smith, R. N., & University of Texas at Austin. (2007). *Extraordinary circumstances: The presidency of Gerald R. Ford.* Austin, TX: Center for American History, University of Texas at Austin.

Reeves, R. (2001). *President Nixon: Alone in the White House.* New York, NY: Simon & Schuster.

Chapter 20

Alesina, A., & Rosenthal, H. (1995). *Partisan politics, divided government, and the economy.* Cambridge, England: Cambridge University Press.

Atkinson, R. (1993). *Crusade: The untold story of the Persian Gulf War.* Boston, MA: Houghton Mifflin.

Bartlett, B. R. (2009). *The new American economy: The failure of Reaganomics and a new way forward.* New York, NY: Palgrave Macmillan.

Laqueur, W. (1989). *The long road to freedom: Russia and Glasnost.* New York, NY: C. Scribner's.

Niskanen, W. A., & Cato Institute. (1988). *Reaganomics: An insider's account of the policies and the people.* New York, NY: Oxford University Press.

Reagan, R., & Brinkley, D. (2007). *The Reagan diaries.* New York, NY: Harper Collins.

Chapter 21

Aberbach, J., & Peele, G. (2011). *Crisis of conservatism?: The Republican Party, the conservative movement and American politics after Bush.* New York, NY: Oxford University Press.

Critchlow, D., & MacLean, N. (2009). *Debating the American conservative movement: 1945 to the present.* Lanham, MD: Rowman and Littlefield.

Hook, S., & Spanier, J. (2004). *American foreign policy since World War II.* Washington, DC: CQ Press.

McLean, B., & Nocera, J. (2010). *All the devils are here: The hidden history of the financial crisis.* New York, NY: Portfolio/Penguin.

Reinhart, C,. & Rogoff, K. (2009). *This time is different: Eight centuries of financial folly.* Princeton, NJ: Princeton University Press.

Shiller, R. (2005). *Irrational exuberance* (2nd ed.). Princeton, NJ: Princeton University Press.

Zelikow, P. (2011). *The 9/11 commission report: The attack from planning to aftermath.* New York, NY: W.W. Norton.

INDEX

A

AAA (Agricultural Adjustment Administration), 231

ABC (American Broadcasting Company), 275

ABM (Anti-Ballistic Missile) Treaty, 331

Abolitionism, 59, 136. *See also* Civil rights; Civil War

Abortion, 286, 344

Acrobat Ranch (TV show), 275

Act Prohibiting the Importation of Slaves, 108

Adams, John
diplomacy in Britain, 61
and drafting of Massachusetts state constitution, 56
in First Continental Congress, 38
involvement in Sons of Liberty, 37
opposition to Stamp Act, 36
presidency, 76–77
role in Federalist Party, 74

Adams, John Quincy
and Monroe Doctrine, 86
presidency, 99–100

Adams, Samuel
in First Continental Congress, 38
involvement in Sons of Liberty, 37

Addams, Jan, 192–193

Adventures of Huckleberry Finn (Twain), 97, 149

The Adventures of Tom Sawyer (Twain), 97, 149

Advertising, 271, 274, 275, 277

Afghanistan, War in, 247, 349

AFL. *See* American Federation of Labor

African Americans. *See also* Civil rights
Andrew Jackson's treatment of, 102
early questions of freedom regarding, 59–60
farming by, 206
housing policies against, 274
Jim Crow laws, 185–186
migration to Northern U.S., 186–187
participation in Revolutionary War, 51
in Progressive era, 190–192
race riots, 300–302
in Reconstruction era, 132–138
settlement in Western U.S., 206
support for Republican Party by, 205
Three-Fifths Compromise, 65, 77
voting rights of, 133, 135, 136, 141, 184, 185, 295–296, 299–300

Age of Exploration, 7–9

The Age of Reason (Paine), 41

"Age of the common man," 99, 102

Agnew, Spiro, 318

Agricultural Adjustment Administration (AAA), 231, 233

Agriculture. *See also* Farm reform
antebellum era, 92–93
and Louisiana Purchase, 82
with Morrill Act, 150
and Republican Party, 75

AIM (American Federation of Labor), 302

Alabama, 120

Alaska, 148–149

Albany Congress, 21–22

Albany Plan of Union, 21, 29

Algonquians, 7

Alien and Sedition Acts, 76

Allen, Ethan, 45

Allied Powers, 212, 214, 216

Allied troops (World War II), 253

Allotment, 158–159

Al Qaeda, 348, 349

American Broadcasting Company (ABC), 275

American Federation of Labor (AFL), 195, 234, 278

American Fur Company, 170

American Indian Movement (AIM), 302

American Medical Association (AMA), 304

American Revolutionary War. *See* Revolutionary War

American Sugar Refining Company, 170

American System, 99–100

Anarchists, 189, 218–220

Anderson, John, 335

Anderson, Robert, 121

Angel Island, 187–188

Anglican Church, 21

Animal Clinic (TV show), 275

Antebellum era, 90–105
agriculture, 92–93
Andrew Jackson's presidency, 100–103
communication, 95
election of 1824, 99
factories, 93–95
John Quincy Adams' presidency, 99–100
Martin Van Buren's presidency, 104–105
nationalism and market society, 90–91

new social structures, 97–98
political culture, 98–99
population growth, 96–97
transportation, 91–92

Anthony, Susan B., 136

Anti-Ballistic Missile (ABM) Treaty, 331

Antifederalists, 65

Anti-Imperialist League, 161

Anti-Saloon League, 183

Antitrust legislation, 170–171, 204

Antiwar protests, 306–308, 313

Apache, 155

Appeasement, 240–245

Appomattox, 127

Arab-Israeli War, 323

Arapaho, 155, 156

Arbella, 12

Arizona, 155

Arkansas, 123, 185

Arms race, 264, 331–332

Arnold, Benedict, 45, 48

Arthur, Chester, 201

Articles of Confederation, 47, 57–58

Asian Americans, 189. *See also* Chinese Americans; Japanese Americans

Assembly lines, 94–95, 199–200

"Assumption plan" (Hamilton's financial plan), 73

Astor, John Jacob, 168, 170

Atlanta Compromise, 190

Atlantic and Gulf Railroad, 174

Atlantic seaboard, 17

Atomic bomb, 248, 254–256

Austria, 244

Austria-Hungary, 212

Automobiles, 274, 277

B

Babbitt (Lewis), 192

Baby boom, 276, 328

Bacon, Nathanial, 14

Bacon's Rebellion, 14, 17

Balloon loans, 224

Baltimore, Maryland, 20, 96

Baltimore and Ohio Railroad, 92

Bank Bill of 1791, 71

Banking system, 212, 229–230

Banks Plan, 136

Bank war, 103

Banneker, Benjamin, 59

Barbary War, 78, 83–84

Barry, Catherine Moore, 45

Base broadening, 327

U

Unemployment
 and mortgage payments, 224
 in 1970s, 323
 in Panic of 1893, 166–167
 and Populist Party, 207
Unilateralism, 347–348
Union (Civil War), 124–127
Union Army, 139
Union Pacific Railroad, 150, 166, 173, 174
Unions, 195–196, 206–207, 218, 233–234, 278
United Kingdom, 264, 314, 351
United Nations, 266, 350
United States Housing Act (USHA), 233
United States Steel Corporation, 170
United States v. Cruikshank, 143
University of California at Berkeley, 306
Urbanization
 in antebellum era, 96
 defined, 91
 and diversity, 196
 small towns vs., 192
Urban slaves, 18
U.S. Constitution. *See* Constitution
U.S. Department of Justice, 141
U.S. Department of the Interior, 203–204
U.S. Postal System, 95
U.S. Steel, 171, 172
U.S. v. E.C. Knight, 170
USHA (United States Housing Act), 233
U.S.S. Chesapeake, 83, 84
USS Cole, 349
Utah, 113
Ute Indians, 155

V

Valley Forge, 44
Vally, 48
Van Buren, Martin
 and Cherokee Indians, 102
 10-hour workday developed by, 95
 presidency, 104–105
Vanderbilt, Cornelius, 168, 174
Vanzetti, Bartolomeo, 219–220
VE Day, 252
Verrazano, Giovanni, 10
Vertical integration, 169, 200
Viet Cong, 290–292
Vietnamization, 292
Vietnam Veterans Against the War, 293

Vietnam War, 290–295
 costs of, 305
 Martin Luther King Jr.'s criticism of, 299
 under Richard Nixon, 314–315
 seeds of, 265, 266
 televising of, 291–292, 313
Virginia
 approval of Constitution by, 65
 ratification of Articles of Confederation by, 56
 religious freedom in, 60
 status in the Union, 121, 123
Virginia City, Nevada, 149
Virginia Company, 13
Virginia Plan, 64–65
Virginia Statute for Religious Freedom, 60
VISTA program, 303
VJ Day, 248
Volcker, Paul, 326
Volunteerism, 227
Von Steuben, Baron, 44
Voting requirements, 98
Voting rights
 of African Americans, 133, 135, 136, 141, 185, 295–296, 299–300
 of women, 184–185, 193, 195, 212, 284
Voting Rights Act, 300

W

Wade, Benjamin F., 132
Wade-Davis Bill, 132
Wage labor, 97, 108
Wagner Act, 234
Walkara, Chief, 152
Walker War, 152
Waltham Plan, 95
War bonds, 252
War of 1812, 83–86
War of Independence. *See* Revolutionary War
War on Terror, 349, 350
Washington, Booker T., 190, 205
Washington, George
 and African-Americans in Revolutionary War, 51
 as commander of Continental Army, 46
 creation of Constitution, 64
 creation of Continental Army under, 44
 fighting in the North, 47, 48
 in First Continental Congress, 39
 freeing of slaves by, 60
 in French and Indian War, 29, 30

 and Newburgh Conspiracy, 58
 presidency, 70, 72–74
 selection as president, 66
Washington D.C.
 abolition of slavery in, 123
 relocation of capital to, 73
Washington Post, 317–318
Washita, Battle of, 156
Watergate scandal, 316–320
Watts Riots, 300
WCTU (Women's Christian Temperance Union), 183, 184
WEAL (Women's Equity Action League), 285
Wealth, distribution of, 98
Weapons of mass destruction (WMDs), 350
Weathermen, 306
Weaver, James, 207
Webster, Daniel, 86, 103, 113
Weimar Republic, 240–242
Welles, Orson, 177
Wells, Ida B., 191–192
Wesley, Charles, 22
Wesley, John, 22
Western United States
 establishment in, 80–83
 in founding of United States, 61
 land disputes over, 58–59
 population growth in, 96
 Revolutionary War fought in, 52
Westmoreland, William, 291
West Virginia, 121, 122
Westward expansion, 17, 112–113, 147–162
 Dawes Severalty Act, 158–159
 Frederick Jackson Turner frontier thesis, 159–160
 gold and silver as motivations in, 148–149
 Homestead Act, 149, 154
 Indian Wars, 153–158
 land grants for, 150–151
 Mormonism, 151–152
 role of manifest destiny, 112–113, 152–153
 Spanish-American War, 160–161
Wheately, Phyllis, 59
Whig Party
 division within, 116
 formation of, 103
 ideology of, 99
Whiskey, 66, 72
Whiskey Ring scandal, 141, 202
White Citizens Councils, 296
Whitefield, George, 22
White House Plumbers, 316
White supremacy, 143
Whitman, Walt, 118

X

Y

Z

Notes

Notes

Notes

Notes

Notes

Notes

Notes

Notes